THE MATHEMATICA® BOOK

STEPHEN WOLFRAM

THE MATHEMATICA® BOOK

Third Edition

WOLFRAM MEDIA

CAMBRIDGE UNIVERSITY PRESS

Library of Congress Cataloging–in–Publication Data

Wolfram, Stephen, 1959 –
    The Mathematica book / Stephen Wolfram. — 3rd ed.
        p.   cm.
    Rev. ed. of: Mathematica. 2nd ed. 1991.
    Includes index.
    ISBN 0–9650532–0–2 (alk. paper). — ISBN 0–9650532–1–0 (pbk.)
    ISBN 0–521–58889–8 (alk. paper). — ISBN 0–521–58888–X (pbk.)
    1. Mathematica (Computer file) 2. Mathematics—Data processing.
I. Wolfram, Stephen. Mathematica. II. Title.
QA76.95.W65   1996
510'.285'53—dc20
                                                                    96–7218
                                                                    CIP

A catalog record for this book is also available from the British Library.

For the latest updates and corrections to this book:
visit http://www.wolfram.com/book–updates *or send blank email to* book–updates–responder@wolfram.com

Comments on this book will be welcomed at:
comments@wolfram.com

In publications that refer to the *Mathematica* system, please cite this book as:
Stephen Wolfram, *The Mathematica Book*, 3rd ed.
(Wolfram Media/Cambridge University Press, 1996)

Previous editions published by Addison-Wesley Publishing Company under the title Mathematica: A System for Doing Mathematics by Computer

Copublishers:

WOLFRAM
MEDIA

ISBN 0–9650532–0–2 Hardback
ISBN 0–9650532–1–0 Paperback

Wolfram Media, Inc.
web: http://www.wolfram–media.com; *email:* info@wolfram–media.com
phone: +1–217–398–9090; *fax:* +1–217–398–9095
mail: 100 Trade Center Drive, Champaign, IL 61820, USA

CAMBRIDGE
UNIVERSITY PRESS

ISBN 0–521–58889–8 Hardback
ISBN 0–521–58888–X Paperback

The Press Syndicate of the University of Cambridge
The Pitt Building, Trumpington Street, Cambridge CB2 1RP, UK
40 West 20th Street, New York, NY 10011–4211, USA
10 Stamford Road, Oakleigh, Melbourne 3166, Australia

Retail and library orders worldwide should be directed to Cambridge University Press and their distributors. Permissions and foreign rights inquiries should be directed to Wolfram Media.

15   14   13   12   11   10   9   8   7   6   5   4   3   2   1

WOLFRAM
RESEARCH

Wolfram Research, Inc.
web: http://www.wolfram.com
email: info@wolfram.com
phone: 217–398–0700
fax: 217–398–0747
mail: 100 Trade Center Drive
 Champaign, IL 61820
 USA

Wolfram Research Europe Ltd.
web: http://www.wolfram.co.uk
email: info@wolfram.co.uk
phone: +44–(0)1993–883400
fax: +44–(0)1993–883800
mail: 10 Blenheim Office Park
 Lower Road, Long Hanborough
 Oxfordshire OX8 8LN
 UNITED KINGDOM

Wolfram Research Asia Ltd.
web: http://www.wolfram.co.jp
email: info@wolfram.co.jp
phone: +81–(0)3–5276–0506
fax: +81–(0)3–5276–0509
mail: Izumi Building 8F
 3–2–15 Misaki-cho
 Chiyoda-ku, Tokyo 101
 JAPAN

MATHEMATICA®

Note: All services are also available at wolfram.co.uk *and* wolfram.co.jp, *as well as at* wolfram.com.

General information:
 info@wolfram.com
 http://www.wolfram.com

Frequently asked technical and other questions:
 http://www.wolfram.com/faq

Central index of *Mathematica*-related material:
 http://www.wolfram.com/central

Current *Mathematica* version information:
 info@wolfram.com
 http://www.wolfram.com/versions

Orders and customer service:
 orders@wolfram.com
 http://www.wolfram.com/orders

User registration and password requests:
 register@wolfram.com
 http://www.wolfram.com/register
 Institutional and other non-owner users are also encouraged to register.

Technical support and bug reports:
 support@wolfram.com
 http://www.wolfram.com/support
 Support is available only to registered users.

Mathematica training information:
 training@wolfram.com
 http://www.wolfram.com/training

Information for educators:
 education@wolfram.com
 http://www.wolfram.com/education

Suggestions:
 suggestions@wolfram.com
 http://www.wolfram.com/suggestions

Comments and feedback:
 comments@wolfram.com
 http://www.wolfram.com/comments
 Information about applications of Mathematica, large and small, is always welcome.

Mathematica Archive:
Wolfram Research maintains an archive of Mathematica-related documents. Publications and other non-proprietary material are welcome at:
 The *Mathematica* Archive
 Wolfram Research, Inc.
 100 Trade Center Drive
 Champaign, IL 61820, USA
 email: archive@wolfram.com
 web: http://www.wolfram.com/archive

Mathematica Products Catalog:
 http://www.wolfram.com/catalog
 To request a current catalog of all Wolfram Research products, use the web site, or send email to info@wolfram.com, *or contact Wolfram Research.*

Mathematica Bookstore:
 http://www.wolfram.com/bookstore
 To request a current list of titles, send blank email to bookstore–responder@wolfram.com.

MathSource Electronic Library:
 http://www.wolfram.com/mathsource
 ftp: mathsource.wolfram.com
 mail server: mathsource@wolfram.com
 administrator: mathsource–admin@wolfram.com

MathUser Newsletter:
 http://www.wolfram.com/mathuser
 To request a free subscription, use the web site, or send email to mathuser@wolfram.com, *or contact Wolfram Research.*

mathgroup news group:
 news: comp.soft–sys.math.mathematica
 http://www.wolfram.com/mathgroup

Book Credits

Editors: Jerome Walsh, George Beck and Joe Grohens • *Typesetters:* Joe Kaiping, Phil Wall and Glenn Scholebo • *Lead proofreader:* Jan Progen • *Proofreaders:* Carol Ordal, Wendy Leung, Angela Latham, Kurt Kessinger, Madhav Chari and John Garvey • *Testers:* Anna Marichev and Kevin Leuthold • *Production programmers:* Jeff Adams and Joe Kaiping • *Formula gallery developer:* Michael Trott • *Cover, part openers and graphics gallery designers:* John Bonadies and Jody Jasinski • *Book designers:* John Bonadies and André Kuzniarek • *Font designer:* André Kuzniarek • *On-line version developers:* Chris LaReau and Robby Villegas • *Project managers:* George Beck and Joe Grohens • *Manufacturing managers:* Jody Jasinski and Rachel Lively • *Business developer:* Dianne Littwin • *Additional content checkers:* Members of Wolfram Research technical support, quality assurance and R&D groups, as well as *Mathematica* beta testers.

For Mathematica software credits, see About Mathematica *in the Mathematica front end.*

About the Author

Stephen Wolfram is the creator of *Mathematica* and is widely regarded as the most important innovator in scientific and technical computing today. Born in London in 1959, he was educated at Eton, Oxford and Caltech. He published his first scientific paper at the age of fifteen, and had received his PhD in theoretical physics from Caltech by the age of twenty. Wolfram's early scientific work was mainly in high-energy physics, quantum field theory and cosmology, and included several now-classic results. Having started to use computers in 1973, Wolfram rapidly became a leader in the emerging field of scientific computing, and in 1979 he began the construction of SMP—the first modern computer algebra system—which he released commercially in 1981.

In recognition of his early work in physics and computing, Wolfram became in 1981 the youngest recipient of a Mac-Arthur Prize Fellowship. Late in 1981, Wolfram then set out on an ambitious new direction in science: to develop a general theory of complexity in nature. Wolfram's key idea was to use computer experiments to study the behavior of simple computer programs known as cellular automata. And in 1982 he made the first in a series of startling discoveries about the origins of complexity. The publication of Wolfram's papers on cellular automata led to a major shift in scientific thinking, and laid the groundwork for a new field of science that Wolfram named "complex systems research".

Through the mid-1980s, Wolfram continued his work on complexity, discovering a number of fundamental connections between computation and nature, and inventing such concepts as computational irreducibility. Wolfram's work led to a wide range of applications—and provided the main scientific foundations for the popular movements known as complexity theory and artificial life. Wolfram himself used his ideas to develop a new randomness generation system and a new approach to computational fluid dynamics—both of which are now in widespread use.

Following his scientific work on complex systems research, Wolfram in 1986 founded the first research center and first journal in the field. Then, after a highly successful career in academia—first at Caltech, then at the Institute for Advanced Study in Princeton, and finally as Professor of Physics, Mathematics and Computer Science at the University of Illinois—Wolfram launched Wolfram Research, Inc.

Wolfram began the development of *Mathematica* in late 1986. The first version of *Mathematica* was released on June 23, 1988, and was immediately hailed as a major advance in the field of computing. In the years that followed, the popularity of *Mathematica* grew rapidly, and Wolfram Research became established as a world leader in the software industry, widely recognized for excellence in both technology and business.

Following the release of *Mathematica* Version 2 in 1991, Wolfram began to divide his time between *Mathematica* development and scientific research. Building on his work from the mid-1980s, Wolfram made a sequence of major discoveries to be described in his forthcoming book *A New Kind of Science*. In addition to solving some fundamental existing scientific problems, Wolfram's recent work points the way to a whole new approach to science and mathematics.

Wolfram has been president and CEO of Wolfram Research since its inception, and remains personally responsible for the design of the core *Mathematica* system.

Other books by Stephen Wolfram:
- *Cellular Automata and Complexity: Collected Papers* (1993)
- *A New Kind of Science* (forthcoming)
  (*For information send email to* info@new–science.com)

Author's web site:
http://www.wolfram.com/s.wolfram

Author's address:
email: s.wolfram@wolfram.com
mail: 100 Trade Center Drive
        Champaign, IL 61820, USA

*For comments on this book or Mathematica
send email to* comments@wolfram.com

About *Mathematica*

Mathematica is the world's only fully integrated environment for technical computing. First released in 1988, it has had a profound effect on the way computers are used in many technical and other fields.

It is often said that the release of *Mathematica* marked the beginning of modern technical computing. Ever since the 1960s individual packages had existed for specific numerical, algebraic, graphical and other tasks. But the visionary concept of *Mathematica* was to create once and for all a single system that could handle all the various aspects of technical computing in a coherent and unified way. The key intellectual advance that made this possible was the invention of a new kind of symbolic computer language that could for the first time manipulate the very wide range of objects involved in technical computing using only a fairly small number of basic primitives.

When *Mathematica* 1.0 was released, the *New York Times* wrote that "the importance of the program cannot be overlooked", and *Business Week* later ranked *Mathematica* among the ten most important new products of the year. *Mathematica* was also hailed in the technical community as a major intellectual and practical revolution.

At first, *Mathematica*'s impact was felt mainly in the physical sciences, engineering and mathematics. But over the years, *Mathematica* has become important in a remarkably wide range of fields. *Mathematica* is used today throughout the sciences—physical, biological, social and other—and counts many of the world's foremost scientists among its enthusiastic supporters. It has played a crucial role in many important discoveries, and has been the basis for thousands of technical papers. In engineering, *Mathematica* has become a standard tool for both development and production, and by now many of the world's important new products rely at one stage or another in their design on *Mathematica*. In commerce, *Mathematica* has played a significant role in the growth of sophisticated financial modeling, as well as being widely used in many kinds of general planning and analysis. *Mathematica* has also emerged as an important tool in computer science and software development: its language component is widely used as a research, prototyping and interface environment.

The largest part of *Mathematica*'s user community consists of technical professionals. But *Mathematica* is also heavily used in education, and there are now many hundreds of courses—from high school to graduate school—based on it. In addition, with the availability of student versions, *Mathematica* has become an important tool for both technical and non-technical students around the world.

The diversity of *Mathematica*'s user base is striking. It spans all continents, ages from below ten up, and includes for example artists, composers, linguists and lawyers. There are also many hobbyists from all walks of life who use *Mathematica* to further their interests in science, mathematics and computing.

Ever since *Mathematica* was first released, its user base has grown steadily, and by now the total number of users is above a million. *Mathematica* has become a standard in a great many organizations, and it is used today in all of the Fortune 50 companies, all of the 15 major departments of the U.S. government, and all of the 50 largest universities in the world.

At a technical level, *Mathematica* is widely regarded as a major feat of software engineering. It is one of the largest single application programs ever developed, and it contains a vast array of novel algorithms and important technical innovations. Among these innovations is the concept of platform-independent interactive documents known as notebooks. Notebooks have already become the standard for many kinds of courseware and reports, and with the new capabilities added in *Mathematica* 3.0 they are poised to emerge as a general standard for publishing technical documents on the web and elsewhere.

The development of *Mathematica* has been carried out at Wolfram Research by a world-class team led by Stephen Wolfram. The success of *Mathematica* has fueled the continuing growth of Wolfram Research, and has allowed a large community of independent *Mathematica*-related businesses to develop. There are today nearly a hundred specialized commercial packages available for *Mathematica*, as well as several periodicals and more than two hundred books devoted to the system.

Some New Features of *Mathematica* 3.0

The first major new version of *Mathematica* in several years, 3.0 strengthens the core computational capabilities of *Mathematica*, and adds some revolutionary new features. Throughout this book, items that are new are indicated by +■ ; those that are changed are indicated by ~■ . Except as noted in Section A.13, 3.0 is fully compatible with earlier versions.

Numerical Computation

- Adaptive precision control to generate results with guaranteed precision.
- High-performance compilation of list-oriented, procedural and functional numerical operations.
- Optimized algorithms for one- and higher-dimensional interpolation.
- Optimized algorithms for solution of differential equations.
- Solution of boundary value ordinary differential equations, and initial value partial differential equations.
- High-dimensional numerical integration.
- Optimized minimization algorithms.
- LU and Jordan decomposition of matrices.
- Numerical differentiation.
- Automatic comparison and manipulation of exact numeric quantities.
- Support for exact implicitly-defined algebraic numbers.
- Support for interval arithmetic.
- Fully adjustable global numerical precision control model.
- New capabilities for extracting segments of digits in exact and inexact numbers.
- Machine-independent mechanisms for input and output of numbers without loss of precision.

Algebraic Computation

- Enhanced and optimized simplification of algebraic expressions.
- Simplification of expressions involving special functions.
- Built-in functions for transformations on trigonometric expressions.
- Greatly extended indefinite and definite symbolic integration.
- Support for principal values and assumptions on parameters in integrals.
- Greatly extended symbolic sums and products.
- Greatly extended symbolic solution of ordinary and partial differential equations.
- Optimized symbolic linear algebra.
- Enhanced handling of exact numerical quantities.
- Generation and system-wide support for algebraic numbers.
- Highly optimized Gröbner basis reduction.

Mathematical Functions

- Faster evaluation of many special functions.
- Fresnel integrals and hyperbolic sine and cosine integrals.
- Inverse error function, gamma function and beta function.
- Product log function.
- $_pF_q$ generalized hypergeometric functions and Meijer G functions.
- Additional Weierstrass, elliptic and related functions.
- Mathieu functions.
- Stieltjes constants.
- Built-in Fibonacci numbers and polynomials.

Graphics

- Full typesetting capabilities for labels and text in plots.
- Automatic conversions to EPS, TIFF, GIF and other formats.
- Kernel control of animation in notebooks.
- Absolute offset specifications in graphics primitives.
- Direct control of final graphics size, resolution, etc.
- Direct generation of text strings for graphics in various formats.

Programming and Core System

- Faster execution speed and lower memory usage for typical kernel operations.
- Dumping of function definitions for optimized loading.

- Powerful new general symbolic programming functions, including `ReplaceList` and `Split`.
- Pattern-based non-local control flow with `Throw` and `Catch`.
- Separate support for verbatim and held patterns.
- Enhanced control of basic evaluation.
- New functions and enhancements for string manipulation.
- Extensive support for manipulation of non-ASCII characters.

Input and Output

- Support for WYSIWYG fully editable two-dimensional typeset input and output.
- Extended *Mathematica* language incorporating special characters and two-dimensional notation.
- Over 700 special characters for mathematical and other notation.
- Support for traditional math textbook notation for output and heuristic input.
- Top-quality typeset output with advanced adjustable layout rules.
- Complete symbolic language for specifying two-dimensional typeset structures.
- Two-dimensional input and manipulation of arrays and matrices.
- Complete support for international character sets and Unicode.
- TEX conversion with line-breaking information.
- Optimized textual import and export of typeset structures.

Notebook Interface

- Programmable documents based on underlying symbolic representation.
- Symbolic language for specifying user interface operations.
- Customizable palettes that can execute any kernel or front end operation.
- Integrated active elements and hyperlinks in notebooks.
- Separate style environments for screen and printing.
- New style sheets for varied document types.
- Language-based control of all features of text, graphics, cells and notebooks.
- In-line typesetting and graphics embedded in text.
- Enhanced text formatting capabilities including full text justification.

- Integrated customizable notebook-based on-line help with hyperlinks and the full text of this book.
- Fully platform-independent notebook file format.
- Notebook conversion to TEX, HTML and other external formats.
- Option inspector for interactive control of all notebooks and front end properties.
- Keyboard commands for editing and notebook navigation; drag and drop.

System Interface

- Additional kernel directory and file manipulation functions.
- Support for multi-platform external program clusters.
- Optimized *MathLink* external program interface.
- Loopback links for storing expressions in external programs.
- Direct support for arrays in external programs.
- Shared libraries for *MathLink*.
- Uniform layout of system files across all platforms.
- Automatic initialization of kernel and front end functionality as well as documentation for add-ons.
- Support for multi-lingual versions and all standard keyboard character encodings.
- Direct CD-ROM executability.
- TCP-based network license server.
- OLE support under Microsoft Windows.

Standard Add-on Packages

- Manipulating and solving algebraic inequalities.
- Symmetric polynomials.
- Manipulating quaternions and elements of Galois fields.
- Complete integrals and differential invariants of nonlinear PDEs.
- Z transforms.
- Primitive roots for arbitrary algebraic extensions.
- Numerical residue and series computations.
- Data smoothing and filtering.
- Classical and robust multivariate descriptive statistics.
- Linear and nonlinear regression with diagnostics.
- Simplified arithmetic and algebra without complex numbers.
- Full on-line documentation of all packages.

The Role of This Book

The Scope of the Book

This book is intended to be a complete introduction to *Mathematica*. It describes essentially all the capabilities of *Mathematica*, and assumes no prior knowledge of the system.

In most uses of *Mathematica*, you will need to know only a small part of the system. This book is organized to make it easy for you to learn the part you need for a particular calculation. In many cases, for example, you may be able to set up your calculation simply by adapting some appropriate examples from the book.

You should understand, however, that the examples in this book are chosen primarily for their simplicity, rather than to correspond to realistic calculations in particular application areas.

There are many other publications that discuss *Mathematica* from the viewpoint of particular classes of applications. In some cases, you may find it better to read one of these publications first, and read this book only when you need a more general perspective on *Mathematica*.

Mathematica is a system built on a fairly small set of very powerful principles. This book describes those principles, but by no means spells out all of their implications. In particular, while the book describes the elements that go into *Mathematica* programs, it does not give detailed examples of complete programs. For those, you should look at other publications.

The Mathematica System Described in the Book

This book describes the standard *Mathematica* kernel, as it exists on all computers that run *Mathematica*. All supported features of the kernel in *Mathematica* Version 3.0 are covered in this book. Most of the important features of the front end are also discussed.

Mathematica is an open software system that can be customized in a wide variety of ways. It is important to realize that this book covers only the full basic *Mathematica* system. If your system is customized in some way, then it may behave differently from what is described in the book.

The most common form of customization is the addition of various *Mathematica* function definitions. These may come, for example, from loading a *Mathematica* package. Some-times the definitions may actually modify the behavior of functions described in this book. In other cases, the definitions may simply add a collection of new functions that are not described in the book. In certain applications, it may be primarily these new functions that you use, rather than the standard ones described in the book.

This book describes what to do when you interact directly with the standard *Mathematica* kernel and notebook front end. Sometimes, however, you may not be using the standard *Mathematica* system directly. Instead, *Mathematica* may be an embedded component of another system that you are using. This system may for example call on *Mathematica* only for certain computations, and may hide the details of those computations from you. Most of what is in this book will only be useful if you can give explicit input to *Mathematica*. If all of your input is substantially modified by the system you are using, then you must rely on the documentation for that system.

Additional Standard Mathematica Documentation

The following are available in printed form for all standard versions of *Mathematica*, and can be ordered from Wolfram Research:

- *Getting Started with Mathematica*: a booklet describing installation, basic operation, and troubleshooting of *Mathematica* on specific computer systems.

- *Standard Add-on Packages*: a book describing standard add-on packages available for *Mathematica*.

Extensive on-line documentation is included with most versions of *Mathematica*. All such documentation can be accessed from the Help Browser in the *Mathematica* notebook front end.

In addition, the following sources of information are available on the web (note that all of these are available at wolfram.co.uk and wolfram.co.jp as well as wolfram.com):

- http://www.wolfram.com: the main Wolfram Research web site, giving extensive information on *Mathematica* and its applications.

- http://www.wolfram.com/faq: answers to frequently asked questions about *Mathematica*.

- http://www.wolfram.com/book–updates: corrections and updates to this book.

Suggestions about Learning *Mathematica*

Getting Started

As with any other computer system, there are a few points that you need to get straight before you can even start using *Mathematica*. For example, you absolutely must know how to type your input to *Mathematica*. To find out these kinds of basic points, you should read at least the first section of Part 1 in this book.

Once you know the basics, you can begin to get a feeling for *Mathematica* by typing in some examples from this book. Always be sure that you type in exactly what appears in the book—do not change any capitalization, bracketing, etc.

After you have tried a few examples from the book, you should start experimenting for yourself. Change the examples slightly, and see what happens. You should look at each piece of output carefully, and try to understand why it came out as it did.

After you have run through some simple examples, you should be ready to take the next step: learning to go through what is needed to solve a complete problem with *Mathematica*.

Solving a Complete Problem

You will probably find it best to start by picking a specific problem to work on. Pick a problem that you understand well—preferably one whose solution you could easily reproduce by hand. Then go through each step in solving the problem, learning what you need to know about *Mathematica* to do it. Always be ready to experiment with simple cases, and understand the results you get with these, before going back to your original problem.

In going through the steps to solve your problem, you will learn about various specific features of *Mathematica*, typically from sections of Part 1. After you have done a few problems with *Mathematica*, you should get a feeling for many of the basic features of the system.

When you have built up a reasonable knowledge of the features of *Mathematica*, you should go back and learn about the overall structure of the *Mathematica* system. You can do this by systematically reading Part 2 of this book. What you will discover is that many of the features that seemed unrelated actually fit together into a coherent overall structure. Knowing this structure will make it much easier for you to understand and remember the specific features you have already learned.

The Principles of Mathematica

You should not try to learn the overall structure of *Mathematica* too early. Unless you have had broad experience with advanced computer languages or pure mathematics, you will probably find Part 2 difficult to understand at first. You will find the structure and principles it describes difficult to remember, and you will always be wondering why particular aspects of them might be useful. However, if you first get some practical experience with *Mathematica*, you will find the overall structure much easier to grasp. You should realize that the principles on which *Mathematica* is built are very general, and it is usually difficult to understand such general principles before you have seen specific examples.

One of the most important aspects of *Mathematica* is that it applies a fairly small number of principles as widely as possible. This means that even though you have used a particular feature only in a specific situation, the principle on which that feature is based can probably be applied in many other situations. One reason it is so important to understand the underlying principles of *Mathematica* is that by doing so you can leverage your knowledge of specific features into a more general context. As an example, you may first learn about transformation rules in the context of algebraic expressions.

But the basic principle of transformation rules applies to any symbolic expression. Thus you can also use such rules to modify the structure of, say, an expression that represents a *Mathematica* graphics object.

Changing the Way You Work

Learning to use *Mathematica* well involves changing the way you solve problems. When you move from pencil and paper to *Mathematica* the balance of what aspects of problem solving are difficult changes. With pencil and paper, you can often get by with a fairly imprecise initial formulation of your problem. Then when you actually do calculations in solving the problem, you can usually fix up the formulation as you go along. However, the calculations you do have to be fairly simple, and you cannot afford to try out many different cases.

When you use *Mathematica*, on the other hand, the initial formulation of your problem has to be quite precise. However, once you have the formulation, you can easily do many different calculations with it. This means that you can effectively carry out many mathematical experiments on your problem. By looking at the results you get, you can then refine the original formulation of your problem.

There are typically many different ways to formulate a given problem in *Mathematica*. In almost all cases, however, the most direct and simple formulations will be best. The more you can formulate your problem in *Mathematica* from the beginning, the better. Often, in fact, you will find that formulating your problem directly in *Mathematica* is better than first trying to set up a traditional mathematical formulation, say an algebraic one. The main point is that *Mathematica* allows you to express not only traditional mathematical operations, but also algorithmic and structural ones. This greater range of possibilities gives you a better chance of being able to find a direct way to represent your original problem.

Writing Programs

For most of the more sophisticated problems that you want to solve with *Mathematica*, you will have to create *Mathematica* programs. *Mathematica* supports several types of programming, and you have to choose which one to use in each case. It turns out that no single type of programming suits all cases well. As a result, it is very important that you learn several different types of programming.

If you already know a traditional programming language such as BASIC, C, Fortran or Pascal, you will probably find it easiest to learn procedural programming in *Mathematica*, using Do, For and so on. But while almost any *Mathematica* program can, in principle, be written in a procedural way, this is rarely the best approach. In a symbolic system like *Mathematica*, functional and rule-based programming typically yields programs that are more efficient, and easier to understand.

If you find yourself using procedural programming a lot, you should make an active effort to convert at least some of your programs to other types. At first, you may find functional and rule-based programs difficult to understand. But after a while, you will find that their global structure is usually much easier to grasp than procedural programs. And as your experience with *Mathematica* grows over a period of months or years, you will probably find that you write more and more of your programs in non-procedural ways.

Learning the Whole System

As you proceed in using and learning *Mathematica*, it is important to remember that *Mathematica* is a large system. Although after a while you should know all of its basic principles, you may never learn the details of all its features. As a result, even after you have had a great deal of experience with *Mathematica*, you will undoubtedly still find it useful to look through this book. When you do so, you are quite likely to notice features that you never noticed before, but that with your experience, you can now see how to use.

How to Read This Book

If at all possible, you should read this book in conjunction with using an actual *Mathematica* system. When you see examples in the book, you should try them out on your computer.

You can get a basic feeling for what *Mathematica* does by looking at "A Tour of *Mathematica*" on page 1, and the "Graphics Gallery" and "Formula Gallery" at the end of the main text in this book. You may also find it useful to try out examples from the Tour with your own copy of *Mathematica*.

Whatever your background, you should make sure to look at the first three or four sections in Part 1 before you start to use *Mathematica* on your own. These sections describe the basics that you need to know in order to use *Mathematica* at any level.

The remainder of Part 1 shows you how to do many different kinds of computations with *Mathematica*. If you are trying to do a specific calculation, you will often find it sufficient just to look at the sections of Part 1 that discuss the features of *Mathematica* you need to use. A good approach is to try and find examples in the book which are close to what you want to do.

The emphasis in Part 1 is on using the basic functions that are built into *Mathematica* to carry out various different kinds of computations.

Part 2, on the other hand, discusses the basic structure and principles that underlie all of *Mathematica*. Rather than describing a sequence of specific features, Part 2 takes a more global approach. If you want to learn how to create your own *Mathematica* functions, you should read Part 2.

Part 3 is intended for those with more sophisticated mathematical interests and knowledge. It covers the more advanced mathematical features of *Mathematica*, as well as describing some features already mentioned in Part 1 in greater mathematical detail.

Each part of the book is divided into sections and subsections. There are two special kinds of subsections, indicated by the following headings:

- **Advanced Topic**: Advanced material which can be omitted on a first reading.

- **Special Topic**: Material relevant only for certain users or certain computer systems.

The main parts in this book are intended to be pedagogical, and can meaningfully be read in a sequential fashion. The Appendix, however, is intended solely for reference purposes. Once you are familiar with *Mathematica*, you will probably find the list of functions in the Appendix the best place to look up details you need.

About the Examples in This Book

All the examples given in this book were generated by running an actual copy of *Mathematica* Version 3.0. If you have a copy of this version, you should be able to reproduce the examples on your computer as they appear in the book.

There are, however, a few points to watch:

- Until you are familiar with *Mathematica*, make sure to type the input *exactly* as it appears in the book. Do not change any of the capital letters or brackets. Later, you will learn what things you can change. When you start out, however, it is important that you do not make any changes; otherwise you may not get the same results as in the book.

- Never type the prompt $In[n]:=$ that begins each input line. Type only the text that follows this prompt.

- You will see that the lines in each dialog are numbered in sequence. Most subsections in the book contain separate dialogs. To make sure you get exactly what the book says, you should start a new *Mathematica* session each time the book does.

- Some "Special Topic" subsections give examples that may be specific to particular computer systems.

- Any examples that involve random numbers will generally give different results than in the book, since the sequence of random numbers produced by *Mathematica* is different in every session.

- Some examples that use machine-precision arithmetic may come out differently on different computer systems. This is a result of differences in floating-point hardware. If you use arbitrary-precision *Mathematica* numbers, you should not see differences.

- Almost all of the examples show output as it would be generated in StandardForm with a notebook interface to *Mathematica*. Output with a text-based interface will look similar, but not identical.

- Almost all of the examples in this book assume that your computer or terminal uses a standard U.S. ASCII character set. If you cannot find some of the characters you need on your keyboard, or if *Mathematica* prints out different characters than you see in the book, you will need to look at your computer documentation to find the correspondence with the character set you are using. The most common problem is that the dollar sign character (SHIFT-4) may come out as your local currency character.

- If the version of *Mathematica* is more recent than the one used to produce this book, then it is possible that some results you get may be different.

- Most of the examples in "A Tour of *Mathematica*", as well as Parts 1 and 2, are chosen so as to be fairly quick to execute. Assuming you have a machine with a clock speed of over about 100 MHz (and most machines produced in 1995 or later do), then few of the examples should take more than a few seconds to execute. If they do, there is probably something wrong. Section 1.3.12 describes how to stop the calculation.

Outline Table of Contents

Table of Contents

+■ a section new in this edition
~■ a section substantially modified in this edition

Part 2. Principles of *Mathematica*

Part 3.   Advanced Mathematics in *Mathematica*

A Tour of Mathematica

The purpose of this Tour is to show examples of a few of the things that Mathematica can do. The Tour is in no way intended to be complete—it is just a sampling of a few of Mathematica's capabilities. It also concentrates only on general features, and does not address how these features can be applied in particular fields. Nevertheless, by reading through the Tour you should get at least some feeling for the basic Mathematica system.

Sometimes, you may be able to take examples from this Tour and immediately adapt them for your own purposes. But more often, you will have to look at some of Part 1, or at on-line Mathematica documentation, before you embark on serious work with Mathematica. If you do try repeating examples from the Tour, it is very important that you enter them exactly as they appear here. Do not change capitalization, types of brackets, etc.

On most versions of Mathematica, you will be able to find this Tour on line as part of the Mathematica help system. Even if you do not have access to a running copy of Mathematica 3.0, you may still be able to try out the examples in this Tour by visiting *http://www.wolfram.com/tour*.

A Tour of *Mathematica*

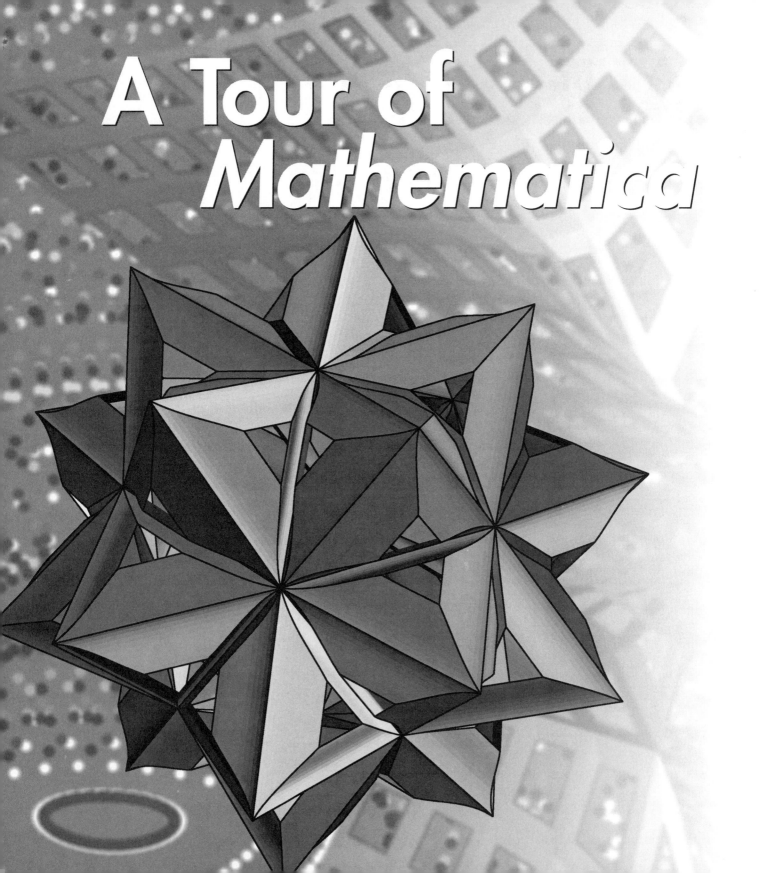

A Tour of *Mathematica*

Mathematica as a Calculator

You can use *Mathematica* just like a calculator: you type
in questions, and *Mathematica* prints back the answers.

*Note: All examples here use
only ordinary keyboard input.
Page 14 shows how to enter
fully formatted input.*

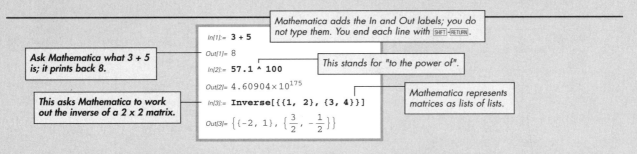

*Mathematica adds the In and Out labels; you do
not type them. You end each line with* SHIFT-RETURN.

In[1]:= **3 + 5**

Out[1]= 8

In[2]:= **57.1 ^ 100**

This stands for "to the power of".

Out[2]= 4.60904×10^{175}

In[3]:= **Inverse[{{1, 2}, {3, 4}}]**

*Mathematica represents
matrices as lists of lists.*

Out[3]= $\left\{ \{-2, 1\}, \left\{ \frac{3}{2}, -\frac{1}{2} \right\} \right\}$

**Ask Mathematica what 3 + 5
is; it prints back 8.**

**This asks Mathematica to work
out the inverse of a 2 x 2 matrix.**

---

*Mathematica can handle formulas
as well as numbers.*

In[1]:= **Integrate[Sqrt[x] Sqrt[1 + x], x]**

*This asks Mathematica to
integrate a simple function.*

Out[1]= $\sqrt{1 + x} \left(\frac{\sqrt{x}}{4} + \frac{x^{3/2}}{2} \right) - \frac{\text{ArcSinh}\left[\sqrt{x}\right]}{4}$

**This asks Mathematica to
solve a quadratic equation.**

In[2]:= **Solve[x^2 + x == a, x]**

This stands for mathematical equality.

Out[2]= $\left\{ \left\{ x \to \frac{1}{2} \left(-1 - \sqrt{1 + 4a} \right) \right\}, \left\{ x \to \frac{1}{2} \left(-1 + \sqrt{1 + 4a} \right) \right\} \right\}$

**The result is a list of rules
for x convenient for use in
other calculations.**

---

*Mathematica can also create two-
and three-dimensional graphics.*

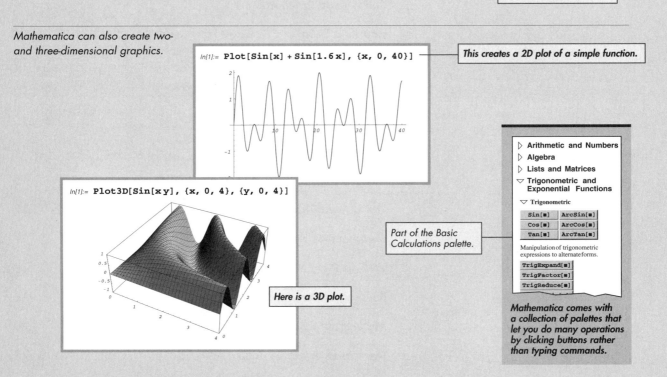

In[1]:= **Plot[Sin[x] + Sin[1.6 x], {x, 0, 40}]**

This creates a 2D plot of a simple function.

In[1]:= **Plot3D[Sin[xy], {x, 0, 4}, {y, 0, 4}]**

Here is a 3D plot.

*Part of the Basic
Calculations palette.*

▷ **Arithmetic and Numbers**
▷ **Algebra**
▷ **Lists and Matrices**
▽ **Trigonometric and
    Exponential Functions**

▽ **Trigonometric**

Sin[■]	ArcSin[■]
Cos[■]	ArcCos[■]
Tan[■]	ArcTan[■]

Manipulation of trigonometric
expressions to alternate forms.

| TrigExpand[■] |
| TrigFactor[■] |
| TrigReduce[■] |

**Mathematica comes with
a collection of palettes that
let you do many operations
by clicking buttons rather
than typing commands.**

Power Computing with *Mathematica*

Even though you can use it as easily as a calculator, *Mathematica* gives you access to immense computational power.

This creates a 100 x 100 matrix of random numbers.

The semicolon tells *Mathematica* not to print the result.

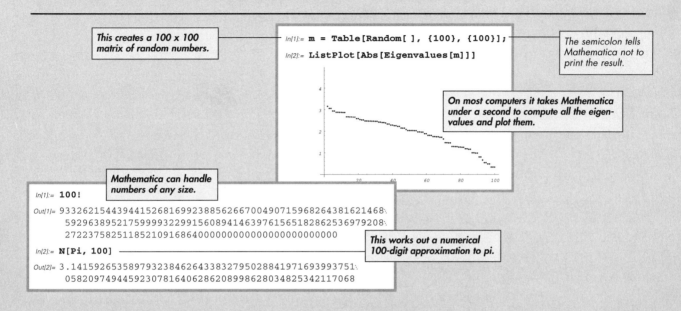

```
In[1]:= m = Table[Random[ ], {100}, {100}];

In[2]:= ListPlot[Abs[Eigenvalues[m]]]
```

On most computers it takes *Mathematica* under a second to compute all the eigenvalues and plot them.

Mathematica can handle numbers of any size.

```
In[1]:= 100!

Out[1]= 9332621544394415268169923885626670049071596826438162146859
        2963895217599993229915608941463976156518286253697920827
        22375825118521091686400000000000000000000000000

In[2]:= N[Pi, 100]

Out[2]= 3.141592653589793238462643383279502884197169399375105820974
        9445923078164062862089986280348253421170668
```

This works out a numerical 100-digit approximation to pi.

Mathematica can work with formulas of any length—solving problems that would have taken years by hand.

This asks *Mathematica* to factor a polynomial.

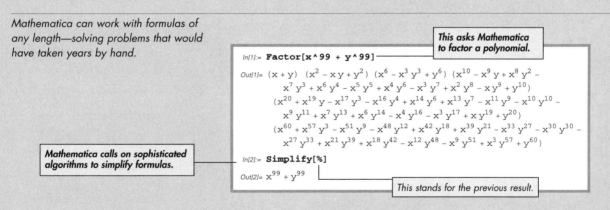

```
In[1]:= Factor[x^99 + y^99]
```

$Out[1]= (x + y) (x^2 - xy + y^2) (x^6 - x^3 y^3 + y^6) (x^{10} - x^9 y + x^8 y^2 - x^7 y^3 + x^6 y^4 - x^5 y^5 + x^4 y^6 - x^3 y^7 + x^2 y^8 - xy^9 + y^{10})$
$(x^{20} + x^{19} y - x^{17} y^3 - x^{16} y^4 + x^{14} y^6 + x^{13} y^7 - x^{11} y^9 - x^{10} y^{10} - x^9 y^{11} + x^7 y^{13} + x^6 y^{14} - x^4 y^{16} - x^3 y^{17} + xy^{19} + y^{20})$
$(x^{60} + x^{57} y^3 - x^{51} y^9 - x^{48} y^{12} + x^{42} y^{18} + x^{39} y^{21} - x^{33} y^{27} - x^{30} y^{30} - x^{27} y^{33} + x^{21} y^{39} + x^{18} y^{42} - x^{12} y^{48} - x^9 y^{51} + x^3 y^{57} + y^{60})$

Mathematica calls on sophisticated algorithms to simplify formulas.

```
In[2]:= Simplify[%]
```
$Out[2]= x^{99} + y^{99}$

This stands for the previous result.

Mathematica has achieved world records—for both size and speed—in many kinds of computations.

This tells *Mathematica* to show only a shortened version of the result.

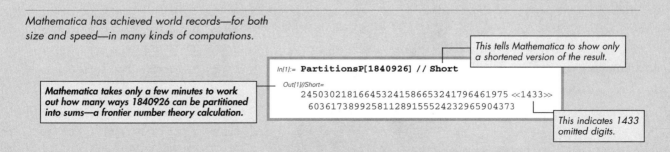

```
In[1]:= PartitionsP[1840926] // Short

Out[1]//Short=
        24503021816645324158665324179646197 5 <<1433>>
        6036173899258112891555242329659043 73
```

Mathematica takes only a few minutes to work out how many ways 1840926 can be partitioned into sums—a frontier number theory calculation.

This indicates 1433 omitted digits.

Accessing Algorithms in *Mathematica*

Whenever you use *Mathematica* you are accessing the
world's largest collection of computational algorithms.

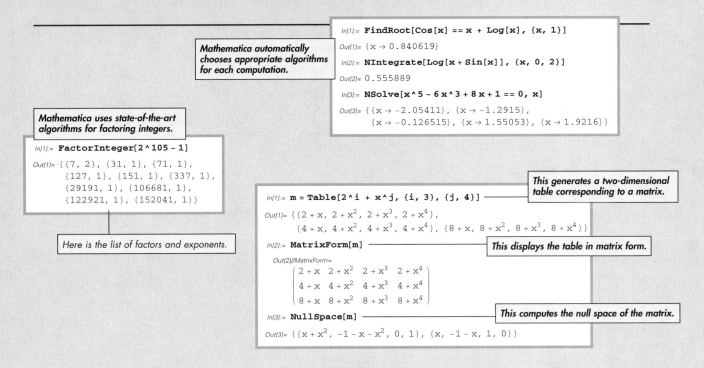

*Mathematica automatically
chooses appropriate algorithms
for each computation.*

```
In[1]:= FindRoot[Cos[x] == x + Log[x], {x, 1}]

Out[1]= {x → 0.840619}

In[2]:= NIntegrate[Log[x + Sin[x]], {x, 0, 2}]

Out[2]= 0.555889

In[3]:= NSolve[x^5 - 6 x^3 + 8 x + 1 == 0, x]

Out[3]= {{x → -2.05411}, {x → -1.2915},
         {x → -0.126515}, {x → 1.55053}, {x → 1.9216}}
```

*Mathematica uses state-of-the-art
algorithms for factoring integers.*

```
In[1]:= FactorInteger[2^105 - 1]

Out[1]= {{7, 2}, {31, 1}, {71, 1},
         {127, 1}, {151, 1}, {337, 1},
         {29191, 1}, {106681, 1},
         {122921, 1}, {152041, 1}}
```

Here is the list of factors and exponents.

*This generates a two-dimensional
table corresponding to a matrix.*

```
In[1]:= m = Table[2^i + x^j, {i, 3}, {j, 4}]

Out[1]= {{2 + x, 2 + x^2, 2 + x^3, 2 + x^4},
         {4 + x, 4 + x^2, 4 + x^3, 4 + x^4}, {8 + x, 8 + x^2, 8 + x^3, 8 + x^4}}

In[2]:= MatrixForm[m]
```

This displays the table in matrix form.

```
Out[2]//MatrixForm=
  ⎛ 2 + x   2 + x^2   2 + x^3   2 + x^4 ⎞
  ⎜ 4 + x   4 + x^2   4 + x^3   4 + x^4 ⎟
  ⎝ 8 + x   8 + x^2   8 + x^3   8 + x^4 ⎠

In[3]:= NullSpace[m]
```

This computes the null space of the matrix.

```
Out[3]= {{x + x^2, -1 - x - x^2, 0, 1}, {x, -1 - x, 1, 0}}
```

*Mathematica can solve differential equations
both symbolically and numerically.*

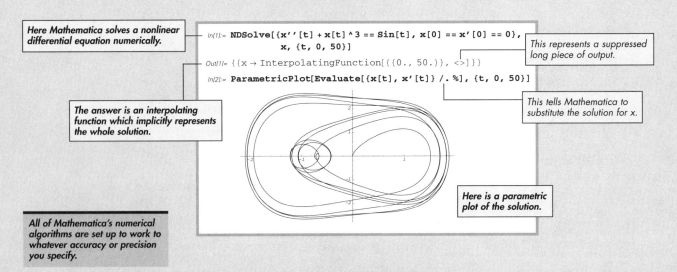

*Here Mathematica solves a nonlinear
differential equation numerically.*

```
In[1]:= NDSolve[{x''[t] + x[t]^3 == Sin[t], x[0] == x'[0] == 0},
        x, {t, 0, 50}]

Out[1]= {{x → InterpolatingFunction[{{0., 50.}}, <>]}}

In[2]:= ParametricPlot[Evaluate[{x[t], x'[t]} /. %], {t, 0, 50}]
```

*This represents a suppressed
long piece of output.*

*This tells Mathematica to
substitute the solution for x.*

*The answer is an interpolating
function which implicitly represents
the whole solution.*

*Here is a parametric
plot of the solution.*

*All of Mathematica's numerical
algorithms are set up to work to
whatever accuracy or precision
you specify.*

Mathematical Knowledge in *Mathematica*

Mathematica incorporates the knowledge from the world's mathematical handbooks—and uses its own revolutionary algorithms to go much further.

Mathematica knows about all the hundreds of special functions in pure and applied mathematics.

> *Mathematica can evaluate special functions with any parameters to any precision.*

In[1]:= **LegendreQ[3, x]**

Out[1]= $\frac{2}{3} - \frac{5 x^2}{2} - \frac{3}{4} x \left(1 - \frac{5 x^2}{3}\right) \text{Log}\left[\frac{1+x}{1-x}\right]$

This stands for $\sqrt{-1}$.

In[2]:= **N[MathieuC[1 + I, 2 I, 3], 50]**

Out[2]= 3.9251311374125198643497646168158379203362717684479 + 1.8988239115433472411052747971439115776785813553761 I

Mathematica is now able to do vastly more integrals than were ever before possible for either humans or computers.

In[1]:= **Integrate[Sqrt[x] ArcTan[x], x]**

Out[1]= $-\frac{4\sqrt{x}}{3} + \frac{1}{3}\sqrt{2} \text{ArcTan}\left[\frac{-\sqrt{2}+2\sqrt{x}}{\sqrt{2}}\right] + \frac{1}{3}\sqrt{2} \text{ArcTan}\left[\frac{\sqrt{2}+2\sqrt{x}}{\sqrt{2}}\right] + \frac{2}{3} x^{3/2} \text{ArcTan}[x] - \frac{\text{Log}\left[-1-x+\sqrt{2x}\right]}{3\sqrt{2}} + \frac{\text{Log}\left[1+x+\sqrt{2x}\right]}{3\sqrt{2}}$

> *Here is a definite integral.*

In[1]:= **Integrate[Log[x] Exp[-x^3], {x, 0, Infinity}]**

Out[1]= $-\frac{1}{54} \text{Gamma}\left[\frac{1}{3}\right] \left(6 \text{EulerGamma} + \sqrt{3}\ \pi + 9 \text{Log}[3]\right)$

In[2]:= **Integrate[Sin[x^2] Exp[-x], {x, 0, Infinity}]**

Out[2]= $-\frac{-\sqrt{\pi} \text{Cos}\left[\frac{1}{4}\right] + \sqrt{2} \text{HypergeometricPFQ}\left[\{1\}, \left\{\frac{3}{4}, \frac{5}{4}\right\}, -\frac{1}{64}\right] - \sqrt{\pi} \text{Sin}\left[\frac{1}{4}\right]}{2\sqrt{2}}$

> *Here is a symbolic sum.*

In[1]:= **Sum[1 / k^6, {k, 1, n}]**

Out[1]= $\frac{\pi^6}{945} - \frac{1}{120} \text{PolyGamma}[5, 1+n]$

> *The results often require special functions.*

> *Mathematica can solve a wide range of ordinary and partial differential equations.*

In[1]:= **DSolve[y''[x] + y'[x] + x y[x] == 0, y[x], x]**

Out[1]= $\left\{\left\{y[x] \to E^{-x/2} \left(\text{AiryBi}\left[(-1)^{1/3}\left(-\frac{1}{4}+x\right)\right] C[1] + \text{AiryAi}\left[(-1)^{1/3}\left(-\frac{1}{4}+x\right)\right] C[2]\right)\right\}\right\}$

> *Mathematica's algorithms can generate a huge range of mathematical results.*

In[1]:= **FullSimplify[Product[Gamma[2 n / 5], {n, 1, 5}]]**

Out[1]= $\frac{12 \pi^2}{25\sqrt{5}}$

In[1]:= **Log[2] < Zeta[3] < Sqrt[2]**

Out[1]= True

In[1]:= **TrigReduce[Cos[x]^4]**

Out[1]= $\frac{1}{8} \left(3 + 4 \text{Cos}[2 x] + \text{Cos}[4 x]\right)$

> *This finds the billionth prime number.*

In[1]:= **Prime[10^9]**

Out[1]= 22801763489

Building Up Computations

Being able to work with formulas lets you easily
integrate all the parts of a computation.

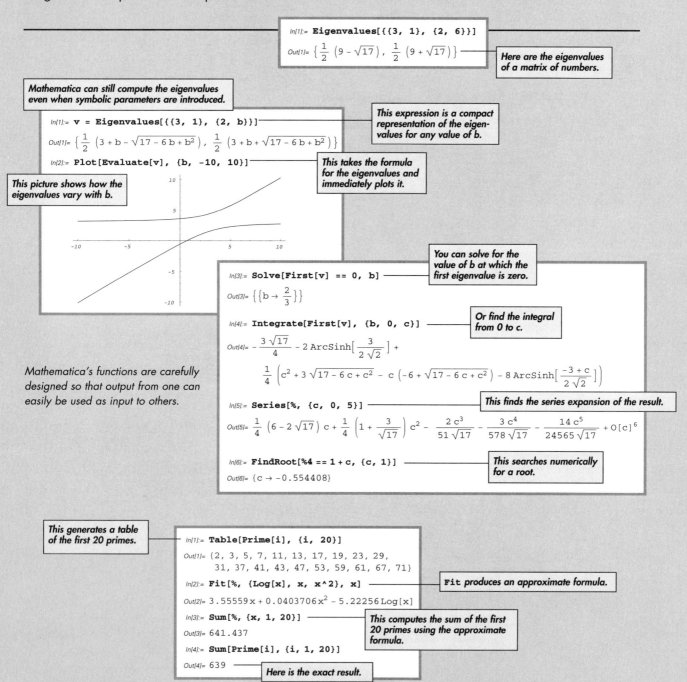

$In[1]:=$ **Eigenvalues[{{3, 1}, {2, 6}}]**

$Out[1]=$ $\left\{ \frac{1}{2} \left(9 - \sqrt{17} \right), \frac{1}{2} \left(9 + \sqrt{17} \right) \right\}$

> Here are the eigenvalues of a matrix of numbers.

> Mathematica can still compute the eigenvalues even when symbolic parameters are introduced.

$In[1]:=$ **v = Eigenvalues[{{3, 1}, {2, b}}]**

$Out[1]=$ $\left\{ \frac{1}{2} \left(3 + b - \sqrt{17 - 6b + b^2} \right), \frac{1}{2} \left(3 + b + \sqrt{17 - 6b + b^2} \right) \right\}$

> This expression is a compact representation of the eigenvalues for any value of b.

$In[2]:=$ **Plot[Evaluate[v], {b, -10, 10}]**

> This takes the formula for the eigenvalues and immediately plots it.

> This picture shows how the eigenvalues vary with b.

> You can solve for the value of b at which the first eigenvalue is zero.

$In[3]:=$ **Solve[First[v] == 0, b]**

$Out[3]=$ $\left\{ \left\{ b \to \frac{2}{3} \right\} \right\}$

$In[4]:=$ **Integrate[First[v], {b, 0, c}]**

> Or find the integral from 0 to c.

$Out[4]=$ $-\frac{3\sqrt{17}}{4} - 2\,\text{ArcSinh}\left[\frac{3}{2\sqrt{2}} \right] +$
$\frac{1}{4} \left(c^2 + 3\sqrt{17 - 6c + c^2} - c\left(-6 + \sqrt{17 - 6c + c^2} \right) - 8\,\text{ArcSinh}\left[\frac{-3 + c}{2\sqrt{2}} \right] \right)$

> Mathematica's functions are carefully designed so that output from one can easily be used as input to others.

$In[5]:=$ **Series[%, {c, 0, 5}]**

> This finds the series expansion of the result.

$Out[5]=$ $\frac{1}{4} \left(6 - 2\sqrt{17} \right) c + \frac{1}{4} \left(1 + \frac{3}{\sqrt{17}} \right) c^2 - \frac{2c^3}{51\sqrt{17}} - \frac{3c^4}{578\sqrt{17}} - \frac{14c^5}{24565\sqrt{17}} + O[c]^6$

$In[6]:=$ **FindRoot[%4 == 1 + c, {c, 1}]**

> This searches numerically for a root.

$Out[6]=$ $\{c \to -0.554408\}$

> This generates a table of the first 20 primes.

$In[1]:=$ **Table[Prime[i], {i, 20}]**

$Out[1]=$ {2, 3, 5, 7, 11, 13, 17, 19, 23, 29,
31, 37, 41, 43, 47, 53, 59, 61, 67, 71}

$In[2]:=$ **Fit[%, {Log[x], x, x^2}, x]**

> Fit produces an approximate formula.

$Out[2]=$ $3.55559x + 0.0403706x^2 - 5.22256\,\text{Log}[x]$

$In[3]:=$ **Sum[%, {x, 1, 20}]**

> This computes the sum of the first 20 primes using the approximate formula.

$Out[3]=$ 641.437

$In[4]:=$ **Sum[Prime[i], {i, 1, 20}]**

$Out[4]=$ 639

> Here is the exact result.

Handling Data

Mathematica lets you import data in any format, then manipulate it using powerful and flexible functions.

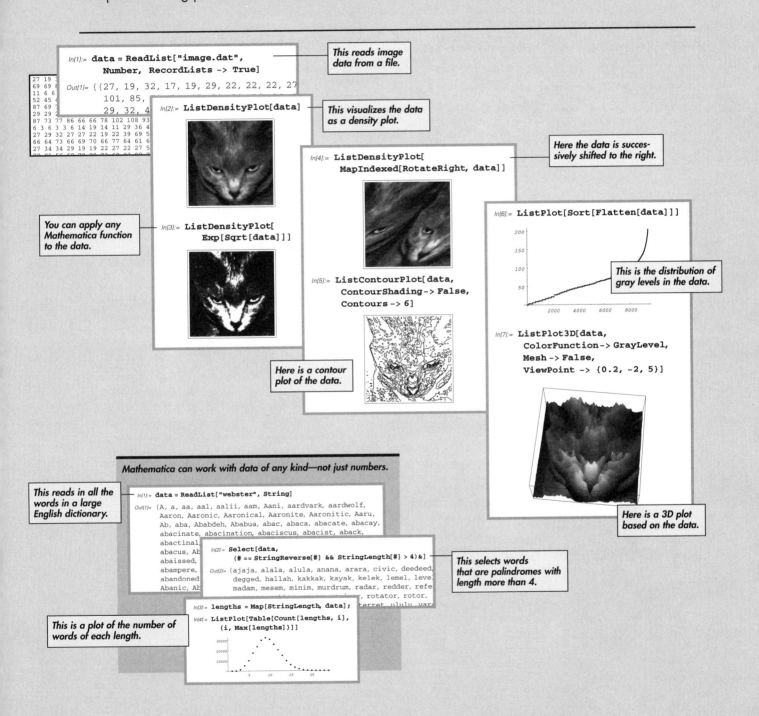

```
In[1]:= data = ReadList["image.dat",
        Number, RecordLists -> True]

Out[1]= {{27, 19, 32, 17, 19, 29, 22, 22, 22, 27
         101, 85,
         29, 32, 4
```

This reads image data from a file.

```
In[2]:= ListDensityPlot[data]
```

This visualizes the data as a density plot.

```
In[4]:= ListDensityPlot[
        MapIndexed[RotateRight, data]]
```

Here the data is successively shifted to the right.

```
In[3]:= ListDensityPlot[
        Exp[Sqrt[data]]]
```

You can apply any Mathematica function to the data.

```
In[5]:= ListContourPlot[data,
        ContourShading-> False,
        Contours -> 6]
```

Here is a contour plot of the data.

```
In[6]:= ListPlot[Sort[Flatten[data]]]
```

This is the distribution of gray levels in the data.

```
In[7]:= ListPlot3D[data,
        ColorFunction-> GrayLevel,
        Mesh -> False,
        ViewPoint -> {0.2, -2, 5}]
```

Here is a 3D plot based on the data.

Mathematica can work with data of any kind—not just numbers.

This reads in all the words in a large English dictionary.

```
In[1]:= data = ReadList["webster", String]

Out[1]= {A, a, aa, aal, aalii, aam, Aani, aardvark, aardwolf,
         Aaron, Aaronic, Aaronical, Aaronite, Aaronitic, Aaru,
         Ab, aba, Ababdeh, Ababua, abac, abaca, abacate, abacay,
         abacinate, abacination, abaciscus, abacist, aback,
         abactinal,
         abacus, Ab
         abaissed,
         abampere,
         abandoned
         Abanic, Ab
```

```
In[2]:= Select[data,
        (# == StringReverse[#] && StringLength[#] > 4)&]

Out[2]= {ajaja, alala, alula, anana, arara, civic, deedeed,
         degged, hallah, kakkak, kayak, kelek, lemel, leve
         madam, mesem, minim, murdrum, radar, redder, refe
                                          rotator, rotor,
                                        terret, ululu, var
```

This selects words that are palindromes with length more than 4.

```
In[3]:= lengths = Map[StringLength, data];
In[4]:= ListPlot[Table[Count[lengths, i],
        {i, Max[lengths]}]]
```

This is a plot of the number of words of each length.

Visualization with *Mathematica*

Mathematica makes it easy to create stunning visual images.

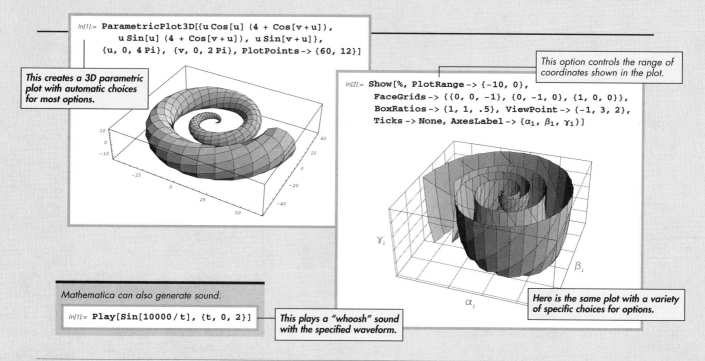

```
In[1]:= ParametricPlot3D[{u Cos[u] (4 + Cos[v + u]),
          u Sin[u] (4 + Cos[v + u]), u Sin[v + u]},
         {u, 0, 4 Pi}, {v, 0, 2 Pi}, PlotPoints -> {60, 12}]
```

This creates a 3D parametric plot with automatic choices for most options.

```
In[2]:= Show[%, PlotRange -> {-10, 0},
          FaceGrids -> {{0, 0, -1}, {0, -1, 0}, {1, 0, 0}},
          BoxRatios -> {1, 1, .5}, ViewPoint -> {-1, 3, 2},
          Ticks -> None, AxesLabel -> {α₁, β₁, γ₁}]
```

This option controls the range of coordinates shown in the plot.

Here is the same plot with a variety of specific choices for options.

Mathematica can also generate sound.

```
In[1]:= Play[Sin[10000 / t], {t, 0, 2}]
```

This plays a "whoosh" sound with the specified waveform.

Mathematica includes primitives from which you can build up 2D and 3D graphics of any complexity.

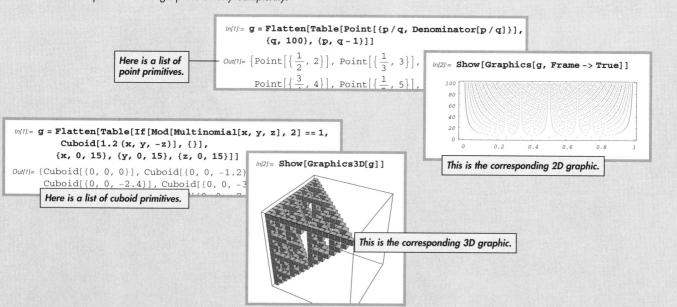

```
In[1]:= g = Flatten[Table[Point[{p / q, Denominator[p / q]}],
          {q, 100}, {p, q - 1}]]
```

Here is a list of point primitives.

$$Out[1]= \left\{ \text{Point}\left[\left\{\frac{1}{2}, 2\right\}\right], \text{Point}\left[\left\{\frac{1}{3}, 3\right\}\right], \right.$$
$$\left. \text{Point}\left[\left\{\frac{3}{4}, 4\right\}\right], \text{Point}\left[\left\{\frac{1}{5}, 5\right\}\right], \right.$$

```
In[2]:= Show[Graphics[g, Frame -> True]]
```

This is the corresponding 2D graphic.

```
In[1]:= g = Flatten[Table[If[Mod[Multinomial[x, y, z], 2] == 1,
          Cuboid[1.2 {x, y, -z}], {}],
         {x, 0, 15}, {y, 0, 15}, {z, 0, 15}]]
```

```
Out[1]= {Cuboid[{0, 0, 0}], Cuboid[{0, 0, -1.2}],
          Cuboid[{0, 0, -2.4}], Cuboid[{0, 0, -3
```

Here is a list of cuboid primitives.

```
In[2]:= Show[Graphics3D[g]]
```

This is the corresponding 3D graphic.

```
In[1]:= Table[Plot3D[Sin[2 x] Sin[2 y] Cos[t],
      {x, 0, Pi}, {y, 0, Pi}, PlotRange -> {-1, 1},
      BoxRatios -> {1, 1, 1}], {t, 0, Pi, Pi / 6}]
```

Mathematica lets you produce animated movies as well as static graphics.

Mathematica has made possible many new kinds of scientific, technical, and artistic images.

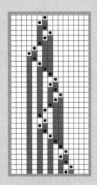

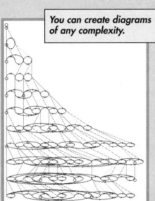

You can create diagrams of any complexity.

You can create representations of abstract mathematical objects.

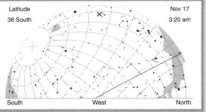

You can visualize structures of any kind.

You can display data in any format.

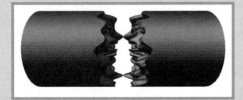

Mathematica **Notebooks**

Every *Mathematica* notebook is a complete interactive document which combines text, tables, graphics, calculations and other elements.

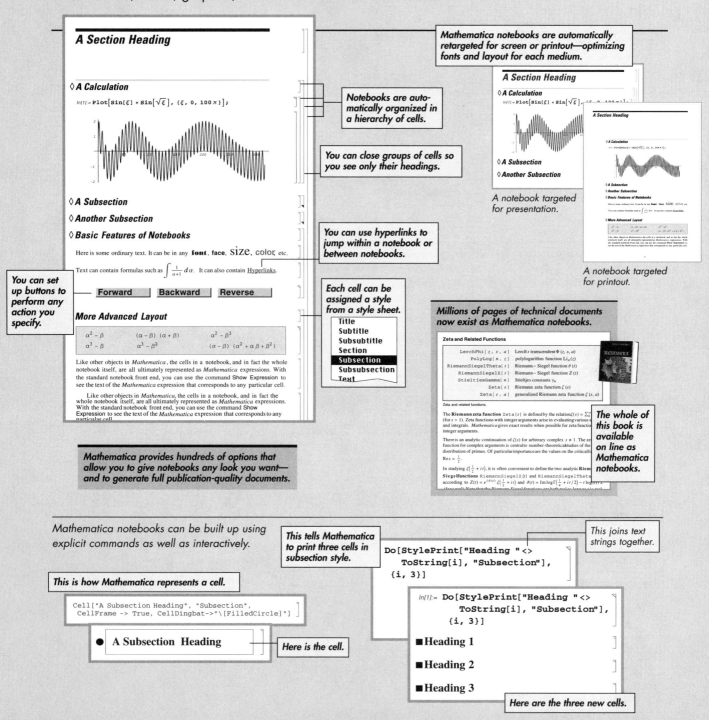

Mathematica notebooks are automatically retargeted for screen or printout—optimizing fonts and layout for each medium.

Notebooks are automatically organized in a hierarchy of cells.

You can close groups of cells so you see only their headings.

You can use hyperlinks to jump within a notebook or between notebooks.

You can set up buttons to perform any action you specify.

Each cell can be assigned a style from a style sheet.

A notebook targeted for presentation.

A notebook targeted for printout.

Millions of pages of technical documents now exist as Mathematica notebooks.

The whole of this book is available on line as *Mathematica* notebooks.

Mathematica provides hundreds of options that allow you to give notebooks any look you want—and to generate full publication-quality documents.

Mathematica notebooks can be built up using explicit commands as well as interactively.

This tells *Mathematica* to print three cells in subsection style.

This joins text strings together.

This is how *Mathematica* represents a cell.

Here is the cell.

Here are the three new cells.

Palettes and Buttons

Palettes and buttons provide a simple but fully customizable point-and-click interface to *Mathematica*.

Mathematica comes with a collection of ready-to-use standard palettes.

The complete Basic Calculations palette is organized as a notebook with palettes inside it.

Part of the standard Basic Calculations palette.

A standard palette for European characters.

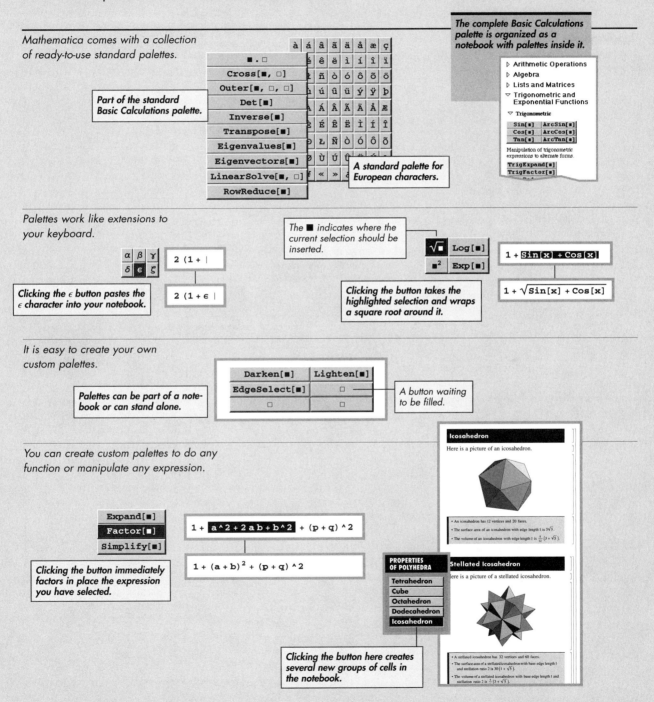

Palettes work like extensions to your keyboard.

Clicking the ϵ button pastes the ϵ character into your notebook.

2 (1 + |

2 (1 + ϵ |

The ■ indicates where the current selection should be inserted.

Clicking the button takes the highlighted selection and wraps a square root around it.

1 + **Sin[x] + Cos[x]**

1 + √Sin[x] + Cos[x]

It is easy to create your own custom palettes.

Palettes can be part of a note-book or can stand alone.

Darken[■] Lighten[■]
EdgeSelect[■] □
□ □

A button waiting to be filled.

You can create custom palettes to do any function or manipulate any expression.

Expand[■]
Factor[■]
Simplify[■]

Clicking the button immediately factors in place the expression you have selected.

1 + **a^2 + 2 a b + b^2** + (p + q) ^ 2

1 + (a + b)² + (p + q) ^ 2

Clicking the button here creates several new groups of cells in the notebook.

Mathematical Notation

Mathematica notebooks fully support standard
mathematical notation—for both output and input.

*Mathematica combines the compactness
of mathematical notation with the precision
of a computer language.*

> Here is an integral input using only
> ordinary keyboard characters.

$In[1]:=$ **Integrate[Log[1 + x] / Sqrt[x], x]**

$Out[1]=$ $-4\sqrt{x} + 4\,\text{ArcTan}\left[\sqrt{x}\right] + 2\sqrt{x}\,\text{Log}[1+x]$

> Here is the same integral entered in two-
> dimensional form with special characters.

> You can enter this form using a
> palette or directly from the keyboard.

$In[1]:=$ $\displaystyle\int \frac{\text{Log}[1+\xi]}{\sqrt{\xi}}\,d\xi$

`:int: Log[1 + :x:]` ESC `/` ESC `2` `:x:` ESC `␣` `:dd: :x:`

> This stands for the ESC key.

> You can use any
> of the notation in this
> palette for input.

$-4\sqrt{\xi} + \left(4\,\text{ArcTan}\left[\sqrt{\xi}\right] + 2\pi\right) + 2\sqrt{\xi}\,\text{Log}[1+\xi]$

> *Mathematica* always lets you edit
> output—and use it again as input.

> *Mathematica* can generate output
> in traditional textbook form.

$In[2]:=$ **TraditionalForm[%]**

$Out[2]//TraditionalForm=$
$4\tan^{-1}\left(\sqrt{\xi}\right) + 2\sqrt{\xi}\,\log(\xi+1) - 4\sqrt{\xi}$

> *Mathematica's StandardForm
> is precise and unambiguous.
> TraditionalForm requires
> heuristics for interpretation.*

> *Mathematica supports over 700 special characters
> with new fonts optimized for both screen and printer.*

Script
Double-struck
Gothic
Greek

> All characters have consistent full names;
> some also have aliases and TEX names.

> *Mathematica produces top-quality
> output for formulas of any size or
> complexity.*

$In[1]:= \displaystyle\sum_{\mu=0}^{\infty} \frac{\varphi^{\mu}\,\text{Cos}\left[\frac{\pi\mu}{4}\right]}{\mu!^2\,(\mu^2+\kappa)\,(\mu^2-\lambda)}$ // **TraditionalForm**

$Out[1]//TraditionalForm=$

$\left(-\lambda\ _1F_2\left(-i\sqrt{\kappa};1,1-i\sqrt{\kappa};e^{-\frac{i\pi}{4}}\varphi\right) - \lambda\ _1F_2\left(i\sqrt{\kappa};1,i\sqrt{\kappa}+1;e^{-\frac{i\pi}{4}}\varphi\right) - \right.$
$\kappa\ _1F_2\left(-\sqrt{\lambda};1,1-\sqrt{\lambda};e^{-\frac{i\pi}{4}}\varphi\right) - \kappa\ _1F_2\left(\sqrt{\lambda};1,\sqrt{\lambda}+1;e^{-\frac{i\pi}{4}}\varphi\right)\right) /$
$4\kappa\left(\sqrt{\kappa}-i\sqrt{\lambda}\right)\left(\sqrt{\kappa}+i\sqrt{\lambda}\right)\lambda +$
$\left(-\lambda\ _1F_2\left(-i\sqrt{\kappa};1,1-i\sqrt{\kappa};e^{\frac{i\pi}{4}}\varphi\right) - \lambda\ _1F_2\left(i\sqrt{\kappa};1,i\sqrt{\kappa}+1;e^{\frac{i\pi}{4}}\varphi\right) - \right.$
$\kappa\ _1F_2\left(-\sqrt{\lambda};1,1-\sqrt{\lambda};e^{\frac{i\pi}{4}}\varphi\right) - \kappa\ _1F_2\left(\sqrt{\lambda};1,\sqrt{\lambda}+1;e^{\frac{i\pi}{4}}\varphi\right)\right) /$

> *Mathematica makes it easy to
> work with abstract notation.*

$In[1]:=$ **Table**$\left[\mathcal{G} \diamond \overline{\alpha_i \oplus \beta_i} \Longrightarrow \genfrac{}{}{0pt}{}{3-i}{i}, \{i, 3\}\right]$

$Out[1]= \left\{\mathcal{G} \diamond \overline{\alpha_1 \oplus \beta_1} \Longrightarrow \genfrac{}{}{0pt}{}{2}{1},\ \mathcal{G} \diamond \overline{\alpha_2 \oplus \beta_2} \Longrightarrow \genfrac{}{}{0pt}{}{1}{2},\ \mathcal{G} \diamond \overline{\alpha_3 \oplus \beta_3} \Longrightarrow \genfrac{}{}{0pt}{}{0}{3}\right\}$

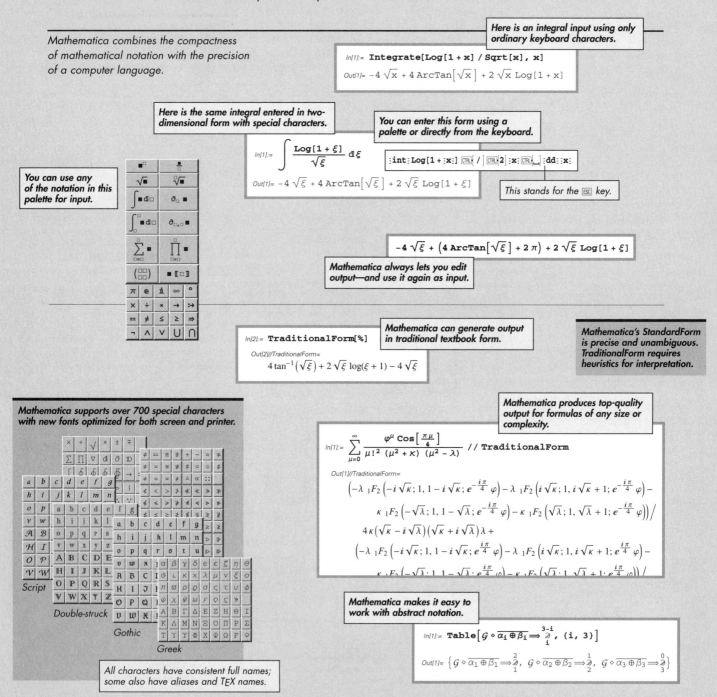

Mathematica and Your Computing Environment

Mathematica runs compatibly across all major computer systems, and lets you exchange data in many standard formats.

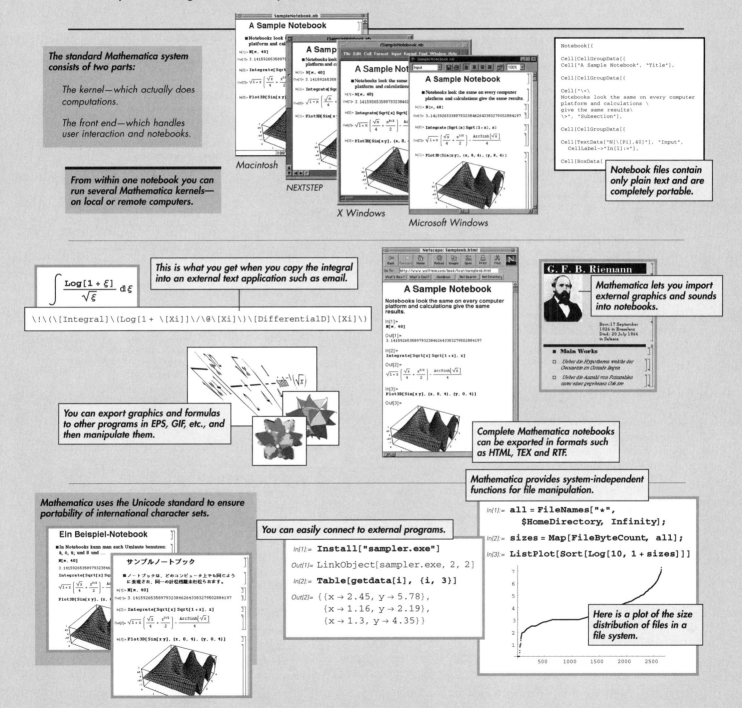

The standard *Mathematica* system consists of two parts:

The kernel—which actually does computations.

The front end—which handles user interaction and notebooks.

From within one notebook you can run several *Mathematica* kernels— on local or remote computers.

Macintosh

NEXTSTEP

X Windows

Microsoft Windows

Notebook files contain only plain text and are completely portable.

This is what you get when you copy the integral into an external text application such as email.

You can export graphics and formulas to other programs in EPS, GIF, etc., and then manipulate them.

Complete Mathematica notebooks can be exported in formats such as HTML, TEX and RTF.

G. F. B. Riemann

Mathematica lets you import external graphics and sounds into notebooks.

Mathematica uses the Unicode standard to ensure portability of international character sets.

Ein Beispiel-Notebook

サンプルノートブック

You can easily connect to external programs.

Mathematica provides system-independent functions for file manipulation.

Here is a plot of the size distribution of files in a file system.

The Unifying Idea of *Mathematica*

Mathematica is built on the powerful unifying idea that
everything can be represented as a symbolic expression.

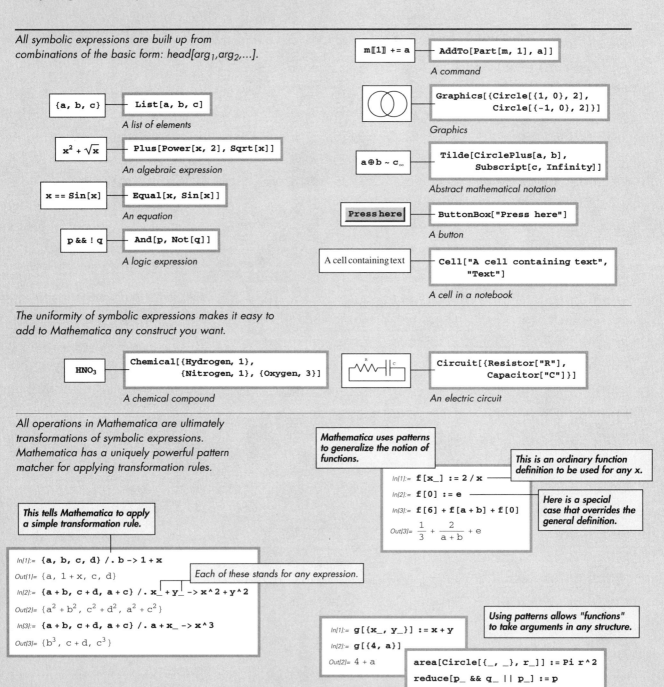

All symbolic expressions are built up from
combinations of the basic form: *head[arg₁,arg₂,...].*

`{a, b, c}` → `List[a, b, c]`	

A list of elements

`x² + √x` → `Plus[Power[x, 2], Sqrt[x]]`

An algebraic expression

`x == Sin[x]` → `Equal[x, Sin[x]]`

An equation

`p && ! q` → `And[p, Not[q]]`

A logic expression

`m[[1]] += a` → `AddTo[Part[m, 1], a]]`

A command

→ `Graphics[{Circle[{1, 0}, 2],`
`        Circle[{-1, 0}, 2]}]`

Graphics

`a⊕b ~ c∞` → `Tilde[CirclePlus[a, b],`
`        Subscript[c, Infinity]]`

Abstract mathematical notation

`Press here` → `ButtonBox["Press here"]`

A button

`A cell containing text` → `Cell["A cell containing text",`
`        "Text"]`

A cell in a notebook

The uniformity of symbolic expressions makes it easy to
add to *Mathematica* any construct you want.

`HNO₃` → `Chemical[{Hydrogen, 1},`
`        {Nitrogen, 1}, {Oxygen, 3}]`

A chemical compound

→ `Circuit[{Resistor["R"],`
`        Capacitor["C"]}]`

An electric circuit

All operations in *Mathematica* are ultimately
transformations of symbolic expressions.
Mathematica has a uniquely powerful pattern
matcher for applying transformation rules.

**Mathematica uses patterns
to generalize the notion of
functions.**

**This is an ordinary function
definition to be used for any x.**

In[1]:= `f[x_] := 2 / x`

In[2]:= `f[0] := e`

In[3]:= `f[6] + f[a + b] + f[0]`

**Here is a special
case that overrides the
general definition.**

Out[3]= $\dfrac{1}{3} + \dfrac{2}{a + b} + e$

**This tells Mathematica to apply
a simple transformation rule.**

In[1]:= `{a, b, c, d} /. b -> 1 + x`

Out[1]= {a, 1 + x, c, d}

Each of these stands for any expression.

In[2]:= `{a + b, c + d, a + c} /. x_ + y_ -> x ^ 2 + y ^ 2`

Out[2]= {a² + b², c² + d², a² + c²}

In[3]:= `{a + b, c + d, a + c} /. a + x_ -> x ^ 3`

Out[3]= {b³, c + d, c³}

**Using patterns allows "functions"
to take arguments in any structure.**

In[1]:= `g[{x_, y_}] := x + y`

In[2]:= `g[{4, a}]`

Out[2]= 4 + a

`area[Circle[{_, _}, r_]] := Pi r^2`

`reduce[p_ && q_ || p_] := p`

Mathematica as a Programming Language

Mathematica is an unprecedentedly flexible and intuitive programming language.

Mathematica incorporates a range of programming paradigms—so you can write every program in its most natural way.

```
In[1]:= z = a;
        Do[Print[z *= z + i], {i, 3}]
        a (1 + a)
        a (1 + a) (2 + a (1 + a))
        a (1 + a) (2 + a (1 + a)) (3 + a (1 + a) (2 + a (1 + a)))
```

Procedural programming

```
In[1]:= 1 + {a, b, c}^2
Out[1]= {1 + a^2, 1 + b^2, 1 + c^2}
In[2]:= Table[i^j, {i, 4}, {j, i}]
Out[2]= {{1}, {2, 4}, {3, 9, 27}, {4, 16, 64, 256}}
In[3]:= Flatten[%]
Out[3]= {1, 2, 4, 3, 9, 27, 4, 16, 64, 256}
In[4]:= Partition[%, 2]
Out[4]= {{1, 2}, {4, 3}, {9, 27}, {4, 16}, {64, 256}}
```

Many operations are automatically threaded over lists.

This flattens out sublists.

This partitions into sublists of length 2.

List-based programming

```
In[1]:= NestList[f, x, 4]
Out[1]= {x, f[x], f[f[x]], f[f[f[x]]], f[f[f[f[x]]]]}
In[2]:= NestList[(1 + #)^2 &, x, 3]
Out[2]= {x, (1 + x)^2, (1 + (1 + x)^2)^2, (1 + (1 + (1 + x)^2)^2)^2}
```

This is a pure function.

Functional programming

```
In[1]:= p[x_ + y_] := p[x] + p[y]
In[2]:= p[a + b + c]
Out[2]= p[a] + p[b] + p[c]
In[3]:= s[{x__, a_, y__}, a_] := {a, x, x, y, y}
In[4]:= s[{1, 2, 3, 4, 5, 6}, 4]
Out[4]= {4, 1, 2, 3, 1, 2, 3, 5, 6, 5, 6}
```

This stands for any sequence of expressions.

Rule-based programming

```
In[1]:= StringReplace["aababbaabaababa ba",
           {"aa" -> "AAA", "ba" -> "V"}]
Out[1]= AAAVbVaVaVVV
```

String-based programming

```
h /: h[x_] + h[y_] := hplus[x, y]
h /: p[h[x_], x_] := hp[x]
h /: f_[h[x_]] := fh[f, x]
```

This associates the definition with the object h.

Here are three definitions to be associated with the object h.

Object-oriented programming

```
f = Factorial
f[n_] := n!
f[n_] := Gamma[n - 1]
f[n_] := n f[n - 1] ; f[1] = 1
f[n_] := Product[i, {i, n}]
f[n_] := Module[{t = 1},
  Do[t = t*i, {i, n}]; t]
f[n_] := Module[{t = 1, i},
  For[i = 1, i <= n, i++, t *= i]; t]
f[n_] := Apply[Times, Range[n]]
f[n_] := Fold[Times, 1, Range[n]]
f[n_] := If[n == 1, 1, n f[n-1]]
f = If[#1 == 1, 1, #1 #0[#1 - 1]]&
f[n_] := Fold[#2[#1]&, 1,
  Array[Function[t, #t]&, n]]
```

A dozen definitions of the factorial function

Mathematica gives you the flexibility to write programs in many different styles.

```
In[1]:= Position[{1, 2, 3, 4, 5} / 2, _Integer]
Out[1]= {{2}, {4}}
In[2]:= MapIndexed[Power, {a, b, c, d}]
Out[2]= {{a}, {b^2}, {c^3}, {d^4}}
In[3]:= FixedPointList[If[EvenQ[#], # / 2, #]&, 10^5]
Out[3]= {100000, 50000, 25000, 12500, 6250, 3125, 3125}
In[4]:= ReplaceList[{a, b, c, d, e},
           {x__, y__} -> {{x}, {y}}]
Out[4]= {{{a}, {b, c, d, e}}, {{a, b}, {c, d, e}},
        {{a, b, c}, {d, e}}, {{a, b, c, d}, {e}}}
```

Many of Mathematica's most powerful functions mix different programming paradigms.

Mixed programming paradigms

Writing Programs in *Mathematica*

Mathematica's high-level programming constructs let you build
sophisticated programs more quickly than ever before.

Single-line *Mathematica* programs can
perform complex operations. This one
produces a one-dimensional random walk.

```
RandomWalk[n_] := NestList[(# + (-1)^Random[Integer])&, 0, n]
```

In[2]:= `ListPlot[RandomWalk[200], PlotJoined -> True]`

Here is a plot of a
200-step random walk.

The directness of *Mathematica* programs makes
them easy to generalize. This one produces a
random walk in d dimensions.

```
RandomWalk[n_, d_] := NestList[
    (# + (-1)^Table[Random[Integer], {d}])&, Table[0, {d}], n]
```

In[2]:= `Show[Graphics3D[
            Line[RandomWalk[1000, 3]]]]`

Here is a plot of a
3D random walk.

Here is a direct program for a step
in the Life cellular automaton.

```
LifeStep[a_List] :=
  MapThread[If[(#1 == 1 && #2 == 4) || #2 == 3, 1, 0]&,
    {a, Sum[RotateLeft[a, {i, j}], {i, -1, 1}, {j, -1, 1}]}, 2]
```

```
LifeStep[list_] :=
  With[{u = Split[Sort[Flatten[Outer[Plus, list, N9], 1]]]},
    Union[Cases[u, {x_, _, _} -> x],
      Intersection[Cases[u, {x_, _, _, _} -> x], list]]]
N9 = Flatten[Array[List, {3, 3}, -1], 1] ;
```

Mathematica's rich structure also makes it easy to
implement this alternative highly optimized algorithm.

Mathematica makes it easy to build
up programs from components.

```
CenterList[n_Integer] :=
  ReplacePart[Table[0, {n}], 1, Ceiling[n / 2]]

ElementaryRule[num_Integer] :=
        IntegerDigits[num, 2, 8]

CAStep[rule_List, a_List] := rule[[
    8 - (RotateLeft[a] + 2 (a + 2 RotateRight[a]))]]

CAEvolveList[rule_List, init_List, t_Integer] :=
  NestList[CAStep[rule, #]&, init, t]

CAGraphics[history_List] :=
  Graphics[Raster[1 - Reverse[history]],
    AspectRatio -> Automatic]
```

Mathematica is a uniquely
scalable language—suitable
for programs of any size.

In[6]:= `Show[CAGraphics[CAEvolveList[
            ElementaryRule[30],
            CenterList[101], 50]]]`

Mathematica has a compiler
for optimizing programs that
work with lists and numbers.

```
Impedance[Resistor[r_], ω_] := r
Impedance[Capacitor[c_], ω_] := 1/(j ω c)
Impedance[Inductor[l_], ω_] := j ω l
Impedance[SeriesElement[e_], ω_] :=
  Apply[Plus, Map[Impedance[#, ω]&, e]]
Impedance[ParallelElement[e_], ω_] :=
  1 / Apply[Plus, 1 / Map[Impedance[#, ω]&, e]]
```

```
g[k_] := 1 + FixedPoint[N[1 / (1 + #), k]&, 1]
g[k_] := FixedPoint[N[Sqrt[1 + #], k]&, 1]
```

Mathematica programs provide
unprecedentedly clear ways to
express algorithms. Both of these
programs approximate the Golden
Ratio to k digits.

```
FareySequence[q_] :=
  Apply[Union, Array[Range[# - 1] / #&, q]]

TransferMatrix[α_, ξ_, p_] :=
  {{ξ + If[1 - α ≤ Mod[p α, 1] < 1, 0, -1], 1}, {1, 0}}

TransferMatrixList[α_, ξ_] :=
  Table[TransferMatrix[α, ξ, p],
    {p, 0, Denominator[α] - 1}]

TransferMatrixProduct[α_, ξ_] :=
  Fold[Expand[Dot[##]]&,
    TransferMatrixList[α,

EnergyPolynomial[α_, ξ_] :=
  Transpose[TransferMatri

Spectrum[α_, ξ_] := ξ /. N
  EnergyPolynomial[α, ξ]
```

In[6]:= `Impedance[SeriesElement[Table[ParallelElement[
            Table[SeriesElement[{Resistor[R_n]}], {n}]],
            {n, 1, 4}]], ω] // Simplify`

Out[6]= $R_1 + \frac{1}{12} (6 R_2 + 4 R_3 + 3 R_4)$

Mathematica programs
are often a direct translation
of material in textbooks.

In[8]:= `Show[Graphics[
            SpectrumData /@
            FareySequence[20]]]`

Mathematica programs can mix
numerical, symbolic and graphics
operations. This short program solves
a sophisticated quantum model.

```
Ω[n_] := Apply[Plus, Map[Last, FactorInteger[n]]]
μ[n_] := MoebiusMu[n]
```

$$p[x_] := -\sum_{k=1}^{\lfloor Log[2,x] \rfloor} \mu[k] \sum_{n=2}^{\lfloor x^{1/k} \rfloor} \mu[n] \, \Omega[n] \left\lfloor \frac{x^{1/k}}{n} \right\rfloor \; /; x > 0$$

Mathematica programs allow a
unique combination of mathematical
and computational notation.

Building Systems with *Mathematica*

Mathematica has everything you need to create complete systems for technical and non-technical applications.

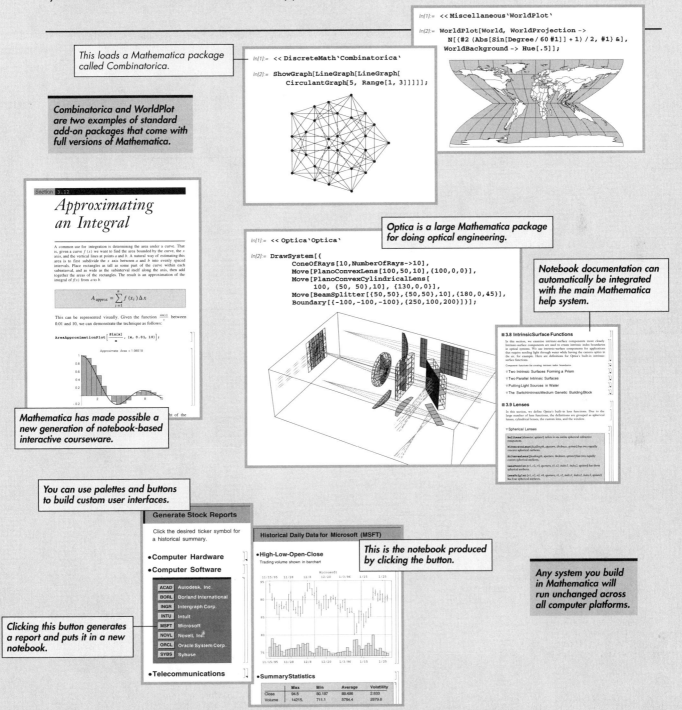

This loads a *Mathematica* package called Combinatorica.

```
In[1]:= << DiscreteMath`Combinatorica`

In[2]:= ShowGraph[LineGraph[LineGraph[
          CirculantGraph[5, Range[1, 3]]]]];
```

```
In[1]:= << Miscellaneous`WorldPlot`

In[2]:= WorldPlot[World, WorldProjection ->
          N[{#2 (Abs[Sin[Degree / 60 #1]] + 1) / 2, #1} &],
          WorldBackground -> Hue[.5]];
```

Combinatorica and WorldPlot are two examples of standard add-on packages that come with full versions of *Mathematica*.

Section 3.12

Approximating an Integral

A common use for integration is determining the area under a curve. That is, given a curve $f(x)$ we want to find the area bounded by the curve, the x axis, and the vertical lines at points a and b. A natural way of estimating this area is to first subdivide the x axis between a and b into evenly spaced intervals. Place rectangles as tall as some part of the curve within each subinterval, and as wide as the subinterval itself along the axis, then add together the areas of the rectangles. The result is an approximation of the integral of $f(x)$ from a to b.

$$A_{approx} = \sum_{i=1}^{n} f(x_i) \Delta x$$

This can be represented visually. Given the function $\frac{\sin[x]}{x}$ between 0.01 and 10, we can demonstrate the technique as follows:

```
AreaApproximationPlot[Sin[x]/x, {x, 0.01, 10}];
```

Approximate Area = 1.98518

Mathematica has made possible a new generation of notebook-based interactive courseware.

Optica is a large *Mathematica* package for doing optical engineering.

```
In[1]:= << Optica`Optica`

In[2]:= DrawSystem[{
          ConeOfRays[10,NumberOfRays->10],
          Move[PlanoConvexLens[100,50,10],{100,0,0}],
          Move[PlanoConvexCylindricalLens[
              100, {50, 50},10], {130,0,0}],
          Move[BeamSplitter[{50,50},{50,50},10],{180,0,45}],
          Boundary[{-100,-100,-100},{250,100,200}]}];
```

Notebook documentation can automatically be integrated with the main *Mathematica* help system.

3.8 IntrinsicSurface Functions

In this section, we examine intrinsic-surface components more closely. Intrinsic-surface components are used to create intrinsic index boundaries in optical systems. We use intrinsic-surface components for applications that require sending light through water while having the camera optics in the air, for example. Here are definitions for Optica's built-in intrinsic-surface functions.

Component functions for creating intrinsic index boundaries

▽ Two Intrinsic Surfaces Forming a Prism
▽ Two Parallel Intrinsic Surfaces
▽ Putting Light Sources in Water
▽ The SwitchIntrinsicMedium Genetic Building Block

3.9 Lenses

In this section, we define Optica's built-in lens functions. Due to the large number of lens functions, the definitions are grouped as spherical lenses, cylindrical lenses, the custom lens, and the window.

▽ Spherical Lenses

You can use palettes and buttons to build custom user interfaces.

Generate Stock Reports

Click the desired ticker symbol for a historical summary.

- •Computer Hardware
- •Computer Software

ACAD	Autodesk, Inc.
BORL	Borland International
INGR	Intergraph Corp.
INTU	Intuit
MSFT	Microsoft
NOVL	Novell, Inc.
ORCL	Oracle System Corp.
SYBS	Sybase

- •Telecommunications

Historical Daily Data for Microsoft (MSFT)

•High-Low-Open-Close
Trading volume shown in barchart

This is the notebook produced by clicking the button.

Clicking this button generates a report and puts it in a new notebook.

•SummaryStatistics

	Max	Min	Average	Volatility
Close	94.5	80.187	88.486	2.833
Volume	14215.	711.1	5784.4	2879.6

Any system you build in *Mathematica* will run unchanged across all computer platforms.

Mathematica as a Software Component

Mathematica has a modular architecture that makes
it easy to use as a highly powerful software component.

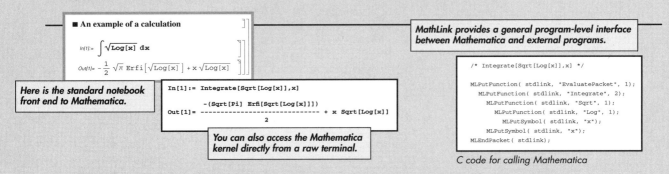

■ An example of a calculation

$In[1]:= \int \sqrt{\text{Log}[x]}\, dx$

$Out[1]= -\dfrac{1}{2}\sqrt{\pi}\ \text{Erfi}\left[\sqrt{\text{Log}[x]}\,\right] + x\sqrt{\text{Log}[x]}$

Here is the standard notebook front end to *Mathematica*.

```
In[1]:= Integrate[Sqrt[Log[x]],x]

               -(Sqrt[Pi]  Erfi[Sqrt[Log[x]]])
Out[1]= ----------------------------------- + x Sqrt[Log[x]]
                        2
```

You can also access the *Mathematica* kernel directly from a raw terminal.

MathLink provides a general program-level interface between *Mathematica* and external programs.

```
/* Integrate[Sqrt[Log[x]],x] */

MLPutFunction( stdlink, "EvaluatePacket", 1);
  MLPutFunction( stdlink, "Integrate", 2);
    MLPutFunction( stdlink, "Sqrt", 1);
      MLPutFunction( stdlink, "Log", 1);
        MLPutSymbol( stdlink, "x");
      MLPutSymbol( stdlink, "x");
MLEndPacket( stdlink);
```

C code for calling *Mathematica*

You can use MathLink to access the *Mathematica*
kernel from many kinds of programs.

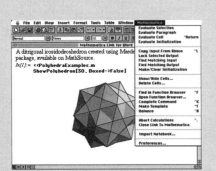

Microsoft Word front end to *Mathematica*

A web site that calls *Mathematica*

Microsoft Excel linked to *Mathematica*

MathLink can also be used to access other
programs from within the *Mathematica* kernel.

```
In[12]:= Map[LinkWrite[#,
          EvaluatePacket[Unevaluated[$System]]]&,
        links];
In[13]:= Map[First[LinkRead[#]], links]
Out[13]= {MicrosoftWindows95,
         Power Macintosh, IBM RISC System / 6000,
         HP - UX PA - RISC, NEXTSTEP Intel,
         DEC OSF / 1 AXP, Li
```

You can use MathLink to communicate between *Mathematica* kernels on different computers across a network.

```
In[1]:= Install["anneal"];
In[2]:= TSPTour[Table[Random[ ], {100}, {2}]]
Out[2]= {10, 7, 34, 30, 46, 40, 43, 38, 65, 57, 28, 23, 8
        78, 94, 6, 92, 32, 18, 26, 98, 56, 31, 97, 37, 4
        27, 49, 11, 84, 44, 96, 16, 76, 82, 68, 55, 36,
        52, 29, 95, 67, 79, 21, 59, 13, 1, 17, 73, 5, 71
        63, 81, 48, 2, 99, 88, 89,
        85, 9, 86, 33, 41, 58, 64,
        60, 66, 22, 50, 69, 72, 61,
        8, 90, 35, 74, 47, 39, 14,
```

Link to a C subroutine library

```
:Begin:
:Function:     anneal
:Pattern:      TSPTour[r:{{_, _}..}]
:Arguments:    {First[Transpose[r]], Last[Transpose[r]],
               Length[r], Range[Length[r]]}
:ArgumentTypes: {RealList, RealList, Integer, IntegerList}
:ReturnType:   Manual
:End:
```

MathLink allows you to set up templates to specify how external programs should be called.

```
ParametricPlot3D[
  {(2 + Cos[u/2] Sin[v] - Sin[u/2] Sin[2v]) Cos[
   (2 + Cos[u/2] Sin[v] - Sin[u/2] Sin[2v]) Sin[
   Sin[u/2] Sin[v] + Cos[u/2] Sin[2v
  {v, 0, 2 Pi}, {u, 0, 2 Pi},
```

Link to a photorealistic renderer

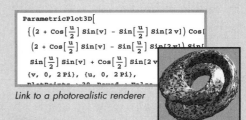

The World of *Mathematica*

With over a million users worldwide, a vast array of
Mathematica products and services now exists.

CALCULUS&*Mathematica*

There are now hundreds
of books in over a
dozen languages about
Mathematica.

Several periodicals
are also devoted to
Mathematica.

There is a growing library of professional
applications based on Mathematica.

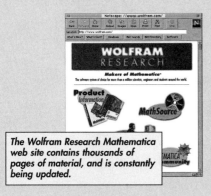

The Wolfram Research Mathematica
web site contains thousands of
pages of material, and is constantly
being updated.

Wolfram Research's MathSource is a
vast repository of Mathematica material.

Hundreds of courses
have been developed
in Mathematica.

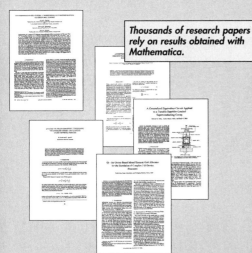

Thousands of research papers
rely on results obtained with
Mathematica.

A vast range of products use
Mathematica in their development or implementation.

Part 1

This part gives a self-contained introduction to Mathematica, concentrating on using Mathematica as an interactive problem-solving system.

When you have read this part, you should have sufficient knowledge of Mathematica to tackle many kinds of practical problems.

You should realize, however, that what is discussed in this part is in many respects just the surface of Mathematica. Underlying all the various features and capabilities that are discussed, there are powerful and general principles. These principles are discussed in Part 2. To get the most out of Mathematica, you will need to understand them.

This part does not assume that you have used a computer before. In addition, most of the material in it requires no knowledge of mathematics beyond high-school level. The more advanced mathematical aspects of Mathematica are discussed in Part 3 of this book.

Part 1

A Practical Introduction to *Mathematica*

1.0 Running *Mathematica*

To find out how to install and run *Mathematica* you should read the documentation that came with your copy of *Mathematica*. The details differ from one computer system to another, and are affected by various kinds of customization that can be done on *Mathematica*. Nevertheless, this section outlines two common cases.

Note that although the details of running *Mathematica* differ from one computer system to another, the structure of *Mathematica* calculations is the same in all cases. You enter input, then *Mathematica* processes it, and returns a result.

■ 1.0.1 Notebook Interfaces

double-click the *Mathematica* icon	a typical graphical action for starting *Mathematica*
mathematica	the operating system command to start *Mathematica*
text ending with SHIFT-RETURN	input for *Mathematica* (SHIFT-ENTER on some keyboards)
choose the Quit menu item	exiting *Mathematica*

Running *Mathematica* with a notebook interface.

On most computer systems, *Mathematica* supports a "notebook" interface in which you interact with *Mathematica* by creating interactive documents.

If you use your computer via a purely graphical interface, you will typically double-click the *Mathematica* icon to start *Mathematica*. If you use your computer via a textually based operating system, you will typically type the command mathematica to start *Mathematica*.

When *Mathematica* starts up, it usually gives you a blank notebook. You enter *Mathematica* input into the notebook, then type SHIFT-RETURN to make *Mathematica* process your input. (To type SHIFT-RETURN, hold down the SHIFT key, then press RETURN.) You can use the standard editing features of your graphical interface to prepare your input, which may go on for several lines. SHIFT-RETURN tells *Mathematica* that you have finished your input.

After you send *Mathematica* input from your notebook, *Mathematica* will label your input with *In[n]:=*. It labels the corresponding output *Out[n]=*.

You type 2 + 2, then end your input with SHIFT-RETURN. *Mathematica* processes the input, then adds the input label *In[1]:=*, and gives the output.

Throughout this book, "dialogs" with *Mathematica* are shown in the following way:

With a notebook interface, you just type in 2 + 2. *Mathematica* then adds the label *In[1]:=*, and prints the result.

In[1]:= 2 + 2

Out[1]= 4

Page xv discusses some important details about reproducing the dialogs on your computer system. Section 1.3 gives more information about *Mathematica* notebooks.

You should realize that notebooks are part of the "front end" to *Mathematica*. The *Mathematica* kernel which actually performs computations may be run either on the same computer as the front end, or on another computer connected via some kind of network or line. In most cases, the kernel is not even started until you actually do a calculation with *Mathematica*.

To exit *Mathematica*, you typically choose the Quit menu item in the notebook interface.

■ 1.0.2 Text-Based Interfaces

math	the operating system command to start *Mathematica*
text ending with SHIFT-RETURN	input for *Mathematica* on all systems
text ending with RETURN	simpler form for input available on some systems
CONTROL-D or Quit[ ]	exiting *Mathematica*

Running *Mathematica* with a text-based interface.

With a text-based interface, you interact with your computer primarily by typing text on the keyboard. This kind of interface is available for *Mathematica* on almost all computer systems.

To start *Mathematica* with a text-based interface, you typically type the command `math` at an operating system prompt. On some systems, you may also be able to start *Mathematica* with a text-based interface by double-clicking on a *Mathematica* Kernel icon.

When *Mathematica* has started, it will print the prompt *In[1]:=*, signifying that it is ready for your input. You can then type your input. On any system, you can tell *Mathematica* that you have finished giving input by typing SHIFT-RETURN. On some systems, typing RETURN or ENTER alone is sufficient.

Mathematica will then process the input, and generate a result. If it prints the result out, it will label it with *Out[1]=*.

Throughout this book, dialogs with *Mathematica* are shown in the following way:

The computer prints *In[1]:=*. You just type in 2 + 2. The line that starts with *Out[1]=* is the result from *Mathematica*.	*In[1]:=* **2 + 2** *Out[1]=* 4

Page xv discusses some important details about reproducing the dialogs on your computer system. Note that you do not explicitly type the *In[n]:=* prompt; only type the text that follows this prompt.

Note also that most of the actual dialogs given in the book show output in the form you get with a notebook interface to *Mathematica*; output with a text-based interface looks similar, but lacks such features as special characters and font size changes.

Section 1.0.1 gives more details on running *Mathematica* with a text-based interface. To exit *Mathematica*, either type CONTROL-D or `Quit[ ]` at an input prompt.

1.1 Numerical Calculations

■ 1.1.1 Arithmetic

You can do arithmetic with *Mathematica* just as you would on an electronic calculator.

This is the sum of two numbers.	*In[1]:=* **2.3 + 5.63**
	Out[1]= 7.93
Here the / stands for division, and the ^ stands for power.	*In[2]:=* **2.4 / 8.9 ^ 2**
	Out[2]= 0.0302992
Spaces denote multiplication in *Mathematica*. You can use a * for multiplication if you want to.	*In[3]:=* **2 3 4**
	Out[3]= 24
You can type arithmetic expressions with parentheses.	*In[4]:=* **(3 + 4) ^ 2 - 2 (3 + 1)**
	Out[4]= 41
Spaces are not needed, though they often make your input easier to read.	*In[5]:=* **(3+4)^2-2(3+1)**
	Out[5]= 41

x^y	power
$-x$	minus
x/y	divide
$x\ y\ z$ or x*y*z	multiply
x+y+z	add

Arithmetic operations in *Mathematica*.

Arithmetic operations in *Mathematica* are grouped according to the standard mathematical conventions. As usual, 2 ^ 3 + 4, for example, means (2 ^ 3) + 4, and not 2 ^ (3 + 4). You can always control grouping by explicitly using parentheses.

This result is given in scientific notation.	*In[6]:=* **2.4 ^ 45**
	Out[6]= 1.28678×10^{17}
You can enter numbers in scientific notation like this.	*In[7]:=* **2.3 10^70**
	Out[7]= 2.3×10^{70}
Or like this.	*In[8]:=* **2.3*^70**
	Out[8]= 2.3×10^{70}

■ 1.1.2 Exact and Approximate Results

A standard electronic calculator does all your calculations to a particular accuracy, say ten decimal digits. With *Mathematica*, however, you can often get *exact* results.

Mathematica gives an *exact* result for 2^{100}, even though it has 31 decimal digits.

```
In[1]:= 2 ^ 100
Out[1]= 1267650600228229401496703205376
```

You can tell *Mathematica* to give you an approximate numerical result, just as a calculator would, by ending your input with //N. The N stands for "numerical". It must be a capital letter. Section 2.1.3 will explain what the // means.

This gives an approximate numerical result.

```
In[2]:= 2 ^ 100 //N
Out[2]= 1.26765×10^30
```

Mathematica can give results in terms of rational numbers.

```
In[3]:= 1/3 + 2/7
Out[3]= 13/21
```

//N always gives the approximate numerical result.

```
In[4]:= 1/3 + 2/7 //N
Out[4]= 0.619048
```

expr //N	give an approximate numerical value for *expr*

Getting numerical approximations.

When you type in an integer like 7, *Mathematica* assumes that it is exact. If you type in a number like 4.5, with an explicit decimal point, *Mathematica* assumes that it is accurate only to a fixed number of decimal places.

This is taken to be an exact rational number, and reduced to its lowest terms.

```
In[5]:= 452/62
Out[5]= 226/31
```

Whenever you give a number with an explicit decimal point, *Mathematica* produces an approximate numerical result.

```
In[6]:= 452.3/62
Out[6]= 7.29516
```

Here again, the presence of the decimal point makes *Mathematica* give you an approximate numerical result.

```
In[7]:= 452./62
Out[7]= 7.29032
```

When any number in an arithmetic expression is given with an explicit decimal point, you get an approximate numerical result for the whole expression.

```
In[8]:= 1. + 452/62
Out[8]= 8.29032
```

■ 1.1.3 Some Mathematical Functions

Mathematica includes a very large collection of mathematical functions. Section 3.2 gives the complete list. Here are a few of the common ones.

Sqrt[x]	square root ($\sqrt{x}$)
Exp[x]	exponential (e^x)
Log[x]	natural logarithm ($\log_e x$)
Log[b, x]	logarithm to base b ($\log_b x$)
Sin[x], Cos[x], Tan[x]	trigonometric functions (with arguments in radians)
ArcSin[x], ArcCos[x], ArcTan[x]	
	inverse trigonometric functions
n!	factorial (product of integers $1, 2, \ldots, n$)
Abs[x]	absolute value
Round[x]	closest integer to x
Mod[n, m]	n modulo m (remainder on division of n by m)
Random[ ]	pseudorandom number between 0 and 1
Max[x, y, ...], Min[x, y, ...]	maximum, minimum of $x, y, \ldots$
FactorInteger[n]	prime factors of n (see page 723)

Some common mathematical functions.

- The arguments of all *Mathematica* functions are enclosed in *square brackets*.

- The names of built-in *Mathematica* functions begin with *capital letters*.

Two important points about functions in *Mathematica*.

It is important to remember that all function arguments in *Mathematica* are enclosed in *square brackets*, not parentheses. Parentheses in *Mathematica* are used only to indicate the grouping of terms, and never to give function arguments.

This gives $\log_e(8.4)$. Notice the capital letter for Log, and the *square brackets* for the argument.

```
In[1]:= Log[8.4]
Out[1]= 2.12823
```

Just as with arithmetic operations, *Mathematica* tries to give exact values for mathematical functions when you give it exact input.

This gives $\sqrt{16}$ as an exact integer.

```
In[2]:= Sqrt[16]
Out[2]= 4
```

This gives an approximate numerical result for $\sqrt{2}$.

```
In[3]:= Sqrt[2] //N
Out[3]= 1.41421
```

The presence of an explicit decimal point tells *Mathematica* to give an approximate numerical result.

```
In[4]:= Sqrt[2.]
Out[4]= 1.41421
```

Since you are not asking for an approximate numerical result, *Mathematica* leaves the number here in an exact symbolic form.

```
In[5]:= Sqrt[2]
Out[5]= √2
```

Here is the exact integer result for $30 \times 29 \times \ldots \times 1$. Computing factorials like this can give you very large numbers. You should be able to calculate up to at least 2000! in a short time.

```
In[6]:= 30!
Out[6]= 265252859812191058636308480000000
```

This gives the approximate numerical value of the factorial.

```
In[7]:= 30! //N
Out[7]= 2.65253×10^32
```

Pi	$\pi \simeq 3.14159$	
E	$e \simeq 2.71828$	
Degree	$\pi/180$: degrees-to-radians conversion factor	
I	$i = \sqrt{-1}$	
Infinity	∞	

Some common mathematical constants.

Notice that the names of these built-in constants all begin with capital letters.

This gives the numerical value of π^2.

```
In[8]:= Pi ^ 2 //N
Out[8]= 9.8696
```

This gives the exact result for $\sin(\pi/2)$. Notice that the arguments to trigonometric functions are always in radians.

```
In[9]:= Sin[Pi/2]
Out[9]= 1
```

This gives the numerical value of sin(20°). Multiplying by the constant Degree converts the argument to radians.	*In[10]:=* **Sin[20 Degree] //N** *Out[10]=* 0.34202
Log[x] gives logarithms to base *e*.	*In[11]:=* **Log[E ^ 5]** *Out[11]=* 5
You can get logarithms in any base *b* using Log[*b*, *x*]. As in standard mathematical notation, the *b* is optional.	*In[12]:=* **Log[2, 256]** *Out[12]=* 8

■ 1.1.4 Arbitrary-Precision Calculations

When you use //N to get a numerical result, *Mathematica* does what a standard calculator would do: it gives you a result to a fixed number of significant figures. You can also tell *Mathematica* exactly how many significant figures to keep in a particular calculation. This allows you to get numerical results in *Mathematica* to any degree of precision.

expr//N or N[*expr*]	approximate numerical value of *expr*
N[*expr*, *n*]	numerical value of *expr* calculated with *n*-digit precision

Numerical evaluation functions.

This gives the numerical value of π to a fixed number of significant digits. Typing N[Pi] is exactly equivalent to Pi //N.	*In[1]:=* **N[Pi]** *Out[1]=* 3.14159
This gives π to 40 digits.	*In[2]:=* **N[Pi, 40]** *Out[2]=* 3.141592653589793238462643383279502884197
Here is $\sqrt{7}$ to 30 digits.	*In[3]:=* **N[Sqrt[7], 30]** *Out[3]=* 2.64575131106459059050161575363

Doing any kind of numerical calculation can introduce small roundoff errors into your results. When you increase the numerical precision, these errors typically become correspondingly smaller. Making sure that you get the same answer when you increase numerical precision is often a good way to check your results.

The quantity $e^{\pi\sqrt{163}}$ turns out to be very close to an integer. To check that the result is not, in fact, an integer, you have to use sufficient numerical precision.	*In[4]:=* **N[Exp[Pi Sqrt[163]], 40]** *Out[4]=* 2.625374126407687439999999999999992500725972 × 10^{17}

■ 1.1.5 Complex Numbers

You can enter complex numbers in *Mathematica* just by including the constant I, equal to $\sqrt{-1}$. Make sure that you type a capital I.

This gives the imaginary number result *2i*.	*In[1]:=* **Sqrt[-4]**
	Out[1]= 2 I
This gives the ratio of two complex numbers.	*In[2]:=* **(4 + 3 I) / (2 - I)**
	Out[2]= 1 + 2 I
Here is the numerical value of a complex exponential.	*In[3]:=* **Exp[2 + 9 I] //N**
	Out[3]= -6.73239 + 3.04517 I

x + I y	the complex number $x + i\,y$
Re[z]	real part
Im[z]	imaginary part
Conjugate[z]	complex conjugate z^* or $\bar{z}$
Abs[z]	absolute value $|z|$
Arg[z]	the argument ϕ in $|z|e^{i\phi}$

Complex number operations.

■ 1.1.6 Getting Used to *Mathematica*

- Arguments of functions are given in *square brackets*.
- Names of built-in functions have their first letters capitalized.
- Multiplication can be represented by a space.
- Powers are denoted by ^.
- Numbers in scientific notation are entered, for example, as 2.5*^-4 or 2.5 10^-4.

Important points to remember in *Mathematica*.

This section has given you a first glimpse of *Mathematica*. If you have used other computer systems before, you will probably have noticed some similarities and some differences. Often you will find the differences the most difficult parts to remember. It may help you, however, to understand a little about *why Mathematica* is set up the way it is, and why such differences exist.

One important feature of *Mathematica* that differs from other computer languages, and from conventional mathematical notation, is that function arguments are enclosed in square brackets, not parentheses. Parentheses in *Mathematica* are reserved specifically for indicating the grouping of terms. There is obviously a conceptual distinction between giving arguments to a function and grouping terms together; the fact that the same notation has often been used for both is largely a consequence of typography and of early computer keyboards. In *Mathematica*, the concepts are distinguished by different notation.

This distinction has several advantages. In parenthesis notation, it is not clear whether $c(1 + x)$ means c[1 + x] or c*(1 + x). Using square brackets for function arguments removes this ambiguity. It also allows multiplication to be indicated without an explicit * or other character. As a result, *Mathematica* can handle expressions like 2x and a x or a (1 + x), treating them just as in standard mathematical notation.

You will have seen in this section that built-in *Mathematica* functions often have quite long names. You may wonder why, for example, the pseudorandom number function is called Random, rather than, say, Rand. The answer, which pervades much of the design of *Mathematica*, is consistency. There is a general convention in *Mathematica* that all function names are spelled out as full English words, unless there is a standard mathematical abbreviation for them. The great advantage of this scheme is that it is *predictable*. Once you know what a function does, you will usually be able to guess exactly what its name is. If the names were abbreviated, you would always have to remember which shortening of the standard English words was used.

Another feature of built-in *Mathematica* names is that they all start with capital letters. In later sections, you will see how to define variables and functions of your own. The capital letter convention makes it easy to distinguish built-in objects. If *Mathematica* used i to represent $\sqrt{-1}$, then you would never be able to use i as the name of one of your variables. In addition, when you read programs written in *Mathematica*, the capitalization of built-in names makes them easier to pick out.

■ 1.1.7 Mathematical Notation in Notebooks

If you use a text-based interface to *Mathematica*, then the input you give must consist only of characters that you can type directly on your computer keyboard. But if you use a notebook interface then other kinds of input become possible.

Usually there are palettes provided which operate like extensions of your keyboard, and which have buttons that you can click to enter particular forms. You can typically access standard palettes using the Palettes submenu of the File menu.

Clicking the π button in this palette
will enter a pi into your notebook.

Clicking the first button in this palette
will create an empty structure for
entering a power. You can use the
mouse to fill in the structure.

You can also give input by using special keys on your keyboard. Pressing one of these keys does
not lead to an ordinary character being entered, but instead typically causes some action to occur or
some structure to be created.

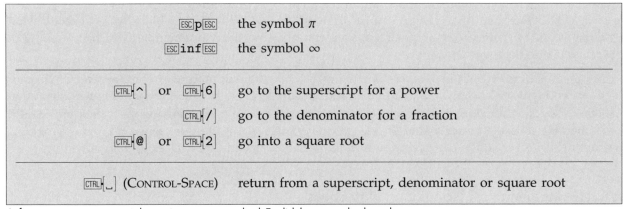

A few ways to enter special notations on a standard English-language keyboard.

Here is a computation entered using
ordinary characters on a keyboard.

$In[1]:=$ **N[Pi^2/6]**

$Out[1]=$ 1.64493

Here is the same computation entered
using a palette or special keys.

$In[2]:=$ **N$\left[\dfrac{\pi^2}{6}\right]$**

$Out[2]=$ 1.64493

Here is an actual sequence of keys that
can be used to enter the input.

$In[3]:=$ **N[** ESC p ESC CTRL ^ 2 CTRL ␣ CTRL / 6 CTRL ␣ **]**

$Out[3]=$ 1.64493

In a traditional computer language such as C or Fortran, the input you give must always consist of
a string of ordinary characters that can be typed directly on a keyboard. But the *Mathematica* language

also allows you to give input that contains special characters, superscripts, built-up fractions, and so on.

The language incorporates many features of traditional mathematical notation. But you should realize that the goal of the language is to provide a precise and consistent way to specify computations. And as a result, it does not follow all of the somewhat haphazard details of traditional mathematical notation.

Nevertheless, as discussed on page 192, it is always possible to get *Mathematica* to produce *output* that imitates every aspect of traditional mathematical notation. And as discussed on page 192, it is also possible for *Mathematica* to import text that uses such notation, and to some extent to translate it into its own more precise language.

1.2 Building Up Calculations

■ 1.2.1 Using Previous Results

In doing calculations, you will often need to use previous results that you have got. In *Mathematica*, % always stands for your last result.

%	the last result generated
%%	the next-to-last result
%% ... % (*k* times)	the *k*[th] previous result
%*n*	the result on output line Out[*n*] (to be used with care)

Ways to refer to your previous results.

Here is the first result.	In[1]:= **77 ^ 2** Out[1]= 5929
This adds 1 to the last result.	In[2]:= **% + 1** Out[2]= 5930
This uses both the last result, and the result before that.	In[3]:= **3 % + % ^ 2 + %%** Out[3]= 35188619

You will have noticed that all the input and output lines in *Mathematica* are numbered. You can use these numbers to refer to previous results.

This adds the results on lines 2 and 3 above.	In[4]:= **%2 + %3** Out[4]= 35194549

If you use a text-based interface to *Mathematica*, then successive input and output lines will always appear in order, as they do in the dialogs in this book. However, if you use a notebook interface to *Mathematica*, as discussed in Section 1.0.1, then successive input and output lines need not appear in order. You can for example "scroll back" and insert your next calculation wherever you want in the notebook. You should realize that % is always defined to be the last result that *Mathematica* generated. This may or may not be the result that appears immediately above your present position in the notebook. With a notebook interface, the only way to tell when a particular result was generated is to look at the Out[*n*] label that it has. Because you can insert and delete anywhere in a notebook, the textual ordering of results in a notebook need have no relation to the order in which the results were generated.

■ 1.2.2 Defining Variables

When you do long calculations, it is often convenient to give *names* to your intermediate results. Just as in standard mathematics, or in other computer languages, you can do this by introducing named *variables*.

This sets the value of the *variable* x to be 5.	*In[1]:=* **x = 5** *Out[1]=* 5
Whenever x appears, *Mathematica* now replaces it with the value 5.	*In[2]:=* **x ^ 2** *Out[2]=* 25
This assigns a new value to x.	*In[3]:=* **x = 7 + 4** *Out[3]=* 11
pi is set to be the numerical value of π to 40-digit accuracy.	*In[4]:=* **pi = N[Pi, 40]** *Out[4]=* 3.141592653589793238462643383279502884197 2
Here is the value you defined for pi.	*In[5]:=* **pi** *Out[5]=* 3.141592653589793238462643383279502884197 2
This gives the numerical value of π^2, to the same accuracy as pi.	*In[6]:=* **pi ^ 2** *Out[6]=* 9.869604401089358618834490999876151135313 7

$x = value$	assign a value to the variable x
$x = y = value$	assign a value to both x and y
$x =.$ or `Clear[x]`	remove any value assigned to x

Assigning values to variables.

It is very important to realize that values you assign to variables are *permanent*. Once you have assigned a value to a particular variable, the value will be kept until you explicitly remove it. The value will, of course, disappear if you start a whole new *Mathematica* session.

Forgetting about definitions you made earlier is the single most common cause of mistakes when using *Mathematica*. If you set x = 5, *Mathematica* assumes that you *always* want x to have the value 5, until or unless you explicitly tell it otherwise. To avoid mistakes, you should remove values you have defined as soon as you have finished using them.

> ■ Remove values you assign to variables as soon as you finish using them.

A useful principle in using *Mathematica*.

The variables you define can have almost any names. There is no limit on the length of their names. One constraint, however, is that variable names can never *start* with numbers. For example, x2 could be a variable, but 2x means 2*x.

Mathematica uses both upper- and lower-case letters. There is a convention that built-in *Mathematica* objects always have names starting with upper-case (capital) letters. To avoid confusion, you should always choose names for your own variables that start with lower-case letters.

aaaaa	a variable name containing only lower-case letters
Aaaaa	a built-in object whose name begins with a capital letter

Naming conventions.

You can type formulas involving variables in *Mathematica* almost exactly as you would in mathematics. There are a few important points to watch, however.

- x y means x times y.
- xy with no space is the variable with name xy.
- 5x means 5 times x.
- x^2y means (x^2) y, not x^(2y).

Some points to watch when using variables in *Mathematica*.

■ 1.2.3 Making Lists of Objects

In doing calculations, it is often convenient to collect together several objects, and treat them as a single entity. *Lists* give you a way to make collections of objects in *Mathematica*. As you will see later, lists are very important and general structures in *Mathematica*.

A list such as {3, 5, 1} is a collection of three objects. But in many ways, you can treat the whole list as a single object. You can, for example, do arithmetic on the whole list at once, or assign the whole list to be the value of a variable.

Here is a list of three numbers.

In[1]:= **{3, 5, 1}**

Out[1]= {3, 5, 1}

This squares each number in the list, and adds 1 to it.

In[2]:= **{3, 5, 1}^2 + 1**

Out[2]= {10, 26, 2}

This takes differences between corresponding elements in the two lists. The lists must be the same length.	*In[3]:=* **{6, 7, 8} - {3.5, 4, 2.5}** *Out[3]=* {2.5, 3, 5.5}
The value of % is the whole list.	*In[4]:=* **%** *Out[4]=* {2.5, 3, 5.5}
You can apply any of the mathematical functions in Section 1.1.3 to whole lists.	*In[5]:=* **Exp[%] // N** *Out[5]=* {12.1825, 20.0855, 244.692}

Just as you can set variables to be numbers, so also you can set them to be lists.

This assigns v to be a list.	*In[6]:=* **v = {2, 4, 3.1}** *Out[6]=* {2, 4, 3.1}
Wherever v appears, it is replaced by the list.	*In[7]:=* **v / (v - 1)** *Out[7]=* $\left\{2, \dfrac{4}{3}, 1.47619\right\}$

■ 1.2.4 Manipulating Elements of Lists

Many of the most powerful list manipulation operations in *Mathematica* treat whole lists as single objects. Sometimes, however, you need to pick out or set individual elements in a list.

You can refer to an element of a *Mathematica* list by giving its "index". The elements are numbered in order, starting at 1.

{*a*, *b*, *c*}	a list
Part[*list*, *i*] or *list*[[*i*]]	the ith element of *list* (the first element is *list*[[1]])
Part[*list*, {*i*, *j*, ... }] or *list*[[{*i*, *j*, ... }]]	a list of the ith, j^{th}, ... elements of *list*

Operations on list elements.

This extracts the second element of the list.	*In[1]:=* **{5, 8, 6, 9}[[2]]** *Out[1]=* 8
This extracts a list of elements.	*In[2]:=* **{5, 8, 6, 9}[[{3, 1, 3, 2, 4}]]** *Out[2]=* {6, 5, 6, 8, 9}
This assigns the value of v to be a list.	*In[3]:=* **v = {2, 4, 7}** *Out[3]=* {2, 4, 7}

You can extract elements of v.

$In[4]:= $ **v[[2]]**

$Out[4]= 4$

By assigning a variable to be a list, you can use *Mathematica* lists much like "arrays" in other computer languages. Thus, for example, you can reset an element of a list by assigning a value to $v[[i]]$.

Part[v, i] or $v[[i]]$	extract the ith element of a list
Part[v, i] = *value* or $v[[i]]$ = *value*	
	reset the ith element of a list

Array-like operations on lists.

Here is a list.

$In[5]:= $ **v = {4, -1, 8, 7}**

$Out[5]= \{4, -1, 8, 7\}$

This resets the third element of the list.

$In[6]:= $ **v[[3]] = 0**

$Out[6]= 0$

Now the list assigned to v has been modified.

$In[7]:= $ **v**

$Out[7]= \{4, -1, 0, 7\}$

■ 1.2.5 The Four Kinds of Bracketing in *Mathematica*

Over the course of the last few sections, we have introduced each of the four kinds of bracketing used in *Mathematica*. Each kind of bracketing has a very different meaning. It is important that you remember all of them.

(*term*)	parentheses for grouping
$f[x]$	square brackets for functions
{a, b, c}	curly braces for lists
$v[[i]]$	double brackets for indexing (Part[v, i])

The four kinds of bracketing in *Mathematica*.

When the expressions you type in are complicated, it is often a good idea to put extra space inside each set of brackets. This makes it somewhat easier for you to see matching pairs of brackets. $v[[\{a, b\}]]$ is, for example, easier to recognize than $v[[\{a, b\}]]$.

■ 1.2.6 Sequences of Operations

In doing a calculation with *Mathematica*, you usually go through a sequence of steps. If you want to, you can do each step on a separate line. Often, however, you will find it convenient to put several steps on the same line. You can do this simply by separating the pieces of input you want to give with semicolons.

$expr_1$; $expr_2$; $expr_3$	do several operations, and give the result of the last one
$expr_1$; $expr_2$;	do the operations, but print no output

Ways to do sequences of operations in *Mathematica*.

This does three operations on the same line. The result is the result from the last operation.

```
In[1]:= x = 4; y = 6; z = y + 6
Out[1]= 12
```

If you end your input with a semicolon, it is as if you are giving a sequence of operations, with an "empty" one at the end. This has the effect of making *Mathematica* perform the operations you specify, but display no output.

$expr$;	do an operation, but display no output

Inhibiting output.

Putting a semicolon at the end of the line tells *Mathematica* to show no output.

```
In[2]:= x = 67 - 5 ;
```

You can still use % to get the output that would have been shown.

```
In[3]:= %
Out[3]= 62
```

1.3 Using the *Mathematica* System

■ 1.3.1 The Structure of *Mathematica*

Mathematica kernel	the part that actually performs computations
Mathematica front end	the part that handles interaction with the user

The basic parts of the *Mathematica* system.

Mathematica is a modular software system in which the *kernel* which actually performs computations is separate from the *front end* which handles interaction with the user.

The most common type of front end for *Mathematica* is based on interactive documents known as *notebooks*. Notebooks mix *Mathematica* input and output with text, graphics, palettes and other material. You can use notebooks either for doing ongoing computations, or as means of presenting or publishing your results.

Notebook interface	interactive documents
Text-based interface	text from the keyboard
MathLink interface	communication with other programs

Common kinds of interfaces to *Mathematica*.

The notebook front end includes many menus and graphical tools for creating and reading notebook documents and for sending and receiving material from the *Mathematica* kernel.

A notebook mixing text, graphics and *Mathematica* input and output.

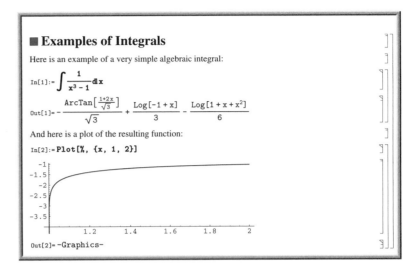

In some cases, you may not need the sophistication of the notebook front end, and you may want instead to interact more directly with the *Mathematica* kernel. You can do this by using a text-based interface, in which text you type on the keyboard goes straight to the kernel.

A dialog with *Mathematica* using a text-based interface.

```
In[1]:= 2^100

Out[1]= 1267650600228229401496703205376

In[2]:= Integrate[1/(x^3 - 1), x]

                   1 + 2 x
             ArcTan[-------]                                 2
                    Sqrt[3]     Log[-1 + x]   Log[1 + x + x ]
Out[2]= -(--------------) + ----------- - ---------------
               Sqrt[3]            3              6
```

An important aspect of *Mathematica* is that it can interact not only with human users but also with other programs. This is achieved primarily through *MathLink*, which is a standardized protocol for two-way communication between external programs and the *Mathematica* kernel.

A fragment of C code that
communicates via *MathLink* with the
Mathematica kernel.

```
MLPutFunction(stdlink,  "EvaluatePacket", 1);

  MLPutFunction(stdlink, "Gamma", 2);
    MLPutReal(stdlink, 2);
    MLPutInteger(stdlink, n);

MLEndPacket(stdlink);
MLCheckFunction(stdlink, "ReturnPacket", &n);

MLGetReal(stdlink, &result);
```

Among the many *MathLink*-compatible programs that are now available, some are set up to serve as complete front ends to *Mathematica*. Often such front ends provide their own special user interfaces, and treat the *Mathematica* kernel purely as an embedded computational engine. If you are using *Mathematica* in this way, then only some parts of the discussion in the remainder of this section will probably be relevant.

■ 1.3.2 Differences between Computer Systems

There are many detailed differences between different kinds of computer systems. But one of the important features of *Mathematica* is that it allows you to work and create material without being concerned about such differences.

In order to fit in as well as possible with particular computer systems, the user interface for *Mathematica* on different systems is inevitably at least slightly different. But the crucial point is that beyond superficial differences, *Mathematica* is set up to work in exactly the same way on every kind of computer system.

- The language used by the *Mathematica* kernel

- The structure of *Mathematica* notebooks

- The *MathLink* communication protocol

Elements of *Mathematica* that are exactly the same on all computer systems.

The commands that you give to the *Mathematica* kernel, for example, are absolutely identical on every computer system. This means that when you write a program using these commands, you can immediately take the program and run it on any computer that supports *Mathematica*.

The structure of *Mathematica* notebooks is also the same on all computer systems. And as a result, if you create a notebook on one computer system, you can immediately take it and use it on any other system.

- The visual appearance of windows, fonts, etc.

- Mechanisms for importing and exporting material from notebooks

- Keyboard shortcuts for menu commands

Elements that can differ from one computer system to another.

Although the underlying structure of *Mathematica* notebooks is always the same, there are often superficial differences in the way notebooks look on different computer systems, and in some of the mechanisms provided for interacting with them.

The goal in each case is to make notebooks work in a way that is as familiar as possible to people who are used to a particular type of computer system.

And in addition, by adapting the details of notebooks to each specific computer system, it becomes easier to exchange material between notebooks and other programs running on that computer system.

The same *Mathematica* notebook on three different computer systems. The underlying structure is exactly the same, but some details of the presentation are different.

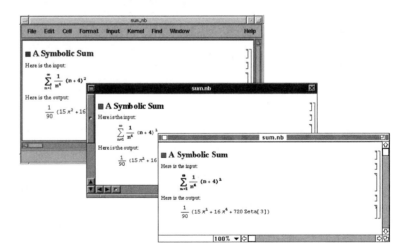

One consequence of the modular nature of the *Mathematica* system is that its parts can be run on different computers. Thus, for example, it is not uncommon to run the front end for *Mathematica* on one computer, while running the kernel on a quite separate computer.

Communications between the kernel and the front end are handled by *MathLink*, using whatever networking mechanisms are available.

■ 1.3.3 Special Topic: Using a Text-Based Interface

With a text-based interface, you interact with *Mathematica* just by typing successive lines of input, and getting back successive lines of output on your screen.

At each stage, *Mathematica* prints a prompt of the form In[*n*]:= to tell you that it is ready to receive input. When you have entered your input, *Mathematica* processes it, and then displays the result with a label of the form Out[*n*]=.

Different text-based interfaces use slightly different schemes for letting *Mathematica* know when you have finished typing your input. With some interfaces you press SHIFT-RETURN, while in others RETURN alone is sufficient.

In interfaces that use SHIFT-RETURN, you can continue your input for several lines by typing RETURN at the end of each line. In interfaces where RETURN is used to signify the end of your input, *Mathematica* will automatically continue reading successive lines until it has received a complete expression. Thus, for example, if you type an opening parenthesis on one line, *Mathematica* will go on reading successive lines of input until it sees the corresponding closing parenthesis. Note that if you enter a completely blank line, *Mathematica* will throw away the lines you have typed so far, and issue a new input prompt.

%*n* or Out[*n*]	the value of the nth output
InString[*n*]	the text of the nth input
In[*n*]	the nth input, for re-evaluation

Retrieving and re-evaluating previous input and output.

With a text-based interface, each line of *Mathematica* input and output appears sequentially. Often your computer system will allow you to scroll backwards to review previous work, and to cut-and-paste previous lines of input.

But whatever kind of computer system you have, you can always use *Mathematica* to retrieve or re-evaluate previous input and output. In general, re-evaluating a particular piece of input or output may give you a different result than when you evaluated it in the first place. The reason is that in between you may have reset the values of variables that are used in that piece of input or output. If you ask for Out[*n*], then *Mathematica* will give you the final form of your n^{th} output. On the other hand, if you ask for In[*n*], then *Mathematica* will take the nth input you gave, and re-evaluate it using whatever current assignments you have given for variables.

◾ 1.3.4 Doing Computations in Notebooks

A typical *Mathematica* notebook containing text, graphics and *Mathematica* expressions. The brackets on the right indicate the extent of each cell.

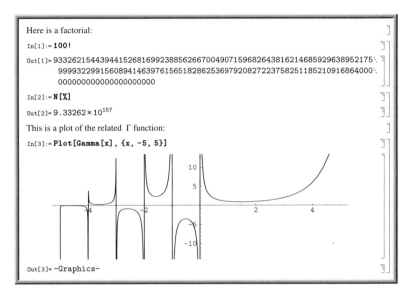

Mathematica notebooks are structured interactive documents that are organized into a sequence of *cells*. Each cell contains material of a definite type—usually text, graphics, sounds or *Mathematica* expressions. When a notebook is displayed on the screen, the extent of each cell is indicated by a bracket on the right.

The notebook front end for *Mathematica* provides many ways to enter and edit the material in a notebook. Some of these ways will be standard to whatever computer system or graphical interface you are using. Others are specific to *Mathematica*.

> SHIFT-RETURN or SHIFT-ENTER   send a cell of input to the *Mathematica* kernel

Doing a computation in a *Mathematica* notebook.

Once you have prepared the material in a cell, you can send it as input to the *Mathematica* kernel simply by pressing SHIFT-RETURN or SHIFT-ENTER. The kernel will send back whatever output is generated, and the front end will create new cells in your notebook to display this output. Note that on systems where both RETURN and ENTER keys are available, ENTER alone is typically equivalent to SHIFT-RETURN.

Here is a cell ready to be sent as input to the *Mathematica* kernel.

```
3^100
```

The output from the computation is inserted in a new cell.

```
In[1]:= 3^100
Out[1]= 515377520732011331036461129765621272702107522001
```

Most kinds of output that you get in *Mathematica* notebooks can readily be edited, just like input. Usually *Mathematica* will make a copy of the output when you first start editing it, so you can keep track of the original output and its edited form.

Once you have done the editing you want, you can typically just press SHIFT-RETURN to send what you have created as input to the *Mathematica* kernel.

Here is a typical computation in a *Mathematica* notebook.

```
In[1]:= Integrate[Sqrt[x + 1] / Sqrt[x - 1], x]
```
$$\text{Out[1]}= \sqrt{-1+x} \ \sqrt{1+x} + 2\,\text{ArcSinh}\left[\frac{\sqrt{-1+x}}{\sqrt{2}}\right]$$

Mathematica will automatically make a copy if you start editing the output.

```
In[1]:= Integrate[Sqrt[x + 1] / Sqrt[x - 1], x]
```
$$\text{Out[1]}= \sqrt{-1+x} \ \sqrt{1+x} + 2\,\text{ArcSinh}\left[\frac{\sqrt{-1+x}}{\sqrt{2}}\right]$$
$$\sqrt{-1+x} \ \sqrt{1+x} + D\left[2\,\text{ArcSinh}\left[\frac{\sqrt{-1+x}}{\sqrt{2}}\right], x\right] \ // \ \text{Simplify}$$

After you have edited the output, you can send it back as further input to the *Mathematica* kernel.

```
In[1]:= Integrate[Sqrt[x + 1] / Sqrt[x - 1], x]
```
$$\text{Out[1]}= \sqrt{-1+x} \ \sqrt{1+x} + 2\,\text{ArcSinh}\left[\frac{\sqrt{-1+x}}{\sqrt{2}}\right]$$
$$\text{In[2]}:= \sqrt{-1+x} \ \sqrt{1+x} + D\left[2\,\text{ArcSinh}\left[\frac{\sqrt{-1+x}}{\sqrt{2}}\right], x\right] \ // \ \text{Simplify}$$
$$\text{Out[2]}= \frac{x^2}{\sqrt{-1+x} \ \sqrt{1+x}}$$

When you do computations in a *Mathematica* notebook, each line of input is typically labeled with $In[n]:=$, while each line of output is labeled with the corresponding $Out[n]=$.

There is no reason, however, that successive lines of input and output should necessarily appear one after the other in your notebook. Often, for example, you will want to go back to an earlier part of your notebook, and re-evaluate some input you gave before.

It is important to realize that wherever a particular expression appears in your notebook, it is the line number given in $In[n]:=$ or $Out[n]=$ which determines when the expression was processed by the *Mathematica* kernel. Thus, for example, the fact that one expression may appear earlier than another in your notebook does not mean that it will have been evaluated first by the kernel. This will only be the case if it has a lower line number.

Each line of input and output is given a label when it is evaluated by the kernel. It is these labels, not the position of the expression in the notebook, that indicate the ordering of evaluation by the kernel.

```
Results:
In[2]:= s^2 + 2
Out[2]= 146
In[4]:= s^2 + 2
Out[4]= 10002
Settings for s:
In[1]:= s = 12
Out[1]= 12
In[3]:= s = 100
Out[3]= 100
```

If you make a mistake and try to enter input that the *Mathematica* kernel does not understand, then the front end will produce a beep. In general, you will get a beep whenever something goes wrong in the front end. You can find out the origin of the beep using the Why the Beep? item in the Help menu.

Animate graphics	double-click the first cell in the sequence of frames
Resize a graphic	click the graphic and move the handles that appear
Find coordinates in a graphic	move around in the graphic holding down the COMMAND or ALT key (or equivalent)
Play a sound	double-click the cell that contains it

Operations on graphics and sounds.

■ 1.3.5 Notebooks as Documents

Mathematica notebooks allow you to create documents that can be viewed interactively on screen or printed on paper.

Particularly in larger notebooks, it is common to have chapters, sections and so on, each represented by groups of cells. The extent of these groups is indicated by a bracket on the right.

The grouping of cells in a notebook is indicated by nested brackets on the right.

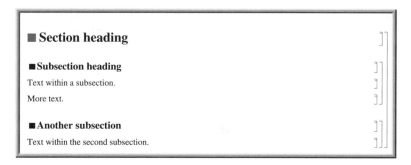

A group of cells can be either *open* or *closed*. When it is open, you can see all the cells in it explicitly. But when it is closed, you see only the first or *heading* cell in the group.

Large notebooks are often distributed with many closed groups of cells, so that when you first look at the notebook, you see just an outline of its contents. You can then open parts you are interested in by double-clicking the appropriate brackets.

Double-clicking the bracket that spans a group of cells closes the group, leaving only the first cell visible.

When a group is closed, the bracket for it has an arrow at the bottom. Double-clicking this arrow opens the group again.

Each cell within a notebook is assigned a particular *style* which indicates its role within the notebook. Thus, for example, material intended as input to be executed by the *Mathematica* kernel is typically in Input style, while text that is intended purely to be read is typically in Text style.

The *Mathematica* front end provides menus and keyboard shortcuts for creating cells with different styles, and for changing styles of existing cells.

This shows cells in various styles. The styles define not only the format of the cell contents, but also their placement and spacing.

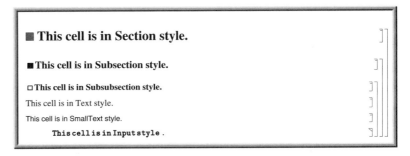

By putting a cell in a particular style, you specify a whole collection of properties for the cell, including for example how large and in what font text should be given.

The *Mathematica* front end allows you to modify such properties, either for complete cells, or for specific material within cells.

Even within a cell of a particular style, the *Mathematica* front end allows a wide range of properties to be modified separately.

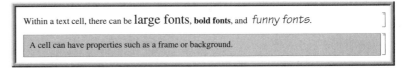

It is worth realizing that in doing different kinds of things with *Mathematica* notebooks, you are using different parts of the *Mathematica* system. Operations such as opening and closing groups of cells, doing animations and playing sounds use only a small part of the *Mathematica* front end, and these operations are supported by a widely available program known as *MathReader* that is typically distributed on the main *Mathematica* CD-ROM.

To be able to create and edit notebooks, you need more of the *Mathematica* front end. And finally, to be able to actually do computations within a *Mathematica* notebook, you need a full *Mathematica* system, with both the front end and the kernel.

MathReader	reading *Mathematica* notebooks
Mathematica front end	creating and editing *Mathematica* notebooks
Mathematica kernel	doing computations in notebooks

Programs required for different kinds of operations with notebooks.

■ 1.3.6 Active Elements in Notebooks

One of the most powerful features of *Mathematica* notebooks is that their actions can be programmed. Thus, for example, you can set up a button in a *Mathematica* notebook which causes various operations to be performed whenever you click it.

Here is a notebook that contains a button.

Click the button to get the current date: | Date[] |

Clicking the button in this case causes the current date to be displayed.

Click the button to get the current date: | Date[] |

{1995, 9, 5, 10, 40, 53}

Later in this book, we will discuss how you can set up buttons and other similar objects in *Mathematica* notebooks. But here suffice it to say that whenever a cell is indicated as *active*, typically by the presence of a stylized "A" in its cell bracket, clicking on active elements within the cell will cause actions that have been programmed for these elements to be performed.

It is common to set up *palettes* which consist of arrays of buttons. Sometimes such palettes appear as cells within a notebook. But more often, a special kind of separate notebook window is used, which can conveniently be placed on the side of your computer screen and used in conjunction with any other notebook.

Palettes consisting of arrays of buttons are often placed in separate notebooks.

In the simplest cases, the buttons in palettes serve essentially like additional keys on your keyboard. Thus, when you press a button, the character or object shown in that button is inserted into your notebook just as if you had typed it.

Here is a palette of Greek letters with buttons that act like additional keys on your keyboard.

Often, however, a button may contain a placeholder indicated by ■. This signifies that when you press the button, whatever is currently selected in your notebook will be inserted at the position of the placeholder.

The buttons here contain placeholders indicated by ■.

Here is a notebook with an expression selected.

$$1 + \left(1 + \overline{\left(1 + (1+x^2)^2\right)^2}\right)^2$$

Pressing the top left button in the palette wraps the selected expression with a square root.

$$1 + \left(1 + \sqrt{\left(1 + (1+x^2)^2\right)^2}\right)^2$$

Sometimes buttons that contain placeholders will be programmed simply to insert a certain expression in your notebook. But more often, they will be programmed to evaluate the result, sending it as input to the *Mathematica* kernel.

These buttons are set up to perform algebraic operations.

Here is a notebook with an expression selected.

$$\frac{2 + 2\cos[2x]}{4} + \frac{1}{32}\,(12 - 16\cos[2x] + 4\cos[4x])$$

Pressing the top left button in the palette causes the selected expression to be simplified.

$$\frac{2 + 2\cos[2x]}{4} + \sin[x]^4$$

There are some situations in which it is convenient to have several placeholders in a single button. Your current selection is typically inserted at the position of the primary placeholder, indicated by ■. Additional placeholders may however be indicated by □, and you can move to the positions of successive placeholders using TAB.

Here is a palette containing buttons with several placeholders.

Here is an expression in a notebook.

$$\frac{\text{Sin}[x]}{1+x}$$

Pressing the top left button in the palette inserts the expression in place of the ■.

$$\int \frac{\text{Sin}[x]}{1+x} d\square$$

You can move to the other placeholders using TAB, and then edit them to insert whatever you want.

$$\int \frac{\text{Sin}[x]}{1+x} dx$$

■ 1.3.7 Special Topic: Hyperlinks and Active Text

The *Mathematica* front end provides a variety of ways to search for particular words or text in *Mathematica* notebooks. But particularly when large documents or collections of documents are involved, it is often convenient to insert *hyperlinks* which immediately take you to a specific point in a notebook.

Hyperlinks are usually indicated by words or phrases that are underlined, and are often in a different color. Clicking on a hyperlink immediately takes you to wherever the hyperlink points.

Here is some text. The text can contain a link, which points elsewhere.

Hyperlinks in notebooks work very much like the buttons discussed in the previous section. And once again, all aspects of hyperlinks are programmable.

Indeed, it is possible to set up active text in notebooks that performs almost any kind of action.

■ 1.3.8 Getting Help in the Notebook Front End

Getting Started	a quick start to using *Mathematica*
Help Browser	looking up specific functions
Mathematica Book	on-line notebook version of this book
Answers	searchable database of common questions and answers

Typical types of help available with the notebook front end.

Included with most versions of the *Mathematica* notebook front end are a wide range of notebooks and other material that you can access to get help while you are using *Mathematica*.

An example of the Help Browser. The basic information is taken from the Reference Guide at the end of this book, supplemented with additional examples.

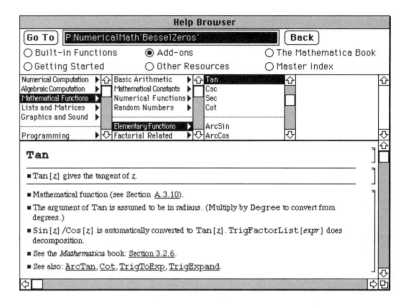

■ 1.3.9 Getting Help with a Text-Based Interface

?Name	show information on *Name*
??Name	show extra information on *Name*
?Aaaa*	show information on all objects whose names begin with *Aaaa*

Ways to get information directly from the *Mathematica* kernel.

This gives information on the built-in function Log.

```
In[1]:= ?Log
Log[z] gives the natural logarithm of z (logarithm to base
     e). Log[b, z] gives the logarithm to base b.
```

You can ask for information about any object, whether it is built into *Mathematica*, has been read in from a *Mathematica* package, or has been introduced by you.

When you use ? to get information, you must make sure that the question mark appears as the first character in your input line. You need to do this so that *Mathematica* can tell when you are requesting information rather than giving ordinary input for evaluation.

You can get extra information by using ??. Attributes will be discussed in Section 2.5.3.

```
In[2]:= ??Log
Log[z] gives the natural logarithm of z (logarithm to base
     e). Log[b, z] gives the logarithm to base b.

Attributes[Log] = {Listable, NumericFunction, Protected}
```

This gives information on all *Mathematica* objects whose names begin with Lo. When there is more than one object, *Mathematica* just lists their names.

```
In[3]:= ?Lo*

Locked       LogGamma        LogIntegral     LowerCaseQ
Log          LogicalExpand   LongForm
```

?Aaaa will give you information on the particular object whose name you specify. Using the "metacharacter" *, however, you can get information on collections of objects with similar names. The rule is that * is a "wild card" that can stand for any sequence of ordinary characters. So, for example, ?Lo* gets information on all objects whose names consist of the letters Lo, followed by any sequence of characters.

You can put * anywhere in the string you ask ? about. For example, ?*Expand would give you all objects whose names *end* with Expand. Similarly, ?x*0 would give you objects whose names start with x, end with 0, and have any sequence of characters in between. (You may notice that the way you use * to specify names in *Mathematica* is similar to the way you use * in Unix and other operating systems to specify file names.)

You can ask for information on most of the special input forms that *Mathematica* uses. This asks for information about the := operator.

```
In[4]:= ?:=

lhs := rhs assigns rhs to be the delayed value of lhs. rhs
    is maintained in an unevaluated form. When lhs appears,
    it is replaced by rhs, evaluated afresh each time.
```

■ 1.3.10 *Mathematica* Packages

One of the most important features of *Mathematica* is that it is an extensible system. There is a certain amount of mathematical and other functionality that is built into *Mathematica*. But by using the *Mathematica* language, it is always possible to add more functionality.

For many kinds of calculations, what is built into the standard version of *Mathematica* will be quite sufficient. However, if you work in a particular specialized area, you may find that you often need to use certain functions that are not built into *Mathematica*.

In such cases, you may well be able to find a *Mathematica* package that contains the functions you need. *Mathematica* packages are files written in the *Mathematica* language. They consist of collections of *Mathematica* definitions which "teach" *Mathematica* about particular application areas.

<<*package*	read in a *Mathematica* package

Reading in *Mathematica* packages.

If you want to use functions from a particular package, you must first read the package into *Mathematica*. The details of how to do this are discussed in Section 1.11. There are various conventions that govern the names you should use to refer to packages.

This command reads in a particular *Mathematica* package.	*In[1]:=* **<< DiscreteMath`CombinatorialFunctions`**
The Subfactorial function is defined in the package.	*In[2]:=* **Subfactorial[10]**
	Out[2]= 1334961

There are a number of subtleties associated with such issues as conflicts between names of functions in different packages. These are discussed in Section 2.6.9. One point to note, however, is that you must not refer to a function that you will read from a package before actually reading in the package. If you do this by mistake, you will have to execute the command Remove["*name*"] to get rid of the function before you read in the package which defines it. If you do not call Remove, *Mathematica* will use "your" version of the function, rather than the one from the package.

Remove["*name*"]   remove a function that has been introduced in error

Making sure that *Mathematica* uses correct definitions from packages.

The fact that *Mathematica* can be extended using packages means that the boundary of exactly what is "part of *Mathematica*" is quite blurred. As far as usage is concerned, there is actually no difference between functions defined in packages and functions that are fundamentally built into *Mathematica*.

In fact, a fair number of the functions described in this book are actually implemented as *Mathematica* packages. However, on most *Mathematica* systems, the necessary packages have been preloaded, so that the functions they define are always present. (On some systems with severe memory limitations, even these packages may be loaded only on request.)

To blur the boundary of what is part of *Mathematica* even further, Section 2.6.11 describes how you can tell *Mathematica* automatically to load a particular package if you ever try to use a certain function. If you never use that function, then it will not be present. But as soon as you try to use it, its definition will be read in from a *Mathematica* package.

As a practical matter, the functions that should be considered "part of *Mathematica*" are probably those that are present in all *Mathematica* systems. It is these functions that are primarily discussed in this book.

Nevertheless, most versions of *Mathematica* come with a standard set of *Mathematica* packages, which contain definitions for many more functions. Some of these functions are mentioned in this book. But to get them, you must usually read in the necessary packages explicitly.

You can use the Help Browser to get information on standard *Mathematica* add-on packages.

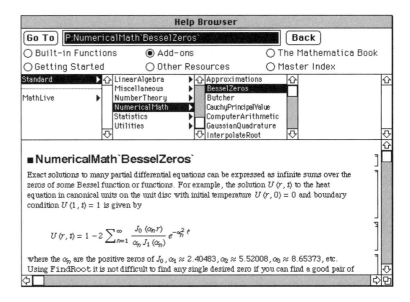

Of course, it is possible to set your *Mathematica* system up so that particular packages are pre-loaded, or are automatically loaded when needed. If you do this, then there may be many functions that appear as standard in your version of *Mathematica*, but which are not documented in this book.

One point that should be mentioned is the relationship between packages and notebooks. Both are stored as files on your computer system, and both can be read into *Mathematica*. However, a notebook is intended to be displayed, typically with a notebook interface, while a package is intended only to be used as *Mathematica* input. Many notebooks in fact contain sections that can be considered as packages, and which contain sequences of definitions intended for input to *Mathematica*.

■ 1.3.11 Warnings and Messages

Mathematica usually goes about its work silently, giving output only when it has finished doing the calculations you asked for.

However, if it looks as if *Mathematica* is doing something you definitely did not intend, *Mathematica* will usually print a message to warn you.

The square root function should have only one argument. *Mathematica* prints a message to warn you that you have given two arguments here.

```
In[1]:= Sqrt[4, 5]

Sqrt::argx:
    Sqrt called with 2 arguments; 1 argument is expected.

Out[1]= Sqrt[4, 5]
```

Each message has a name. You can switch off messages using Off.

```
In[2]:= Off[Sqrt::argx]
```

The message Sqrt::argx has now
been switched off, and will no longer
appear.

In[3]:= **Sqrt[4, 5]**

Out[3]= Sqrt[4, 5]

This switches Sqrt::argx back on
again.

In[4]:= **On[Sqrt::argx]**

Off[*Function*::*tag*]	switch off (suppress) a message
On[*Function*::*tag*]	switch on a message

Functions for controlling message output.

■ 1.3.12 Interrupting Calculations

There will probably be times when you want to stop *Mathematica* in the middle of a calculation.
Perhaps you realize that you asked *Mathematica* to do the wrong thing. Or perhaps the calculation is
just taking a long time, and you want to find out what is going on.

The way that you interrupt a *Mathematica* calculation depends on what kind of interface you are
using.

COMMAND-COMMA or ALT-COMMA	notebook interfaces
CONTROL-C	text-based interfaces

Typical keys to interrupt calculations in *Mathematica*.

On some computer systems, it may take *Mathematica* some time to respond to your interrupt. When
Mathematica does respond, it will typically give you a menu of possible things to do.

continue	continue the calculation
show	show what *Mathematica* is doing
inspect	inspect the current state of your calculation
abort	abort this particular calculation
exit	exit *Mathematica* completely

Some typical options available when you interrupt a calculation in *Mathematica*.

1.4 Algebraic Calculations

■ 1.4.1 Symbolic Computation

One of the most important features of *Mathematica* is that it can do *symbolic*, as well as *numerical* calculations. This means that it can handle algebraic formulas as well as numbers.

Here is a typical numerical computation.

In[1]:= **3 + 62 - 1**

Out[1]= 64

This is a symbolic computation.

In[2]:= **3x - x + 2**

Out[2]= $2 + 2x$

Numerical computation	3 + 62 - 1	$\longrightarrow$ 64
Symbolic computation	3x - x + 2	$\longrightarrow$ $2 + 2x$

Numerical and symbolic computations.

You can type any algebraic expression into *Mathematica*.

In[3]:= **-1 + 2x + x^3**

Out[3]= $-1 + 2x + x^3$

Mathematica automatically carries out basic algebraic simplifications. Here it combines x^2 and $-4x^2$ to get $-3x^2$.

In[4]:= **x^2 + x - 4 x^2**

Out[4]= $x - 3x^2$

You can type in any algebraic expression, using the operators listed on page 29. You can use spaces to denote multiplication. Be careful not to forget the space in x y. If you type in xy with no space, *Mathematica* will interpret this as a single symbol, with the name xy, not as a product of the two symbols x and y.

Mathematica rearranges and combines terms using the standard rules of algebra.

In[5]:= **x y + 2 x^2 y + y^2 x^2 - 2 y x**

Out[5]= $-xy + 2x^2y + x^2y^2$

Here is another algebraic expression.

In[6]:= **(x + 2y + 1)(x - 2)^2**

Out[6]= $(-2 + x)^2 (1 + x + 2y)$

The function Expand multiplies out products and powers.

In[7]:= **Expand[%]**

Out[7]= $4 - 3x^2 + x^3 + 8y - 8xy + 2x^2y$

Factor does essentially the inverse of Expand.

In[8]:= **Factor[%]**

Out[8]= $(-2 + x)^2 (1 + x + 2y)$

When you type in more complicated expressions, it is important that you put parentheses in the right places. Thus, for example, you have to give the expression x^{4y} in the form x^(4y). If you leave out the parentheses, you get $x^4 y$ instead. It never hurts to put in too many parentheses, but to find out exactly when you need to use parentheses, look at Section A.2.

Here is a more complicated formula, requiring several parentheses.	*In[9]:=* `Sqrt[2]/9801 (4n)! (1103 + 26390 n) / (n!^4 396^(4n))`

$$Out[9]= \frac{\sqrt{2}\; 396^{-4n}\, (1103 + 26390\,n)\, (4\,n)!}{9801\, n!^4}$$

When you type in an expression, *Mathematica* automatically applies its large repertoire of rules for transforming expressions. These rules include the standard rules of algebra, such as $x - x = 0$, together with much more sophisticated rules involving higher mathematical functions.

Mathematica uses standard rules of algebra to replace $(\sqrt{1+x})^4$ by $(1+x)^2$.	*In[10]:=* `Sqrt[1 + x]^4`
	$Out[10]= (1+x)^2$

Mathematica knows no rules for this expression, so it leaves the expression in the original form you gave.	*In[11]:=* `Log[1 + Cos[x]]`
	$Out[11]= \mathrm{Log}[1 + \mathrm{Cos}[x]]$

The notion of transformation rules is a very general one. In fact, you can think of the whole of *Mathematica* as simply a system for applying a collection of transformation rules to many different kinds of expressions.

The general principle that *Mathematica* follows is simple to state. It takes any expression you input, and gets results by applying a succession of transformation rules, stopping when it knows no more transformation rules that can be applied.

■ Take any expression, and apply transformation rules until the result no longer changes.

The fundamental principle of *Mathematica*.

■ 1.4.2 Values for Symbols

When *Mathematica* transforms an expression such as x + x into 2x, it is treating the variable x in a purely symbolic or formal fashion. In such cases, x is a symbol which can stand for any expression.

Often, however, you need to replace a symbol like x with a definite "value". Sometimes this value will be a number; often it will be another expression.

To take an expression such as 1 + 2x and replace the symbol x that appears in it with a definite value, you can create a *Mathematica* transformation rule, and then apply this rule to the expression. To replace x with the value 3, you would create the transformation rule x -> 3. You must type -> as a pair of characters, with no space in between. You can think of x -> 3 as being a rule in which "x goes to 3".

To apply a transformation rule to a particular *Mathematica* expression, you type *expr* /. *rule*. The "replacement operator" /. is typed as a pair of characters, with no space in between.

<table>
<tr><td>This uses the transformation rule x->3 in the expression 1 + 2x.</td><td>In[1]:= 1 + 2x /. x -> 3
Out[1]= 7</td></tr>
<tr><td>You can replace x with any expression. Here every occurrence of x is replaced by 2 - y.</td><td>In[2]:= 1 + x + x^2 /. x -> 2 - y
Out[2]= $3 + (2-y)^2 - y$</td></tr>
<tr><td>Here is a transformation rule. Mathematica treats it like any other symbolic expression.</td><td>In[3]:= x -> 3 + y
Out[3]= $x \to 3 + y$</td></tr>
<tr><td>This applies the transformation rule on the previous line to the expression x^2 - 9.</td><td>In[4]:= x^2 - 9 /. %
Out[4]= $-9 + (3+y)^2$</td></tr>
</table>

expr /. *x -> value*	replace *x* by *value* in the expression *expr*
expr /. {*x -> xval* , *y -> yval*}	perform several replacements

Replacing symbols by values in expressions.

<table>
<tr><td>You can apply rules together by putting the rules in a list.</td><td>In[5]:= (x + y) (x - y)^2 /. {x -> 3, y -> 1 - a}
Out[5]= $(4-a)(2+a)^2$</td></tr>
</table>

The replacement operator /. allows you to apply transformation rules to a particular expression. Sometimes, however, you will want to define transformation rules that should *always* be applied. For example, you might want to replace x with 3 whenever x occurs.

As discussed in Section 1.2.2, you can do this by *assigning* the value 3 to x using x = 3. Once you have made the assignment x = 3, x will always be replaced by 3, whenever it appears.

<table>
<tr><td>This assigns the value 3 to x.</td><td>In[6]:= x = 3
Out[6]= 3</td></tr>
<tr><td>Now x will automatically be replaced by 3 wherever it appears.</td><td>In[7]:= x^2 - 1
Out[7]= 8</td></tr>
<tr><td>This assigns the expression 1 + a to be the value of x.</td><td>In[8]:= x = 1 + a
Out[8]= $1 + a$</td></tr>
<tr><td>Now x is replaced by 1 + a.</td><td>In[9]:= x^2 - 1
Out[9]= $-1 + (1+a)^2$</td></tr>
</table>

You can define the value of a symbol to be any expression, not just a number. You should realize that once you have given such a definition, the definition will continue to be used whenever the symbol appears, until you explicitly change or remove the definition. For most people, forgetting to remove values you have assigned to symbols is the single most common source of mistakes in using *Mathematica*.

x = value	define a value for *x* which will always be used
x =.	remove any value defined for *x*

Assigning values to symbols.

The symbol x still has the value you assigned to it above.	*In[10]:=* **x + 5 - 2x**
	Out[10]= $6 + a - 2(1 + a)$
This removes the value you assigned to x.	*In[11]:=* **x =.**
Now x has no value defined, so it can be used as a purely symbolic variable.	*In[12]:=* **x + 5 - 2x**
	Out[12]= $5 - x$

A symbol such as x can serve many different purposes in *Mathematica*, and in fact, much of the flexibility of *Mathematica* comes from being able to mix these purposes at will. However, you need to keep some of the different uses of x straight in order to avoid making mistakes. The most important distinction is between the use of x as a name for another expression, and as a symbolic variable that stands only for itself.

Traditional programming languages that do not support symbolic computation allow variables to be used only as names for objects, typically numbers, that have been assigned as values for them. In *Mathematica*, however, x can also be treated as a purely formal variable, to which various transformation rules can be applied. Of course, if you explicitly give a definition, such as x = 3, then x will always be replaced by 3, and can no longer serve as a formal variable.

You should understand that explicit definitions such as x = 3 have a global effect. On the other hand, a replacement such as *expr /. x->3* affects only the specific expression *expr*. It is usually much easier to keep things straight if you avoid using explicit definitions except when absolutely necessary.

You can always mix replacements with assignments. With assignments, you can give names to expressions in which you want to do replacements, or to rules that you want to use to do the replacements.

This assigns a value to the symbol t.	*In[13]:=* **t = 1 + x^2**
	Out[13]= $1 + x^2$
This finds the value of t, and then replaces x by 2 in it.	*In[14]:=* **t /. x -> 2**
	Out[14]= 5
This finds the value of t for a different value of x.	*In[15]:=* **t /. x -> 5a**
	Out[15]= $1 + 25a^2$

This finds the value of t when x is
replaced by Pi, and then evaluates the
result numerically.

In[16]:= **t /. x -> Pi //N**

Out[16]= 10.8696

■ 1.4.3 Transforming Algebraic Expressions

There are often many different ways to write the same algebraic expression. As one example, the expression $(1 + x)^2$ can be written as $1 + 2x + x^2$. *Mathematica* provides a large collection of functions for converting between different forms of algebraic expressions.

Expand[*expr*]	multiply out products and powers, writing the result as a sum of terms
Factor[*expr*]	write *expr* as a product of minimal factors

Two common functions for transforming algebraic expressions.

Expand gives the "expanded form",
with products and powers multiplied
out.

In[1]:= **Expand[(1 + x)^2]**

Out[1]= $1 + 2x + x^2$

Factor recovers the original form.

In[2]:= **Factor[%]**

Out[2]= $(1 + x)^2$

It is easy to generate complicated
expressions with Expand.

In[3]:= **Expand[(1 + x + 3 y)^4]**

Out[3]= $1 + 4x + 6x^2 + 4x^3 + x^4 + 12y + 36xy + 36x^2y + 12x^3y +$
$54y^2 + 108xy^2 + 54x^2y^2 + 108y^3 + 108xy^3 + 81y^4$

Factor often gives you simpler
expressions.

In[4]:= **Factor[%]**

Out[4]= $(1 + x + 3y)^4$

There are some cases, though, where
Factor can give you more complicated
expressions.

In[5]:= **Factor[x^10 - 1]**

Out[5]= $(-1 + x)(1 + x)(1 - x + x^2 - x^3 + x^4)(1 + x + x^2 + x^3 + x^4)$

In this case, Expand gives the
"simpler" form.

In[6]:= **Expand[%]**

Out[6]= $-1 + x^{10}$

■ 1.4.4 Simplifying Algebraic Expressions

There are many situations where you want to write a particular algebraic expression in the simplest possible form. Although it is difficult to know exactly what one means in all cases by the "simplest form", a worthwhile practical procedure is to look at many different forms of an expression, and pick out the one that involves the smallest number of parts.

`Simplify[`*expr*`]`	try to find the simplest form of *expr* by applying various standard algebraic transformations
`FullSimplify[`*expr*`]`	try to find the simplest form by applying a wide range of transformations

Simplifying algebraic expressions.

Simplify writes $x^2 + 2x + 1$ in factored form.

```
In[1]:= Simplify[x^2 + 2x + 1]
```
$$Out[1]= (1 + x)^2$$

Simplify leaves $x^{10} - 1$ in expanded form, since for this expression, the factored form is larger.

```
In[2]:= Simplify[x^10 - 1]
```
$$Out[2]= -1 + x^{10}$$

You can often use `Simplify` to "clean up" complicated expressions that you get as the results of computations.

Here is the integral of $1/(x^4 - 1)$. Integrals are discussed in more detail in Section 1.5.3.

```
In[3]:= Integrate[1/(x^4-1), x]
```
$$Out[3]= -\frac{ArcTan[x]}{2} + \frac{Log[-1 + x]}{4} - \frac{Log[1 + x]}{4}$$

Differentiating the result from `Integrate` should give back your original expression. In this case, as is common, you get a more complicated version of the expression.

```
In[4]:= D[%, x]
```
$$Out[4]= \frac{1}{4(-1 + x)} - \frac{1}{4(1 + x)} - \frac{1}{2(1 + x^2)}$$

Simplify succeeds in getting back the original, more simple, form of the expression.

```
In[5]:= Simplify[%]
```
$$Out[5]= \frac{1}{-1 + x^4}$$

`Simplify` is set up to try various standard algebraic transformations on the expressions you give. Sometimes, however, it can take more sophisticated transformations to make progress in finding the simplest form of an expression.

`FullSimplify` tries a much wider range of transformations, involving not only algebraic functions, but also many other kinds of functions.

Simplify does nothing to this expression.

```
In[6]:= Simplify[Gamma[x] Gamma[1 - x]]
```
$$Out[6]= Gamma[1 - x] Gamma[x]$$

FullSimplify, however, transforms it to a simpler form.

```
In[7]:= FullSimplify[Gamma[x] Gamma[1 - x]]
```
$$Out[7]= \pi Csc[\pi x]$$

For fairly small expressions, `FullSimplify` will often succeed in making some remarkable simplifications. But for larger expressions, it often becomes unmanageably slow.

The reason for this is that to do its job, FullSimplify effectively has to try combining every part of an expression with every other, and for large expressions the number of cases that it has to consider can be astronomically large.

Simplify also has a difficult task to do, but it is set up to avoid some of the most time-consuming transformations that are tried by FullSimplify. For simple algebraic calculations, therefore, you may often find it convenient to apply Simplify quite routinely to your results.

In more complicated calculations, however, even Simplify, let alone FullSimplify, may end up needing to try a very large number of different forms, and therefore taking a long time. In such cases, you typically need to do more controlled simplification, and use your knowledge of the form you want to get to guide the process.

■ 1.4.5 Advanced Topic: Putting Expressions into Different Forms

Complicated algebraic expressions can usually be written in many different ways. *Mathematica* provides a variety of functions for converting expressions from one form to another.

In many applications, the most common of these functions are Expand, Factor and Simplify. However, particularly when you have rational expressions that contain quotients, you may need to use other functions.

Expand[*expr*]	multiply out products and powers
ExpandAll[*expr*]	apply Expand everywhere
Factor[*expr*]	reduce to a product of factors
Together[*expr*]	put all terms over a common denominator
Apart[*expr*]	separate into terms with simple denominators
Cancel[*expr*]	cancel common factors between numerators and denominators
Simplify[*expr*]	try a sequence of algebraic transformations and give the smallest form of *expr* found

Functions for transforming algebraic expressions.

Here is a rational expression that can be written in many different forms.

$In[1]:= e = (x - 1)^2 (2 + x) / ((1 + x) (x - 3)^2)$

$$Out[1]= \frac{(-1+x)^2 (2+x)}{(-3+x)^2 (1+x)}$$

Expand expands out the numerator, but leaves the denominator in factored form.

$In[2]:=$ **Expand[e]**

$$Out[2]= \frac{2}{(-3+x)^2\,(1+x)} - \frac{3\,x}{(-3+x)^2\,(1+x)} + \frac{x^3}{(-3+x)^2\,(1+x)}$$

ExpandAll expands out everything, including the denominator.

$In[3]:=$ **ExpandAll[e]**

$$Out[3]= \frac{2}{9+3\,x-5\,x^2+x^3} - \frac{3\,x}{9+3\,x-5\,x^2+x^3} + \frac{x^3}{9+3\,x-5\,x^2+x^3}$$

Together collects all the terms together over a common denominator.

$In[4]:=$ **Together[%]**

$$Out[4]= \frac{2-3\,x+x^3}{9+3\,x-5\,x^2+x^3}$$

Apart breaks the expression apart into terms with simple denominators.

$In[5]:=$ **Apart[%]**

$$Out[5]= 1 + \frac{5}{(-3+x)^2} + \frac{19}{4\,(-3+x)} + \frac{1}{4\,(1+x)}$$

Factor factors everything, in this case reproducing the original form.

$In[6]:=$ **Factor[%]**

$$Out[6]= \frac{(-1+x)^2\,(2+x)}{(-3+x)^2\,(1+x)}$$

According to Simplify, this is the simplest way to write the original expression.

$In[7]:=$ **Simplify[e]**

$$Out[7]= \frac{(-1+x)^2\,(2+x)}{(-3+x)^2\,(1+x)}$$

Getting expressions into the form you want is something of an art. In most cases, it is best simply to experiment, trying different transformations until you get what you want. Often you will be able to use palettes in the front end to do this.

When you have an expression with a single variable, you can choose to write it as a sum of terms, a product, and so on. If you have an expression with several variables, there is an even wider selection of possible forms. You can, for example, choose to group terms in the expression so that one or another of the variables is "dominant".

Collect[*expr*, *x*]	group together powers of *x*
FactorTerms[*expr*, *x*]	pull out factors that do not depend on *x*

Rearranging expressions in several variables.

Here is an algebraic expression in two variables.

$In[8]:=$ **v = Expand[(3 + 2 x)^2 (x + 2 y)^2]**

$$Out[8]= 9\,x^2 + 12\,x^3 + 4\,x^4 + 36\,x\,y + 48\,x^2\,y + 16\,x^3\,y + 36\,y^2 + 48\,x\,y^2 + 16\,x^2\,y^2$$

This groups together terms in v that involve the same power of x.	$In[9]:=$ **Collect[v, x]**
	$Out[9]=$ $4x^4 + 36y^2 + x^3(12 + 16y) + x^2(9 + 48y + 16y^2) + $ $x(36y + 48y^2)$

This groups together powers of y.	$In[10]:=$ **Collect[v, y]**
	$Out[10]=$ $9x^2 + 12x^3 + 4x^4 + (36x + 48x^2 + 16x^3)y + $ $(36 + 48x + 16x^2)y^2$

This factors out the piece that does not depend on y.	$In[11]:=$ **FactorTerms[v, y]**
	$Out[11]=$ $(9 + 12x + 4x^2)(x^2 + 4xy + 4y^2)$

As we have seen, even when you restrict yourself to polynomials and rational expressions, there are many different ways to write any particular expression. If you consider more complicated expressions, involving, for example, higher mathematical functions, the variety of possible forms becomes still greater. As a result, it is totally infeasible to have a specific function built into *Mathematica* to produce each possible form. Rather, *Mathematica* allows you to construct arbitrary sets of transformation rules for converting between different forms. Many *Mathematica* packages include such rules; the details of how to construct them for yourself are given in Section 2.4.

There are nevertheless a few additional built-in *Mathematica* functions for transforming expressions.

+	TrigExpand[*expr*]	expand out trigonometric expressions into a sum of terms
+	TrigFactor[*expr*]	factor trigonometric expressions into products of terms
+	TrigReduce[*expr*]	reduce trigonometric expressions using multiple angles
+	TrigToExp[*expr*]	convert trigonometric functions to exponentials
+	ExpToTrig[*expr*]	convert exponentials to trigonometric functions
	ComplexExpand[*expr*]	perform expansions assuming that all variables are real
	PowerExpand[*expr*]	transform $(xy)^p$ into $x^p y^p$, etc.

Some other functions for transforming expressions.

This expands out the trigonometric expression, writing it so that all functions have argument x.	$In[12]:=$ **TrigExpand[Tan[x] Cos[2x]]**
	$Out[12]=$ $Cos[x] Sin[x] - Sin[x]^2 Tan[x]$

This uses trigonometric identities to generate a factored form of the expression.	$In[13]:=$ **TrigFactor[%]**
	$Out[13]=$ $(Cos[x] - Sin[x])(Cos[x] + Sin[x]) Tan[x]$

This reduces the expression by using multiple angles.	$In[14]:=$ **TrigReduce[%]**
	$Out[14]=$ $Sec[x]\left(-\dfrac{Sin[x]}{2} + \dfrac{Sin[3x]}{2}\right)$

This expands the sine assuming that x and y are both real.	*In[15]:=* **ComplexExpand[Sin[x + I y]]**
	Out[15]= Cosh[y] Sin[x] + I Cos[x] Sinh[y]
This does the expansion allowing x and y to be complex.	*In[16]:=* **ComplexExpand[Sin[x + I y], {x, y}]**
	Out[16]= -Cosh[Im[x] + Re[y]] Sin[Im[y] - Re[x]] + I Cos[Im[y] - Re[x]] Sinh[Im[x] + Re[y]]

The transformations on expressions done by functions like Expand and Factor are always correct, whatever values the symbolic variables in the expressions may have. Sometimes, however, it is useful to perform transformations which are correct only if certain assumptions are made about the possible values of symbolic variables. One such transformation is performed by PowerExpand.

Mathematica does not automatically expand out non-integer powers of products.	*In[17]:=* **Sqrt[x y]**
	Out[17]= $\sqrt{xy}$
PowerExpand does the expansion.	*In[18]:=* **PowerExpand[%]**
	Out[18]= $\sqrt{x} \sqrt{y}$
The expansion is guaranteed to be correct if x and y are both non-negative.	*In[19]:=* **{Sqrt[x y], Sqrt[x] Sqrt[y]} /. {x -> -1, y -> -1}**
	Out[19]= {1, -1}

■ 1.4.6 Picking Out Pieces of Algebraic Expressions

Coefficient[*expr*, *form*]	coefficient of *form* in *expr*
Exponent[*expr*, *form*]	maximum power of *form* in *expr*
Part[*expr*, *n*] or *expr*[[*n*]]	n^{th} term of *expr*

Functions to pick out pieces of polynomials.

Here is an algebraic expression.	*In[1]:=* **e = Expand[(1 + 3x + 4y^2)^2]**
	Out[1]= $1 + 6x + 9x^2 + 8y^2 + 24xy^2 + 16y^4$
This gives the coefficient of x in e.	*In[2]:=* **Coefficient[e, x]**
	Out[2]= $6 + 24y^2$
Exponent[*expr*, *y*] gives the highest power of *y* that appears in *expr*.	*In[3]:=* **Exponent[e, y]**
	Out[3]= 4
This gives the fourth term in e.	*In[4]:=* **Part[e, 4]**
	Out[4]= $8y^2$

You may notice that the function Part[*expr*, *n*] used to pick out the nth term in a sum is the same as the function described in Section 1.2.4 for picking out elements in lists. This is no coincidence. In fact, as discussed in Section 2.1.5, every *Mathematica* expression can be manipulated structurally much like a list. However, as discussed in Section 2.1.5, you must be careful, because *Mathematica* often shows algebraic expressions in a form that is different from the way it treats them internally.

Coefficient works even with polynomials that are not explicitly expanded out.	*In[5]:=* **Coefficient[(1 + 3x + 4y^2)^2, x]** *Out[5]=* $6 + 24\,y^2$

Numerator[*expr*]	numerator of *expr*
Denominator[*expr*]	denominator of *expr*

Functions to pick out pieces of rational expressions.

Here is a rational expression.	*In[6]:=* **r = (1 + x)/(2 (2 - y))** *Out[6]=* $\dfrac{1+x}{2\,(2-y)}$
Denominator picks out the denominator.	*In[7]:=* **Denominator[%]** *Out[7]=* $2\,(2-y)$
Denominator gives 1 for expressions that are not quotients.	*In[8]:=* **Denominator[1/x + 2/y]** *Out[8]=* 1

■ 1.4.7 Controlling the Display of Large Expressions

When you do symbolic calculations, it is quite easy to end up with extremely complicated expressions. Often, you will not even want to *see* the complete result of a computation.

If you end your input with a semicolon, *Mathematica* will do the computation you asked for, but will not display the result. You can nevertheless use % or Out[*n*] to refer to the result.

Even though you may not want to see the *whole* result from a computation, you often do need to see its basic form. You can use Short to display the *outline* of an expression, omitting some of the terms.

Ending your input with ; stops *Mathematica* from displaying the complicated result of the computation.	*In[1]:=* **Expand[(x + 5 y + 10)^8] ;**
You can still refer to the result as %. //Short displays a one-line outline of the result. The <<*n*>> stands for *n* terms that have been left out.	*In[2]:=* **% //Short** *Out[2]//Short=* $100000000 + \langle\langle 43 \rangle\rangle + 390625\,y^8$

This shows a three-line version of the expression. More parts are now visible.	$In[3]:=$ **Short[%, 3]**

$Out[3]//Short=$ $100000000 + 80000000 x + 28000000 x^2 +$
$5600000 x^3 + \ll 37 \gg + 437500 x^2 y^6 +$
$6250000 y^7 + 625000 x y^7 + 390625 y^8$

This gives the total number of terms in the sum.	$In[4]:=$ **Length[%]**

$Out[4]=$ 45

command ;	execute *command*, but do not print the result
expr // Short	show a one-line outline form of *expr*
Short[*expr*, *n*]	show an *n*-line outline of *expr*

Some ways to shorten your output.

■ 1.4.8 The Limits of *Mathematica*

In just one *Mathematica* command, you can easily specify a calculation that is far too complicated for any computer to do. For example, you could ask for Expand[(1+x)^(10^100)]. The result of this calculation would have $10^{100} + 1$ terms—more than the total number of particles in the universe.

You should have no trouble working out Expand[(1+x)^100] on any computer that can run *Mathematica*. But as you increase the exponent of (1+x), the results you get will eventually become too big for your computer's memory to hold. Exactly at what point this happens depends not only on the total amount of memory your computer has, but often also on such details as what other jobs happen to be running on your computer when you try to do your calculation.

If your computer does run out of memory in the middle of a calculation, most versions of *Mathematica* have no choice but to stop immediately. As a result, it is important to plan your calculations so that they never need more memory than your computer has.

Even if the result of an algebraic calculation is quite simple, the intermediate expressions that you generate in the course of the calculation can be very complicated. This means that even if the final result is small, the intermediate parts of a calculation can be too big for your computer to handle. If this happens, you can usually break your calculation into pieces, and succeed in doing each piece on its own. You should know that the internal scheme which *Mathematica* uses for memory management is such that once part of a calculation is finished, the memory used to store intermediate expressions that arose is immediately made available for new expressions.

Memory space is the most common limiting factor in *Mathematica* calculations. Time can also, however, be a limiting factor. You will usually be prepared to wait a second, or even a minute, for the result of a calculation. But you will less often be prepared to wait an hour or a day, and you will almost never be able to wait a year.

One class of calculations where time is often the limiting factor is those that effectively involve searching or testing a large number of possibilities. Integer factorization is a classic example. At some level, the problem of factoring an integer always seems to boil down to something related to testing a large number of candidate factors. As far as one knows now, the number of cases to test can increase almost as fast as the exponential of the number of digits in the integer we are trying to factor. As a result, the time needed to factor integers can increase very rapidly with the size of the integers you try to factor. In practice, you will find that `FactorInteger[`k`]` will give a result almost immediately when k has fewer than about 25 digits. But when k has 50 digits, `FactorInteger[`k`]` will often take an unmanageably long time.

In the field of computation theory, a distinction is typically drawn between algorithms which are "polynomial time", and those which are not. A polynomial time algorithm can always be executed in a time that increases only like a polynomial in the length of the input. Non-polynomial time algorithms may take times that increase exponentially with the length of their input.

The internal code of *Mathematica* typically uses polynomial time algorithms whenever it is feasible. There are some problems, however, for which no polynomial time algorithms are known. In such cases, *Mathematica* has no choice but to use non-polynomial time algorithms, which may take times that increase exponentially with the length of their input. Integer factorization is one such case. Other cases include factoring polynomials and solving equations when the number of variables involved becomes large.

Even when the time needed to do a computation does not increase exponentially, there will always come a point where the computation is too large or time-consuming to do on your particular computer system. As you work with *Mathematica*, you should develop some feeling for the limits on the kinds of calculations you can do in your particular application area.

- Doing arithmetic with numbers containing a few tens of thousands of digits.

- Expanding out a polynomial that gives a few hundred thousand terms.

- Factoring a polynomial in three variables with a few hundred terms.

- Applying a recursive rule a few hundred thousand times.

- Finding the numerical inverse of a 150×150 matrix.

- Finding the determinant of a 100×100 integer matrix.

- Finding the determinant of an 8×8 symbolic matrix.

- Finding numerical roots of a polynomial of degree 50.

- Rendering a few hundred thousand graphics primitives.

- Sorting a list of a few million elements.

- Searching a string that is a few million characters long.

- Formatting ten pages of `TraditionalForm` output.

Some operations that typically take a few seconds on a 1995 vintage workstation.

■ 1.4.9 Using Symbols to Tag Objects

There are many ways to use symbols in *Mathematica*. So far, we have concentrated on using symbols to store values and to represent mathematical variables. This section describes another way to use symbols in *Mathematica*.

The idea is to use symbols as "tags" for different types of objects.

Working with physical units gives one simple example. When you specify the length of an object, you want to give not only a number, but also the units in which the length is measured. In standard notation, you might write a length as 12 meters.

You can imitate this notation almost directly in *Mathematica*. You can for example simply use a symbol `meters` to indicate the units of our measurement.

The symbol `meters` here acts as a tag, which indicates the units used.	*In[1]:=* `12 meters` *Out[1]=* 12meters
You can add lengths like this.	*In[2]:=* `% + 5.3 meters` *Out[2]=* 17.3meters
This gives a speed.	*In[3]:=* `% / (25 seconds)` *Out[3]=* $\dfrac{0.692\text{meters}}{\text{seconds}}$

This converts to a speed in feet per second. | *In[4]:=* **% /. meters -> 3.28084 feet**

$$Out[4]= \frac{2.27034\,\text{feet}}{\text{seconds}}$$

There is in fact a standard *Mathematica* package that allows you to work with units. The package defines many symbols that represent standard types of units.

Load the *Mathematica* package for handling units.

In[5]:= **<<Miscellaneous`Units`**

The package uses standardized names for units.

In[6]:= **12 Meter/Second**

$$Out[6]= \frac{12\,\text{Meter}}{\text{Second}}$$

The function Convert[*expr, units*] converts to the specified units.

In[7]:= **Convert[%, Mile/Hour]**

$$Out[7]= \frac{26.8432\,\text{Mile}}{\text{Hour}}$$

Usually you have to give prefixes for units as separate words.

In[8]:= **Convert[3 Kilo Meter / Hour, Inch / Minute]**

$$Out[8]= \frac{1968.5\,\text{Inch}}{\text{Minute}}$$

1.5 Symbolic Mathematics

■ 1.5.1 Basic Operations

Mathematica's ability to deal with symbolic expressions, as well as numbers, allows you to use it for many kinds of mathematics.

Calculus is one example. With *Mathematica*, you can differentiate an expression *symbolically*, and get a formula for the result.

This finds the derivative of x^n.

    In[1]:= **D[x^n, x]**

    Out[1]= $n x^{-1+n}$

Here is a slightly more complicated example.

    In[2]:= **D[x^2 Log[x + a], x]**

    Out[2]= $\dfrac{x^2}{a+x} + 2 x \, Log[a+x]$

D[f, x**]**	the (partial) derivative $\frac{\partial f}{\partial x}$
Integrate[f, x**]**	the indefinite integral $\int f \, dx$
Sum[f, {i, *imin*, *imax*}**]**	the sum $\sum_{i=imin}^{imax} f$
Solve[lhs==rhs, x**]**	solution to an equation for x
Series[f, {x, x_0, *order*}**]**	a power series expansion of f about the point $x = x_0$
Limit[f, x->x_0**]**	the limit $\lim_{x \to x_0} f$

Some symbolic mathematical operations.

Getting formulas as the results of computations is usually desirable when it is possible. There are however many circumstances where it is mathematically impossible to get an explicit formula as the result of a computation. This happens, for example, when you try to solve an equation for which there is no "closed form" solution. In such cases, you must resort to numerical methods and approximations. These are discussed in Section 1.6.

■ 1.5.2 Differentiation

Here is the derivative of x^n with respect to x.

    In[1]:= **D[x^n, x]**

    Out[1]= $n x^{-1+n}$

Mathematica knows the derivatives of all the standard mathematical functions.	$In[2]:=$ **D[ArcTan[x], x]** $Out[2]= \dfrac{1}{1+x^2}$
This differentiates three times with respect to x.	$In[3]:=$ **D[x^n, {x, 3}]** $Out[3]= (-2+n)\,(-1+n)\,n\,x^{-3+n}$

The function D[x^n, x] really gives a *partial* derivative, in which n is assumed not to depend on x. *Mathematica* has another function, called Dt, which finds *total* derivatives, in which all variables are assumed to be related. In mathematical notation, D[f, x] is like $\frac{\partial f}{\partial x}$, while Dt[$f$, x] is like $\frac{df}{dx}$. You can think of Dt as standing for "derivative total".

Dt gives a *total derivative*, which assumes that n can depend on x. Dt[n, x] stands for $\frac{dn}{dx}$.	$In[4]:=$ **Dt[x^n, x]** $Out[4]= n\,x^{-1+n} + x^n\,Dt[n, x]\,Log[x]$
This gives the total differential $d(x^n)$. Dt[x] is the differential dx.	$In[5]:=$ **Dt[x^n]** $Out[5]= n\,x^{-1+n}\,Dt[x] + x^n\,Dt[n]\,Log[x]$

D[f, x]	partial derivative $\frac{\partial}{\partial x} f$
D[f, x_1, x_2, ...]	multiple derivative $\frac{\partial}{\partial x_1}\frac{\partial}{\partial x_2} ... f$
D[f, $\{x, n\}$]	repeated derivative $\frac{\partial^n f}{\partial x^n}$
Dt[f]	total differential df
Dt[f, x]	total derivative $\frac{d}{dx} f$

Some differentiation functions.

As well as treating variables like x symbolically, you can also treat functions in *Mathematica* symbolically. Thus, for example, you can find formulas for derivatives of f[x], without specifying any explicit form for the function f.

Mathematica does not know how to differentiate f, so it gives you back a symbolic result in terms of f'.	$In[6]:=$ **D[f[x], x]** $Out[6]= f'[x]$
Mathematica uses the chain rule to simplify derivatives.	$In[7]:=$ **D[2 x f[x^2], x]** $Out[7]= 2\,f[x^2] + 4\,x^2\,f'[x^2]$

■ 1.5.3 Integration

Here is the integral $\int x^n\, dx$ in *Mathematica*.

$In[1]:=$ **Integrate[x^n, x]**

$Out[1]=$ $\dfrac{x^{1+n}}{1+n}$

Here is a slightly more complicated example.

$In[2]:=$ **Integrate[1/(x^4 - a^4), x]**

$Out[2]=$ $-\dfrac{ArcTan\left[\frac{x}{a}\right]}{2\,a^3} + \dfrac{Log[a-x]}{4\,a^3} - \dfrac{Log[a+x]}{4\,a^3}$

Mathematica knows how to do almost any integral that can be done in terms of standard mathematical functions. But you should realize that even though an integrand may contain only fairly simple functions, its integral may involve much more complicated functions—or may not be expressible at all in terms of standard mathematical functions.

Here is a fairly straightforward integral.

$In[3]:=$ **Integrate[Log[1 - x^2], x]**

$Out[3]=$ $-2x - Log[-1+x] + Log[1+x] + x\,Log[1-x^2]$

This integral can be done only in terms of a dilogarithm function.

$In[4]:=$ **Integrate[Log[1 - x^2]/x, x]**

$Out[4]=$ $-\dfrac{1}{2}\,PolyLog[2, x^2]$

This integral involves Erf.

$In[5]:=$ **Integrate[Exp[1 - x^2], x]**

$Out[5]=$ $\dfrac{1}{2}\,E\,\sqrt{\pi}\,Erf[x]$

And this one involves a Fresnel function.

$In[6]:=$ **Integrate[Sin[x^2], x]**

$Out[6]=$ $\sqrt{\dfrac{\pi}{2}}\;FresnelS\left[\sqrt{\dfrac{2}{\pi}}\,x\right]$

Even this integral requires a hypergeometric function.

$In[7]:=$ **Integrate[(1 - x^2)^n, x]**

$Out[7]=$ $x\,Hypergeometric2F1\left[\dfrac{1}{2}, -n, \dfrac{3}{2}, x^2\right]$

This integral simply cannot be done in terms of standard mathematical functions. As a result, *Mathematica* just leaves it undone.

$In[8]:=$ **Integrate[x^x, x]**

$Out[8]=$ $\int x^x dx$

$$\texttt{Integrate[}f, x\texttt{]} \quad \text{the indefinite integral } \int f\, dx$$

$$\texttt{Integrate[}f, x, y\texttt{]} \quad \text{the multiple integral } \int dx\, dy\, f$$

$$\texttt{Integrate[}f, \{x, xmin, xmax\}\texttt{]} \quad \text{the definite integral } \int_{xmin}^{xmax} f\, dx$$

$$\texttt{Integrate[}f, \{x, xmin, xmax\}, \{y, ymin, ymax\}\texttt{]}$$
$$\text{the multiple integral } \int_{xmin}^{xmax} dx \int_{ymin}^{ymax} dy\, f$$

Integration.

Here is the definite integral $\int_a^b \log(x)\, dx$.	`In[9]:= Integrate[ Log[x], {x, a, b} ]` `Out[9]= -a (-1 + Log[a]) + b (-1 + Log[b])`
Here is another definite integral.	`In[10]:= Integrate[Exp[-x^2], {x, 0, Infinity}]` `Out[10]=` $\dfrac{\sqrt{\pi}}{2}$
Mathematica cannot give you a formula for this definite integral.	`In[11]:= Integrate[ x^x, {x, 0, 1} ]` `Out[11]=` $\displaystyle\int_0^1 x^x\, dx$
You can still get a numerical result, though.	`In[12]:= N[ % ]` `Out[12]= 0.78343`
This evaluates the multiple integral $\int_0^1 dx \int_0^x dy\,(x^2 + y^2)$. The range of the outermost integration variable appears first.	`In[13]:= Integrate[ x^2 + y^2, {x, 0, 1}, {y, 0, x} ]` `Out[13]=` $\dfrac{1}{3}$

■ 1.5.4 Sums and Products

This constructs the sum $\sum_{i=1}^7 \frac{x^i}{i}$.	`In[1]:= Sum[x^i/i, {i, 1, 7}]` `Out[1]=` $x + \dfrac{x^2}{2} + \dfrac{x^3}{3} + \dfrac{x^4}{4} + \dfrac{x^5}{5} + \dfrac{x^6}{6} + \dfrac{x^7}{7}$
You can leave out the lower limit if it is equal to 1.	`In[2]:= Sum[x^i/i, {i, 7}]` `Out[2]=` $x + \dfrac{x^2}{2} + \dfrac{x^3}{3} + \dfrac{x^4}{4} + \dfrac{x^5}{5} + \dfrac{x^6}{6} + \dfrac{x^7}{7}$
This makes *i* increase in steps of 2, so that only odd-numbered values are included.	`In[3]:= Sum[x^i/i, {i, 1, 5, 2}]` `Out[3]=` $x + \dfrac{x^3}{3} + \dfrac{x^5}{5}$

Products work just like sums.

$In[4]:=$ **Product[x + i, {i, 1, 4}]**

$Out[4]=$ $(1 + x) (2 + x) (3 + x) (4 + x)$

Sum[f, {i, $imin$, $imax$}]	the sum $\sum_{i=imin}^{imax} f$
Sum[f, {i, $imin$, $imax$, di}]	the sum with i increasing in steps of di
Sum[f, {i, $imin$, $imax$}, {j, $jmin$, $jmax$}]	
	the nested sum $\sum_{i=imin}^{imax} \sum_{j=jmin}^{jmax} f$
Product[f, {i, $imin$, $imax$}]	the product $\prod_{i=imin}^{imax} f$

Sums and products.

This sum is computed symbolically as a function of n.

$In[5]:=$ **Sum[i^2, {i, 1, n}]**

$Out[5]=$ $\dfrac{1}{6} n (1 + n) (1 + 2n)$

Mathematica can also give an exact result for this infinite sum.

$In[6]:=$ **Sum[1/i^4, {i, 1, Infinity}]**

$Out[6]=$ $\dfrac{\pi^4}{90}$

As with integrals, simple sums can lead to complicated results.

$In[7]:=$ **Sum[1/(i^4 + 2), {i, 1, Infinity}]**

$Out[7]=$ $(3 \text{Cos}[2^{3/4} \pi] - 3 \text{Cosh}[2^{3/4} \pi] -$
$2\, 2^{3/4} \pi \text{Sin}[2^{3/4} \pi] - 2\, 2^{3/4} \pi \text{Sinh}[2^{3/4} \pi]) /$
$(16 (\text{Cos}[2^{3/4} \pi] - \text{Cosh}[2^{3/4} \pi]))$

This sum cannot be evaluated exactly using standard mathematical functions.

$In[8]:=$ **Sum[1/(i! + (2i)!), {i, 1, Infinity}]**

$Out[8]=$ $\displaystyle\sum_{i=1}^{\infty} \dfrac{1}{i! + (2i)!}$

You can nevertheless find a numerical approximation to the result.

$In[9]:=$ **N[%]**

$Out[9]=$ 0.373197

Mathematica also has a notation for multiple sums and products.
Sum[f, {i, $imin$, $imax$}, {j, $jmin$, $jmax$}] represents a sum over i and j, which would be written in standard mathematical notation as $\sum_{i=imin}^{imax} \sum_{j=jmin}^{jmax} f$. Notice that in *Mathematica* notation, as in standard mathematical notation, the range of the *outermost* variable is given *first*.

This is the multiple sum $\sum_{i=1}^{3} \sum_{j=1}^{i} x^i y^j$. Notice that the outermost sum over i is given first, just as in the mathematical notation.

$In[10]:=$ **Sum[x^i y^j, {i, 1, 3}, {j, 1, i}]**

$Out[10]=$ $x y + x^2 y + x^3 y + x^2 y^2 + x^3 y^2 + x^3 y^3$

The way the ranges of variables are specified in Sum and Product is an example of the rather general *iterator notation* that *Mathematica* uses. You will see this notation again when we discuss generating tables and lists using Table (Section 1.8.2), and when we describe Do loops (Section 1.7.3).

$\{imax\}$	iterate *imax* times, without incrementing any variables
$\{i, imax\}$	*i* goes from 1 to *imax* in steps of 1
$\{i, imin, imax\}$	*i* goes from *imin* to *imax* in steps of 1
$\{i, imin, imax, di\}$	*i* goes from *imin* to *imax* in steps of *di*
$\{i, imin, imax\}, \{j, jmin, jmax\}, ...$	*i* goes from *imin* to *imax*, and for each such value, *j* goes from *jmin* to *jmax*, etc.

Mathematica iterator notation.

■ 1.5.5 Equations

Section 1.2.2 discussed *assignments* such as $x = y$ which *set* x equal to y. This section discusses *equations*, which *test* equality. The equation $x == y$ *tests* whether x is equal to y.

This *tests* whether 2 + 2 and 4 are equal. The result is the symbol True.

```
In[1]:= 2 + 2 == 4
Out[1]= True
```

It is very important that you do not confuse $x = y$ with $x == y$. While $x = y$ is an *imperative* statement that actually causes an assignment to be done, $x == y$ merely *tests* whether x and y are equal, and causes no explicit action. If you have used the C programming language, you will recognize that the notation for assignment and testing in *Mathematica* is the same as in C.

$x = y$	assigns x to have value y
$x == y$	tests whether x and y are equal

Assignments and tests.

This *assigns* x to have value 4.

```
In[2]:= x = 4
Out[2]= 4
```

If you ask for x, you now get 4.

```
In[3]:= x
Out[3]= 4
```

This *tests* whether x is equal to 4. In this case, it is.

```
In[4]:= x == 4
Out[4]= True
```

x is equal to 4, not 6.	*In[5]:=* **x == 6**
	Out[5]= False
This removes the value assigned to x.	*In[6]:=* **x =.**

The tests we have used so far involve only numbers, and always give a definite answer, either **True** or **False**. You can also do tests on symbolic expressions.

Mathematica cannot get a definite result for this test unless you give x a specific numerical value.	*In[7]:=* **x == 5**
	Out[7]= $x == 5$
If you replace x by the specific numerical value 4, the test gives False.	*In[8]:=* **% /. x -> 4**
	Out[8]= False

Even when you do tests on symbolic expressions, there are some cases where you can get definite results. An important one is when you test the equality of two expressions that are *identical*. Whatever the numerical values of the variables in these expressions may be, *Mathematica* knows that the expressions must always be equal.

The two expressions are *identical*, so the result is **True**, whatever the value of x may be.	*In[9]:=* **2 x + x^2 == 2 x + x^2**
	Out[9]= True
Mathematica does not try to tell whether these expressions are equal. In this case, using **Expand** would make them have the same form.	*In[10]:=* **2 x + x^2 == x (2 + x)**
	Out[10]= $2x + x^2 == x(2 + x)$

Expressions like x == 4 represent *equations* in *Mathematica*. There are many functions in *Mathematica* for manipulating and solving equations.

This is an *equation* in *Mathematica*. Subsection 1.5.7 will discuss how to solve it for x.	*In[11]:=* **x^2 + 2 x - 7 == 0**
	Out[11]= $-7 + 2x + x^2 == 0$
You can assign a name to the equation.	*In[12]:=* **eqn = %**
	Out[12]= $-7 + 2x + x^2 == 0$
If you ask for eqn, you now get the equation.	*In[13]:=* **eqn**
	Out[13]= $-7 + 2x + x^2 == 0$

■ 1.5.6 Relational and Logical Operators

$x == y$	equal (also input as $x = y$)
$x \mathrel{!}= y$	unequal (also input as $x \neq y$)
$x > y$	greater than
$x >= y$	greater than or equal to (also input as $x \geq y$)
$x < y$	less than
$x <= y$	less than or equal to (also input as $x \leq y$)
$x == y == z$	all equal
$x \mathrel{!}= y \mathrel{!}= z$	all unequal (distinct)
$x > y > z$, etc.	strictly decreasing, etc.

Relational operators.

This tests whether 10 is less than 7. The result is False.

```
In[1]:= 10 < 7
Out[1]= False
```

Not all of these numbers are unequal, so this gives False.

```
In[2]:= 3 != 2 != 3
Out[2]= False
```

You can mix < and <=.

```
In[3]:= 3 < 5 <= 6
Out[3]= True
```

Since both of the quantities involved are numeric, *Mathematica* can determine that this is true.

```
In[4]:= Pi^E < E^Pi
Out[4]= True
```

Mathematica does not know whether this is true or false.

```
In[5]:= x > y
Out[5]= x > y
```

!p	not (also input as ¬p)
p && q && ...	and (also input as $p \wedge q \wedge$ ...)
p || q || ...	or (also input as $p \vee q \vee$ ...)
Xor[p, q, ...]	exclusive or
If[p, *then*, *else*]	give *then* if p is True, and *else* if p is False
LogicalExpand[*expr*]	expand out logical expressions

Logical operations.

Both tests give True, so the result is True.

```
In[6]:= 7 > 4 && 2 != 3
Out[6]= True
```

You should remember that the logical operations ==, && and \|\| are all *double characters* in *Mathematica*. If you have used the C programming language, you will recognize this notation as being the same as in C.

Mathematica does not know whether this is true or false.

```
In[7]:= p && q
Out[7]= p && q
```

Mathematica leaves this expression unchanged.

```
In[8]:= (p || q) && !(r || s)
Out[8]= (p || q) && !(r || s)
```

You can use LogicalExpand to expand out the terms.

```
In[9]:= LogicalExpand[ % ]
Out[9]= p && !r && !s || q && !r && !s
```

■ 1.5.7 Solving Equations

An expression like x^2 + 2 x - 7 == 0 represents an *equation* in *Mathematica*. You will often need to *solve* equations like this, to find out for what values of x they are true.

This gives the two solutions to the quadratic equation $x^2 + 2x - 7 = 0$. The solutions are given as replacements for x.

```
In[1]:= Solve[x^2 + 2x - 7 == 0, x]
Out[1]= {{x → -1 - 2√2 }, {x → -1 + 2√2 }}
```

Here are the numerical values of the solutions.

```
In[2]:= N[ % ]
Out[2]= {{x → -3.82843}, {x → 1.82843}}
```

You can get a list of the actual solutions for x by applying the rules generated by Solve to x using the replacement operator.

```
In[3]:= x /. %
Out[3]= {-3.82843, 1.82843}
```

You can equally well apply the rules to any other expression involving x.

In[4]:= **x^2 + 3 x /. %%**

Out[4]= {3.17157, 8.82843}

Solve[*lhs* == *rhs*, *x*]	solve an equation, giving a list of rules for *x*
x /. *solution*	use the list of rules to get values for *x*
expr /. *solution*	use the list of rules to get values for an expression

Finding and using solutions to equations.

Solve always tries to give you explicit *formulas* for the solutions to equations. However, it is a basic mathematical result that, for sufficiently complicated equations, explicit algebraic formulas cannot be given. If you have an algebraic equation in one variable, and the highest power of the variable is at most four, then *Mathematica* can always give you formulas for the solutions. However, if the highest power is five or more, it may be mathematically impossible to give explicit algebraic formulas for all the solutions.

Mathematica can always solve algebraic equations in one variable when the highest power is less than five.

In[5]:= **Solve[x^4 - 5 x^2 - 3 == 0, x]**

$$Out[5]= \left\{ \left\{ x \to -\frac{1}{2} I \sqrt{2 \left(-5 + \sqrt{37}\right)} \right\}, \right.$$
$$\left\{ x \to \frac{1}{2} I \sqrt{2 \left(-5 + \sqrt{37}\right)} \right\}, \left\{ x \to -\sqrt{\frac{1}{2} \left(5 + \sqrt{37}\right)} \right\},$$
$$\left. \left\{ x \to \sqrt{\frac{1}{2} \left(5 + \sqrt{37}\right)} \right\} \right\}$$

It can solve some equations that involve higher powers.

In[6]:= **Solve[x^6 == 1, x]**

$$Out[6]= \left\{ \{x \to -1\}, \{x \to 1\}, \left\{x \to -(-1)^{1/3}\right\}, \right.$$
$$\left. \left\{x \to (-1)^{1/3}\right\}, \left\{x \to -(-1)^{2/3}\right\}, \left\{x \to (-1)^{2/3}\right\} \right\}$$

There are some equations, however, for which it is mathematically impossible to find explicit formulas for the solutions. *Mathematica* uses **Root** objects to represent the solutions in this case.

In[7]:= **Solve[2 - 4 x + x^5 == 0, x]**

$$Out[7]= \{\{x \to Root[2 - 4\#1 + \#1^5\&, 1]\},$$
$$\{x \to Root[2 - 4\#1 + \#1^5\&, 2]\},$$
$$\{x \to Root[2 - 4\#1 + \#1^5\&, 3]\},$$
$$\{x \to Root[2 - 4\#1 + \#1^5\&, 4]\},$$
$$\{x \to Root[2 - 4\#1 + \#1^5\&, 5]\}\}$$

Even though you cannot get explicit formulas, you can still find the solutions numerically.

In[8]:= **N[%]**

$$Out[8]= \{\{x \to -1.51851\}, \{x \to 0.508499\},$$
$$\{x \to 1.2436\}, \{x \to -0.116792 - 1.43845 I\},$$
$$\{x \to -0.116792 + 1.43845 I\}\}$$

In addition to being able to solve purely algebraic equations, *Mathematica* can also solve some equations involving other functions.

After printing a warning, *Mathematica* returns one solution to this equation.

In[9]:= **Solve[Sin[x] == a, x]**

Solve::ifun:
    Inverse functions are being used by Solve, so some
        solutions may not be found.

Out[9]= {{x → ArcSin[a]}}

It is important to realize that an equation such as sin(*x*) = *a* actually has an infinite number of possible solutions, in this case differing by multiples of 2π. However, Solve by default returns just one solution, but prints a message telling you that other solutions may exist. Section 3.4.5 discusses this in more detail.

There is no explicit "closed form" solution for a transcendental equation like this.

In[10]:= **Solve[Cos[x] == x, x]**

Solve::tdep:
    The equations appear to involve transcendental
        functions of the variables in an essentially
        non-algebraic way.

Out[10]= Solve[Cos[x] == x, x]

You can find an approximate numerical solution using FindRoot, and giving a starting value for x.

In[11]:= **FindRoot[Cos[x] == x, {x, 1}]**

Out[11]= {x → 0.739085}

Solve can also handle equations involving symbolic functions. In such cases, it again prints a warning, then gives results in terms of formal inverse functions.

Mathematica returns a result in terms of the formal inverse function of f.

In[12]:= **Solve[f[x^2] == a, x]**

InverseFunction::ifun:
    Warning: Inverse functions are being used. Values may
        be lost for multivalued inverses.

Out[12]= $\left\{\left\{x \to -\sqrt{f^{(-1)}[a]}\right\}, \left\{x \to \sqrt{f^{(-1)}[a]}\right\}\right\}$

Solve[{*lhs₁*==*rhs₁*, *lhs₂*==*rhs₂*, ... }, {*x, y, ...* }]
   solve a set of simultaneous equations for *x, y, ...*

Solving sets of simultaneous equations.

You can also use *Mathematica* to solve sets of simultaneous equations. You simply give the list of equations, and specify the list of variables to solve for.

Here is a list of two simultaneous equations, to be solved for the variables *x* and *y*.

In[13]:= **Solve[{a x + y == 0, 2 x + (1-a) y == 1}, {x, y}]**

Out[13]= $\left\{\left\{x \to -\dfrac{1}{-2+a-a^2}, y \to -\dfrac{a}{2-a+a^2}\right\}\right\}$

Here are some more complicated simultaneous equations. The two solutions are given as two lists of replacements for x and y.

$In[14]:=$ **Solve[{x^2 + y^2 == 1, x + 3 y == 0}, {x, y}]**

$Out[14]= \left\{\left\{x \to -\dfrac{3}{\sqrt{10}}, y \to \dfrac{1}{\sqrt{10}}\right\}, \left\{x \to \dfrac{3}{\sqrt{10}}, y \to -\dfrac{1}{\sqrt{10}}\right\}\right\}$

This uses the solutions to evaluate the expression x + y.

$In[15]:=$ **x + y /. %**

$Out[15]= \left\{-\sqrt{\dfrac{2}{5}}, \sqrt{\dfrac{2}{5}}\right\}$

Mathematica can solve any set of simultaneous *linear* equations. It can also solve a large class of simultaneous polynomial equations. Even when it does not manage to solve the equations explicitly, *Mathematica* will still usually reduce them to a much simpler form.

When you are working with sets of equations in several variables, it is often convenient to reorganize the equations by eliminating some variables between them.

This eliminates y between the two equations, giving a single equation for x.

$In[16]:=$ **Eliminate[{a x + y == 0, 2 x + (1-a) y == 1}, y]**

$Out[16]= -1 + 2x - ax + a^2 x == 0$

If you have several equations, there is no guarantee that there exists *any* consistent solution for a particular variable.

There is no consistent solution to these equations, so *Mathematica* returns {}, indicating that the set of solutions is empty.

$In[17]:=$ **Solve[{x==1, x==2}, x]**

$Out[17]= \{\}$

There is also no consistent solution to these equations for almost all values of a.

$In[18]:=$ **Solve[{x==1, x==a}, x]**

$Out[18]= \{\}$

The general question of whether a set of equations has any consistent solution is quite a subtle one. For example, for most values of a, the equations {x==1, x==a} are inconsistent, so there is no possible solution for x. However, if a is equal to 1, then the equations *do* have a solution. Solve is set up to give you *generic* solutions to equations. It discards any solutions that exist only when special constraints between parameters are satisfied.

If you use Reduce instead of Solve, *Mathematica* will however keep *all* the possible solutions to a set of equations, including those that require special conditions on parameters.

This shows that the equations have a solution only when a==1. The notation x==1 && a==1 represents the requirement that *both* x==1 *and* a==1 should be True.

$In[19]:=$ **Reduce[{x==1, x==a}, x]**

$Out[19]= x == 1 \,\&\&\, a == 1$

This gives the complete set of possible solutions to the equation. The answer is stated in terms of a combination of simpler equations. **&&** indicates equations that must simultaneously be true; **||** indicates alternatives.

```
In[20]:= Reduce[a x - b == 0, x]
```

$$Out[20]= b == 0 \&\& a == 0 \; || \; a \neq 0 \&\& x == \frac{b}{a}$$

This gives a more complicated combination of equations.

```
In[21]:= Reduce[a x^2 - b == 0, x]
```

$$Out[21]= b == 0 \&\& a == 0 \; ||$$

$$a \neq 0 \&\& x == -\frac{\sqrt{b}}{\sqrt{a}} \; || \; a \neq 0 \&\& x == \frac{\sqrt{b}}{\sqrt{a}}$$

Solve[*lhs*==*rhs*, *x*]	solve an equation for *x*
Solve[{*lhs*₁==*rhs*₁, *lhs*₂==*rhs*₂, ... }, {*x*, *y*, ... }]	solve a set of simultaneous equations for *x*, *y*, ...
Eliminate[{*lhs*₁==*rhs*₁, *lhs*₂==*rhs*₂, ... }, {*x*, ... }]	eliminate *x*, ... in a set of simultaneous equations
Reduce[{*lhs*₁==*rhs*₁, *lhs*₂==*rhs*₂, ... }, {*x*, *y*, ... }]	give a set of simplified equations, including all possible solutions

Functions for solving and manipulating equations.

■ 1.5.8 Differential Equations

DSolve[*eqns*, *y*[*x*], *x*]	solve a differential equation for *y*[*x*], taking *x* as the independent variable
DSolve[*eqns*, *y*, *x*]	give a solution for *y* in pure function form

Solving an ordinary differential equation.

Here is the solution to the differential equation $y'(x) = ay(x) + 1$. C[1] is a coefficient which must be determined from boundary conditions.

```
In[1]:= DSolve[ y'[x] == a y[x] + 1, y[x], x ]
```

$$Out[1]= \left\{\left\{y[x] \to -\frac{1}{a} + E^{ax} C[1]\right\}\right\}$$

If you include an appropriate initial condition, there are no undetermined coefficients in the solution.

```
In[2]:= DSolve[ {y'[x] == a y[x] + 1, y[0] == 0}, y[x], x ]
```

$$Out[2]= \left\{\left\{y[x] \to \frac{-1 + E^{ax}}{a}\right\}\right\}$$

Whereas algebraic equations such as $x^2 + x = 1$ are equations for *variables*, differential equations such as $y''(x) + y'(x) = y(x)$ are equations for *functions*. In *Mathematica*, you must always give differential equations explicitly in terms of functions such as y[x], and you must specify the variables such as x on which the functions depend. As a result, you must write an equation such as $y''(x) + y'(x) = y(x)$ in the form y''[x] + y'[x] == y[x]. You cannot write it as y'' + y' == y.

Mathematica can solve both linear and nonlinear ordinary differential equations, as well as lists of simultaneous equations. If you do not specify enough initial or boundary conditions, *Mathematica* will give solutions that involve an appropriate number of undetermined coefficients. Each time you use DSolve, it names the undetermined coefficients C[1], C[2], etc.

Here is a pair of simultaneous differential equations, with no initial or boundary conditions. The solution you get involves two undetermined coefficients.

$In[3]:=$ **DSolve[{x'[t] == y[t], y'[t] == x[t]},**
                                          {x[t], y[t]}, t]

$Out[3]=$ {{x[t] → -E^{-t} C[1] + E^t C[2],
             y[t] → E^{-t} C[1] + E^t C[2]}}

When you ask DSolve to get you a solution for y[x], the rules it returns specify how to replace y[x] in any expression. However, these rules do not specify how to replace objects such as y'[x]. If you want to manipulate solutions that you get from DSolve, you will often find it better to ask for solutions for y, rather than for y[x].

This gives the solution for y as a "pure function".

$In[4]:=$ **DSolve[y'[x] == x + y[x], y, x]**

$Out[4]=$ {{y → (-1 + E$^{\#1}$ C[1] – #1&)}}

You can now use the replacement operator to apply this solution to expressions involving y.

$In[5]:=$ **y''[x] + y[x] /. %**

$Out[5]=$ {-1 – x + 2E^x C[1]}

Section 2.2.5 explains how the "pure function" indicated by & that appears in the result from DSolve works.

■ 1.5.9 Power Series

The mathematical operations we have discussed so far are *exact*. Given precise input, their results are exact formulas.

In many situations, however, you do not need an exact result. It may be quite sufficient, for example, to find an *approximate* formula that is valid, say, when the quantity x is small.

This gives a power series approximation to $(1 + x)^n$ for x close to 0, up to terms of order x^3.

$In[1]:=$ **Series[(1 + x)^n, {x, 0, 3}]**

$Out[1]=$ $1 + nx + \dfrac{1}{2}(-1 + n)nx^2 +$

          $\dfrac{1}{6}(-2 + n)(-1 + n)nx^3 + O[x]^4$

Mathematica knows the power series expansions for many mathematical functions.

$In[2]:=$ **Series[Exp[-a t] (1 + Sin[2 t]), {t, 0, 4}]**

$Out[2]= 1 + (2 - a) t + \left(-2a + \dfrac{a^2}{2}\right) t^2 +$

$\left(-\dfrac{4}{3} + a^2 - \dfrac{a^3}{6}\right) t^3 + \left(\dfrac{4a}{3} - \dfrac{a^3}{3} + \dfrac{a^4}{24}\right) t^4 + O[t]^5$

If you give it a function that it does not know, Series writes out the power series in terms of derivatives.

$In[3]:=$ **Series[1 + f[t], {t, 0, 3}]**

$Out[3]= 1 + f[0] + f'[0] t + \dfrac{1}{2} f''[0] t^2 + \dfrac{1}{6} f^{(3)}[0] t^3 + O[t]^4$

Power series are approximate formulas that play much the same role with respect to algebraic expressions as approximate numbers play with respect to numerical expressions. *Mathematica* allows you to perform operations on power series, in all cases maintaining the appropriate order or "degree of precision" for the resulting power series.

Here is a simple power series, accurate to order x^5.

$In[4]:=$ **Series[Exp[x], {x, 0, 5}]**

$Out[4]= 1 + x + \dfrac{x^2}{2} + \dfrac{x^3}{6} + \dfrac{x^4}{24} + \dfrac{x^5}{120} + O[x]^6$

When you do operations on a power series, the result is computed only to the appropriate order in x.

$In[5]:=$ **%^2 (1 + %)**

$Out[5]= 2 + 5x + \dfrac{13x^2}{2} + \dfrac{35x^3}{6} + \dfrac{97x^4}{24} + \dfrac{55x^5}{24} + O[x]^6$

This turns the power series back into an ordinary expression.

$In[6]:=$ **Normal[%]**

$Out[6]= 2 + 5x + \dfrac{13x^2}{2} + \dfrac{35x^3}{6} + \dfrac{97x^4}{24} + \dfrac{55x^5}{24}$

Now the square is computed *exactly*.

$In[7]:=$ **%^2**

$Out[7]= \left(2 + 5x + \dfrac{13x^2}{2} + \dfrac{35x^3}{6} + \dfrac{97x^4}{24} + \dfrac{55x^5}{24}\right)^2$

Applying Expand gives a result with eleven terms.

$In[8]:=$ **Expand[%]**

$Out[8]= 4 + 20x + 51x^2 + \dfrac{265x^3}{3} + \dfrac{467x^4}{4} + \dfrac{1505x^5}{12} +$

$\dfrac{7883x^6}{72} + \dfrac{1385x^7}{18} + \dfrac{24809x^8}{576} + \dfrac{5335x^9}{288} + \dfrac{3025x^{10}}{576}$

Series[*expr*, {*x*, x_0, *n*}]	find the power series expansion of *expr* about the point $x = x_0$ to at most n^{th} order
Normal[*series*]	truncate a power series to give an ordinary expression

Power series operations.

■ 1.5.10 Limits

Here is the expression $\sin(x)/x$.	`In[1]:= t = Sin[x]/x`
	$$Out[1]= \frac{Sin[x]}{x}$$
If you replace x by 0, the expression becomes 0/0, and you get an indeterminate result.	`In[2]:= t /. x->0`
	`Power::infy: Infinite expression` $\frac{1}{0}$ `encountered.`
	`Infinity::indet:` `Indeterminate expression 0 ComplexInfinity encountered.`
	`Out[2]= Indeterminate`
If you find the numerical value of $\sin(x)/x$ for x close to 0, however, you get a result that is close to 1.	`In[3]:= t /. x->0.01`
	`Out[3]= 0.999983`
This finds the *limit* of $\sin(x)/x$ as x approaches 0. The result is indeed 1.	`In[4]:= Limit[t, x->0]`
	`Out[4]= 1`

`Limit[`*expr*`, x->`x_0`]`	the limit of *expr* as x approaches x_0

Limits.

■ 1.5.11 Packages for Symbolic Mathematics

There are many *Mathematica* packages which implement symbolic mathematical operations. This section describes a few examples drawn from the standard set of packages distributed with *Mathematica*. As discussed in Section 1.3.10, some copies of *Mathematica* may be set up so that the functions described here are automatically loaded into *Mathematica* if they are ever needed.

Laplace Transforms

`<<Calculus`LaplaceTransform``	load the Laplace transform package
`LaplaceTransform[`*expr*`, t, s]`	find the Laplace transform of *expr*
`InverseLaplaceTransform[`*expr*`, s, t]`	
	find the inverse Laplace transform of *expr*

Laplace transforms.

This loads the Laplace transform package. In some versions of *Mathematica*, you may not need to load this package explicitly.

In[1]:= `<<Calculus`LaplaceTransform``

This evaluates a Laplace transform.

In[2]:= `LaplaceTransform[ t^3 Exp[a t], t, s ]`

$$Out[2]= \frac{6}{(-a+s)^4}$$

Here is the inverse transform.

In[3]:= `InverseLaplaceTransform[%, s, t]`

Out[3]= $E^{a t} t^3$

Fourier Transforms

`<<Calculus`FourierTransform``	load the symbolic Fourier transform package
`FourierTransform[`*expr*`, `*t*`, `*s*`]`	find the symbolic Fourier transform of *expr*
`InverseFourierTransform[`*expr*`, `*s*`, `*t*`]`	find the inverse Fourier transform of *expr*

Fourier transforms.

This loads the symbolic Fourier transform package.

In[1]:= `<<Calculus`FourierTransform``

This evaluates a Fourier transform.

In[2]:= `FourierTransform[ t^2 Sin[t], t, w ]`

Out[2]= $-I \pi (\text{DiracDelta}''[1-w] - \text{DiracDelta}''[1+w])$

Vector Analysis

`<<Calculus`VectorAnalysis``	load the vector analysis package
`SetCoordinates[`*system*`[`*names*`]]`	
	specify the coordinate system to be used (`Cartesian`, `Cylindrical`, `Spherical`, etc.), giving the names of the coordinates in that system
`Grad[`*f*`]`	evaluate the gradient ∇f of f in the coordinate system chosen
`Div[`*f*`]`	evaluate the divergence $\nabla \cdot f$ of the list f
`Curl[`*f*`]`	evaluate the curl $\nabla \times f$ of the list f
`Laplacian[`*f*`]`	evaluate the Laplacian $\nabla^2 f$ of f

Vector analysis.

This loads the vector analysis package. In some versions of *Mathematica*, you may not need to load the package explicitly.

```
In[1]:= <<Calculus`VectorAnalysis`
```

This specifies that a spherical coordinate system with coordinate names r, theta and phi should be used.

```
In[2]:= SetCoordinates[Spherical[r, theta, phi]]
Out[2]= Spherical[r, theta, phi]
```

This evaluates the gradient of $r^2 \sin(\theta)$ in the spherical coordinate system.

```
In[3]:= Grad[r^2 Sin[theta]]
Out[3]= {2 r Sin[theta], r Cos[theta], 0}
```

■ 1.5.12 Advanced Topic: Generic and Non-Generic Cases

This gives a result for the integral of x^n that is valid for almost all values of n.

```
In[1]:= Integrate[x^n, x]
```
$$Out[1]= \frac{x^{1+n}}{1+n}$$

For the special case of x^{-1}, however, the correct result is different.

```
In[2]:= Integrate[x^-1, x]
Out[2]= Log[x]
```

The overall goal of symbolic computation is typically to get formulas that are valid for many possible values of the variables that appear in them. It is however often not practical to try to get formulas that are valid for absolutely every possible value of each variable.

Mathematica always replaces $0/x$ by 0.

```
In[3]:= 0 / x
Out[3]= 0
```

If x is equal to 0, however, then the true result is not 0.

```
In[4]:= 0 / 0
                                       1
Power::infy: Infinite expression  - encountered.
                                       0
Infinity::indet:
    Indeterminate expression 0 ComplexInfinity encountered.
Out[4]= Indeterminate
```

This construct treats both cases, but would be quite unwieldy to use.

```
In[5]:= If[x != 0, 0, Indeterminate]
Out[5]= If[x ≠ 0, 0, Indeterminate]
```

If *Mathematica* did not automatically replace $0/x$ by 0, then few symbolic computations would get very far. But you should realize that the practical necessity of making such replacements can cause misleading results to be obtained when exceptional values of parameters are used.

The basic operations of *Mathematica* are nevertheless carefully set up so that whenever possible the results obtained will be valid for almost all values of each variable.

$\sqrt{x^2}$ is not automatically replaced by x.

```
In[6]:= Sqrt[x^2]
Out[6]= √x²
```

If it were, then the result here would be -2, which is incorrect.

```
In[7]:= % /. x -> -2
Out[7]= 2
```

This makes the assumption that x is a positive real variable, and does the replacement.

```
In[8]:= PowerExpand[Sqrt[x^2]]
Out[8]= x
```

■ 1.5.13 Mathematical Notation in Notebooks

If you use the notebook front end for *Mathematica*, then you can enter some of the operations discussed in this section in special ways.

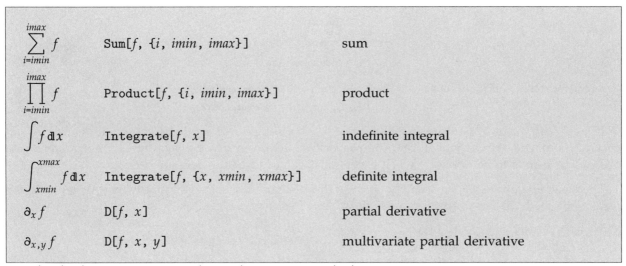

$\sum_{i=imin}^{imax} f$	Sum[f, {i, $imin$, $imax$}]	sum
$\prod_{i=imin}^{imax} f$	Product[f, {i, $imin$, $imax$}]	product
$\int f\, dx$	Integrate[f, x]	indefinite integral
$\int_{xmin}^{xmax} f\, dx$	Integrate[f, {x, $xmin$, $xmax$}]	definite integral
$\partial_x f$	D[f, x]	partial derivative
$\partial_{x,y} f$	D[f, x, y]	multivariate partial derivative

Special and ordinary ways to enter mathematical operations in notebooks.

This shows part of the standard palette for entering mathematical operations. When you press a button in the palette, the form shown in the button is inserted into your notebook, with the black square replaced by whatever you had selected in the notebook.

ESC `sum` ESC	summation sign $\sum$	
ESC `prod` ESC	product sign $\prod$	
ESC `int` ESC	integral sign $\int$	
ESC `dd` ESC	special differential $\mathbb{d}$ for use in integrals	
ESC `pd` ESC	partial derivative ∂	
CTRL `_` or CTRL `-`	move to the subscript position or lower limit of an integral	
CTRL `^` or CTRL `6`	move to the superscript position or upper limit of an integral	
CTRL `+` or CTRL `=`	move to the underscript position or lower limit of a sum or product	
CTRL `&` or CTRL `7`	move to the overscript position or upper limit of a sum or product	
CTRL `%` or CTRL `5`	switch between upper and lower positions	
CTRL `␣` (CONTROL-SPACE)	return from upper or lower positions	

Ways to enter special notations on a standard English-language keyboard.

You can enter an integral like this. Be sure to use the special differential $\mathbb{d}$ entered as ESC `dd` ESC, not just an ordinary d.

$$In[1]:= \int x^n \, \mathbb{d}x$$

$$Out[1]= \frac{x^{1+n}}{1+n}$$

Here is the actual key sequence you type to get the input.

$$In[2]:= \text{ESC}\,\mathbf{int}\,\text{ESC}\,\mathbf{x}\,\text{CTRL}\,\mathbf{^}\,\mathbf{n}\,\text{CTRL}\,\mathbf{␣}\,\text{ESC}\,\mathbf{dd}\,\text{ESC}\,\mathbf{x}$$

$$Out[2]= \frac{x^{1+n}}{1+n}$$

1.6 Numerical Mathematics

■ 1.6.1 Basic Operations

Exact symbolic results are usually very desirable when they can be found. In many calculations, however, it is not possible to get symbolic results. In such cases, you must resort to numerical methods.

$N[expr]$	numerical value of an expression (see Section 1.1)
$NIntegrate[f, \{x, xmin, xmax\}]$	numerical approximation to $\int_{xmin}^{xmax} f \, dx$
$NSum[f, \{i, imin, Infinity\}]$	numerical approximation to $\sum_{imin}^{\infty} f$
$NSolve[lhs==rhs, x]$	numerical approximation to the solutions of a polynomial equation
$FindRoot[lhs==rhs, \{x, x_0\}]$	search for a numerical solution to an equation, starting with $x = x_0$
$FindMinimum[f, \{x, x_0\}]$	search for a minimum of f, starting with $x = x_0$

Basic numerical operations.

Mathematica maintains this expression in an exact, symbolic, form.

```
In[1]:= (3 + Sqrt[2])^3
```
$$Out[1]= \left(3 + \sqrt{2}\right)^3$$

You can even use standard symbolic operations on it.

```
In[2]:= Expand[ % ]
```
$$Out[2]= 45 + 29\sqrt{2}$$

$N[expr]$ gives you a numerical approximation.

```
In[3]:= N[ % ]
```
$$Out[3]= 86.0122$$

Functions such as Integrate always try to get exact results for computations. When they cannot get exact results, they typically return unevaluated. You can then find numerical approximations by explicitly applying N. Functions such as NIntegrate do the calculations numerically from the start, without first trying to get an exact result.

There is no exact formula for this integral, so Mathematica returns it unevaluated.

```
In[4]:= Integrate[Sin[Sin[x]], {x, 1, 2}]
```
$$Out[4]= \int_1^2 Sin[Sin[x]]dx$$

You can use N to get an approximate numerical result.

```
In[5]:= N[ % ]
```
$$Out[5]= 0.81645$$

NIntegrate does the integral numerically from the start.

In[6]:= **NIntegrate[Sin[Sin[x]], {x, 1, 2}]**

Out[6]= 0.81645

■ 1.6.2 Numerical Sums, Products and Integrals

NSum[*f*, {*i*, *imin*, Infinity}]	numerical approximation to $\sum_{imin}^{\infty} f$
NProduct[*f*, {*i*, *imin*, Infinity}]	
	numerical approximation to $\prod_{imin}^{\infty} f$
NIntegrate[*f*, {*x*, *xmin*, *xmax*}]	
	numerical approximation to $\int_{xmin}^{xmax} f \, dx$
NIntegrate[*f*, {*x*, *xmin*, *xmax*}, {*y*, *ymin*, *ymax*}]	
	the multiple integral $\int_{xmin}^{xmax} dx \int_{ymin}^{ymax} dy \, f$

Numerical sums, products and integrals.

Here is a numerical approximation to $\sum_{i=1}^{\infty} \frac{1}{i^3}$.

In[1]:= **NSum[1/i^3, {i, 1, Infinity}]**

Out[1]= 1.20206

NIntegrate can handle singularities at the end points of the integration region.

In[2]:= **NIntegrate[1/Sqrt[x (1-x)], {x, 0, 1}]**

Out[2]= 3.14159

You can do numerical integrals over infinite regions.

In[3]:= **NIntegrate[Exp[-x^2], {x, -Infinity, Infinity}]**

Out[3]= 1.77245

Here is a double integral over a triangular domain. Note the order in which the variables are given.

In[4]:= **NIntegrate[Sin[x y], {x, 0, 1}, {y, 0, x}]**

Out[4]= 0.119906

■ 1.6.3 Numerical Equation Solving

NSolve[*lhs*==*rhs*, *x*]	solve a polynomial equation numerically
NSolve[{*lhs*₁==*rhs*₁, *lhs*₂==*rhs*₂, ... }, {*x*, *y*, ... }]	
	solve a system of polynomial equations numerically
FindRoot[*lhs*==*rhs*, {*x*, x_0}]	search for a numerical solution to an equation, starting at $x = x_0$
FindRoot[{*lhs*₁==*rhs*₁, *lhs*₂==*rhs*₂, ... }, {*x*, x_0}, {*y*, y_0}, ...]	
	search for numerical solutions to simultaneous equations

Numerical root finding and minimization.

NSolve gives you numerical approximations to all the roots of a polynomial equation.

```
In[1]:= NSolve[ x^5 + x + 1 == 0, x ]
Out[1]= {{x → -0.754878}, {x → -0.5 - 0.866025 I},
          {x → -0.5 + 0.866025 I}, {x → 0.877439 - 0.744862 I},
          {x → 0.877439 + 0.744862 I}}
```

You can also use NSolve to solve sets of simultaneous equations numerically.

```
In[2]:= NSolve[{x + y == 2, x - 3 y + z == 3, x - y + z == 0},
              {x, y, z}]
Out[2]= {{x → 3.5, y → -1.5, z → -5.}}
```

If your equations involve only linear functions or polynomials, then you can use NSolve to get numerical approximations to all the solutions. However, when your equations involve more complicated functions, there is in general no systematic procedure for finding all solutions, even numerically. In such cases, you can use FindRoot to search for solutions. You have to give FindRoot a place to start its search.

This searches for a numerical solution, starting at $x = 1$.

```
In[3]:= FindRoot[ 3 Cos[x] == Log[x], {x, 1} ]
Out[3]= {x → 1.44726}
```

The equation has several solutions. If you start at a different x, FindRoot may return a different solution.

```
In[4]:= FindRoot[ 3 Cos[x] == Log[x], {x, 10} ]
Out[4]= {x → 13.1064}
```

You can search for solutions to sets of equations. Here the solution involves complex numbers.

```
In[5]:= FindRoot[{x==Log[y], y==Log[x]}, {x, I}, {y, 2}]
Out[5]= {x → 0.318131 + 1.33724 I, y → 0.318131 + 1.33724 I}
```

■ 1.6.4 Numerical Differential Equations

> NDSolve[*eqns*, *y*, {*x*, *xmin*, *xmax*}]
>   solve numerically for the function *y*, with the independent variable *x* in the range *xmin* to *xmax*
>
> NDSolve[*eqns*, {*y*₁, *y*₂, ... }, {*x*, *xmin*, *xmax*}]
>   solve a system of equations for the y_i

Numerical solution of ordinary differential equations.

This generates a numerical solution to the equation $y'(x) = y(x)$ with $0 < x < 2$. The result is given in terms of an InterpolatingFunction.

```
In[1]:= NDSolve[{y'[x] == y[x], y[0] == 1}, y, {x, 0, 2}]
Out[1]= {{y → InterpolatingFunction[{{0., 2.}}, <>]}}
```

Here is the value of $y(1.5)$.

```
In[2]:= y[1.5] /. %
Out[2]= {4.48171}
```

With an algebraic equation such as $x^2 + 3x + 1 = 0$, each solution for x is simply a single number. For a differential equation, however, the solution is a *function*, rather than a single number. For example, in the equation $y'(x) = y(x)$, you want to get an approximation to the function $y(x)$ as the independent variable x varies over some range.

Mathematica represents numerical approximations to functions as InterpolatingFunction objects. These objects are functions which, when applied to a particular x, return the approximate value of $y(x)$ at that point. The InterpolatingFunction effectively stores a table of values for $y(x_i)$, then interpolates this table to find an approximation to $y(x)$ at the particular x you request.

$y[x]$ /. *solution*	use the list of rules for the function y to get values for $y[x]$
InterpolatingFunction[*data*][x]	
	evaluate an interpolated function at the point x
Plot[Evaluate[$y[x]$ /. *solution*], {x, *xmin*, *xmax*}]	
	plot the solution to a differential equation

Using results from NDSolve.

This solves a system of two coupled differential equations.

```
In[3]:= NDSolve[ {y'[x] == z[x], z'[x] == -y[x], y[0] == 0,
               z[0] == 1}, {y, z}, {x, 0, Pi} ]

Out[3]= {{y → InterpolatingFunction[{{0., 3.14159}}, <>],
           z → InterpolatingFunction[{{0., 3.14159}}, <>]}}
```

Here is the value of z[2] found from the solution.

```
In[4]:= z[2] /. %
Out[4]= {-0.416147}
```

Here is a plot of the solution for z[x] found on line 3. Plot is discussed in Section 1.9.1.

```
In[5]:= Plot[Evaluate[z[x] /. %3], {x, 0, Pi}]
```

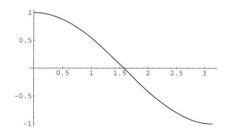

■ 1.6.5 Numerical Optimization

`ConstrainedMin[f, ineqs, {x, y, ... }]`	minimize the linear function f subject to the linear constraints *ineqs*
`FindMinimum[f, {x, x0}]`	search for a local minimum of the arbitrary function f, starting at $x = x_0$
`FindMinimum[f, {x, x0}, {y, y0}, ... ]`	search for a local minimum in several variables

Numerical minimization functions.

The function `ConstrainedMin` allows you to solve linear programming problems in which you give a linear function f, then find its minimum over a domain specified by a list of linear inequalities. `ConstrainedMin` assumes that all the variables you give are constrained to be non-negative.

This gives the minimum value of $x - y - z$ in the specified domain, followed by the values of x, y and z at which the value is attained.

```
In[1]:= ConstrainedMin[x - y - z, {y + z < 3, x > 7},
                                                  {x, y, z}]

Out[1]= {4, {x → 7, y → 3, z → 0}}
```

When the function you want to minimize is linear, you can always use `ConstrainedMin` to find its global minimum. For more complicated functions, however, there is usually no systematic way to find a global minimum. Instead, you can use `FindMinimum` to search for local minima.

This searches for a local minimum of $x \cos(x)$, starting at $x = 1$.

```
In[2]:= FindMinimum[x Cos[x], {x, 1}]
Out[2]= {-3.28837, {x → 3.42562}}
```

With a different starting point, you may reach a different local minimum.

```
In[3]:= FindMinimum[x Cos[x], {x, 10}]
Out[3]= {-9.47729, {x → 9.52933}}
```

This finds a minimum of $\sin(xy)$.

```
In[4]:= FindMinimum[Sin[x y], {x, 2}, {y, 2}]
Out[4]= {-1., {x → 2.1708, y → 2.1708}}
```

■ 1.6.6 Manipulating Numerical Data

When you have numerical data, it is often convenient to find a simple formula that approximates it. For example, you can try to "fit" a line or curve through the points in your data.

$\text{Fit}[\{y_1, y_2, \dots \}, \{f_1, f_2, \dots \}, x]$

fit the values y_n to a linear combination of functions f_i

$\text{Fit}[\{\{x_1, y_1\}, \{x_2, y_2\}, \dots \}, \{f_1, f_2, \dots \}, x]$

fit the points (x_n, y_n) to a linear combination of the f_i

Functions for fitting curves.

This generates a table of the numerical values of the exponential function. Table will be discussed in Section 1.8.2.	`In[1]:= data = Table[ Exp[x/5.] , {x, 7}]`
	
	`Out[1]= {1.2214, 1.49182, 1.82212, 2.22554,`
	`        2.71828, 3.32012, 4.0552}`

This finds a least-squares fit to data of the form $c_1 + c_2 x + c_3 x^2$. The elements of data are assumed to correspond to values 1, 2, ... of x.	`In[2]:= Fit[data, {1, x, x^2}, x]` `Out[2]= 1.09428 + 0.0986337 x + 0.0459482 x`^{2}
This finds a fit of the form $c_1 + c_2 x + c_3 x^3 + c_4 x^5$.	`In[3]:= Fit[data, {1, x, x^3, x^5}, x]` `Out[3]= 0.96806 + 0.246829 x + 0.00428281 x`^{3}` - 6.57948 × 10`$^{-6}$` x`^{5}

This gives a table of x, y pairs.	`In[4]:= data = Table[ {x, Exp[Sin[x]]} , {x, 0., 1., 0.2}]`
	
	`Out[4]= {{0., 1.}, {0.2, 1.21978}, {0.4, 1.47612},`
	`        {0.6, 1.75882}, {0.8, 2.04901}, {1., 2.31978}}`

This finds a fit to the new data, of the form $c_1 + c_2 \sin(x) + c_3 \sin(2x)$.	`In[5]:= Fit[%, {1, Sin[x], Sin[2x]}, x]`
	
	`Out[5]= 0.989559 + 2.04199 Sin[x] - 0.418176 Sin[2x]`

One common way of picking out "signals" in numerical data is to find the *Fourier transform*, or frequency spectrum, of the data.

`Fourier[`*data*`]`	numerical Fourier transform
`InverseFourier[`*data*`]`	inverse Fourier transform

Fourier transforms.

Here is a simple square pulse.	`In[6]:= data = {1, 1, 1, 1, -1, -1, -1, -1}`
	
	`Out[6]= {1, 1, 1, 1, -1, -1, -1, -1}`

This takes the Fourier transform of the pulse.	`In[7]:= Fourier[data]`
	
	`Out[7]= {0. + 0. I, 0.707107 + 1.70711 I,`
	`        0. + 0. I, 0.707107 + 0.292893 I,`
	`        0. + 0. I, 0.707107 - 0.292893 I,`
	`        0. + 0. I, 0.707107 - 1.70711 I}`

Note that the `Fourier` function in *Mathematica* is defined with the sign convention typically used in the physical sciences—opposite to the one often used in electrical engineering. Section 3.8.3 gives more details.

■ 1.6.7 Statistics Packages

The standard set of packages distributed with *Mathematica* includes several for doing statistical analyses of data.

`Statistics`DescriptiveStatistics``	descriptive statistics functions
`Statistics`MultivariateDescriptiveStatistics``	multivariate descriptive statistics functions
`Statistics`ContinuousDistributions``	properties of continuous statistical distributions
`Statistics`DiscreteDistributions``	properties of discrete statistical distributions
`Statistics`HypothesisTests``	hypothesis tests based on the normal distribution
`Statistics`ConfidenceIntervals``	confidence intervals derived from the normal distribution
`Statistics`MultinormalDistribution``	properties of distributions based on the multivariate normal distribution
`Statistics`LinearRegression``	linear regression analysis
`Statistics`NonlinearFit``	nonlinear fitting of data
`Statistics`DataSmoothing``	smoothing of data
`Statistics`DataManipulation``	utilities for data manipulation

Some standard statistical analysis packages.

```
<<Statistics`DescriptiveStatistics`
                           load the descriptive statistics package
```

Mean[*data*]	mean (average value)
Median[*data*]	median (central value)
Variance[*data*]	variance
StandardDeviation[*data*]	standard deviation
LocationReport[*data*], DispersionReport[*data*], ShapeReport[*data*]	give lists of quantities characterizing the statistical distribution of data

Basic descriptive statistics.

This loads the descriptive statistics package. In some versions of *Mathematica*, you may not need to load this package explicitly.

```
In[1]:= <<Statistics`DescriptiveStatistics`
```

Here is some "data".

```
In[2]:= data = {4.3, 7.2, 8.4, 5.8, 9.2, 3.9}
Out[2]= {4.3, 7.2, 8.4, 5.8, 9.2, 3.9}
```

This gives the mean of your data.

```
In[3]:= Mean[data]
Out[3]= 6.46667
```

Here is the variance.

```
In[4]:= Variance[data]
Out[4]= 4.69467
```

This gives a list of rules for various quantities that characterize the dispersion of your data.

```
In[5]:= DispersionReport[data]
Out[5]= {Variance → 4.69467,
          StandardDeviation → 2.16672, SampleRange → 5.3,
          MeanDeviation → 1.8, MedianDeviation → 2.05,
          QuartileDeviation → 2.05}
```

1.7 Functions and Programs

■ 1.7.1 Defining Functions

In this part of the book, we have seen many examples of functions that are built into *Mathematica*. In this section, we discuss how you can add your own simple functions to *Mathematica*. Part 2 will describe in much greater detail the mechanisms for adding functions to *Mathematica*.

As a first example, consider adding a function called f which squares its argument. The *Mathematica* command to define this function is f[x_] := x^2. The _ (referred to as "blank") on the left-hand side is very important; what it means will be discussed below. For now, just remember to put a _ on the left-hand side, but not on the right-hand side, of your definition.

This defines the function f. Notice the _ on the left-hand side.	`In[1]:= f[x_] := x^2`
f squares its argument.	`In[2]:= f[a+1]` $Out[2]= (1+a)^2$
The argument can be a number.	`In[3]:= f[4]` $Out[3]= 16$
Or it can be a more complicated expression.	`In[4]:= f[3x + x^2]` $Out[4]= (3x + x^2)^2$
You can use f in a calculation.	`In[5]:= Expand[f[(x+1+y)]]` $Out[5]= 1 + 2x + x^2 + 2y + 2xy + y^2$

This shows the definition you made for f.	`In[6]:= ?f`
	`Global'f`
	`f[x_] := x^2`

`f[x_] := x^2`	define the function f
`?f`	show the definition of *f*
`Clear[f]`	clear all definitions for *f*

Defining a function in *Mathematica*.

The names like f that you use for functions in *Mathematica* are just symbols. Because of this, you should make sure to avoid using names that begin with capital letters, to prevent confusion with built-in *Mathematica* functions. You should also make sure that you have not used the names for anything else earlier in your session.

Mathematica functions can have any number of arguments.

In[7]:= **hump[x_, xmax_] := (x - xmax)^2 / xmax**

You can use the hump function just as you would any of the built-in functions.

In[8]:= **2 + hump[x, 3.5]**

Out[8]= $2 + 0.285714 (-3.5 + x)^2$

This gives a new definition for hump, which overwrites the previous one.

In[9]:= **hump[x_, xmax_] := (x - xmax)^4**

The new definition is displayed.

In[10]:= **?hump**

Global`hump

hump[x_, xmax_] := (x - xmax)^4

This clears all definitions for hump.

In[11]:= **Clear[hump]**

When you have finished with a particular function, it is always a good idea to clear definitions you have made for it. If you do not do this, then you will run into trouble if you try to use the same function for a different purpose later in your *Mathematica* session. You can clear all definitions you have made for a function or symbol *f* by using Clear[*f*].

■ 1.7.2 Functions as Procedures

In many kinds of calculations, you may find yourself typing the same input to *Mathematica* over and over again. You can save yourself a lot of typing by defining a *function* that contains your input commands.

This constructs a product of three terms, and expands out the result.

In[1]:= **Expand[Product[x + i, {i, 3}]]**

Out[1]= $6 + 11 x + 6 x^2 + x^3$

This does the same thing, but with four terms.

In[2]:= **Expand[Product[x + i, {i, 4}]]**

Out[2]= $24 + 50 x + 35 x^2 + 10 x^3 + x^4$

This defines a function exprod which constructs a product of *n* terms, then expands it out.

In[3]:= **exprod[n_] := Expand[Product[x + i, {i, 1, n}]]**

Every time you use the function, it will execute the Product and Expand operations.

In[4]:= **exprod[5]**

Out[4]= $120 + 274 x + 225 x^2 + 85 x^3 + 15 x^4 + x^5$

The functions you define in *Mathematica* are essentially procedures that execute the commands you give. You can have several steps in your procedures, separated by semicolons.

The result you get from the whole function is simply the last expression in the procedure. Notice that you have to put parentheses around the procedure when you define it like this.

In[5]:= **cex[n_, i_] := (t = exprod[n]; Coefficient[t, x^i])**

This "runs" the procedure.   *In[6]:=* **cex[5, 3]**

                                              Out[6]= 85

$expr_1$; $expr_2$; ...	a sequence of expressions to evaluate
Module[{a, b, ... }, $proc$]	a procedure with local variables a, b, ...

Constructing procedures.

When you write procedures in *Mathematica*, it is usually a good idea to make variables you use inside the procedures *local*, so that they do not interfere with things outside the procedures. You can do this by setting up your procedures as *modules*, in which you give a list of variables to be treated as local.

The function cex defined above is not a module, so the value of t "escapes", and exists even after the function returns.

In[7]:= **t**

Out[7]= $120 + 274 x + 225 x^2 + 85 x^3 + 15 x^4 + x^5$

This function is defined as a module with local variable u.

In[8]:= **ncex[n_, i_] :=**
                 Module[{u}, u = exprod[n]; Coefficient[u, x^i]]

The function gives the same result as before.

In[9]:= **ncex[5, 3]**

Out[9]= 85

Now, however, the value of u does not escape from the function.

In[10]:= **u**

Out[10]= u

■ 1.7.3 Repetitive Operations

In using *Mathematica*, you sometimes need to repeat an operation many times. There are many ways to do this. Often the most natural is in fact to set up a structure such as a list with many elements, and then apply your operation to each of the elements.

Another approach is to use the *Mathematica* function Do, which works much like the iteration constructs in languages such as C and Fortran. Do uses the standard *Mathematica* iterator notation introduced for Sum and Product in Section 1.5.4.

Do[*expr*, {*i, imax*}]	evaluate *expr* with *i* running from 1 to *imax*
Do[*expr*, {*i, imin, imax, di*}]	evaluate *expr* with *i* running from *imin* to *imax* in steps of *di*
Print[*expr*]	print *expr*
Table[*expr*, {*i, imax*}]	make a list of the values of *expr* with *i* running from 1 to *imax*

Implementing repetitive operations.

This prints out the values of the first five factorials.

In[1]:= **Do[Print[i!], {i, 5}]**

```
1
2
6
24
120
```

It is often more useful to have a list of results, which you can then manipulate further.

In[2]:= **Table[i!, {i, 5}]**

Out[2]= {1, 2, 6, 24, 120}

If you do not give an iteration variable, *Mathematica* simply repeats the operation you have specified, without changing anything.

In[3]:= **r = 1; Do[r = 1/(1 + r), {100}]; r**

$$Out[3]= \frac{573147844013817084101}{927372692193078999176}$$

■ 1.7.4 Transformation Rules for Functions

Section 1.4.2 discussed how you can use transformation rules of the form *x -> value* to replace symbols by values. The notion of transformation rules in *Mathematica* is, however, quite general. You can set up transformation rules not only for symbols, but for any *Mathematica* expression.

Applying the transformation rule x -> 3 replaces x by 3.

In[1]:= **1 + f[x] + f[y] /. x -> 3**

Out[1]= 1 + f[3] + f[y]

You can also use a transformation rule for f[x]. This rule does not affect f[y].

In[2]:= **1 + f[x] + f[y] /. f[x] -> p**

Out[2]= 1 + p + f[y]

f[t_] is a *pattern* that stands for f with any argument.

In[3]:= **1 + f[x] + f[y] /. f[t_] -> t^2**

Out[3]= $1 + x^2 + y^2$

Probably the most powerful aspect of transformation rules in *Mathematica* is that they can involve not only literal expressions, but also *patterns*. A pattern is an expression such as f[t_] which contains a blank (underscore). The blank can stand for any expression. Thus, a transformation rule for f[t_] specifies how the function f with *any* argument should be transformed. Notice that, in contrast, a transformation rule for f[x] without a blank, specifies only how the literal expression f[x] should be transformed, and does not, for example, say anything about the transformation of f[y].

When you give a function definition such as f[t_] := t^2, all you are doing is telling *Mathematica* to automatically apply the transformation rule f[t_] -> t^2 whenever possible.

You can set up transformation rules for expressions of any form.	*In[4]:=* **f[a b] + f[c d] /. f[x_ y_] -> f[x] + f[y]**
	Out[4]= f[a] + f[b] + f[c] + f[d]
This uses a transformation rule for x^p_.	*In[5]:=* **1 + x^2 + x^4 /. x^p_ -> f[p]**
	Out[5]= 1 + f[2] + f[4]

Sections 2.3 and 2.4 will explain in detail how to set up patterns and transformation rules for any kind of expression. Suffice it to say here that in *Mathematica* all expressions have a definite symbolic structure; transformation rules allow you to transform parts of that structure.

1.8 Lists

■ 1.8.1 Collecting Objects Together

We first encountered lists in Section 1.2.3 as a way of collecting numbers together. In this section, we shall see many different ways to use lists. You will find that lists are some of the most flexible and powerful objects in *Mathematica*. You will see that lists in *Mathematica* represent generalizations of several standard concepts in mathematics and computer science.

At a basic level, what a *Mathematica* list essentially does is to provide a way for you to collect together several expressions of any kind.

Here is a list of numbers.

```
In[1]:= {2, 3, 4}
Out[1]= {2, 3, 4}
```

This gives a list of symbolic expressions.

```
In[2]:= x^% - 1
Out[2]= {-1 + x^2, -1 + x^3, -1 + x^4}
```

You can differentiate these expressions.

```
In[3]:= D[%, x]
Out[3]= {2x, 3x^2, 4x^3}
```

And then you can find values when x is replaced with 3.

```
In[4]:= % /. x -> 3
Out[4]= {6, 27, 108}
```

The mathematical functions that are built into *Mathematica* are mostly set up to be "listable" so that they act separately on each element of a list. This is, however, not true of all functions in *Mathematica*. Unless you set it up specially, a new function f that you introduce will treat lists just as single objects. Sections 2.2.4 and 2.2.10 will describe how you can use Map and Thread to apply a function like this separately to each element in a list.

■ 1.8.2 Making Tables of Values

You can use lists as tables of values. You can generate the tables, for example, by evaluating an expression for a sequence of different parameter values.

This gives a table of the values of i^2, with i running from 1 to 6.

```
In[1]:= Table[i^2, {i, 6}]
Out[1]= {1, 4, 9, 16, 25, 36}
```

Here is a table of $\sin(n/5)$ for n from 0 to 4.

```
In[2]:= Table[Sin[n/5], {n, 0, 4}]
```
$$Out[2]= \left\{0, \, \text{Sin}\left[\frac{1}{5}\right], \, \text{Sin}\left[\frac{2}{5}\right], \, \text{Sin}\left[\frac{3}{5}\right], \, \text{Sin}\left[\frac{4}{5}\right]\right\}$$

This gives the numerical values.

```
In[3]:= N[%]
Out[3]= {0, 0.198669, 0.389418, 0.564642, 0.717356}
```

You can also make tables of formulas.

In[4]:= **Table[x^i + 2i, {i, 5}]**

Out[4]= $\{2 + x, \ 4 + x^2, \ 6 + x^3, \ 8 + x^4, \ 10 + x^5\}$

Table uses exactly the same iterator notation as the functions Sum and Product, which were discussed in Section 1.5.4.

In[5]:= **Product[x^i + 2i, {i, 5}]**

Out[5]= $(2 + x) \ (4 + x^2) \ (6 + x^3) \ (8 + x^4) \ (10 + x^5)$

This makes a table with values of x running from 0 to 1 in steps of 0.25.

In[6]:= **Table[Sqrt[x], {x, 0, 1, 0.25}]**

Out[6]= {0, 0.5, 0.707107, 0.866025, 1.}

You can perform other operations on the lists you get from Table.

In[7]:= **%^2 + 3**

Out[7]= {3, 3.25, 3.5, 3.75, 4.}

TableForm displays lists in a "tabular" format. Notice that both words in the name TableForm begin with capital letters.

In[8]:= **% // TableForm**

```
                      3
                      3.25
Out[8]//TableForm=    3.5
                      3.75
                      4.
```

All the examples so far have been of tables obtained by varying a single parameter. You can also make tables that involve several parameters. These multidimensional tables are specified using the standard *Mathematica* iterator notation, discussed in Section 1.5.4.

This makes a table of $x^i + y^j$ with i running from 1 to 3 and j running from 1 to 2.

In[9]:= **Table[x^i + y^j, {i, 3}, {j, 2}]**

Out[9]= $\{\{x + y, \ x + y^2\}, \ \{x^2 + y, \ x^2 + y^2\}, \ \{x^3 + y, \ x^3 + y^2\}\}$

The table in this example is a *list of lists*. The elements of the outer list correspond to successive values of *i*. The elements of each inner list correspond to successive values of *j*, with *i* fixed.

Sometimes you may want to generate a table by evaluating a particular expression many times, without incrementing any variables.

This creates a list containing four copies of the symbol x.

In[10]:= **Table[x, {4}]**

Out[10]= {x, x, x, x}

This gives a list of four pseudorandom numbers. Table re-evaluates Random[ ] for each element in the list, so that you get a different pseudorandom number.

In[11]:= **Table[Random[ ], {4}]**

Out[11]= {0.0560708, 0.6303, 0.359894, 0.871377}

Table[f, {$imax$}]	give a list of $imax$ values of f
Table[f, {i, $imax$}]	give a list of the values of f as i runs from 1 to $imax$
Table[f, {i, $imin$, $imax$}]	give a list of values with i running from $imin$ to $imax$
Table[f, {i, $imin$, $imax$, di}]	use steps of di
Table[f, {i, $imin$, $imax$}, {j, $jmin$, $jmax$}, ...]	
	generate a multidimensional table
TableForm[$list$]	display a list in tabular form

Functions for generating tables.

You can use the operations discussed in Section 1.2.4 to extract elements of the table.

This creates a 2×2 table, and gives it the name m.

In[12]:= **m = Table[i - j, {i, 2}, {j, 2}]**

Out[12]= {{0, -1}, {1, 0}}

This extracts the first sublist from the list of lists that makes up the table.

In[13]:= **m[[1]]**

Out[13]= {0, -1}

This extracts the second element of that sublist.

In[14]:= **%[[2]]**

Out[14]= -1

This does the two operations together.

In[15]:= **m[[1,2]]**

Out[15]= -1

This displays m in a "tabular" form.

In[16]:= **TableForm[m]**

$$
Out[16]//TableForm= \begin{matrix} 0 & -1 \\ 1 & 0 \end{matrix}
$$

t[[i]] or Part[t, i]	give the ith sublist in t (also input as t[[i]])
t[[{i_1, i_2, ... }]] or Part[t, {i_1, i_2, ... }]	
	give a list of the $i_1{}^{\text{th}}$, $i_2{}^{\text{th}}$, ... parts of t
t[[i, j, ...]] or Part[t, i, j, ...]	
	give the part of t corresponding to t[[i]][[j]] ...

Ways to extract parts of tables.

As we mentioned in Section 1.2.4, you can think of lists in *Mathematica* as being analogous to "arrays". Lists of lists are then like two-dimensional arrays. When you lay them out in a tabular form, the two indices of each element are like its x and y coordinates.

You can use **Table** to generate arrays with any number of dimensions.

This generates a three-dimensional $2 \times 2 \times 2$ array. It is a list of lists of lists.	*In[17]:=* **Table[i j^2 k^3, {i, 2}, {j, 2}, {k, 2}]** *Out[17]=* {{{1, 8}, {4, 32}}, {{2, 16}, {8, 64}}}

■ 1.8.3 Vectors and Matrices

Vectors and matrices in *Mathematica* are simply represented by lists and by lists of lists, respectively.

$$\{a, b, c\} \quad \text{vector } (a, b, c)$$

$$\{\{a, b\}, \{c, d\}\} \quad \text{matrix } \begin{pmatrix} a & b \\ c & d \end{pmatrix}$$

The representation of vectors and matrices by lists.

This is a 2×2 matrix.	*In[1]:=* **m = {{a, b}, {c, d}}** *Out[1]=* {{a, b}, {c, d}}
Here is the first row.	*In[2]:=* **m[[1]]** *Out[2]=* {a, b}
Here is the element m_{12}.	*In[3]:=* **m[[1,2]]** *Out[3]=* b
This is a two-component vector.	*In[4]:=* **v = {x, y}** *Out[4]=* {x, y}
The objects p and q are treated as scalars.	*In[5]:=* **p v + q** *Out[5]=* {q + p x, q + p y}
Vectors are added component by component.	*In[6]:=* **v + {xp, yp} + {xpp, ypp}** *Out[6]=* {x + xp + xpp, y + yp + ypp}
This takes the dot ("scalar") product of two vectors.	*In[7]:=* **{x, y} . {xp, yp}** *Out[7]=* x xp + y yp
You can also multiply a matrix by a vector.	*In[8]:=* **m . v** *Out[8]=* {a x + b y, c x + d y}
Or a matrix by a matrix.	*In[9]:=* **m . m** *Out[9]=* {{a^2 + b c, a b + b d}, {a c + c d, b c + d^2}}

Or a vector by a matrix.

In[10]:= **v . m**

Out[10]= {a x + c y, b x + d y}

This combination makes a scalar.

In[11]:= **v . m . v**

Out[11]= x (a x + c y) + y (b x + d y)

Because of the way *Mathematica* uses lists to represent vectors and matrices, you never have to distinguish between "row" and "column" vectors.

Table[f, {i, n}]	build a length-n vector by evaluating f with i = 1, 2, ... , n
Array[a, n]	build a length-n vector of the form {a[1], a[2], ... }
Range[n]	create the list {1, 2, 3, ... , n}
Range[n_1, n_2]	create the list {n_1, n_1+1, ... , n_2}
Range[n_1, n_2, dn]	create the list {n_1, n_1+dn, ... , n_2}
list[[i]] or Part[*list*, i]	give the ith element in the vector *list*
Length[*list*]	give the number of elements in *list*
ColumnForm[*list*]	display the elements of *list* in a column
$c\,v$	multiply by a scalar
a . b	vector dot product
Cross[a, b]	vector cross product (also input as $a \times b$)

Functions for vectors.

Table[f, {i, m}, {j, n}]	build an $m \times n$ matrix by evaluating f with i ranging from 1 to m and j ranging from 1 to n
Array[a, {m, n}]	build an $m \times n$ matrix with i, j^{th} element a[i, j]
IdentityMatrix[n]	generate an $n \times n$ identity matrix
DiagonalMatrix[*list*]	generate a square matrix with the elements in *list* on the diagonal
list[[i]] or Part[*list*, i]	give the ith row in the matrix *list*
list[[i, j]] or Part[*list*, i, j]	give the i, j^{th} element in matrix *list*
Dimensions[*list*]	give the dimensions of a matrix represented by *list*
MatrixForm[*list*]	display *list* in matrix form

Functions for matrices.

This builds a 3×3 matrix s with elements $s_{ij} = i + j$.

```
In[12]:= s = Table[i+j, {i, 3}, {j, 3}]
Out[12]= {{2, 3, 4}, {3, 4, 5}, {4, 5, 6}}
```

This displays s in standard two-dimensional matrix format.

```
In[13]:= MatrixForm[s]
```

$$Out[13]//MatrixForm= \begin{pmatrix} 2 & 3 & 4 \\ 3 & 4 & 5 \\ 4 & 5 & 6 \end{pmatrix}$$

This gives a vector with symbolic elements. You can use this in deriving general formulas that are valid with any choice of vector components.

```
In[14]:= Array[a, 4]
Out[14]= {a[1], a[2], a[3], a[4]}
```

This gives a 3×2 matrix with symbolic elements. Section 2.2.6 will discuss how you can produce other kinds of elements with Array.

```
In[15]:= Array[p, {3, 2}]
Out[15]= {{p[1, 1], p[1, 2]}, {p[2, 1], p[2, 2]},
          {p[3, 1], p[3, 2]}}
```

Here are the dimensions of the matrix on the previous line.

```
In[16]:= Dimensions[%]
Out[16]= {3, 2}
```

This generates a 3×3 diagonal matrix.

```
In[17]:= DiagonalMatrix[{a, b, c}]
Out[17]= {{a, 0, 0}, {0, b, 0}, {0, 0, c}}
```

$c\ m$	multiply by a scalar
$a\ .\ b$	matrix product
Inverse[m]	matrix inverse
MatrixPower[m, n]	n^{th} power of a matrix
Det[m]	determinant
Transpose[m]	transpose
Eigenvalues[m]	eigenvalues
Eigenvectors[m]	eigenvectors
Eigenvalues[N[m]], Eigenvectors[N[m]]	numerical eigenvalues and eigenvectors

Some mathematical operations on matrices.

Here is the 2×2 matrix of symbolic variables that was defined above.

```
In[18]:= m
Out[18]= {{a, b}, {c, d}}
```

This gives its determinant.	*In[19]:=* **Det[m]**
	Out[19]= -bc + ad
Here is the transpose of m.	*In[20]:=* **Transpose[m]**
	Out[20]= {{a, c}, {b, d}}
This gives the inverse of m in symbolic form.	*In[21]:=* **Inverse[m]**
	Out[21]= $\left\{\left\{\dfrac{d}{-bc+ad}, -\dfrac{b}{-bc+ad}\right\}, \left\{-\dfrac{c}{-bc+ad}, \dfrac{a}{-bc+ad}\right\}\right\}$
Here is a particular 3×3 rational matrix known as a "Hilbert matrix".	*In[22]:=* **h = Table[1/(i+j-1), {i, 3}, {j, 3}]**
	Out[22]= $\left\{\left\{1, \dfrac{1}{2}, \dfrac{1}{3}\right\}, \left\{\dfrac{1}{2}, \dfrac{1}{3}, \dfrac{1}{4}\right\}, \left\{\dfrac{1}{3}, \dfrac{1}{4}, \dfrac{1}{5}\right\}\right\}$
This gives its inverse.	*In[23]:=* **Inverse[h]**
	Out[23]= {{9, -36, 30}, {-36, 192, -180}, {30, -180, 180}}
Taking the dot product of the inverse with the original matrix gives the identity matrix.	*In[24]:=* **% . h**
	Out[24]= {{1, 0, 0}, {0, 1, 0}, {0, 0, 1}}
Here is a 3×3 matrix.	*In[25]:=* **r = Table[i+j+1, {i, 3}, {j, 3}]**
	Out[25]= {{3, 4, 5}, {4, 5, 6}, {5, 6, 7}}
Eigenvalues gives the eigenvalues of the matrix.	*In[26]:=* **Eigenvalues[r]**
	Out[26]= $\left\{0, \dfrac{1}{2}\left(15 - \sqrt{249}\right), \dfrac{1}{2}\left(15 + \sqrt{249}\right)\right\}$
This gives a numerical approximation to the matrix.	*In[27]:=* **rn = N[r]**
	Out[27]= {{3., 4., 5.}, {4., 5., 6.}, {5., 6., 7.}}
Here are numerical approximations to the eigenvalues.	*In[28]:=* **Eigenvalues[rn]**
	Out[28]= {15.3899, -0.389867, 1.37205×10^{-15}}

Section 3.7 discusses other matrix operations that are built into *Mathematica*.

~■ 1.8.4 Getting Pieces of Lists

First[*list*]	the first element in *list*
Last[*list*]	the last element
Part[*list*, *n*] or *list*[[*n*]]	the nth element
Part[*list*, -*n*] or *list*[[-*n*]]	the nth element from the end
Part[*list*, {n_1, n_2, ... }] or *list*[[{n_1, n_2, ... }]]	the list of elements at positions n_1, n_2, ...

Picking out elements of lists.

We will use this list for the examples.	In[1]:= **t = {a,b,c,d,e,f,g}**
	Out[1]= {a, b, c, d, e, f, g}
Here is the last element of t.	In[2]:= **Last[t]**
	Out[2]= g
This gives the third element.	In[3]:= **t[[3]]**
	Out[3]= c
This gives a list of the first and fourth elements.	In[4]:= **t[[{1, 4}]]**
	Out[4]= {a, d}

Take[*list*, *n*]	the first *n* elements in *list*
Take[*list*, -*n*]	the last *n* elements
Take[*list*, {*m*, *n*}]	elements *m* through *n* (inclusive)
Rest[*list*]	*list* with its first element dropped
Drop[*list*, *n*]	*list* with its first *n* elements dropped
Drop[*list*, -*n*]	*list* with its last *n* elements dropped
Drop[*list*, {*m*, *n*}]	*list* with elements *m* through *n* dropped

Picking out sequences in lists.

This gives the first three elements of the list t defined above.	In[5]:= **Take[t, 3]**
	Out[5]= {a, b, c}

This gives the last three elements.

In[6]:= **Take[t, -3]**

Out[6]= {e, f, g}

This gives elements 2 through 5 inclusive.

In[7]:= **Take[t, {2, 5}]**

Out[7]= {b, c, d, e}

This gives t with the first element dropped.

In[8]:= **Rest[t]**

Out[8]= {b, c, d, e, f, g}

This gives t with its first three elements dropped.

In[9]:= **Drop[t, 3]**

Out[9]= {d, e, f, g}

This gives t with only its third element dropped.

In[10]:= **Drop[t, {3, 3}]**

Out[10]= {a, b, d, e, f, g}

Part[*list*, i, j, ...]   or   *list*[[i, j, ...]]
   the element *list*[[i]][[j]] ...

Part[*list*, {i_1, i_2, ... }, {j_1, j_2, ... }, ...]   or   *list*[[{i_1, i_2, ... }, {j_1, j_2, ... }, ...]]
   the list of elements obtained by picking out parts i_1, i_2, ...
   at the first level, etc.

Extracting parts of nested lists.

Here is a list of lists.

In[11]:= **t = {{a, b, c}, {d, e, f}}**

Out[11]= {{a, b, c}, {d, e, f}}

This picks out the first sublist.

In[12]:= **t[[1]]**

Out[12]= {a, b, c}

This picks out the second element in the first sublist.

In[13]:= **t[[1, 2]]**

Out[13]= b

This is equivalent to t[[1, 2]], but is clumsier to write.

In[14]:= **t[[1]][[2]]**

Out[14]= b

This gives a list containing two copies of the second part of t, followed by one copy of the first part.

In[15]:= **t[[{2, 2, 1}]]**

Out[15]= {{d, e, f}, {d, e, f}, {a, b, c}}

For each of the parts picked out on the previous line, this gives a list of their second and third parts.

```
In[16]:= t[[{2, 2, 1}, {2, 3}]]
Out[16]= {{e, f}, {e, f}, {b, c}}
```

+	Extract[*list*, {*i*, *j*, ... }]	the element at position {*i*, *j*, ... } in *list*
+	Extract[*list*, {{*i*₁, *j*₁, ... }, {*i*₂, *j*₂, ... }, ... }]	
		the list of elements at positions {i_1, j_1, ... }, {i_2, j_2, ... }, ...

Another way to extract parts of nested lists.

This extracts the element at position {2, 1} in t.

```
In[17]:= Extract[t, {2, 1}]
Out[17]= d
```

This extracts a list of three elements from t.

```
In[18]:= Extract[t, {{1, 1}, {2, 2}, {2, 3}}]
Out[18]= {a, e, f}
```

Section 2.1.5 will show how all the functions in this section can be generalized to work not only on lists, but on any *Mathematica* expressions.

The functions in this section allow you to pick out pieces that occur at particular positions in lists. Section 2.3.2 will show how you can use functions like `Select` and `Cases` to pick out elements of lists based not on their positions, but instead on their properties.

■ 1.8.5 Testing and Searching List Elements

Position[*list*, *form*]	the positions at which *form* occurs in *list*
Count[*list*, *form*]	the number of times *form* appears as an element of *list*
MemberQ[*list*, *form*]	test whether *form* is an element of *list*
FreeQ[*list*, *form*]	test whether *form* occurs nowhere in *list*

Testing and searching for elements of lists.

The previous section discussed how to extract pieces of lists based on their positions or indices. *Mathematica* also has functions that search and test for elements of lists, based on the values of those elements.

This gives a list of the positions at which a appears in the list.

```
In[1]:= Position[{a, b, c, a, b}, a]
Out[1]= {{1}, {4}}
```

Count counts the number of occurrences of a.	*In[2]:=* **Count[{a, b, c, a, b}, a]**
	Out[2]= 2
This shows that a is an element of {a, b, c}.	*In[3]:=* **MemberQ[{a, b, c}, a]**
	Out[3]= True
On the other hand, d is not.	*In[4]:=* **MemberQ[{a, b, c}, d]**
	Out[4]= False
This assigns m to be the 3×3 identity matrix.	*In[5]:=* **m = IdentityMatrix[3]**
	Out[5]= {{1, 0, 0}, {0, 1, 0}, {0, 0, 1}}
This shows that 0 does occur *somewhere* in m.	*In[6]:=* **FreeQ[m, 0]**
	Out[6]= False
This gives a list of the positions at which 0 occurs in m.	*In[7]:=* **Position[m, 0]**
	Out[7]= {{1, 2}, {1, 3}, {2, 1}, {2, 3}, {3, 1}, {3, 2}}
Extract takes the list of positions and shows that the element at each position is indeed 0.	*In[8]:=* **Extract[m, %]**
	Out[8]= {0, 0, 0, 0, 0, 0}

As discussed in Section 2.3.2, the functions Count and Position, as well as MemberQ and FreeQ, can be used not only to search for *particular* list elements, but also to search for classes of elements which match specific "patterns".

■ 1.8.6 Adding, Removing and Modifying List Elements

Prepend[*list*, *element*]	add *element* at the beginning of *list*
Append[*list*, *element*]	add *element* at the end of *list*
Insert[*list*, *element*, *i*]	insert *element* at position *i* in *list*
Insert[*list*, *element*, *-i*]	insert at position *i* counting from the end of *list*
Insert[*list*, *element*, {*i*, *j*, ... }]	insert at position *i*, *j*, ... in *list*
Delete[*list*, *i*]	delete the element at position *i* in *list*
Delete[*list*, {*i*, *j*, ... }]	delete at position *i*, *j*, ... in *list*

Functions for adding and deleting elements in lists.

This gives a list with x prepended.	*In[1]:=* **Prepend[{a, b, c}, x]**
	Out[1]= {x, a, b, c}

This adds x at the end.	*In[2]:=* **Append[{a, b, c}, x]**
	Out[2]= {a, b, c, x}
This inserts x so that it becomes element number 2.	*In[3]:=* **Insert[{a, b, c}, x, 2]**
	Out[3]= {a, x, b, c}
Negative numbers count from the end of the list.	*In[4]:=* **Insert[{a, b, c}, x, -2]**
	Out[4]= {a, b, x, c}
Delete removes an element from the list.	*In[5]:=* **Delete[{a, b, c, d}, 3]**
	Out[5]= {a, b, d}

ReplacePart[*list*, *element*, *i*]	replace the element at position *i* in *list*
ReplacePart[*list*, *element*, -*i*]	replace at position *i* counting from the end
ReplacePart[*list*, *element*, {*i*, *j*, ... }]	replace *list*[[*i*, *j*, ...]]
ReplacePart[*list*, *element*, {{i_1, j_1, ... }, {i_2, ... }, ... }]	replace all parts *list*[[i_k, j_k, ...]] with the same element
ReplacePart[*list*, *element*, {{i_1, ... }, ... }, {n_1, n_2, ... }]	replace part *list*[[i_k, ...]] with *element*[[n_k]]

Modifying parts of lists.

This replaces the third element in the list with x.	*In[6]:=* **ReplacePart[{a, b, c, d}, x, 3]**
	Out[6]= {a, b, x, d}
This replaces the first and fourth parts of the list. Notice the need for double lists in specifying multiple parts to replace.	*In[7]:=* **ReplacePart[{a, b, c, d}, x, {{1}, {4}}]**
	Out[7]= {x, b, c, x}
Here is a 3 × 3 identity matrix.	*In[8]:=* **IdentityMatrix[3]**
	Out[8]= {{1, 0, 0}, {0, 1, 0}, {0, 0, 1}}
This replaces the (2, 2) component of the matrix by x.	*In[9]:=* **ReplacePart[%, x, {2, 2}]**
	Out[9]= {{1, 0, 0}, {0, x, 0}, {0, 0, 1}}

■ 1.8.7 Combining Lists

Join[*list*₁, *list*₂, ...]	concatenate lists together
Union[*list*₁, *list*₂, ...]	combine lists, removing repeated elements and sorting the result

Functions for combining lists.

Join concatenates any number of lists together.

In[1]:= **Join[{a, b, c}, {x, y}, {c, {d, e}, a}]**

Out[1]= {a, b, c, x, y, c, {d, e}, a}

Union combines lists, keeping only distinct elements.

In[2]:= **Union[{a, b, c}, {c, a, d}, {a, d}]**

Out[2]= {a, b, c, d}

■ 1.8.8 Advanced Topic: Lists as Sets

Mathematica usually keeps the elements of a list in exactly the order you originally entered them. If you want to treat a *Mathematica* list like a mathematical *set*, however, you may want to ignore the order of elements in the list.

Union[*list*₁, *list*₂, ...]	give a list of the distinct elements in the *list*ᵢ
Intersection[*list*₁, *list*₂, ...]	give a list of the elements that are common to all the *list*ᵢ
Complement[*universal*, *list*₁, ...]	give a list of the elements that are in *universal*, but not in any of the *list*ᵢ

Set theoretical functions.

Union gives the elements that occur in *any* of the lists.

In[1]:= **Union[{c, a, b}, {d, a, c}, {a, e}]**

Out[1]= {a, b, c, d, e}

Intersection gives only elements that occur in *all* the lists.

In[2]:= **Intersection[{a, c, b}, {b, a, d, a}]**

Out[2]= {a, b}

Complement gives elements that occur in the first list, but not in any of the others.

In[3]:= **Complement[{a, b, c, d}, {a, d}]**

Out[3]= {b, c}

■ 1.8.9 Rearranging Lists

Sort[*list*]	sort the elements of *list* into a standard order
Union[*list*]	sort elements, removing any duplicates
Reverse[*list*]	reverse the order of elements in *list*
RotateLeft[*list*, *n*]	rotate the elements of *list* *n* places to the left
RotateRight[*list*, *n*]	rotate *n* places to the right
RotateLeft[*list*], RotateRight[*list*]	
	rotate by one position

Functions for rearranging lists.

This sorts the elements of a list into a standard order. In simple cases like this, the order is alphabetical or numerical.

```
In[1]:= Sort[{b, a, c, a, b}]
Out[1]= {a, a, b, b, c}
```

This sorts the elements, removing any duplicates.

```
In[2]:= Union[{b, a, c, a, b}]
Out[2]= {a, b, c}
```

This reverses the list.

```
In[3]:= Reverse[{a, b, c, d}]
Out[3]= {d, c, b, a}
```

This rotates ("shifts") the elements in the list two places to the left.

```
In[4]:= RotateLeft[{a, b, c, d, e}, 2]
Out[4]= {c, d, e, a, b}
```

You can rotate to the right by giving a negative displacement, or by using RotateRight.

```
In[5]:= RotateLeft[{a, b, c, d, e}, -2]
Out[5]= {d, e, a, b, c}
```

■ 1.8.10 Grouping Together Elements of Lists

Partition[*list*, *n*]	partition *list* into *n* element pieces
Partition[*list*, *n*, *d*]	use offset *d* for successive pieces
Split[*list*]	split *list* into pieces consisting of runs of identical elements

Functions for grouping together elements of lists.

Here is a list.

```
In[1]:= t = {a, b, c, d, e, f, g}
Out[1]= {a, b, c, d, e, f, g}
```

This groups the elements of the list in pairs, and in this case throws away the single element which is left at the end.

In[2]:= **Partition[t, 2]**

Out[2]= {{a, b}, {c, d}, {e, f}}

This groups elements in triples. There is no overlap between the triples.

In[3]:= **Partition[t, 3]**

Out[3]= {{a, b, c}, {d, e, f}}

This makes triples of elements, with each successive triple offset by just one element.

In[4]:= **Partition[t, 3, 1]**

Out[4]= {{a, b, c}, {b, c, d}, {c, d, e}, {d, e, f}, {e, f, g}}

This splits up the list into runs of identical elements.

In[5]:= **Split[{a, a, b, b, b, a, a, a, b}]**

Out[5]= {{a, a}, {b, b, b}, {a, a, a}, {b}}

■ 1.8.11 Mathematical Operations on Lists

Section 2.2.3 will discuss in detail how to do mathematical operations on lists. Here are a couple of cases that often occur in practice; Section 2.2.3 will give many generalizations.

Apply[Plus, *list*] or Plus @@ *list*
    add together all the elements in *list*

Apply[Times, *list*] or Times @@ *list*
    multiply together all the elements in *list*

Simple mathematical operations on lists.

This adds all the elements in a list.

In[1]:= **Apply[Plus, {a, b, c, d}]**

Out[1]= a + b + c + d

■ 1.8.12 Advanced Topic: Rearranging Nested Lists

You will encounter nested lists if you use matrices or generate multidimensional arrays and tables. Rearranging nested lists can be a complicated affair, and you will often have to experiment to get the right combination of commands.

Transpose[*list*]	interchange the top two levels of lists
Transpose[*list*, {*m*, *n*, ... }]	put first level at level *m*, second level at level *n*, ...
Flatten[*list*]	flatten out all levels in *list*
Flatten[*list*, *n*]	flatten out the top *n* levels in *list*
FlattenAt[*list*, *i*]	flatten out a sublist that appears at position *i*
FlattenAt[*list*, {*i*, *j*, ... }]	flatten out a sublist at position *i*, *j*, ...
FlattenAt[*list*, {{i_1, j_1, ... }, {i_2, ... }, ... }]	flatten out several sublists
RotateLeft[*list*, {n_1, n_2, ... }]	rotate successive levels by n_i places
Partition[*list*, {n_1, n_2, ... }, {d_1, d_2, ... }]	partition successive levels into n_i element pieces with offsets d_i

Functions for rearranging nested lists.

Here is a 3×2 array.

```
In[1]:= t = {{a, b}, {c, d}, {e, f}}
Out[1]= {{a, b}, {c, d}, {e, f}}
```

You can rearrange it to get a 2×3 array.

```
In[2]:= Transpose[t]
Out[2]= {{a, c, e}, {b, d, f}}
```

This "flattens out" sublists. You can think of it as effectively just removing the inner sets of braces.

```
In[3]:= Flatten[t]
Out[3]= {a, b, c, d, e, f}
```

Here is a $2 \times 2 \times 2$ array.

```
In[4]:= t = Table[i^2 +j^2 +k^2, {i, 2}, {j, 2}, {k, 2}]
Out[4]= {{{3, 6}, {6, 9}}, {{6, 9}, {9, 12}}}
```

This flattens out all the levels.

```
In[5]:= Flatten[t]
Out[5]= {3, 6, 6, 9, 6, 9, 9, 12}
```

This flattens only the first level of sublists.

```
In[6]:= Flatten[t, 1]
Out[6]= {{3, 6}, {6, 9}, {6, 9}, {9, 12}}
```

This flattens out only the sublist that appears at position 2.

```
In[7]:= FlattenAt[{{a, b}, {c, d}}, 2]
Out[7]= {{a, b}, c, d}
```

There are many other operations you can perform on nested lists. We will discuss some more of them when we look at Map, Apply, Scan and Level in Part 2.

■ 1.8.13 Advanced Topic: Combinatorial Operations

You can use lists to set up many kinds of combinatorial calculations. Here are a few examples.

Permutations[*list*]	give all possible orderings of *list*
Outer[List, *list*₁, *list*₂]	give lists of elements in *list*₁ and *list*₂ combined in all possible ways
Outer[List, *list*₁, *list*₂, *n*]	combine only elements on the top *n* levels
OrderedQ[*list*]	give True if the elements of *list* are in order
Signature[*list*]	give the signature of the permutation needed to put *list* into standard order

Some combinatorial operations on lists.

This gives the 3! = 6 possible permutations of three elements.

```
In[1]:= Permutations[{a,b,c}]
Out[1]= {{a, b, c}, {a, c, b}, {b, a, c}, {b, c, a},
          {c, a, b}, {c, b, a}}
```

This combines the list elements in all possible ways. This operation is analogous to a mathematical "outer product" (see Section 3.7.11).

```
In[2]:= Outer[List, {a, b}, {c, d}]
Out[2]= {{{a, c}, {a, d}}, {{b, c}, {b, d}}}
```

1.9 Graphics and Sound

■ 1.9.1 Basic Plotting

Plot[*f*, {*x*, *xmin*, *xmax*}]	plot *f* as a function of *x* from *xmin* to *xmax*
Plot[{*f₁*, *f₂*, ... }, {*x*, *xmin*, *xmax*}]	
	plot several functions together

Basic plotting functions.

This plots a graph of sin(*x*) as a function of *x* from 0 to 2π.

In[1]:= **Plot[Sin[x], {x, 0, 2Pi}]**

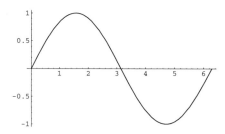

You can plot functions that have singularities. *Mathematica* will try to choose appropriate scales.

In[2]:= **Plot[Tan[x], {x, -3, 3}]**

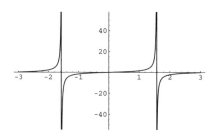

You can give a list of functions to plot.   *In[3]:=* `Plot[{Sin[x], Sin[2x], Sin[3x]}, {x, 0, 2Pi}]`

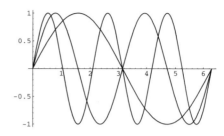

To get smooth curves, *Mathematica* has to evaluate functions you plot at a large number of points. As a result, it is important that you set things up so that each function evaluation is as quick as possible.

When you ask *Mathematica* to plot an object, say *f*, as a function of *x*, there are two possible approaches it can take. One approach is first to try and evaluate *f*, presumably getting a symbolic expression in terms of *x*, and then subsequently evaluate this expression numerically for the specific values of *x* needed in the plot. The second approach is first to work out what values of *x* are needed, and only subsequently to evaluate *f* with those values of *x*.

If you type `Plot[f, {x, xmin, xmax}]` it is the second of these approaches that is used. This has the advantage that *Mathematica* only tries to evaluate *f* for specific numerical values of *x*; it does not matter whether sensible values are defined for *f* when *x* is symbolic.

There are, however, some cases in which it is much better to have *Mathematica* evaluate *f* before it starts to make the plot. A typical case is when *f* is actually a command that generates a table of functions. You want to have *Mathematica* first produce the table, and then evaluate the functions, rather than trying to produce the table afresh for each value of *x*. You can do this by typing `Plot[Evaluate[f], {x, xmin, xmax}]`.

This makes a plot of the Bessel functions $J_n(x)$ with *n* running from 1 to 4. The `Evaluate` tells *Mathematica* *first* to make the table of functions, and only *then* to evaluate them for particular values of **x**.

In[4]:= `Plot[Evaluate[Table[BesselJ[n, x], {n, 4}]], {x, 0, 10}]`

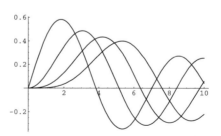

This finds the numerical solution to a differential equation, as discussed in Section 1.6.4.

In[5]:= `NDSolve[{y'[x] == Sin[y[x]], y[0] == 1}, y, {x, 0, 4}]`

Out[5]= `{{y → InterpolatingFunction[{{0., 4.}}, <>]}}`

Here is a plot of the solution. The Evaluate tells *Mathematica* to first set up an InterpolatingFunction object, then evaluate this at a sequence of x values.

In[6]:= **Plot[Evaluate[y[x] /. %], {x, 0, 4}]**

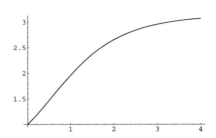

Plot[*f*, {*x*, *xmin*, *xmax*}]	*first* choose specific numerical values for *x*, then evaluate *f* for each value of *x*
Plot[Evaluate[*f*], {*x*, *xmin*, *xmax*}]	*first* evaluate *f*, then choose specific numerical values of *x*
Plot[Evaluate[Table[*f*, ...]], {*x*, *xmin*, *xmax*}]	generate a list of functions, and then plot them
Plot[Evaluate[*y*[*x*] /. *solution*], {*x*, *xmin*, *xmax*}]	plot a numerical solution to a differential equation obtained from NDSolve

Methods for setting up objects to plot.

■ 1.9.2 Special Topic: How Graphics Are Output

The details of how *Mathematica* outputs graphics vary between different computer systems and different *Mathematica* interfaces. The documentation that came with your copy of *Mathematica* should tell you what is relevant in your case.

With text-based *Mathematica* interfaces, each piece of graphics output typically fills your complete screen, or causes a new window to be created which is then filled with graphics. The details of how you get rid of the graphics vary from one system to another. Note that when you start *Mathematica* with a text-based interface, you may have to load a *Mathematica* package to tell *Mathematica* how you want graphics output to be done. The details of this should be described in the documentation that came with your copy of *Mathematica*.

With a notebook-based *Mathematica* interface, each piece of graphics is placed in a cell in your notebook. The *Mathematica* front end allows you to manipulate the graphics in several ways, for example by resizing them, or redisplaying them with different options.

Many *Mathematica* systems allow you to collect together sequences of graphic images and display them in quick succession to produce an animated "movie". Notebook-based interfaces typically allow you to select a sequence of cells to serve as the frames in your animation. Many text-based interfaces also provide animation capabilities; typically the function `ShowAnimation[{`g_1`, `g_2`, ... }]`, where the g_i are pieces of graphics output, generates a movie.

You should understand that when *Mathematica* produces any kind of graphics output, it does so in three stages. The first stage is to execute commands like `Plot` to produce a sequence of *Mathematica* graphics primitives. These primitives, to be discussed in Section 2.9, represent objects such as lines, points and polygons as *Mathematica* expressions. The second stage of producing graphics output is to convert these graphics primitives to a standardized device-independent representation of your graphical image. *Mathematica* generates this representation in the PostScript page description language.

The final stage of graphics output is to take the PostScript description of a graphical image, and render it on the particular device you want. In a notebook-based interface, the *Mathematica* front end performs this rendering. On other systems, the rendering is usually done by an external program which is automatically called from within *Mathematica*.

The importance of using PostScript as a graphics description language is that it can be rendered on many different kinds of devices, including both displays and printers, and it can be imported into many kinds of programs. Specific versions of *Mathematica* come with various conversion utilities to produce Encapsulated PostScript form, and other standard graphics formats.

With text-based *Mathematica* interfaces, the command `PSPrint[`*graphics*`]` is typically set up to print a piece of graphics. The command `Display["`*file*`", `*graphics*`, "EPS"]` saves the encapsulated PostScript representation of the graphics in a file.

Although most graphics from *Mathematica* are first converted to PostScript, and then rendered on particular devices, there are some cases where it is more convenient to render directly from the original *Mathematica* form. One example is on systems that manipulate images of three-dimensional objects in real time. On such systems, the function `Live[`*graphics*`]` is typically set up to produce a "live" version of a piece of *Mathematica* graphics, which can then be manipulated directly using the various tools available on the particular computer system.

■ 1.9.3 Options

When *Mathematica* plots a graph for you, it has to make many choices. It has to work out what the scales should be, where the function should be sampled, how the axes should be drawn, and so on. Most of the time, *Mathematica* will probably make pretty good choices. However, if you want to get the very best possible pictures for your particular purposes, you may have to help *Mathematica* in making some of its choices.

There is a general mechanism for specifying "options" in *Mathematica* functions. Each option has a definite name. As the last arguments to a function like `Plot`, you can include a sequence of rules of the form *name->value*, to specify the values for various options. Any option for which you do not give an explicit rule is taken to have its "default" value.

Plot[*f*, {*x*, *xmin*, *xmax*}, *option->value*]
                                  make a plot, specifying a particular value for an option

Choosing an option for a plot.

A function like Plot has many options that you can set. Usually you will need to use at most a few of them at a time. If you want to optimize a particular plot, you will probably do best to experiment, trying a sequence of different settings for various options.

Each time you produce a plot, you can specify options for it. Section 1.9.4 will also discuss how you can change some of the options, even after you have produced the plot.

option name	default value	
AspectRatio	1/GoldenRatio	the height-to-width ratio for the plot; Automatic sets it from the absolute x and y coordinates
Axes	Automatic	whether to include axes
AxesLabel	None	labels to be put on the axes: *ylabel* specifies a label for the y axis, {*xlabel*, *ylabel*} for both axes
AxesOrigin	Automatic	the point at which axes cross
TextStyle	$TextStyle	the default style to use for text in the plot
FormatType	StandardForm	the default format type to use for text in the plot
DisplayFunction	$DisplayFunction	how to display graphics; Identity causes no display
Frame	False	whether to draw a frame around the plot
FrameLabel	None	labels to be put around the frame; give a list in clockwise order starting with the lower x axis
FrameTicks	Automatic	what tick marks to draw if there is a frame; None gives no tick marks
GridLines	None	what grid lines to include: Automatic includes a grid line for every major tick mark
PlotLabel	None	an expression to be printed as a label for the plot
PlotRange	Automatic	the range of coordinates to include in the plot: All includes all points
Ticks	Automatic	what tick marks to draw if there are axes; None gives no tick marks

Some of the options for Plot. These can also be used in Show.

Here is a plot with all options having their default values.

$In[1]:=$ **Plot[Sin[x^2], {x, 0, 3}]**

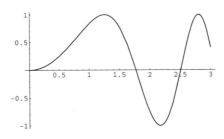

This draws axes on a frame around the plot.

$In[2]:=$ **Plot[Sin[x^2], {x, 0, 3}, Frame->True]**

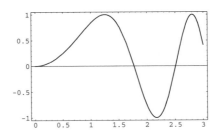

This specifies labels for the *x* and *y* axes. The expressions you give as labels are printed just as they would be if they appeared as *Mathematica* output. You can give any piece of text by putting it inside a pair of double quotes.

$In[3]:=$ **Plot[Sin[x^2], {x, 0, 3},**
            AxesLabel -> {"x value", "Sin[x^2]"}]

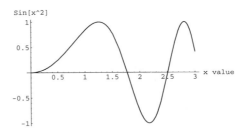

You can give several options at the same time, in any order.

In[4]:= **Plot[Sin[x^2], {x, 0, 3}, Frame -> True,**
GridLines -> Automatic]

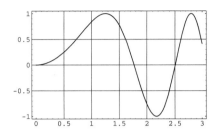

Setting the AspectRatio option changes the whole shape of your plot. AspectRatio gives the ratio of width to height. Its default value is the inverse of the Golden Ratio—supposedly the most pleasing shape for a rectangle.

In[5]:= **Plot[Sin[x^2], {x, 0, 3}, AspectRatio -> 1]**

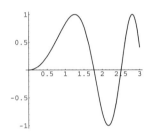

Automatic	use internal algorithms
None	do not include this
All	include everything
True	do this
False	do not do this

Some common settings for various options.

When *Mathematica* makes a plot, it tries to set the x and y scales to include only the "interesting" parts of the plot. If your function increases very rapidly, or has singularities, the parts where it gets too large will be cut off. By specifying the option PlotRange, you can control exactly what ranges of x and y coordinates are included in your plot.

Automatic	show at least a large fraction of the points, including the "interesting" region (the default setting)
All	show all points
{ymin, ymax}	show a specific range of y values
{xrange, yrange}	show the specified ranges of x and y values

Settings for the option PlotRange.

The setting for the option PlotRange gives explicit y limits for the graph. With the y limits specified here, the bottom of the curve is cut off.

In[6]:= Plot[Sin[x^2], {x, 0, 3}, PlotRange -> {0, 1.2}]

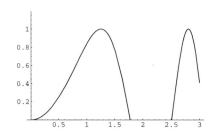

Mathematica always tries to plot functions as smooth curves. As a result, in places where your function wiggles a lot, Mathematica will use more points. In general, Mathematica tries to *adapt* its sampling of your function to the form of the function. There is, however, a limit, which you can set, to how finely Mathematica will ever sample a function.

The function $\sin(\frac{1}{x})$ wiggles infinitely often when $x \simeq 0$. Mathematica tries to sample more points in the region where the function wiggles a lot, but it can never sample the infinite number that you would need to reproduce the function exactly. As a result, there are slight glitches in the plot.

In[7]:= Plot[Sin[1/x], {x, -1, 1}]

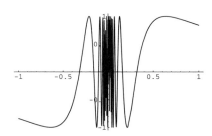

option name	default value	
PlotStyle	Automatic	a list of lists of graphics primitives to use for each curve (see Section 2.9.3)
PlotPoints	25	the minimum number of points at which to sample the function
MaxBend	10.	the maximum kink angle between successive segments of a curve
PlotDivision	20.	the maximum factor by which to subdivide in sampling the function
Compiled	True	whether to compile the function being plotted

More options for Plot. These cannot be used in Show.

It is important to realize that since *Mathematica* can only sample your function at a limited number of points, it can always miss features of the function. By increasing PlotPoints, you can make *Mathematica* sample your function at a larger number of points. Of course, the larger you set PlotPoints to be, the longer it will take *Mathematica* to plot *any* function, even a smooth one.

Since Plot needs to evaluate your function many times, it is important to make each evaluation as quick as possible. As a result, *Mathematica* usually *compiles* your function into a low-level pseudocode that can be executed very efficiently. One potential problem with this, however, is that the pseudocode allows only machine-precision numerical operations. If the function you are plotting requires higher-precision operations, you may have to switch off compilation in Plot. You can do this by setting the option Compiled -> False. Note that *Mathematica* can only compile "in-line code"; it cannot for example compile functions that you have defined. As a result, you should, when possible, use Evaluate as described on page 129 to evaluate any such definitions and get a form that the *Mathematica* compiler can handle.

■ 1.9.4 Redrawing and Combining Plots

Mathematica saves information about every plot you produce, so that you can later redraw it. When you redraw plots, you can change some of the options you use.

Show[*plot*]	redraw a plot
Show[*plot*, *option->value*]	redraw with options changed
Show[*plot₁*, *plot₂*, ...]	combine several plots
Show[GraphicsArray[{{*plot₁*, *plot₂*, ... }, ... }]]	
	draw an array of plots
InputForm[*plot*]	show the information that is saved about a plot

Functions for manipulating plots.

Here is a simple plot. -Graphics- is usually printed on the output line to stand for the information that *Mathematica* saves about the plot.

In[1]:= **Plot[ChebyshevT[7, x], {x, -1, 1}]**

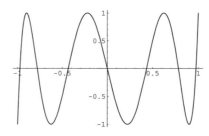

This redraws the plot from the previous line.

In[2]:= **Show[%]**

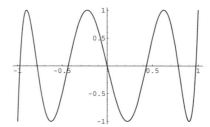

When you redraw the plot, you can change some of the options. This changes the choice of *y* scale.

In[3]:= **Show[%, PlotRange -> {-1, 2}]**

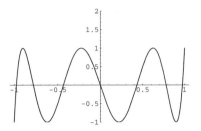

This takes the plot from the previous line, and changes another option in it.

In[4]:= **Show[%, PlotLabel -> "A Chebyshev Polynomial"]**

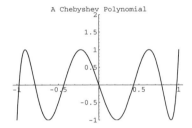

By using **Show** with a sequence of different options, you can look at the same plot in many different ways. You may want to do this, for example, if you are trying to find the best possible setting of options.

You can also use **Show** to combine plots. It does not matter whether the plots have the same scales: *Mathematica* will always choose new scales to include the points you want.

This sets **gj0** to be a plot of $J_0(x)$ from *x* = 0 to 10.

In[5]:= **gj0 = Plot[BesselJ[0, x], {x, 0, 10}]**

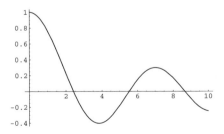

Here is a plot of $Y_1(x)$ from $x = 1$ to 10.

In[6]:= **gy1 = Plot[BesselY[1, x], {x, 1, 10}]**

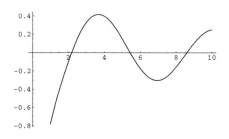

This shows the previous two plots combined into one. Notice that the scale is adjusted appropriately.

In[7]:= **gjy = Show[gj0, gy1]**

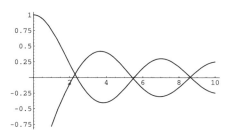

Using Show[*plot₁*, *plot₂*, ...] you can combine several plots into one. GraphicsArray allows you to draw several plots in an array.

Show[GraphicsArray[{*plot₁*, *plot₂*, ... }]]
                  draw several plots side by side

Show[GraphicsArray[{{*plot₁*}, {*plot₂*}, ... }]]
                  draw a column of plots

Show[GraphicsArray[{{*plot₁₁*, *plot₁₂*, ... }, ... }]]
                  draw a rectangular array of plots

Show[GraphicsArray[*plots*, GraphicsSpacing -> {*h*, *v*}]]
                  put the specified horizontal and vertical spacing between the plots

---

Drawing arrays of plots.

This shows the plots given above in an array.

$In[8]:=$ **Show[GraphicsArray[{{gj0, gjy}, {gy1, gjy}}]]**

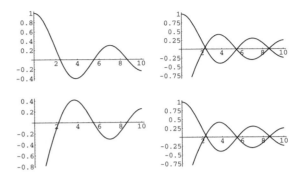

If you redisplay an array of plots using Show, any options you specify will be used for the whole array, rather than for individual plots.

$In[9]:=$ **Show[%, Frame->True, FrameTicks->None]**

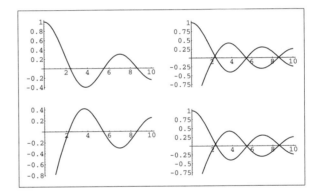

Here is a way to change options for all   In[10]:= **Show[% /. (Ticks -> Automatic) -> (Ticks -> None)]**
the plots in the array.

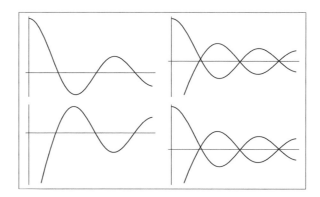

GraphicsArray by default puts a narrow border around each of the plots in the array it gives. You can change the size of this border by setting the option **GraphicsSpacing -> {h, v}**. The parameters *h* and *v* give the horizontal and vertical spacings to be used, as fractions of the width and height of the plots.

This increases the horizontal spacing,   In[11]:= **Show[%, GraphicsSpacing -> {0.3, 0}]**
but decreases the vertical spacing
between the plots in the array.

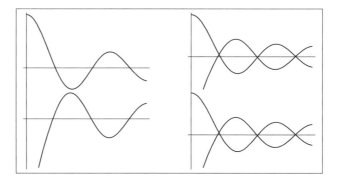

When you make a plot, *Mathematica* saves the list of points it used, together with some other information. Using what is saved, you can redraw plots in many different ways with **Show**. However, you should realize that no matter what options you specify, **Show** still has the same basic set of points to work with. So, for example, if you set the options so that *Mathematica* displays a small portion of your original plot magnified, you will probably be able to see the individual sample points that **Plot** used. Options like **PlotPoints** can only be set in the original **Plot** command itself. (*Mathematica* always plots the actual points it has; it avoids using smoothed or splined curves, which can give misleading results in mathematical graphics.)

Here is a simple plot.   *In[12]:=* **Plot[Cos[x], {x, -Pi, Pi}]**

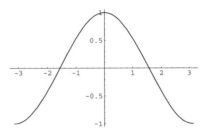

This shows a small region of the plot   *In[13]:=* **Show[%, PlotRange -> {{0, .3}, {.92, 1}}]**
in a magnified form. At this
resolution, you can see the individual
line segments that were produced by
the original **Plot** command.

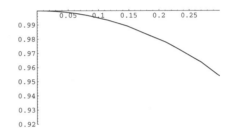

■ 1.9.5 Advanced Topic: Manipulating Options

There are a number of functions built into *Mathematica* which, like **Plot**, have various options you can set. *Mathematica* provides some general mechanisms for handling such options.

If you do not give a specific setting for an option to a function like **Plot**, then *Mathematica* will automatically use a default value for the option. The function **Options[***function***, ***option***]** allows you to find out the default value for a particular option. You can reset the default using **SetOptions[***function***, ***option***->***value***]**. Note that if you do this, the default value you have given will stay until you explicitly change it.

Options[*function***]**	give a list of the current default settings for all options
Options[*function***, ***option***]**	give the default setting for a particular option
SetOptions[*function***, ***option***->***value***, ...]**	
	reset defaults

Manipulating default settings for options.

Here is the default setting for the PlotRange option of Plot.

In[1]:= **Options[Plot, PlotRange]**

Out[1]= {PlotRange → Automatic}

This resets the default for the PlotRange option. The semicolon stops *Mathematica* from printing out the rather long list of options for Plot.

In[2]:= **SetOptions[Plot, PlotRange->All]** ;

Until you explicitly reset it, the default for the PlotRange option will now be All.

In[3]:= **Options[Plot, PlotRange]**

Out[3]= {PlotRange → All}

The graphics objects that you get from Plot or Show store information on the options they use. You can get this information by applying the Options function to these graphics objects.

Options[*plot*]	show all the options used for a particular plot
Options[*plot*, *option*]	show the setting for a specific option
FullOptions[*plot*, *option*]	show the actual form used for a specific option, even if the setting for the option is Automatic or All

Getting information on options used in plots.

Here is a plot, with default settings for all options.

In[4]:= **g = Plot[SinIntegral[x], {x, 0, 20}]**

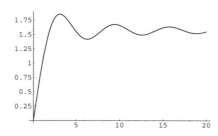

The setting used for the PlotRange option was All.

In[5]:= **Options[g, PlotRange]**

Out[5]= {PlotRange → All}

FullOptions gives the *actual* automatically chosen values used for PlotRange.

In[6]:= **FullOptions[g, PlotRange]**

Out[6]= {{-0.499999, 20.5}, {-0.0462976, 1.89823}}

■ 1.9.6 Contour and Density Plots

ContourPlot[*f*, {*x*, *xmin*, *xmax*}, {*y*, *ymin*, *ymax*}]
                      make a contour plot of *f* as a function of *x* and *y*

DensityPlot[*f*, {*x*, *xmin*, *xmax*}, {*y*, *ymin*, *ymax*}]
                      make a density plot of *f*

Contour and density plots.

This gives a contour plot of the function $\sin(x)\sin(y)$.

In[1]:= **ContourPlot[Sin[x] Sin[y], {x, -2, 2}, {y, -2, 2}]**

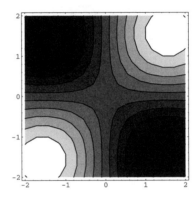

A contour plot gives you essentially a "topographic map" of a function. The contours join points on the surface that have the same height. The default is to have contours corresponding to a sequence of equally spaced *z* values. Contour plots produced by *Mathematica* are by default shaded, in such a way that regions with higher *z* values are lighter.

option name	default value	
ColorFunction	Automatic	what colors to use for shading; Hue uses a sequence of hues
Contours	10	the total number of contours, or the list of z values for contours
PlotRange	Automatic	the range of values to be included; you can specify {*zmin*, *zmax*}, All or Automatic
ContourShading	True	whether to use shading
PlotPoints	15	number of evaluation points in each direction
Compiled	True	whether to compile the function being plotted

Some options for ContourPlot. The first set can also be used in Show.

Particularly if you use a display or printer that does not handle gray levels well, you may find it better to switch off shading in contour plots.

In[2]:= **Show[%, ContourShading -> False]**

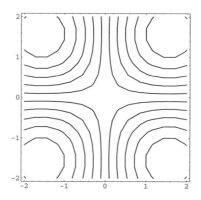

You should realize that if you do not evaluate your function on a fine enough grid, there may be inaccuracies in your contour plot. One point to notice is that whereas a curve generated by Plot may be inaccurate if your function varies too quickly in a particular region, the shape of contours can be inaccurate if your function varies too slowly. A rapidly varying function gives a regular pattern of contours, but a function that is almost flat can give irregular contours. You can typically overcome such problems by increasing the value of PlotPoints.

Density plots show the values of your function at a regular array of points. Lighter regions are higher.

In[3]:= **DensityPlot[Sin[x] Sin[y], {x, -2, 2}, {y, -2, 2}]**

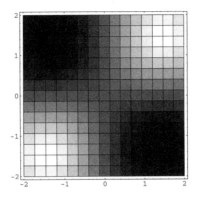

You can get rid of the mesh like this. But unless you have a very large number of regions, plots usually look better when you include the mesh.

In[4]:= **Show[%, Mesh -> False]**

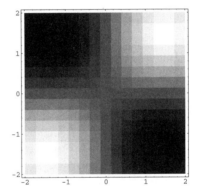

option name	default value	
ColorFunction	Automatic	what colors to use for shading; Hue uses a sequence of hues
Mesh	True	whether to draw a mesh
PlotPoints	15	number of evaluation points in each direction
Compiled	True	whether to compile the function being plotted

Some options for DensityPlot. The first set can also be used in Show.

■ 1.9.7 Three-Dimensional Surface Plots

Plot3D[*f*, {*x*, *xmin*, *xmax*}, {*y*, *ymin*, *ymax*}]
make a three-dimensional plot of *f* as a function of the variables *x* and *y*

Basic 3D plotting function.

This makes a three-dimensional plot of the function sin(*xy*).

In[1]:= **Plot3D[Sin[x y], {x, 0, 3}, {y, 0, 3}]**

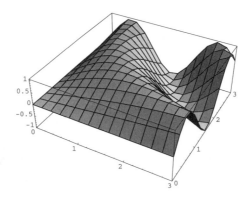

There are many options for three-dimensional plots in *Mathematica*. Some will be discussed in this section; others will be described in Section 2.9.

The first set of options for three-dimensional plots is largely analogous to those provided in the two-dimensional case.

option name	default value	
Axes	True	whether to include axes
AxesLabel	None	labels to be put on the axes: *zlabel* specifies a label for the *z* axis, {*xlabel*, *ylabel*, *zlabel*} for all axes
Boxed	True	whether to draw a three-dimensional box around the surface
ColorFunction	Automatic	what colors to use for shading; Hue uses a sequence of hues
TextStyle	$TextStyle	the default style to use for text in the plot
FormatType	StandardForm	the default format type to use for text in the plot
DisplayFunction	$DisplayFunction	how to display graphics; Identity causes no display
FaceGrids	None	how to draw grids on faces of the bounding box; All draws a grid on every face
HiddenSurface	True	whether to draw the surface as solid
Lighting	True	whether to color the surface using simulated lighting
Mesh	True	whether an *xy* mesh should be drawn on the surface
PlotRange	Automatic	the range of coordinates to include in the plot: you can specify All, {*zmin*, *zmax*} or {{*xmin*,*xmax*},{*ymin*,*ymax*},{*zmin*,*zmax*}}
Shading	True	whether the surface should be shaded or left white
ViewPoint	{1.3, -2.4, 2}	the point in space from which to look at the surface
PlotPoints	15	the number of points in each direction at which to sample the function; {n_x, n_y} specifies different numbers in the *x* and *y* directions
Compiled	True	whether to compile the function being plotted

Some options for Plot3D. The first set can also be used in Show.

This redraws the plot on the previous line, with options changed. With this setting for PlotRange, only the part of the surface in the range $-0.5 \le z \le 0.5$ is shown.

In[2]:= **Show[%, PlotRange -> {-0.5, 0.5}]**

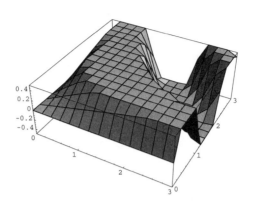

When you make the original plot, you can choose to sample more points. You will need to do this to get good pictures of functions that wiggle a lot.

In[3]:= **Plot3D[10 Sin[x + Sin[y]], {x, -10, 10}, {y, -10, 10},**
                          PlotPoints -> 40]

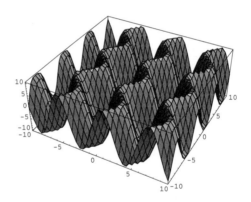

Here is the same plot, with labels for the axes, and grids added to each face.

In[4]:= **Show[%, AxesLabel -> {"Time", "Depth", "Value"},**
                                              FaceGrids -> All]

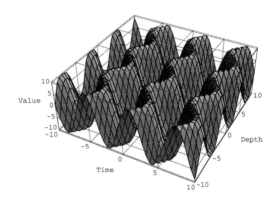

Probably the single most important issue in plotting a three-dimensional surface is specifying where you want to look at the surface from. The **ViewPoint** option for **Plot3D** and **Show** allows you to specify the point {x, y, z} in space from which you view a surface. The details of how the coordinates for this point are defined will be discussed in Section 2.9.10. In many versions of *Mathematica*, there are ways to choose three-dimensional view points interactively, then get the coordinates to give as settings for the **ViewPoint** option.

Here is a surface, viewed from the default view point {1.3, -2.4, 2}. This view point is chosen to be "generic", so that visually confusing coincidental alignments between different parts of your object are unlikely.

In[5]:= **Plot3D[Sin[x y], {x, 0, 3}, {y, 0, 3}]**

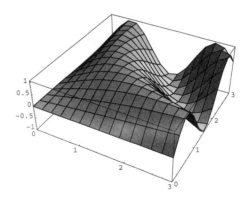

This redraws the picture, with the view point directly in front. Notice the perspective effect that makes the back of the box look much smaller than the front.

`In[6]:= Show[%, ViewPoint -> {0, -2, 0}]`

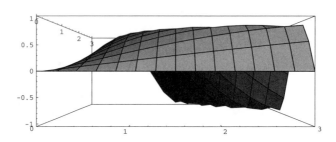

{1.3, -2.4, 2}	default view point
{0, -2, 0}	directly in front
{0, -2, 2}	in front and up
{0, -2, -2}	in front and down
{-2, -2, 0}	left-hand corner
{2, -2, 0}	right-hand corner
{0, 0, 2}	directly above

Typical choices for the `ViewPoint` option.

The human visual system is not particularly good at understanding complicated mathematical surfaces. As a result, you need to generate pictures that contain as many clues as possible about the form of the surface.

View points slightly above the surface usually work best. It is generally a good idea to keep the view point close enough to the surface that there is some perspective effect. Having a box explicitly drawn around the surface is helpful in recognizing the orientation of the surface.

Here is a plot with the default settings for surface rendering options.

In[7]:= **g = Plot3D[Exp[-(x^2+y^2)], {x, -2, 2}, {y, -2, 2}]**

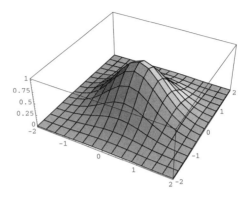

This shows the surface without the mesh drawn. It is usually much harder to see the form of the surface if the mesh is not there.

In[8]:= **Show[g, Mesh -> False]**

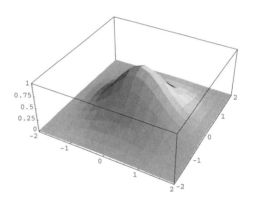

This shows the surface with no   *In[9]:=* **Show[g, Shading -> False]**
shading. Some display devices may
not be able to show shading.

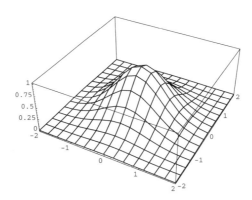

The inclusion of shading and a mesh are usually great assets in understanding the form of a surface. On some vector graphics output devices, however, you may not be able to get shading. You should also realize that when shading is included, it may take a long time to render the surface on your output device.

To add an extra element of realism to three-dimensional graphics, *Mathematica* by default colors three-dimensional surfaces using a simulated lighting model. In the default case, *Mathematica* assumes that there are three light sources shining on the object from the upper right of the picture. Section 2.9.12 describes how you can set up other light sources, and how you can specify the reflection properties of an object.

While in most cases, particularly with color output devices, simulated lighting is an asset, it can sometimes be confusing. If you set the option **Lighting -> False**, then *Mathematica* will not use simulated lighting, but will instead shade all surfaces with gray levels determined by their height.

Plot3D usually colors surfaces using a   *In[10]:=* **Plot3D[Sin[x y], {x, 0, 3}, {y, 0, 3}]**
simulated lighting model.

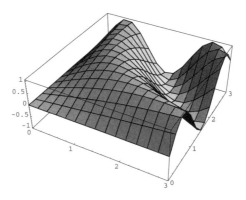

Lighting -> False switches off the simulated lighting, and instead shades surfaces with gray levels determined by height.

In[11]:= **Show[%, Lighting -> False]**

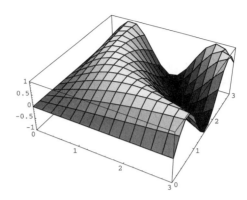

With Lighting -> False, *Mathematica* shades surfaces according to height. You can also tell *Mathematica* explicitly how to shade each element of a surface. This allows you effectively to use shading to display an extra coordinate at each point on your surface.

Plot3D[{*f*, GrayLevel[*s*]}, {*x*, *xmin*, *xmax*}, {*y*, *ymin*, *ymax*}]
          plot a surface corresponding to *f*, shaded in gray according to the function *s*

Plot3D[{*f*, Hue[*s*]}, {*x*, *xmin*, *xmax*}, {*y*, *ymin*, *ymax*}]
          shade by varying color hue rather than gray level

Specifying shading functions for surfaces.

This shows a surface whose height is determined by the function Sin[x y], but whose shading is determined by GrayLevel[x/3].

In[12]:= **Plot3D[{Sin[x y], GrayLevel[x/3]},**
                      {x, 0, 3}, {y, 0, 3}]

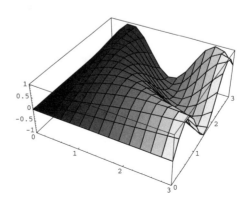

■ 1.9.8 Converting between Types of Graphics

Contour, density and surface plots are three different ways to display essentially the same information about a function. In all cases, you need the values of a function at a grid of points.

The *Mathematica* functions `ContourPlot`, `DensityPlot` and `Plot3D` all produce *Mathematica* graphics objects that include a list of the values of your function on a grid. As a result, having used any one of these functions, *Mathematica* can easily take its output and use it to produce another type of graphics.

Here is a surface plot.   *In[1]:=* `Plot3D[BesselJ[nu, 3x], {nu, 0, 3}, {x, 0, 3}]`

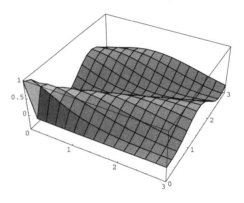

This converts the object produced by   *In[2]:=* `Show[ ContourGraphics[ % ] ]`
Plot3D into a contour plot.

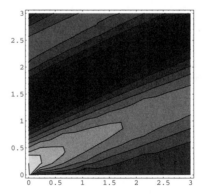

Show[ContourGraphics[*g*]]	convert to a contour plot
Show[DensityGraphics[*g*]]	convert to a density plot
Show[SurfaceGraphics[*g*]]	convert to a surface plot
Show[Graphics[*g*]]	convert to a two-dimensional image

Conversions between types of graphics.

You can use GraphicsArray to show different types of graphics together.

In[3]:= **Show[GraphicsArray[{%, %%}]]**

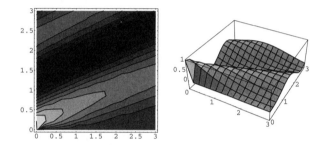

■ 1.9.9 Plotting Lists of Data

So far, we have discussed how you can use *Mathematica* to make plots of *functions*. You give *Mathematica* a function, and it builds up a curve or surface by evaluating the function at many different points.

This section describes how you can make plots from lists of data, instead of functions. (Section 1.11.3 discusses how to read data from external files and programs.) The *Mathematica* commands for plotting lists of data are direct analogs of the ones discussed above for plotting functions.

ListPlot[{y_1, y_2, ... }]   plot y_1, y_2, ... at x values 1, 2, ...

ListPlot[{{x_1, y_1}, {x_2, y_2}, ... }]

plot points (x_1, y_1), ...

ListPlot[*list*, PlotJoined -> True]

join the points with lines

ListPlot3D[{{z_{11}, z_{12}, ... }, {z_{21}, z_{22}, ... }, ... }]

make a three-dimensional plot of the array of heights z_{yx}

ListContourPlot[*array*]   make a contour plot from an array of heights

ListDensityPlot[*array*]   make a density plot

Functions for plotting lists of data.

Here is a list of values.

In[1]:= **t = Table[i^2, {i, 10}]**

Out[1]= {1, 4, 9, 16, 25, 36, 49, 64, 81, 100}

This plots the values.

In[2]:= **ListPlot[t]**

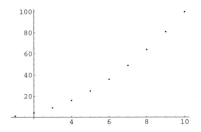

This joins the points with lines.

In[3]:= **ListPlot[t, PlotJoined -> True]**

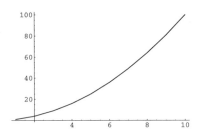

This gives a list of *x, y* pairs.

In[4]:= **Table[{i^2, 4 i^2 + i^3}, {i, 10}]**

Out[4]= {{1, 5}, {4, 24}, {9, 63}, {16, 128},
{25, 225}, {36, 360}, {49, 539}, {64, 768},
{81, 1053}, {100, 1400}}

This plots the points.

In[5]:= **ListPlot[%]**

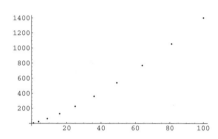

This gives a rectangular array of values. The array is quite large, so we end the input with a semicolon to stop the result from being printed out.

In[6]:= **t3 = Table[Mod[x, y], {y, 20}, {x, 30}] ;**

This makes a three-dimensional plot of the array of values.

In[7]:= **ListPlot3D[t3]**

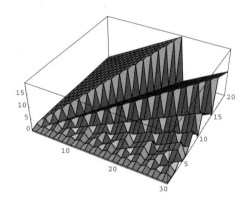

You can redraw the plot using Show, as usual.

In[8]:= **Show[%, ViewPoint -> {1.5, -0.5, 0}]**

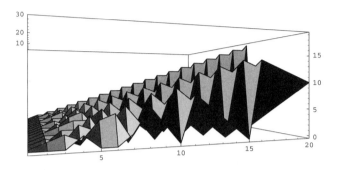

This gives a density plot of the array of values.

In[9]:= **ListDensityPlot[t3]**

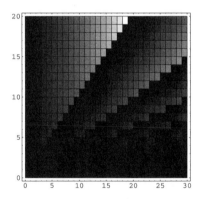

■ 1.9.10 Parametric Plots

Section 1.9.1 described how to plot curves in *Mathematica* in which you give the *y* coordinate of each point as a function of the *x* coordinate. You can also use *Mathematica* to make *parametric* plots. In a parametric plot, you give both the *x* and *y* coordinates of each point as a function of a third parameter, say *t*.

ParametricPlot[{f_x, f_y}, {*t*, *tmin*, *tmax*}]
    make a parametric plot

ParametricPlot[{{f_x, f_y}, {g_x, g_y}, ... }, {*t*, *tmin*, *tmax*}]
    plot several parametric curves together

ParametricPlot[{f_x, f_y}, {*t*, *tmin*, *tmax*}, AspectRatio -> Automatic]
    attempt to preserve the shapes of curves

Functions for generating parametric plots.

Here is the curve made by taking the *x* coordinate of each point to be Sin[t] and the *y* coordinate to be Sin[2t].

In[1]:= **ParametricPlot[{Sin[t], Sin[2t]}, {t, 0, 2Pi}]**

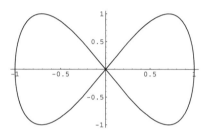

The "shape" of the curve produced depends on the ratio of height to width for the whole plot.

In[2]:= **ParametricPlot[{Sin[t], Cos[t]}, {t, 0, 2Pi}]**

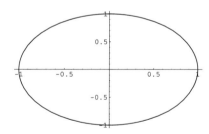

Setting the option AspectRatio to
Automatic makes *Mathematica* preserve
the "true shape" of the curve, as
defined by the actual coordinate values
it involves.

In[3]:= **Show[%, AspectRatio -> Automatic]**

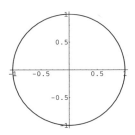

ParametricPlot3D[{f_x, f_y, f_z}, {t, *tmin*, *tmax*}]
              make a parametric plot of a three-dimensional curve

ParametricPlot3D[{f_x, f_y, f_z}, {t, *tmin*, *tmax*}, {u, *umin*, *umax*}]
              make a parametric plot of a three-dimensional surface

ParametricPlot3D[{f_x, f_y, f_z, s}, ...]
              shade the parts of the parametric plot according to the
              function s

ParametricPlot3D[{{f_x, f_y, f_z}, {g_x, g_y, g_z}, ... }, ...]
              plot several objects together

Three-dimensional parametric plots.

ParametricPlot3D[{f_x, f_y, f_z}, {t, *tmin*, *tmax*}] is the direct analog in three dimensions of
ParametricPlot[{f_x, f_y}, {t, *tmin*, *tmax*}] in two dimensions. In both cases, *Mathematica* effectively
generates a sequence of points by varying the parameter t, then forms a curve by joining these
points. With ParametricPlot, the curve is in two dimensions; with ParametricPlot3D, it is in three
dimensions.

This makes a parametric plot of a helical curve. Varying t produces circular motion in the x, y plane, and linear motion in the z direction.

In[4]:= **ParametricPlot3D[{Sin[t], Cos[t], t/3}, {t, 0, 15}]**

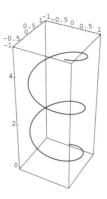

ParametricPlot3D[$\{f_x, f_y, f_z\}$, $\{t, tmin, tmax\}$, $\{u, umin, umax\}$] creates a surface, rather than a curve. The surface is formed from a collection of quadrilaterals. The corners of the quadrilaterals have coordinates corresponding to the values of the f_i when t and u take on values in a regular grid.

Here the x and y coordinates for the quadrilaterals are given simply by t and u. The result is a surface plot of the kind that can be produced by Plot3D.

In[5]:= **ParametricPlot3D[{t, u, Sin[t u]},**
{t, 0, 3}, {u, 0, 3}]

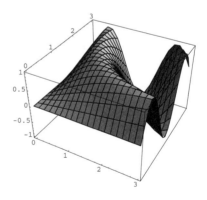

This shows the same surface as before, but with the *y* coordinates distorted by a quadratic transformation.

In[6]:= **ParametricPlot3D[{t, u^2, Sin[t u]},
                {t, 0, 3}, {u, 0, 3}]**

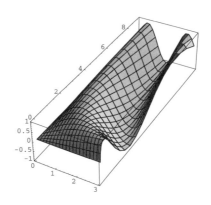

This produces a helicoid surface by taking the helical curve shown above, and at each section of the curve drawing a quadrilateral.

In[7]:= **ParametricPlot3D[{u Sin[t], u Cos[t], t/3},
                {t, 0, 15}, {u, -1, 1}]**

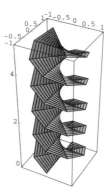

In general, it is possible to construct many complicated surfaces using **ParametricPlot3D**. In each case, you can think of the surfaces as being formed by "distorting" or "rolling up" the *t*, *u* coordinate grid in a certain way.

This produces a cylinder. Varying the
t parameter yields a circle in the *x*, *y*
plane, while varying u moves the
circles in the *z* direction.

In[8]:= **ParametricPlot3D[{Sin[t], Cos[t], u},**
             {t, 0, 2Pi}, {u, 0, 4}]

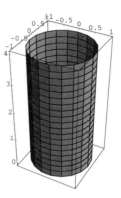

This produces a torus. Varying u
yields a circle, while varying t rotates
the circle around the *z* axis to form the
torus.

In[9]:= **ParametricPlot3D[**
         {Cos[t] (3 + Cos[u]), Sin[t] (3 + Cos[u]), Sin[u]},
             {t, 0, 2Pi}, {u, 0, 2Pi}]

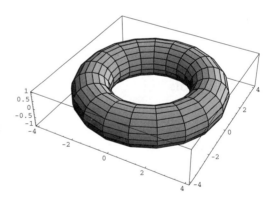

This produces a sphere.
```
In[10]:= ParametricPlot3D[
                {Cos[t] Cos[u], Sin[t] Cos[u], Sin[u]},
                {t, 0, 2Pi}, {u, -Pi/2, Pi/2}]
```

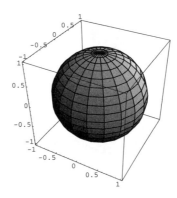

You should realize that when you draw surfaces with `ParametricPlot3D`, the exact choice of parametrization is often crucial. You should be careful, for example, to avoid parametrizations in which all or part of your surface is covered more than once. Such multiple coverings often lead to discontinuities in the mesh drawn on the surface, and may make `ParametricPlot3D` take much longer to render the surface.

■ 1.9.11 Some Special Plots

As discussed in Section 2.9, *Mathematica* includes a full graphics programming language. In this language, you can set up many different kinds of plots. A few of the common ones are included in standard *Mathematica* packages.

`<<Graphics`	load a package to set up additional graphics functions
`LogPlot[f, {x, xmin, xmax}]`	generate a log-linear plot
`LogLogPlot[f, {x, xmin, xmax}]`	generate a log-log plot
`LogListPlot[list]`	generate a log-linear plot from a list of data
`LogLogListPlot[list]`	generate a log-log plot from a list of data
`PolarPlot[r, {t, tmin, tmax}]`	generate a polar plot of the radius r as a function of angle t
`ErrorListPlot[{{x_1, y_1, dy_1}, ... }]`	generate a plot of data with error bars
`TextListPlot[{{x_1, y_1, "s_1"}, ... }]`	plot a list of data with each point given by the text string s_i
`BarChart[list]`	plot a list of data as a bar chart
`PieChart[list]`	plot a list of data as a pie chart
`PlotVectorField[{f_x, f_y}, {x, xmin, xmax}, {y, ymin, ymax}]`	plot the vector field corresponding to the vector function f
`ListPlotVectorField[list]`	plot the vector field corresponding to the two-dimensional array of vectors in *list*
`SphericalPlot3D[r, {theta, min, max}, {phi, min, max}]`	generate a three-dimensional spherical plot

Some special plotting functions defined in standard *Mathematica* packages.

This loads a standard *Mathematica* package to set up additional graphics functions.

`In[1]:= <<Graphics`

This generates a log-linear plot.

`In[2]:= LogPlot[ Exp[-x] + 4 Exp[-2x], {x, 0, 6} ]`

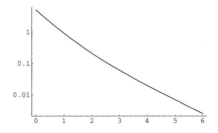

Here is a list of the first 10 primes.

```
In[3]:= p = Table[Prime[n], {n, 10}]
Out[3]= {2, 3, 5, 7, 11, 13, 17, 19, 23, 29}
```

This plots the primes using the integers 1, 2, 3, ... as plotting symbols.

```
In[4]:= TextListPlot[p]
```

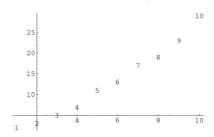

Here is a bar chart of the primes.

```
In[5]:= BarChart[p]
```

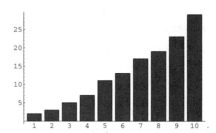

This gives a pie chart.

```
In[6]:= PieChart[p]
```

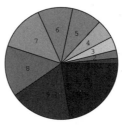

■ 1.9.12 Special Topic: Animated Graphics

On many computer systems, *Mathematica* can produce not only static images, but also animated graphics or "movies".

The basic idea in all cases is to generate a sequence of "frames" which can be displayed in rapid succession. You can use the standard *Mathematica* graphics functions described above to produce each frame. The mechanism for displaying the frames as a movie depends on the *Mathematica* interface you are using. With a notebook-based interface, you typically put the frames in a sequence of cells, then select the cells and choose a command to animate them. With text-based interfaces, there is often an external program provided for displaying animated graphics. The program can typically be accessed from inside *Mathematica* using the function `Animate`.

`<<Graphics'Animation'`	load the animation package (if necessary)
`Animate[plot, {t, tmin, tmax}]`	execute the graphics command *plot* for a sequence of values of t, and animate the resulting sequence of frames
`ShowAnimation[{$g_1$, $g_2$, ... }]`	produce an animation from a sequence of graphics objects

Typical ways to produce animated graphics.

When you produce a sequence of frames for a movie, it is important that different frames be consistent. Thus, for example, you should typically give an explicit setting for the `PlotRange` option, rather than using the default `Automatic` setting, in order to ensure that the scales used in different frames are the same. If you have three-dimensional graphics with different view points, you should similarly set `SphericalRegion -> True` in order to ensure that the scaling of different plots is the same.

This generates a list of graphics objects. Setting `DisplayFunction -> Identity` stops `Plot3D` from rendering the graphics it produces. Explicitly setting `PlotRange` ensures that the scale is the same in each piece of graphics.

```
In[1]:= Table[ Plot3D[ BesselJ[0, Sqrt[x^2 + y^2] + t],
            {x, -10, 10}, {y, -10, 10}, Axes -> False,
            PlotRange -> {-0.5, 1.0},
            DisplayFunction -> Identity ],
       {t, 0, 8} ] // Short
Out[1]//Short= {-SurfaceGraphics-, <<7>>, -SurfaceGraphics-}
```

On an appropriate computer system, `ShowAnimation[%]` would animate the graphics. This partitions the graphics into three rows, and shows the resulting array of images.

In[2]:= **Show[GraphicsArray[Partition[%, 3]]]**

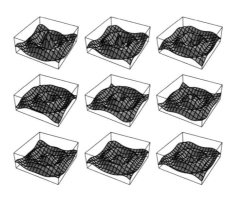

■ 1.9.13 Sound

On most computer systems, *Mathematica* can produce not only graphics but also sound. *Mathematica* treats graphics and sound in a closely analogous way.

For example, just as you can use `Plot[f, {x, xmin, xmax}]` to plot a function, so also you can use `Play[f, {t, 0, tmax}]` to "play" a function. Play takes the function to define the waveform for a sound: the values of the function give the amplitude of the sound as a function of time.

`Play[f, {t, 0, tmax}]`	play a sound with amplitude *f* as a function of time *t* in seconds

Playing a function.

On a suitable computer system, this plays a pure tone with a frequency of 440 hertz for one second.

In[1]:= **Play[Sin[2Pi 440 t], {t, 0, 1}]**

Out[1]= -Sound-

Sounds produced by Play can have any waveform. They do not, for example, have to consist of a collection of harmonic pieces. In general, the amplitude function you give to Play specifies the instantaneous signal associated with the sound. This signal is typically converted to a voltage, and ultimately to a displacement. Note that *amplitude* is sometimes defined to be the *peak* signal associated with a sound; in *Mathematica*, it is always the *instantaneous* signal as a function of time.

This plays a more complex sound.

In[2]:= **Play[Sin[700 t + 25 t Sin[350 t]], {t, 0, 4}]**

Out[2]= -Sound-

Play is set up so that the time variable that appears in it is always measured in absolute seconds. When a sound is actually played, its amplitude is sampled a certain number of times every second. You can specify the sample rate by setting the option SampleRate.

Play[f, {t, 0, *tmax*}, SampleRate -> r]	play a sound, sampling it r times a second

Specifying the sample rate for a sound.

In general, the higher the sample rate, the better high-frequency components in the sound will be rendered. A sample rate of r typically allows frequencies up to $r/2$ hertz. The human auditory system can typically perceive sounds in the frequency range 20 to 22000 hertz (depending somewhat on age and sex). The fundamental frequencies for the 88 notes on a piano range from 27.5 to 4096 hertz.

The standard sample rate used for compact disc players is 44100. The effective sample rate in a typical telephone system is around 8000. On most computer systems, the default sample rate used by *Mathematica* is around 8000.

You can use Play[{f_1, f_2}, ...] to produce stereo sound. In general, *Mathematica* supports any number of sound channels.

ListPlay[{a_1, a_2, ... }, SampleRate -> r]	play a sound with a sequence of amplitude levels

Playing sampled sounds.

The function ListPlay allows you simply to give a list of values which are taken to be sound amplitudes sampled at a certain rate.

When sounds are actually rendered by *Mathematica*, only a certain range of amplitudes is allowed. The option PlayRange in Play and ListPlay specifies how the amplitudes you give should be scaled to fit in the allowed range. The settings for this option are analogous to those for the PlotRange graphics option discussed on page 136.

PlayRange -> Automatic (default)	use an internal procedure to scale amplitudes
PlayRange -> All	scale so that all amplitudes fit in the allowed range
PlayRange -> {*amin*, *amax*}	make amplitudes between *amin* and *amax* fit in the allowed range, and clip others

Specifying the scaling of sound amplitudes.

While it is often convenient to use the default setting PlayRange -> Automatic, you should realize that Play may run significantly faster if you give an explicit PlayRange specification, so it does not have to derive one.

Show[*sound*]	replay a sound object

Replaying a sound object.

Both Play and ListPlay return Sound objects which contain procedures for synthesizing sounds. You can replay a particular Sound object using the function Show that is also used for redisplaying graphics.

The internal structure of Sound objects is discussed in Section 2.9.18.

1.10 Input and Output in Notebooks

■ 1.10.1 Entering Greek Letters

click on α	use a button in a palette
`\[Alpha]`	use a full name
ESC**a**ESC or ESC`alpha`ESC	use a standard alias (shown below as ⋮`a`⋮)
ESC`\alpha`ESC	use a TeX alias
ESC`&agr`ESC	use an SGML alias

Ways to enter Greek letters in a notebook.

Here is a palette for entering common Greek letters.

α	β	γ	δ	ϵ	ζ	η
θ	κ	λ	μ	ν	ξ	π
ρ	σ	τ	ϕ	χ	ψ	ω
Α	Β	Γ	Δ	Ε	Ζ	Η
Θ	Λ	Ξ	Φ	Χ	Ψ	Ω

You can use Greek letters just like the ordinary letters that you type on your keyboard.

```
In[1]:= Expand[(α + β)^3]
```

Out[1]= $\alpha^3 + 3\alpha^2\beta + 3\alpha\beta^2 + \beta^3$

There are several ways to enter Greek letters. This input uses full names.

```
In[2]:= Expand[(\[Alpha] + \[Beta])^3]
```

Out[2]= $\alpha^3 + 3\alpha^2\beta + 3\alpha\beta^2 + \beta^3$

	full name	aliases		full name	aliases
α	\[Alpha]	:a:, :alpha:	Γ	\[CapitalGamma]	:G:, :Gamma:
β	\[Beta]	:b:, :beta:	Δ	\[CapitalDelta]	:D:, :Delta:
γ	\[Gamma]	:g:, :gamma:	Θ	\[CapitalTheta]	:Q:, :Th:, :Theta:
δ	\[Delta]	:d:, :delta:	Λ	\[CapitalLambda]	:L:, :Lambda:
ϵ	\[Epsilon]	:e:, :epsilon:	Π	\[CapitalPi]	:P:, :Pi:
ζ	\[Zeta]	:z:, :zeta:	Σ	\[CapitalSigma]	:S:, :Sigma:
η	\[Eta]	:h:, :et:, :eta:	Υ	\[CapitalUpsilon]	:U:, :Upsilon:
θ	\[Theta]	:q:, :th:, :theta:	Φ	\[CapitalPhi]	:F:, :Ph:, :Phi:
κ	\[Kappa]	:k:, :kappa:	X	\[CapitalChi]	:C:, :Ch:, :Chi:
λ	\[Lambda]	:l:, :lambda:	Ψ	\[CapitalPsi]	:Y:, :Ps:, :Psi:
μ	\[Mu]	:m:, :mu:	Ω	\[CapitalOmega]	:O:, :W:, :Omega:
ν	\[Nu]	:n:, :nu:			
ξ	\[Xi]	:x:, :xi:			
π	\[Pi]	:p:, :pi:			
ρ	\[Rho]	:r:, :rho:			
σ	\[Sigma]	:s:, :sigma:			
τ	\[Tau]	:t:, :tau:			
ϕ	\[Phi]	:f:, :ph:, :phi:			
φ	\[CurlyPhi]	:j:, :cph:, :cphi:			
χ	\[Chi]	:c:, :ch:, :chi:			
ψ	\[Psi]	:y:, :ps:, :psi:			
ω	\[Omega]	:o:, :w:, :omega:			

Commonly used Greek letters. In aliases : stands for the key [ESC]. TEX aliases are not listed explicitly.

Note that in *Mathematica* the letter π stands for Pi. None of the other Greek letters have special meanings.

π stands for Pi.

```
In[3]:= N[π]
Out[3]= 3.14159
```

You can use Greek letters either on their own or with other letters.

```
In[4]:= Expand[(Rαβ + Ξ)^4]
```
$Out[4]= R\alpha\beta^4 + 4R\alpha\beta^3\,\Xi + 6R\alpha\beta^2\,\Xi^2 + 4R\alpha\beta\,\Xi^3 + \Xi^4$

The symbol $\pi\alpha$ is not related to the symbol π.

```
In[5]:= Factor[πα^4 - 1]
```
$Out[5]= (-1 + \pi\alpha)\,(1 + \pi\alpha)\,(1 + \pi\alpha^2)$

■ 1.10.2 Entering Two-Dimensional Input

When *Mathematica* reads the text x^y, it interprets it as x raised to the power y.

$In[1]:= \mathbf{x\char94 y}$

$Out[1]= x^y$

In a notebook, you can also give the two-dimensional input x^y directly. *Mathematica* again interprets this as a power.

$In[2]:= \mathbf{x^y}$

$Out[2]= x^y$

One way to enter a two-dimensional form such as x^y into a *Mathematica* notebook is to copy this form from a palette by clicking the appropriate button in the palette.

Here is a palette for entering some common two-dimensional notations.

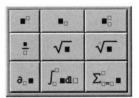

There are also several ways to enter two-dimensional forms directly from the keyboard.

x [CTRL][^] y [CTRL][␣]	use control keys that exist on most keyboards
x [CTRL][6] y [CTRL][␣]	use control keys that should exist on all keyboards
\!\(x\^y\) followed by Make 2D	use only ordinary printable characters

Ways to enter a superscript directly from the keyboard. [CTRL][␣] stands for CONTROL-SPACE.

You type [CTRL][^] by holding down the CONTROL key, then hitting the ^ key. As soon as you do this, your cursor will jump to a superscript position. You can then type anything you want and it will appear in that position.

When you have finished, press [CTRL][␣] to move back down from the superscript position. [CTRL][␣] stands for CONTROL-SPACE; you type it by holding down the CONTROL key, then pressing the space bar.

This sequence of keystrokes enters x^y.

$In[3]:= \mathbf{x}\ [CTRL][^]\ \mathbf{y}$

$Out[3]= x^y$

Here the whole expression y+z is in the superscript.

$In[4]:= \mathbf{x}\ [CTRL][^]\ \mathbf{y + z}$

$Out[4]= x^{y+z}$

Pressing [CTRL][␣] (CONTROL-SPACE) takes you down from the superscript.

$In[5]:= \mathbf{x}\ [CTRL][^]\ \mathbf{y}\ [CTRL][␣]\ \mathbf{+ z}$

$Out[5]= x^y + z$

You can remember the fact that $\boxed{\text{CTRL}}\boxed{\char`^}$ gives you a superscript by thinking of $\boxed{\text{CTRL}}\boxed{\char`^}$ as just a more immediate form of $\char`^$. When you type x^y, *Mathematica* will leave this one-dimensional form unchanged until you explicitly process it. But if you type x $\boxed{\text{CTRL}}\boxed{\char`^}$ y then *Mathematica* will immediately give you a superscript.

On a standard English-language keyboard, the character $\char`^$ appears as the shifted version of 6. *Mathematica* therefore accepts $\boxed{\text{CTRL}}\boxed{6}$ as an alternative to $\boxed{\text{CTRL}}\boxed{\char`^}$. Note that if you are using something other than a standard English-language keyboard, *Mathematica* will almost always accept $\boxed{\text{CTRL}}\boxed{6}$ but may not accept $\boxed{\text{CTRL}}\boxed{\char`^}$.

This is an alternative input form that avoids the use of control characters.	In[6]:= \!\(x \^ y \) Out[6]= x^y
With this input form, *Mathematica* automatically understands that the + z does not go in the superscript.	In[7]:= \!\(x \^ y + z \) Out[7]= $x^y + z$

Using control characters minimizes the number of keystrokes that you need to type in order to enter a superscript. But particularly if you want to save your input in a file, or send it to another program, it is often more convenient to use a form that does not involve control characters. You can do this using \! sequences.

If you copy a \! sequence into *Mathematica*, it will automatically jump into two-dimensional form. But if you enter the sequence directly from the keyboard, you explicitly need to choose the Make 2D menu item in order to get the two-dimensional form.

When entered from the keyboard \(... \) sequences are shown in literal form.	\!\(x\^y + z\)
Choosing the Make 2D item in the Edit menu converts these sequences into two-dimensional forms.	$x^y + z$

---

x $\boxed{\text{CTRL}}\boxed{\_}$ y $\boxed{\text{CTRL}}\boxed{\;}$	use control keys that exist on most keyboards
x $\boxed{\text{CTRL}}\boxed{-}$ y $\boxed{\text{CTRL}}\boxed{\;}$	use control keys that should exist on all keyboards
\!\(x_y\) followed by Make 2D	use only ordinary printable characters

Ways to enter a subscript directly from the keyboard.

Subscripts in *Mathematica* work very much like superscripts. However, whereas *Mathematica* automatically interprets x^y as x raised to the power y, it has no similar interpretation for x_y. Instead, it just treats x_y as a purely symbolic object.

This enters y as a subscript.	*In[8]:=* **x** [CTRL]-[_] **y**
	Out[8]= x_y
Here is another way to enter y as a subscript.	*In[9]:=* \!\(**x** _ **y** \)
	Out[9]= x_y

---

x [CTRL]-[/] y [CTRL]-[␣]   use control keys

\!\(x\/y\) followed by Make 2D   use only ordinary printable characters

Ways to enter a built-up fraction directly from the keyboard.

This enters the built-up fraction $\frac{x}{y}$.	*In[10]:=* **x** [CTRL]-[/] **y**
	Out[10]= $\dfrac{x}{y}$
Here the whole y + z goes into the denominator.	*In[11]:=* **x** [CTRL]-[/] **y** + **z**
	Out[11]= $\dfrac{x}{y+z}$
But pressing CONTROL-SPACE takes you out of the denominator, so the + z does not appear in the denominator.	*In[12]:=* **x** [CTRL]-[/] **y** [CTRL]-[␣] + **z**
	Out[12]= $\dfrac{x}{y} + z$
Mathematica automatically interprets a built-up fraction as a division.	*In[13]:=* $\dfrac{\mathbf{8888}}{\mathbf{2222}}$
	Out[13]= 4
Here is another way to enter a built-up fraction.	*In[14]:=* \!\(**8888** \/ **2222** \)
	Out[14]= 4

[CTRL]-[@] x [CTRL]-[␣]   use control keys that exist on most keyboards

[CTRL]-[2] x [CTRL]-[␣]   use control keys that should exist on all keyboards

\!\(\@x\) followed by Make 2D   use only ordinary printable characters

Ways to enter a square root directly from the keyboard.

This enters a square root.	*In[15]:=* [CTRL]-[@] **x** + **y**
	Out[15]= $\sqrt{x+y}$
CONTROL-SPACE takes you out of the square root.	*In[16]:=* [CTRL]-[@] **x** [CTRL]-[␣] + **y**
	Out[16]= $\sqrt{x} + y$

Here is a form without control characters.

$In[17]:= \ \!\(\@ x + y \)$

$Out[17]= \sqrt{x} + y$

And here is the usual one-dimensional *Mathematica* input that gives the same output expression.

$In[18]:= \textbf{Sqrt[x] + y}$

$Out[18]= \sqrt{x} + y$

CTRL ^ or CTRL 6	go to the superscript position	
CTRL _ or CTRL -	go to the subscript position	
CTRL @ or CTRL 2	go into a square root	
CTRL % or CTRL 5	go from subscript to superscript or vice versa, or to the exponent position in a root	
CTRL /	go to the denominator for a fraction	
CTRL ␣	return from a special position (CONTROL-SPACE)	

Special input forms based on control characters. The second forms given should work on any keyboard.

This puts both a subscript and a superscript on x.

$In[19]:= \textbf{x}$ CTRL ^ $\textbf{y}$ CTRL % $\textbf{z}$

$Out[19]= x_z^y$

Here is another way to enter the same expression.

$In[20]:= \textbf{x}$ CTRL _ $\textbf{z}$ CTRL % $\textbf{y}$

$Out[20]= x_z^y$

\!\(... \)	all two-dimensional input and grouping within it
x \^ y	superscript x^y within \!\(... \)
x _ y	subscript x_y within \!\(... \)
x \^ y \% z	subscript and superscript x_z^y within \!\(... \)
\@ x	square root $\sqrt{x}$ within \!\(... \)
x \/ y	built-up fraction $\frac{x}{y}$ within \!\(... \)

Special input forms that generate two-dimensional input with the Make 2D menu item.

You must preface the outermost \(
with \!.

$In[21]:= \!\(a \/ b + \@ c \) + d$

$Out[21]= \frac{a}{b} + \sqrt{c} + d$

You can use \(and \) to indicate the
grouping of elements in an expression
without introducing explicit
parentheses.

$In[22]:= \!\(a \/ \(b + \@ c \) \) + d$

$Out[22]= \frac{a}{b + \sqrt{c}} + d$

In addition to subscripts and superscripts, *Mathematica* also supports the notion of underscripts and overscripts—elements that go directly underneath or above. Among other things, you can use underscripts and overscripts to enter the limits of sums and products.

x CTRL[+] y CTRL[␣] or x CTRL[=] y CTRL[␣]	create an underscript $\underset{y}{x}$
\!\(x\+y\) followed by Make 2D	create an underscript $\underset{y}{x}$
x CTRL[&] y CTRL[␣] or x CTRL[7] y CTRL[␣]	create an overscript $\overset{y}{x}$
\!\(x\&y\) followed by Make 2D	create an overscript $\overset{y}{x}$

Creating underscripts and overscripts.

+ ■ 1.10.3 Editing and Evaluating Two-Dimensional Expressions

When you see a two-dimensional expression on the screen, you can edit it much as you would edit text. You can for example place your cursor somewhere and start typing. Or you can select a part of the expression, then remove it using the DELETE key, or insert a new version by typing it in.

In addition to ordinary text editing features, there are some keys that you can use to move around in two-dimensional expressions.

CTRL[.]	select the next larger subexpression
CTRL[␣]	move to the right of the current structure
→	move to the next character
←	move to the previous character

Ways to move around in two-dimensional expressions.

This shows the sequence of subexpressions selected by repeatedly typing CTRL . .

$$-\frac{\text{ArcTan}\left[\frac{1+2x}{\sqrt{3}}\right]}{\sqrt{3}}+\frac{\text{Log}[-1+x]}{3}-\frac{\text{Log}[1+x+x^2]}{6}+\frac{\text{Log}[-1+x+x^2+x^3]}{9}$$

$$-\frac{\text{ArcTan}\left[\frac{1+2x}{\sqrt{3}}\right]}{\sqrt{3}}+\frac{\text{Log}[-1+x]}{3}-\frac{\text{Log}[1+x+x^2]}{6}+\frac{\text{Log}[-1+x+x^2+x^3]}{9}$$

$$-\frac{\text{ArcTan}\left[\frac{1+2x}{\sqrt{3}}\right]}{\sqrt{3}}+\frac{\text{Log}[-1+x]}{3}-\frac{\text{Log}[1+x+x^2]}{6}+\frac{\text{Log}[-1+x+x^2+x^3]}{9}$$

$$-\frac{\text{ArcTan}\left[\frac{1+2x}{\sqrt{3}}\right]}{\sqrt{3}}+\frac{\text{Log}[-1+x]}{3}-\frac{\text{Log}[1+x+x^2]}{6}+\frac{\text{Log}[-1+x+x^2+x^3]}{9}$$

$$-\frac{\text{ArcTan}\left[\frac{1+2x}{\sqrt{3}}\right]}{\sqrt{3}}+\frac{\text{Log}[-1+x]}{3}-\frac{\text{Log}[1+x+x^2]}{6}+\frac{\text{Log}[-1+x+x^2+x^3]}{9}$$

$$-\frac{\text{ArcTan}\left[\frac{1+2x}{\sqrt{3}}\right]}{\sqrt{3}}+\frac{\text{Log}[-1+x]}{3}-\frac{\text{Log}[1+x+x^2]}{6}+\frac{\text{Log}[-1+x+x^2+x^3]}{9}$$

SHIFT-RETURN	evaluate the whole current cell
COMMAND-RETURN or ALT-RETURN	evaluate only the selected subexpression

Ways to evaluate two-dimensional expressions.

In most computations, you will want to go from one step to the next by taking the whole expression that you have generated, and then evaluating it. But if for example you are trying to manipulate a single formula to put it into a particular form, you may instead find it more convenient to perform a sequence of operations separately on different parts of the expression.

You do this by selecting each part you want to operate on, then inserting the operation you want to perform, then using COMMAND-RETURN.

Here is an expression with one part selected.

```
{Factor[x^4 - 1], Factor[x^5 - 1], Factor[x^6 - 1], Factor[x^7 - 1]}
```

Pressing COMMAND-RETURN evaluates the selected part.

```
{Factor[x^4 - 1], (-1 + x) (1 + x + x^2 + x^3 + x^4), Factor[x^6 - 1], Factor[x^7 - 1]}
```

∎ 1.10.4 Entering Formulas

character	short form	long form	symbol
π	⸬p⸬	\[Pi]	Pi
∞	⸬inf⸬	\[Infinity]	Infinity
°	⸬deg⸬	\[Degree]	Degree

Special forms for some common symbols. ⸬ stands for the key ESC.

This is equivalent to Sin[60 Degree].

$In[1]:=$ **Sin[60°]**

$Out[1]=$ $\dfrac{\sqrt{3}}{2}$

Here is the long form of the input.

$In[2]:=$ **Sin[60 \[Degree]]**

$Out[2]=$ $\dfrac{\sqrt{3}}{2}$

You can enter the same input like this.

$In[3]:=$ **Sin[60 ⸬deg⸬]**

$Out[3]=$ $\dfrac{\sqrt{3}}{2}$

Here the angle is in radians.

$In[4]:=$ **Sin$\left[\dfrac{\pi}{3}\right]$**

$Out[4]=$ $\dfrac{\sqrt{3}}{2}$

special characters	short form	long form	ordinary characters
$x \le y$	x ⸬<=⸬ y	x \[LessEqual] y	x <= y
$x \ge y$	x ⸬>=⸬ y	x \[GreaterEqual] y	x >= y
$x \ne y$	x ⸬!=⸬ y	x \[NotEqual] y	x != y
$x \to y$	x ⸬->⸬ y	x \[Rule] y	x -> y

Special forms for a few operators. Pages 970–975 give a complete list.

Here the replacement rule is entered using two ordinary characters, as ->.

$In[5]:=$ **x/(x+1) /. x -> 3 + y**

$Out[5]=$ $\dfrac{3+y}{4+y}$

This means exactly the same.

In[6]:= **x/(x+1) /. x \[Rule] 3 + y**

Out[6]= $\dfrac{3+y}{4+y}$

As does this.

In[7]:= **x/(x+1) /. x → 3 + y**

Out[7]= $\dfrac{3+y}{4+y}$

Or this.

In[8]:= **x/(x+1) /. x :->: 3 + y**

Out[8]= $\dfrac{3+y}{4+y}$

The special arrow form → is by default also used for output.

In[9]:= **Solve[x^2 == 1, x]**

Out[9]= **{{x → -1}, {x → 1}}**

special characters	short form	long form	ordinary characters
$x \div y$	x :div: y	x \[Divide] y	x / y
$x \times y$	x :*: y	x \[Times] y	x * y
$x \times y$	x :cross: y	x \[Cross] y	Cross[x, y]
$x == y$	x :==: y	x \[Equal] y	x == y
$x \wedge y$	x :&&: y	x \[And] y	x && y
$x \vee y$	x :||: y	x \[Or] y	x || y
$\neg x$	:!: x	\[Not] x	!x
$x \Rightarrow y$	x :=>: y	x \[Implies] y	Implies[x, y]
$x \cup y$	x :un: y	x \[Union] y	Union[x, y]
$x \cap y$	x :inter: y	x \[Intersection] y	Intersection[x, y]
xy	x :,: y	x \[InvisibleComma] y	x,y

Some operators with special forms used for input but not output.

Mathematica understands ÷, but does not use it by default for output.

In[10]:= **x ÷ y**

Out[10]= $\dfrac{x}{y}$

The forms of input discussed so far in this section use special characters, but otherwise just consist of ordinary one-dimensional lines of text. *Mathematica* notebooks, however, also make it possible to use two-dimensional forms of input.

two-dimensional	one-dimensional	
x^y	x ^ y	power
$\dfrac{x}{y}$	x / y	division
$\sqrt{x}$	Sqrt[x]	square root
$\sqrt[n]{x}$	x ^ (1/n)	n^{th} root
$\displaystyle\sum_{i=imin}^{imax} f$	Sum[f, {i, imin, imax}]	sum
$\displaystyle\prod_{i=imin}^{imax} f$	Product[f, {i, imin, imax}]	product
$\displaystyle\int f\,dx$	Integrate[f, x]	indefinite integral
$\displaystyle\int_{xmin}^{xmax} f\,dx$	Integrate[f, {x, xmin, xmax}]	definite integral
$\partial_x f$	D[f, x]	partial derivative
$\partial_{x,y} f$	D[f, x, y]	multivariate partial derivative

Some two-dimensional forms that can be used in *Mathematica* notebooks.

You can enter two-dimensional forms using any of the mechanisms discussed on pages 175–179. Note that upper and lower limits for sums and products must be entered as overscripts and underscripts—not superscripts and subscripts.

This enters an indefinite integral. Note the use of ⦂dd⦂ to enter the "differential d".

In[11]:= ⦂int⦂ **f[x]** ⦂dd⦂ **x**

Out[11]= $\displaystyle\int$ **f[x]** d**x**

Here is an indefinite integral that can be explicitly evaluated.

In[12]:= $\displaystyle\int$ **Exp[-x²]** d**x**

Out[12]= $\dfrac{1}{2}\,\sqrt{\pi}$ **Erf[x]**

Here is the usual *Mathematica* input for this integral.

In[13]:= **Integrate[Exp[-x^2], x]**

Out[13]= $\frac{1}{2} \sqrt{\pi} \ \text{Erf}[x]$

This enters exactly the same integral.

In[14]:= **\!\(\[Integral] Exp[-x\^2] \[DifferentialD]x \)**

Out[14]= $\frac{1}{2} \sqrt{\pi} \ \text{Erf}[x]$

short form	long form	
:sum:	\[Sum]	summation sign Σ
:prod:	\[Product]	product sign Π
:int:	\[Integral]	integral sign $\int$
:dd:	\[DifferentialD]	special ⅆ for use in integrals
:pd:	\[PartialD]	partial derivative operator ∂

Some special characters used in entering formulas. Section 3.10 gives a complete list.

You should realize that even though a summation sign can look almost identical to a capital sigma it is treated in a very different way by *Mathematica*. The point is that a sigma is just a letter; but a summation sign is an operator which tells *Mathematica* to perform a Sum operation.

Capital sigma is just a letter.

In[15]:= **a + \[CapitalSigma]^2**

Out[15]= $a + \Sigma^2$

A summation sign, on the other hand, is an operator.

In[16]:= [ESC]**sum**[ESC] [CTRL][+] **n=0** [CTRL][%] **m** [CTRL][␣] **1/f[n]**

Out[16]= $\displaystyle\sum_{n=0}^{m} \frac{1}{f[n]}$

Here is another way to enter the same input.

In[17]:= **\!\(\[Sum] \+ \(n = 0 \) \% m 1 \/ f[n] \)**

Out[17]= $\displaystyle\sum_{n=0}^{m} \frac{1}{f[n]}$

Much as *Mathematica* distinguishes between a summation sign and a capital sigma, it also distinguishes between an ordinary d and the special "differential d" ⅆ that is used in the standard notation for integrals. It is crucial that you use this differential ⅆ—entered as [ESC]dd[ESC]—when you type in an integral. If you try to use an ordinary d, *Mathematica* will just interpret this as a symbol called d—it will not understand that you are entering the second part of an integration operator.

This computes the derivative of x^n.

In[18]:= **∂ₓ xⁿ**

Out[18]= $n \, x^{-1+n}$

Here is the same derivative specified in ordinary one-dimensional form.

$In[19]:=$ **D[x^n, x]**

$Out[19]=$ $n\,x^{-1+n}$

This computes the third derivative.

$In[20]:=$ $\partial_{x,x,x}\,x^n$

$Out[20]=$ $(-2+n)\,(-1+n)\,n\,x^{-3+n}$

Here is the equivalent one-dimensional input form.

$In[21]:=$ **D[x^n, x, x, x]**

$Out[21]=$ $(-2+n)\,(-1+n)\,n\,x^{-3+n}$

■ 1.10.5 Entering Tables and Matrices

The *Mathematica* front end typically provides a Create Table/Matrix/Palette menu item which allows you to create a blank array with any specified number of rows and columns. Once you have such an array, you can then edit it to fill in whatever elements you want.

Mathematica treats an array like this as a matrix represented by a list of lists.

$In[1]:=$ $\begin{array}{ccc} a & b & c \\ 1 & 2 & 3 \end{array}$

$Out[1]=$ {{a, b, c}, {1, 2, 3}}

Putting parentheses around the array makes it look more like a matrix, but does not affect its interpretation.

$In[2]:=$ $\begin{pmatrix} a & b & c \\ 1 & 2 & 3 \end{pmatrix}$

$Out[2]=$ {{a, b, c}, {1, 2, 3}}

Using MatrixForm tells *Mathematica* to display the result of the Transpose as a matrix.

$In[3]:=$ **MatrixForm** $\left[\text{Transpose} \left[\begin{pmatrix} a & b & c \\ 1 & 2 & 3 \end{pmatrix} \right] \right]$

$Out[3]//MatrixForm=$ $\begin{pmatrix} a & 1 \\ b & 2 \\ c & 3 \end{pmatrix}$

CTRL[,]	add a column
CTRL[↵] (CONTROL-RETURN)	add a row
TAB	go to the next □ or ■ element
CTRL[⎵] (CONTROL-SPACE)	move out of the table or matrix

Entering tables and matrices.

Note that you can use CTRL[,] and CTRL[↵] to start building up an array, and particularly for small arrays this is often more convenient than using the Create Table/Matrix/Palette menu item.

Page 428 will describe how to adjust many aspects of the appearance of arrays you create in *Mathematica*. The Create Table/Matrix/Palette menu item typically allows you to make basic adjustments, such as drawing lines between rows or columns.

+■ 1.10.6 Subscripts, Bars and Other Modifiers

Here is a typical palette of modifiers.

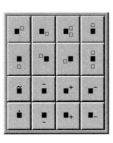

Mathematica allows you to use any expression as a subscript.

$In[1]:=$ **Expand$\left[(1 + x_{1+n})^4\right]$**

$Out[1]=$ $1 + 4 x_{1+n} + 6 x_{1+n}^2 + 4 x_{1+n}^3 + x_{1+n}^4$

Unless you specifically tell it otherwise, Mathematica will interpret a superscript as a power.

$In[2]:=$ **Factor$[x_n^4 - 1]$**

$Out[2]=$ $(-1 + x_n) (1 + x_n) (1 + x_n^2)$

$\boxed{\text{CTRL}}\boxed{\_}$ or $\boxed{\text{CTRL}}\boxed{-}$	go to the position for a subscript
$\boxed{\text{CTRL}}\boxed{+}$ or $\boxed{\text{CTRL}}\boxed{=}$	go to the position underneath
$\boxed{\text{CTRL}}\boxed{\char94}$ or $\boxed{\text{CTRL}}\boxed{6}$	go to the position for a superscript
$\boxed{\text{CTRL}}\boxed{\&}$ or $\boxed{\text{CTRL}}\boxed{7}$	go to the position on top
$\boxed{\text{CTRL}}\boxed{\ }$	return from a special position (CONTROL-SPACE)

Special input forms based on control characters. The second forms given should work on any keyboard.

This enters a subscript using control keys.

$In[3]:=$ **Expand[(1 + x $\boxed{\text{CTRL}}\boxed{\_}$ 1+n $\boxed{\text{CTRL}}\boxed{\ }$)^4]**

$Out[3]=$ $1 + 4 x_{1+n} + 6 x_{1+n}^2 + 4 x_{1+n}^3 + x_{1+n}^4$

Just as $\boxed{\text{CTRL}}\boxed{\char94}$ and $\boxed{\text{CTRL}}\boxed{\_}$ go to superscript and subscript positions, so also $\boxed{\text{CTRL}}\boxed{\&}$ and $\boxed{\text{CTRL}}\boxed{=}$ can be used to go to positions directly above and below. With the layout of a standard English-language keyboard $\boxed{\text{CTRL}}\boxed{\&}$ is directly to the right of $\boxed{\text{CTRL}}\boxed{\char94}$ while $\boxed{\text{CTRL}}\boxed{=}$ is directly to the right of $\boxed{\text{CTRL}}\boxed{\_}$.

key sequence	displayed form	expression form
x CTRL $\&$ _	$\bar{x}$	OverBar[x]
x CTRL $\&$: vec :	$\vec{x}$	OverVector[x]
x CTRL $\&$ ~	$\tilde{x}$	OverTilde[x]
x CTRL $\&$ ^	$\hat{x}$	OverHat[x]
x CTRL $\&$.	$\dot{x}$	OverDot[x]
x CTRL $=$ _	$\underline{x}$	UnderBar[x]

Ways to enter some common modifiers using control keys.

Here is $\bar{x}$.

$In[4]:=$ **x** CTRL $\&$ _ CTRL ⌴

$Out[4]=$ $\bar{x}$

You can use $\bar{x}$ as a variable.

$In[5]:=$ **Solve[a^2 == %, a]**

$Out[5]=$ $\{\{a \rightarrow -\sqrt{\bar{x}}\}, \{a \rightarrow \sqrt{\bar{x}}\}\}$

key sequence	displayed form	expression form
x _ y	x_y	Subscript[x, y]
x \+ y	$\underset{y}{x}$	Underscript[x, y]
x \^ y	x^y	Superscript[x, y] (interpreted as Power[x, y])
x \& y	$\overset{y}{x}$	Overscript[x, y]
x \&_	$\bar{x}$	OverBar[x]
x \&\[RightVector]	$\vec{x}$	OverVector[x]
x \&~	$\tilde{x}$	OverTilde[x]
x \&^	$\hat{x}$	OverHat[x]
x \&.	$\dot{x}$	OverDot[x]
x \+_	$\underline{x}$	UnderBar[x]

Ways to enter modifiers without control keys. All these forms can be used only inside \!\(... \).

⁺■ **1.10.7 Special Topic: Non-English Characters and Keyboards**

If you enter text in languages other than English, you will typically need to use various additional accented and other characters. If your computer system is set up in an appropriate way, then you will often be able to enter such characters directly using standard keys on your keyboard. But however your system is set up, *Mathematica* always provides a uniform way to handle such characters.

	full name	*alias*		*full name*	*alias*
à	\[AGrave]	⋮a'⋮	ø	\[OSlash]	⋮o/⋮
å	\[ARing]	⋮ao⋮	ö	\[ODoubleDot]	⋮o"⋮
ä	\[ADoubleDot]	⋮a"⋮	ù	\[UGrave]	⋮u'⋮
ç	\[CCedilla]	⋮c,⋮	ü	\[UDoubleDot]	⋮u"⋮
č	\[CHacek]	⋮cv⋮	ß	\[SZ]	⋮sz⋮, ⋮ss⋮
é	\[EAcute]	⋮e'⋮	Å	\[CapitalARing]	⋮Ao⋮
è	\[EGrave]	⋮e'⋮	Ä	\[CapitalADoubleDot]	⋮A"⋮
í	\[IAcute]	⋮i'⋮	Ö	\[CapitalODoubleDot]	⋮O"⋮
ñ	\[NTilde]	⋮n~⋮	Ü	\[CapitalUDoubleDot]	⋮U"⋮
ò	\[OGrave]	⋮o'⋮			

Some common European characters.

Here is a function whose name involves an accented character.

In[1]:= **Lam\[EAcute][x, y]**

Out[1]= Lamé[x, y]

This is another way to enter the same input.

In[2]:= **Lam⋮e'⋮[x, y]**

Out[2]= Lamé[x, y]

You should realize that there is no uniform standard for computer keyboards around the world, and as a result it is inevitable that some details of what has been said in this chapter may not apply to your keyboard.

In particular, the identification for example of [CTRL]6 with [CTRL][^] is valid only for keyboards on which ^ appears as Shift-6. On other keyboards, *Mathematica* uses [CTRL]6 to go to a superscript position, but not necessarily [CTRL][^].

Regardless of how your keyboard is set up you can always use palettes or menu items to set up superscripts and other kinds of notation. And assuming you have some way to enter characters such as \, you can always give input using full names such as \[Infinity] and textual forms such as \(x\/y\).

⁺■ **1.10.8 Other Mathematical Notation**

Mathematica supports an extremely wide range of mathematical notation, although often it does not assign a pre-defined meaning to it. Thus, for example, you can enter an expression such as x ⊕ y, but *Mathematica* will not initially make any assumption about what you mean by ⊕.

Mathematica knows that ⊕ is an operator, but it does not initially assign any specific meaning to it.	*In[1]:=* **{17 ⊕ 5, 8 ⊕ 3}** *Out[1]=* {17⊕5, 8⊕3}
This gives *Mathematica* a definition for what the ⊕ operator does.	*In[2]:=* **x_ ⊕ y_ := Mod[x + y, 2]**
Now *Mathematica* can evaluate ⊕ operations.	*In[3]:=* **{17 ⊕ 5, 8 ⊕ 3}** *Out[3]=* {0, 1}

	full name	*alias*		*full name*	*alias*
⊕	\[CirclePlus]	⁚c+⁚	⟶	\[LongRightArrow]	⁚-->⁚
⊗	\[CircleTimes]	⁚c*⁚	↔	\[LeftRightArrow]	⁚<->⁚
±	\[PlusMinus]	⁚+-⁚	↑	\[UpArrow]	
∧	\[Wedge]	⁚^⁚	⇌	\[Equilibrium]	⁚equi⁚
∨	\[Vee]	⁚v⁚	⊢	\[RightTee]	
≃	\[TildeEqual]	⁚~=⁚	⊃	\[Superset]	⁚sup⁚
≈	\[TildeTilde]	⁚~~⁚	⊓	\[SquareIntersection]	
∼	\[Tilde]	⁚~⁚	∈	\[Element]	⁚elem⁚
∝	\[Proportional]	⁚prop⁚	∉	\[NotElement]	⁚!elem⁚
≡	\[Congruent]	⁚===⁚	∘	\[SmallCircle]	⁚sc⁚
≳	\[GreaterTilde]	⁚>~⁚	∴	\[Therefore]	
≫	\[GreaterGreater]				\[VerticalSeparator]	⁚|⁚
≻	\[Succeeds]				\[VerticalBar]	⁚_|⁚
▷	\[RightTriangle]		\	\[Backslash]	⁚\⁚

A few of the operators whose input is supported by *Mathematica*.

Mathematica assigns built-in meanings to ≥ and ≽, but not to ≳ or ≫.	*In[4]:=* **{3 ≥ 4, 3 ≽ 4, 3 ≳ 4, 3 ≫ 4}** *Out[4]=* {False, False, 3 ≳ 4, 3 ≫ 4}

There are some forms which look like characters on a standard keyboard, but which are interpreted in a different way by *Mathematica*. Thus, for example, \[Backslash] or ⁚\⁚ displays as \ but is not interpreted in the same way as a \ typed directly on the keyboard.

The \ and ∧ characters used here are different from the \ and ^ you would type directly on a keyboard.

$In[5]:=$ **{a :\: b, a :^: b}**

$Out[5]=$ {a \ b, a ∧ b}

Most operators work like ⊕ and go in between their operands. But some operators can go in other places. Thus, for example, :<: and :>: or \[LeftAngleBracket] and \[RightAngleBracket] are effectively operators which go around their operand.

The elements of the angle bracket operator go around their operand.

$In[6]:=$ **\[LeftAngleBracket] 1 + x \[RightAngleBracket]**

$Out[6]=$ ⟨1 + x⟩

	full name	alias			full name	alias
ℓ	\[ScriptL]	:scl:		Å	\[Angstrom]	:Ang:
ℰ	\[ScriptCapitalE]	:scE:		ℏ	\[HBar]	:hb:
ℜ	\[GothicCapitalR]	:goR:		£	\[Sterling]	
ℤ	\[DoubleStruckCapitalZ]	:dsZ:		∠	\[Angle]	
ℵ	\[Aleph]	:al:		•	\[Bullet]	:bu:
∅	\[EmptySet]	:es:		†	\[Dagger]	:dg:
μ	\[Micro]	:mi:		♮	\[Natural]	

Some additional letters and letter-like forms.

You can use letters and letter-like forms anywhere in symbol names.

$In[7]:=$ **{R∅, \[Angle]ABC}**

$Out[7]=$ {R∅, ∠ABC}

∅ is assumed to be a symbol, and so is just multiplied by a and b.

$In[8]:=$ **a ∅ b**

$Out[8]=$ a b ∅

+■ 1.10.9 Forms of Input and Output

Mathematica notebooks allow you to give input and get output in a variety of different forms. Typically the front end provides menu commands for converting cells from one form to another.

InputForm	a form that can be typed directly using characters on a standard keyboard
OutputForm	a form for output only that uses just characters on a standard keyboard
StandardForm	a form for input and output that makes use of special characters and positioning
TraditionalForm	a form primarily for output that imitates all aspects of traditional mathematical notation

Forms of input and output.

The input here works in both InputForm and StandardForm.

$In[1]:=$ **x^2 + y^2/z**

$Out[1]= x^2 + \dfrac{y^2}{z}$

Here is a version of the input appropriate for StandardForm.

$In[2]:= \mathbf{x^2 + \dfrac{y^2}{z}}$

$Out[2]= x^2 + \dfrac{y^2}{z}$

InputForm is the most general form of input for *Mathematica*: it works whether you are using a notebook interface or a text-based interface.

With a notebook interface, output is by default produced in StandardForm.

$In[3]:=$ **Sqrt[x] + 1/(2 + Sqrt[y])**

$Out[3]= \sqrt{x} + \dfrac{1}{2 + \sqrt{y}}$

With a text-based interface, OutputForm is used instead.

$In[4]:=$ **Sqrt[x] + 1/(2 + Sqrt[y]) // OutputForm**

$Out[4]//OutputForm= Sqrt[x] + \dfrac{1}{2 + Sqrt[y]}$

With a notebook interface, the default form for both input and output is StandardForm.

The basic idea of StandardForm is to provide a precise but elegant representation of *Mathematica* expressions, making use of special characters, two-dimensional positioning, and so on.

Both input and output are given here in StandardForm.

$$In[5]:= \int \frac{1}{(x^3+1)}\,dx$$

$$Out[5]= \frac{\text{ArcTan}\left[\frac{-1+2x}{\sqrt{3}}\right]}{\sqrt{3}} + \frac{1}{3}\,\text{Log}[1+x] - \frac{1}{6}\,\text{Log}[1-x+x^2]$$

An important feature of StandardForm is that any output you get in this form you can also directly use as input.

$$In[6]:= \frac{\text{ArcTan}\left[\frac{-1+2x}{\sqrt{3}}\right]}{\sqrt{3}} + \frac{1}{3}\,\text{Log}[1+x] - \frac{1}{6}\,\text{Log}[1-x+x^2]$$

$$Out[6]= \frac{\text{ArcTan}\left[\frac{-1+2x}{\sqrt{3}}\right]}{\sqrt{3}} + \frac{1}{3}\,\text{Log}[1+x] - \frac{1}{6}\,\text{Log}[1-x+x^2]$$

The precise nature of StandardForm prevents it from following all of the somewhat haphazard conventions of traditional mathematical notation. *Mathematica* however also supports TraditionalForm, which uses a large collection of rules to give a rather complete rendition of traditional mathematical notation.

TraditionalForm uses lower-case names for functions, and puts their arguments in parentheses rather than square brackets.

$$In[7]:= \int \frac{1}{(x^3+1)}\,dx \text{ // TraditionalForm}$$

$$Out[7]//TraditionalForm= \frac{\tan^{-1}\left(\frac{2x-1}{\sqrt{3}}\right)}{\sqrt{3}} + \frac{1}{3}\log(x+1) - \frac{1}{6}\log(x^2-x+1)$$

Here are a few transformations made by TraditionalForm.

$$In[8]:= \{\text{Abs}[x], \text{ArcTan}[x], \text{BesselJ}[0, x], \text{Binomial}[i, j]\} \text{ // TraditionalForm}$$

$$Out[8]//TraditionalForm= \left\{|x|, \tan^{-1}(x), J_0(x), \binom{i}{j}\right\}$$

TraditionalForm is often useful for generating output that can be inserted directly into documents which use traditional mathematical notation. But you should understand that TraditionalForm is intended primarily for output: it does not have the kind of precision that is needed to provide reliable input to *Mathematica*.

Thus, for example, in TraditionalForm, Ci(*x*) is the representation for both Ci[*x*] and CosIntegral[*x*], so if this form appears on its own as input, *Mathematica* will have no idea which of the two interpretations is the correct one.

In StandardForm, these three expressions are all displayed in a unique and unambiguous way.

$$In[9]:= \{\text{Ci}[1+x], \text{CosIntegral}[1+x], \text{Ci}(1+x)\} \text{ // StandardForm}$$

$$Out[9]//StandardForm= \{\text{Ci}[1+x], \text{CosIntegral}[1+x], \text{Ci}(1+x)\}$$

In TraditionalForm, however, the first two are impossible to distinguish, and the third differs only in the presence of an extra space.

$$In[10]:= \{\text{Ci}[1+x], \text{CosIntegral}[1+x], \text{Ci}(1+x)\} \text{ // TraditionalForm}$$

$$Out[10]//TraditionalForm= \{\text{Ci}(x+1), \text{Ci}(x+1), \text{Ci}(x+1)\}$$

The ambiguities of TraditionalForm make it in general unsuitable for specifying input to the *Mathematica* kernel. But at least for sufficiently simple cases, *Mathematica* does include various heuristic rules for trying to interpret TraditionalForm expressions as *Mathematica* input.

Cells intended for input to the kernel are assumed by default to contain StandardForm expressions.

$$\text{In[1]:= } c\left(\sqrt{x} + \frac{1}{x}\right) + \Gamma(x)$$

$$\text{Out[1]= } c\left(\frac{1}{x} + \sqrt{x}\right) + x\,\Gamma$$

Here the front end was specifically told that input would be given in TraditionalForm. The cell bracket has a jagged line to indicate the difficulties involved.

$$\text{In[1]:= } c\left(\sqrt{x} + \frac{1}{x}\right) + \Gamma(x)$$

$$\text{Out[1]= } c\left[\frac{1}{x} + \sqrt{x}\right] + \text{Gamma}[x]$$

- The input is a copy or simple edit of previous output.
- The input has been converted from StandardForm, perhaps with simple edits.
- The input contains explicit hidden information giving its interpretation.
- The input contains only the simplest and most familiar notations.

Some situations in which TraditionalForm input can be expected to work.

Whenever *Mathematica* generates an expression in TraditionalForm, it automatically inserts various hidden tags so that the expression can later be interpreted unambiguously if it is given as input. And even if you edit the expression, the tags will often be left sufficiently undisturbed that unambiguous interpretation will still be possible.

This generates output in TraditionalForm.

In[11]:= **Exp[I Pi x] // TraditionalForm**

Out[11]//TraditionalForm= $e^{i\pi x}$

Mathematica was told to expect TraditionalForm input here. The input was copied from the previous output line, and thus contains hidden tags that ensure the correct interpretation.

In[12]:= $e^{i\pi x}$ **// StandardForm**

Out[12]//StandardForm= $\text{E}^{\text{I}\pi x}$

Simple editing often does not disturb the hidden tags.

In[13]:= $e^{2i\pi x}$ **// StandardForm**

Out[13]//StandardForm= $\text{E}^{2\text{I}\pi x}$

If you enter a TraditionalForm expression from scratch, or import it from outside *Mathematica*, then *Mathematica* will still do its best to guess what the expression means. When there are ambiguities, what it typically does is to assume that you are using notation in whatever way is more common in elementary mathematical applications.

In `TraditionalForm` input, this is interpreted as a derivative.

$In[14]:= \dfrac{\partial\, y(x)}{\partial\, x}$ // **StandardForm**

Out[14]//StandardForm= y'[x]

This is interpreted as an arc tangent.

$In[15]:=$ **tan**$^{-1}(x)$ // **StandardForm**

Out[15]//StandardForm= ArcTan[x]

This is interpreted as the square of a tangent.

$In[16]:=$ **tan**$^2(x)$ // **StandardForm**

Out[16]//StandardForm= Tan[x]^2

There is no particularly standard traditional interpretation for this; *Mathematica* assumes that it is 1/Tan[x]^2.

$In[17]:=$ **tan**$^{-2}(x)$ // **StandardForm**

Out[17]//StandardForm= Cot[x]^2

You should realize that `TraditionalForm` does not provide any kind of precise or complete way of specifying *Mathematica* expressions. Nevertheless, for some elementary purposes it may be sufficient, particularly if you use a few additional tricks.

- Use $x(y)$ for functions; $x\ (y)$ for multiplication

- Use ꞉ee꞉ for the exponential constant E

- Use ꞉ii꞉ or ꞉jj꞉ for the imaginary unit I

- Use ꞉dd꞉ for differential operators in integrals and derivatives

---

A few tricks for `TraditionalForm` input.

With a space f (1 + x) is interpreted as multiplication. Without a space, g(1 + x) is interpreted as a function.

$In[18]:= f\,(1+x) + g(1+x)$ // **StandardForm**

Out[18]//StandardForm= f[1 + x] + g[1 + x]

The ordinary e is interpreted as a symbol e. The special "exponential e", entered as ꞉ee꞉, is interpreted as the exponential constant.

$In[19]:= \{e^{3.7},\ e^{3.7}\}$ // **StandardForm**

Out[19]//StandardForm= {e$^{3.7}$, 40.4473}

◼ 1.10.10 Mixing Text and Formulas

The simplest way to mix text and formulas in a *Mathematica* notebook is to put each kind of material in a separate cell. Sometimes, however, you may want to embed a formula within a cell of text.

CTRL (or CTRL 9	begin entering a formula
CTRL) or CTRL 0	end entering a formula

Entering a formula within text.

Here is a notebook with formulas embedded in a text cell.

This is a text cell, but it can contain formulas such as $\int \frac{1}{x^3-1} dx$ or $-\frac{\log(x^2+x+1)}{6} - \tan^{-1}\frac{\left(\frac{2x+1}{\sqrt{3}}\right)}{\sqrt{3}} + \frac{\log(x-1)}{3}$. The formulas flow with the text.

Mathematica notebooks often contain both formulas that are intended for actual evaluation by *Mathematica*, and ones that are intended just to be read in a more passive way.

You can use exactly the same mechanisms for entering formulas, whether or not they will ultimately be given as *Mathematica* input.

You should realize, however, that to make the detailed typography of typical formulas look as good as possible, *Mathematica* automatically does things such as inserting spaces around certain operators. But these kinds of adjustments can potentially be inappropriate if you use notation in very different ways from the ones *Mathematica* is expecting.

In such cases, you may have to make detailed typographical adjustments by hand, using the mechanisms discussed on page 428.

■ 1.10.11 Displaying and Printing *Mathematica* Notebooks

Depending on the purpose for which you are using a *Mathematica* notebook, you may want to change its overall appearance. The front end allows you to specify independently the styles to be used for display on the screen and for printing. Typically you can do this by choosing appropriate items in the Format menu.

`ScreenStyleEnvironment`	styles to be used for screen display
`PrintingStyleEnvironment`	styles to be used for printed output
`Working`	standard style definitions for screen display
`Presentation`	style definitions for presentations
`Condensed`	style definitions for high display density
`Printing`	style definitions for printed output

Front end settings that define the global appearance of a notebook.

Here is a typical notebook as it appears in working form on the screen.

■ A Symbolic Sum

Here is the input:

$$\sum_{n=1}^{\infty} \frac{1}{n(n+4)^2}$$

Here is the output:

$$(615 + 1435\,m + 1090\,m^2 + 332\,m^3 + 35\,m^4 - 72\,\pi^2 - 150\,m\,\pi^2 - 105\,m^2\,\pi^2 - 30\,m^3\,\pi^2 - 3\,m^4\,\pi^2)\,/\,(72\,(1+m)\,(2+m)\,(3+m)\,(4+m)) + \frac{\text{PolyGamma}[1,\,5+m]}{4}$$

Here is the same notebook with condensed styles.

■ A Symbolic Sum

Here is the input:

$$\sum_{n=1}^{\infty} \frac{1}{n(n+4)^2}$$

Here is the output:

$$\frac{615 + 1435\,m + 1090\,m^2 + 332\,m^3 + 35\,m^4 - 72\,\pi^2 - 150\,m\,\pi^2 - 105\,m^2\,\pi^2 - 30\,m^3\,\pi^2 - 3\,m^4\,\pi^2}{72\,(1+m)\,(2+m)\,(3+m)\,(4+m)} + \frac{\text{PolyGamma}[1,\,5+m]}{4}$$

Here is a preview of how the notebook would appear when printed out.

■ A Symbolic Sum

Here is the input:

$$\sum_{n=1}^{\infty} \frac{1}{n(n+4)^2}$$

Here is the output:

$$\frac{615 + 1435\,m + 1090\,m^2 + 332\,m^3 + 35\,m^4 - 72\,\pi^2 - 150\,m\,\pi^2 - 105\,m^2\,\pi^2 - 30\,m^3\,\pi^2 - 3\,m^4\,\pi^2}{72\,(1+m)\,(2+m)\,(3+m)\,(4+m)} + \frac{\text{PolyGamma}[1,\,5+m]}{4}$$

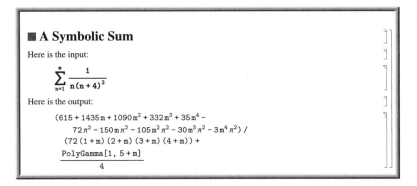

+■ 1.10.12 Creating Your Own Palettes

The *Mathematica* notebook front end comes with a collection of standard palettes. But it also allows you to create your own palettes.

> ■ Set up a blank palette using Create Table/Matrix/Palette under the Input menu
>
> ■ Fill in the contents
>
> ■ Make the palette active using Generate Palette from Selection under the File menu

The basic steps in creating a palette.

Create Table/Matrix/Palette will create a blank palette.

You can then insert whatever you want into each button.

The menu item Generate Palette makes a separate active palette.

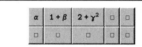

Clicking on a button in the palette now inserts its contents into your notebook.

$$x + y + \frac{1}{2 + \gamma^2}$$

Create Table/Matrix/Palette	set up a blank palette
Generate Palette from Selection	make a separate active palette
Generate Notebook from Palette	convert a palette back into an editable notebook
Edit Button	edit the script associated with a palette or button

Menu items for setting up palettes.

When you are creating a palette, you can use the same mechanisms to add columns and rows as you can when you are creating any other kind of table, matrix or grid. Thus CTRL [,] will add a new column of buttons, and CTRL ↵ (CONTROL-RETURN) will add a new row.

button contents	action
X	replace current selection by X
text containing X■Y	replace current selection S by XSY

Contents of buttons.

In the simplest case, when you press a button in a palette what will happen is that the contents of the button will be inserted into your notebook, replacing whatever your current selection was.

Sometimes however you may not simply want to overwrite your current selection, but rather you may want to modify the selection in some way. As an example, you might want to wrap a function like Expand around your current selection.

You can do this by setting up a button with contents Expand[■]. The ■ can be entered as ∶spl∶ or \[SelectionPlaceholder]. In general, ■ serves as a placeholder for your current selection. When you press a button that contains ■, the ■ is first replaced by your current selection, and only then is the result inserted into your notebook.

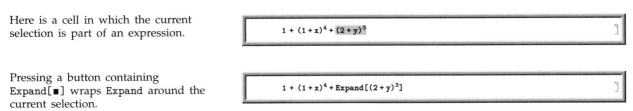

Here is a cell in which the current selection is part of an expression.

$1 + (1+x)^4 + (2+y)^3$

Pressing a button containing Expand[■] wraps Expand around the current selection.

$1 + (1+x)^4 + \text{Expand}[(2+y)^3]$

Mathematica allows you to associate any action you want with a button. You can set up some common actions by using the Edit Button menu, having selected either a single button or a whole palette.

Paste	paste the contents of the button (default)
Evaluate	paste then evaluate in place what has been pasted
EvaluateCell	paste then evaluate the whole cell
CopyEvaluate	copy the current selection into a new cell, then paste and evaluate in place
CopyEvaluateCell	copy the current selection into a new cell, then paste and evaluate the whole cell

Typical actions for buttons.

With the default `Paste` setting for a button action, pressing the button modifies the contents of a cell but does no evaluation. By choosing other button actions, however, you can tell *Mathematica* to perform an evaluation every time you press the button.

With the button action `Evaluate` the result of this evaluation is made to overwrite your current selection. This is useful if you want to set up a button which modifies parts of an expression in place, say by applying `Expand[■]` to them.

The button action `Evaluate` performs evaluation only on whatever was pasted into your current cell. The button action `EvaluateCell`, on the other hand, performs evaluation on the whole cell, generating a new cell to show the result.

Here is an expression with a part
selected.

$$1 + (1+x)^4 + (2+y)^3$$

This shows the result of pressing a
button containing `Expand[■]` with an
`EvaluateCell` button action.

$$1 + (1+x)^4 + \text{Expand}[(2+y)^3]$$
$$9 + (1+x)^4 + 12y + 6y^2 + y^3$$

Sometimes it is useful to be able to extract the current selection from a cell, and then operate on it in a new cell. You can do this using the button actions `CopyEvaluate` and `CopyEvaluateCell`.

Here is an expression with a part
selected.

$$1 + (1+x)^4 + (2+y)^3$$

A button with a `CopyEvaluateCell`
button action copies the current
selection into a new cell, then pastes
the contents of the button, and then
performs an evaluation, putting the
result into a new cell.

$$1 + (1+x)^4 + (2+y)^3$$
$$\text{In[1]:= Expand}[(2+y)^3]$$
$$\text{Out[1]= } 8 + 12y + 6y^2 + y^3$$

Create Table/Matrix/Palette	set up a blank palette
Create Button	set up a single button not in a palette
Generate Palette from Selection	make a separate window
Cell Active	activate buttons within a cell in a notebook

Ways to create active elements in the front end.

Mathematica allows you to set up a wide range of active elements in the notebook front end. In the most common case, you have a palette which consists of an array of buttons in a separate window. But you can also have arrays of buttons, or even single buttons, within the cells of an ordinary notebook.

In addition, you can make a button execute any action you want—performing computations in the *Mathematica* kernel, or changing the configuration of notebooks in the front end. Section 2.10.6 discusses how to do this.

■ 1.10.13 Setting Up Hyperlinks

Create Hyperlink	set up the destination for a hyperlink
Paste	insert a hyperlink in text

Menu items for setting up hyperlinks.

A hyperlink is a special kind of button which jumps to another part of a notebook when it is pressed. Typically hyperlinks are indicated in *Mathematica* by blue or underlined text.

To set up a hyperlink, you first go to wherever you want the destination of the hyperlink to be. Then you choose the menu item Create Hyperlink. This places on the clipboard a specification of the hyperlink.

You can then go to another part of your notebook, and paste this specification, thereby setting up a hyperlink.

+■ 1.10.14 Automatic Numbering

- ■ Choose a cell style such as `NumberedEquation`
- ■ Use the Create Automatic Numbering Object menu, with a counter name such as `Section`

Two ways to set up automatic numbering in a *Mathematica* notebook.

The input for each cell here is exactly the same, but the cells contain an element that displays as a progressively larger number as one goes through the notebook.

> ■ **1. A Section**
>
> ■ **2. A Section**
>
> ■ **3. A Section**

These cells are in `NumberedEquation` style.

$$\int \frac{x}{x+1} dx \qquad\qquad (1)$$

$$\int \frac{\text{Sin}[x]}{x+1} dx \qquad\qquad (2)$$

$$\int \frac{\text{Log}[x] + \text{Exp}[x]}{x+1} dx \qquad\qquad (3)$$

+■ 1.10.15 Exposition in *Mathematica* Notebooks

Mathematica notebooks provide the basic technology that you need to be able to create a very wide range of sophisticated interactive documents. But to get the best out of this technology you need to develop an appropriate style of exposition.

Many people at first tend to use *Mathematica* notebooks either as simple worksheets containing a sequence of input and output lines, or as on-screen versions of traditional books and other printed material. But the most effective and productive uses of *Mathematica* notebooks tend to lie at neither one of these extremes, and instead typically involve a fine-grained mixing of *Mathematica* input and output with explanatory text. In most cases the single most important factor in obtaining such fine-grained mixing is uniform use of the *Mathematica* language.

One might think that there would tend to be three kinds of material in a *Mathematica* notebook: plain text, mathematical formulas, and computer code. But one of the key ideas of *Mathematica* is to provide a single language that offers the best of both traditional mathematical formulas and computer code.

In `StandardForm`, *Mathematica* expressions have the same kind of compactness and elegance as traditional mathematical formulas. But unlike such formulas, *Mathematica* expressions are set up in a completely consistent and uniform way. As a result, if you use *Mathematica* expressions, then regardless of your subject matter, you never have to go back and reexplain your basic notation: it is always just the notation of the *Mathematica* language. In addition, if you set up your explanations in terms of *Mathematica* expressions, then a reader of your notebook can immediately take what you have given, and actually execute it as *Mathematica* input.

If one has spent many years working with traditional mathematical notation, then it takes a little time to get used to seeing mathematical facts presented as StandardForm *Mathematica* expressions. Indeed, at first one often has a tendency to try to use TraditionalForm whenever possible, perhaps with hidden tags to indicate its interpretation. But quite soon one tends to evolve to a mixture of StandardForm and TraditionalForm. And in the end it becomes clear that StandardForm alone is for most purposes the most effective form of presentation.

In traditional mathematical exposition, there are many tricks for replacing chunks of text by fragments of formulas. In StandardForm many of these same tricks can be used. But the fact that *Mathematica* expressions can represent not only mathematical objects but also procedures and algorithms increases greatly the extent to which chunks of text can be replaced by shorter and more precise material.

1.11 Files and External Operations

■ 1.11.1 Reading and Writing *Mathematica* Files

You can use files on your computer system to store definitions and results from *Mathematica*. The most general approach is to store everything as plain text that is appropriate for input to *Mathematica*. With this approach, a version of *Mathematica* running on one computer system produces files that can be read by a version running on any computer system. In addition, such files can be manipulated by other standard programs, such as text editors.

<< *name*	read in a *Mathematica* input file
expr >> *name*	output *expr* to a file as plain text
expr >>> *name*	append *expr* to a file
!!*name*	display the contents of a plain text file

Reading and writing files.

This expands $(x + y)^3$, and outputs the result to a file called tmp.	$In[1]:=$ **Expand[(x + y)^3] >> tmp**
Here are the contents of tmp. They can be used directly as input for *Mathematica*.	$In[2]:=$ **!!tmp** x^3 + 3*x^2*y + 3*x*y^2 + y^3
This reads in tmp, evaluating the *Mathematica* input it contains.	$In[3]:=$ **<<tmp** $Out[3]=$ $x^3 + 3x^2y + 3xy^2 + y^3$

If you are familiar with Unix or MS-DOS operating systems, you will recognize the *Mathematica* redirection operators >>, >>> and << as being analogous to the shell operators >, >> and <.

The redirection operators >> and >>> are convenient for storing results you get from *Mathematica*. The function Save["*name*", *f*, *g*, ...] allows you to save definitions for variables and functions.

Save["*name*", *f*, *g*, ...]	save definitions for variables or functions in a file

Saving definitions in plain text files.

Here is a definition for a function f.	$In[4]:=$ **f[x_] := x^2 + c**
This gives c the value 17.	$In[5]:=$ **c = 17** $Out[5]=$ 17

This saves the definition of f in the file ftmp.	*In[6]:=* **Save["ftmp", f]**
Mathematica automatically saves both the actual definition of f, and the definition of c on which it depends.	*In[7]:=* **!!ftmp** f[x_] := x^2 + c c = 17
This clears the definitions of f and c.	*In[8]:=* **Clear[f, c]**
You can reinstate the definitions you saved simply by reading in the file ftmp.	*In[9]:=* **<<ftmp** *Out[9]=* 17

file.m	*Mathematica* expression file in plain text format
file.nb	*Mathematica* notebook file
file.mx	*Mathematica* definitions in DumpSave format

Typical names of *Mathematica* files.

If you use a notebook interface to *Mathematica*, then the *Mathematica* front end allows you to save complete notebooks, including not only *Mathematica* input and output, but also text, graphics and other material.

It is conventional to give *Mathematica* notebook files names that end in .nb, and most versions of *Mathematica* enforce this convention.

When you open a notebook in the *Mathematica* front end, *Mathematica* will immediately display the contents of the notebook, but it will not normally send any of these contents to the kernel for evaluation until you explicitly request this to be done.

Within a *Mathematica* notebook, however, you can use the Cell menu in the front end to identify certain cells as *initialization cells*, and if you do this, then the contents of these cells will automatically be evaluated whenever you open the notebook.

The I in the cell bracket indicates that the second cell is an initialization cell that will be evaluated whenever the notebook is opened.	■ **Implementation** ⟧ f[x_] := Log[x] + Log[1 - x] ⟧

It is sometimes convenient to maintain *Mathematica* material both in a notebook which contains explanatory text, and in a package which contains only raw *Mathematica* definitions. You can do this by putting the *Mathematica* definitions into opening auto-evaluate cells in the notebook. Every time you save the notebook, the front end will then allow you to save an associated .m file which contains only the raw *Mathematica* definitions.

■ 1.11.2 Advanced Topic: Finding and Manipulating Files

Although the details of how files are named and organized differ from one computer system to another, *Mathematica* provides some fairly general mechanisms for finding and handling files.

Mathematica assumes that files on your computer system are organized in a collection of *directories*. At any point, you have a *current working directory*. You can always refer to files in this directory just by giving their names.

`Directory[ ]`	give your current working directory
`SetDirectory["`*dir*`"]`	set your current working directory
`FileNames[ ]`	list the files in your current working directory
`FileNames["`*form*`"]`	list the files whose names match a certain form
`<<`*name*	read in a file with the specified name
`<<`*context*`	read in a file corresponding to the specified context
`CopyFile["`*file₁*`", "`*file₂*`"]`	copy *file₁* to *file₂*
`DeleteFile["`*file*`"]`	delete a file

Functions for finding and manipulating files.

This is the current working directory. The form it has differs from one computer system to another.

```
In[1]:= Directory[ ]
Out[1]= /users/sw
```

This resets the current working directory.

```
In[2]:= SetDirectory["Examples"]
Out[2]= /users/sw/Examples
```

This gives a list of all files in your current working directory whose names match the form Test*.m.

```
In[3]:= FileNames["Test*.m"]
Out[3]= {Test1.m, Test2.m, TestFinal.m}
```

Although you usually want to create files only in your current working directory, you often need to read in files from other directories. As a result, when you ask *Mathematica* to read in a file with a particular name, *Mathematica* automatically searches a list of directories (specified by the value of the search path variable $Path) to try and find a file with that name.

One issue in handling files in *Mathematica* is that the form of file and directory names varies between computer systems. This means for example that names of files which contain standard *Mathematica* packages may be quite different on different systems. Through a sequence of conventions, it is however possible to read in a standard *Mathematica* package with the same command on all systems. The way this works is that each package defines a so-called *Mathematica* context, of the form *name`name`*. On each system, all files are named in correspondence with the contexts they define. Then when you use the command <<*name`name`* *Mathematica* automatically translates the context name into the file name appropriate for your particular computer system.

FindList["*file*", "*text*"]	give a list of all lines in a file that contain the specified text
FindList[FileNames[ ], "*text*"]	search in all files in your current directory

Searching for text in files.

This searches all lines in the file index containing Laplace.

In[1]:= **FindList["index", "Laplace"]**

Out[1]= {Laplace transforms: Calculus`LaplaceTransform`,
                  Inverse Laplace transforms:
                       Calculus`LaplaceTransform`}

■ 1.11.3 Reading Data Files

ReadList["*file*", Number]	read numbers from a file, and return a *Mathematica* list of them
ReadList["*file*", Number, RecordLists->True]	read numbers from a file, making a separate list for each line in the file

Reading numerical data files.

If you have a table of numbers in a file, generated for example by an external program, you can read them into *Mathematica* using ReadList. The numbers in your file can be given in C or Fortran-like form, as 2.3E5 and so on. ReadList converts all numbers to the appropriate *Mathematica* form.

This shows the contents of the file rand.dat.

In[1]:= **!!rand.dat**

```
3.4    -5.7E-2    8.4E+2
4.5    -7.8E-2    1.9E+3
6.4    -0.1       4.7E+4
```

This reads the file rand.dat, and returns a list of the numbers in the file.

In[2]:= **ReadList["rand.dat", Number]**

Out[2]= {3.4, -0.057, 840., 4.5, -0.078, 1900.,
                  6.4, -0.1, 47000.}

This reads the numbers making a separate list for each line in the file.

In[3]:= **ReadList["rand.dat", Number, RecordLists -> True]**

Out[3]= {{3.4, -0.057, 840.}, {4.5, -0.078, 1900.},
                  {6.4, -0.1, 47000.}}

Mathematica allows you to read files in many different ways. For example, instead of reading numbers, you can read strings or "words". In addition, you can use Find to search for particular parts of files to read. These possibilities are discussed in Section 2.11.7.

■ 1.11.4 Generating C and Fortran Expressions

If you have special-purpose programs written in C or Fortran, you may want to take formulas you have generated in *Mathematica* and insert them into the source code of your programs. *Mathematica* allows you to convert mathematical expressions into C and Fortran expressions.

CForm[*expr*]	write out *expr* so it can be used in a C program
FortranForm[*expr*]	write out *expr* for Fortran

Mathematica output for programming languages.

Here is an expression, written out in standard *Mathematica* form.

$In[1]:=$ **Expand[(1 + x + y)^2]**

$Out[1]= 1 + 2x + x^2 + 2y + 2xy + y^2$

Here is the expression in Fortran form.

$In[2]:=$ **FortranForm[%]**

$Out[2]//FortranForm= 1 + 2*x + x**2 + 2*y + 2*x*y + y**2$

Here is the same expression in C form. Macros for objects like Power are defined in the C header file mdefs.h that comes with most versions of *Mathematica*.

$In[3]:=$ **CForm[%]**

$Out[3]//CForm= 1 + 2*x + Power(x,2) + 2*y + 2*x*y + Power(y,2)$

You should realize that there are many differences between *Mathematica* and C or Fortran. As a result, expressions you translate may not work exactly the same as they do in *Mathematica*. In addition, there are so many differences in programming constructs that no attempt is made to translate these automatically.

Compile[*x*, *expr*]	compile an expression into efficient internal code

A way to compile *Mathematica* expressions.

One of the common motivations for converting *Mathematica* expressions into C or Fortran is to try to make them faster to evaluate numerically. But the single most important reason that C and Fortran can potentially be more efficient than *Mathematica* is that in these languages one always specifies up front what type each variable one uses will be—integer, real number, array, and so on.

The *Mathematica* function `Compile` makes such assumptions within *Mathematica*, and generates highly efficient internal code. Usually this code runs not much if at all slower than custom C or Fortran.

■ 1.11.5 Exporting Graphics

Mathematica provides a variety of mechanisms for exporting graphics that you generate to printers and other programs.

If you use the notebook front end for *Mathematica*, then you can typically just copy and paste graphics directly using the standard mechanism available on your computer system.

`Display["`*file*`",` *graphics*`, "`*format*`"]`	export *graphics* to a file in the specified format
`Display["!`*command*`",` *graphics*`, "`*format*`"]`	send graphics to an external command

Ways to export *Mathematica* graphics.

The command `Display` allows you systematically to send graphics from *Mathematica* to external files and programs.

This generates a plot.　　　　　　　　　*In[1]:=* `Plot[Sin[x] + Sin[Sqrt[2] x], {x, 0, 10}]`

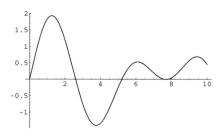

This saves the plot in a file in　　　　　*In[2]:=* `Display["sinplot.eps", %, "EPS"]`
Encapsulated PostScript format.　　　　*Out[2]=* -Graphics-

Here is a typical command for printing　*In[3]:=* `Display["!lpr", %, "EPS"]`
the plot on a Unix system.　　　　　　*Out[3]=* -Graphics-

"MPS"	*Mathematica* abbreviated PostScript
"EPS"	Encapsulated PostScript
"PDF"	Adobe Acrobat portable document format
"Illustrator"	Adobe Illustrator format
"PICT"	Macintosh PICT
"Metafile"	Microsoft Windows metafile
"TIFF"	TIFF
"GIF"	GIF
"PSImage"	PostScript image format
"XBitmap"	X Windows bitmap
"PCL"	Hewlett-Packard printer control language
"PBM"	portable bitmap
"MGF"	*Mathematica* system-independent raster graphics format

Typical graphics formats supported by *Mathematica*. The first group are resolution independent.

When you export a graphic outside of *Mathematica*, you usually have to specify the absolute size at which the graphic should be rendered. You can do this using the ImageSize option to Display.

ImageSize->*x* makes the width of the graphic be *x* printer's points; ImageSize->72 *xi* thus makes the width *xi* inches. The default is to produce an image that is four inches wide.

+ ImageSize	Automatic	absolute image size in printer's points
+ ImageRotated	False	whether to rotate the image (landscape mode)
+ ImageResolution	Automatic	resolution in dpi for the image

Options for Display.

Within *Mathematica* graphics are manipulated in a way that is completely independent of the resolution of the computer screen or other output device on which the graphics will eventually be rendered.

Many programs and devices accept graphics in resolution-independent formats such as Encapsulated PostScript (EPS). But some require that the graphics be converted to rasters or bitmaps with a specific resolution. The `ImageResolution` option for `Display` allows you to determine what resolution in dots per inch (dpi) should be used. The lower you set this resolution, the lower the quality of the image you will get, but also the less memory the image will take to store. For screen display, typical resolutions are 72 dpi and above; for printers 300 dpi and above.

■ 1.11.6 Exporting Formulas from Notebooks

Here is a cell containing a formula.

$$-\frac{\text{ArcTan}\left[\frac{1+2x}{\sqrt{3}}\right]}{\sqrt{3}} + \frac{\text{Log}[-1+x]}{3} - \frac{\text{Log}[1+x+x^2]}{6}$$

This is what you get if you copy the formula and paste it into an external text-based program.

```
\!\(-\(ArcTan[\(1 + 2 x\)\/\@3]\/\@3\) + Log[-1 + x]\/3
 - Log[1 + x + x\^2]\/6\)
```

Pasting the text back into a notebook immediately reproduces the original formula.

$$-\frac{\text{ArcTan}\left[\frac{1+2x}{\sqrt{3}}\right]}{\sqrt{3}} + \frac{\text{Log}[-1+x]}{3} - \frac{\text{Log}[1+x+x^2]}{6}$$

Mathematica allows you to export formulas both textually and visually. You can use `Display` to tell *Mathematica* to write a visual representation of a formula into a file.

`Display["`*file*`.eps", ToBoxes[`*expr*`], "EPS"]`	save the visual form of *expr* to a file in EPS format
`Display["`*file*`", ToBoxes[`*expr*`], "`*format*`"]`	save the visual form of *expr* in the specified format

Exporting expressions in visual form.

■ 1.11.7 Generating TₑX

Mathematica notebooks provide a sophisticated environment for creating technical documents. But particularly if you want to merge your work with existing material in TₑX, you may find it convenient to use `TeXForm` to convert expressions in *Mathematica* into a form suitable for input to TₑX.

TeXForm[*expr*]	print *expr* in TeX input form

Mathematica output for TeX.

Here is an expression, printed in standard *Mathematica* form.

$In[1]:= $ **(x + y)^2 / Sqrt[x y]**

$$Out[1]= \frac{(x+y)^2}{\sqrt{xy}}$$

Here is the expression in TeX input form.

$In[2]:= $ **TeXForm[%]**

$Out[2]//TeXForm=$ {{{{\left(x + y \right) }^2}}\over {{\sqrt{x\,y}}}}

+ TeXSave["*file*.tex"]	save your complete current notebook in TeX input form
+ TeXSave["*file*.tex", "*source*.nb"]	
	save a TeX version of the notebook *source*.nb

Converting complete notebooks to TeX.

In addition to being able to convert individual expressions to TeX, *Mathematica* also provides capabilities for translating complete notebooks. These capabilites can usually be accessed from the Save As Special menu in the notebook front end, where various options can be set.

+■ 1.11.8 Converting Notebooks to HTML

+ HTMLSave["*file*.html"]	save your complete current notebook in HTML form
+ HTMLSave["*file*.html", "*source*.nb"]	
	save an HTML version of the notebook *source*.nb

Converting notebooks to HTML.

■ 1.11.9 Splicing *Mathematica* Output into External Files

If you want to make use of *Mathematica* output in an external file such as a program or document, you will often find it useful to "splice" the output automatically into the file.

Splice["*file*.mx"]	splice *Mathematica* output into an external file named *file*.mx, putting the results in the file *file*.x
Splice["*infile*", "*outfile*"]	splice *Mathematica* output into *infile*, sending the output to *outfile*

Splicing *Mathematica* output into files.

The basic idea is to set up the definitions you need in a particular *Mathematica* session, then run Splice to use the definitions you have made to produce the appropriate output to insert into the external files.

```
#include "mdefs.h"

double f(x)
double x;
{
double y;

y = <* Integrate[Sin[x]^5, x] *> ;

return(2*y - 1) ;
}
```

A simple C program containing a *Mathematica* formula.

```
#include "mdefs.h"

double f(x)
double x;
{
double y;

y = -5*Cos(x)/8 + 5*Cos(3*x)/48 - Cos(5*x)/80 ;

return(2*y - 1) ;
}
```

The C program after processing with Splice.

■ 1.11.10 Running External Programs

Although *Mathematica* does many things well, there are some things that are inevitably better done by external programs. You can use *Mathematica* to control the external programs, or to analyze output they generate.

On almost all computer systems, it is possible to run external programs directly from within *Mathematica*. *Mathematica* communicates with the external programs through interprocess communication mechanisms such as pipes.

In the simplest cases, the only communication you need is to send and receive plain text. You can prepare input in *Mathematica*, then give it as the standard input for the external program. Or you can take the standard output of the external program, and use it as input to *Mathematica*.

In general, *Mathematica* allows you to treat streams of data exchanged with external programs just like files. In place of a file name, you give the external command to run, prefaced by an exclamation point.

`<<`*file*	read in a file
`<<"!`*command*`"`	run an external command, and read in the output it produces
expr `>> "!`*command*`"`	feed the textual form of *expr* to an external command
`ReadList["!`*command*`", Number]`	run an external command, and read in a list of the numbers it produces

Some ways to communicate with external programs.

This feeds the expression x^2 + y^2 as input to the external command lpr, which, on a typical Berkeley Unix system, sends output to a printer.

```
In[1]:= x^2 + y^2 >> "!lpr"
```

With a text-based interface, putting ! at the beginning of a line causes the remainder of the line to be executed as an external command. squares is an external program which prints numbers and their squares.

```
In[2]:= !squares 4
1    1
2    4
3    9
4    16
```

This runs the external command squares 4, then reads numbers from the output it produces.

```
In[3]:= ReadList["!squares 4", Number, RecordLists->True]
Out[3]= {{1, 1}, {2, 4}, {3, 9}, {4, 16}}
```

■ 1.11.11 *MathLink*

The previous section discussed how to exchange plain text with external programs. In many cases, however, you will find it convenient to communicate with external programs at a higher level, and to exchange more structured data with them.

On almost all computer systems, *Mathematica* supports the *MathLink* communication standard, which allows higher-level communication between *Mathematica* and external programs. In order to use *MathLink*, an external program has to include some special source code, which is usually distributed with *Mathematica*.

MathLink allows external programs both to call *Mathematica*, and to be called by *Mathematica*. Section 2.12 discusses some of the details of *MathLink*. By using *MathLink*, you can, for example, treat *Mathematica* essentially like a subroutine embedded inside an external program. Or you can create a front end that implements your own user interface, and communicates with the *Mathematica* kernel via *MathLink*.

You can also use *MathLink* to let *Mathematica* call individual functions inside an external program. As described in Section 2.12, you can set up a *MathLink* template file to specify how particular functions in *Mathematica* should call functions inside your external program. From the *MathLink* template file, you can generate source code to include in your program. Then when you start your program, the appropriate *Mathematica* definitions are automatically made, and when you call a particular *Mathematica* function, code in your external program is executed.

`Install["`*command*`"]`	start an external program and install *Mathematica* definitions to call functions it contains
`Uninstall[`*link*`]`	terminate an external program and uninstall definitions for functions in it

Calling functions in external programs.

This starts the external program simul, and installs *Mathematica* definitions to call various functions in it.

```
In[1]:= Install["simul"]

Out[1]= LinkObject[simul, 5, 4]
```

Here is a usage message for a function that was installed in *Mathematica* to call a function in the external program.

```
In[2]:= ?srun

srun[{a, r, gamma}, x] performs a simulation  with the
   specified parameters.
```

When you call this function, it executes code in the external program.

```
In[3]:= srun[{3, 0, 7}, 5]

Out[3]= 6.781241
```

This terminates the simul program.

```
In[4]:= Uninstall["simul"]

Out[4]= simul
```

1.12 Special Topic: The Internals of *Mathematica*

■ 1.12.1 Why You Do Not Usually Need to Know about Internals

Most of this book is concerned with explaining *what Mathematica* does, not *how* it does it. But the purpose of this chapter is to say at least a little about how *Mathematica* does what it does. Appendix A.9 gives some more details.

You should realize at the outset that while knowing about the internals of *Mathematica* may be of intellectual interest, it is usually much less important in practice than one might at first suppose.

Indeed, one of the main points of *Mathematica* is that it provides an environment where you can perform mathematical and other operations without having to think in detail about how these operations are actually carried out inside your computer.

Thus, for example, if you want to factor the polynomial $x^{15} - 1$, you can do this just by giving *Mathematica* the command Factor[x^15 - 1]; you do not have to know the fairly complicated details of how such a factorization is actually carried out by the internal code of *Mathematica*.

Indeed, in almost all practical uses of *Mathematica*, issues about how *Mathematica* works inside turn out to be largely irrelevant. For most purposes it suffices to view *Mathematica* simply as an abstract system which performs certain specified mathematical and other operations.

You might think that knowing how *Mathematica* works inside would be necessary in determining what answers it will give. But this is only very rarely the case. For the vast majority of the computations that *Mathematica* does are completely specified by the definitions of mathematical or other operations.

Thus, for example, 3^40 will always be 12157665459056928801, regardless of how *Mathematica* internally computes this result.

There are some situations, however, where several different answers are all equally consistent with the formal mathematical definitions. Thus, for example, in computing symbolic integrals, there are often several different expressions which all yield the same derivative. Which of these expressions is actually generated by Integrate can then depend on how Integrate works inside.

Here is the answer generated by Integrate.	$In[1]:=$ **Integrate[1/x + 1/x^2, x]**
	$Out[1]= -\dfrac{1}{x} + \text{Log}[x]$
This is an equivalent expression that might have been generated if Integrate worked differently inside.	$In[2]:=$ **Together[%]**
	$Out[2]= \dfrac{-1 + x\,\text{Log}[x]}{x}$

In numerical computations, a similar phenomenon occurs. Thus, for example, `FindRoot` gives you a root of a function. But if there are several roots, which root is actually returned depends on the details of how `FindRoot` works inside.

This finds a particular root of $\cos(x) + \sin(x)$.

```
In[3]:= FindRoot[Cos[x] + Sin[x], {x, 10.5}]
Out[3]= {x → 14.9226}
```

With a different starting point, a different root is found. Which root is found with each starting point depends in detail on the internal algorithm used.

```
In[4]:= FindRoot[Cos[x] + Sin[x], {x, 10.8}]
Out[4]= {x → 11.781}
```

The dependence on the details of internal algorithms can be more significant if you push approximate numerical computations to the limits of their validity.

Thus, for example, if you give `NIntegrate` a pathological integrand, whether it yields a meaningful answer or not can depend on the details of the internal algorithm that it uses.

`NIntegrate` knows that this result is unreliable, and can depend on the details of the internal algorithm, so it prints warning messages.

```
In[5]:= NIntegrate[Sin[1/x], {x, 0, 1}]

NIntegrate::slwcon:
    Numerical integration converging too slowly; suspect
      one of the following: singularity, oscillatory
      integrand, or insufficient WorkingPrecision. If your
      integrand is oscillatory try using the option
      Method->Oscillatory in NIntegrate.

NIntegrate::ncvb:
    NIntegrate failed to converge to prescribed accuracy
      after 7 recursive bisections in x near x = 0.0035126
      8.

Out[5]= 0.504894
```

Traditional numerical computation systems have tended to follow the idea that all computations should yield results that at least nominally have the same precision. A consequence of this idea is that it is not sufficient just to look at a result to know whether it is accurate; you typically also have to analyze the internal algorithm by which the result was found. This fact has tended to make people believe that it is always important to know internal algorithms for numerical computations.

But with the approach that *Mathematica* takes, this is rarely the case. For *Mathematica* can usually use its arbitrary-precision numerical computation capabilities to give results where every digit that is generated follows the exact mathematical specification of the operation being performed.

Even though this is an approximate numerical computation, every digit is determined by the mathematical definition for π.

```
In[6]:= N[Pi, 30]
Out[6]= 3.14159265358979323846264338279
```

Once again, every digit here is determined by the mathematical definition for $\sin(x)$.

```
In[7]:= N[Sin[10^50], 20]
Out[7]= -0.78967249342931008271
```

If you use machine-precision numbers, *Mathematica* cannot give a reliable result, and the answer depends on the details of the internal algorithm used.	*In[8]:=* **Sin[10.^50]** *Out[8]=* -0.4805

It is a general characteristic that whenever the results you get can be affected by the details of internal algorithms, you should not depend on these results. For if nothing else, different versions of *Mathematica* may exhibit differences in these results, either because the algorithms operate slightly differently on different computer systems, or because fundamentally different algorithms are used in versions released at different times.

This is the result for $\sin(10^{50})$ on one type of computer.	*In[1]:=* **Sin[10.^50]** *Out[1]=* -0.4805

Here is the same calculation on another type of computer.	*In[1]:=* **Sin[10.^50]** *Out[1]=* -0.0528229

And here is the result obtained in *Mathematica* Version 1.0.	*In[1]:=* **Sin[10.^50]** *Out[1]=* 0.0937538

Particularly in more advanced applications of *Mathematica*, it may sometimes seem worthwhile to try to analyze internal algorithms in order to predict which way of doing a given computation will be the most efficient. And there are indeed occasionally major improvements that you will be able to make in specific computations as a result of such analyses.

But most often the analyses will not be worthwhile. For the internals of *Mathematica* are quite complicated, and even given a basic description of the algorithm used for a particular purpose, it is usually extremely difficult to reach a reliable conclusion about how the detailed implementation of this algorithm will actually behave in particular circumstances.

A typical problem is that *Mathematica* has many internal optimizations, and the efficiency of a computation can be greatly affected by whether the details of the computation do or do not allow a given internal optimization to be used.

■ 1.12.2 Basic Internal Architecture

numbers	sequences of binary digits
strings	sequences of character code bytes or byte pairs
symbols	pointers to the central table of symbols
general expressions	sequences of pointers to the head and elements

Internal representations used by *Mathematica*.

When you type input into *Mathematica*, a data structure is created in the memory of your computer to represent the expression you have entered.

In general, different pieces of your expression will be stored at different places in memory. Thus, for example, for a list such as {2, x, y + z} the "backbone" of the list will be stored at one place, while each of the actual elements will be stored at a different place.

The backbone of the list then consists just of three "pointers" that specify the addresses in computer memory at which the actual expressions that form the elements of the list are to be found. These expressions then in turn contain pointers to their subexpressions. The chain of pointers ends when one reaches an object such as a number or a string, which is stored directly as a pattern of bits in computer memory.

Crucial to the operation of *Mathematica* is the notion of symbols such as x. Whenever x appears in an expression, *Mathematica* represents it by a pointer. But the pointer is always to the same place in computer memory—an entry in a central table of all symbols defined in your *Mathematica* session.

This table is a repository of all information about each symbol. It contains a pointer to a string giving the symbol's name, as well as pointers to expressions which give rules for evaluating the symbol.

- Recycle memory as soon as the data in it is no longer referenced.

The basic principle of *Mathematica* memory management.

Every piece of memory used by *Mathematica* maintains a count of how many pointers currently point to it. When this count drops to zero, *Mathematica* knows that the piece of memory is no longer being referenced, and immediately makes the piece of memory available for something new.

This strategy essentially ensures that no memory is ever wasted, and that any piece of memory that *Mathematica* uses is actually storing data that you need to access in your *Mathematica* session.

- Create an expression corresponding to the input you have given.
- Process the expression using all rules known for the objects in it.
- Generate output corresponding to the resulting expression.

The basic actions of *Mathematica*.

At the heart of *Mathematica* is a conceptually simple procedure known as the *evaluator* which takes every function that appears in an expression and evaluates that function.

When the function is one of the thousand or so that are built into *Mathematica*, what the evaluator does is to execute directly internal code in the *Mathematica* system. This code is set up to perform the operations corresponding to the function, and then to build a new expression representing the result.

> ■ The built-in functions of *Mathematica* support universal computation.

The basic feature that makes *Mathematica* a self-contained system.

A crucial feature of the built-in functions in *Mathematica* is that they support *universal computation*. What this means is that out of these functions you can construct programs that perform absolutely any kinds of operation that are possible for a computer.

As it turns out, small subsets of *Mathematica*'s built-in functions would be quite sufficient to support universal computation. But having the whole collection of functions makes it in practice easier to construct the programs one needs.

The underlying point, however, is that because *Mathematica* supports universal computation you never have to modify its built-in functions: all you have to do to perform a particular task is to combine these functions in an appropriate way.

Universal computation is the basis for all standard computer languages. But many of these languages rely on the idea of *compilation*. If you use C or Fortran, for example, you first write your program, then you compile it to generate machine code that can actually be executed on your computer.

Mathematica does not require you to go through the compilation step: once you have input an expression, the functions in the expression can immediately be executed.

Often *Mathematica* will preprocess expressions that you enter, arranging things so that subsequent execution will be as efficient as possible. But such preprocessing never affects the results that are generated, and can rarely be seen explicitly.

■ 1.12.3 The Algorithms of *Mathematica*

The built-in functions of *Mathematica* implement a very large number of algorithms from computer science and mathematics. Some of these algorithms are fairly old, but the vast majority had to be created or at least modified specifically for *Mathematica*. Most of the more mathematical algorithms in *Mathematica* ultimately carry out operations which at least at some time in the past were performed by hand. In almost all cases, however, the algorithms use methods very different from those common in hand calculation.

Symbolic integration provides an example. In hand calculation, symbolic integration is typically done by a large number of tricks involving changes of variables and the like.

But in *Mathematica* symbolic integration is performed by a fairly small number of very systematic procedures. For indefinite integration, the idea of these procedures is to find the most general form of the integral, then to differentiate this and try to match up undetermined coefficients.

Often this procedure produces at an intermediate stage immensely complicated algebraic expressions, and sometimes very sophisticated kinds of mathematical functions. But the great advantage of the procedure is that it is completely systematic, and its operation requires no special cleverness of the kind that only a human could be expected to provide.

In having *Mathematica* do integrals, therefore, one can be confident that it will systematically get results, but one cannot expect that the way these results are derived will have much at all to do with the way they would be derived by hand.

The same is true with most of the mathematical algorithms in *Mathematica*. One striking feature is that even for operations that are simple to describe, the systematic algorithms to perform these operations in *Mathematica* involve fairly advanced mathematical or computational ideas.

Thus, for example, factoring a polynomial in x is first done modulo a prime such as 17 by finding the null space of a matrix obtained by reducing high powers of x modulo the prime and the original polynomial. Then factorization over the integers is achieved by "lifting" modulo successive powers of the prime using a collection of intricate theorems in algebra and analysis.

The use of powerful systematic algorithms is important in making the built-in functions in *Mathematica* able to handle difficult and general cases. But for easy cases that may be fairly common in practice it is often possible to use simpler and more efficient algorithms.

As a result, built-in functions in *Mathematica* often have large numbers of extra pieces that handle various kinds of special cases. These extra pieces can contribute greatly to the complexity of the internal code, often taking what would otherwise be a five-page algorithm and making it hundreds of pages long.

Most of the algorithms in *Mathematica*, including all their special cases, were explicitly constructed by hand. But some algorithms were instead effectively created automatically by computer.

Many of the algorithms used for machine-precision numerical evaluation of mathematical functions are examples. The main parts of such algorithms are formulas which are as short as possible but which yield the best numerical approximations.

Most such formulas used in *Mathematica* were actually derived by *Mathematica* itself. Often many months of computation were required, but the result was a short formula that can be used to evaluate functions in an optimal way.

■ 1.12.4 The Software Engineering of *Mathematica*

Mathematica is one of the more complex software systems ever constructed. Its source code is written in a combination of C and *Mathematica*, and for Version 3.0, the code for the kernel consists of about

500,000 lines of C and 80,000 lines of *Mathematica*. This corresponds to roughly 15 megabytes of data, or some 15,000 printed pages.

The C code in *Mathematica* is actually written in a custom extension of C which supports certain memory management and object-oriented features. The *Mathematica* code is optimized using `Share` and `DumpSave`.

In the *Mathematica* kernel the breakdown of different parts of the code is roughly as follows: language and system: 30%; numerical computation: 25%; algebraic computation: 25%; graphics and kernel output: 20%.

Most of this code is fairly dense and algorithmic: those parts that are in effect simple procedures or tables use minimal code since they tend to be written at a higher level—often directly in *Mathematica*.

The source code for the kernel, save a fraction of a percent, is identical for all computer systems on which *Mathematica* runs.

For the front end, however, a significant amount of specialized code is needed to support each different type of user interface environment. The front end contains about 175,000 lines of system-independent C source code, of which roughly 60,000 lines are concerned with expression formatting. Then there are between 20,000 and 50,000 lines of specific code that is customized for each user interface environment.

Mathematica uses a client-server model of computing. The front end and kernel are connected via *MathLink*—the same system as is used to communicate with other programs.

Within the C code portion of the *Mathematica* kernel, modularity and consistency are achieved by having different parts communicate primarily by exchanging complete *Mathematica* expressions.

But it should be noted that even though different parts of the system are quite independent at the level of source code, they have many algorithmic interdependencies. Thus, for example, it is common for numerical functions to make extensive use of algebraic algorithms, or for graphics code to use fairly advanced mathematical algorithms embodied in quite different *Mathematica* functions.

Since the beginning of its development in 1986, the effort spent directly on creating the source code for *Mathematica* is a substantial fraction of a thousand man-years. In addition, a comparable or somewhat larger effort has been spent on testing and verification.

The source code of *Mathematica* has changed greatly since Version 1.0 was released. The total number of lines of code in the kernel grew from 150,000 in Version 1.0 to 350,000 in Version 2.0 and nearly 600,000 in Version 3.0. In addition, at every stage existing code has been revised—so that Version 3.0 has only a few percent of its code in common with Version 1.0.

Despite these changes in internal code, however, the user-level design of *Mathematica* has remained compatible from Version 1.0 on. Much functionality has been added, but programs created for *Mathematica* Version 1.0 will almost always run absolutely unchanged under Version 3.0.

+■ 1.12.5 Testing and Verification

Every version of *Mathematica* is subjected to a large amount of testing before it is released. The vast majority of this testing is done by an automated system that is written in *Mathematica*.

The automated system feeds millions of pieces of input to *Mathematica*, and checks that the output obtained from them is correct. Often there is some subtlety in doing such checking: one must account for different behavior of randomized algorithms and for such issues as differences in machine-precision arithmetic on different computers.

The test inputs used by the automated system are obtained in several ways:

■ For every *Mathematica* function, inputs are devised that exercise both common and extreme cases.

■ Inputs are devised to exercise each feature of the internal code.

■ All the examples in this book and in other books about *Mathematica* are used.

■ Standard numerical tables are optically scanned for test inputs.

■ Formulas from all standard mathematical tables are entered.

■ Exercises from textbooks are entered.

■ For pairs of functions such as `Integrate` and `D` or `Factor` and `Expand`, random expressions are generated and tested.

When tests are run, the automated testing system checks not only the results, but also side effects such as messages, as well as memory usage and speed.

There is also a special instrumented version of *Mathematica* which is set up to perform internal consistency tests. This version of *Mathematica* runs at a small fraction of the speed of the real *Mathematica*, but at every step it checks internal memory consistency, interruptibility, and so on.

The instrumented version of *Mathematica* also records which pieces of *Mathematica* source code have been accessed, allowing one to confirm that all of the various internal functions in *Mathematica* have been exercised by the tests given.

All standard *Mathematica* tests are routinely run on each version of *Mathematica*, on each different computer system. Depending on the speed of the computer system, these tests take a few days to a few weeks of computer time.

In addition, huge numbers of tests based on random inputs are run for the equivalent of many years of computer time on a sampling of different computer systems.

Even with all this testing, however, it is inevitable in a system as complex as *Mathematica* that errors will remain.

The standards of correctness for *Mathematica* are certainly much higher than for typical mathematical proofs. But just as long proofs will inevitably contain errors that go undetected for many years, so also a complex software system such as *Mathematica* will contain errors that go undetected even after millions of people have used it.

Nevertheless, particularly after all the testing that has been done on it, the probability that you will actually discover an error in *Mathematica* in the course of your work is extremely low.

Doubtless there will be times when *Mathematica* does things you do not expect. But you should realize that the probabilities are such that it is vastly more likely that there is something wrong with your input to *Mathematica* or your understanding of what is happening than with the internal code of the *Mathematica* system itself.

If you do believe that you have found a genuine error in *Mathematica*, then you should contact Wolfram Research at the addresses given in the front of this book so that the error can be corrected in future versions.

Part 2

Part 1 introduced Mathematica by showing you how to use some of its more common features. This part looks at Mathematica in a different way. Instead of discussing individual features, it concentrates on the global structure of Mathematica, and describes the framework into which all the features fit.

When you first start doing calculations with Mathematica, you will probably find it sufficient just to read the relevant parts of Part 1. However, once you have some general familiarity with the Mathematica system, you should make a point of reading this part.

This part describes the basic structure of the Mathematica language, with which you can extend Mathematica, adding your own functions, objects or other constructs. This part shows how Mathematica uses a fairly small number of very powerful symbolic programming methods to allow you to build up many different kinds of programs.

Most of this part assumes no specific prior knowledge of computer science. Nevertheless, some of it ventures into some fairly complicated issues. You can probably ignore these issues unless they specifically affect programs you are writing.

If you are an expert on computer languages, you may be able to glean some understanding of Mathematica by looking at the Reference Guide at the end of this book. Nevertheless, to get a real appreciation for the principles of Mathematica, you will have to read this part.

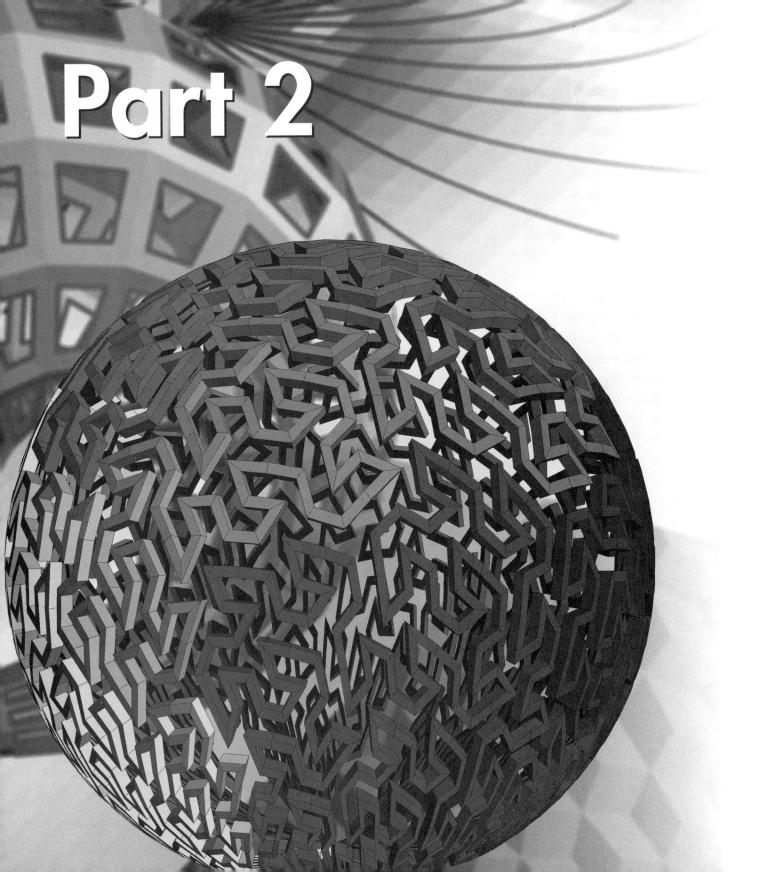

Part 2

Principles of *Mathematica*

2.1 Expressions

■ 2.1.1 Everything Is an Expression

Mathematica handles many different kinds of things: mathematical formulas, lists and graphics, to name a few. Although they often look very different, *Mathematica* represents all of these things in one uniform way. They are all *expressions*.

A prototypical example of a *Mathematica* expression is f[x, y]. You might use f[x, y] to represent a mathematical function $f(x, y)$. The function is named f, and it has two arguments, x and y.

You do not always have to write expressions in the form $f[x, y, \dots]$. For example, x + y is also an expression. When you type in x + y, *Mathematica* converts it to the standard form Plus[x, y]. Then, when it prints it out again, it gives it as x + y.

The same is true of other "operators", such as ^ (Power) and / (Divide).

In fact, everything you type into *Mathematica* is treated as an expression.

x + y + z	Plus[x, y, z]
x y z	Times[x, y, z]
x^n	Power[x, n]
{a, b, c}	List[a, b, c]
a -> b	Rule[a, b]
a = b	Set[a, b]

Some examples of *Mathematica* expressions.

You can see the full form of any expression by using FullForm[*expr*].

Here is an expression.

```
In[1]:= x + y + z
Out[1]= x + y + z
```

This is the full form of the expression.

```
In[2]:= FullForm[%]
Out[2]//FullForm= Plus[x, y, z]
```

Here is another expression.

```
In[3]:= 1 + x^2 + (y + z)^2
```
$$Out[3]= 1 + x^2 + (y + z)^2$$

Its full form has several nested pieces.

```
In[4]:= FullForm[%]
Out[4]//FullForm= Plus[1, Power[x, 2], Power[Plus[y, z], 2]]
```

The object *f* in an expression *f*[*x*, *y*, ...] is known as the *head* of the expression. You can extract it using `Head[`*expr*`]`. Particularly when you write programs in *Mathematica*, you will often want to test the head of an expression to find out what kind of thing the expression is.

Head gives the "function name" f.

In[5]:= **Head[f[x, y]]**

Out[5]= f

Here Head gives the name of the "operator".

In[6]:= **Head[a + b + c]**

Out[6]= Plus

Everything has a head.

In[7]:= **Head[{a, b, c}]**

Out[7]= List

Numbers also have heads.

In[8]:= **Head[23432]**

Out[8]= Integer

You can distinguish different kinds of numbers by their heads.

In[9]:= **Head[345.6]**

Out[9]= Real

`Head[`*expr*`]`	give the head of an expression: the *f* in *f*[*x*, *y*]
`FullForm[`*expr*`]`	display an expression in the full form used by *Mathematica*

Functions for manipulating expressions.

■ 2.1.2 The Meaning of Expressions

The notion of expressions is a crucial unifying principle in *Mathematica*. It is the fact that every object in *Mathematica* has the same underlying structure that makes it possible for *Mathematica* to cover so many areas with a comparatively small number of basic operations.

Although all expressions have the same basic structure, there are many different ways that expressions can be used. Here are a few of the interpretations you can give to the parts of an expression.

meaning of f	meaning of x, y, ...	examples
Function	arguments or parameters	`Sin[x]`, `f[x, y]`
Command	arguments or parameters	`Expand[(x + 1)^2]`
Operator	operands	`x + y`, `a = b`
Head	elements	`{a, b, c}`
Object type	contents	`RGBColor[r, g, b]`

Some interpretations of parts of expressions.

Expressions in *Mathematica* are often used to specify operations. So, for example, typing in 2 + 3 causes 2 and 3 to be added together, while `Factor[x^6 - 1]` performs factorization.

Perhaps an even more important use of expressions in *Mathematica*, however, is to maintain a structure, which can then be acted on by other functions. An expression like `{a, b, c}` does not specify an operation. It merely maintains a list structure, which contains a collection of three elements. Other functions, such as `Reverse` or `Dot`, can act on this structure.

The full form of the expression `{a, b, c}` is `List[a, b, c]`. The head `List` performs no operations. Instead, its purpose is to serve as a "tag" to specify the "type" of the structure.

You can use expressions in *Mathematica* to create your own structures. For example, you might want to represent points in three-dimensional space, specified by three coordinates. You could give each point as `point[x, y, z]`. The "function" `point` again performs no operation. It serves merely to collect the three coordinates together, and to label the resulting object as a `point`.

You can think of expressions like `point[x, y, z]` as being "packets of data", tagged with a particular head. Even though all expressions have the same basic structure, you can distinguish different "types" of expressions by giving them different heads. You can then set up transformation rules and programs which treat different types of expressions in different ways.

■ 2.1.3 Special Ways to Input Expressions

Mathematica allows you to use special notation for many common operators. For example, although internally *Mathematica* represents a sum of two terms as `Plus[x, y]`, you can enter this expression in the much more convenient form $x + y$.

The *Mathematica* language has a definite grammar which specifies how your input should be converted to internal form. One aspect of the grammar is that it specifies how pieces of your input should be grouped. For example, if you enter an expression such as `a + b ^ c`, the *Mathematica* grammar specifies that this should be considered, following standard mathematical notation, as `a + (b ^ c)` rather than `(a + b) ^ c`. *Mathematica* chooses this grouping because it treats the operator `^` as having a higher *precedence* than +. In general, the arguments of operators with higher precedence are grouped before those of operators with lower precedence.

You should realize that absolutely every special input form in *Mathematica* is assigned a definite precedence. This includes not only the traditional mathematical operators, but also forms such as ->, := or the semicolons used to separate expressions in a *Mathematica* program.

The table on pages 972–977 gives all the operators of *Mathematica* in order of decreasing precedence. The precedence is arranged, where possible, to follow standard mathematical usage, and to minimize the number of parentheses that are usually needed.

You will find, for example, that relational operators such as < have lower precedence than arithmetic operators such as +. This means that you can write expressions such as x + y > 7 without using parentheses.

There are nevertheless many cases where you do have to use parentheses. For example, since ; has a lower precedence than =, you need to use parentheses to write x = (a ; b). *Mathematica* interprets the expression x = a ; b as (x = a) ; b. In general, it can never hurt to include extra parentheses, but it can cause a great deal of trouble if you leave parentheses out, and *Mathematica* interprets your input in a way you do not expect.

$f[x, y]$	standard form for $f[x, y]$
$f @ x$	prefix form for $f[x]$
$x // f$	postfix form for $f[x]$
$x \sim f \sim y$	infix form for $f[x, y]$

Four ways to write expressions in *Mathematica*.

There are several common types of operators in *Mathematica*. The + in $x + y$ is an "infix" operator. The − in $-p$ is a "prefix" operator. Even when you enter an expression such as $f[x, y, \dots]$ *Mathematica* allows you to do it in ways that mimic infix, prefix and postfix forms.

This "postfix form" is exactly equivalent to f[x + y].	*In[1]:=* **x + y //f** *Out[1]=* f[x + y]
You will often want to add functions like N as "afterthoughts", and give them in postfix form.	*In[2]:=* **3^(1/4) + 1 //N** *Out[2]=* 2.31607
It is sometimes easier to understand what a function is doing when you write it in infix form.	*In[3]:=* **{a, b, c} ~Join~ {d, e}** *Out[3]=* {a, b, c, d, e}

You should notice that // has very low precedence. If you put //*f* at the end of any expression containing arithmetic or logical operators, the *f* is applied to the *whole expression*. So, for example, x+y //f means f[x+y], not x+f[y].

The prefix form @ has a much higher precedence. f @ x + y is equivalent to f[x] + y, not f[x + y]. You can write f[x + y] in prefix form as f @ (x + y).

■ 2.1.4 Parts of Expressions

Since lists are just a particular kind of expression, it will come as no surprise that you can refer to parts of any expression much as you refer to parts of a list.

This gets the second element in the list {a, b, c}.	*In[1]:=* **{a, b, c}[[2]]**
	Out[1]= b
You can use the same method to get the second element in the sum x + y + z.	*In[2]:=* **(x + y + z)[[2]]**
	Out[2]= y
This gives the last element in the sum.	*In[3]:=* **(x + y + z)[[-1]]**
	Out[3]= z
Part 0 is the head.	*In[4]:=* **(x + y + z)[[0]]**
	Out[4]= Plus

You can refer to parts of an expression such as *f*[*g*[*a*], *g*[b]] just as you refer to parts of nested lists.

This is part 1.	*In[5]:=* **f[g[a], g[b]] [[1]]**
	Out[5]= g[a]
This is part {1,1}.	*In[6]:=* **f[g[a], g[b]] [[1, 1]]**
	Out[6]= a
This extracts part {2,1} of the expression 1 + x^2.	*In[7]:=* **(1 + x^2) [[2, 1]]**
	Out[7]= x
To see what part is {2,1}, you can look at the full form of the expression.	*In[8]:=* **FullForm[1 + x^2]**
	Out[8]//FullForm= Plus[1, Power[x, 2]]

You should realize that the assignment of indices to parts of expressions is done on the basis of the internal *Mathematica* forms of the expression, as shown by FullForm. These forms do not always correspond directly with what you see printed out. This is particularly true for algebraic expressions, where *Mathematica* uses a standard internal form, but prints the expressions in special ways.

Here is the internal form of x / y.	*In[9]:=* **FullForm[x / y]**
	Out[9]//FullForm= Times[x, Power[y, -1]]

It is the internal form that is used in specifying parts.

In[10]:= **(x / y)[[2]]**

$$Out[10]= \frac{1}{y}$$

You can manipulate parts of expressions just as you manipulate parts of lists.

This replaces the third part of a + b + c + d by x^2. Note that the sum is automatically rearranged when the replacement is done.

In[11]:= **ReplacePart[a + b + c + d, x^2, 3]**

Out[11]= $a + b + d + x^2$

Here is an expression.

In[12]:= **t = 1 + (3 + x)^2 / y**

$$Out[12]= 1 + \frac{(3+x)^2}{y}$$

This is the full form of t.

In[13]:= **FullForm[t]**

Out[13]//FullForm= Plus[1, Times[Power[Plus[3, x], 2], Power[y, -1]]]

This resets a part of the expression t.

In[14]:= **t[[2, 1, 1]] = x**

Out[14]= x

Now the form of t has been changed.

In[15]:= **t**

$$Out[15]= 1 + \frac{x^2}{y}$$

Part[*expr*, *n*] or *expr*[[*n*]]   the nth part of *expr*

Part[*expr*, {*n*$_1$, *n*$_2$, ... }] or *expr*[[{*n*$_1$, *n*$_2$, ... }]]
a combination of parts of an expression

ReplacePart[*expr*, *elem*, *n*]   replace the nth part of *expr* by *elem*

Functions for manipulating parts of expressions.

Section 1.2.4 discussed how you can use lists of indices to pick out several elements of a list at a time. You can use the same procedure to pick out several parts in an expression at a time.

This picks out elements 2 and 4 in the list, and gives a list of these elements.

In[16]:= **{a, b, c, d, e}[[{2, 4}]]**

Out[16]= {b, d}

This picks out parts 2 and 4 of the sum, and gives a *sum* of these elements.

In[17]:= **(a + b + c + d + e)[[{2, 4}]]**

Out[17]= b + d

Any part in an expression can be viewed as being an argument of some function. When you pick out several parts by giving a list of indices, the parts are combined using the same function as in the expression.

■ 2.1.5 Manipulating Expressions like Lists

You can use most of the list operations discussed in Section 1.8 on any kind of *Mathematica* expression. By using these operations, you can manipulate the structure of expressions in many ways.

Here is an expression that corresponds to a sum of terms.	*In[1]:=* **t = 1 + x + x^2 + y^2** *Out[1]=* $1 + x + x^2 + y^2$
Take[t, 2] takes the first two elements from t, just as if t were a list.	*In[2]:=* **Take[t, 2]** *Out[2]=* $1 + x$
Length gives the number of elements in t.	*In[3]:=* **Length[t]** *Out[3]=* 4
You can use FreeQ[*expr*, *form*] to test whether *form* appears nowhere in *expr*.	*In[4]:=* **FreeQ[t, x]** *Out[4]=* False
This gives a list of the positions at which x appears in t.	*In[5]:=* **Position[t, x]** *Out[5]=* {{2}, {3, 1}}

You should remember that all functions which manipulate the structure of expressions act on the internal forms of these expressions. You can see these forms using FullForm[*expr*]. They may not be what you would expect from the printed versions of the expressions.

Here is a function with four arguments.	*In[6]:=* **f[a, b, c, d]** *Out[6]=* f[a, b, c, d]
You can add an argument using Append.	*In[7]:=* **Append[%, e]** *Out[7]=* f[a, b, c, d, e]
This reverses the arguments.	*In[8]:=* **Reverse[%]** *Out[8]=* f[e, d, c, b, a]

There are a few extra functions that can be used with expressions, as discussed in Section 2.2.10.

■ 2.1.6 Expressions as Trees

Here is an expression in full form.	*In[1]:=* **FullForm[x^3 + (1 + x)^2]** *Out[1]//FullForm=* Plus[Power[x, 3], Power[Plus[1, x], 2]]
TreeForm prints out expressions to show their "tree" structure.	*In[2]:=* **TreeForm[x^3 + (1 + x)^2]** *Out[2]//TreeForm=* Plus[...]

$$Out[2]//TreeForm= \text{Plus}\left[\begin{array}{cc} | & | \\ \text{Power[x, 3]} & \text{Power}\left[\begin{array}{cc} | & , 2 \\ \text{Plus[1, x]} & \end{array}\right] \end{array}\right]$$

You can think of any *Mathematica* expression as a tree. In the expression above, the top node in the tree consists of a Plus. From this node come two "branches", x^3 and (1 + x)^2. From the x^3 node, there are then two branches, x and 3, which can be viewed as "leaves" of the tree.

This matrix is a simple tree with just two levels.	*In[3]:=* **TreeForm[{{a, b}, {c, d}}]**

$$Out[3]//TreeForm= \text{List} \left[\underset{\text{List}[a, b]}{\mid} , \underset{\text{List}[c, d]}{\mid} \right]$$

Here is a more complicated expression.	*In[4]:=* **{{a b, c d^2}, {x^3 y^4}}**

$$Out[4]= \{\{a\,b, c\,d^2\}, \{x^3\,y^4\}\}$$

The tree for this expression has several levels. The representation of the tree here was too long to fit on a single line, so it had to be broken onto two lines.

In[5]:= **TreeForm[%]**

$$Out[5]//TreeForm= \text{List} \left[\mid \underset{\underset{\text{Times}[a, b]}{\text{List}\left[\mid , \mid \underset{\text{Power}[d, 2]}{\text{Times}\left[c, \mid\right]}\right]}}{} , \right.$$

$$\left. \underset{\text{List}\left[\mid \underset{\underset{\text{Power}[x, 3]}{\text{Times}\left[\mid , \mid \right]}}{}\right]}{\mid} \underset{\text{Power}[y, 4]}{} \right]$$

The indices that label each part of an expression have a simple interpretation in terms of trees. Descending from the top node of the tree, each index specifies which branch to take in order to reach the part you want.

■ 2.1.7 Levels in Expressions

The **Part** function allows you to access specific parts of *Mathematica* expressions. But particularly when your expressions have fairly uniform structure, it is often convenient to be able to refer to a whole collection of parts at the same time.

Levels provide a general way of specifying collections of parts in *Mathematica* expressions. Many *Mathematica* functions allow you to specify the levels in an expression on which they should act.

Here is a simple expression, displayed in tree form.	*In[1]:=* **(t = {x, {x, y}, y}) // TreeForm**

$$Out[1]//TreeForm= \text{List} \left[x, \underset{\text{List}[x, y]}{\mid} , y \right]$$

This searches for x in the expression t down to level 1. It finds only one occurrence.	*In[2]:=* **Position[t, x, 1]**

$$Out[2]= \{\{1\}\}$$

This searches down to level 2. Now it finds both occurrences of x.	*In[3]:=* **Position[t, x, 2]** *Out[3]=* {{1}, {2, 1}}
This searches only at level 2. It finds just one occurrence of x.	*In[4]:=* **Position[t, x, {2}]** *Out[4]=* {{2, 1}}

Position[*expr*, *form*, *n*]	give the positions at which *form* occurs in *expr* down to level *n*
Position[*expr*, *form*, {*n*}]	give the positions exactly at level *n*

Controlling Position using levels.

You can think of levels in expressions in terms of trees. The level of a particular part in an expression is simply the distance down the tree at which that part appears, with the top of the tree considered as level 0.

It is equivalent to say that the parts which appear at level *n* are those that can be specified by a sequence of exactly *n* indices.

n	levels 1 through *n*
Infinity	all levels (except 0)
{*n*}	level *n* only
{n_1, n_2}	levels n_1 through n_2
Heads -> True	include heads
Heads -> False	exclude heads

Level specifications.

Here is an expression, displayed in tree form.	*In[5]:=* **(u = f[f[g[a], a], a, h[a], f]) // TreeForm** *Out[5]//TreeForm=* f[, a, , f] f[, a] h[a] g[a]
This searches for a at levels from 2 downwards.	*In[6]:=* **Position[u, a, {2, Infinity}]** *Out[6]=* {{1, 1, 1}, {1, 2}, {3, 1}}
This shows where f appears other than in the head of an expression.	*In[7]:=* **Position[u, f, Heads->False]** *Out[7]=* {{4}}

This includes occurrences of f in heads of expressions.

In[8]:= **Position[u, f, Heads->True]**

Out[8]= {{0}, {1, 0}, {4}}

Level[*expr, lev***]**	a list of the parts of *expr* at the levels specified by *lev*
Depth[*expr***]**	the total number of levels in *expr*

Testing and extracting levels.

This gives a list of all parts of u that occur down to level 2.

In[9]:= **Level[u, 2]**

Out[9]= {g[a], a, f[g[a], a], a, a, h[a], f}

Here are the parts specifically at level 2.

In[10]:= **Level[u, {2}]**

Out[10]= {g[a], a, a}

When you have got the hang of ordinary levels, you can try thinking about *negative levels*. Negative levels label parts of expressions starting at the *bottom* of the tree. Level -1 contains all the leaves of the tree: objects like symbols and numbers.

This shows the parts of u at level -1.

In[11]:= **Level[u, {-1}]**

Out[11]= {a, a, a, a, f}

You can think of expressions as having a "depth", which is equal to the maximum number of levels shown by **TreeForm**. In general, level -*n* in an expression is defined to consist of all subexpressions whose depth is *n*.

The depth of g[a] is 2.

In[12]:= **Depth[g[a]]**

Out[12]= 2

The parts of u at level -2 are those that have depth exactly 2.

In[13]:= **Level[u, {-2}]**

Out[13]= {g[a], h[a]}

2.2 Functional Operations

■ 2.2.1 Function Names as Expressions

In an expression like $f[x]$, the "function name" f is itself an expression, and you can treat it as you would any other expression.

You can replace names of functions using transformation rules.	`In[1]:= f[x] + f[1 - x]  /.  f -> g` `Out[1]= g[1 - x] + g[x]`
Any assignments you have made are used on function names.	`In[2]:= p1 = p2; p1[x, y]` `Out[2]= p2[x, y]`
This defines a function which takes a function name as an argument.	`In[3]:= pf[f_, x_] := f[x] + f[1 - x]`
This gives Log as the function name to use.	`In[4]:= pf[Log, q]` `Out[4]= Log[1 - q] + Log[q]`

The ability to treat the names of functions just like other kinds of expressions is an important consequence of the symbolic nature of the *Mathematica* language. It makes possible the whole range of *functional operations* discussed in the sections that follow.

Ordinary *Mathematica* functions such as Log or Integrate typically operate on data such as numbers and algebraic expressions. *Mathematica* functions that represent functional operations, however, can operate not only on ordinary data, but also on functions themselves. Thus, for example, the functional operation InverseFunction takes a *Mathematica* function name as an argument, and represents the inverse of that function.

InverseFunction is a functional operation: it takes a *Mathematica* function as an argument, and returns another function which represents its inverse.	`In[5]:= InverseFunction[ArcSin]` `Out[5]= Sin`
The result obtained from InverseFunction is a function which you can apply to data.	`In[6]:= %[x]` `Out[6]= Sin[x]`
You can also use InverseFunction in a purely symbolic way.	`In[7]:= InverseFunction[f] [x]` `Out[7]= f^{(-1)} [x]`

There are many kinds of functional operations in *Mathematica*. Some represent mathematical operations; others represent various kinds of procedures and algorithms.

Unless you are familiar with advanced symbolic languages, you will probably not recognize most of the functional operations discussed in the sections that follow. At first, the operations may seem difficult to understand. But it is worth persisting. Functional operations provide one of the most conceptually and practically efficient ways to use *Mathematica*.

■ 2.2.2 Applying Functions Repeatedly

Nest[*f*, *x*, *n*]	apply the function *f* nested *n* times to *x*
NestList[*f*, *x*, *n*]	generate the list {*x*, *f*[*x*], *f*[*f*[*x*]], ... }, where *f* is nested up to *n* deep
FixedPoint[*f*, *x*]	apply the function *f* repeatedly until the result no longer changes
FixedPointList[*f*, *x*]	generate the list {*x*, *f*[*x*], *f*[*f*[*x*]], ... }, stopping when the elements no longer change
FixedPoint[*f*, *x*, SameTest -> *comp*]	stop when the function *comp* applied to two successive results yields True

Ways to apply functions of one argument repeatedly.

Nest[*f*, *x*, *n*] takes the "name" *f* of a function, and applies the function *n* times to *x*.

In[1]:= **Nest[f, x, 4]**

Out[1]= f[f[f[f[x]]]]

This makes a list of each successive nesting.

In[2]:= **NestList[f, x, 4]**

Out[2]= {x, f[x], f[f[x]], f[f[f[x]]], f[f[f[f[x]]]]}

Here is a simple function.

In[3]:= **recip[x_] := 1/(1 + x)**

You can iterate the function using Nest.

In[4]:= **Nest[recip, x, 3]**

$$Out[4]= \cfrac{1}{1 + \cfrac{1}{1 + \cfrac{1}{1+x}}}$$

Many programs you write will involve operations that need to be iterated several times. Nest and NestList are powerful constructs for doing this.

Here is a function that takes one step in Newton's approximation to $\sqrt{3}$.

In[5]:= **newton3[x_] := N[1/2 (x + 3/x)]**

Here are five successive iterates of the function, starting at *x* = 1.

In[6]:= **NestList[newton3, 1.0, 5]**

Out[6]= {1., 2., 1.75, 1.73214, 1.73205, 1.73205}

Using the function FixedPoint, you can automatically continue applying newton3 until the result no longer changes.

In[7]:= **FixedPoint[newton3, 1.0]**

Out[7]= 1.73205

Here is the sequence of results.	*In[8]:=* **FixedPointList[newton3, 1.0]**
	Out[8]= {1., 2., 1.75, 1.73214, 1.73205, 1.73205, 1.73205}
You control when FixedPointList stops by giving a function with which to compare successive results.	*In[9]:=* **FixedPointList[newton3, 1.0,** **SameTest -> (Abs[#1 - #2] < 10.^-4 &)]**
	Out[9]= {1., 2., 1.75, 1.73214, 1.73205}

The functional operations Nest and NestList take a function *f* of one argument, and apply it repeatedly. At each step, they use the result of the previous step as the new argument of *f*.

It is important to generalize this notion to functions of two arguments. You can again apply the function repeatedly, but now each result you get supplies only one of the new arguments you need. A convenient approach is to get the other argument at each step from the successive elements of a list.

FoldList[*f*, *x*, {*a*, *b*, ... }]	create the list {*x*, *f*[*x*, *a*], *f*[*f*[*x*, *a*], *b*], ... }
Fold[*f*, *x*, {*a*, *b*, ... }]	give the last element of the list produced by FoldList[*f*, *x*, {*a*, *b*, ... }]

Ways to repeatedly apply functions of two arguments.

Here is an example of what FoldList does.	*In[10]:=* **FoldList[f, x, {a, b, c}]**
	Out[10]= {x, f[x, a], f[f[x, a], b], f[f[f[x, a], b], c]}
Fold gives the last element of the list produced by FoldList.	*In[11]:=* **Fold[f, x, {a, b, c}]**
	Out[11]= f[f[f[x, a], b], c]
This gives a list of cumulative sums.	*In[12]:=* **FoldList[Plus, 0, {a, b, c}]**
	Out[12]= {0, a, a + b, a + b + c}

Using Fold and FoldList you can write many elegant and efficient programs in *Mathematica*. In some cases, you may find it helpful to think of Fold and FoldList as producing a simple nesting of a family of functions indexed by their first argument.

This defines a function nextdigit.	*In[13]:=* **nextdigit[a_, b_] := 10 a + b**
Here is a rather elegant definition of a function that gives the number corresponding to a list of digits in base 10.	*In[14]:=* **tonumber[digits_] := Fold[nextdigit, 0, digits]**
Here is an example of tonumber in action.	*In[15]:=* **tonumber[{1, 3, 7, 2, 9, 1}]**
	Out[15]= 137291

■ 2.2.3 Applying Functions to Lists and Other Expressions

In an expression like f[{a, b, c}] you are giving a list as the argument to a function. Often you need instead to apply a function directly to the elements of a list, rather than to the list as a whole. You can do this in *Mathematica* using Apply.

This makes each element of the list an argument of the function f.	In[1]:= **Apply[f, {a, b, c}]**
	Out[1]= f[a, b, c]
This gives Plus[a, b, c] which yields the sum of the elements in the list.	In[2]:= **Apply[Plus, {a, b, c}]**
	Out[2]= a + b + c
Here is the definition of the statistical mean, written using Apply.	In[3]:= **mean[list_] := Apply[Plus, list] / Length[list]**

Apply[*f*, {*a*, *b*, ... }]	apply *f* to a list, giving *f*[*a*, *b*, ...]
Apply[*f*, *expr*] or *f* @@ *expr*	apply *f* to the top level of an expression
Apply[*f*, *expr*, *lev*]	apply *f* at the specified levels in an expression

Applying functions to lists and other expressions.

What Apply does in general is to replace the head of an expression with the function you specify. Here it replaces Plus by List.	In[4]:= **Apply[List, a + b + c]**
	Out[4]= {a, b, c}
Here is a matrix.	In[5]:= **m = {{a, b, c}, {b, c, d}}**
	Out[5]= {{a, b, c}, {b, c, d}}
Using Apply without an explicit level specification replaces the top-level list with f.	In[6]:= **Apply[f, m]**
	Out[6]= f[{a, b, c}, {b, c, d}]
This applies f only to parts of m at level 1.	In[7]:= **Apply[f, m, {1}]**
	Out[7]= {f[a, b, c], f[b, c, d]}
This applies f at levels 0 through 1.	In[8]:= **Apply[f, m, {0, 1}]**
	Out[8]= f[f[a, b, c], f[b, c, d]]

■ 2.2.4 Applying Functions to Parts of Expressions

If you have a list of elements, it is often important to be able to apply a function separately to each of the elements. You can do this in *Mathematica* using Map.

This applies f separately to each element in a list.	In[1]:= **Map[f, {a, b, c}]**
	Out[1]= {f[a], f[b], f[c]}
This defines a function which takes the first two elements from a list.	In[2]:= **take2[list_] := Take[list, 2]**
You can use Map to apply take2 to each element of a list.	In[3]:= **Map[take2, {{1, 3, 4}, {5, 6, 7}, {2, 1, 6, 6}}]**
	Out[3]= {{1, 3}, {5, 6}, {2, 1}}

> Map[*f*, {*a*, *b*, ... }]   apply *f* to each element in a list, giving {*f*[*a*], *f*[*b*], ... }

Applying a function to each element in a list.

What Map[*f*, *expr*] effectively does is to "wrap" the function *f* around each element of the expression *expr*. You can use Map on any expression, not just a list.

This applies f to each element in the sum.	In[4]:= **Map[f, a + b + c]**
	Out[4]= f[a] + f[b] + f[c]
This applies Sqrt to each argument of g.	In[5]:= **Map[Sqrt, g[x^2, x^3]]**
	Out[5]= g[$\sqrt{x^2}$, $\sqrt{x^3}$]

Map[*f*, *expr*] applies *f* to the first level of parts in *expr*. You can use MapAll[*f*, *expr*] to apply *f* to *all* the parts of *expr*.

This defines a 2 × 2 matrix m.	In[6]:= **m = {{a, b}, {c, d}}**
	Out[6]= {{a, b}, {c, d}}
Map applies f to the first level of m, in this case the rows of the matrix.	In[7]:= **Map[f, m]**
	Out[7]= {f[{a, b}], f[{c, d}]}
MapAll applies f at *all* levels in m. If you look carefully at this expression, you will see an f wrapped around every part.	In[8]:= **MapAll[f, m]**
	Out[8]= f[{{f[{f[a], f[b]}], f[{f[c], f[d]}]}}]

In general, you can use level specifications as described on page 236 to tell Map to which parts of an expression to apply your function.

This applies f only to the parts of m at level 2.	In[9]:= **Map[f, m, {2}]**
	Out[9]= {{f[a], f[b]}, {f[c], f[d]}}
Setting the option Heads->True wraps f around the head of each part, as well as its elements.	In[10]:= **Map[f, m, Heads->True]**
	Out[10]= f[List][f[{a, b}], f[{c, d}]]

`Map[f, expr]` or `f /@ expr`	apply *f* to the first-level parts of *expr*
`MapAll[f, expr]` or `f //@ expr`	apply *f* to all parts of *expr*
`Map[f, expr, lev]`	apply *f* to each part of *expr* at levels specified by *lev*

Ways to apply a function to different parts of expressions.

Level specifications allow you to tell `Map` to which levels of parts in an expression you want a function applied. With `MapAt`, however, you can instead give an explicit list of parts where you want a function applied. You specify each part by giving its indices, as discussed in Section 2.1.4.

Here is a 2×3 matrix.

In[11]:= `mm = {{a, b, c}, {b, c, d}}`

Out[11]= {{a, b, c}, {b, c, d}}

This applies f to parts {1, 2} and {2, 3}.

In[12]:= `MapAt[f, mm, {{1, 2}, {2, 3}}]`

Out[12]= {{a, f[b], c}, {b, c, f[d]}}

This gives a list of the positions at which b occurs in mm.

In[13]:= `Position[mm, b]`

Out[13]= {{1, 2}, {2, 1}}

You can feed the list of positions you get from `Position` directly into `MapAt`.

In[14]:= `MapAt[f, mm, %]`

Out[14]= {{a, f[b], c}, {f[b], c, d}}

To avoid ambiguity, you must put each part specification in a list, even when it involves only one index.

In[15]:= `MapAt[f, {a, b, c, d}, {{2}, {3}}]`

Out[15]= {a, f[b], f[c], d}

`MapAt[f, expr, {part₁, part₂, ... }]`	
	apply *f* to specified parts of *expr*

Applying a function to specific parts of an expression.

Here is an expression.

In[16]:= `t = 1 + (3 + x)^2 / x`

Out[16]= $1 + \dfrac{(3+x)^2}{x}$

This is the full form of t.

In[17]:= `FullForm[ t ]`

Out[17]//FullForm= Plus[1, Times[Power[x, -1], Power[Plus[3, x], 2]]]

You can use `MapAt` on any expression. Remember that parts are numbered on the basis of the full forms of expressions.

In[18]:= `MapAt[f, t, {{2, 1, 1}, {2, 2}}]`

Out[18]= $1 + \dfrac{f\left[(3+x)^2\right]}{f[x]}$

MapIndexed[*f*, *expr*]	apply *f* to the elements of an expression, giving the part specification of each element as a second argument to *f*
MapIndexed[*f*, *expr*, *lev*]	apply *f* to parts at specified levels, giving the list of indices for each part as successive arguments to *f*

Applying a function to parts and their indices.

This applies f to each element in a list, giving the index of the element as a second argument to f.

```
In[19]:= MapIndexed[f, {a, b, c}]
Out[19]= {f[a, {1}], f[b, {2}], f[c, {3}]}
```

This applies f to both levels in a matrix.

```
In[20]:= MapIndexed[f, {{a, b}, {c, d}}, 2]
Out[20]= {f[{f[a, {1, 1}], f[b, {1, 2}]}, {1}],
          f[{f[c, {2, 1}], f[d, {2, 2}]}, {2}]}
```

Map allows you to apply a function of one argument to parts of an expression. Sometimes, however, you may instead want to apply a function of several arguments to corresponding parts of several different expressions. You can do this using MapThread.

MapThread[*f*, {*expr*$_1$, *expr*$_2$, ... }]	apply *f* to corresponding elements in each of the *expr*$_i$
MapThread[*f*, {*expr*$_1$, *expr*$_2$, ... }, *lev*]	apply *f* to parts of the *expr*$_i$ at the specified level

Applying a function to several expressions at once.

This applies f to corresponding pairs of list elements.

```
In[21]:= MapThread[f, {{a, b, c}, {ap, bp, cp}}]
Out[21]= {f[a, ap], f[b, bp], f[c, cp]}
```

MapThread works with any number of expressions, so long as they have the same structure.

```
In[22]:= MapThread[f, {{a, b}, {ap, bp}, {app, bpp}}]
Out[22]= {f[a, ap, app], f[b, bp, bpp]}
```

Functions like Map allow you to create expressions with parts modified. Sometimes you simply want to go through an expression, and apply a particular function to some parts of it, without building a new expression. A typical case is when the function you apply has certain "side effects", such as making assignments, or generating output.

Scan[*f*, *expr*]	evaluate *f* applied to each element of *expr* in turn
Scan[*f*, *expr*, *lev*]	evaluate *f* applied to parts of *expr* on levels specified by *lev*

Evaluating functions on parts of expressions.

Map constructs a new list in which f has been applied to each element of the list.

```
In[23]:= Map[f, {a, b, c}]
Out[23]= {f[a], f[b], f[c]}
```

Scan evaluates the result of applying a function to each element, but does not construct a new expression.

```
In[24]:= Scan[Print, {a, b, c}]
a
b
c
```

Scan visits the parts of an expression in a depth-first walk, with the leaves visited first.

```
In[25]:= Scan[Print, 1 + x^2, Infinity]
1
x
2
 2
x
```

■ 2.2.5 Pure Functions

Function[x, *body*]	a pure function in which x is replaced by any argument you provide
Function[{x_1, x_2, ... }, *body*]	a pure function that takes several arguments
body &	a pure function in which arguments are specified as # or #1, #2, #3, etc.

Pure functions.

When you use functional operations such as Nest and Map, you always have to specify a function to apply. In all the examples above, we have used the "name" of a function to specify the function. Pure functions allow you to give functions which can be applied to arguments, without having to define explicit names for the functions.

This defines a function h.

```
In[1]:= h[x_] := f[x] + g[x]
```

Having defined h, you can now use its name in Map.

```
In[2]:= Map[h, {a, b, c}]
Out[2]= {f[a] + g[a], f[b] + g[b], f[c] + g[c]}
```

Here is a way to get the same result using a pure function.

```
In[3]:= Map[ f[#] + g[#] &, {a, b, c} ]
Out[3]= {f[a] + g[a], f[b] + g[b], f[c] + g[c]}
```

There are several equivalent ways to write pure functions in *Mathematica*. The idea in all cases is to construct an object which, when supplied with appropriate arguments, computes a particular function. Thus, for example, if *fun* is a pure function, then *fun*[*a*] evaluates the function with argument *a*.

Here is a pure function which represents the operation of squaring.

```
In[4]:= Function[x, x^2]
Out[4]= Function[x, x²]
```

Supplying the argument n to the pure function yields the square of n.

```
In[5]:= %[n]
Out[5]= n²
```

You can use a pure function wherever you would usually give the name of a function.

You can use a pure function in Map. | *In[6]:=* **Map[Function[x, x^2], a + b + c]**

Out[6]= $a^2 + b^2 + c^2$

Or in Nest. | *In[7]:=* **Nest[Function[q, 1/(1+q)], x, 3]**

Out[7]= $\dfrac{1}{1 + \dfrac{1}{1 + \frac{1}{1+x}}}$

This sets up a pure function with two arguments and then applies the function to the arguments a and b. | *In[8]:=* **Function[{x, y}, x^2 + y^3] [a, b]**

Out[8]= $a^2 + b^3$

If you are going to use a particular function repeatedly, then you can define the function using $f[x\_] := body$, and refer to the function by its name f. On the other hand, if you only intend to use a function once, you will probably find it better to give the function in pure function form, without ever naming it.

If you are familiar with formal logic or the LISP programming language, you will recognize *Mathematica* pure functions as being like λ expressions or anonymous functions. Pure functions are also close to the pure mathematical notion of operators.

#	the first variable in a pure function
#*n*	the nth variable in a pure function
##	the sequence of all variables in a pure function
##*n*	the sequence of variables starting with the nth one

Short forms for pure functions.

Just as the name of a function is irrelevant if you do not intend to refer to the function again, so also the names of arguments in a pure function are irrelevant. *Mathematica* allows you to avoid using explicit names for the arguments of pure functions, and instead to specify the arguments by giving "slot numbers" #*n*. In a *Mathematica* pure function, #*n* stands for the nth argument you supply. # stands for the first argument.

#^2 & is a short form for a pure function that squares its argument. | *In[9]:=* **Map[#^2 &, a + b + c]**

Out[9]= $a^2 + b^2 + c^2$

This applies a function that takes the first two elements from each list. By using a pure function, you avoid having to define the function separately. | *In[10]:=* **Map[Take[#, 2]&, {{2, 1, 7}, {4, 1, 5}, {3, 1, 2}}]**

Out[10]= {{2, 1}, {4, 1}, {3, 1}}

Using short forms for pure functions, you can simplify the definition of tonumber given on page 240.	`In[11]:= tonumber[digits_] := Fold[(10 #1 + #2)&, 0, digits]`

When you use short forms for pure functions, it is very important that you do not forget the ampersand. If you leave the ampersand out, *Mathematica* will not know that the expression you give is to be used as a pure function.

When you use the ampersand notation for pure functions, you must be careful about the grouping of pieces in your input. As shown on page 977 the ampersand notation has fairly low precedence, which means that you can type expressions like #1 + #2 & without parentheses. On the other hand, if you want, for example, to set an option to be a pure function, you need to use parentheses, as in *option -> (fun &)*.

Pure functions in *Mathematica* can take any number of arguments. You can use ## to stand for all the arguments that are given, and ##*n* to stand for the *n*th and subsequent arguments.

## stands for all arguments.	`In[12]:= f[##, ##]& [x, y]`
	`Out[12]= f[x, y, x, y]`
##2 stands for all arguments except the first one.	`In[13]:= Apply[f[##2, #1]&, {{a, b, c}, {ap, bp}}, {1}]`
	`Out[13]= {f[b, c, a], f[bp, ap]}`

■ 2.2.6 Building Lists from Functions

`Array[f, n]`	generate a length n list of the form $\{f[1], f[2], \dots\}$
`Array[f, {n_1, n_2, \dots}]`	generate an $n_1 \times n_2 \times \dots$ nested list, each of whose entries consists of f applied to its indices
`NestList[f, x, n]`	generate a list of the form $\{x, f[x], f[f[x]], \dots\}$, where f is nested up to n deep
`FoldList[f, x, {a, b, \dots}]`	generate a list of the form $\{x, f[x, a], f[f[x, a], b], \dots\}$
`ComposeList[{f_1, f_2, \dots}, x]`	generate a list of the form $\{x, f_1[x], f_2[f_1[x]], \dots\}$

Making lists from functions.

This makes a list of 5 elements, each of the form p[*i*].	`In[1]:= Array[p, 5]`
	`Out[1]= {p[1], p[2], p[3], p[4], p[5]}`
Here is another way to produce the same list.	`In[2]:= Table[p[i], {i, 5}]`
	`Out[2]= {p[1], p[2], p[3], p[4], p[5]}`
This produces a list whose elements are $i + i^2$.	`In[3]:= Array[ # + #^2 &, 5]`
	`Out[3]= {2, 6, 12, 20, 30}`

This generates a 2×3 matrix whose entries are m[i, j].

```
In[4]:= Array[m, {2, 3}]
Out[4]= {{m[1, 1], m[1, 2], m[1, 3]},
          {m[2, 1], m[2, 2], m[2, 3]}}
```

This generates a 3×3 matrix whose elements are the squares of the sums of their indices.

```
In[5]:= Array[Plus[##]^2 &, {3, 3}]
Out[5]= {{4, 9, 16}, {9, 16, 25}, {16, 25, 36}}
```

NestList and **FoldList** were discussed in Section 2.2.2. Particularly by using them with pure functions, you can construct some very elegant and efficient *Mathematica* programs.

This gives a list of results obtained by successively differentiating x^n with respect to x.

```
In[6]:= NestList[ D[#, x]&, x^n, 3 ]
Out[6]= {x^n, n x^{-1+n}, (-1+n) n x^{-2+n}, (-2+n) (-1+n) n x^{-3+n}}
```

■ 2.2.7 Selecting Parts of Expressions with Functions

Section 1.2.4 showed how you can pick out elements of lists based on their *positions*. Often, however, you will need to select elements based not on *where* they are, but rather on *what* they are.

Select[*list*, *f***]** selects elements of *list* using the function *f* as a criterion. Select applies *f* to each element of *list* in turn, and keeps only those for which the result is True.

This selects the elements of the list for which the pure function yields True, i.e., those numerically greater than 4.

```
In[1]:= Select[{2, 15, 1, a, 16, 17}, # > 4 &]
Out[1]= {15, 16, 17}
```

You can use **Select** to pick out pieces of any expression, not just elements of a list.

This gives a sum of terms involving x, y and z.

```
In[2]:= t = Expand[(x + y + z)^2]
Out[2]= x^2 + 2 x y + y^2 + 2 x z + 2 y z + z^2
```

You can use **Select** to pick out only those terms in the sum that do not involve the symbol x.

```
In[3]:= Select[t, FreeQ[#, x]&]
Out[3]= y^2 + 2 y z + z^2
```

Select[*expr*, *f*]	select the elements in *expr* for which the function *f* gives True
Select[*expr*, *f*, *n*]	select the first *n* elements in *expr* for which the function *f* gives True

Selecting pieces of expressions.

Section 2.3.5 discusses some "predicates" that are often used as criteria in **Select**.

This gives the first element which satisfies the criterion you specify.

```
In[4]:= Select[{-1, 3, 10, 12, 14}, # > 3 &, 1]
Out[4]= {10}
```

■ 2.2.8 Expressions with Heads That Are Not Symbols

In most cases, you want the head *f* of a *Mathematica* expression like $f[x]$ to be a single symbol. There are, however, some important applications of heads that are not symbols.

This expression has f[3] as a head. You can use heads like this to represent "indexed functions".	*In[1]:=* **f[3][x, y]** *Out[1]=* f[3][x, y]

You can use any expression as a head. Remember to put in the necessary parentheses.	*In[2]:=* **(a + b)[x]** *Out[2]=* (a + b)[x]

One case where we have already encountered the use of complicated expressions as heads is in working with pure functions in Section 2.2.5. By giving Function[*vars*, *body*] as the head of an expression, you specify a function of the arguments to be evaluated.

With the head Function[x, x^2], the value of the expression is the square of the argument.	*In[3]:=* **Function[x, x^2] [a + b]** *Out[3]=* $(a+b)^2$

There are several constructs in *Mathematica* which work much like pure functions, but which represent specific kinds of functions, typically numerical ones. In all cases, the basic mechanism involves giving a head which contains complete information about the function you want to use.

Function[*vars*, *body*][*args*]	pure function
InterpolatingFunction[*data*][*args*]	
	approximate numerical function (generated by Interpolation and NDSolve)
CompiledFunction[*data*][*args*]	compiled numerical function (generated by Compile)

Some expressions which have heads that are not symbols.

NDSolve returns a list of rules that give y as an InterpolatingFunction object.	*In[4]:=* **NDSolve[{y''[x] == y[x], y[0]==y'[0]==1}, y, {x, 0, 5}]** *Out[4]=* {{y → InterpolatingFunction[{{0., 5.}}, <>]}}

Here is the InterpolatingFunction object.	*In[5]:=* **y /. First[%]** *Out[5]=* InterpolatingFunction[{{0., 5.}}, <>]

You can use the InterpolatingFunction object as a head to get numerical approximations to values of the function y.	*In[6]:=* **% [3.8]** *Out[6]=* 44.7015

Another important use of more complicated expressions as heads is in implementing *functionals* and *functional operators* in mathematics.

As one example, consider the operation of differentiation. As will be discussed in Section 3.5.4, an expression like `f'` represents a *derivative function*, obtained from `f` by applying a functional operator to it. In *Mathematica*, `f'` is represented as `Derivative[1][f]`: the "functional operator" `Derivative[1]` is applied to `f` to give another function, represented as `f'`.

This expression has a head which represents the application of the "functional operator" `Derivative[1]` to the "function" `f`.	*In[7]:=* `f'[x] // FullForm` *Out[7]//FullForm=* `Derivative[1][f][x]`
You can replace the head `f'` with another head, such as `fp`. This effectively takes `fp` to be a "derivative function" obtained from `f`.	*In[8]:=* `% /. f' -> fp` *Out[8]=* `fp[x]`

■ 2.2.9 Advanced Topic: Working with Operators

You can think of an expression like $f[x]$ as being formed by applying an *operator* f to the expression x. You can think of an expression like $f[g[x]]$ as the result of *composing* the operators f and g, and applying the result to x.

`Composition[`f, g, ... `]`	the composition of functions f, g, ...
`InverseFunction[`f`]`	the inverse of a function f
`Identity`	the identity function

Some functional operations.

This represents the composition of the functions f, g and h.	*In[1]:=* `Composition[f, g, h]` *Out[1]=* `Composition[f, g, h]`
You can manipulate compositions of functions symbolically.	*In[2]:=* `InverseFunction[Composition[%, q]]` *Out[2]=* `Composition[q`$^{(-1)}$`, h`$^{(-1)}$`, g`$^{(-1)}$`, f`$^{(-1)}$`]`
The composition is evaluated explicitly when you supply a specific argument.	*In[3]:=* `%[x]` *Out[3]=* `q`$^{(-1)}$`[h`$^{(-1)}$`[g`$^{(-1)}$`[f`$^{(-1)}$`[x]]]]`

You can get the sum of two expressions in *Mathematica* just by typing $x + y$. Sometimes it is also worthwhile to consider performing operations like addition on *operators*.

You can think of this as containing a sum of two operators f and g.	*In[4]:=* `(f + g)[x]` *Out[4]=* `(f + g)[x]`
Using `Through`, you can convert the expression to a more explicit form.	*In[5]:=* `Through[%, Plus]` *Out[5]=* `f[x] + g[x]`

This corresponds to the mathematical operator $1 + \frac{\partial}{\partial x}$.

In[6]:= **Identity + (D[#, x]&)**

Out[6]= Identity + (∂_x #1&)

Mathematica does not automatically apply the separate pieces of the operator to an expression.

In[7]:= **% [x^2]**

Out[7]= (Identity + (∂_x #1&)) [x²]

You can use Through to apply the operator.

In[8]:= **Through[%, Plus]**

Out[8]= 2 x + x²

Identity[*expr*]	the identity function
Through[$p[f_1, f_2][x]$, q]	give $p[f_1[x], f_2[x]]$ if p is the same as q
Operate[p, $f[x]$]	give $p[f][x]$
Operate[p, $f[x]$, n]	apply p at level n in f
MapAll[p, *expr*, Heads->True]	apply p to all parts of *expr*, including heads

Operations for working with operators.

This has a complicated expression as a head.

In[9]:= **t = ((1 + a)(1 + b))[x]**

Out[9]= ((1 + a) (1 + b)) [x]

Functions like Expand do not automatically go inside heads of expressions.

In[10]:= **Expand[%]**

Out[10]= ((1 + a) (1 + b)) [x]

With the Heads option set to True, MapAll goes inside heads.

In[11]:= **MapAll[Expand, t, Heads->True]**

Out[11]= (1 + a + b + a b) [x]

The replacement operator /. does go inside heads of expressions.

In[12]:= **t /. a->1**

Out[12]= (2 (1 + b)) [x]

You can use Operate to apply a function specifically to the head of an expression.

In[13]:= **Operate[p, t]**

Out[13]= p[(1 + a) (1 + b)] [x]

■ 2.2.10 Structural Operations

Mathematica contains some powerful primitives for making structural changes to expressions. You can use these primitives both to implement mathematical properties such as associativity and distributivity, and to provide the basis for some succinct and efficient programs.

This section describes various operations that you can explicitly perform on expressions. Section 2.5.3 will describe how some of these operations can be performed automatically on all expressions with a particular head by assigning appropriate attributes to that head.

You can use the *Mathematica* function Sort[*expr*] to sort elements not only of lists, but of expressions with any head. In this way, you can implement the mathematical properties of commutativity or symmetry for arbitrary functions.

You can use Sort to put the arguments of any function into a standard order.	*In[1]:=* **Sort[f[c, a, b]]**
	Out[1]= f[a, b, c]

Sort[*expr*]	sort the elements of a list or other expression into a standard order
Sort[*expr*, *pred*]	sort using the function *pred* to determine whether pairs are in order
OrderedQ[*expr*]	give True if the elements of *expr* are in standard order, and False otherwise
Order[*expr₁*, *expr₂*]	give 1 if *expr₁* comes before *expr₂* in standard order, and −1 if it comes after

Sorting into order.

The second argument to Sort is a function used to determine whether pairs are in order. This sorts numbers into descending order.	*In[2]:=* **Sort[{5, 1, 8, 2}, (#2 < #1)&]**
	Out[2]= {8, 5, 2, 1}

This sorting criterion puts elements that do not depend on x before those that do.	*In[3]:=* **Sort[{x^2, y, x+y, y-2}, FreeQ[#1, x]&]**
	Out[3]= {y, −2 + y, x + y, x²}

Flatten[*expr*]	flatten out all nested functions with the same head as *expr*
Flatten[*expr*, *n*]	flatten at most *n* levels of nesting
Flatten[*expr*, *n*, *h*]	flatten functions with head *h*
FlattenAt[*expr*, *i*]	flatten only the *i*ᵗʰ element of *expr*

Flattening out expressions.

Flatten removes nested occurrences of a function.	*In[4]:=* **Flatten[f[a, f[b, c], f[f[d]]]]**
	Out[4]= f[a, b, c, d]

You can use Flatten to "splice" sequences of elements into lists or other expressions.

```
In[5]:= Flatten[ {a, f[b, c], f[a, b, d]}, 1, f ]
Out[5]= {a, b, c, a, b, d}
```

You can use Flatten to implement the mathematical property of associativity. The function Distribute allows you to implement properties such as distributivity and linearity.

Distribute[*f*[*a* + *b* + ... , ...]]	distribute *f* over sums to give *f*[*a*, ...] + *f*[*b*, ...] + ...
Distribute[*f*[*args*], *g*]	distribute *f* over any arguments which have head *g*
Distribute[*expr*, *g*, *f*]	distribute only when the head is *f*
Distribute[*expr*, *g*, *f*, *gp*, *fp*]	distribute *f* over *g*, replacing them with *fp* and *gp*, respectively

Applying distributive laws.

This "distributes" f over a + b.

```
In[6]:= Distribute[ f[a + b] ]
Out[6]= f[a] + f[b]
```

Here is a more complicated example.

```
In[7]:= Distribute[ f[a + b, c + d] ]
Out[7]= f[a, c] + f[a, d] + f[b, c] + f[b, d]
```

In general, if *f* is distributive over Plus, then an expression like *f*[*a* + *b*] can be "expanded" to give *f*[*a*] + *f*[*b*]. The function Expand does this kind of expansion for standard algebraic operators such as Times. Distribute allows you to perform the same kind of expansion for arbitrary operators.

Expand uses the distributivity of Times over Plus to perform algebraic expansions.

```
In[8]:= Expand[ (a + b) (c + d) ]
Out[8]= a c + b c + a d + b d
```

This applies distributivity over lists, rather than sums. The result contains all possible pairs of arguments.

```
In[9]:= Distribute[ f[{a, b}, {c, d}], List ]
Out[9]= {f[a, c], f[a, d], f[b, c], f[b, d]}
```

This distributes over lists, but does so only if the head of the whole expression is f.

```
In[10]:= Distribute[ f[{a, b}, {c, d}], List, f ]
Out[10]= {f[a, c], f[a, d], f[b, c], f[b, d]}
```

This distributes over lists, making sure that the head of the whole expression is f. In the result, it uses gp in place of List, and fp in place of f.

```
In[11]:= Distribute[ f[{a, b}, {c, d}], List, f, gp, fp ]
Out[11]= gp[fp[a, c], fp[a, d], fp[b, c], fp[b, d]]
```

Related to Distribute is the function Thread. What Thread effectively does is to apply a function in parallel to all the elements of a list or other expression.

Thread[$f[\{a_1, a_2\}, \{b_1, b_2\}]$]	thread f over lists to give $\{f[a_1, b_1], f[a_2, b_2]\}$
Thread[$f[args]$, g]	thread f over objects with head g in *args*

Functions for threading expressions.

Here is a function whose arguments are lists.

```
In[12]:= f[{a1, a2}, {b1, b2}]
Out[12]= f[{a1, a2}, {b1, b2}]
```

Thread applies the function "in parallel" to each element of the lists.

```
In[13]:= Thread[%]
Out[13]= {f[a1, b1], f[a2, b2]}
```

Arguments that are not lists get repeated.

```
In[14]:= Thread[ f[{a1, a2}, {b1, b2}, c, d] ]
Out[14]= {f[a1, b1, c, d], f[a2, b2, c, d]}
```

As mentioned in Section 1.8.1, and discussed in more detail in Section 2.5.3, many built-in *Mathematica* functions have the property of being "listable", so that they are automatically threaded over any lists that appear as arguments.

Built-in mathematical functions such as Log are listable, so that they are automatically threaded over lists.

```
In[15]:= Log[{a, b, c}]
Out[15]= {Log[a], Log[b], Log[c]}
```

Log is, however, not automatically threaded over equations.

```
In[16]:= Log[x == y]
Out[16]= Log[x == y]
```

You can use Thread to get functions applied to both sides of an equation.

```
In[17]:= Thread[%, Equal]
Out[17]= Log[x] == Log[y]
```

Outer[f, $list_1$, $list_2$]	generalized outer product
Inner[f, $list_1$, $list_2$, g]	generalized inner product

Generalized outer and inner products.

Outer[f, $list_1$, $list_2$, ...] takes all possible combinations of elements from the $list_i$, and combines them with f. Outer can be viewed as a generalization of a Cartesian product for tensors, as discussed in Section 3.7.11.

Outer forms all possible combinations of elements, and applies f to them.

```
In[18]:= Outer[f, {a, b}, {1, 2, 3}]
Out[18]= {{f[a, 1], f[a, 2], f[a, 3]},
          {f[b, 1], f[b, 2], f[b, 3]}}
```

Here Outer produces a lower-triangular Boolean matrix.

```
In[19]:= Outer[ Greater, {1, 2, 3}, {1, 2, 3} ]
Out[19]= {{False, False, False}, {True, False, False},
          {True, True, False}}
```

You can use Outer on any sequence of expressions with the same head.

In[20]:= `Outer[ g, f[a, b], f[c, d] ]`

Out[20]= f[f[g[a, c], g[a, d]], f[g[b, c], g[b, d]]]

Outer, like Distribute, constructs all possible combinations of elements. On the other hand, Inner, like Thread, constructs only combinations of elements that have corresponding positions in the expressions it acts on.

Here is a structure built by Inner.

In[21]:= `Inner[f, {a, b}, {c, d}, g]`

Out[21]= g[f[a, c], f[b, d]]

Inner is a generalization of Dot.

In[22]:= `Inner[Times, {a, b}, {c, d}, Plus]`

Out[22]= a c + b d

■ 2.2.11 Sequences

The function Flatten allows you to explicitly flatten out all sublists.

In[1]:= `Flatten[{a, {b, c}, {d, e}}]`

Out[1]= {a, b, c, d, e}

FlattenAt lets you specify at what positions you want sublists flattened.

In[2]:= `FlattenAt[{a, {b, c}, {d, e}}, 2]`

Out[2]= {a, b, c, {d, e}}

Sequence objects automatically get spliced in, and do not require any explicit flattening.

In[3]:= `{a, Sequence[b, c], Sequence[d, e]}`

Out[3]= {a, b, c, d, e}

Sequence[e_1, e_2, ...]	a sequence of arguments that will automatically be spliced into any function

Representing sequences of arguments in functions.

Sequence works in any function.

In[4]:= `f[Sequence[a, b], c]`

Out[4]= f[a, b, c]

This includes functions with special input forms.

In[5]:= `a == Sequence[b, c]`

Out[5]= a == b == c

Here is a common way that Sequence is used.

In[6]:= `{a, b, f[x, y], g[w], f[z, y]} /. f->Sequence`

Out[6]= {a, b, x, y, g[w], z, y}

2.3 Patterns

■ 2.3.1 Introduction

Patterns are used throughout *Mathematica* to represent classes of expressions. A simple example of a pattern is the expression f[x_]. This pattern represents the class of expressions with the form f[*anything*].

The main power of patterns comes from the fact that many operations in *Mathematica* can be done not only with single expressions, but also with patterns that represent whole classes of expressions.

You can use patterns in transformation rules to specify how classes of expressions should be transformed.	*In[1]:=* **f[a] + f[b] /. f[x_] -> x^2** *Out[1]=* $a^2 + b^2$
You can use patterns to find the positions of all expressions in a particular class.	*In[2]:=* **Position[{f[a], g[b], f[c]}, f[x_]]** *Out[2]=* {{1}, {3}}

The basic object that appears in almost all *Mathematica* patterns is _ (traditionally called "blank" by *Mathematica* programmers). The fundamental rule is simply that _ *stands for any expression*. On most keyboards the _ underscore character appears as the shifted version of the - dash character.

Thus, for example, the pattern f[_] stands for any expression of the form f[*anything*]. The pattern f[x_] also stands for any expression of the form f[*anything*], but gives the name x to the expression *anything*, allowing you to refer to it on the right-hand side of a transformation rule.

You can put blanks anywhere in an expression. What you get is a pattern which matches all expressions that can be made by "filling in the blanks" in any way.

f[n_]	f with any argument, named n
f[n_, m_]	f with two arguments, named n and m
x^n_	x to any power, with the power named n
x_^n_	any expression to any power
a_ + b_	a sum of two expressions
{a1_, a2_}	a list of two expressions
f[n_, n_]	f with two *identical* arguments

Some examples of patterns.

You can construct patterns for expressions with any structure.	*In[3]:=* **f[{a, b}] + f[c] /. f[{x_, y_}] -> p[x + y]** *Out[3]=* f[c] + p[a + b]

One of the most common uses of patterns is for "destructuring" function arguments. If you make a definition for f[list_], then you need to use functions like Part explicitly in order to pick out elements of the list. But if you know for example that the list will always have two elements, then it is usually much more convenient instead to give a definition instead for f[{x_, y_}]. Then you can refer to the elements of the list directly as x and y. In addition, *Mathematica* will not use the definition you have given unless the argument of f really is of the required form of a list of two expressions.

Here is one way to define a function which takes a list of two elements, and evaluates the first element raised to the power of the second element.

`In[4]:= g[list_] := Part[list, 1] ^ Part[list, 2]`

Here is a much more elegant way to make the definition, using a pattern.

`In[5]:= h[{x_, y_}] := x ^ y`

A crucial point to understand is that *Mathematica* patterns represent classes of expressions with a given *structure*. One pattern will match a particular expression if the structure of the pattern is the same as the structure of the expression, in the sense that by filling in blanks in the pattern you can get the expression. Even though two expressions may be *mathematically equal*, they cannot be represented by the same *Mathematica* pattern unless they have the same structure.

Thus, for example, the pattern (1 + x_)^2 can stand for expressions like (1 + a)^2 or (1 + b^3)^2 that have the same *structure*. However, it cannot stand for the expression 1 + 2 a + a^2. Although this expression is *mathematically equal* to (1 + a)^2, it does not have the same *structure* as the pattern (1 + x_)^2.

The fact that patterns in *Mathematica* specify the *structure* of expressions is crucial in making it possible to set up transformation rules which change the *structure* of expressions, while leaving them mathematically equal.

It is worth realizing that in general it would be quite impossible for *Mathematica* to match patterns by mathematical, rather than structural, equivalence. In the case of expressions like (1 + a)^2 and 1 + 2 a + a^2, you can determine equivalence just by using functions like Expand and Factor. But, as discussed on page 307 there is no general way to find out whether an arbitrary pair of mathematical expressions are equal.

As another example, the pattern x^_ will match the expression x^2. It will not, however, match the expression 1, even though this could be considered as x^0. Section 2.3.9 will discuss how to construct a pattern for which this particular case will match. But you should understand that in all cases pattern matching in *Mathematica* is fundamentally structural.

The x^n_ matches only x^2 and x^3. 1 and x can mathematically be written as x^n, but do not have the same structure.

`In[6]:= {1, x, x^2, x^3} /. x^n_ -> r[n]`

`Out[6]= {1, x, r[2], r[3]}`

Another point to realize is that the structure *Mathematica* uses in pattern matching is the full form of expressions printed by FullForm. Thus, for example, an object such as 1/x, whose full form is Power[x, -1] will be matched by the pattern x_^n_, but not by the pattern x_/y_, whose full form is

`Times[x_, Power[y_, -1]]`. Again, Section 2.3.9 will discuss how you can construct patterns which can match all these cases.

The expressions in the list contain explicit powers of b, so the transformation rule can be applied.	`In[7]:= {a/b, 1/b^2, 2/b^2} /. b^n_ -> d[n]` `Out[7]= {ad[-1], d[-2], 2d[-2]}`

Here is the full form of the list.	`In[8]:= FullForm[{a/b, 1/b^2, 2/b^2}]`
	`Out[8]//FullForm= List[Times[a, Power[b, -1]], Power[b, -2],`
	`                    Times[2, Power[b, -2]]]`

Although *Mathematica* does not use mathematical equivalences such as $x^1 = x$ when matching patterns, it does use certain structural equivalences. Thus, for example, *Mathematica* takes account of properties such as commutativity and associativity in pattern matching.

To apply this transformation rule, *Mathematica* makes use of the commutativity and associativity of addition.	`In[9]:= f[a + b] + f[a + c] + f[b + d] /.`
	`               f[a + x_] + f[c + y_] -> p[x, y]`
	`Out[9]= f[b+d] + p[b, a]`

The discussion so far has considered only pattern objects such as `x_` which can stand for any single expression. In later subsections, we discuss the constructs that *Mathematica* uses to extend and restrict the classes of expressions represented by patterns.

■ 2.3.2 Finding Expressions That Match a Pattern

`Cases[`*list*`, `*form*`]`	give the elements of *list* that match *form*
`Count[`*list*`, `*form*`]`	give the number of elements in *list* that match *form*
`Position[`*list*`, `*form*`, {1}]`	give the positions of elements in *list* that match *form*
`Select[`*list*`, `*test*`]`	give the elements of *list* on which *test* gives True

Picking out elements that match a pattern.

This gives the elements of the list which match the pattern x^_.	`In[1]:= Cases[ {3, 4, x, x^2, x^3}, x^_ ]` `Out[1]= {x`^{2}`, x`^{3}`}`
Here is the total number of elements which match the pattern.	`In[2]:= Count[ {3, 4, x, x^2, x^3}, x^_ ]` `Out[2]= 2`

You can apply functions like `Cases` not only to lists, but to expressions of any kind. In addition, you can specify the level of parts at which you want to look.

Cases[*expr*, *lhs->rhs*]	find elements of *expr* that match *lhs*, and give a list of the results of applying the transformation rule to them
Cases[*expr*, *lhs->rhs*, *lev*]	test parts of *expr* at levels specified by *lev*
Count[*expr*, *form*, *lev*]	give the total number of parts that match *form* at levels specified by *lev*
Position[*expr*, *form*, *lev*]	give the positions of parts that match *form* at levels specified by *lev*

Searching for parts of expressions that match a pattern.

This returns a list of the exponents n.

In[3]:= **Cases[{3, 4, x, x^2, x^3}, x^n_ -> n]**
Out[3]= {2, 3}

The pattern _Integer matches any integer. This gives a list of integers appearing at any level.

In[4]:= **Cases[{3, 4, x, x^2, x^3}, _Integer, Infinity]**
Out[4]= {3, 4, 2, 3}

Cases[*expr*, *form*, *lev*, *n*]	find only the first *n* parts that match *form*
Position[*expr*, *form*, *lev*, *n*]	give the positions of the first *n* parts that match *form*

Limiting the number of parts to search for.

This gives the positions of the first two powers of x appearing at any level.

In[5]:= **Position[{4, 4 + x^a, x^b, 6 + x^5}, x^_, Infinity, 2]**
Out[5]= {{2, 2}, {3}}

The positions are specified in exactly the form used by functions such as Extract and ReplacePart discussed in Section 1.8.

In[6]:= **ReplacePart[{4, 4 + x^a, x^b, 6 + x^5}, zzz, %]**
Out[6]= {4, 4 + zzz, zzz, 6 + x^5}

DeleteCases[*expr*, *form*]	delete elements of *expr* that match *form*
DeleteCases[*expr*, *form*, *lev*]	delete parts of *expr* that match *form* at levels specified by *lev*

Deleting parts of expressions that match a pattern.

This deletes the elements which match x^n_.

In[7]:= **DeleteCases[{3, 4, x, x^2, x^3}, x^n_]**
Out[7]= {3, 4, x}

This deletes all integers appearing at any level.

In[8]:= **DeleteCases[{3, 4, x, 2+x, 3+x}, _Integer, Infinity]**
Out[8]= {x, x, x}

+	`ReplaceList[`*expr*`, `*lhs* `-> ` *rhs*`]`	find all ways that *expr* can match *lhs*

Finding arrangements of an expression that match a pattern.

This finds all ways that the sum can be written in two parts.

```
In[9]:= ReplaceList[a + b + c, x_ + y_ -> g[x, y]]

Out[9]= {g[a, b+c], g[b, a+c], g[c, a+b], g[a+b, c],
          g[a+c, b], g[b+c, a]}
```

This finds all pairs of identical elements. The pattern `___` stands for any sequence of elements.

```
In[10]:= ReplaceList[{a, b, b, b, c, c, a},
                      {___, x_, x_, ___} -> x]

Out[10]= {b, b, c}
```

■ 2.3.3 Naming Pieces of Patterns

Particularly when you use transformation rules, you often need to name pieces of patterns. An object like `x_` stands for any expression, but gives the expression the name `x`. You can then, for example, use this name on the right-hand side of a transformation rule.

An important point is that when you use `x_`, *Mathematica* requires that all occurrences of blanks with the same name `x` in a particular expression must stand for the same expression.

Thus `f[x_, x_]` can only stand for expressions in which the two arguments of `f` are exactly the same. `f[_, _]`, on the other hand, can stand for any expression of the form `f[`*x*`, `*y*`]`, where `x` and `y` need not be the same.

The transformation rule applies only to cases where the two arguments of `f` are identical.

```
In[1]:= {f[a, a], f[a, b]} /. f[x_, x_] -> p[x]

Out[1]= {p[a], f[a, b]}
```

Mathematica allows you to give names not just to single blanks, but to any piece of a pattern. The object `x`:*pattern* in general represents a pattern which is assigned the name `x`. In transformation rules, you can use this mechanism to name exactly those pieces of a pattern that you need to refer to on the right-hand side of the rule.

	`_`	any expression
	`x_`	any expression, to be named *x*
	`x`:*pattern*	an expression to be named *x*, matching *pattern*

Patterns with names.

This gives a name to the complete form _^_ so you can refer to it as a whole on the right-hand side of the transformation rule.

In[2]:= **f[a^b] /. f[x:_^_] -> p[x]**

Out[2]= p[a^b]

Here the exponent is named n, while the whole object is x.

In[3]:= **f[a^b] /. f[x:_^n_] -> p[x, n]**

Out[3]= p[a^b, b]

When you give the same name to two pieces of a pattern, you constrain the pattern to match only those expressions in which the corresponding pieces are identical.

Here the pattern matches both cases.

In[4]:= **{f[h[4], h[4]], f[h[4], h[5]]} /. f[h[_], h[_]] -> q**

Out[4]= {q, q}

Now both arguments of f are constrained to be the same, and only the first case matches.

In[5]:= **{f[h[4], h[4]], f[h[4], h[5]]} /. f[x:h[_], x_] -> r[x]**

Out[5]= {r[h[4]], f[h[4], h[5]]}

■ 2.3.4 Specifying Types of Expression in Patterns

You can tell a lot about what "type" of expression something is by looking at its head. Thus, for example, an integer has head Integer, while a list has head List.

In a pattern, _h and x_h represent expressions that are constrained to have head h. Thus, for example, _Integer represents any integer, while _List represents any list.

*x*_h	an expression with head *h*
*x*_Integer	an integer
*x*_Real	an approximate real number
*x*_Complex	a complex number
*x*_List	a list
*x*_Symbol	a symbol

Patterns for objects with specified heads.

This replaces just those elements that are integers.

In[1]:= **{a, 4, 5, b} /. x_Integer -> p[x]**

Out[1]= {a, p[4], p[5], b}

You can think of making an assignment for f[x_Integer] as like defining a function f that must take an argument of "type" Integer.

This defines a value for the function gamma when its argument is an integer.

In[2]:= **gamma[n_Integer] := (n - 1)!**

The definition applies only when the argument of gamma is an integer.	*In[3]:=* **gamma[4] + gamma[x]**
	Out[3]= 6 + gamma[x]
The object 4. has head Real, so the definition does not apply.	*In[4]:=* **gamma[4.]**
	Out[4]= gamma[4.]
This defines values for expressions with integer exponents.	*In[5]:=* **d[x_^n_Integer] := n x^(n-1)**
The definition is used only when the exponent is an integer.	*In[6]:=* **d[x^4] + d[(a+b)^3] + d[x^(1/2)]**
	Out[6]= $3 (a + b)^2 + 4 x^3 + d\left[\sqrt{x}\,\right]$

■ 2.3.5 Putting Constraints on Patterns

Mathematica provides a general mechanism for specifying constraints on patterns. All you need do is to put /; *condition* at the end of a pattern to signify that it applies only when the specified condition is True. You can read the operator /; as "slash-semi", "whenever" or "provided that".

pattern /; *condition*	a pattern that matches only when a condition is satisfied
lhs :> *rhs* /; *condition*	a rule that applies only when a condition is satisfied
lhs := *rhs* /; *condition*	a definition that applies only when a condition is satisfied

Putting conditions on patterns and transformation rules.

This gives a definition for fac that applies only when its argument n is positive.	*In[1]:=* **fac[n_ /; n > 0] := n!**
The definition for fac is used only when the argument is positive.	*In[2]:=* **fac[6] + fac[-4]**
	Out[2]= 720 + fac[-4]
This gives the negative elements in the list.	*In[3]:=* **Cases[{3, -4, 5, -2}, x_ /; x < 0]**
	Out[3]= {-4, -2}

You can use /; on whole definitions and transformation rules, as well as on individual patterns. In general, you can put /; *condition* at the end of any := definition or :> rule to tell *Mathematica* that the definition or rule applies only when the specified condition holds. Note that /; conditions should not usually be put at the end of = definitions or -> rules, since they will then be evaluated immediately, as discussed in Section 2.4.8.

Here is another way to give a definition which applies only when its argument n is positive.	*In[4]:=* **fac2[n_] := n! /; n > 0**

Once again, the factorial functions evaluate only when their arguments are positive.

In[5]:= **fac2[6] + fac2[-4]**

Out[5]= 720 + fac2[-4]

You can use the **/;** operator to implement arbitrary mathematical constraints on the applicability of rules. In typical cases, you give patterns which *structurally* match a wide range of expressions, but then use *mathematical* constraints to reduce the range of expressions to a much smaller set.

This rule applies only to expressions that have the structure v[x_, 1 - x_].

In[6]:= **v[x_, 1 - x_] := p[x]**

This expression has the appropriate structure, so the rule applies.

In[7]:= **v[a^2, 1 - a^2]**

Out[7]= p[a^2]

This expression, while mathematically of the correct form, does not have the appropriate structure, so the rule does not apply.

In[8]:= **v[4, -3]**

Out[8]= v[4, -3]

This rule applies to any expression of the form w[x_, y_], with the added restriction that y == 1 - x.

In[9]:= **w[x_, y_] := p[x] /; y == 1 - x**

The new rule does apply to this expression.

In[10]:= **w[4, -3]**

Out[10]= p[4]

In setting up patterns and transformation rules, there is often a choice of where to put **/;** conditions. For example, you can put a **/;** condition on the right-hand side of a rule in the form *lhs :> rhs /; condition*, or you can put it on the left-hand side in the form *lhs /; condition -> rhs*. You may also be able to insert the condition inside the expression *lhs*. The only constraint is that all the names of patterns that you use in a particular condition must appear in the pattern to which the condition is attached. If this is not the case, then some of the names needed to evaluate the condition may not yet have been "bound" in the pattern-matching process. If this happens, then *Mathematica* uses the global values for the corresponding variables, rather than the values determined by pattern matching.

Thus, for example, the condition in f[x_, y_] /; (x + y < 2) will use values for x and y that are found by matching f[x_, y_], but the condition in f[x_ /; x + y < 2, y_] will use the global value for y, rather than the one found by matching the pattern.

As long as you make sure that the appropriate names are defined, it is usually most efficient to put **/;** conditions on the smallest possible parts of patterns. The reason for this is that *Mathematica* matches pieces of patterns sequentially, and the sooner it finds a **/;** condition which fails, the sooner it can reject a match.

Putting the **/;** condition around the x_ is slightly more efficient than putting it around the whole pattern.

In[11]:= **Cases[{z[1, 1], z[-1, 1], z[-2, 2]}, z[x_ /; x < 0, y_]]**

Out[11]= {z[-1, 1], z[-2, 2]}

You need to put parentheses around the /; piece in a case like this.

```
In[12]:= {1 + a, 2 + a, -3 + a} /. (x_ /; x < 0) + a -> p[x]
Out[12]= {1 + a, 2 + a, p[-3]}
```

It is common to use /; to set up patterns and transformation rules that apply only to expressions with certain properties. There is a collection of functions built into *Mathematica* for testing the properties of expressions. It is a convention that functions of this kind have names that end with the letter Q, indicating that they "ask a question".

IntegerQ[*expr*]	integer
EvenQ[*expr*]	even number
OddQ[*expr*]	odd number
PrimeQ[*expr*]	prime number
NumberQ[*expr*]	explicit number of any kind
NumericQ[*expr*]	numeric quantity
PolynomialQ[*expr*, {x_1, x_2, ... }]	
	polynomial in x_1, x_2, ...
VectorQ[*expr*]	a list representing a vector
MatrixQ[*expr*]	a list of lists representing a matrix
VectorQ[*expr*, NumberQ], MatrixQ[*expr*, NumberQ]	
	vectors and matrices where all elements are numbers
VectorQ[*expr*, *test*], MatrixQ[*expr*, *test*]	
	vectors and matrices for which the function *test* yields True when applied to any element

Some functions for testing mathematical properties of expressions.

The rule applies to all elements of the list that are numbers.

```
In[13]:= {2.3, 4, 7/8, a, b} /. (x_ /; NumberQ[x]) -> x^2
```
$$Out[13]= \left\{5.29, 16, \frac{49}{64}, a, b\right\}$$

This definition applies only to vectors of integers.

```
In[14]:= mi[list_] := list^2 /; VectorQ[list, IntegerQ]
```

The definition is now used only in the first case.

```
In[15]:= {mi[{2, 3}], mi[{2.1, 2.2}], mi[{a, b}]}
Out[15]= {{4, 9}, mi[{2.1, 2.2}], mi[{a, b}]}
```

An important feature of all the *Mathematica* property-testing functions whose names end in Q is that they always return **False** if they cannot determine whether the expression you give has a particular property.

4561 is an integer, so this returns True.	*In[16]:=* **IntegerQ[4561]**
	Out[16]= True
This returns False, since x is not known to be an integer.	*In[17]:=* **IntegerQ[x]**
	Out[17]= False

In some cases, you can explicitly specify the results that property-testing functions should give. Thus, with a definition such as x /: IntegerQ[x] = True, as discussed in Section 2.4.10, *Mathematica* will assume that x is an integer. This means that if you explicitly ask for IntegerQ[x], you will now get True, rather than False. However, *Mathematica* does not automatically propagate assertions, so it cannot determine for example that IntegerQ[x^2] is True. You must load an appropriate *Mathematica* package to make this possible.

SameQ[x, y] or $x === y$	x and y are identical
UnsameQ[x, y] or $x =!= y$	x and y are not identical
OrderedQ[{a, b, ... }]	a, b, ... are in standard order
MemberQ[*expr*, *form*]	*form* matches an element of *expr*
FreeQ[*expr*, *form*]	*form* matches nothing in *expr*
MatchQ[*expr*, *form*]	*expr* matches the pattern *form*
ValueQ[*expr*]	a value has been defined for *expr*
AtomQ[*expr*]	*expr* has no subexpressions

Some functions for testing structural properties of expressions.

With ==, the equation remains in symbolic form; === yields False unless the expressions are manifestly equal.	*In[18]:=* **{x == y, x === y}**
	Out[18]= {x == y, False}
The expression n is not a *member* of the list {x, x^n}.	*In[19]:=* **MemberQ[{x, x^n}, n]**
	Out[19]= False
However, {x, x^n} is not completely free of n.	*In[20]:=* **FreeQ[{x, x^n}, n]**
	Out[20]= False
You can use FreeQ to define a "linearity" rule for h.	*In[21]:=* **h[a_ b_, x_] := a h[b, x] /; FreeQ[a, x]**
Terms free of x are pulled out of each h.	*In[22]:=* **h[a b x, x] + h[2 (1+x) x^2, x]**
	Out[22]= a b h[x, x] + 2 h[x^2 (1 + x), x]

pattern **?** *test*	a pattern which matches an expression only if *test* yields True when applied to the expression

Another way to constrain patterns.

The construction *pattern* **/;** *condition* allows you to evaluate a condition involving pattern names to determine whether there is a match. The construction *pattern* **?** *test* instead applies a function *test* to the whole expression matched by *pattern* to determine whether there is a match. Using **?** instead of **/;** sometimes leads to more succinct definitions.

With this definition matches for x_ are tested with the function NumberQ.

```
In[23]:= p[x_?NumberQ] := x^2
```

The definition applies only when p has a numerical argument.

```
In[24]:= p[4.5] + p[3/2] + p[u]

Out[24]= 22.5 + p[u]
```

Here is a more complicated definition. Do not forget the parentheses around the pure function.

```
In[25]:= q[{x_Integer, y_Integer} ?
                    (Function[v, v.v > 4])] := qp[x + y]
```

The definition applies only in certain cases.

```
In[26]:= {q[{3, 4}], q[{1, 1}], q[{-5, -7}]}

Out[26]= {qp[7], q[{1, 1}], qp[-12]}
```

■ 2.3.6 Patterns Involving Alternatives

patt$_1$ **|** *patt*$_2$ **|** ...	a pattern that can have one of several forms

Specifying patterns that involve alternatives.

This defines h to give p when its argument is either a or b.

```
In[1]:= h[a | b] := p
```

The first two cases give p.

```
In[2]:= {h[a], h[b], h[c], h[d]}

Out[2]= {p, p, h[c], h[d]}
```

You can also use alternatives in transformation rules.

```
In[3]:= {a, b, c, d} /. (a | b) -> p

Out[3]= {p, p, c, d}
```

Here is another example, in which one of the alternatives is itself a pattern.

```
In[4]:= {1, x, x^2, x^3, y^2} /. (x | x^_) -> q

Out[4]= {1, q, q, q, y^2}
```

When you use alternatives in patterns, you should make sure that the same set of names appear in each alternative. When a pattern like (a[x_] | b[x_]) matches an expression, there will always be a definite expression that corresponds to the object x. On the other hand, if you try to match a pattern like (a[x_] | b[y_]), then there will be a definite expression corresponding either to x, or to y, but not to both. As a result, you cannot use x and y to refer to definite expressions, for example on the right-hand side of a transformation rule.

Here f is used to name the head, which can be either a or b.	*In[5]:=* `{a[2], b[3], c[4], a[5]} /. (f:(a|b))[x_] -> r[f, x]`
	Out[5]= `{r[a, 2], r[b, 3], c[4], r[a, 5]}`

■ 2.3.7 Flat and Orderless Functions

Although *Mathematica* matches patterns in a purely structural fashion, its notion of structural equivalence is quite sophisticated. In particular, it takes account of properties such as commutativity and associativity in functions like Plus and Times.

This means, for example, that *Mathematica* considers the expressions $x + y$ and $y + x$ equivalent for the purposes of pattern matching. As a result, a pattern like g[x_ + y_, x_] can match not only g[a + b, a], but also g[a + b, b].

This expression has exactly the same form as the pattern.	*In[1]:=* `g[a + b, a] /. g[x_ + y_, x_] -> p[x, y]`
	Out[1]= `p[a, b]`

In this case, the expression has to be put in the form g[b + a, b] in order to have the same structure as the pattern.	*In[2]:=* `g[a + b, b] /. g[x_ + y_, x_] -> p[x, y]`
	Out[2]= `p[b, a]`

Whenever *Mathematica* encounters an *orderless* or *commutative* function such as Plus or Times in a pattern, it effectively tests all the possible orders of arguments to try and find a match. Sometimes, there may be several orderings that lead to matches. In such cases, *Mathematica* just uses the first ordering it finds. For example, h[x_ + y_, x_ + z_] could match h[a + b, a + b] with x→a, y→b, z→b or with x→b, y→a, z→a. *Mathematica* tries the case x→a, y→b, z→b first, and so uses this match.

This can match either with x → a or with x → b. *Mathematica* tries x → a first, and so uses this match.	*In[3]:=* `h[a + b, a + b] /. h[x_ + y_, x_ + z_] -> p[x, y, z]`
	Out[3]= `p[a, b, b]`

ReplaceList shows both possible matches.	*In[4]:=* `ReplaceList[h[a + b, a + b],`
	`          h[x_ + y_, x_ + z_] -> p[x, y, z]]`
	Out[4]= `{p[a, b, b], p[b, a, a]}`

As discussed in Section 2.5.3, *Mathematica* allows you to assign certain attributes to functions, which specify how those functions should be treated in evaluation and pattern matching. Functions can for example be assigned the attribute Orderless, which specifies that they should be treated as commutative or symmetric, and allows their arguments to be rearranged in trying to match patterns.

Orderless	commutative function: $f[b, c, a]$, etc., are equivalent to $f[a, b, c]$
Flat	associative function: $f[f[a], b]$, etc., are equivalent to $f[a, b]$
OneIdentity	$f[f[a]]$, etc., are equivalent to a
Attributes[f]	give the attributes assigned to f
SetAttributes[f, *attr*]	add *attr* to the attributes of f
ClearAttributes[f, *attr*]	remove *attr* from the attributes of f

Some attributes that can be assigned to functions.

Plus has attributes Orderless and Flat, as well as others.

```
In[5]:= Attributes[Plus]
Out[5]= {Flat, Listable, NumericFunction, OneIdentity,
             Orderless, Protected}
```

This defines q to be an orderless or commutative function.

```
In[6]:= SetAttributes[q, Orderless]
```

The arguments of q are automatically sorted into order.

```
In[7]:= q[b, a, c]
Out[7]= q[a, b, c]
```

Mathematica rearranges the arguments of q functions to find a match.

```
In[8]:= f[q[a, b], q[b, c]] /.
             f[q[x_, y_], q[x_, z_]] -> p[x, y, z]
Out[8]= p[b, a, c]
```

In addition to being orderless, functions like Plus and Times also have the property of being *flat* or *associative*. This means that you can effectively "parenthesize" their arguments in any way, so that, for example, x + (y + z) is equivalent to x + y + z, and so on.

Mathematica takes account of flatness in matching patterns. As a result, a pattern like g[x_ + y_] can match g[a + b + c], with x → a and y → (b + c).

The argument of g is written as a + (b + c) so as to match the pattern.

```
In[9]:= g[a + b + c] /. g[x_ + y_] -> p[x, y]
Out[9]= p[a, b+c]
```

If there are no other constraints, *Mathematica* will match x_ to the first element of the sum.

```
In[10]:= g[a + b + c + d] /. g[x_ + y_] -> p[x, y]
Out[10]= p[a, b+c+d]
```

This shows all the possible matches.

```
In[11]:= ReplaceList[g[a + b + c], g[x_ + y_] -> p[x, y]]
Out[11]= {p[a, b+c], p[b, a+c], p[c, a+b], p[a+b, c],
             p[a+c, b], p[b+c, a]}
```

Here x_ is forced to match b + d.

In[12]:= **g[a + b + c + d, b + d] /. g[x_ + y_, x_] -> p[x, y]**

Out[12]= p[b+d, a+c]

Mathematica can usually apply a transformation rule to a function only if the pattern in the rule covers all the arguments in the function. However, if you have a flat function, it is sometimes possible to apply transformation rules even though not all the arguments are covered.

This rule applies even though it does not cover all the terms in the sum.	*In[13]:=* **a + b + c /. a + c -> p** *Out[13]=* b+p
This combines two of the terms in the sum.	*In[14]:=* **u[a] + u[b] + v[c] + v[d] /. u[x_] + u[y_] -> u[x + y]** *Out[14]=* u[a+b] +v[c] +v[d]

Functions like Plus and Times are both flat and orderless. There are, however, some functions, such as Dot, which are flat, but not orderless.

Both x_ and y_ can match any sequence of terms in the dot product.	*In[15]:=* **a . b . c . d . a . b /. x_ . y_ . x_ -> p[x, y]** *Out[15]=* p[a.b, c.d]
This assigns the attribute Flat to the function r.	*In[16]:=* **SetAttributes[r, Flat]**
Mathematica writes the expression in the form r[r[a, b], r[a, b]] to match the pattern.	*In[17]:=* **r[a, b, a, b] /. r[x_, x_] -> rp[x]** *Out[17]=* rp[r[a, b]]
Mathematica writes this expression in the form r[a, r[r[b], r[b]], c] to match the pattern.	*In[18]:=* **r[a, b, b, c] /. r[x_, x_] -> rp[x]** *Out[18]=* r[a, rp[r[b]], c]

In an ordinary function that is not flat, a pattern such as x_ matches an individual argument of the function. But in a function *f[a, b, c, ...]* that is flat, x_ can match objects such as *f[b, c]* which effectively correspond to a sequence of arguments. However, in the case where x_ matches a single argument in a flat function, the question comes up as to whether the object it matches is really just the argument *a* itself, or *f[a]*. *Mathematica* chooses the first of these cases if the function carries the attribute OneIdentity, and chooses the second case otherwise.

This adds the attribute OneIdentity to the function r.	*In[19]:=* **SetAttributes[r, OneIdentity]**
Now x_ matches individual arguments, without r wrapped around them.	*In[20]:=* **r[a, b, b, c] /. r[x_, x_] -> rp[x]** *Out[20]=* r[a, rp[b], c]

The functions Plus, Times and Dot all have the attribute OneIdentity, reflecting the fact that Plus[*x*] is equivalent to *x*, and so on. However, in representing mathematical objects, it is often convenient to deal with flat functions that do not have the attribute OneIdentity.

■ 2.3.8 Functions with Variable Numbers of Arguments

Unless *f* is a flat function, a pattern like *f*[*x*_, *y*_] stands only for instances of the function with exactly two arguments. Sometimes you need to set up patterns that can allow any number of arguments.

You can do this using *multiple blanks*. While a single blank such as x_ stands for a single *Mathematica* expression, a double blank such as x__ stands for a sequence of one or more expressions.

Here x__ stands for the sequence of expressions (a, b, c).	*In[1]:=* **f[a, b, c] /. f[x__] -> p[x, x, x]** *Out[1]=* p[a, b, c, a, b, c, a, b, c]
Here is a more complicated definition, which picks out pairs of duplicated elements in h.	*In[2]:=* **h[a___, x_, b___, x_, c___] := hh[x] h[a, b, c]**
The definition is applied twice, picking out the two paired elements.	*In[3]:=* **h[2, 3, 2, 4, 5, 3]** *Out[3]=* h[4, 5] hh[2] hh[3]

"Double blanks" __ stand for sequences of one or more expressions. "Triple blanks" ___ stand for sequences of zero or more expressions. You should be very careful whenever you use triple blank patterns. It is easy to make a mistake that can lead to an infinite loop. For example, if you define p[x_, y___] := p[x] q[y], then typing in p[a] will lead to an infinite loop, with y repeatedly matching a sequence with zero elements. Unless you are sure you want to include the case of zero elements, you should always use double blanks rather than triple blanks.

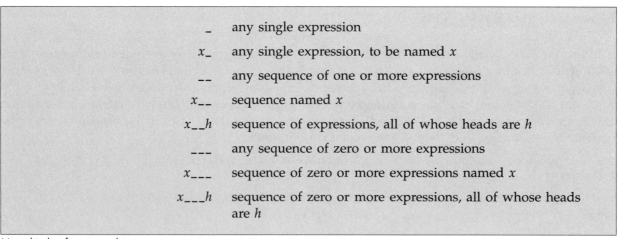

_	any single expression
*x*_	any single expression, to be named *x*
__	any sequence of one or more expressions
*x*__	sequence named *x*
*x*__*h*	sequence of expressions, all of whose heads are *h*
___	any sequence of zero or more expressions
*x*___	sequence of zero or more expressions named *x*
*x*___*h*	sequence of zero or more expressions, all of whose heads are *h*

More kinds of pattern objects.

Notice that with flat functions such as Plus and Times, *Mathematica* automatically handles variable numbers of arguments, so you do not explicitly need to use double or triple blanks, as discussed in Section 2.3.7.

When you use multiple blanks, there are often several matches that are possible for a particular expression. In general, *Mathematica* tries first those matches that assign the shortest sequences of arguments to the first multiple blanks that appear in the pattern.

This gives a list of all the matches that *Mathematica* tries.

```
In[4]:= ReplaceList[f[a, b, c, d], f[x__, y__] -> g[{x}, {y}]]
Out[4]= {g[{a}, {b, c, d}], g[{a, b}, {c, d}],
          g[{a, b, c}, {d}]}
```

Many kinds of enumeration can be done by using `ReplaceList` with various kinds of patterns.

```
In[5]:= ReplaceList[f[a, b, c, d], f[___, x__] -> g[x]]
Out[5]= {g[a, b, c, d], g[b, c, d], g[c, d], g[d]}
```

This effectively enumerates all sublists with at least one element.

```
In[6]:= ReplaceList[f[a, b, c, d], f[___, x__, ___] -> g[x]]
Out[6]= {g[a], g[a, b], g[b], g[a, b, c], g[b, c], g[c],
          g[a, b, c, d], g[b, c, d], g[c, d], g[d]}
```

■ 2.3.9 Optional and Default Arguments

Sometimes you may want to set up functions where certain arguments, if omitted, are given "default values". The pattern $x\_:v$ stands for an object that can be omitted, and if so, will be replaced by the default value v.

This defines a function j with a required argument x, and optional arguments y and z, with default values 1 and 2, respectively.

```
In[1]:= j[x_, y_:1, z_:2] := jp[x, y, z]
```

The default value of z is used here.

```
In[2]:= j[a, b]
Out[2]= jp[a, b, 2]
```

Now the default values of both y and z are used.

```
In[3]:= j[a]
Out[3]= jp[a, 1, 2]
```

$x\_:v$	an expression which, if omitted, is taken to have default value v
$x\_h:v$	an expression with head h and default value v
$x\_.$	an expression with a built-in default value

Pattern objects with default values.

Some common *Mathematica* functions have built-in default values for their arguments. In such cases, you need not explicitly give the default value in $x\_:v$, but instead you can use the more convenient notation $x\_.$ in which a built-in default value is assumed.

x_ + y_.	default for y is 0
x_ y_.	default for y is 1
x_^y_.	default for y is 1

Some patterns with optional pieces.

Here a matches the pattern x_ + y_.
with y taken to have the default
value 0.

In[4]:= {f[a], f[a + b]} /. f[x_ + y_.] -> p[x, y]

Out[4]= {p[a, 0], p[b, a]}

Because Plus is a flat function, a pattern such as x_ + y_ can match a sum with any number of terms. This pattern cannot, however, match a single term such as a. However, the pattern x_ + y_. contains an optional piece, and can match either an explicit sum of terms in which both x_ and y_ appear, or a single term x_, with y taken to be 0.

Using constructs such as $x_.$, you can easily construct single patterns that match expressions with several different structures. This is particularly useful when you want to match several mathematically equal forms that do not have the same structure.

The pattern matches g[a^2], but not
g[a + b].

In[5]:= {g[a^2], g[a + b]} /. g[x_^n_] -> p[x, n]

Out[5]= {p[a, 2], g[a + b]}

By giving a pattern in which the
exponent is optional, you can match
both cases.

In[6]:= {g[a^2], g[a + b]} /. g[x_^n_.] -> p[x, n]

Out[6]= {p[a, 2], p[a + b, 1]}

The pattern a_. + b_. x_ matches any
linear function of x_.

In[7]:= lin[a_. + b_. x_, x_] := p[a, b]

In this case, b → 1.

In[8]:= lin[1 + x, x]

Out[8]= p[1, 1]

Here b → 1 and a → 0.

In[9]:= lin[y, y]

Out[9]= p[0, 1]

Standard *Mathematica* functions such as Plus and Times have built-in default values for their arguments. You can also set up defaults for your own functions, as described in Section A.5.1.

■ 2.3.10 Setting Up Functions with Optional Arguments

When you define a complicated function, you will often want to let some of the arguments of the function be "optional". If you do not give those arguments explicitly, you want them to take on certain "default" values.

Built-in *Mathematica* functions use two basic methods for dealing with optional arguments. You can choose between the same two methods when you define your own functions in *Mathematica*.

The first method is to have the meaning of each argument determined by its position, and then to allow one to drop arguments, replacing them by default values. Almost all built-in *Mathematica* functions that use this method drop arguments from the end. For example, the built-in function Flatten[*list*, *n*] allows you to drop the second argument, which is taken to have a default value of Infinity.

You can implement this kind of "positional" argument using _: patterns.

$f[x\_,\ k\_:kdef]\ :=\ value$	a typical definition for a function whose second argument is optional, with default value *kdef*

Defining a function with positional arguments.

This defines a function with an optional second argument. When the second argument is omitted, it is taken to have the default value Infinity.	*In[1]:=* **f[list_, n_:Infinity] := f0[list, n]**
Here is a function with two optional arguments.	*In[2]:=* **fx[list_, n1_:1, n2_:2] := fx0[list, n1, n2]**
Mathematica assumes that arguments are dropped from the end. As a result m here gives the value of n1, while n2 has its default value of 2.	*In[3]:=* **fx[k, m]** *Out[3]=* fx0[k, m, 2]

The second method that built-in *Mathematica* functions use for dealing with optional arguments is to give explicit names to the optional arguments, and then to allow their values to be given using transformation rules. This method is particularly convenient for functions like Plot which have a very large number of optional parameters, only a few of which usually need to be set in any particular instance.

The typical arrangement is that values for "named" optional arguments can be specified by including the appropriate transformation rules at the end of the arguments to a particular function. Thus, for example, the rule PlotJoined->True, which specifies the setting for the named optional argument PlotJoined, could appear as ListPlot[*list*, PlotJoined->True].

When you set up named optional arguments for a function *f*, it is conventional to store the default values of these arguments as a list of transformation rules assigned to Options[*f*].

f[*x_*, *opts___*] := *value*	a typical definition for a function with zero or more named optional arguments
name /. {*opts*} /. Options[*f*]	replacements used to get the value of a named optional argument in the body of the function

Named arguments.

This sets up default values for two named optional arguments opt1 and opt2 in the function fn.

In[4]:= **Options[fn] = { opt1 -> 1, opt2 -> 2 }**

Out[4]= {opt1 → 1, opt2 → 2}

This gives the default value for opt1.

In[5]:= **opt1 /. Options[fn]**

Out[5]= 1

The rule opt1->3 is applied first, so the default rule for opt1 in Options[fn] is not used.

In[6]:= **opt1 /. opt1->3 /. Options[fn]**

Out[6]= 3

Here is the definition for a function fn which allows zero or more named optional arguments to be specified.

In[7]:= **fn[x_, opts___] := k[x, opt2/.{opts}/.Options[fn]]**

With no optional arguments specified, the default rule for opt2 is used.

In[8]:= **fn[4]**

Out[8]= k[4, 2]

If you explicitly give a rule for opt2, it will be used before the default rules stored in Options[fn] are tried.

In[9]:= **fn[4, opt2->7]**

Out[9]= k[4, 7]

■ 2.3.11 Repeated Patterns

expr..	a pattern or other expression repeated one or more times
expr...	a pattern or other expression repeated zero or more times

Repeated patterns.

Multiple blanks such as *x__* allow you to give patterns in which sequences of arbitrary expressions can occur. The *Mathematica pattern repetition operators* .. and ... allow you to construct patterns in which particular forms can be repeated any number of times. Thus, for example, f[a..] represents any expression of the form f[a], f[a, a], f[a, a, a] and so on.

The pattern f[a..] allows the argument a to be repeated any number of times.

In[1]:= **Cases[{ f[a], f[a, b, a], f[a, a, a] }, f[a..]]**

Out[1]= {f[a], f[a, a, a]}

This pattern allows any number of a arguments, followed by any number of b arguments.	`In[2]:= Cases[{ f[a], f[a, a, b], f[a, b, a], f[a, b, b] }, f[a.., b..]]`
	`Out[2]= {f[a, a, b], f[a, b, b]}`

Here each argument can be either a or b.	`In[3]:= Cases[{ f[a], f[a, b, a], f[a, c, a] }, f[(a | b)..]]`
	`Out[3]= {f[a], f[a, b, a]}`

You can use `..` and `...` to represent repetitions of any pattern. If the pattern contains named parts, then each instance of these parts must be identical.

This defines a function whose argument must consist of a list of pairs.	`In[4]:= v[x:{{_, _}..}] := Transpose[x]`

The definition applies in this case.	`In[5]:= v[{{a1, b1}, {a2, b2}, {a3, b3}}]`
	`Out[5]= {{a1, a2, a3}, {b1, b2, b3}}`

With this definition, the second elements of all the pairs must be the same.	`In[6]:= vn[x:{{_, n_}..}] := Transpose[x]`

The definition applies in this case.	`In[7]:= vn[{{a, 2}, {b, 2}, {c, 2}}]`
	`Out[7]= {{a, b, c}, {2, 2, 2}}`

⁺■ 2.3.12 Verbatim Patterns

⁺	`Verbatim[`*expr*`]`	an expression that must be matched verbatim

Verbatim patterns.

Here the `x_` in the rule matches any expression.	`In[1]:= {f[2], f[a], f[x_], f[y_]} /. f[x_] -> x^2`
	`Out[1]= {4, a`^{2}`, x_`^{2}`, y_`^{2}`}`

The `Verbatim` tells *Mathematica* that only the exact expression `x_` should be matched.	`In[2]:= {f[2], f[a], f[x_], f[y_]} /. f[Verbatim[x_]] -> x^2`
	`Out[2]= {f[2], f[a], x`^{2}`, f[y_]}`

■ 2.3.13 Patterns for Some Common Types of Expression

Using the objects described above, you can set up patterns for many kinds of expressions. In all cases, you must remember that the patterns must represent the structure of the expressions in *Mathematica* internal form, as shown by `FullForm`.

Especially for some common kinds of expressions, the standard output format used by *Mathematica* is not particularly close to the full internal form. But it is the internal form that you must use in setting up patterns.

*n*_Integer	an integer *n*
*x*_Real	an approximate real number *x*
*z*_Complex	a complex number *z*
Complex[*x*_, *y*_]	a complex number *x* + *iy*
Complex[*x*_Integer, *y*_Integer]	a complex number where both real and imaginary parts are integers
(*r*_Rational | *r*_Integer)	rational number or integer *r*
Rational[*n*_, *d*_]	a rational number $\frac{n}{d}$
(*x*_ /; NumberQ[*x*] && Im[*x*]==0)	a real number of any kind
(*x*_ /; NumberQ[*x*])	a number of any kind

Some typical patterns for numbers.

Here are the full forms of some numbers.

```
In[1]:= {2, 2.5, 2.5 + I, 2/7} // FullForm
Out[1]//FullForm= List[2, 2.5, Complex[2.5, 1], Rational[2, 7]]
```

The rule picks out each piece of the complex numbers.

```
In[2]:= {2.5 - I, 3 + I} /. Complex[x_, y_] -> p[x, y]
Out[2]= {p[2.5, -1], p[3, 1]}
```

The fact that these expressions have different full forms means that you cannot use *x*_ + I *y*_ to match a complex number.

```
In[3]:= {2.5 - I, x + I y} // FullForm
Out[3]//FullForm= List[Complex[2.5, -1],
                Plus[x, Times[Complex[0, 1], y]]]
```

The pattern here matches both ordinary integers, and complex numbers where both the real and imaginary parts are integers.

```
In[4]:= Cases[ {2.5 - I, 2, 3 + I, 2 - 0.5 I, 2 + 2 I},
               _Integer | Complex[_Integer, _Integer] ]
Out[4]= {2, 3 + I, 2 + 2 I}
```

As discussed in Section 1.4.1, *Mathematica* puts all algebraic expressions into a standard form, in which they are written essentially as a sum of products of powers. In addition, ratios are converted into products of powers, with denominator terms having negative exponents, and differences are converted into sums with negated terms. To construct patterns for algebraic expressions, you must use this standard form. This form often differs from the way *Mathematica* prints out the algebraic expressions. But in all cases, you can find the full internal form using FullForm[*expr*].

Here is a typical algebraic expression.

```
In[5]:= -1/z^2 - z/y + 2 (x z)^2 y
```

$$Out[5]= -\frac{1}{z^2} - \frac{z}{y} + 2 x^2 y z^2$$

This is the full internal form of the expression.

In[6]:= **FullForm[%]**

Out[6]//FullForm= Plus[Times[-1, Power[z, -2]],
                Times[-1, Power[y, -1], z],
                Times[2, Power[x, 2], y, Power[z, 2]]]]

This is what you get by applying a transformation rule to all powers in the expression.

In[7]:= **% /. x_^n_ -> e[x, n]**

Out[7]= -z e[y, -1] - e[z, -2] + 2 y e[x, 2] e[z, 2]

$x\_ + y\_$	a sum of two or more terms
$x\_ + y\_.$	a single term or a sum of terms
$n\_\text{Integer } x\_$	an expression with an explicit integer multiplier
$a\_. + b\_. \; x\_$	a linear expression $a + bx$
$x\_ \char94 n\_$	x^n with $n \neq 0, 1$
$x\_ \char94 n\_.$	x^n with $n \neq 0$
$a\_. + b\_. \; x\_ + c\_. \; x\_\char94 2$	a quadratic expression with non-zero linear term

Some typical patterns for algebraic expressions.

This pattern picks out linear functions of x.

In[8]:= **{1, a, x, 2 x, 1 + 2 x} /. a_. + b_. x -> p[a, b]**

Out[8]= {1, a, p[0, 1], p[0, 2], p[1, 2]}

x_List or $x:\{\_\_\_\}$	a list
$x\_\text{List} \; /; \; \text{VectorQ}[x]$	a vector containing no sublists
$x\_\text{List} \; /; \; \text{VectorQ}[x, \text{NumberQ}]$	a vector of numbers
$x:\{\_\_\_\text{List}\}$ or $x:\{\{\_\_\_\}...\}$	a list of lists
$x\_\text{List} \; /; \; \text{MatrixQ}[x]$	a matrix containing no sublists
$x\_\text{List} \; /; \; \text{MatrixQ}[x, \text{NumberQ}]$	a matrix of numbers
$x:\{\{\_, \_\}...\}$	a list of pairs

Some typical patterns for lists.

This defines a function whose argument must be a list containing lists with either one or two elements.

In[9]:= **h[x:{ ({_} | {_, _})... }] := q**

The definition applies in the second and third cases.

In[10]:= **{h[{a, b}], h[{{a}, {b}}], h[{{a}, {b, c}}]}**

Out[10]= {h[{a, b}], q, q}

■ 2.3.14 An Example: Defining Your Own Integration Function

Now that we have introduced the basic features of patterns in *Mathematica*, we can use them to give a more or less complete example. We will show how you could define your own simple integration function in *Mathematica*.

From a mathematical point of view, the integration function is defined by a sequence of mathematical relations. By setting up transformation rules for patterns, you can implement these mathematical relations quite directly in *Mathematica*.

mathematical form	*Mathematica definition*
$\int (y+z)\,dx = \int y\,dx + \int z\,dx$	`integrate[y_ + z_, x_] :=` `    integrate[y, x] + integrate[z, x]`
$\int c\,y\,dx = c \int y\,dx$ (*c* independent of *x*)	`integrate[c_ y_, x_] :=` `    c integrate[y, x] /; FreeQ[c, x]`
$\int c\,dx = c\,x$	`integrate[c_, x_] := c x /; FreeQ[c, x]`
$\int x^n\,dx = \frac{x^{(n+1)}}{n+1}, n \neq -1$	`integrate[x_^n_., x_] := x^(n+1)/(n+1) /;` `    FreeQ[n, x] && n != -1`
$\int \frac{1}{ax+b}\,dx = \frac{\log(ax+b)}{a}$	`integrate[1/(a_. x_ + b_.), x_] :=` `    Log[a x + b]/a /; FreeQ[{a,b}, x]`
$\int e^{ax+b}\,dx = \frac{1}{a}\,e^{ax+b}$	`integrate[Exp[a_. x_ + b_.], x_] :=` `    Exp[a x + b]/a /; FreeQ[{a,b}, x]`

Definitions for an integration function.

This implements the linearity relation for integrals:
$\int (y+z)\,dx = \int y\,dx + \int z\,dx$.

```
In[1]:= integrate[y_ + z_, x_] :=
                integrate[y, x] + integrate[z, x]
```

The associativity of Plus makes the linearity relation work with any number of terms in the sum.

```
In[2]:= integrate[a x + b x^2 + 3, x]
```
```
Out[2]= integrate[3, x] + integrate[a x, x] +
            integrate[b x², x]
```

This makes integrate pull out factors that are independent of the integration variable x.

```
In[3]:= integrate[c_ y_, x_] := c integrate[y, x] /; FreeQ[c, x]
```

Mathematica tests each term in each product to see whether it satisfies the FreeQ condition, and so can be pulled out.

```
In[4]:= integrate[a x + b x^2 + 3, x]
```
```
Out[4]= integrate[3, x] + a integrate[x, x] +
            b integrate[x², x]
```

This gives the integral $\int c\,dx = c\,x$ of a constant.

```
In[5]:= integrate[c_, x_] := c x /; FreeQ[c, x]
```

Now the constant term in the sum can be integrated.

```
In[6]:= integrate[a x + b x^2 + 3, x]
Out[6]= 3 x + a integrate[x, x] + b integrate[x^2, x]
```

This gives the standard formula for the integral of x^n. By using the pattern x_^n_., rather than x_^n_, we include the case of $x^1 = x$.

```
In[7]:= integrate[x_^n_., x_] :=
            x^(n+1)/(n+1) /; FreeQ[n, x] && n != -1
```

Now this integral can be done completely.

```
In[8]:= integrate[a x + b x^2 + 3, x]
```
$$Out[8]= 3x + \frac{a x^2}{2} + \frac{b x^3}{3}$$

Of course, the built-in integration function Integrate (with a capital I) could have done the integral anyway.

```
In[9]:= Integrate[a x + b x^2 + 3, x]
```
$$Out[9]= 3x + \frac{a x^2}{2} + \frac{b x^3}{3}$$

Here is the rule for integrating the reciprocal of a linear function. The pattern a_. x_ + b_. stands for any linear function of x.

```
In[10]:= integrate[1/(a_. x_ + b_.), x_] :=
             Log[a x + b]/a /; FreeQ[{a,b}, x]
```

Here both a and b take on their default values.

```
In[11]:= integrate[1/x, x]
Out[11]= Log[x]
```

Here is a more complicated case. The symbol a now matches 2 p.

```
In[12]:= integrate[1/(2 p x - 1), x]
```
$$Out[12]= \frac{Log[-1 + 2 p x]}{2 p}$$

You can go on and add many more rules for integration. Here is a rule for integrating exponentials.

```
In[13]:= integrate[Exp[a_. x_ + b_.], x_] :=
             Exp[a x + b]/a /; FreeQ[{a,b}, x]
```

2.4 Transformation Rules and Definitions

■ 2.4.1 Applying Transformation Rules

expr /. *lhs* -> *rhs*	apply a transformation rule to *expr*
expr /. {*lhs$_1$* -> *rhs$_1$*, *lhs$_2$* -> *rhs$_2$*, ... }	
	try a sequence of rules on each part of *expr*

Applying transformation rules.

<table>
<tr><td>The replacement operator /.
(pronounced "slash-dot") applies rules
to expressions.</td><td>In[1]:= x + y /. x -> 3
Out[1]= 3 + y</td></tr>
<tr><td>You can give a list of rules to apply.
Each rule will be tried once on each
part of the expression.</td><td>In[2]:= x + y /. {x -> a, y -> b}
Out[2]= a + b</td></tr>
</table>

expr /. {*rules$_1$*, *rules$_2$*, ... }	give a list of the results from applying each of the *rules$_i$* to *expr*

Applying lists of transformation rules.

<table>
<tr><td>If you give a list of lists of rules, you
get a list of results.</td><td>In[3]:= x + y /. {{x -> 1, y -> 2}, {x -> 4, y -> 2}}
Out[3]= {3, 6}</td></tr>
<tr><td>Functions such as Solve and NSolve
return lists whose elements are lists of
rules, each representing a solution.</td><td>In[4]:= Solve[x^3 - 5x^2 +2x + 8 == 0, x]
Out[4]= {{x → -1}, {x → 2}, {x → 4}}</td></tr>
<tr><td>When you apply these rules, you get a
list of results, one corresponding to
each solution.</td><td>In[5]:= x^2 + 6 /. %
Out[5]= {7, 10, 22}</td></tr>
</table>

When you use *expr* /. *rules*, each rule is tried in turn on each part of *expr*. As soon as a rule applies, the appropriate transformation is made, and the resulting part is returned.

<table>
<tr><td>The rule for x^3 is tried first; if it does
not apply, the rule for x^n_ is used.</td><td>In[6]:= {x^2, x^3, x^4} /. {x^3 -> u, x^n_ -> p[n]}
Out[6]= {p[2], u, p[4]}</td></tr>
<tr><td>A result is returned as soon as the rule
has been applied, so the inner instance
of h is not replaced.</td><td>In[7]:= h[x + h[y]] /. h[u_] -> u^2
Out[7]= $(x + h[y])^2$</td></tr>
</table>

The replacement *expr* /. *rules* tries each rule just once on each part of *expr*.

Since each rule is tried just once, this serves to swap x and y.	*In[8]:=* **{x^2, y^3} /. {x -> y, y -> x}**
	Out[8]= {y^2, x^3}
You can use this notation to apply one set of rules, followed by another.	*In[9]:=* **x^2 /. x -> (1 + y) /. y -> b**
	Out[9]= (1 + b)^2

Sometimes you may need to go on applying rules over and over again, until the expression you are working on no longer changes. You can do this using the repeated replacement operation *expr //. rules* (or **ReplaceRepeated[***expr*, *rules***]**).

expr /. rules	try rules once on each part of *expr*
expr //. rules	try rules repeatedly until the result no longer changes

Single and repeated rule application.

With the single replacement operator /. each rule is tried only once on each part of the expression.	*In[10]:=* **x^2 + y^6 /. {x -> 2 + a, a -> 3}**
	Out[10]= (2 + a)^2 + y^6
With the repeated replacement operator //. the rules are tried repeatedly until the expression no longer changes.	*In[11]:=* **x^2 + y^6 //. {x -> 2 + a, a -> 3}**
	Out[11]= 25 + y^6
Here the rule is applied only once.	*In[12]:=* **log[a b c d] /. log[x_ y_] -> log[x] + log[y]**
	Out[12]= log[a] + log[b c d]
With the repeated replacement operator, the rule is applied repeatedly, until the result no longer changes.	*In[13]:=* **log[a b c d] //. log[x_ y_] -> log[x] + log[y]**
	Out[13]= log[a] + log[b] + log[c] + log[d]

When you use //. (pronounced "slash-slash-dot"), *Mathematica* repeatedly passes through your expression, trying each of the rules given. It goes on doing this until it gets the same result on two successive passes.

If you give a set of rules that is circular, then //. can keep on getting different results forever. In practice, the maximum number of passes that //. makes on a particular expression is determined by the setting for the option **MaxIterations**. If you want to keep going for as long as possible, you can use **ReplaceRepeated[***expr*, *rules*, **MaxIterations -> Infinity]**. You can always stop by explicitly interrupting *Mathematica*.

By setting the option **MaxIterations**, you can explicitly tell **ReplaceRepeated** how many times to try the rules you give.	*In[14]:=* **ReplaceRepeated[x, x -> x + 1, MaxIterations -> 1000]**
	ReplaceRepeated::rrlim:
	Exiting after x scanned 1000 times.
	Out[14]= 1000 + x

The replacement operators /. and //. share the feature that they try each rule on every subpart of your expression. On the other hand, Replace[*expr*, *rules*] tries the rules only on the whole of *expr*, and not on any of its subparts.

You can use Replace, together with functions like Map and MapAt, to control exactly which parts of an expression a replacement is applied to. Remember that you can use the function ReplacePart[*expr*, *new*, *pos*] to replace part of an expression with a specific object.

The operator /. applies rules to all subparts of an expression.	*In[15]:=* **x^2 /. x -> a** *Out[15]=* a^2
Replace applies rules only to the whole expression.	*In[16]:=* **Replace[x^2, x^2 -> b]** *Out[16]=* b
No replacement is done here.	*In[17]:=* **Replace[x^2, x -> a]** *Out[17]=* x^2

expr /. *rules*	apply rules to all subparts of *expr*
Replace[*expr*, *rules*]	apply rules to the whole of *expr* only

Applying rules to whole expressions.

Replace returns the result from using the first rule that applies.	*In[18]:=* **Replace[f[u], {f[x_] -> x^2, f[x_] -> x^3}]** *Out[18]=* u^2
ReplaceList gives a list of the results from every rule that applies.	*In[19]:=* **ReplaceList[f[u], {f[x_] -> x^2, f[x_] -> x^3}]** *Out[19]=* $\{u^2, u^3\}$
If a single rule can be applied in several ways, ReplaceList gives a list of all the results.	*In[20]:=* **ReplaceList[a + b + c, x_ + y_ -> g[x, y]]** *Out[20]=* $\{g[a, b+c], g[b, a+c], g[c, a+b], g[a+b, c],$ $g[a+c, b], g[b+c, a]\}$
This gives a list of ways of breaking the original list in two.	*In[21]:=* **ReplaceList[{a, b, c, d}, {x__, y__} -> g[{x}, {y}]]** *Out[21]=* $\{g[\{a\}, \{b, c, d\}], g[\{a, b\}, \{c, d\}],$ $g[\{a, b, c\}, \{d\}]\}$
This finds all sublists that are flanked by the same element.	*In[22]:=* **ReplaceList[{a, b, c, a, d, b, d},** **{___, x_, y__, x_, ___} -> g[x, {y}]]** *Out[22]=* $\{g[a, \{b, c\}], g[b, \{c, a, d\}], g[d, \{b\}]\}$

Replace[*expr*, *rules*]	apply *rules* in one way only
ReplaceList[*expr*, *rules*]	apply *rules* in all possible ways

Applying rules in one way or all possible ways.

■ 2.4.2 Manipulating Sets of Transformation Rules

You can manipulate lists of transformation rules in *Mathematica* just like other symbolic expressions. It is common to assign a name to a rule or set of rules.

This assigns the "name" sinexp to the trigonometric expansion rule.	*In[1]:=* `sinexp = Sin[2 x_] -> 2 Sin[x] Cos[x]` *Out[1]=* $\text{Sin}[2\text{x}\_] \to 2\,\text{Cos}[\text{x}]\,\text{Sin}[\text{x}]$
You can now request the rule "by name".	*In[2]:=* `Sin[2 (1 + x)^2] /. sinexp` *Out[2]=* $2\,\text{Cos}\big[(1+\text{x})^2\big]\,\text{Sin}\big[(1+\text{x})^2\big]$

You can use lists of rules to represent mathematical and other relations. Typically you will find it convenient to give names to the lists, so that you can easily specify the list you want in a particular case.

In most situations, it is only one rule from any given list that actually applies to a particular expression. Nevertheless, the /. operator tests each of the rules in the list in turn. If the list is very long, this process can take a long time.

Mathematica allows you to preprocess lists of rules so that /. can operate more quickly on them. You can take any list of rules and apply the function `Dispatch` to them. The result is a representation of the original list of rules, but including dispatch tables which allow /. to "dispatch" to potentially applicable rules immediately, rather than testing all the rules in turn.

Here is a list of rules for the first five factorials.	*In[3]:=* `facs = Table[f[i] -> i!, {i, 5}]` *Out[3]=* $\{\text{f}[1] \to 1,\ \text{f}[2] \to 2,\ \text{f}[3] \to 6,\ \text{f}[4] \to 24,\ \text{f}[5] \to 120\}$

This sets up dispatch tables that make the rules faster to use.	*In[4]:=* `dfacs = Dispatch[facs]`
	 Out[4]= `Dispatch[{f[1] → 1, f[2] → 2,`
	 `f[3] → 6, f[4] → 24, f[5] → 120},`
	 `-DispatchTables -]`

You can apply the rules using the /. operator.	*In[5]:=* `f[4] /. dfacs` *Out[5]=* `24`

`Dispatch[`*rules*`]`	create a representation of a list of rules that includes dispatch tables
expr `/.` *drules*	apply rules that include dispatch tables

Creating and using dispatch tables.

For long lists of rules, you will find that setting up dispatch tables makes replacement operations much faster. This is particularly true when your rules are for individual symbols or other expressions that do not involve pattern objects. Once you have built dispatch tables in such cases, you will find that the /. operator takes a time that is more or less independent of the number of rules you have. Without dispatch tables, however, /. will take a time directly proportional to the total number of rules.

■ 2.4.3 Making Definitions

The replacement operator / . allows you to apply transformation rules to a specific expression. Often, however, you want to have transformation rules automatically applied whenever possible.

You can do this by assigning explicit values to *Mathematica* expressions and patterns. Each assignment specifies a transformation rule to be applied whenever an expression of the appropriate form occurs.

expr / . *lhs* -> *rhs*	apply a transformation rule to a specific expression
lhs = *rhs*	assign a value which defines a transformation rule to be used whenever possible

Manual and automatic application of transformation rules.

This applies a transformation rule for x to a specific expression.	$In[1]:= (1 + x)^6 / . x \to 3 - a$ $Out[1]= (4-a)^6$
By assigning a value to x, you tell *Mathematica* to apply a transformation rule for x whenever possible.	$In[2]:= x = 3 - a$ $Out[2]= 3-a$
Now x is transformed automatically.	$In[3]:= (1 + x)^7$ $Out[3]= (4-a)^7$

You should realize that except inside constructs like `Module` and `Block`, all assignments you make in a *Mathematica* session are *permanent*. They continue to be used for the duration of the session, unless you explicitly clear or overwrite them.

The fact that assignments are permanent means that they must be made with care. Probably the single most common mistake in using *Mathematica* is to make an assignment for a variable like x at one point in your session, and then later to use x having forgotten about the assignment you made.

There are several ways to avoid this kind of mistake. First, you should avoid using assignments whenever possible, and instead use more controlled constructs such as the / . replacement operator. Second, you should explicitly use the deassignment operator =. or the function `Clear` to remove values you have assigned when you have finished with them.

Another important way to avoid mistakes is to think particularly carefully before assigning values to variables with common or simple names. You will often want to use a variable such as x as a symbolic parameter. But if you make an assignment such as x = 3, then x will be replaced by 3 whenever it occurs, and you can no longer use x as a symbolic parameter.

In general, you should be sure not to assign permanent values to any variables that you might want to use for more than one purpose. If at one point in your session you wanted the variable c to stand for the speed of light, you might assign it a value such as 3.*10^8. But then you cannot use c later in your session to stand, say, for an undetermined coefficient. One way to avoid this kind of problem is to make assignments only for variables with more explicit names, such as `SpeedOfLight`.

x =.	remove the value assigned to the object *x*
`Clear[`*x*, *y*, ... `]`	clear all the values of *x*, *y*, ...

Removing assignments.

This does not give what you might expect, because x still has the value you assigned it above.

In[4]:= `Factor[ x^2 - 1 ]`

Out[4]= $(-4+a)(-2+a)$

This removes any value assigned to x.

In[5]:= `Clear[x]`

Now this gives the result you expect.

In[6]:= `Factor[ x^2 - 1 ]`

Out[6]= $(-1+x)(1+x)$

■ 2.4.4 Special Forms of Assignment

Particularly when you write procedural programs in *Mathematica*, you will often need to modify the value of a particular variable repeatedly. You can always do this by constructing the new value and explicitly performing an assignment such as *x* = *value*. *Mathematica*, however, provides special notations for incrementing the values of variables, and for some other common cases.

i++	increment the value of *i* by 1
i--	decrement *i*
++*i*	pre-increment *i*
--*i*	pre-decrement *i*
i += *di*	add *di* to the value of *i*
i -= *di*	subtract *di* from *i*
x *= *c*	multiply *x* by *c*
x /= *c*	divide *x* by *c*

Modifying values of variables.

This assigns the value 7x to the variable t.

In[1]:= `t = 7x`

Out[1]= $7x$

This increments the value of t by 18x.	*In[2]:=* **t += 18x**
	Out[2]= 25 x
The value of t has been modified.	*In[3]:=* **t**
	Out[3]= 25 x
This sets t to 8, multiplies its value by 7, then gives the final value of t.	*In[4]:=* **t = 8; t *= 7; t**
	Out[4]= 56
The value of i++ is the value of i *before* the increment is done.	*In[5]:=* **i=5; Print[i++]; Print[i]**
	5
	6
The value of ++i is the value of i *after* the increment.	*In[6]:=* **i=5; Print[++i]; Print[i]**
	6
	6

$x = y = value$	assign the same value to both x and y
$\{x, y\} = \{value_1, value_2\}$	assign different values to x and y
$\{x, y\} = \{y, x\}$	interchange the values of x and y

Assigning values to several variables at a time.

This assigns the value 5 to x and 8 to y.	*In[7]:=* **{x, y} = {5, 8}**
	Out[7]= {5, 8}
This interchanges the values of x and y.	*In[8]:=* **{x, y} = {y, x}**
	Out[8]= {8, 5}
Now x has value 8.	*In[9]:=* **x**
	Out[9]= 8
And y has value 5.	*In[10]:=* **y**
	Out[10]= 5
You can use assignments to lists to permute values of variables in any way.	*In[11]:=* **{a, b, c} = {1, 2, 3}; {b, a, c} = {a, c, b}; {a, b, c}**
	Out[11]= {3, 1, 2}

When you write programs in *Mathematica*, you will sometimes find it convenient to take a list, and successively add elements to it. You can do this using the functions PrependTo and AppendTo.

PrependTo[*v*, *elem*]	prepend *elem* to the value of *v*
AppendTo[*v*, *elem*]	append *elem*
v = {*v*, *elem*}	make a nested list containing *elem*

Assignments for modifying lists.

This assigns the value of v to be the list {5, 7, 9}.

In[12]:= **v = {5, 7, 9}**

Out[12]= {5, 7, 9}

This appends the element 11 to the value of v.

In[13]:= **AppendTo[v, 11]**

Out[13]= {5, 7, 9, 11}

Now the value of v has been modified.

In[14]:= **v**

Out[14]= {5, 7, 9, 11}

Although AppendTo[*v*, *elem*] is always equivalent to *v* = Append[*v*, *elem*], it is often a convenient notation. However, you should realize that because of the way *Mathematica* stores lists, it is usually less efficient to add a sequence of elements to a particular list than to create a nested structure that consists, for example, of lists of length 2 at each level. When you have built up such a structure, you can always reduce it to a single list using Flatten.

This sets up a nested list structure for w.

In[15]:= **w = {1}; Do[w = {w, k^2}, {k, 1, 4}]; w**

Out[15]= {{{{1}, 1}, 4}, 9}, 16}

You can use Flatten to unravel the structure.

In[16]:= **Flatten[w]**

Out[16]= {1, 1, 4, 9, 16}

■ 2.4.5 Making Definitions for Indexed Objects

In many kinds of calculations, you need to set up "arrays" which contain sequences of expressions, each specified by a certain index. One way to implement arrays in *Mathematica* is by using lists. You can define a list, say *a* = {*x*, *y*, *z*, ... }, then access its elements using *a*[[*i*]], or modify them using *a*[[*i*]] = *value*. This approach has a drawback, however, in that it requires you to fill in all the elements when you first create the list.

Often, it is more convenient to set up arrays in which you can fill in only those elements that you need at a particular time. You can do this by making definitions for expressions such as *a*[*i*].

This defines a value for a[1].

In[1]:= **a[1] = 9**

Out[1]= 9

This defines a value for a[2].

In[2]:= **a[2] = 7**

Out[2]= 7

This shows all the values you have defined for expressions associated with a so far.

```
In[3]:= ?a
Global`a
a[1] = 9
a[2] = 7
```

You can define a value for a[5], even though you have not yet given values to a[3] and a[4].

```
In[4]:= a[5] = 0
Out[4]= 0
```

This generates a list of the values of the a[*i*].

```
In[5]:= Table[a[i], {i, 5}]
Out[5]= {9, 7, a[3], a[4], 0}
```

You can think of the expression a[*i*] as being like an "indexed" or "subscripted" variable.

$a[i]$ = *value*	add or overwrite a value
$a[i]$	access a value
$a[i]$ =.	remove a value
?*a*	show all defined values
Clear[*a*]	clear all defined values
Table[*a*[i], {i, 1, *n*}] or Array[*a*, *n*]	convert to an explicit List

Manipulating indexed variables.

When you have an expression of the form $a[i]$, there is no requirement that the "index" i be a number. In fact, *Mathematica* allows the index to be any expression whatsoever. By using indices that are symbols, you can for example build up simple databases in *Mathematica*.

This defines the "object" area with "index" square to have value 1.

```
In[6]:= area[square] = 1
Out[6]= 1
```

This adds another result to the area "database".

```
In[7]:= area[triangle] = 1/2
Out[7]= 1/2
```

Here are the entries in the area database so far.

```
In[8]:= ?area
Global`area
area[square] = 1
area[triangle] = 1/2
```

You can use these definitions wherever you want. You have not yet assigned a value for area[pentagon].

```
In[9]:= 4 area[square] + area[pentagon]
Out[9]= 4 + area[pentagon]
```

■ 2.4.6 Making Definitions for Functions

Section 1.7.1 discussed how you can define functions in *Mathematica*. In a typical case, you would type in f[x_] = x^2 to define a function f. (Actually, the definitions in Section 1.7.1 used the := operator, rather than the = one. Section 2.4.8 will explain exactly when to use each of the := and = operators.)

The definition f[x_] = x^2 specifies that whenever *Mathematica* encounters an expression which matches the pattern f[x_], it should replace the expression by x^2. Since the pattern f[x_] matches all expressions of the form f[*anything*], the definition applies to functions f with any "argument".

Function definitions like f[x_] = x^2 can be compared with definitions like f[a] = b for indexed variables discussed in the previous subsection. The definition f[a] = b specifies that whenever the *particular* expression f[a] occurs, it is to be replaced by b. But the definition says nothing about expressions such as f[y], where f appears with another "index".

To define a "function", you need to specify values for expressions of the form f[*x*], where the argument *x* can be anything. You can do this by giving a definition for the pattern f[x_], where the pattern object x_ stands for any expression.

f[*x*] = *value*	definition for a *specific expression x*
f[x_] = *value*	definition for *any expression*, referred to as *x*

The difference between defining an indexed variable and a function.

Making definitions for f[2] or f[a] can be thought of as being like giving values to various elements of an "array" named f. Making a definition for f[x_] is like giving a value for a set of "array elements" with arbitrary "indices". In fact, you can actually think of any function as being like an array with an arbitrarily variable index.

In mathematical terms, you can think of f as a *mapping*. When you define values for, say, f[1] and f[2], you specify the image of this mapping for various discrete points in its domain. Defining a value for f[x_] specifies the image of f on a continuum of points.

This defines a transformation rule for the *specific expression* f[x].

In[1]:= **f[x] = u**

Out[1]= u

When the specific expression f[x] appears, it is replaced by u. Other expressions of the form f[*argument*] are, however, not modified.

In[2]:= **f[x] + f[y]**

Out[2]= u + f[y]

This defines a value for f with *any expression* as an "argument".

In[3]:= **f[x_] = x^2**

Out[3]= x^2

The old definition for the *specific expression* f[x] is still used, but the new general definition for f[x_] is now used to find a value for f[y].

In[4]:= **f[x] + f[y]**

Out[4]= $u + y^2$

This removes all definitions for f.

In[5]:= **Clear[f]**

Mathematica allows you to define transformation rules for any expression or pattern. You can mix definitions for specific expressions such as f[1] or f[a] with definitions for patterns such as f[x_].

Many kinds of mathematical functions can be set up by mixing specific and general definitions in *Mathematica*. As an example, consider the factorial function. This particular function is in fact built into *Mathematica* (it is written $n!$). But you can use *Mathematica* definitions to set up the function for yourself.

The standard mathematical definition for the factorial function can be entered almost directly into *Mathematica*, in the form: f[n_] := n f[n-1]; f[1] = 1. This definition specifies that for any n, f[n] should be replaced by n f[n-1], except that when n is 1, f[1] should simply be replaced by 1.

Here is the value of the factorial function with argument 1.

In[6]:= **f[1] = 1**

Out[6]= 1

Here is the general recursion relation for the factorial function.

In[7]:= **f[n_] := n f[n-1]**

Now you can use these definitions to find values for the factorial function.

In[8]:= **f[10]**

Out[8]= 3628800

The results are the same as you get from the built-in version of factorial.

In[9]:= **10!**

Out[9]= 3628800

■ 2.4.7 The Ordering of Definitions

When you make a sequence of definitions in *Mathematica*, some may be more general than others. *Mathematica* follows the principle of trying to put more general definitions after more specific ones. This means that special cases of rules are typically tried before more general cases.

This behavior is crucial to the factorial function example given in the previous section. Regardless of the order in which you entered them, *Mathematica* will always put the rule for the special case f[1] ahead of the rule for the general case f[n_]. This means that when *Mathematica* looks for the value of an expression of the form f[n], it tries the special case f[1] first, and only if this does not apply, it tries the general case f[n_]. As a result, when you ask for f[5], *Mathematica* will keep on using the general rule until the "end condition" rule for f[1] applies.

■ *Mathematica* tries to put specific definitions before more general definitions.

Treatment of definitions in *Mathematica*.

If *Mathematica* did not follow the principle of putting special rules before more general ones, then the special rules would always be "shadowed" by more general ones. In the factorial example, if the rule for `f[n_]` was ahead of the rule for `f[1]`, then even when *Mathematica* tried to evaluate `f[1]`, it would use the general `f[n_]` rule, and it would never find the special `f[1]` rule.

Here is a general definition for `f[n_]`.	`In[1]:= f[n_] := n f[n-1]`
Here is a definition for the special case `f[1]`.	`In[2]:= f[1] = 1` `Out[2]= 1`

Mathematica puts the special case before the general one.	`In[3]:= ?f`
	`Global'f`
	`f[1] = 1`
	`f[n_] := n*f[n - 1]`

In the factorial function example used above, it is clear which rule is more general. Often, however, there is no definite ordering in generality of the rules you give. In such cases, *Mathematica* simply tries the rules in the order you give them.

These rules have no definite ordering in generality.	`In[4]:= log[x_ y_] := log[x] + log[y] ; log[x_^n_] := n log[x]`

Mathematica stores the rules in the order you gave them.	`In[5]:= ?log`
	`Global'log`
	`log[(x_)*(y_)] := log[x] + log[y]`
	`log[(x_)^(n_)] := n*log[x]`

This rule is a special case of the rule for `log[x_ y_]`.	`In[6]:= log[2 x_] := log[x] + log2`

Mathematica puts the special rule before the more general one.	`In[7]:= ?log`
	`Global'log`
	`log[2*(x_)] := log[x] + log2`
	`log[(x_)*(y_)] := log[x] + log[y]`
	`log[(x_)^(n_)] := n*log[x]`

Although in many practical cases, *Mathematica* can recognize when one rule is more general than another, you should realize that this is not always possible. For example, if two rules both contain complicated `/;` conditions, it may not be possible to work out which is more general, and, in fact, there may not be a definite ordering. Whenever the appropriate ordering is not clear, *Mathematica* stores rules in the order you give them.

■ 2.4.8 Immediate and Delayed Definitions

You may have noticed that there are two different ways to make assignments in *Mathematica*: *lhs* = *rhs* and *lhs* := *rhs*. The basic difference between these forms is *when* the expression *rhs* is evaluated. *lhs* = *rhs* is an *immediate assignment*, in which *rhs* is evaluated at the time when the assignment is made. *lhs* := *rhs*, on the other hand, is a *delayed assignment*, in which *rhs* is not evaluated when the assignment is made, but is instead evaluated each time the value of *lhs* is requested.

lhs = *rhs* (immediate assignment)	*rhs* is evaluated when the assignment is made
lhs := *rhs* (delayed assignment)	*rhs* is evaluated each time the value of *lhs* is requested

The two types of assignments in *Mathematica*.

This uses the := operator to define the function ex.	`In[1]:= ex[x_] := Expand[(1 + x)^2]`

Because := was used, the definition is maintained in an unevaluated form.	`In[2]:= ?ex`
	
	`Global'ex`
	
	`ex[x_] := Expand[(1 + x)^2]`

When you make an assignment with the = operator, the right-hand side is evaluated immediately.	`In[3]:= iex[x_] = Expand[(1 + x)^2]` $Out[3]= 1 + 2x + x^2$

The definition now stored is the result of the Expand command.	`In[4]:= ?iex`
	
	`Global'iex`
	
	`iex[x_] = 1 + 2*x + x^2`

When you execute ex, the Expand is performed.	`In[5]:= ex[y + 2]` $Out[5]= 9 + 6y + y^2$
iex simply substitutes its argument into the already expanded form, giving a different answer.	`In[6]:= iex[y + 2]` $Out[6]= 1 + 2(2 + y) + (2 + y)^2$

As you can see from the example above, both = and := can be useful in defining functions, but they have different meanings, and you must be careful about which one to use in a particular case.

One rule of thumb is the following. If you think of an assignment as giving the final "value" of an expression, use the = operator. If instead you think of the assignment as specifying a "command" for finding the value, use the := operator. If in doubt, it is usually better to use the := operator than the = one.

lhs = *rhs*	*rhs* is intended to be the "final value" of *lhs* (e.g., `f[x_] = 1 - x^2`)
lhs := *rhs*	*rhs* gives a "command" or "program" to be executed whenever you ask for the value of *lhs* (e.g., `f[x_] := Expand[1 - x^2]`)

Interpretations of assignments with the `=` and `:=` operators.

Although `:=` is probably used more often than `=` in defining functions, there is one important case in which you must use `=` to define a function. If you do a calculation, and get an answer in terms of a symbolic parameter x, you often want to go on and find results for various specific values of x. One way to do this is to use the `/.` operator to apply appropriate rules for x in each case. It is usually more convenient however, to use `=` to define a function whose argument is x.

Here is an expression involving x.	`In[7]:= D[Log[Sin[x]]^2, x]`
	`Out[7]= 2 Cot[x] Log[Sin[x]]`
This defines a function whose argument is the value to be taken for x.	`In[8]:= dlog[x_] = %`
	`Out[8]= 2 Cot[x] Log[Sin[x]]`
Here is the result when x is taken to be 1 + a.	`In[9]:= dlog[1 + a]`
	`Out[9]= 2 Cot[1 + a] Log[Sin[1 + a]]`

An important point to notice in the example above is that there is nothing special about the name `x` that appears in the `x_` pattern. It is just a symbol, indistinguishable from an `x` that appears in any other expression.

`f[x_] = expr`	define a function which gives the value *expr* for any particular value of x

Defining functions for evaluating expressions.

You can use `=` and `:=` not only to define functions, but also to assign values to variables. If you type x = *value*, then *value* is immediately evaluated, and the result is assigned to x. On the other hand, if you type x := *value*, then *value* is not immediately evaluated. Instead, it is maintained in an unevaluated form, and is evaluated afresh each time x is used.

This evaluates `Random[ ]` to find a pseudorandom number, then assigns this number to `r1`.	`In[10]:= r1 = Random[ ]`
	`Out[10]= 0.0560708`
Here `Random[ ]` is maintained in an unevaluated form, to be evaluated afresh each time `r2` is used.	`In[11]:= r2 := Random[ ]`

Here are values for r1 and r2.	`In[12]:= {r1, r2}`
	`Out[12]= {0.0560708, 0.6303}`

The value of r1 never changes. Every time r2 is used, however, a new pseudorandom number is generated.	`In[13]:= {r1, r2}`
	`Out[13]= {0.0560708, 0.359894}`

The distinction between immediate and delayed assignments is particularly important when you set up chains of assignments.

This defines a to be 1.	`In[14]:= a = 1`
	`Out[14]= 1`

Here a + 2 is evaluated to give 3, and the result is assigned to be the value of ri.	`In[15]:= ri = a + 2`
	`Out[15]= 3`

Here a + 2 is maintained in an unevaluated form, to be evaluated every time the value of rd is requested.	`In[16]:= rd := a + 2`

In this case, ri and rd give the same values.	`In[17]:= {ri, rd}`
	`Out[17]= {3, 3}`

Now the value of a is changed.	`In[18]:= a = 2`
	`Out[18]= 2`

Now rd uses the new value for a, while ri keeps its original value.	`In[19]:= {ri, rd}`
	`Out[19]= {3, 4}`

You can use delayed assignments such as $t := rhs$ to set up variables whose values you can find in a variety of different "environments". Every time you ask for t, the expression rhs is evaluated using the current values of the objects on which it depends.

The right-hand side of the delayed assignment is maintained in an unevaluated form.	`In[20]:= t := {a, Factor[x^a - 1]}`

This sets a to 4, then finds the value of t.	`In[21]:= a = 4; t`
	`Out[21]= {4, (-1 + x) (1 + x) (1 + x^2)}`

Here a is 6.	`In[22]:= a = 6; t`
	`Out[22]= {6, (-1 + x) (1 + x) (1 - x + x^2) (1 + x + x^2)}`

In the example above, the symbol a acts as a "global variable", whose value affects the value of t. When you have a large number of parameters, many of which change only occasionally, you may find this kind of setup convenient. However, you should realize that implicit or hidden dependence of one variable on others can often become quite confusing. When possible, you should make all dependencies explicit, by defining functions which take all necessary parameters as arguments.

lhs -> *rhs*	*rhs* is evaluated when the rule is given
lhs :> *rhs*	*rhs* is evaluated when the rule is used

Two types of transformation rules in *Mathematica*.

Just as you can make immediate and delayed assignments in *Mathematica*, so you can also set up immediate and delayed transformation rules.

The right-hand side of this rule is evaluated when you give the rule.	*In[23]:=* **f[x_] -> Expand[(1 + x)^2]**
	Out[23]= f[x_] → 1 + 2 x + x²
A rule like this is probably not particularly useful.	*In[24]:=* **f[x_] -> Expand[x]**
	Out[24]= f[x_] → x
Here the right-hand side of the rule is maintained in an unevaluated form, to be evaluated every time the rule is used.	*In[25]:=* **f[x_] :> Expand[x]**
	Out[25]= f[x_] :→ Expand[x]
Applying the rule causes the expansion to be done.	*In[26]:=* **f[(1 + p)^2] /. f[x_] :> Expand[x]**
	Out[26]= 1 + 2 p + p²

In analogy with assignments, you should typically use -> when you want to replace an expression with a definite value, and you should use :> when you want to give a command for finding the value.

■ 2.4.9 Functions That Remember Values They Have Found

When you make a function definition using :=, the value of the function is recomputed every time you ask for it. In some kinds of calculations, you may end up asking for the same function value many times. You can save time in these cases by having *Mathematica* remember all the function values it finds. Here is an "idiom" for defining a function that does this.

f[*x*_] := f[*x*] = *rhs*	define a function which remembers values that it finds

Defining a function that remembers values it finds.

This defines a function f which stores all values that it finds.	*In[1]:=* **f[x_] := f[x] = f[x - 1] + f[x - 2]**
Here are the end conditions for the recursive function f.	*In[2]:=* **f[0] = f[1] = 1**
	Out[2]= 1

Here is the original definition of f.

```
In[3]:= ?f
Global`f

f[0] = 1

f[1] = 1

f[x_] := f[x] = f[x - 1] + f[x - 2]
```

This computes f[5]. The computation involves finding the sequence of values f[5], f[4], ... f[2].

```
In[4]:= f[5]
Out[4]= 8
```

All the values of f found so far are explicitly stored.

```
In[5]:= ?f
Global`f

f[0] = 1

f[1] = 1

f[2] = 2

f[3] = 3

f[4] = 5

f[5] = 8

f[x_] := f[x] = f[x - 1] + f[x - 2]
```

If you ask for f[5] again, *Mathematica* can just look up the value immediately; it does not have to recompute it.

```
In[6]:= f[5]
Out[6]= 8
```

You can see how a definition like f[x_] := f[x] = f[x-1] + f[x-2] works. The function f[x_] is defined to be the "program" f[x] = f[x-1] + f[x-2]. When you ask for a value of the function f, the "program" is executed. The program first calculates the value of f[x-1] + f[x-2], then saves the result as f[x].

It is often a good idea to use functions that remember values when you implement mathematical *recursion relations* in *Mathematica*. In a typical case, a recursion relation gives the value of a function f with an integer argument x in terms of values of the same function with arguments $x - 1$, $x - 2$, etc. The Fibonacci function definition $f(x) = f(x - 1) + f(x - 2)$ used above is an example of this kind of recursion relation. The point is that if you calculate say $f(10)$ by just applying the recursion relation over and over again, you end up having to recalculate quantities like $f(5)$ many times. In a case like this, it is therefore better just to *remember* the value of $f(5)$, and look it up when you need it, rather than having to recalculate it.

There is of course a trade-off involved in remembering values. It is faster to find a particular value, but it takes more memory space to store all of them. You should usually define functions to remember values only if the total number of different values that will be produced is comparatively small, or the expense of recomputing them is very great.

■ 2.4.10 Associating Definitions with Different Symbols

When you make a definition in the form *f*[*args*] = *rhs* or *f*[*args*] := *rhs*, *Mathematica* associates your definition with the object *f*. This means, for example, that such definitions are displayed when you type ?*f*. In general, definitions for expressions in which the symbol *f* appears as the head are termed *downvalues* of *f*.

Mathematica however also supports *upvalues*, which allow definitions to be associated with symbols that do not appear directly as their head.

Consider for example a definition like `Exp[g[x_]]` := *rhs*. One possibility is that this definition could be associated with the symbol `Exp`, and considered as a downvalue of `Exp`. This is however probably not the best thing either from the point of view of organization or efficiency.

Better is to consider `Exp[g[x_]]` := *rhs* to be associated with g, and to correspond to an upvalue of g.

f[*args*] := *rhs*	define a downvalue for *f*
f[*g*[*args*], ...] ^:= *rhs*	define an upvalue for *g*

Associating definitions with different symbols.

This is taken to define a downvalue for f.	*In[1]:=* **f[g[x_]] := fg[x]**
You can see the definition when you ask about f.	*In[2]:=* **?f**
	Global`f
	f[g[x_]] := fg[x]
This defines an upvalue for g.	*In[3]:=* **g/: Exp[g[x_]] := expg[x]**
The definition is associated with g.	*In[4]:=* **?g**
	Global`g
	Exp[g[x_]] ^:= expg[x]
It is not associated with Exp.	*In[5]:=* **?Exp**
	Exp[z] is the exponential function.
The definition is used to evaluate this expression.	*In[6]:=* **Exp[g[5]]**
	Out[6]= expg[5]

In simple cases, you will get the same answers to calculations whether you give a definition for *f*[*g*[*x*]] as a downvalue for *f* or an upvalue for *g*. However, one of the two choices is usually much more natural and efficient than the other.

A good rule of thumb is that a definition for *f*[*g*[*x*]] should be given as an upvalue for *g* in cases where the function *f* is more common than *g*. Thus, for example, in the case of `Exp[g[x]]`, Exp is a built-in *Mathematica* function, while g is presumably a function you have added. In such a case, you will typically think of definitions for Exp[g[x]] as giving relations satisfied by g. As a result, it is more natural to treat the definitions as upvalues for g than as downvalues for Exp.

This gives the definition as an upvalue for g.	In[7]:= **g/: g[x_] + g[y_] := gplus[x, y]**

Here are the definitions for g so far.

In[8]:= **?g**

Global`g

Exp[g[x_]] ^:= expg[x]

g[x_] + g[y_] ^:= gplus[x, y]

The definition for a sum of g's is used whenever possible.	In[9]:= **g[5] + g[7]**
	Out[9]= gplus[5, 7]

Since the full form of the pattern g[x_] + g[y_] is Plus[g[x_], g[y_]], a definition for this pattern could be given as a downvalue for Plus. It is almost always better, however, to give the definition as an upvalue for g.

In general, whenever *Mathematica* encounters a particular function, it tries all the definitions you have given for that function. If you had made the definition for g[x_] + g[y_] a downvalue for Plus, then *Mathematica* would have tried this definition whenever Plus occurs. The definition would thus be tested every time *Mathematica* added expressions together, making this very common operation slower in all cases.

However, by giving a definition for g[x_] + g[y_] as an upvalue for g, you associate the definition with g. In this case, *Mathematica* only tries the definition when it finds a g inside a function such as Plus. Since g presumably occurs much less frequently than Plus, this is a much more efficient procedure.

$f[g]$ ^= *value*   or $f[g[args]]$ ^= *value*
　　　　　　　　　　make assignments to be associated with g, rather than f

$f[g]$ ^:= *value*   or $f[g[args]]$ ^:= *value*
　　　　　　　　　　make delayed assignments associated with g

$f[arg_1, arg_2, \ldots]$ ^= *value*   make assignments associated with the heads of *all* the arg_i

---

Shorter ways to define upvalues.

A typical use of upvalues is in setting up a "database" of properties of a particular object. With upvalues, you can associate each definition you make with the object that it concerns, rather than with the property you are specifying.

This defines an upvalue for square which gives its area.	In[10]:= **area[square] ^= 1**
	Out[10]= 1

This adds a definition for the perimeter.

In[11]:= **perimeter[square] ^= 4**

Out[11]= 4

Both definitions are now associated with the object square.

In[12]:= **?square**

Global`square

area[square] ^= 1

perimeter[square] ^= 4

In general, you can associate definitions for an expression with any symbol that occurs at a sufficiently high level in the expression. With an expression of the form $f[args]$, you can define an upvalue for a symbol g so long as either g itself, or an object with head g, occurs in *args*. If g occurs at a lower level in an expression, however, you cannot associate definitions with it.

g occurs as the head of an argument, so you can associate a definition with it.

In[13]:= **g/: h[w[x_], g[y_]] := hwg[x, y]**

Here g appears too deep in the left-hand side for you to associate a definition with it.

In[14]:= **g/: h[w[g[x_]], y_] := hw[x, y]**

TagSetDelayed::tagpos:
    Tag g in h[w[g[x_]], y_]
        is too deep for an assigned rule to be found.

Out[14]= $Failed

$$f[\ \ldots\ ] := rhs \qquad \text{downvalue for } f$$
$$f/: f[g[\ \ldots\ ]][\ \ldots\ ] := rhs \qquad \text{downvalue for } f$$
$$g/: f[\ \ldots\ , g, \ \ldots\ ] := rhs \qquad \text{upvalue for } g$$
$$g/: f[\ \ldots\ , g[\ \ldots\ ], \ \ldots\ ] := rhs \qquad \text{upvalue for } g$$

Possible positions for symbols in definitions.

As discussed in Section 2.1.2, you can use *Mathematica* symbols as "tags", to indicate the "type" of an expression. For example, complex numbers in *Mathematica* are represented internally in the form Complex[x, y], where the symbol Complex serves as a tag to indicate that the object is a complex number.

Upvalues provide a convenient mechanism for specifying how operations act on objects that are tagged to have a certain type. For example, you might want to introduce a class of abstract mathematical objects of type quat. You can represent each object of this type by a *Mathematica* expression of the form quat[*data*].

In a typical case, you might want quat objects to have special properties with respect to arithmetic operations such as addition and multiplication. You can set up such properties by defining upvalues for quat with respect to Plus and Times.

This defines an upvalue for quat with respect to Plus.	`In[15]:= quat[x_] + quat[y_] ^:= quat[x + y]`

The upvalue you have defined is used to simplify this expression.	`In[16]:= quat[a] + quat[b] + quat[c]` `Out[16]= quat[a + b + c]`

When you define an upvalue for quat with respect to an operation like Plus, what you are effectively doing is to extend the domain of the Plus operation to include quat objects. You are telling *Mathematica* to use special rules for addition in the case where the things to be added together are quat objects.

In defining addition for quat objects, you could always have a special addition operation, say quatPlus, to which you assign an appropriate downvalue. It is usually much more convenient, however, to use the standard *Mathematica* Plus operation to represent addition, but then to "overload" this operation by specifying special behavior when quat objects are encountered.

You can think of upvalues as a way to implement certain aspects of object-oriented programming. A symbol like quat represents a particular type of object. Then the various upvalues for quat specify "methods" that define how quat objects should behave under certain operations, or on receipt of certain "messages".

■ 2.4.11 Defining Numerical Values

If you make a definition such as f[x_] := *value*, *Mathematica* will use the value you give for any f function it encounters. In some cases, however, you may want to define a value that is to be used specifically when you ask for numerical values.

expr = *value*	define a value to be used whenever possible
N[*expr*] = *value*	define a value to be used for numerical approximation

Defining ordinary and numerical values.

This defines a numerical value for the function f.	`In[1]:= N[f[x_]] := Sum[x^-i/i^2, {i, 20}]`

Defining the numerical value does not tell *Mathematica* anything about the ordinary value of f.	`In[2]:= f[2] + f[5]` `Out[2]= f[2] + f[5]`

If you ask for a numerical approximation, however, *Mathematica* uses the numerical values you have defined.	`In[3]:= N[%]` `Out[3]= 0.793244`

You can define numerical values for both functions and symbols. The numerical values are used by all numerical *Mathematica* functions, including NIntegrate, FindRoot and so on.

N[*expr*] = *value*	define a numerical value to be used when default numerical precision is requested
N[*expr*, *n*] = *value*	define a numerical value to be used when *n*-digit precision is requested

Defining numerical values that depend on numerical precision.

This defines a numerical value for the symbol const, using 4n + 5 terms in the product for n-digit precision.	*In[4]:=* **N[const, n_] := Product[1 - 2^-i, {i, 2, 4n + 5}]**
Here is the value of const, computed to 30-digit precision using the value you specified.	*In[5]:=* **N[const, 30]** *Out[5]=* 0.577576190173204842557799443585

Mathematica treats numerical values essentially like upvalues. When you define a numerical value for *f*, *Mathematica* effectively enters your definition as an upvalue for f with respect to the numerical evaluation operation N.

■ 2.4.12 Modifying Built-in Functions

Mathematica allows you to define transformation rules for any expression. You can define such rules not only for functions that you add to *Mathematica*, but also for intrinsic functions that are already built into *Mathematica*. As a result, you can enhance, or modify, the features of built-in *Mathematica* functions.

This capability is powerful, but potentially dangerous. *Mathematica* will always follow the rules you give it. This means that if the rules you give are incorrect, then *Mathematica* will give you incorrect answers.

To avoid the possibility of changing built-in functions by mistake, *Mathematica* "protects" all built-in functions from redefinition. If you want to give a definition for a built-in function, you have to remove the protection first. After you give the definition, you should usually restore the protection, to prevent future mistakes.

Unprotect[*f*]	remove protection
Protect[*f*]	add protection

Protection for functions.

Built-in functions are usually "protected", so you cannot redefine them.

```
In[1]:= Log[7] = 2
Set::write: Tag Log in Log[7] is Protected.
Out[1]= 2
```

This removes protection for Log.

```
In[2]:= Unprotect[Log]
Out[2]= {Log}
```

Now you can give your own definitions for Log. This particular definition is not mathematically correct, but *Mathematica* will still allow you to give it.

```
In[3]:= Log[7] = 2
Out[3]= 2
```

Mathematica will use your definitions whenever it can, whether they are mathematically correct or not.

```
In[4]:= Log[7] + Log[3]
Out[4]= 2 + Log[3]
```

This removes the incorrect definition for Log.

```
In[5]:= Log[7] =.
```

This restores the protection for Log.

```
In[6]:= Protect[Log]
Out[6]= {Log}
```

Definitions you give can override built-in features of *Mathematica*. In general, *Mathematica* tries to use your definitions before it uses built-in definitions.

The rules that are built into *Mathematica* are intended to be appropriate for the broadest range of calculations. In specific cases, however, you may not like what the built-in rules do. In such cases, you can give your own rules to override the ones that are built in.

There is a built-in rule for simplifying Exp[Log[*expr*]].

```
In[7]:= Exp[Log[y]]
Out[7]= y
```

You can give your own rule for Exp[Log[*expr*]], overriding the built-in rule.

```
In[8]:= (
        Unprotect[Exp] ;
        Exp[Log[expr_]] := explog[expr] ;
        Protect[Exp] ;
        )
```

Now your rule is used, rather than the built-in one.

```
In[9]:= Exp[Log[y]]
Out[9]= explog[y]
```

■ 2.4.13 Advanced Topic: Manipulating Value Lists

DownValues[*f*]	give the list of downvalues of *f*
UpValues[*f*]	give the list of upvalues of *f*
DownValues[*f*] = *rules*	set the downvalues of *f*
UpValues[*f*] = *rules*	set the upvalues of *f*

Finding and setting values of symbols.

Mathematica effectively stores all definitions you give as lists of transformation rules. When a particular symbol is encountered, the lists of rules associated with it are tried.

Under most circumstances, you do not need direct access to the actual transformation rules associated with definitions you have given. Instead, you can simply use *lhs* = *rhs* and *lhs* =. to add and remove rules. In some cases, however, you may find it useful to have direct access to the actual rules.

Here is a definition for f.   *In[1]:=* **f[x_] := x^2**

This gives the explicit rule corresponding to the definition you made for f.

In[2]:= **DownValues[f]**

Out[2]= {HoldPattern[f[x_]] :→ x²}

Notice that the rules returned by DownValues and UpValues are set up so that neither their left- nor right-hand sides get evaluated. The left-hand sides are wrapped in HoldPattern, and the rules are delayed, so that the right-hand sides are not immediately evaluated.

As discussed in Section 2.4.6, *Mathematica* tries to order definitions so that more specific ones appear before more general ones. In general, however, there is no unique way to make this ordering, and you may want to choose a different ordering from the one that *Mathematica* chooses by default. You can do this by reordering the list of rules obtained from DownValues or UpValues.

Here are some definitions for the object g.

In[3]:= **g[x_ + y_] := gp[x, y] ; g[x_ y_] := gm[x, y]**

This shows the default ordering used for the definitions.

In[4]:= **DownValues[g]**

Out[4]= {HoldPattern[g[x_ + y_]] :→ gp[x, y],
                 HoldPattern[g[x_ y_]] :→ gm[x, y]}

This reverses the order of the definitions for g.

In[5]:= **DownValues[g] = Reverse[DownValues[g]]**

Out[5]= {HoldPattern[g[x_ y_]] :→ gm[x, y],
                 HoldPattern[g[x_ + y_]] :→ gp[x, y]}

2.5 Evaluation of Expressions

■ 2.5.1 Principles of Evaluation

The fundamental operation that *Mathematica* performs is *evaluation*. Whenever you enter an expression, *Mathematica* evaluates the expression, then returns the result.

Evaluation in *Mathematica* works by applying a sequence of definitions. The definitions can either be ones you explicitly entered, or ones that are built into *Mathematica*.

Thus, for example, *Mathematica* evaluates the expression 6 + 7 using a built-in procedure for adding integers. Similarly, *Mathematica* evaluates the algebraic expression x - 3x + 1 using a built-in simplification procedure. If you had made the definition x = 5, then *Mathematica* would use this definition to reduce x - 3x + 1 to -9.

The two most central concepts in *Mathematica* are probably *expressions* and *evaluation*. Section 2.1 discussed how all the different kinds of objects that *Mathematica* handles are represented in a uniform way using expressions. This section describes how all the operations that *Mathematica* can perform can also be viewed in a uniform way as examples of evaluation.

Computation	$5 + 6$	$\longrightarrow$ 11
Simplification	$x - 3x + 1$	$\longrightarrow$ $1 - 2x$
Execution	$x = 5$	$\longrightarrow$ 5

Some interpretations of evaluation.

Mathematica is an *infinite evaluation* system. When you enter an expression, *Mathematica* will keep on using definitions it knows until it gets a result to which no definitions apply.

This defines x1 in terms of x2, and then defines x2.	`In[1]:= x1 = x2 + 2 ; x2 = 7` `Out[1]= 7`
If you ask for x1, *Mathematica* uses all the definitions it knows to give you a result.	`In[2]:= x1` `Out[2]= 9`
Here is a recursive definition in which the factorial function is defined in terms of itself.	`In[3]:= fac[1] = 1 ; fac[n_] := n fac[n-1]`
If you ask for fac[10], *Mathematica* will keep on applying the definitions you have given until the result it gets no longer changes.	`In[4]:= fac[10]` `Out[4]= 3628800`

When *Mathematica* has used all the definitions it knows, it gives whatever expression it has obtained as the result. Sometimes the result may be an object such as a number. But usually the result is an expression in which some objects are represented in a symbolic form.

Mathematica uses its built-in definitions for simplifying sums, but knows no definitions for f[3], so leaves this in symbolic form.	*In[5]:=* **f[3] + 4f[3] + 1** *Out[5]=* $1 + 5 f[3]$

Mathematica follows the principle of applying definitions until the result it gets no longer changes. This means that if you take the final result that *Mathematica* gives, and enter it as *Mathematica* input, you will get back the same result again. (There are some subtle cases discussed in Section 2.5.12 in which this does not occur.)

If you type in a result from *Mathematica*, you get back the same expression again.	*In[6]:=* **1 + 5 f[3]** *Out[6]=* $1 + 5 f[3]$

At any given time, *Mathematica* can only use those definitions that it knows at that time. If you add more definitions later, however, *Mathematica* will be able to use these. The results you get from *Mathematica* may change in this case.

Here is a new definition for the function f.	*In[7]:=* **f[x_] = x^2** *Out[7]=* x^2

With the new definition, the results you get can change.	*In[8]:=* **1 + 5 f[3]** *Out[8]=* 46

The simplest examples of evaluation involve using definitions such as f[x_] = x^2 which transform one expression directly into another. But evaluation is also the process used to execute programs written in *Mathematica*. Thus, for example, if you have a procedure consisting of a sequence of *Mathematica* expressions, some perhaps representing conditionals and loops, the execution of this procedure corresponds to the evaluation of these expressions. Sometimes the evaluation process may involve evaluating a particular expression several times, as in a loop.

The expression Print[zzzz] is evaluated three times during the evaluation of the Do expression.	*In[9]:=* **Do[Print[zzzz], {3}]** zzzz zzzz zzzz

■ 2.5.2 Reducing Expressions to Their Standard Form

The built-in functions in *Mathematica* operate in a wide variety of ways. But many of the mathematical functions share an important approach: they are set up so as to reduce classes of mathematical expressions to standard forms.

The built-in definitions for the Plus function, for example, are set up to write any sum of terms in a standard unparenthesized form. The associativity of addition means that expressions like (a + b) + c, a + (b + c) and a + b + c are all equivalent. But for many purposes it is convenient for all these forms to be reduced to the single standard form a + b + c. The built-in definitions for Plus are set up to do this.

Through the built-in definitions for   `In[1]:= (a + b) + c`
Plus, this expression is reduced to a
standard unparenthesized form.   `Out[1]= a + b + c`

Whenever *Mathematica* knows that a function is associative, it tries to remove parentheses (or nested invocations of the function) to get the function into a standard "flattened" form.

A function like addition is not only associative, but also commutative, which means that expressions like a + c + b and a + b + c with terms in different orders are equal. Once again, *Mathematica* tries to put all such expressions into a "standard" form. The standard form it chooses is the one in which all the terms are in a definite order, corresponding roughly to alphabetical order.

Mathematica sorts the terms in this sum   `In[2]:= c + a + b`
into a standard order.   `Out[2]= a + b + c`

flat (associative)	$f[f[a, b], c]$ is equivalent to $f[a, b, c]$, etc.
orderless (commutative)	$f[b, a]$ is equivalent to $f[a, b]$, etc.

Two important properties that *Mathematica* uses in reducing certain functions to standard form.

There are several reasons to try to put expressions into standard forms. The most important is that if two expressions are really in standard form, it is obvious whether or not they are equal.

When the two sums are put into   `In[3]:= f[a + c + b] - f[c + a + b]`
standard order, they are immediately
seen to be equal, so that two f's   `Out[3]= 0`
cancel, leaving the result 0.

You could imagine finding out whether a + c + b was equal to c + a + b by testing all possible orderings of each sum. It is clear that simply reducing both sums to standard form is a much more efficient procedure.

One might think that *Mathematica* should somehow automatically reduce *all* mathematical expressions to a single standard canonical form. With all but the simplest kinds of expressions, however, it is quite easy to see that you do not want the *same* standard form for all purposes.

For polynomials, for example, there are two obvious standard forms, which are good for different purposes. The first standard form for a polynomial is a simple sum of terms, as would be generated in *Mathematica* by applying the function Expand. This standard form is most appropriate if you need to add and subtract polynomials.

There is, however, another possible standard form that you can use for polynomials. By applying Factor, you can write any polynomial as a product of irreducible factors. This canonical form is useful if you want to do operations like division.

Expanded and factored forms are in a sense both equally good standard forms for polynomials. Which one you decide to use simply depends on what you want to use it for. As a result, *Mathematica* does not automatically put polynomials into one of these two forms. Instead, it gives you functions like `Expand` and `Factor` that allow you explicitly to put polynomials in whatever form you want.

Here is a list of two polynomials that are mathematically equal.	*In[4]:=* **t = {x^2 - 1, (x + 1)(x - 1)}**
	Out[4]= $\{-1 + x^2, \ (-1 + x)\,(1 + x)\}$
You can write both of them in expanded form just by applying `Expand`. In this form, the equality of the polynomials is obvious.	*In[5]:=* **Expand[t]**
	Out[5]= $\{-1 + x^2, \ -1 + x^2\}$
You can also see that the polynomials are equal by writing them both in factored form.	*In[6]:=* **Factor[t]**
	Out[6]= $\{(-1 + x)\,(1 + x), \ (-1 + x)\,(1 + x)\}$

Although it is clear that you do not always want expressions reduced to the *same* standard form, you may wonder whether it is at least *possible* to reduce all expressions to *some* standard form.

There is a basic result in the mathematical theory of computation which shows that this is, in fact, not always possible. You cannot guarantee that any finite sequence of transformations will take any two arbitrarily chosen expressions to a standard form.

In a sense, this is not particularly surprising. If you could in fact reduce all mathematical expressions to a standard form, then it would be quite easy to tell whether any two expressions were equal. The fact that so many of the difficult problems of mathematics can be stated as questions about the equality of expressions suggests that this can in fact be difficult.

■ 2.5.3 Attributes

Definitions such as `f[x_] = x^2` specify *values* for functions. Sometimes, however, you need to specify general properties of functions, without necessarily giving explicit values.

Mathematica provides a selection of *attributes* that you can use to specify various properties of functions. For example, you can use the attribute `Flat` to specify that a particular function is "flat", so that nested invocations are automatically flattened, and it behaves as if it were associative.

This assigns the attribute `Flat` to the function `f`.	*In[1]:=* **SetAttributes[f, Flat]**
Now `f` behaves as a flat, or associative, function, so that nested invocations are automatically flattened.	*In[2]:=* **f[f[a, b], c]**
	Out[2]= f[a, b, c]

Attributes like `Flat` can affect not only evaluation, but also operations such as pattern matching. If you give definitions or transformation rules for a function, you must be sure to have specified the attributes of the function first.

Here is a definition for the flat function f.

```
In[3]:= f[x_, x_] := f[x]
```

Because f is flat, the definition is automatically applied to every subsequence of arguments.

```
In[4]:= f[a, a, a, b, b, b, c, c]
Out[4]= f[a, b, c]
```

Attributes[f]	give the attributes of f
Attributes[f] = {$attr_1$, $attr_2$, ... }	set the attributes of f
Attributes[f] = {}	set f to have no attributes
SetAttributes[f, $attr$]	add $attr$ to the attributes of f
ClearAttributes[f, $attr$]	remove $attr$ from the attributes of f

Manipulating attributes of symbols.

This shows the attributes assigned to f.

```
In[5]:= Attributes[f]
Out[5]= {Flat}
```

This removes the attributes assigned to f.

```
In[6]:= Attributes[f] = { }
Out[6]= {}
```

	Orderless	orderless, commutative function (arguments are sorted into standard order)
	Flat	flat, associative function (arguments are "flattened out")
	OneIdentity	$f[f[a]]$, etc. are equivalent to a for pattern matching
	Listable	f is automatically "threaded" over lists that appear as arguments (e.g., $f[\{a,b\}]$ becomes $\{f[a], f[b]\}$)
	Constant	all derivatives of f are zero
+	NumericFunction	f is assumed to have a numerical value when its arguments are numeric quantities
	Protected	values of f cannot be changed
	Locked	attributes of f cannot be changed
	ReadProtected	values of f cannot be read
	HoldFirst	the first argument of f is not evaluated
	HoldRest	all but the first argument of f is not evaluated
	HoldAll	none of the arguments of f are evaluated
+	HoldAllComplete	the arguments of f are treated as completely inert
+	NHoldFirst	the first argument of f is not affected by N
+	NHoldRest	all but the first argument of f is not affected by N
+	NHoldAll	none of the arguments of f are affected by N
+	SequenceHold	Sequence objects appearing in the arguments of f are not flattened out
	Temporary	f is a local variable, removed when no longer used
	Stub	Needs is automatically called if f is ever explicitly input

The complete list of attributes for symbols in *Mathematica*.

Here are the attributes for the built-in function Plus.

```
In[7]:= Attributes[Plus]

Out[7]= {Flat, Listable, NumericFunction, OneIdentity,
         Orderless, Protected}
```

An important attribute assigned to built-in mathematical functions in *Mathematica* is the attribute Listable. This attribute specifies that a function should automatically be distributed or "threaded" over lists that appear as its arguments. This means that the function effectively gets applied separately to each element in any lists that appear as its arguments.

| The built-in Log function is Listable. | *In[8]:=* **Log[{5, 8, 11}]** |
| | *Out[8]=* {Log[5], Log[8], Log[11]} |

| This defines the function p to be listable. | *In[9]:=* **SetAttributes[p, Listable]** |

| Now p is automatically threaded over lists that appear as its arguments. | *In[10]:=* **p[{a, b, c}, d]** |
| | *Out[10]=* {p[a, d], p[b, d], p[c, d]} |

Many of the attributes you can assign to functions in *Mathematica* directly affect the evaluation of those functions. Some attributes, however, affect only other aspects of the treatment of functions. For example, the attribute OneIdentity affects only pattern matching, as discussed in Section 2.3.7. Similarly, the attribute Constant is only relevant in differentiation, and operations that rely on differentiation.

The Protected attribute affects assignments. *Mathematica* does not allow you to make any definition associated with a symbol that carries this attribute. The functions Protect and Unprotect discussed in Section 2.4.12 can be used as alternatives to SetAttributes and ClearAttributes to set and clear this attribute. As discussed in Section 2.4.12 most built-in *Mathematica* objects are initially protected so that you do not make definitions for them by mistake.

| Here is a definition for the function g. | *In[11]:=* **g[x_] = x + 1** |
| | *Out[11]=* 1 + x |

| This sets the Protected attribute for g. | *In[12]:=* **Protect[g]** |
| | *Out[12]=* {g} |

Now you cannot modify the definition of g.	*In[13]:=* **g[x_] = x**
	Set::write: Tag g in g[x_] is Protected.
	Out[13]= x

You can usually see the definitions you have made for a particular symbol by typing *?f*, or by using a variety of built-in *Mathematica* functions. However, if you set the attribute ReadProtected, *Mathematica* will not allow you to look at the definition of a particular symbol. It will nevertheless continue to use the definitions in performing evaluation.

Although you cannot modify it, you can still look at the definition of g.	*In[14]:=* **?g**
	Global`g
	Attributes[g] = {Protected}
	g[x_] = 1 + x

| This sets the ReadProtected attribute for g. | *In[15]:=* **SetAttributes[g, ReadProtected]** |

Now you can no longer read the definition of g.	*In[16]:=* **?g**
	Global`g
	Attributes[g] = {Protected, ReadProtected}

Functions like `SetAttributes` and `ClearAttributes` usually allow you to modify the attributes of a symbol in any way. However, if you once set the `Locked` attribute on a symbol, then *Mathematica* will not allow you to modify the attributes of that symbol for the remainder of your *Mathematica* session. Using the `Locked` attribute in addition to `Protected` or `ReadProtected`, you can arrange for it to be impossible for users to modify or read definitions.

`Clear[`*f*`]`	remove values for *f*, but not attributes
`ClearAll[`*f*`]`	remove both values and attributes of *f*

Clearing values and attributes.

This clears values and attributes of p which was given attribute `Listable` above.	*In[17]:=* `ClearAll[p]`
Now p is no longer listable.	*In[18]:=* `p[{a, b, c}, d]`
	Out[18]= p[{a, b, c}, d]

By defining attributes for a function you specify properties that *Mathematica* should assume whenever that function appears. Often, however, you want to assume the properties only in a particular instance. In such cases, you will be better off not to use attributes, but instead to call a particular function to implement the transformation associated with the attributes.

By explicitly calling `Thread`, you can implement the transformation that would be done automatically if p were listable.	*In[19]:=* `Thread[p[{a, b, c}, d]]`
	Out[19]= {p[a, d], p[b, d], p[c, d]}

`Orderless`	`Sort[`*f*`[`*args*`]]`
`Flat`	`Flatten[`*f*`[`*args*`]]`
`Listable`	`Thread[`*f*`[`*args*`]]`
`Constant`	`Dt[`*expr*`, Constants->`*f*`]`

Functions that perform transformations associated with some attributes.

Attributes in *Mathematica* can only be permanently defined for single symbols. However, *Mathematica* also allows you to set up pure functions which behave as if they carry attributes.

> Function[*vars*, *body*, {*attr*₁, ... }]
>
> a pure function with attributes $attr_1, \ldots$

Pure functions with attributes.

This pure function applies p to the whole list.	*In[20]:=* **Function[{x}, p[x]] [{a, b, c}]** *Out[20]=* p[{a, b, c}]
By adding the attribute Listable, the function gets distributed over the elements of the list before applying p.	*In[21]:=* **Function[{x}, p[x], {Listable}] [{a, b, c}]** *Out[21]=* {p[a], p[b], p[c]}

■ 2.5.4 The Standard Evaluation Procedure

This section describes the standard procedure used by *Mathematica* to evaluate expressions. This procedure is the one followed for most kinds of expressions. There are however some kinds of expressions, such as those used to represent *Mathematica* programs and control structures, which are evaluated in a non-standard way. The treatment of such expressions is discussed in the sections that follow this one.

In the standard evaluation procedure, *Mathematica* first evaluates the head of an expression, and then evaluates each element of the expressions. These elements are in general themselves expressions, to which the same evaluation procedure is recursively applied.

The three Print functions are evaluated in turn, each printing its argument, then returning the value Null.	*In[1]:=* **{Print[1], Print[2], Print[3]}** 1 2 3 *Out[1]=* {Null, Null, Null}
This assigns the symbol ps to be Plus.	*In[2]:=* **ps = Plus** *Out[2]=* Plus
The head ps is evaluated first, so this expression behaves just like a sum of terms.	*In[3]:=* **ps[ps[a, b], c]** *Out[3]=* a + b + c

As soon as *Mathematica* has evaluated the head of an expression, it sees whether the head is a symbol that has attributes. If the symbol has the attributes Orderless, Flat or Listable, then immediately after evaluating the elements of the expression *Mathematica* performs the transformations associated with these attributes.

The next step in the standard evaluation procedure is to use definitions that *Mathematica* knows for the expression it is evaluating. *Mathematica* first tries to use definitions that you have made, and if there are none that apply, it tries built-in definitions.

If *Mathematica* finds a definition that applies, it performs the corresponding transformation on the expression. The result is another expression, which must then in turn be evaluated according to the standard evaluation procedure.

- Evaluate the head of the expression.

- Evaluate each element in turn.

- Apply transformations associated with the attributes `Orderless`, `Listable` and `Flat`.

- Apply any definitions that you have given.

- Apply any built-in definitions.

- Evaluate the result.

The standard evaluation procedure.

As discussed in Section 2.5.1, *Mathematica* follows the principle that each expression is evaluated until no further definitions apply. This means that *Mathematica* must continue re-evaluating results until it gets an expression which remains unchanged through the evaluation procedure.

Here is an example that shows how the standard evaluation procedure works on a simple expression. We assume that a = 7.

`2 a x + a^2 + 1`	here is the original expression
`Plus[Times[2, a, x], Power[a, 2], 1]`	
	this is the internal form
`Times[2, a, x]`	this is evaluated first
`Times[2, 7, x]`	a is evaluated to give 7
`Times[14, x]`	built-in definitions for `Times` give this result
`Power[a, 2]`	this is evaluated next
`Power[7, 2]`	here is the result after evaluating a
`49`	built-in definitions for `Power` give this result
`Plus[Times[14, x], 49, 1]`	here is the result after the arguments of `Plus` have been evaluated
`Plus[50, Times[14, x]]`	built-in definitions for `Plus` give this result
`50 + 14 x`	the result is printed like this

A simple example of evaluation in *Mathematica*.

Mathematica provides various ways to "trace" the evaluation process, as discussed in Section 2.5.10. The function Trace[*expr*] gives a nested list showing each subexpression generated during evaluation. (Note that the standard evaluation traverses the expression tree in a depth-first way, so that the smallest subparts of the expression appear first in the results of Trace.)

First set a to 7.

In[4]:= **a = 7**

Out[4]= 7

This gives a nested list of all the subexpressions generated during the evaluation of the expression.

In[5]:= **Trace[2 a x + a^2 + 1]**

Out[5]= {{{a, 7}, 27x, 14x}, {{a, 7}, 7^2, 49},

14x + 49 + 1, 50 + 14x}

The order in which *Mathematica* applies different kinds of definitions is important. The fact that *Mathematica* applies definitions you have given before it applies built-in definitions means that you can give definitions which override the built-in ones, as discussed in Section 2.4.12.

This expression is evaluated using the built-in definition for ArcSin.

In[6]:= **ArcSin[1]**

Out[6]= $\dfrac{\pi}{2}$

You can give your own definitions for ArcSin. You need to remove the protection attribute first.

In[7]:= **Unprotect[ArcSin]; ArcSin[1] = 5Pi/2;**

Your definition is used before the one that is built in.

In[8]:= **ArcSin[1]**

Out[8]= $\dfrac{5\pi}{2}$

As discussed in Section 2.4.10, you can associate definitions with symbols either as upvalues or downvalues. *Mathematica* always tries upvalue definitions before downvalue ones.

If you have an expression like *f*[*g*[*x*]], there are in general two sets of definitions that could apply: downvalues associated with *f*, and upvalues associated with *g*. *Mathematica* tries the definitions associated with *g* before those associated with *f*.

This ordering follows the general strategy of trying specific definitions before more general ones. By applying upvalues associated with arguments before applying downvalues associated with a function, *Mathematica* allows you to make definitions for special arguments which override the general definitions for the function with any arguments.

This defines a rule for f[g[x_]], to be associated with f.

In[9]:= **f/: f[g[x_]] := frule[x]**

This defines a rule for f[g[x_]], to be associated with g.

In[10]:= **g/: f[g[x_]] := grule[x]**

The rule associated with g is tried before the rule associated with f.

In[11]:= **f[g[2]]**

Out[11]= grule[2]

If you remove rules associated with g, the rule associated with f is used.	*In[12]:=* **Clear[g] ; f[g[1]]**
	Out[12]= frule[1]

■ Definitions associated with *g* are applied before definitions associated with *f* in the expression *f*[*g*[*x*]].

The order in which definitions are applied.

Most functions such as **Plus** that are built into *Mathematica* have downvalues. There are, however, some objects in *Mathematica* which have built-in upvalues. For example, **SeriesData** objects, which represent power series, have built-in upvalues with respect to various mathematical operations.

For an expression like *f*[*g*[*x*]], the complete sequence of definitions that are tried in the standard evaluation procedure is:

■ Definitions you have given associated with *g*;

■ Built-in definitions associated with *g*;

■ Definitions you have given associated with *f*;

■ Built-in definitions associated with *f*.

The fact that upvalues are used before downvalues is important in many situations. In a typical case, you might want to define an operation such as composition. If you give upvalues for various objects with respect to composition, these upvalues will be used whenever such objects appear. However, you can also give a general procedure for composition, to be used if no special objects are present. You can give this procedure as a downvalue for composition. Since downvalues are tried after upvalues, the general procedure will be used only if no objects with upvalues are present.

Here is a definition associated with q for composition of "q objects".	*In[13]:=* **q/: comp[q[x_], q[y_]] := qcomp[x, y]**
Here is a general rule for composition, associated with comp.	*In[14]:=* **comp[f_[x_], f_[y_]] := gencomp[f, x, y]**
If you compose two q objects, the rule associated with q is used.	*In[15]:=* **comp[q[1], q[2]]**
	Out[15]= qcomp[1, 2]
If you compose r objects, the general rule associated with comp is used.	*In[16]:=* **comp[r[1], r[2]]**
	Out[16]= gencomp[r, 1, 2]

In general, there can be several objects that have upvalues in a particular expression. *Mathematica* first looks at the head of the expression, and tries any upvalues associated with it. Then it successively looks at each element of the expression, trying any upvalues that exist. *Mathematica* performs this procedure first for upvalues that you have explicitly defined, and then for upvalues that are built in.

The procedure means that in a sequence of elements, upvalues associated with earlier elements take precedence over those associated with later elements.

This defines an upvalue for p with respect to c.	*In[17]:=* **p/: c[1___, p[x_], r___] := cp[x, {1, r}]**

This defines an upvalue for q.	*In[18]:=* **q/: c[1___, q[x_], r___] := cq[x, {1, r}]**

Which upvalue is used depends on which occurs first in the sequence of arguments to c.	*In[19]:=* **{c[p[1], q[2]], c[q[1], p[2]]}** *Out[19]=* **{cp[1, {q[2]}], cq[1, {p[2]}]}**

■ 2.5.5 Non-Standard Evaluation

While most built-in *Mathematica* functions follow the standard evaluation procedure, some important ones do not. For example, most of the *Mathematica* functions associated with the construction and execution of programs use non-standard evaluation procedures. In typical cases, the functions either never evaluate some of their arguments, or do so in a special way under their own control.

$x = y$	do not evaluate the left-hand side
If[p, a, b]	evaluate a if p is True, and b if it is False
Do[*expr*, {n}]	evaluate *expr* n times
Plot[f, {x, ... }]	evaluate f with a sequence of numerical values for x
Function[{x}, *body*]	do not evaluate until the function is applied

Some functions that use non-standard evaluation procedures.

When you give a definition such as a = 1, *Mathematica* does not evaluate the a that appears on the left-hand side. You can see that there would be trouble if the a was evaluated. The reason is that if you had previously set a = 7, then evaluating a in the definition a = 1 would put the definition into the nonsensical form 7 = 1.

In the standard evaluation procedure, each argument of a function is evaluated in turn. This is prevented by setting the attributes HoldFirst, HoldRest and HoldAll. These attributes make *Mathematica* "hold" particular arguments in an unevaluated form.

HoldFirst	do not evaluate the first argument
HoldRest	evaluate only the first argument
HoldAll	evaluate none of the arguments

Attributes for holding function arguments in unevaluated form.

With the standard evaluation procedure, all arguments to a function are evaluated.	*In[1]:=* **f[1 + 1, 2 + 4]**
	Out[1]= f[2, 6]
This assigns the attribute HoldFirst to h.	*In[2]:=* **SetAttributes[h, HoldFirst]**
The first argument to h is now held in an unevaluated form.	*In[3]:=* **h[1 + 1, 2 + 4]**
	Out[3]= h[1 + 1, 6]
When you use the first argument to h like this, it will get evaluated.	*In[4]:=* **h[1 + 1, 2 + 4] /. h[x_, y_] -> x^y**
	Out[4]= 64
Built-in functions like Set carry attributes such as HoldFirst.	*In[5]:=* **Attributes[Set]**
	Out[5]= {HoldFirst, Protected, SequenceHold}

Even though a function may have attributes which specify that it should hold certain arguments unevaluated, you can always explicitly tell *Mathematica* to evaluate those arguments by giving the arguments in the form Evaluate[*arg*].

Evaluate effectively overrides the HoldFirst attribute, and causes the first argument to be evaluated.	*In[6]:=* **h[Evaluate[1 + 1], 2 + 4]**
	Out[6]= h[2, 6]

f[Evaluate[*arg*]]	evaluate *arg* immediately, even though attributes of *f* may specify that it should be held

Forcing the evaluation of function arguments.

By holding its arguments, a function can control when those arguments are evaluated. By using Evaluate, you can force the arguments to be evaluated immediately, rather than being evaluated under the control of the function. This capability is useful in a number of circumstances.

One example discussed on page 129 occurs when plotting graphs of expressions. The *Mathematica* Plot function holds unevaluated the expression you are going to plot, then evaluates it at a sequence of numerical positions. In some cases, you may instead want to evaluate the expression immediately, and have Plot work with the evaluated form. For example, if you want to plot a list of functions generated by `Table`, then you will want the `Table` operation done immediately, rather than being done every time a point is to be plotted.

Evaluate causes the list of functions to be constructed immediately, rather than being constructed at each value of x chosen by `Plot`.

```
In[7]:= Plot[
          Evaluate[Table[Sin[n x], {n, 1, 3}]],
                       {x, 0, 2Pi} ]
```

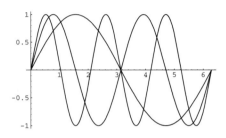

There are a number of built-in *Mathematica* functions which, like `Plot`, are set up to hold some of their arguments. You can always override this behavior using `Evaluate`.

The *Mathematica* `Set` function holds its first argument, so the symbol a is not evaluated in this case.

```
In[8]:= a = b
Out[8]= b
```

You can make `Set` evaluate its first argument using `Evaluate`. In this case, the result is the object which is the *value* of a, namely b is set to 6.

```
In[9]:= Evaluate[a] = 6
Out[9]= 6
```

b has now been set to 6.

```
In[10]:= b
Out[10]= 6
```

In most cases, you want all expressions you give to *Mathematica* to be evaluated. Sometimes, however, you may want to prevent the evaluation of certain expressions. For example, if you want to manipulate pieces of a *Mathematica* program symbolically, then you must prevent those pieces from being evaluated while you are manipulating them.

You can use the functions `Hold` and `HoldForm` to keep expressions unevaluated. These functions work simply by carrying the attribute `HoldAll`, which prevents their arguments from being evaluated. The functions provide "wrappers" inside which expressions remain unevaluated.

The difference between `Hold[`*expr*`]` and `HoldForm[`*expr*`]` is that in standard *Mathematica* output format, `Hold` is printed explicitly, while `HoldForm` is not. If you look at the full internal *Mathematica* form, you can however see both functions.

`Hold` maintains expressions in an unevaluated form.

```
In[11]:= Hold[1 + 1]
Out[11]= Hold[1 + 1]
```

HoldForm also keeps expressions unevaluated, but is invisible in standard *Mathematica* output format.

In[12]:= **HoldForm[1 + 1]**

Out[12]= 1 + 1

HoldForm is still present internally.

In[13]:= **FullForm[%]**

Out[13]//FullForm= HoldForm[Plus[1, 1]]

The function ReleaseHold removes Hold and HoldForm, so the expressions they contain get evaluated.

In[14]:= **ReleaseHold[%]**

Out[14]= 2

Hold[*expr*]	keep *expr* unevaluated
HoldComplete[*expr*]	keep *expr* unevaluated and prevent upvalues associated with *expr* from being used
HoldForm[*expr*]	keep *expr* unevaluated, and print without HoldForm
ReleaseHold[*expr*]	remove Hold and HoldForm in *expr*
Extract[*expr*, *index*, Hold]	get a part of *expr*, wrapping it with Hold to prevent evaluation
ReplacePart[*expr*, Hold[*value*], *index*, 1]	replace part of *expr*, extracting *value* without evaluating it

Functions for handling unevaluated expressions.

Parts of expressions are usually evaluated as soon as you extract them.

In[15]:= **Extract[Hold[1 + 1, 2 + 3], 2]**

Out[15]= 5

This extracts a part and immediately wraps it with Hold, so it does not get evaluated.

In[16]:= **Extract[Hold[1 + 1, 2 + 3], 2, Hold]**

Out[16]= Hold[2 + 3]

The last argument of 1 tells ReplacePart to extract the first part of Hold[7 + 8] before inserting it.

In[17]:= **ReplacePart[Hold[1 + 1, 2 + 3], Hold[7 + 8], 2, 1]**

Out[17]= Hold[1 + 1, 7 + 8]

f[... , Unevaluated[*expr*], ...]	give *expr* unevaluated as an argument to *f*

Temporary prevention of argument evaluation.

1 + 1 evaluates to 2, and Length[2] gives 0.

In[18]:= **Length[1 + 1]**

Out[18]= 0

This gives the unevaluated form 1 + 1   *In[19]:=* **Length[Unevaluated[1 + 1]]**
as the argument of Length.
                                             Out[19]= 2

Unevaluated[*expr*] effectively works by temporarily giving a function an attribute like HoldFirst, and then supplying *expr* as an argument to the function.

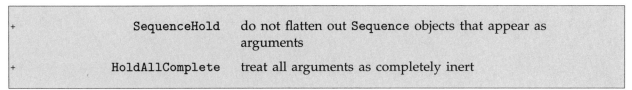

+	SequenceHold	do not flatten out Sequence objects that appear as arguments
+	HoldAllComplete	treat all arguments as completely inert

Attributes for preventing other aspects of evaluation.

By setting the attribute HoldAll, you can prevent *Mathematica* from evaluating the arguments of a function. But even with this attribute set, *Mathematica* will still do some transformations on the arguments. By setting SequenceHold you can prevent it from flattening out Sequence objects that appear in the arguments. And by setting HoldAllComplete you can also inhibit the stripping of Unevaluated, and prevent *Mathematica* from using any upvalues it finds associated with the arguments.

■ 2.5.6 Evaluation in Patterns, Rules and Definitions

There are a number of important interactions in *Mathematica* between evaluation and pattern matching. The first observation is that pattern matching is usually done on expressions that have already been at least partly evaluated. As a result, it is usually appropriate that the patterns to which these expressions are matched should themselves be evaluated.

The fact that the pattern is evaluated   *In[1]:=* **f[k^2] /. f[x_^(1 + 1)] -> p[x]**
means that it matches the expression
given.   *Out[1]=* p[k]

The right-hand side of the /; condition   *In[2]:=* **f[{a, b}] /. f[list_ /; Length[list] > 1] -> list^2**
is not evaluated until it is used during
pattern matching.   *Out[2]=* {a^2, b^2}

There are some cases, however, where you may want to keep all or part of a pattern unevaluated. You can do this by wrapping the parts you do not want to evaluate with HoldPattern. In general, whenever HoldPattern[*patt*] appears within a pattern, this form is taken to be equivalent to *patt* for the purpose of pattern matching, but the expression *patt* is maintained unevaluated.

+	HoldPattern[*patt*]	equivalent to *patt* for pattern matching, with *patt* kept unevaluated

Preventing evaluation in patterns.

One application for `HoldPattern` is in specifying patterns which can apply to unevaluated expressions, or expressions held in an unevaluated form.

`HoldPattern` keeps the 1 + 1 from being evaluated, and allows it to match the 1 + 1 on the left-hand side of the `/.` operator.	*In[3]:=* `Hold[u[1 + 1]] /. HoldPattern[1 + 1] -> x` *Out[3]=* `Hold[u[x]]`

Notice that while functions like `Hold` prevent evaluation of expressions, they do not affect the manipulation of parts of those expressions with `/.` and other operators.

This defines values for `r` whenever its argument is not an atomic object.	*In[4]:=* `r[x_] := x^2 /; !AtomQ[x]`
According to the definition, expressions like `r[3]` are left unchanged.	*In[5]:=* `r[3]` *Out[5]=* `r[3]`
However, the pattern `r[x_]` is transformed according to the definition for `r`.	*In[6]:=* `r[x_]` *Out[6]=* $x\_^2$
You need to wrap `HoldPattern` around `r[x_]` to prevent it from being evaluated.	*In[7]:=* `{r[3], r[5]} /. HoldPattern[r[x_]] -> x` *Out[7]=* `{3, 5}`

As illustrated above, the left-hand sides of transformation rules such as *lhs* -> *rhs* are usually evaluated immediately, since the rules are usually applied to expressions which have already been evaluated. The right-hand side of *lhs* -> *rhs* is also evaluated immediately. With the delayed rule *lhs* :> *rhs*, however, the expression *rhs* is not evaluated.

The right-hand side is evaluated immediately in -> but not :> rules.	*In[8]:=* `{{x -> 1 + 1}, {x :> 1 + 1}}` *Out[8]=* `{{x → 2}, {x :→ 1 + 1}}`
Here are the results of applying the rules. The right-hand side of the :> rule gets inserted inside the `Hold` without evaluation.	*In[9]:=* `{x^2, Hold[x]} /. %` *Out[9]=* `{{4, Hold[2]}, {4, Hold[1 + 1]}}`

lhs -> *rhs*	evaluate both *lhs* and *rhs*
lhs :> *rhs*	evaluate *lhs* but not *rhs*

Evaluation in transformation rules.

While the left-hand sides of transformation rules are usually evaluated, the left-hand sides of definitions are usually not. The reason for the difference is as follows. Transformation rules are typically applied using `/.` to expressions that have already been evaluated. Definitions, however, are used during the evaluation of expressions, and are applied to expressions that have not yet been completely evaluated. To work on such expressions, the left-hand sides of definitions must be maintained in a form that is at least partially unevaluated.

Definitions for symbols are the simplest case. As discussed in the previous section, a symbol on the left-hand side of a definition such as *x = value* is not evaluated. If *x* had previously been assigned a value *y*, then if the left-hand side of *x = value* were evaluated, it would turn into the quite unrelated definition *y = value*.

Here is a definition. The symbol on the left-hand side is not evaluated.	*In[10]:=* **k = w[3]** *Out[10]=* w[3]
This redefines the symbol.	*In[11]:=* **k = w[4]** *Out[11]=* w[4]
If you evaluate the left-hand side, then you define not the symbol k, but the *value* w[4] of the symbol k.	*In[12]:=* **Evaluate[k] = w[5]** *Out[12]=* w[5]
Now w[4] has value w[5].	*In[13]:=* **w[4]** *Out[13]=* w[5]

Although individual symbols that appear on the left-hand sides of definitions are not evaluated, more complicated expressions are partially evaluated. In an expression such as *f[args]* on the left-hand side of a definition, the *args* are evaluated.

The 1 + 1 is evaluated, so that a value is defined for g[2].	*In[14]:=* **g[1 + 1] = 5** *Out[14]=* 5
This shows the value defined for g.	*In[15]:=* **?g** Global'g g[2] = 5

You can see why the arguments of a function that appears on the left-hand side of a definition must be evaluated by considering how the definition is used during the evaluation of an expression. As discussed in Section 2.5.1, when *Mathematica* evaluates a function, it first evaluates each of the arguments, then tries to find definitions for the function. As a result, by the time *Mathematica* applies any definition you have given for a function, the arguments of the function must already have been evaluated. An exception to this occurs when the function in question has attributes which specify that it should hold some of its arguments unevaluated.

symbol = *value*	*symbol* is not evaluated; *value* is evaluated
symbol := *value*	neither *symbol* nor *value* is evaluated
f[*args*] = *value*	*args* are evaluated; left-hand side as a whole is not
f[HoldPattern[*arg*]] = *value*	*f*[*arg*] is assigned, without evaluating *arg*
Evaluate[*lhs*] = *value*	left-hand side is evaluated completely

Evaluation in definitions.

While in most cases it is appropriate for the arguments of a function that appears on the left-hand side of a definition to be evaluated, there are some situations in which you do not want this to happen. In such cases, you can wrap HoldPattern around the parts that you do not want to be evaluated.

■ 2.5.7 Evaluation in Iteration Functions

The built-in *Mathematica* iteration functions such as Table and Sum, as well as Plot and Plot3D, evaluate their arguments in a slightly special way.

When evaluating an expression like Table[*f*, {*i*, *imax*}], the first step, as discussed on page 369, is to make the value of *i* local. Next, the limit *imax* in the iterator specification is evaluated. The expression *f* is maintained in an unevaluated form, but is repeatedly evaluated as a succession of values are assigned to *i*. When this is finished, the global value of *i* is restored.

The function Random[ ] is evaluated four separate times here, so four different pseudorandom numbers are generated.

In[1]:= **Table[Random[ ], {4}]**

Out[1]= {0.0560708, 0.6303, 0.359894, 0.871377}

This evaluates Random[ ] before feeding it to Table. The result is a list of four identical numbers.

In[2]:= **Table[Evaluate[Random[ ]], {4}]**

Out[2]= {0.858645, 0.858645, 0.858645, 0.858645}

In most cases, it is convenient for the function *f* in an expression like Table[*f*, {*i*, *imax*}] to be maintained in an unevaluated form until specific values have been assigned to *i*. This is true in particular if a complete symbolic form for *f* valid for any *i* cannot be found.

This defines fac to give the factorial when it has an integer argument, and to give NaN (standing for "Not a Number") otherwise.

In[3]:= **fac[n_Integer] := n! ; fac[x_] := NaN**

In this form, fac[i] is not evaluated until an explicit integer value has been assigned to i.

In[4]:= **Table[fac[i], {i, 5}]**

Out[4]= {1, 2, 6, 24, 120}

Using `Evaluate` forces `fac[i]` to be evaluated with `i` left as a symbolic object.

In[5]:= **Table[Evaluate[fac[i]], {i, 5}]**

Out[5]= {NaN, NaN, NaN, NaN, NaN}

In cases where a complete symbolic form for *f* with arbitrary *i* in expressions such as `Table[`*f*`, {`*i*`, `*imax*`}]` *can* be found, it is often more efficient to compute this form first, and then feed it to `Table`. You can do this using `Table[Evaluate[`*f*`], {`*i*`, `*imax*`}]`.

The `Sum` in this case is evaluated separately for each value of `i`.

In[6]:= **Table[Sum[i^k, {k, 4}], {i, 8}]**

Out[6]= {4, 30, 120, 340, 780, 1554, 2800, 4680}

It is however possible to get a symbolic formula for the sum, valid for any value of `i`.

In[7]:= **Sum[i^k, {k, 4}]**

Out[7]= $i + i^2 + i^3 + i^4$

By inserting `Evaluate`, you tell *Mathematica* first to evaluate the sum symbolically, then to iterate over `i`.

In[8]:= **Table[Evaluate[Sum[i^k, {k, 4}]], {i, 8}]**

Out[8]= {4, 30, 120, 340, 780, 1554, 2800, 4680}

`Table[`*f*`, {`*i*`, `*imax*`}]`	keep *f* unevaluated until specific values are assigned to *i*
`Table[Evaluate[`*f*`], {`*i*`, `*imax*`}]`	evaluate *f* first with *i* left symbolic

Evaluation in iteration functions.

As discussed on page 129, it is convenient to use `Evaluate` when you plot a graph of a function or a list of functions. This causes the symbolic form of the function or list to be found first, before the iteration begins.

■ 2.5.8 Conditionals

Mathematica provides various ways to set up *conditionals*, which specify that particular expressions should be evaluated only if certain conditions hold.

lhs := *rhs* /; *test*	use the definition only if *test* evaluates to True
If[*test*, *then*, *else*]	evaluate *then* if *test* is True, and *else* if it is False
Which[*test*₁, *value*₁, *test*₂, ...]	evaluate the *test*ᵢ in turn, giving the value associated with the first one that is True
Switch[*expr*, *form*₁, *value*₁, *form*₂, ...]	compare *expr* with each of the *form*ᵢ, giving the value associated with the first form it matches
Switch[*expr*, *form*₁, *value*₁, *form*₂, ... , _, *def*]	use *def* as a default value

Conditional constructs.

The test gives False, so the *"else"* expression y is returned.	*In[1]:=* **If[7 > 8, x, y]**
	Out[1]= y
Only the *"else"* expression is evaluated in this case.	*In[2]:=* **If[7 > 8, Print[x], Print[y]]**
	y

When you write programs in *Mathematica*, you will often have a choice between making a single definition whose right-hand side involves several branches controlled by If functions, or making several definitions, each controlled by an appropriate /; condition. By using several definitions, you can often produce programs that are both clearer, and easier to modify.

This defines a step function, with value 1 for x > 0, and −1 otherwise.	*In[3]:=* **f[x_] := If[x > 0, 1, -1]**
This defines the positive part of the step function using a /; condition.	*In[4]:=* **g[x_] := 1 /; x > 0**
Here is the negative part of the step function.	*In[5]:=* **g[x_] := -1 /; x <= 0**
This shows the complete definition using /; conditions.	*In[6]:=* **?g**
	Global'g
	g[x_] := 1 /; x > 0
	g[x_] := -1 /; x <= 0

The function If provides a way to choose between two alternatives. Often, however, there will be more than two alternatives. One way to handle this is to use a nested set of If functions. Usually, however, it is instead better to use functions like Which and Switch.

This defines a function with three regions. Using True as the third test makes this the default case.	*In[7]:=* **h[x_] := Which[x < 0, x^2, x > 5, x^3, True, 0]**

| This uses the first case in the Which. | *In[8]:=* **h[-5]** |
| | *Out[8]=* 25 |

| This uses the third case. | *In[9]:=* **h[2]** |
| | *Out[9]=* 0 |

| This defines a function that depends on the values of its argument modulo 3. | *In[10]:=* **r[x_] := Switch[Mod[x, 3], 0, a, 1, b, 2, c]** |

| Mod[7, 3] is 1, so this uses the second case in the Switch. | *In[11]:=* **r[7]** |
| | *Out[11]=* b |

| 17 matches neither 0 nor 1, but does match _. | *In[12]:=* **Switch[17, 0, a, 1, b, _, q]** |
| | *Out[12]=* q |

An important point about symbolic systems such as *Mathematica* is that the conditions you give may yield neither True nor False. Thus, for example, the condition x == y does not yield True or False unless x and y have specific values, such as numerical ones.

| In this case, the test gives neither True nor False, so both branches in the If remain unevaluated. | *In[13]:=* **If[x == y, a, b]** |
| | *Out[13]=* If[x == y, a, b] |

| You can add a special fourth argument to If, which is used if the test does not yield True or False. | *In[14]:=* **If[x == y, a, b, c]** |
| | *Out[14]=* c |

If[*test*, *then*, *else*, *unknown*]	a form of If which includes the expression to use if *test* is neither True nor False
TrueQ[*expr*]	give True if *expr* is True, and False otherwise
lhs === *rhs* or SameQ[*lhs*, *rhs*]	give True if *lhs* and *rhs* are identical, and False otherwise
lhs =!= *rhs* or UnsameQ[*lhs*, *rhs*]	give True if *lhs* and *rhs* are not identical, and False otherwise
MatchQ[*expr*, *form*]	give True if the pattern *form* matches *expr*, and give False otherwise

Functions for dealing with symbolic conditions.

| *Mathematica* leaves this as a symbolic equation. | *In[15]:=* **x == y** |
| | *Out[15]=* x == y |

| Unless *expr* is manifestly True, TrueQ[*expr*] effectively assumes that *expr* is False. | *In[16]:=* **TrueQ[x == y]** |
| | *Out[16]=* False |

Unlike ==, === tests whether two expressions are manifestly identical. In this case, they are not.	*In[17]:=* **x === y**
	Out[17]= False

The main difference between *lhs* === *rhs* and *lhs* == *rhs* is that === always returns True or False, whereas == can leave its input in symbolic form, representing a symbolic equation, as discussed in Section 1.5.5. You should typically use === when you want to test the *structure* of an expression, and == if you want to test mathematical equality. The *Mathematica* pattern matcher effectively uses === to determine when one literal expression matches another.

You can use === to test the structure of expressions.	*In[18]:=* **Head[a + b + c] === Times**
	Out[18]= False

The == operator gives a less useful result.	*In[19]:=* **Head[a + b + c] == Times**
	Out[19]= Plus == Times

In setting up conditionals, you will often need to use combinations of tests, such as $test_1$ && $test_2$ && ... . An important point is that the result from this combination of tests will be False if *any* of the $test_i$ yield False. *Mathematica* always evaluates the $test_i$ in turn, stopping if any of the $test_i$ yield False.

$expr_1$ && $expr_2$ && $expr_3$	evaluate until one of the $expr_i$ is found to be **False**
$expr_1$ || $expr_2$ || $expr_3$	evaluate until one of the $expr_i$ is found to be **True**

Evaluation of logical expressions.

This function involves a combination of two tests.	*In[20]:=* **t[x_] := (x != 0 && 1/x < 3)**

Here both tests are evaluated.	*In[21]:=* **t[2]**
	Out[21]= True

Here the first test yields False, so the second test is not tried. The second test would involve 1/0, and would generate an error.	*In[22]:=* **t[0]**
	Out[22]= False

The way that *Mathematica* evaluates logical expressions allows you to combine sequences of tests where later tests may make sense only if the earlier ones are satisfied. The behavior, which is analogous to that found in languages such as C, is convenient in constructing many kinds of *Mathematica* programs.

■ 2.5.9 Loops and Control Structures

The execution of a *Mathematica* program involves the evaluation of a sequence of *Mathematica* expressions. In simple programs, the expressions to be evaluated may be separated by semicolons, and evaluated one after another. Often, however, you need to evaluate expressions several times, in some kind of "loop".

Do[*expr*, {*i*, *imax*}]	evaluate *expr* repetitively, with *i* varying from 1 to *imax* in steps of 1
Do[*expr*, {*i*, *imin*, *imax*, *di*}]	evaluate *expr* with *i* varying from *imin* to *imax* in steps of *di*
Do[*expr*, {*n*}]	evaluate *expr* *n* times

Simple looping constructs.

This evaluates `Print[i^2]`, with i running from 1 to 4.

$In[1]:=$ `Do[Print[i^2], {i, 4}]`

```
1
4
9
16
```

This executes an assignment for t in a loop with k running from 2 to 6 in steps of 2.

$In[2]:=$ `t = x; Do[t = 1/(1 + k t), {k, 2, 6, 2}]; t`

$$Out[2]= \cfrac{1}{1+\cfrac{6}{1+\frac{4}{1+2x}}}$$

The way iteration is specified in Do is exactly the same as in functions like Table and Sum. Just as in those functions, you can set up several nested loops by giving a sequence of iteration specifications to Do.

This loops over values of i from 1 to 4, and for each value of i, loops over j from 1 to i-1.

$In[3]:=$ `Do[Print[{i,j}], {i, 4}, {j, i-1}]`

```
{2, 1}
{3, 1}
{3, 2}
{4, 1}
{4, 2}
{4, 3}
```

Sometimes you may want to repeat a particular operation a certain number of times, without changing the value of an iteration variable. You can specify this kind of repetition in Do just as you can in Table and other iteration functions.

This repeats the assignment t = 1/(1+t) three times.

$In[4]:=$ `t = x; Do[t = 1/(1+t), {3}]; t`

$$Out[4]= \cfrac{1}{1+\cfrac{1}{1+\frac{1}{1+x}}}$$

You can put a procedure inside Do.

$In[5]:=$ `t = 67; Do[Print[t]; t = Floor[t/2], {3}]`

```
67
33
16
```

Nest[*f*, *expr*, *n*]	apply *f* to *expr* *n* times
FixedPoint[*f*, *expr*]	start with *expr*, and apply *f* repeatedly until the result no longer changes
FixedPoint[*f*, *expr*, SameTest -> *comp*]	
	stop when the function *comp* applied to two successive results yields True

Applying functions repetitively.

Do allows you to repeat operations by evaluating a particular expression many times with different values for iteration variables. Often, however, you can make more elegant and efficient programs using the functional programming constructs discussed in Section 2.2.2. Nest[*f*, *x*, *n*], for example, allows you to apply a function repeatedly to an expression.

This nests f three times.

$In[6]:=$ **Nest[f, x, 3]**

$Out[6]=$ f[f[f[x]]]

By nesting a pure function, you can get the same result as in the example with Do above.

$In[7]:=$ **Nest[Function[t, 1/(1+t)], x, 3]**

$$Out[7]= \frac{1}{1 + \frac{1}{1+\frac{1}{1+x}}}$$

Nest allows you to apply a function a specified number of times. Sometimes, however, you may simply want to go on applying a function until the results you get no longer change. You can do this using FixedPoint[*f*, *x*].

FixedPoint goes on applying a function until the result no longer changes.

$In[8]:=$ **FixedPoint[Function[t, Print[t]; Floor[t/2]], 67]**

```
67
33
16
8
4
2
1
0
```

$Out[8]=$ 0

You can use FixedPoint to imitate the evaluation process in *Mathematica*, or the operation of functions such as *expr* //. *rules*. In general, FixedPoint goes on until two successive results it gets are the same. By default, FixedPoint uses SameQ to test whether results are the same. You can specify an alternative function to use by setting the SameTest option.

Catch[*expr*]	evaluate *expr* until Throw[*value*] is encountered, then return *value*
+ Catch[*expr*, *form*]	evaluate *expr* until Throw[*value*, *tag*] is encountered, where *form* matches *tag*
+ Catch[*expr*, *form*, *f*]	return *f*[*value*, *tag*] instead of *value*

Non-local control of evaluation.

When the Throw is encountered, evaluation stops, and the current value of i is returned as the value of the enclosing Catch.

```
In[9]:= Catch[Do[Print[i]; If[i > 3, Throw[i]], {i, 10}]]

1
2
3
4

Out[9]= 4
```

Throw and Catch provide a flexible way to control the process of evaluation in *Mathematica*. The basic idea is that whenever a Throw is encountered, the evaluation that is then being done is stopped, and *Mathematica* immediately returns to the nearest appropriate enclosing Catch.

Scan applies the function Print to each successive element in the list, and in the end just returns Null.

```
In[10]:= Scan[Print, {7, 6, 5, 4}]

7
6
5
4
```

The evaluation of Scan stops as soon as Throw is encountered, and the enclosing Catch returns as its value the argument of Throw.

```
In[11]:= Catch[Scan[(Print[#];
                If[# < 6, Throw[#]])&, {7, 6, 5, 4}]]

7
6
5

Out[11]= 5
```

The same result is obtained with Map, even though Map would have returned a list if its evaluation had not been stopped by encountering a Throw.

```
In[12]:= Catch[Map[(Print[#];
                If[# < 6, Throw[#]])&, {7, 6, 5, 4}]]

7
6
5

Out[12]= 5
```

You can use Throw and Catch to divert the operation of functional programming constructs, allowing for example the evaluation of such constructs to continue only until some condition has been met. Note that if you stop evaluation using Throw, then the structure of the result you get may be quite different from what you would have got if you had allowed the evaluation to complete.

Here is a list generated by repeated application of a function.

```
In[13]:= NestList[1/(# + 1)&, -2.5, 6]
Out[13]= {-2.5, -0.666667, 3., 0.25, 0.8,
          0.555555, 0.642857}
```

Since there is no Throw encountered, the result here is just as before.

In[14]:= `Catch[ NestList[1/(# + 1)&, -2.5, 6] ]`

Out[14]= {-2.5, -0.666667, 3., 0.25, 0.8, 0.555555, 0.642857}

Now the evaluation of the NestList is diverted, and the single number given as the argument of Throw is returned.

In[15]:= `Catch[ NestList`
`[If[# > 1, Throw[#], 1/(# + 1)]&, -2.5, 6] ]`

Out[15]= 3.

Throw and Catch operate in a completely global way: it does not matter how or where a Throw is generated—it will always stop evaluation and return to the enclosing Catch.

The Throw stops the evaluation of f, and causes the Catch to return just a, with no trace of f left.

In[16]:= `Catch[ f[ Throw[ a ] ] ]`

Out[16]= a

This defines a function which generates a Throw when its argument is larger than 10.

In[17]:= `g[x_] := If[x > 10, Throw[overflow], x!]`

No Throw is generated here.

In[18]:= `Catch[ g[4] ]`

Out[18]= 24

But here the Throw generated inside the evaluation of g returns to the enclosing Catch.

In[19]:= `Catch[ g[40] ]`

Out[19]= overflow

In small programs, it is often adequate to use Throw[*value*] and Catch[*expr*] in their simplest form. But particularly if you write larger programs that contain many separate pieces, it is usually much better to use Throw[*value*, *tag*] and Catch[*expr*, *form*]. By keeping the expressions *tag* and *form* local to a particular piece of your program, you can then ensure that your Throw and Catch will also operate only within that piece.

Here the Throw is caught by the inner Catch.

In[20]:= `Catch[ f [ Catch[ Throw[x, a], a ] ], b ]`

Out[20]= f[x]

But here it is caught only by the outer Catch.

In[21]:= `Catch[ f [ Catch[ Throw[x, b], a ] ], b ]`

Out[21]= x

You can use patterns in specifying the tags which a particular Catch should catch.

In[22]:= `Catch[ Throw[x, a], a | b ]`

Out[22]= x

This keeps the tag a completely local.

In[23]:= `Module[{a}, Catch[ Throw[x, a], a] ]`

Out[23]= x

You should realize that there is no need for the tag that appears in Throw to be a constant; in general it can be any expression.

Here the inner Catch catches all throws
with tags less than 4, and continues
the Do. But as soon as the tag reaches
4, the outer Catch is needed.

In[24]:= **Catch[Do[Catch[Throw[i^2, i], n_ /; n < 4],**
                                {i, 10}], _]

Out[24]= 16

When you use Catch[*expr*, *form*] with Throw[*value*, *tag*], the value returned by Catch is simply
the expression *value* given in the Throw. If you use Catch[*expr*, *form*, *f*], however, then the value
returned by Catch is instead *f*[*value*, *tag*].

Here f is applied to the value and tag
in the Throw.

In[25]:= **Catch[Throw[x, a], a, f]**

Out[25]= f[x, a]

If there is no Throw, f is never used.

In[26]:= **Catch[x, a, f]**

Out[26]= x

While[*test*, *body*]	evaluate *body* repetitively, so long as *test* is True
For[*start*, *test*, *incr*, *body*]	evaluate *start*, then repetitively evaluate *body* and *incr*, until *test* fails

General loop constructs.

Functions like Do, Nest and FixedPoint provide structured ways to make loops in *Mathematica*
programs, while Throw and Catch provide opportunities for modifying this structure. Sometimes,
however, you may want to create loops that even from the outset have less structure. And in such
cases, you may find it convenient to use the functions While and For, which perform operations
repeatedly, stopping when a specified condition fails to be true.

The While loop continues until the
condition fails.

In[27]:= **n = 17; While[(n = Floor[n/2]) != 0, Print[n]]**

```
8
4
2
1
```

The functions While and For in *Mathematica* are similar to the control structures while and for in
languages such as C. Notice, however, that there are a number of important differences. For example,
the roles of comma and semicolon are reversed in *Mathematica* For loops relative to C language ones.

This is a very common form for a For
loop. i++ increments the value of i.

In[28]:= **For[i=1, i < 4, i++, Print[i]]**

```
1
2
3
```

Here is a more complicated For loop.
Notice that the loop terminates as soon
as the test i^2 < 10 fails.

In[29]:= **For[i=1; t=x, i^2 < 10, i++, t = t^2 + i;**
                        Print[t]]

$$1 + x^2$$
$$2 + (1 + x^2)^2$$
$$3 + (2 + (1 + x^2)^2)^2$$

In *Mathematica*, both While and For always evaluate the loop test before evaluating the body of the loop. As soon as the loop test fails to be True, While and For terminate. The body of the loop is thus only evaluated in situations where the loop test is True.

The loop test fails immediately, so the body of the loop is never evaluated.

In[30]:= **While[False, Print[x]]**

In a While or For loop, or in general in any *Mathematica* procedure, the *Mathematica* expressions you give are evaluated in a definite sequence. You can think of this sequence as defining the "flow of control" in the execution of a *Mathematica* program.

In most cases, you should try to keep the flow of control in your *Mathematica* programs as simple as possible. The more the flow of control depends for example on specific values generated during the execution of the program, the more difficult you will typically find it to understand the structure and operation of the program.

Functional programming constructs typically involve very simple flow of control. While and For loops are always more complicated, since they are set up to make the flow of control depend on the values of the expressions given as tests. Nevertheless, even in such loops, the flow of control does not usually depend on the values of expressions given in the body of the loop.

In some cases, however, you may need to construct *Mathematica* programs in which the flow of control is affected by values generated during the execution of a procedure or of the body of a loop. One way to do this, which fits in with functional programming ideas, is to use Throw and Catch. But *Mathematica* also provides various functions for modifying the flow of control which work like in languages such as C.

Break[ ]	exit the nearest enclosing loop
Continue[ ]	go to the next step in the current loop
Return[*expr*]	return the value *expr*, exiting all procedures and loops in a function
Goto[*name*]	go to the element Label[*name*] in the current procedure
Throw[*value*]	return *value* as the value of the nearest enclosing Catch (non-local return)

Control flow functions.

The Break[ ] causes the loop to terminate as soon as t exceeds 19.

In[31]:= **t = 1; Do[t *= k; Print[t];**
                If[t > 19, Break[]], {k, 10}]

```
1
2
6
24
```

When k < 3, the Continue[ ] causes the loop to be continued, without executing t += 2.

```
In[32]:= t = 1; Do[t *= k; Print[t];
                If[k < 3, Continue[]]; t += 2, {k, 10}]
1
2
6
32
170
1032
7238
57920
521298
5213000
```

Return[*expr*] allows you to exit a particular function, returning a value. You can think of Throw as a kind of non-local return which allows you to exit a whole sequence of nested functions. Such behavior can be convenient for handling certain error conditions.

Here is an example of the use of Return. This particular procedure could equally well have been written without using Return.

```
In[33]:= f[x_] :=
            (If[x > 5, Return[big]]; t = x^3; Return[t - 7])
```

When the argument is greater than 5, the first Return in the procedure is used.

```
In[34]:= f[10]

Out[34]= big
```

This function "throws" error if its argument is negative.

```
In[35]:= h[x_] := If[x < 0, Throw[error], Sqrt[x]]
```

No Throw is generated here.

```
In[36]:= Catch[ h[6] + 2 ]

Out[36]= 2 + √6
```

But in this case a Throw is generated, and the whole Catch returns the value error.

```
In[37]:= Catch[ h[-6] + 2 ]

Out[37]= error
```

Functions like Continue[ ] and Break[ ] allow you to "transfer control" to the beginning or end of a loop in a *Mathematica* program. Sometimes you may instead need to transfer control to a particular element in a *Mathematica* procedure. If you give a Label as an element in a procedure, you can use Goto to transfer control to this element.

This goes on looping until q exceeds 6.

```
In[38]:= (q = 2; Label[begin]; Print[q]; q += 3;
                If[q < 6, Goto[begin]])
2
5
```

Note that you can use Goto in a particular *Mathematica* procedure only when the Label it specifies occurs as an element of the same *Mathematica* procedure. In general, use of Goto reduces the degree of structure that can readily be perceived in a program, and therefore makes the operation of the program more difficult to understand.

■ 2.5.10 Tracing Evaluation

The standard way in which *Mathematica* works is to take any expression you give as input, evaluate the expression completely, and then return the result. When you are trying to understand what *Mathematica* is doing, however, it is often worthwhile to look not just at the final result of evaluation, but also at intermediate steps in the evaluation process.

Trace[*expr*]	generate a list of all expressions used in the evaluation of *expr*
Trace[*expr*, *form*]	include only expressions which match the pattern *form*

Tracing the evaluation of expressions.

The expression 1 + 1 is evaluated immediately to 2.	*In[1]:=* **Trace[1 + 1]** *Out[1]=* {1 + 1, 2}
The 2^3 is evaluated before the addition is done.	*In[2]:=* **Trace[2^3 + 4]** *Out[2]=* {{2^3, 8}, 8 + 4, 12}
The evaluation of each subexpression is shown in a separate sublist.	*In[3]:=* **Trace[2^3 + 4^2 + 1]** *Out[3]=* {{2^3, 8}, {4^2, 16}, 8 + 16 + 1, 25}

Trace[*expr*] gives a list which includes *all* the intermediate expressions involved in the evaluation of *expr*. Except in rather simple cases, however, the number of intermediate expressions generated in this way is typically very large, and the list returned by Trace is difficult to understand.

Trace[*expr*, *form*] allows you to "filter" the expressions that Trace records, keeping only those which match the pattern *form*.

Here is a recursive definition of a factorial function.	*In[4]:=* **fac[n_] := n fac[n-1]; fac[1] = 1** *Out[4]=* 1

This gives *all* the intermediate expressions generated in the evaluation of fac[3]. The result is quite complicated.	*In[5]:=* **Trace[fac[3]]**
	Out[5]= {fac[3], 3 fac[3 - 1], {{3 - 1, 2}, fac[2],
	      2 fac[2 - 1], {{2 - 1, 1}, fac[1], 1}, 21, 2},
	      32, 6}

This shows only intermediate expressions of the form fac[n_].	*In[6]:=* **Trace[fac[3], fac[n_]]** *Out[6]=* {fac[3], {fac[2], {fac[1]}}}
You can specify any pattern in Trace.	*In[7]:=* **Trace[fac[10], fac[n_/;n > 5]]** *Out[7]=* {fac[10], {fac[9], {fac[8], {fac[7], {fac[6]}}}}}

Trace[*expr*, *form*] effectively works by intercepting every expression that is about to be evaluated during the evaluation of *expr*, and picking out those that match the pattern *form*.

If you want to trace "calls" to a function like `fac`, you can do so simply by telling `Trace` to pick out expressions of the form `fac[n_]`. You can also use patterns like `f[n_, 2]` to pick out calls with particular argument structure.

A typical *Mathematica* program, however, consists not only of "function calls" like `fac[n]`, but also of other elements, such as assignments to variables, control structures, and so on. All of these elements are represented as expressions. As a result, you can use patterns in `Trace` to pick out any kind of *Mathematica* program element. Thus, for example, you can use a pattern like `k = _` to pick out all assignments to the symbol `k`.

This shows the sequence of assignments made for `k`.	`In[8]:= Trace[(k=2; For[i=1, i<4, i++, k = i/k]; k), k=_]`
	$Out[8]= \left\{\{k = 2\}, \left\{\left\{k = \frac{1}{2}\right\}, \{k = 4\}, \left\{k = \frac{3}{4}\right\}\right\}\right\}$

`Trace[`*expr, form*`]` can pick out expressions that occur at any time in the evaluation of *expr*. The expressions need not, for example, appear directly in the form of *expr* that you give. They may instead occur, say, during the evaluation of functions that are called as part of the evaluation of *expr*.

Here is a function definition.	`In[9]:= h[n_] := (k=n/2; Do[k = i/k, {i, n}]; k)`
You can look for expressions generated during the evaluation of `h`.	`In[10]:= Trace[h[3], k=_]`
	$Out[10]= \left\{\left\{k = \frac{3}{2}\right\}, \left\{\left\{k = \frac{2}{3}\right\}, \{k = 3\}, \{k = 1\}\right\}\right\}$

`Trace` allows you to monitor intermediate steps in the evaluation not only of functions that you define, but also of some functions that are built into *Mathematica*. You should realize, however, that the specific sequence of intermediate steps followed by built-in *Mathematica* functions depends in detail on their implementation and optimization in a particular version of *Mathematica*.

`Trace[`*expr*, *f*`[___]]`	show all calls to the function *f*
`Trace[`*expr*, *i* = _`]`	show assignments to *i*
`Trace[`*expr*, _ = _`]`	show all assignments
`Trace[`*expr*, `Message[___]]`	show messages generated

Some ways to use Trace.

The function `Trace` returns a list that represents the "history" of a *Mathematica* computation. The expressions in the list are given in the order that they were generated during the computation. In most cases, the list returned by `Trace` has a nested structure, which represents the "structure" of the computation.

The basic idea is that each sublist in the list returned by `Trace` represents the "evaluation chain" for a particular *Mathematica* expression. The elements of this chain correspond to different forms of the same expression. Usually, however, the evaluation of one expression requires the evaluation of a number of other expressions, often subexpressions. Each subsidiary evaluation is represented by a sublist in the structure returned by Trace.

Here is a sequence of assignments.	*In[11]:=* **a[1] = a[2]; a[2] = a[3]; a[3] = a[4]**
	Out[11]= a[4]

This yields an evaluation chain reflecting the sequence of transformations for a[*i*] used.	*In[12]:=* **Trace[a[1]]**
	Out[12]= {a[1], a[2], a[3], a[4]}

The successive forms generated in the simplification of y + x + y show up as successive elements in its evaluation chain.	*In[13]:=* **Trace[y + x + y]**
	Out[13]= {y + x + y, x + y + y, x + 2y}

Each argument of the function f has a separate evaluation chain, given in a sublist.	*In[14]:=* **Trace[f[1 + 1, 2 + 3, 4 + 5]]**
	Out[14]= {{1 + 1, 2}, {2 + 3, 5}, {4 + 5, 9}, f[2, 5, 9]}

The evaluation chain for each subexpression is given in a separate sublist.	*In[15]:=* **Trace[x x + y y]**
	Out[15]= {{x x, x^2}, {y y, y^2}, $x^2 + y^2$}

Tracing the evaluation of a nested expression yields a nested list.	*In[16]:=* **Trace[f[f[f[1 + 1]]]]**
	Out[16]= {{{{1 + 1, 2}, f[2]}, f[f[2]]}, f[f[f[2]]]}

There are two basic ways that subsidiary evaluations can be required during the evaluation of a *Mathematica* expression. The first way is that the expression may contain subexpressions, each of which has to be evaluated. The second way is that there may be rules for the evaluation of the expression that involve other expressions which themselves must be evaluated. Both kinds of subsidiary evaluations are represented by sublists in the structure returned by Trace.

The subsidiary evaluations here come from evaluation of the arguments of f and g.	*In[17]:=* **Trace[f[g[1 + 1], 2 + 3]]**
	Out[17]= {{{1 + 1, 2}, g[2]}, {2 + 3, 5}, f[g[2], 5]}

Here is a function with a condition attached.	*In[18]:=* **fe[n_] := n + 1 /; EvenQ[n]**

The evaluation of fe[6] involves a subsidiary evaluation associated with the condition.	*In[19]:=* **Trace[fe[6]]**
	Out[19]= {fe[6], {{EvenQ[6], True}, RuleCondition[
	$ConditionHold[$ConditionHold[6 + 1]], True],
	$ConditionHold[$ConditionHold[6 + 1]]},
	6 + 1, 7}

You often get nested lists when you trace the evaluation of functions that are defined "recursively" in terms of other instances of themselves. The reason is typically that each new instance of the function appears as a subexpression in the expressions obtained by evaluating previous instances of the function.

Thus, for example, with the definition `fac[n_] := n fac[n-1]`, the evaluation of `fac[6]` yields the expression `6 fac[5]`, which contains `fac[5]` as a subexpression.

The successive instances of `fac` generated appear in successively nested sublists.

```
In[20]:= Trace[fac[6], fac[_]]
Out[20]= {fac[6], {fac[5],
                {fac[4], {fac[3], {fac[2], {fac[1]}}}}}}
```

With this definition, `fp[n-1]` is obtained directly as the value of `fp[n]`.

```
In[21]:= fp[n_] := fp[n - 1] /; n > 1
```

`fp[n]` never appears in a subexpression, so no sublists are generated.

```
In[22]:= Trace[fp[6], fp[_]]
Out[22]= {fp[6], fp[6 - 1], fp[5], fp[5 - 1], fp[4], fp[4 - 1],
              fp[3], fp[3 - 1], fp[2], fp[2 - 1], fp[1]}
```

Here is the recursive definition of the Fibonacci numbers.

```
In[23]:= fib[n_] := fib[n - 1] + fib[n - 2]
```

Here are the end conditions for the recursion.

```
In[24]:= fib[0] = fib[1] = 1
Out[24]= 1
```

This shows all the steps in the recursive evaluation of `fib[5]`.

```
In[25]:= Trace[fib[5], fib[_]]
Out[25]= {fib[5], {fib[4], {fib[3],
              {fib[2], {fib[1]}, {fib[0]}}, {fib[1]}},
              {fib[2], {fib[1]}, {fib[0]}}},
              {fib[3], {fib[2], {fib[1]}, {fib[0]}}, {fib[1]}}}
```

Each step in the evaluation of any *Mathematica* expression can be thought of as the result of applying a particular transformation rule. As discussed in Section 2.4.10, all the rules that *Mathematica* knows are associated with specific symbols or "tags". You can use `Trace[`*expr*`, `*f*`]` to see all the steps in the evaluation of *expr* that are performed using transformation rules associated with the symbol *f*. In this case, `Trace` gives not only the expressions to which each rule is applied, but also the results of applying the rules.

In general, `Trace[`*expr*`, `*form*`]` picks out all the steps in the evaluation of *expr* where *form* matches *either* the expression about to be evaluated, *or* the tag associated with the rule used.

Trace[*expr*, *f*]	show all evaluations which use transformation rules associated with the symbol *f*
Trace[*expr*, *f* | *g*]	show all evaluations associated with either *f* or *g*

Tracing evaluations associated with particular tags.

This shows only intermediate expressions that match `fac[_]`.

```
In[26]:= Trace[fac[3], fac[_]]
Out[26]= {fac[3], {fac[2], {fac[1]}}}
```

This shows all evaluations that use transformation rules associated with the symbol `fac`.	*In[27]:=* **Trace[fac[3], fac]** *Out[27]=* {fac[3], 3 fac[3 - 1], {fac[2], 2 fac[2 - 1], {fac[1], 1}}}
Here is a rule for the `log` function.	*In[28]:=* **log[x_ y_] := log[x] + log[y]**
This traces the evaluation of `log[a b c d]`, showing all transformations associated with `log`.	*In[29]:=* **Trace[log[a b c d], log]** *Out[29]=* {log[a b c d], log[a] + log[b c d], {log[b c d], log[b] + log[c d], {log[c d], log[c] + log[d]}}}

`Trace[`*expr*, *form*, `TraceOn ->` *oform*`]`	switch on tracing only within forms matching *oform*
`Trace[`*expr*, *form*, `TraceOff ->` *oform*`]`	switch off tracing within any form matching *oform*

Switching off tracing inside certain forms.

`Trace[`*expr*, *form*`]` allows you to trace expressions matching *form* generated at any point in the evaluation of *expr*. Sometimes, you may want to trace only expressions generated during certain parts of the evaluation of *expr*.

By setting the option `TraceOn ->` *oform*, you can specify that tracing should be done only during the evaluation of forms which match *oform*. Similarly, by setting `TraceOff ->` *oform*, you can specify that tracing should be switched off during the evaluation of forms which match *oform*.

This shows all steps in the evaluation.	*In[30]:=* **Trace[log[fac[2] x]]**
	
	Out[30]= {{{fac[2], 2 fac[2 - 1],
	          {{2 - 1, 1}, fac[1], 1}, 21, 2}, 2 x},
	          log[2 x], log[2] + log[x]}

This shows only those steps that occur during the evaluation of `fac`.	*In[31]:=* **Trace[log[fac[2] x], TraceOn -> fac]** *Out[31]=* {{{fac[2], 2 fac[2 - 1], {{2 - 1, 1}, fac[1], 1}, 21, 2}}}
This shows only those steps that do not occur during the evaluation of `fac`.	*In[32]:=* **Trace[log[fac[2] x], TraceOff -> fac]** *Out[32]=* {{{fac[2], 2}, 2 x}, log[2 x], log[2] + log[x]}

`Trace[`*expr*, *lhs* `->` *rhs*`]`	find all expressions matching *lhs* that arise during the evaluation of *expr*, and replace them with *rhs*

Applying rules to expressions encountered during evaluation.

This tells Trace to return only the arguments of fib used in the evaluation of fib[5].	*In[33]:=* **Trace[fib[5], fib[n_] -> n]** *Out[33]=* {5, {4, {3, {2, {1}, {0}}, {1}}, {2, {1}, {0}}}, {3, {2, {1}, {0}}, {1}}}

A powerful aspect of the *Mathematica* Trace function is that the object it returns is basically a standard *Mathematica* expression which you can manipulate using other *Mathematica* functions. One important point to realize, however, is that Trace wraps all expressions that appear in the list it produces with HoldForm to prevent them from being evaluated. The HoldForm is not displayed in standard *Mathematica* output format, but it is still present in the internal structure of the expression.

This shows the expressions generated at intermediate stages in the evaluation process.	*In[34]:=* **Trace[1 + 3^2]** *Out[34]=* {{3^2, 9}, 1 + 9, 10}
The expressions are wrapped with HoldForm to prevent them from evaluating.	*In[35]:=* **Trace[1 + 3^2] // InputForm** *Out[35]//InputForm=* {{HoldForm[3^2], HoldForm[9]}, HoldForm[1 + 9], HoldForm[10]}
In standard *Mathematica* output format, it is sometimes difficult to tell which lists are associated with the structure returned by Trace, and which are expressions being evaluated.	*In[36]:=* **Trace[{1 + 1, 2 + 3}]** *Out[36]=* {{1 + 1, 2}, {2 + 3, 5}, {2, 5}}
Looking at the input form resolves any ambiguities.	*In[37]:=* **InputForm[%]** *Out[37]//InputForm=* {{HoldForm[1 + 1], HoldForm[2]}, {HoldForm[2 + 3], HoldForm[5]}, HoldForm[{2, 5}]}
When you use a transformation rule in Trace, the result is evaluated before being wrapped with HoldForm.	*In[38]:=* **Trace[fac[4], fac[n_] -> n + 1]** *Out[38]=* {5, {4, {3, {2}}}}

For sophisticated computations, the list structures returned by Trace can be quite complicated. When you use Trace[*expr*, *form*], Trace will include as elements in the lists only those expressions which match the pattern *form*. But whatever pattern you give, the nesting structure of the lists remains the same.

This shows all occurrences of fib[_] in the evaluation of fib[3].	*In[39]:=* **Trace[fib[3], fib[_]]** *Out[39]=* {fib[3], {fib[2], {fib[1]}, {fib[0]}}, {fib[1]}}
This shows only occurrences of fib[1], but the nesting of the lists is the same as for fib[_].	*In[40]:=* **Trace[fib[3], fib[1]]** *Out[40]=* {{{fib[1]}}, {fib[1]}}

You can set the option TraceDepth -> *n* to tell Trace to include only lists nested at most *n* levels deep. In this way, you can often pick out the "big steps" in a computation, without seeing the details. Note that by setting TraceDepth or TraceOff you can avoid looking at many of the steps in a computation, and thereby significantly speed up the operation of Trace for that computation.

This shows only steps that appear in lists nested at most two levels deep.	*In[41]:=* **Trace[fib[3], fib[_], TraceDepth->2]**
	Out[41]= {fib[3], {fib[2]}, {fib[1]}}

Trace[*expr*, *form*, TraceDepth -> *n*]
              trace the evaluation of *expr*, ignoring steps that lead to lists nested more than *n* levels deep

Restricting the depth of tracing.

When you use Trace[*expr*, *form*], you get a list of all the expressions which match *form* produced during the evaluation of *expr*. Sometimes it is useful to see not only these expressions, but also the results that were obtained by evaluating them. You can do this by setting the option TraceForward -> True in Trace.

This shows not only expressions which match fac[_], but also the results of evaluating those expressions.	*In[42]:=* **Trace[fac[4], fac[_], TraceForward->True]**
	Out[42]= {fac[4], {fac[3], {fac[2], {fac[1], 1}, 2}, 6}, 24}

Expressions picked out using Trace[*expr*, *form*] typically lie in the middle of an evaluation chain. By setting TraceForward -> True, you tell Trace to include also the expression obtained at the end of the evaluation chain. If you set TraceForward -> All, Trace will include *all* the expressions that occur after the expression matching *form* on the evaluation chain.

With TraceForward->All, all elements on the evaluation chain after the one that matches fac[_] are included.	*In[43]:=* **Trace[fac[4], fac[_], TraceForward->All]**
	Out[43]= {fac[4], 4 fac[4 - 1], {fac[3], 3 fac[3 - 1],
	{fac[2], 2 fac[2 - 1], {fac[1], 1}, 21, 2}, 32, 6},
	46, 24}

By setting the option TraceForward, you can effectively see what happens to a particular form of expression during an evaluation. Sometimes, however, you want to find out not what happens to a particular expression, but instead how that expression was generated. You can do this by setting the option TraceBackward. What TraceBackward does is to show you what *preceded* a particular form of expression on an evaluation chain.

This shows that the number 120 came from the evaluation of fac[5] during the evaluation of fac[10].	*In[44]:=* **Trace[fac[10], 120, TraceBackward->True]**
	Out[44]= {{{{{{fac[5], 120}}}}}}
Here is the whole evaluation chain associated with the generation of the number 120.	*In[45]:=* **Trace[fac[10], 120, TraceBackward->All]**
	Out[45]= {{{{{{fac[5], 5 fac[5 - 1], 5 24, 120}}}}}}

TraceForward and TraceBackward allow you to look forward and backward in a particular evaluation chain. Sometimes, you may also want to look at the evaluation chains within which the particular evaluation chain occurs. You can do this using TraceAbove. If you set the option TraceAbove -> True, then Trace will include the initial and final expressions in all the relevant evaluation chains. With TraceAbove -> All, Trace includes all the expressions in all these evaluation chains.

This includes the initial and final expressions in all evaluation chains which contain the chain that contains 120.

```
In[46]:= Trace[fac[7], 120, TraceAbove->True]
Out[46]= {fac[7], {fac[6], {fac[5], 120}, 720}, 5040}
```

This shows all the ways that fib[2] is generated during the evaluation of fib[5].

```
In[47]:= Trace[fib[5], fib[2], TraceAbove->True]
Out[47]= {fib[5], {fib[4],
             {fib[3], {fib[2], 2}, 3}, {fib[2], 2}, 5},
             {fib[3], {fib[2], 2}, 3}, 8}
```

Trace[*expr*, *form*, *opts*]	trace the evaluation of *expr* using the specified options
TraceForward -> True	include the final expression in the evaluation chain containing *form*
TraceForward -> All	include all expressions following *form* in the evaluation chain
TraceBackward -> True	include the first expression in the evaluation chain containing *form*
TraceBackward -> All	include all expressions preceding *form* in the evaluation chain
TraceAbove -> True	include the first and last expressions in all evaluation chains which contain the chain containing *form*
TraceAbove -> All	include all expressions in all evaluation chains which contain the chain containing *form*

Option settings for including extra steps in trace lists.

The basic way that Trace[*expr*, ...] works is to intercept each expression encountered during the evaluation of *expr*, and then to use various criteria to determine whether this expression should be recorded. Normally, however, Trace intercepts expressions only *after* function arguments have been evaluated. By setting TraceOriginal -> True, you can get Trace also to look at expressions *before* function arguments have been evaluated.

This includes expressions which match fac[_] both before and after argument evaluation.

```
In[48]:= Trace[fac[3], fac[_], TraceOriginal -> True]
Out[48]= {fac[3], {fac[3 - 1], fac[2], {fac[2 - 1], fac[1]}}}
```

The list structure produced by Trace normally includes only expressions that constitute steps in non-trivial evaluation chains. Thus, for example, individual symbols that evaluate to themselves are not normally included. Nevertheless, if you set TraceOriginal -> True, then Trace looks at absolutely every expression involved in the evaluation process, including those that have trivial evaluation chains.

In this case, Trace includes absolutely all expressions, even those with trivial evaluation chains.

In[49]:= **Trace[fac[1], TraceOriginal -> True]**

Out[49]= {fac[1], {fac}, {1}, fac[1], 1}

option name	default value	
TraceForward	False	whether to show expressions following *form* in the evaluation chain
TraceBackward	False	whether to show expressions preceding *form* in the evaluation chain
TraceAbove	False	whether to show evaluation chains leading to the evaluation chain containing *form*
TraceOriginal	False	whether to look at expressions before their heads and arguments are evaluated

Additional options for Trace.

When you use Trace to study the execution of a program, there is an issue about how local variables in the program should be treated. As discussed in Section 2.6.3, *Mathematica* scoping constructs such as Module create symbols with new names to represent local variables. Thus, even if you called a variable x in the original code for your program, the variable may effectively be renamed x$*nnn* when the program is executed.

Trace[*expr*, *form*] is set up so that by default a symbol x that appears in *form* will match all symbols with names of the form x$*nnn* that arise in the execution of *expr*. As a result, you can for example use Trace[*expr*, x = _] to trace assignment to all variables, local and global, that were named x in your original program.

Trace[*expr*, *form*, MatchLocalNames -> False]	
	include all steps in the execution of *expr* that match *form*, with no replacements for local variable names allowed

Preventing the matching of local variables.

In some cases, you may want to trace only the global variable x, and not any local variables that were originally named x. You can do this by setting the option MatchLocalNames -> False.

This traces assignments to all variables with names of the form x$*nnn*.	*In[50]:=* **Trace[Module[{x}, x = 5], x = _]** *Out[50]=* **{{x$1 = 5}}**
This traces assignments only to the specific global variable *x*.	*In[51]:=* **Trace[Module[{x}, x = 5], x = _,** **MatchLocalNames -> False]** *Out[51]=* **{}**

The function **Trace** performs a complete computation, then returns a structure which represents the history of the computation. Particularly in very long computations, it is however sometimes useful to see traces of the computation as it proceeds. The function **TracePrint** works essentially like **Trace**, except that it prints expressions when it encounters them, rather than saving up all of the expressions to create a list structure.

This prints expressions encountered in the evaluation of fib[3].	*In[52]:=* **TracePrint[fib[3], fib[_]]**
	
	    fib[3]
	     fib[3 - 1]
	    fib[2]
	      fib[2 - 1]
	     fib[1]
	      fib[2 - 2]
	     fib[0]
	    fib[3 - 2]
	    fib[1]
	
	Out[52]= 3

The sequence of expressions printed by **TracePrint** corresponds to the sequence of expressions given in the list structure returned by **Trace**. Indentation in the output from **TracePrint** corresponds to nesting in the list structure from **Trace**. You can use the **Trace** options **TraceOn**, **TraceOff** and **TraceForward** in **TracePrint**. However, since **TracePrint** produces output as it goes, it cannot support the option **TraceBackward**. In addition, **TracePrint** is set up so that **TraceOriginal** is effectively always set to **True**.

Trace[*expr*, ...]	trace the evaluation of *expr*, returning a list structure containing the expressions encountered
TracePrint[*expr*, ...]	trace the evaluation of *expr*, printing the expressions encountered
TraceDialog[*expr*, ...]	trace the evaluation of *expr*, initiating a dialog when each specified expression is encountered
TraceScan[*f*, *expr*, ...]	trace the evaluation of *expr*, applying *f* to HoldForm of each expression encountered

Functions for tracing evaluation.

This enters a dialog when fac[5] is encountered during the evaluation of fac[10].

```
In[53]:= TraceDialog[fac[10], fac[5]]

TraceDialog::dgbgn: Entering Dialog; use Return[] to exit.

Out[54]= fac[5]
```

Inside the dialog you can for example find out where you are by looking at the "stack".

```
In[55]:= Stack[ ]
Out[55]= {TraceDialog, Times, Times, Times,
              Times, Times, fac}
```

This returns from the dialog, and gives the final result from the evaluation of fac[10].

```
In[56]:= Return[ ]

TraceDialog::dgend: Exiting Dialog.

Out[53]= 3628800
```

The function TraceDialog effectively allows you to stop in the middle of a computation, and interact with the *Mathematica* environment that exists at that time. You can for example find values of intermediate variables in the computation, and even reset those values. There are however a number of subtleties, mostly associated with pattern and module variables.

What TraceDialog does is to call the function Dialog on a sequence of expressions. The Dialog function is discussed in detail in Section 2.13.2. When you call Dialog, you are effectively starting a subsidiary *Mathematica* session with its own sequence of input and output lines.

In general, you may need to apply arbitrary functions to the expressions you get while tracing an evaluation. TraceScan[*f*, *expr*, ...] applies *f* to each expression that arises. The expression is wrapped with HoldForm to prevent it from evaluating.

In TraceScan[*f*, *expr*, ...], the function *f* is applied to expressions before they are evaluated. TraceScan[*f*, *expr*, *patt*, *fp*] applies *f* before evaluation, and *fp* after evaluation.

■ 2.5.11 Advanced Topic: The Evaluation Stack

Throughout any computation, *Mathematica* maintains an *evaluation stack* containing the expressions it is currently evaluating. You can use the function Stack to look at the stack. This means, for example, that if you interrupt *Mathematica* in the middle of a computation, you can use Stack to find out what *Mathematica* is doing.

The expression that *Mathematica* most recently started to evaluate always appears as the last element of the evaluation stack. The previous elements of the stack are the other expressions whose evaluation is currently in progress.

Thus at the point when x is being evaluated, the stack associated with the evaluation of an expression like $f[g[x]]$ will have the form $\{f[g[x]], g[x], x\}$.

Stack[_] gives the expressions that are being evaluated at the time when it is called, in this case including the Print function.	`In[1]:= f[g[ Print[Stack[_]] ]] ;`
	
	`{f[g[Print[Stack[_]]]]; , f[g[Print[Stack[_]]]],`
	
	` g[Print[Stack[_]]], Print[Stack[_]]}`

Stack[ ] gives the tags associated with the evaluations that are being done when it is called.	`In[2]:= f[g[ Print[Stack[ ]] ]] ;`
	
	`{CompoundExpression, f, g, Print}`

In general, you can think of the evaluation stack as showing what functions called what other functions to get to the point *Mathematica* is at in your computation. The sequence of expressions corresponds to the first elements in the successively nested lists returned by Trace with the option TraceAbove set to True.

Stack[ ]	give a list of the tags associated with evaluations that are currently being done
Stack[_]	give a list of all expressions currently being evaluated
Stack[*form*]	include only expressions which match *form*

Looking at the evaluation stack.

It is rather rare to call Stack directly in your main *Mathematica* session. More often, you will want to call Stack in the middle of a computation. Typically, you can do this from within a dialog, or subsidiary session, as discussed in Section 2.13.2.

Here is the standard recursive definition of the factorial function.	`In[3]:= fac[1] = 1; fac[n_] := n fac[n-1]`

This evaluates fac[10], starting a dialog when it encounters fac[4].	`In[4]:= TraceDialog[fac[10], fac[4]]`
	
	`TraceDialog::dgbgn: Entering Dialog; use Return[] to exit.`
	
	`Out[5]= fac[4]`

This shows what objects were being evaluated when the dialog was started.	*In[6]:=* **Stack[ ]**
	Out[6]= {TraceDialog, Times, Times, Times, Times, Times, Times, fac}

This ends the dialog.	*In[7]:=* **Return[ ]**
	TraceDialog::dgend: Exiting Dialog.
	Out[4]= 3628800

In the simplest cases, the *Mathematica* evaluation stack is set up to record *all* expressions currently being evaluated. Under some circumstances, however, this may be inconvenient. For example, executing Print[Stack[ ]] will always show a stack with Print as the last function.

The function StackInhibit allows you to avoid this kind of problem. StackInhibit[*expr*] evaluates *expr* without modifying the stack.

StackInhibit prevents Print from being included on the stack.	*In[5]:=* **f[g[StackInhibit[Print[Stack[ ]]]]] ;**
	{CompoundExpression, f, g}

Functions like TraceDialog automatically call StackInhibit each time they start a dialog. This means that Stack does not show functions that are called within the dialog, only those outside.

StackInhibit[*expr*]	evaluate *expr* without modifying the stack
StackBegin[*expr*]	evaluate *expr* with a fresh stack
StackComplete[*expr*]	evaluate *expr* with intermediate expressions in evaluation chains included on the stack

Controlling the evaluation stack.

By using StackInhibit and StackBegin, you can control which parts of the evaluation process are recorded on the stack. StackBegin[*expr*] evaluates *expr*, starting a fresh stack. This means that during the evaluation of *expr*, the stack does not include anything outside the StackBegin. Functions like TraceDialog[*expr*, ...] call StackBegin before they begin evaluating *expr*, so that the stack shows how *expr* is evaluated, but not how TraceDialog was called.

StackBegin[*expr*] uses a fresh stack in the evaluation of *expr*.	*In[6]:=* **f[StackBegin[g[h[StackInhibit[Print[Stack[ ]]]]]]]**
	{g, h}
	Out[6]= f[g[h[Null]]]

Stack normally shows you only those expressions that are currently being evaluated. As a result, it includes only the latest form of each expression. Sometimes, however, you may find it useful also to see earlier forms of the expressions. You can do this using StackComplete.

What StackComplete[*expr*] effectively does is to keep on the stack the complete evaluation chain for each expression that is currently being evaluated. In this case, the stack corresponds to the sequence of expressions obtained from `Trace` with the option `TraceBackward -> All` as well as `TraceAbove -> True`.

■ 2.5.12 Advanced Topic: Controlling Infinite Evaluation

The general principle that *Mathematica* follows in evaluating expressions is to go on applying transformation rules until the expressions no longer change. This means, for example, that if you make an assignment like x = x + 1, *Mathematica* should go into an infinite loop. In fact, *Mathematica* stops after a definite number of steps, determined by the value of the global variable `$RecursionLimit`. You can always stop *Mathematica* earlier by explicitly interrupting it.

<table>
<tr>
<td>This assignment could cause an infinite loop. Mathematica stops after a number of steps determined by <code>$RecursionLimit</code>.</td>
<td>

`In[1]:= x = x + 1`

`$RecursionLimit::reclim: Recursion depth of 256 exceeded.`

`Out[1]= 255 + Hold[1 + x]`
</td>
</tr>
<tr>
<td>When Mathematica stops without finishing evaluation, it returns a held result. You can continue the evaluation by explicitly calling <code>ReleaseHold</code>.</td>
<td>

`In[2]:= ReleaseHold[%]`

`$RecursionLimit::reclim: Recursion depth of 256 exceeded.`

`Out[2]= 510 + Hold[1 + x]`
</td>
</tr>
</table>

`$RecursionLimit`	maximum depth of the evaluation stack
`$IterationLimit`	maximum length of an evaluation chain

Global variables that limit infinite evaluation.

<table>
<tr>
<td>Here is a circular definition, whose evaluation is stopped by <code>$IterationLimit</code>.</td>
<td>

`In[3]:= {a, b} = {b, a}`

`$IterationLimit::itlim: Iteration limit of 4096 exceeded.`

`$IterationLimit::itlim: Iteration limit of 4096 exceeded.`

`Out[3]= {Hold[b], Hold[a]}`
</td>
</tr>
</table>

The variables `$RecursionLimit` and `$IterationLimit` control the two basic ways that an evaluation can become infinite in *Mathematica*. `$RecursionLimit` limits the maximum depth of the evaluation stack, or equivalently, the maximum nesting depth that would occur in the list structure produced by `Trace`. `$IterationLimit` limits the maximum length of any particular evaluation chain, or the maximum length of any single list in the structure produced by `Trace`.

Functions such as `FixedPoint`, `Do` and `ReplaceRepeated` (the `//.` operator) use the global value of `$IterationLimit` as the default setting for their own `IterationLimit` option, which determines the maximum number of iterations they will allow.

`$RecursionLimit` and `$IterationLimit` are by default set to values that are appropriate for most computations, and most computer systems. You can, however, reset these variables to any integer (above a lower limit), or to `Infinity`. Note that on most computer systems, you should never set `$RecursionLimit = Infinity`, as discussed on page 687.

This resets $RecursionLimit and $IterationLimit to 20.	`In[4]:= $RecursionLimit = $IterationLimit = 20`
	
	`Out[4]= 20`

Now infinite definitions like this are stopped after just 20 steps.

`In[5]:= t = {t}`

`$RecursionLimit::reclim: Recursion depth of 20 exceeded.`

`Out[5]= {{{{{{{{{{{{{{{{{{{Hold[{t}]}}}}}}}}}}}}}}}}}}}}`

Without an end condition, this recursive definition leads to infinite computations.

`In[6]:= fn[n_] := {fn[n-1], n}`

A fairly large structure is built up before the computation is stopped.

`In[7]:= fn[10]`

`$RecursionLimit::reclim: Recursion depth of 20 exceeded.`

```
Out[7]= {{{{{{{{{{{{{{{{{{{{{Hold[fn[-8 - 1]], -8}, -7},
                               -6}, -5}, -4}, -3}, -2},
                          -1}, 0}, 1},
                     2},
                    3},
                   4},
                  5},
                 6},
                7},
               8},
              9},
             10}
```

Here is another recursive definition.

`In[8]:= fm[n_] := fm[n - 1]`

In this case, no complicated structure is built up, and the computation is stopped by $IterationLimit.

`In[9]:= fm[0]`

`$IterationLimit::itlim: Iteration limit of 20 exceeded.`

`Out[9]= Hold[fm[-19 - 1]]`

It is important to realize that infinite loops can take up not only time but also computer memory. Computations limited by `$IterationLimit` do not normally build up large intermediate structures. But those limited by `$RecursionLimit` often do. In many cases, the size of the structures produced is a linear function of the value of `$RecursionLimit`. But in some cases, the size can grow exponentially, or worse, with `$RecursionLimit`.

An assignment like x = x + 1 is obviously circular. When you set up more complicated recursive definitions, however, it can be much more difficult to be sure that the recursion terminates, and that you will not end up in an infinite loop. The main thing to check is that the right-hand sides of your transformation rules will always be different from the left-hand sides. This ensures that evaluation will always "make progress", and *Mathematica* will not simply end up applying the same transformation rule to the same expression over and over again.

Some of the trickiest cases occur when you have rules that depend on complicated /; conditions (see Section 2.3.5). One particularly awkward case is when the condition involves a "global variable". *Mathematica* may think that the evaluation is finished because the expression did not change. However, a side effect of some other operation could change the value of the global variable, and so should lead to a new result in the evaluation. The best way to avoid this kind of difficulty is not to use global variables in /; conditions. If all else fails, you can type Update[*s*] to tell *Mathematica* to update all expressions involving *s*. Update[ ] tells *Mathematica* to update absolutely all expressions.

■ 2.5.13 Advanced Topic: Interrupts and Aborts

Section 1.3.12 described how you can interrupt a *Mathematica* computation by pressing appropriate keys on your keyboard.

In some cases, you may want to simulate such interrupts from within a *Mathematica* program. In general, executing Interrupt[ ] has the same effect as pressing interrupt keys. On a typical system, a menu of options is displayed, as discussed in Section 1.3.12.

Interrupt[ ]	interrupt a computation
Abort[ ]	abort a computation
CheckAbort[*expr*, *failexpr*]	evaluate *expr* and return the result, or *failexpr* if an abort occurs
AbortProtect[*expr*]	evaluate *expr*, masking the effect of aborts until the evaluation is complete

Interrupts and aborts.

The function Abort[ ] has the same effect as interrupting a computation, and selecting the abort option in the interrupt menu.

You can use Abort[ ] to implement an "emergency stop" in a program. In almost all cases, however, you should try to use functions like Return and Throw, which lead to more controlled behavior.

Abort terminates the computation, so only the first Print is executed.

```
In[1]:= Print[a]; Abort[ ]; Print[b]

a

Out[1]= $Aborted
```

If you abort at any point during the evaluation of a *Mathematica* expression, *Mathematica* normally abandons the evaluation of the whole expression, and returns the value $Aborted.

You can, however, "catch" aborts using the function CheckAbort. If an abort occurs during the evaluation of *expr* in CheckAbort[*expr*, *failexpr*], then CheckAbort returns *failexpr*, but the abort propagates no further. Functions like Dialog use CheckAbort in this way to contain the effect of aborts.

CheckAbort catches the abort, prints c and returns the value aborted.	`In[2]:= CheckAbort[Print[a]; Abort[ ]; Print[b], Print[c]; aborted]` a c *Out[2]=* aborted
The effect of the Abort is contained by CheckAbort, so b is printed.	`In[3]:= CheckAbort[Print[a]; Abort[ ], Print[c]; aborted]; Print[b]` a c b

When you construct sophisticated programs in *Mathematica*, you may sometimes want to guarantee that a particular section of code in a program cannot be aborted, either interactively or by calling Abort. The function AbortProtect allows you to evaluate an expression, saving up any aborts until after the evaluation of the expression is complete.

The Abort is saved up until AbortProtect is finished.	`In[4]:= AbortProtect[Abort[ ]; Print[a]]; Print[b]` a *Out[4]=* $Aborted
The CheckAbort sees the abort, but does not propagate it further.	`In[5]:= AbortProtect[Abort[ ]; CheckAbort[Print[a], x]]; Print[b]` b

Even inside AbortProtect, CheckAbort will see any aborts that occur, and will return the appropriate *failexpr*. Unless this *failexpr* itself contains Abort[ ], the aborts will be "absorbed" by the CheckAbort.

■ 2.5.14 Compiling *Mathematica* Expressions

If you make a definition like f[x_] := x Sin[x], *Mathematica* will store the expression x Sin[x] in a form that can be evaluated for any x. Then when you give a particular value for x, *Mathematica* substitutes this value into x Sin[x], and evaluates the result. The internal code that *Mathematica* uses to perform this evaluation is set up to work equally well whether the value you give for x is a number, a list, an algebraic object, or any other kind of expression.

Having to take account of all these possibilities inevitably makes the evaluation process slower. However, if *Mathematica* could *assume* that x will be a machine number, then it could avoid many steps, and potentially evaluate an expression like x Sin[x] much more quickly.

Using Compile, you can construct *compiled functions* in *Mathematica*, which evaluate *Mathematica* expressions assuming that all the parameters which appear are numbers (or logical variables). Compile[{x_1, x_2, ... }, *expr*] takes an expression *expr* and returns a "compiled function" which evaluates this expression when given arguments x_1, x_2, ...

In general, `Compile` creates a `CompiledFunction` object which contains a sequence of simple instructions for evaluating the compiled function. The instructions are chosen to be close to those found in the machine code of a typical computer, and can thus be executed quickly.

`Compile[{`x_1`, `x_2`, ... }, ` *expr*`]`	create a compiled function which evaluates *expr* for numerical values of the x_i

Creating compiled functions.

This defines f to be a pure function which evaluates x Sin[x] for any x.

```
In[1]:= f = Function[{x}, x Sin[x]]
Out[1]= Function[{x}, x Sin[x]]
```

This creates a compiled function for evaluating x Sin[x].

```
In[2]:= fc = Compile[{x}, x Sin[x]]
Out[2]= CompiledFunction[{x}, x Sin[x], -CompiledCode-]
```

f and fc yield the same results, but fc runs faster when the argument you give is a number.

```
In[3]:= {f[2.5], fc[2.5]}
Out[3]= {1.49618, 1.49618}
```

`Compile` is useful in situations where you have to evaluate a particular numerical or logical expression many times. By taking the time to call `Compile`, you can get a compiled function which can be executed more quickly than an ordinary *Mathematica* function.

For simple expressions such as x Sin[x], there is usually little difference between the execution speed for ordinary and compiled functions. However, as the size of the expressions involved increases, the advantage of compilation also increases. For large expressions, compilation can speed up execution by a factor as large as 20.

Compilation makes the biggest difference for expressions containing a large number of simple, say arithmetic, functions. For more complicated functions, such as `BesselK` or `Eigenvalues`, most of the computation time is spent executing internal *Mathematica* algorithms, on which compilation has no effect.

This creates a compiled function for finding values of the tenth Legendre polynomial. The `Evaluate` tells *Mathematica* to construct the polynomial explicitly before doing compilation.

```
In[4]:= pc = Compile[{x}, Evaluate[LegendreP[10, x]]]
```
$$Out[4]= CompiledFunction\Big[\{x\}, -\frac{63}{256} + \frac{3465\,x^2}{256} - \frac{15015\,x^4}{128} + \frac{45045\,x^6}{128} - \frac{109395\,x^8}{256} + \frac{46189\,x^{10}}{256},$$
$$-CompiledCode-\Big]$$

This finds the value of the tenth Legendre polynomial with argument 0.4.

```
In[5]:= pc[0.4]
Out[5]= 0.0968391
```

This uses built-in numerical code.

```
In[6]:= LegendreP[10, 0.4]
Out[6]= 0.0968391
```

Even though you can use compilation to speed up numerical functions that you write, you should still try to use built-in *Mathematica* functions whenever possible. Built-in functions will usually run faster than any compiled *Mathematica* programs you can create. In addition, they typically use more extensive algorithms, with more complete control over numerical precision and so on.

You should realize that built-in *Mathematica* functions quite often themselves use `Compile`. Thus, for example, `NIntegrate` by default automatically uses `Compile` on the expression you tell it to integrate. Similarly, functions like `Plot` and `Plot3D` use `Compile` on the expressions you ask them to plot. Built-in functions that use `Compile` typically have the option `Compiled`. Setting `Compiled -> False` tells the functions not to use `Compile`.

`Compile[{{`x_1`, `t_1`}, {`x_2`, `t_2`}, ... }, `*expr*`]`	compile *expr* assuming that x_i is of type t_i
`Compile[{{`x_1`, `t_1`, `n_1`}, {`x_2`, `t_2`, `n_2`}, ... }, `*expr*`]`	compile *expr* assuming that x_i is a rank n_i array of objects each of type t_i
`Compile[`*vars*`, `*expr*`, {{`p_1`, `pt_1`}, ... }]`	compile *expr*, assuming that subexpressions which match p_i are of type pt_i

`_Integer`	machine-size integer
`_Real`	machine-precision approximate real number
`_Complex`	machine-precision approximate complex number
`True	False`	logical variable

Specifying types for compilation.

`Compile` works by making assumptions about the types of objects that occur in evaluating the expression you give. The default assumption is that all variables in the expression are approximate real numbers.

`Compile` nevertheless also allows integers, complex numbers and logical variables (`True` or `False`), as well as arrays of numbers. You can specify the type of a particular variable by giving a pattern which matches only values that have that type. Thus, for example, you can use the pattern `_Integer` to specify the integer type. Similarly, you can use `True | False` to specify a logical variable that must be either `True` or `False`.

This compiles the expression 5 i + j with the assumption that i and j are integers.

```
In[7]:= Compile[{{i, _Integer}, {j, _Integer}}, 5 i + j]

Out[7]= CompiledFunction[{i, j}, 5 i + j, -CompiledCode-]
```

This yields an integer result.	*In[8]:=* **%[8, 7]**
	Out[8]= 47

This compiles an expression that performs an operation on a matrix of integers.	*In[9]:=* **Compile[{{m, _Integer, 2}}, Apply[Plus, Flatten[m]]]**
	Out[9]= CompiledFunction[{m}, Plus@@Flatten[m],
	-CompiledCode-]

The list operations are now carried out in a compiled way, and the result is an integer.	*In[10]:=* **%[{{1, 2, 3}, {7, 8, 9}}]**
	Out[10]= 30

The types that `Compile` handles correspond essentially to the types that computers typically handle at a machine-code level. Thus, for example, `Compile` can handle approximate real numbers that have machine precision, but it cannot handle arbitrary-precision numbers. In addition, if you specify that a particular variable is an integer, `Compile` generates code only for the case when the integer is of "machine size", typically between $\pm 2^{31}$.

When the expression you ask to compile involves only standard arithmetic and logical operations, `Compile` can deduce the types of objects generated at every step simply from the types of the input variables. However, if you call other functions, `Compile` will typically not know what type of value they return. If you do not specify otherwise, `Compile` assumes that any other function yields an approximate real number value. You can, however, also give an explicit list of patterns, specifying what type to assume for an expression that matches a particular pattern.

This defines a function which yields an integer result when given an integer argument.	*In[11]:=* **com[i_] := Binomial[2i, i]**

This compiles x^com[i] using the assumption that com[_] is always an integer.	*In[12]:=* **Compile[{x, {i, _Integer}}, x^com[i],**
	{{com[_], _Integer}}]
	Out[12]= CompiledFunction[{x, i}, $x^{com[i]}$, -CompiledCode-]

This evaluates the compiled function.	*In[13]:=* **%[5.6, 1]**
	Out[13]= 31.36

The idea of `Compile` is to create a function which is optimized for certain types of arguments. `Compile` is nevertheless set up so that the functions it creates work with whatever types of arguments they are given. When the optimization cannot be used, a standard *Mathematica* expression is evaluated to find the value of the function.

Here is a compiled function for taking the square root of a variable.	*In[14]:=* **sq = Compile[{x}, Sqrt[x]]**
	Out[14]= CompiledFunction[{x}, $\sqrt{x}$, -CompiledCode-]

If you give a real number argument, optimized code is used.	*In[15]:=* **sq[4.5]**
	Out[15]= 2.12132

The compiled code cannot be used, so *Mathematica* prints a warning, then just evaluates the original symbolic expression.

```
In[16]:= sq[1 + u]
```

CompiledFunction::cfr:
    Cannot use compiled code; Argument 1 + u at position 1
        should be a machine-size real number.

$$Out[16]= \sqrt{1+u}$$

The compiled code generated by `Compile` must make assumptions not only about the types of arguments you will supply, but also about the types of all objects that arise during the execution of the code. Sometimes these types depend on the actual *values* of the arguments you specify. Thus, for example, `Sqrt[`x`]` yields a real number result for real x if x is not negative, but yields a complex number if x is negative.

`Compile` always makes a definite assumption about the type returned by a particular function. If this assumption turns out to be invalid in a particular case when the code generated by `Compile` is executed, then *Mathematica* simply abandons the compiled code in this case, and evaluates an ordinary *Mathematica* expression to get the result.

The compiled code does not expect a complex number, so *Mathematica* has to revert to explicitly evaluating the original symbolic expression.

```
In[17]:= sq[-4.5]
```

CompiledFunction::cfn:
    Numerical error encountered at instruction 3;
        proceeding with uncompiled evaluation.

$$Out[17]= 0. + 2.12132 I$$

An important feature of `Compile` is that it can handle not only mathematical expressions, but also various simple *Mathematica* programs. Thus, for example, `Compile` can handle conditionals and control flow structures.

In all cases, `Compile[`*vars*`, `*expr*`]` holds its arguments unevaluated. This means that you can explicitly give a "program" as the expression to compile.

This creates a compiled version of a *Mathematica* program which implements Newton's approximation to square roots.

```
In[18]:= newt = Compile[ {x, {n, _Integer}},
                Module[{t}, t = x; Do[t = (t + x/t)/2, {n}]; t]
            ]
```

$$Out[18]= \text{CompiledFunction}\Big[\{x, n\}, \text{Module}\Big[\{t\}, t = x;$$
$$\text{Do}\Big[t = \frac{1}{2}\Big(t + \frac{x}{t}\Big), \{n\}\Big];$$
$$t\Big], -\text{CompiledCode}-\Big]$$

This executes the compiled code.

```
In[19]:= newt[2.4, 6]
```

$$Out[19]= 1.54919$$

■ 2.5.15 Advanced Topic: Manipulating Compiled Code

If you use compiled code created by Compile only within *Mathematica* itself, then you should never need to know the details of its internal form. Nevertheless, the compiled code can be represented by an ordinary *Mathematica* expression, and it is sometimes useful to manipulate it.

For example, you can take compiled code generated by Compile, and feed it to external programs or devices. You can also create CompiledFunction objects yourself, then execute them in *Mathematica*.

In all of these cases, you need to know the internal form of CompiledFunction objects. The first element of a CompiledFunction object is always a list of patterns which specifies the types of arguments accepted by the object. The fourth element of a CompiledFunction object is a *Mathematica* pure function that is used if the compiled code instruction stream fails for any reason to give a result.

CompiledFunction[$\{arg_1, arg_2, \dots\}$, $\{n_i, n_r, n_c, n_l\}$, *instr*, *func*]
　　　　　　　　compiled code taking arguments of type arg_i and executing
　　　　　　　　the instruction stream *instr* using n_k registers of type k

---

The structure of a compiled code object.

This shows the explicit form of the compiled code generated by Compile.

```
In[1]:= Compile[{x}, x^2] // InputForm

Out[1]//InputForm=
            CompiledFunction[{_Real}, {0, 0, 3, 0, 0},
        {{1, 2}, {4, 1, 0}, {20, 0, 1}, {38, 1, 1, 2}, {9, 2}},
        Function[{x}, x^2]]
```

The instruction stream in a CompiledFunction object consists of a list of instructions for a simple idealized computer. The computer is assumed to have numbered "registers", on which operations can be performed. There are four basic types of registers: integer, real, complex and logical. For each of these basic types it is then possible to have either a single scalar register or an array of registers of any rank. A list of the total number of registers of each type required to evaluate a particular CompiledFunction object is given as the second element of the object.

The actual instructions in the compiled code object are given as lists. The first element is an integer "opcode" which specifies what operation should be performed. Subsequent elements are either the numbers of registers of particular types, or literal constants. Typically the last element of the list is the number of a "destination register", into which the result of the operation should be put.

2.6 Modularity and the Naming of Things

■ 2.6.1 Modules and Local Variables

Mathematica normally assumes that all your variables are *global*. This means that every time you use a name like x, *Mathematica* normally assumes that you are referring to the *same* object.

Particularly when you write programs, however, you may not want all your variables to be global. You may, for example, want to use the name x to refer to two quite different variables in two different programs. In this case, you need the x in each program to be treated as a *local* variable.

You can set up local variables in *Mathematica* using *modules*. Within each module, you can give a list of variables which are to be treated as local to the module.

Module[{x, y, ... }, *body*]	a module with local variables *x, y, ...*

Creating modules in *Mathematica*.

This defines the global variable t to have value 17.	*In[1]:=* **t = 17**
	Out[1]= 17
The t inside the module is local, so it can be treated independently of the global t.	*In[2]:=* **Module[{t}, t=8; Print[t]]**
	8
The global t still has value 17.	*In[3]:=* **t**
	Out[3]= 17

The most common way that modules are used is to set up temporary or intermediate variables inside functions you define. It is important to make sure that such variables are kept local. If they are not, then you will run into trouble whenever their names happen to coincide with the names of other variables.

The intermediate variable t is specified to be local to the module.	*In[4]:=* **f[v_] := Module[{t}, t = (1 + v)^2; t = Expand[t]]**
This runs the function f.	*In[5]:=* **f[a + b]**
	Out[5]= $1 + 2a + a^2 + 2b + 2ab + b^2$
The global t still has value 17.	*In[6]:=* **t**
	Out[6]= 17

You can treat local variables in modules just like other symbols. Thus, for example, you can use them as names for local functions, you can assign attributes to them, and so on.

This sets up a module which defines a local function f.	*In[7]:=* **gfac10[k_] :=** **Module[{f, n}, f[1] = 1; f[n_] := k + n f[n-1]; f[10]]**
In this case, the local function f is just an ordinary factorial.	*In[8]:=* **gfac10[0]** *Out[8]=* 3628800
In this case, f is set up as a generalized factorial.	*In[9]:=* **gfac10[2]** *Out[9]=* 8841802

When you set up a local variable in a module, *Mathematica* initially assigns no value to the variable. This means that you can use the variable in a purely symbolic way, even if there was a global value defined for the variable outside the module.

This uses the global value of t defined above, and so yields a number.	*In[10]:=* **Expand[(1 + t)^3]** *Out[10]=* 5832
Here Length simply receives a number as its argument.	*In[11]:=* **Length[Expand[(1 + t)^3]]** *Out[11]=* 0
The local variable t has no value, so it acts as a symbol, and Expand produces the anticipated algebraic result.	*In[12]:=* **Module[{t}, Length[Expand[(1 + t)^3]]]** *Out[12]=* 4

> **Module[{$x = x_0$, $y = y_0$, ... }, *body*]**
>   a module with initial values for local variables

Assigning initial values to local variables.

This specifies t to be a local variable, with initial value u.	*In[13]:=* **g[u_] := Module[{ t = u }, t += t/(1 + u)]**
This uses the definition of g.	*In[14]:=* **g[a]** *Out[14]=* $a + \dfrac{a}{1 + a}$

You can define initial values for any of the local variables in a module. The initial values are always evaluated before the module is executed. As a result, even if a variable x is defined as local to the module, the global x will be used if it appears in an expression for an initial value.

The initial value of u is taken to be the global value of t.	*In[15]:=* **Module[{t = 6, u = t}, u^2]** *Out[15]=* 289

> ***lhs* := Module[*vars*, *rhs* /; *cond*]**   share local variables between *rhs* and *cond*

Using local variables in definitions with conditions.

When you set up /; conditions for definitions, you often need to introduce temporary variables. In many cases, you may want to share these temporary variables with the body of the right-hand side of the definition. *Mathematica* allows you to enclose the whole right-hand side of your definition in a module, including the condition.

This defines a function with a condition attached.	*In[16]:=* **h[x_] := Module[{t}, t^2 - 1 /; (t = x - 4) > 1]**
Mathematica shares the value of the local variable t between the condition and the body of the right-hand side.	*In[17]:=* **h[10]** *Out[17]=* 35

■ 2.6.2 Local Constants

With[{*x* = *x*$_0$, *y* = *y*$_0$, ... }, *body*]
   define local constants *x*, *y*, ...

Defining local constants.

Module allows you to set up local *variables*, to which you can assign any sequence of values. Often, however, all you really need are local *constants*, to which you assign a value only once. The *Mathematica* With construct allows you to set up such local constants.

This defines a global value for t.	*In[1]:=* **t = 17** *Out[1]=* 17
This defines a function using t as a local constant.	*In[2]:=* **w[x_] := With[{t = x + 1}, t + t^3]**
This uses the definition of w.	*In[3]:=* **w[a]** *Out[3]=* $1 + a + (1 + a)^3$
t still has its global value.	*In[4]:=* **t** *Out[4]=* 17

Just as in Module, the initial values you define in With are evaluated before the With is executed.

The expression t + 1 which gives the value of the local constant t is evaluated using the global t.	*In[5]:=* **With[{t = t + 1}, t^2]** *Out[5]=* 324

The way With[{*x* = *x*$_0$, ... }, *body*] works is to take *body*, and replace every occurrence of *x*, etc. in it by *x*$_0$, etc. You can think of With as a generalization of the /. operator, suitable for application to *Mathematica* code instead of other expressions.

This replaces x with a.	*In[6]:=* **With[{x = a}, x = 5]** *Out[6]=* 5

After the replacement, the body of the With is a = 5, so a gets the global value 5.	*In[7]:=* **a** *Out[7]=* 5
This clears the value of a.	*In[8]:=* **Clear[a]**

In some respects, With is like a special case of Module, in which each local variable is assigned a value exactly once.

One of the main reasons for using With rather than Module is that it typically makes the *Mathematica* programs you write easier to understand. In a module, if you see a local variable x at a particular point, you potentially have to trace through all of the code in the module to work out the value of x at that point. In a With construct, however, you can always find out the value of a local constant simply by looking at the initial list of values, without having to trace through specific code.

If you have several With constructs, it is always the innermost one for a particular variable that is in effect. You can mix Module and With. The general rule is that the innermost one for a particular variable is the one that is in effect.

With nested With constructs, the innermost one is always the one in effect.	*In[9]:=* **With[{t = 8}, With[{t = 9}, t^2]]** *Out[9]=* 81
You can mix Module and With constructs.	*In[10]:=* **Module[{t = 8}, With[{t = 9}, t^2]]** *Out[10]=* 81
Local variables in inner constructs do not mask ones outside unless the names conflict.	*In[11]:=* **With[{t = a}, With[{u = b}, t + u]]** *Out[11]=* a + b

Except for the question of when x and *body* are evaluated, With[$\{x = x_0\}$, *body*] works essentially like *body* /. x -> x_0. However, With behaves in a special way when the expression *body* itself contains With or Module constructs. The main issue is to prevent the local constants in the various With constructs from conflicting with each other, or with global objects. The details of how this is done are discussed in Section 2.6.3.

The y in the inner With is renamed to prevent it from conflicting with the global y.	*In[12]:=* **With[{x = 2 + y}, Hold[With[{y = 4}, x + y]]]** *Out[12]=* Hold[With[{y\$ = 4}, (2 + y) + y\$]]

■ 2.6.3 How Modules Work

The way modules work in *Mathematica* is basically very simple. Every time any module is used, a new symbol is created to represent each of its local variables. The new symbol is given a unique name which cannot conflict with any other names. The name is formed by taking the name you specify for the local variable, followed by \$, with a unique "serial number" appended.

The serial number is found from the value of the global variable \$ModuleNumber. This variable counts the total number of times any Module of any form has been used.

> ■ `Module` generates symbols with names of the form *x$nnn* to represent each local variable.

The basic principle of modules in *Mathematica*.

This shows the symbol generated for t within the module.	`In[1]:= Module[{t}, Print[t]]` `t$1`

The symbols are different every time any module is used.	`In[2]:= Module[{t, u}, Print[t]; Print[u]]`
	`t$2`
	`u$2`

For most purposes, you will never have to deal directly with the actual symbols generated inside modules. However, if for example you start up a dialog while a module is being executed, then you will see these symbols. The same is true whenever you use functions like `Trace` to watch the evaluation of modules.

You see the symbols that are generated inside modules when you use `Trace`.	`In[3]:= Trace[ Module[{t}, t = 3] ]` `Out[3]= {Module[{t}, t = 3], {t$3 = 3, 3}, 3}`
This starts a dialog inside a module.	`In[4]:= Module[{t}, t = 6; Dialog[ ]]`

Inside the dialog, you see the symbols generated for local variables such as t.	`In[5]:= Stack[_]`
	`Out[5]= {Module[{t}, t = 6;`
	`            Dialog[]], t$4 = 6;`
	`            Dialog[], Dialog[]}`

You can work with these symbols as you would with any other symbols.	`In[6]:= t$4 + 1` `Out[6]= 7`
This returns from the dialog.	`In[7]:= Return[t$4 ^ 2]` `Out[4]= 36`

Under some circumstances, it is convenient explicitly to return symbols that are generated inside modules.

You can explicitly return symbols that are generated inside modules.	`In[5]:= Module[{t}, t]` `Out[5]= t$6`
You can treat these symbols as you would any others.	`In[6]:= %^2 + 1` `Out[6]= 1 + t$6`^{2}

`Unique[x]`	generate a new symbol with a unique name of the form *x$nnn*
`Unique[{x, y, ... }]`	generate a list of new symbols

Generating new symbols with unique names.

The function `Unique` allows you to generate new symbols in the same way as `Module` does. Each time you call `Unique`, `$ModuleNumber` is incremented, so that the names of new symbols are guaranteed to be unique.

This generates a unique new symbol whose name starts with x.	`In[7]:= Unique[x]`
	`Out[7]= x$7`

Each time you call Unique you get a symbol with a larger serial number.	`In[8]:= {Unique[x], Unique[x], Unique[x]}`
	`Out[8]= {x$8, x$9, x$10}`

If you call Unique with a list of names, you get the same serial number for each of the symbols.	`In[9]:= Unique[{x, xa, xb}]`
	`Out[9]= {x$11, xa$11, xb$11}`

You can use the standard *Mathematica* *?name* mechanism to get information on symbols that were generated inside modules or by the function `Unique`.

Executing this module generates the symbol q$*nnn*.	`In[10]:= Module[{q}, q^2 + 1]`
	`Out[10]= 1 + q$12`^{2}

You can see the generated symbol here.	`In[11]:= ?q*`
	`q        q$12`

Symbols generated by `Module` and `Unique` behave in exactly the same way as other symbols for the purposes of evaluation. However, these symbols carry the attribute `Temporary`, which specifies that they should be removed completely from the system when they are no longer used. Thus most symbols that are generated inside modules are removed when the execution of those modules is finished. The symbols survive only if they are explicitly returned.

This shows a new q variable generated inside a module.	`In[12]:= Module[{q}, Print[q]]`
	`q$13`

The new variable is removed when the execution of the module is finished, so it does not show up here.	`In[13]:= ?q*`
	`q        q$12`

You should realize that the use of names such as *x$nnn* for generated symbols is purely a convention. You can in principle give any symbol a name of this form. But if you do, the symbol may collide with one that is produced by `Module` or `Unique`.

An important point to note is that symbols generated by `Module` and `Unique` are in general unique only within a particular *Mathematica* session. The variable `$ModuleNumber` which determines the serial numbers for these symbols is always reset at the beginning of each session.

This means in particular that if you save expressions containing generated symbols in a file, and then read them into another session, there is no guarantee that conflicts will not occur.

One way to avoid such conflicts is explicitly to set `$ModuleNumber` differently at the beginning of each session. In particular, if you set `$ModuleNumber = 10^10 $SessionID`, you should avoid any conflicts. The global variable `$SessionID` should give a unique number which characterizes a particular *Mathematica* session on a particular computer. The value of this variable is determined from such quantities as the absolute date and time, the ID of your computer, and, if appropriate, the ID of the particular *Mathematica* process.

`$ModuleNumber`	the serial number for symbols generated by `Module` and `Unique`
`$SessionID`	a number that should be different for every *Mathematica* session

Variables to be used in determining serial numbers for generated symbols.

Having generated appropriate symbols to represent the local variables you have specified, `Module[`*vars*`, `*body*`]` then has to evaluate *body* using these symbols. The first step is to take the actual expression *body* as it appears inside the module, and effectively to use `With` to replace all occurrences of each local variable name with the appropriate generated symbol. After this is done, `Module` actually performs the evaluation of the resulting expression.

An important point to note is that `Module[`*vars*`, `*body*`]` inserts generated symbols only into the actual expression *body*. It does not, for example, insert such symbols into code that is called from *body*, but does not explicitly appear in *body*.

Section 2.6.6 will discuss how you can use `Block` to set up "local values" which work in a different way.

Since x does not appear explicitly in the body of the module, the local value is not used.

$$In[14]:= \texttt{tmp = x\^2 + 1; Module[\{x = 4\}, tmp]}$$

$$Out[14]= 1 + x^2$$

Most of the time, you will probably set up modules by giving explicit *Mathematica* input of the form `Module[`*vars*`, `*body*`]`. Since the function `Module` has the attribute `HoldAll`, the form of *body* will usually be kept unevaluated until the module is executed.

It is, however, possible to build modules dynamically in *Mathematica*. The generation of new symbols, and their insertion into *body* are always done only when a module is actually executed, not when the module is first given as *Mathematica* input.

This evaluates the body of the module immediately, making x appear explicitly.

$$In[15]:= \texttt{tmp = x\^2 + 1; Module[\{x = 4\}, Evaluate[tmp]]}$$

$$Out[15]= 17$$

■ 2.6.4 Advanced Topic: Variables in Pure Functions and Rules

`Module` and `With` allow you to give a specific list of symbols whose names you want to treat as local. In some situations, however, you want to automatically treat certain symbol names as local.

For example, if you use a pure function such as `Function[{x}, x + a]`, you want x to be treated as a "formal parameter", whose specific name is local. The same is true of the x that appears in a rule like `f[x_] -> x^2`, or a definition like `f[x_] := x^2`.

Mathematica uses a uniform scheme to make sure that the names of formal parameters which appear in constructs like pure functions and rules are kept local, and are never confused with global names. The basic idea is to replace formal parameters when necessary by symbols with names of the form $x\$$. By convention, $x\$$ is never used as a global name.

Here is a nested pure function.

`In[1]:= Function[{x}, Function[{y}, x + y]]`

`Out[1]= Function[{x}, Function[{y}, x + y]]`

Mathematica renames the formal parameter y in the inner function to avoid conflict with the global object y.

`In[2]:= %[2y]`

`Out[2]= Function[{y$}, 2 y + y$]`

The resulting pure function behaves as it should.

`In[3]:= %[a]`

`Out[3]= a + 2 y`

In general, *Mathematica* renames the formal parameters in an object like `Function[`*vars*`, `*body*`]` whenever *body* is modified in any way by the action of another pure function.

The formal parameter y is renamed because the body of the inner pure function was changed.

`In[4]:= Function[{x}, Function[{y}, x + y]] [a]`

`Out[4]= Function[{y$}, a + y$]`

Since the body of the inner function does not change, the formal parameter is not renamed.

`In[5]:= Function[{x}, x + Function[{y}, y^2]] [a]`

`Out[5]= a + Function[{y}, y²]`

Mathematica renames formal parameters in pure functions more liberally than is strictly necessary. In principle, renaming could be avoided if the names of the formal parameters in a particular function do not actually conflict with parts of expressions substituted into the body of the pure function. For uniformity, however, *Mathematica* still renames formal parameters even in such cases.

In this case, the formal parameter x in the inner function shields the body of the function, so no renaming is needed.

`In[6]:= Function[{x}, Function[{x}, x + y]] [a]`

`Out[6]= Function[{x}, x + y]`

Here are three nested functions.

`In[7]:= Function[{x}, Function[{y}, Function[{z}, x + y + z]]]`

`Out[7]= Function[{x}, Function[{y},`
`            Function[{z}, x + y + z]]]`

Both inner functions are renamed in this case.

`In[8]:= %[a]`

`Out[8]= Function[{y$}, Function[{z$}, a + y$ + z$]]`

As mentioned on page 246, pure functions in *Mathematica* are like λ expressions in formal logic. The renaming of formal parameters allows *Mathematica* pure functions to reproduce all the semantics of standard λ expressions faithfully.

`Function[{`x`, ... }, `*body*`]`	local parameters
lhs `->` *rhs* and *lhs* `:>` *rhs*	local pattern names
lhs `=` *rhs* and *lhs* `:=` *rhs*	local pattern names
`With[{`$x = x_0$`, ... }, `*body*`]`	local constants
`Module[{`x`, ... }, `*body*`]`	local variables

Scoping constructs in *Mathematica*.

Mathematica has several "scoping constructs" in which certain names are treated as local. When you mix these constructs in any way, *Mathematica* does appropriate renamings to avoid conflicts.

Mathematica renames the formal parameter of the pure function to avoid a conflict.

```
In[9]:= With[{x = a}, Function[{a}, a + x]]
Out[9]= Function[{a$}, a$ + a]
```

Here the local constant in the inner With is renamed to avoid a conflict.

```
In[10]:= With[{x = y}, Hold[With[{y = 4}, x + y]]]
Out[10]= Hold[With[{y$ = 4}, y + y$]]
```

There is no conflict between names in this case, so no renaming is done.

```
In[11]:= With[{x = y}, Hold[With[{z = x + 2}, z + 2]]]
Out[11]= Hold[With[{z = y + 2}, z + 2]]
```

The local variable y in the module is renamed to avoid a conflict.

```
In[12]:= With[{x = y}, Hold[Module[{y}, x + y]]]
Out[12]= Hold[Module[{y$}, y + y$]]
```

If you execute the module, however, the local variable is renamed again to make its name unique.

```
In[13]:= ReleaseHold[%]
Out[13]= y + y$1
```

Mathematica treats transformation rules as scoping constructs, in which the names you give to patterns are local. You can set up named patterns either using $x\_$, $x\_\_$ and so on, or using $x:patt$.

The x in the h goes with the x_, and is considered local to the rule.

```
In[14]:= With[{x = 5}, g[x_, x] -> h[x]]
Out[14]= g[x_, 5] -> h[x]
```

In a rule like `f[x_] -> x + y`, the x which appears on the right-hand side goes with the name of the x_ pattern. As a result, this x is treated as a variable local to the rule, and cannot be modified by other scoping constructs.

The y, on the other hand, is not local to the rule, and *can* be modified by other scoping constructs. When this happens, *Mathematica* renames the patterns in the rule to prevent the possibility of a conflict.

Mathematica renames the x in the rule to prevent a conflict.	*In[15]:=* **With[{w = x}, f[x_] -> w + x]**
	Out[15]= f[x\$_] → x + x\$

When you use **With** on a scoping construct, *Mathematica* automatically performs appropriate renamings. In some cases, however, you may want to make substitutions inside scoping constructs, without any renaming. You can do this using the **/.** operator.

When you substitute for y using **With**, the x in the pure function is renamed to prevent a conflict.	*In[16]:=* **With[{y = x + a}, Function[{x}, x + y]]**
	Out[16]= Function[{x\$}, x\$ + (a + x)]

If you use **/.** rather than **With**, no such renaming is done.	*In[17]:=* **Function[{x}, x + y] /. y -> a + x**
	Out[17]= Function[{x}, x + (a + x)]

When you apply a rule such as $f[x\_] \rightarrow rhs$, or use a definition such as $f[x\_] := rhs$, *Mathematica* implicitly has to substitute for x everywhere in the expression *rhs*. It effectively does this using the **/.** operator. As a result, such substitution does not respect scoping constructs. However, when the insides of a scoping construct are modified by the substitution, the other variables in the scoping construct are renamed.

This defines a function for creating pure functions.	*In[18]:=* **mkfun[var_, body_] := Function[{var}, body]**

The x and x^2 are explicitly inserted into the pure function, effectively by using the **/.** operator.	*In[19]:=* **mkfun[x, x^2]**
	Out[19]= Function[{x}, x^2]

This defines a function that creates a pair of nested pure functions.	*In[20]:=* **mkfun2[var_, body_] := Function[{x},**
	Function[{var}, body + x]]

The x in the outer pure function is renamed in this case.	*In[21]:=* **mkfun2[x, x^2]**
	Out[21]= Function[{x\$}, Function[{x}, $x^2 + x\$$]]

■ 2.6.5 Dummy Variables in Mathematics

When you set up mathematical formulas, you often have to introduce various kinds of local objects or "dummy variables". You can treat such dummy variables using modules and other *Mathematica* scoping constructs.

Integration variables are a common example of dummy variables in mathematics. When you write down a formal integral, conventional notation requires you to introduce an integration variable with a definite name. This variable is essentially "local" to the integral, and its name, while arbitrary, must not conflict with any other names in your mathematical expression.

Here is a function for evaluating an integral.	*In[1]:=* **p[n_] := Integrate[f[s] s^n, {s, 0, 1}]**

The s here conflicts with the integration variable.	$In[2]:= $ **p[s + 1]**
	$Out[2]= \int_0^1 s^{1+s} f[s] ds$
Here is a definition with the integration variable specified as local to a module.	$In[3]:= $ **pm[n_] := Module[{s}, Integrate[f[s] s^n, {s, 0, 1}]]**
Since you have used a module, *Mathematica* automatically renames the integration variable to avoid a conflict.	$In[4]:= $ **pm[s + 1]**
	$Out[4]= \int_0^1 s\$11^{1+s} f[s\$11] ds\$11$

In many cases, the most important issue is that dummy variables should be kept local, and should not interfere with other variables in your mathematical expression. In some cases, however, what is instead important is that different uses of the *same* dummy variable should not conflict.

Repeated dummy variables often appear in products of vectors and tensors. With the "summation convention", any vector or tensor index that appears exactly twice is summed over all its possible values. The actual name of the repeated index never matters, but if there are two separate repeated indices, it is essential that their names do not conflict.

This sets up the repeated index j as a dummy variable.	$In[5]:= $ **q[i_] := Module[{j}, a[i, j] b[j]]**
The module gives different instances of the dummy variable different names.	$In[6]:= $ **q[i1] q[i2]**
	$Out[6]= $ a[i1, j\$17] a[i2, j\$18] b[j\$17] b[j\$18]

There are many situations in mathematics where you need to have variables with unique names. One example is in representing solutions to equations. With an equation like $\sin(x) = 0$, there are an infinite number of solutions, each of the form $x = n\pi$, where n is a dummy variable that can be equal to any integer. If you generate solutions to the equation on two separate occasions, there is no guarantee that the value of n should be the same in both cases. As a result, you must set up the solution so that the object n is different every time.

This defines a value for sinsol, with n as a dummy variable.	$In[7]:= $ **sinsol := Module[{n}, n Pi]**
Different occurrences of the dummy variable are distinguished.	$In[8]:= $ **sinsol - sinsol**
	$Out[8]= $ n\$19 π - n\$20 π

Another place where unique objects are needed is in representing "constants of integration". When you do an integral, you are effectively solving an equation for a derivative. In general, there are many possible solutions to the equation, differing by additive "constants of integration". The standard *Mathematica* Integrate function always returns a solution with no constant of integration. But if you were to introduce constants of integration, you would need to use modules to make sure that they are always unique.

■ 2.6.6 Blocks and Local Values

Modules in *Mathematica* allow you to treat the *names* of variables as local. Sometimes, however, you want the names to be global, but *values* to be local. You can do this in *Mathematica* using `Block`.

`Block[{x, y, ... }, body]`	evaluate *body* using local values for $x, y, ...$
`Block[{x = x_0, y = y_0, ... }, body]`	assign initial values to $x, y, ...$

Setting up local values.

Here is an expression involving x.

$In[1]:=$ **x^2 + 3**

$Out[1]=$ $3 + x^2$

This evaluates the previous expression, using a local value for x.

$In[2]:=$ **Block[{x = a + 1}, %]**

$Out[2]=$ $3 + (1 + a)^2$

There is no global value for x.

$In[3]:=$ **x**

$Out[3]=$ x

As described in the sections above, the variable x in a module such as `Module[{x}, body]` is always set up to refer to a unique symbol, different each time the module is used, and distinct from the global symbol x. The x in a block such as `Block[{x}, body]` is, however, taken to be the global symbol x. What the block does is to make the *value* of x local. The value x had when you entered the block is always restored when you exit the block. And during the execution of the block, x can take on any value.

This sets the symbol t to have value 17.

$In[4]:=$ **t = 17**

$Out[4]=$ 17

Variables in modules have unique local names.

$In[5]:=$ **Module[{t}, Print[t]]**

t$1

In blocks, variables retain their global names, but can have local values.

$In[6]:=$ **Block[{t}, Print[t]]**

t

t is given a local value inside the block.

$In[7]:=$ **Block[{t}, t = 6; t^4 + 1]**

$Out[7]=$ 1297

When the execution of the block is over, the previous value of t is restored.

$In[8]:=$ **t**

$Out[8]=$ 17

Blocks in *Mathematica* effectively allow you to set up "environments" in which you can temporarily change the values of variables. Expressions you evaluate at any point during the execution of a block will use the values currently defined for variables in the block. This is true whether the expressions appear directly as part of the body of the block, or are produced at any point in its evaluation.

This defines a delayed value for the symbol u.	*In[9]:=* **u := x^2 + t^2**

If you evaluate u outside a block, the global value for t is used.	*In[10]:=* **u**
	Out[10]= $289 + x^2$

You can specify a temporary value for t to use inside the block.	*In[11]:=* **Block[{t = 5}, u + 7]**
	Out[11]= $32 + x^2$

An important implicit use of Block in *Mathematica* is for iteration constructs such as Do, Sum and Table. *Mathematica* effectively uses Block to set up local values for the iteration variables in all of these constructs.

Sum automatically makes the value of the iterator t local.	*In[12]:=* **Sum[t^2, {t, 10}]**
	Out[12]= 385

The local values in iteration constructs are slightly more general than in Block. They handle variables such as a[1], as well as pure symbols.	*In[13]:=* **Sum[a[1]^2, {a[1], 10}]**
	Out[13]= 385

When you set up functions in *Mathematica*, it is sometimes convenient to have "global variables" which can affect the functions without being given explicitly as arguments. Thus, for example, *Mathematica* itself has a global variable $RecursionLimit which affects the evaluation of all functions, but is never explicitly given as an argument.

Mathematica will usually keep any value you define for a global variable until you explicitly change it. Often, however, you want to set up values which last only for the duration of a particular computation, or part of a computation. You can do this by making the values local to a *Mathematica* block.

This defines a function which depends on the "global variable" t.	*In[14]:=* **f[x_] := x^2 + t**

In this case, the global value of t is used.	*In[15]:=* **f[a]**
	Out[15]= $17 + a^2$

Inside a block, you can set up a local value for t.	*In[16]:=* **Block[{t = 2}, f[b]]**
	Out[16]= $2 + b^2$

You can use global variables not only to set parameters in functions, but also to accumulate results from functions. By setting up such variables to be local to a block, you can arrange to accumulate results only from functions called during the execution of the block.

This function increments the global variable t, and returns its current value.	*In[17]:=* **h[x_] := (t += x^2)**

If you do not use a block, evaluating h[a] changes the global value of t.	*In[18]:=* **h[a]**
	Out[18]= $17 + a^2$
With a block, only the local value of t is affected.	*In[19]:=* **Block[{t = 0}, h[c]]**
	Out[19]= c^2
The global value of t remains unchanged.	*In[20]:=* **t**
	Out[20]= $17 + a^2$

When you enter a block such as Block[{x}, *body*], any value for x is removed. This means that you can in principle treat x as a "symbolic variable" inside the block. However, if you explicitly return x from the block, it will be replaced by its value outside the block as soon as it is evaluated.

The value of t is removed when you enter the block.	*In[21]:=* **Block[{t}, Print[Expand[(t + 1)^2]]]**
	$1 + 2 t + t^2$
If you return an expression involving t, however, it is evaluated using the global value for t.	*In[22]:=* **Block[{t}, t^2 - 3]**
	Out[22]= $-3 + (17 + a^2)^2$

■ 2.6.7 Blocks Compared with Modules

When you write a program in *Mathematica*, you should always try to set it up so that its parts are as independent as possible. In this way, the program will be easier for you to understand, maintain and add to.

One of the main ways to ensure that different parts of a program do not interfere is to give their variables only a certain "scope". *Mathematica* provides two basic mechanisms for limiting the scope of variables: modules and blocks.

In writing actual programs, modules are far more common than blocks. When scoping is needed in interactive calculations, however, blocks are often convenient.

Module[*vars*, *body*]	lexical scoping
Block[*vars*, *body*]	dynamic scoping

Mathematica variable scoping mechanisms.

Most traditional computer languages use a so-called "lexical scoping" mechanism for variables, which is analogous to the module mechanism in *Mathematica*. Some symbolic computer languages such as LISP also allow "dynamic scoping", analogous to *Mathematica* blocks.

When lexical scoping is used, variables are treated as local to a particular section of the *code* in a program. In dynamic scoping, the values of variables are local to a part of the *execution history* of the program.

In compiled languages like C, there is a very clear distinction between "code" and "execution history". The symbolic nature of *Mathematica* makes this distinction slightly less clear, since "code" can in principle be built up dynamically during the execution of a program.

What `Module[`*vars*`, `*body*`]` does is to treat the form of the expression *body* at the time when the module is executed as the "code" of a *Mathematica* program. Then when any of the *vars* explicitly appears in this "code", they are considered to be local.

`Block[`*vars*`, `*body*`]` does not look at the *form* of the expression *body*. Instead, throughout the evaluation of *body*, the block uses local values for the *vars*.

This defines m in terms of i.	`In[1]:= m = i^2`
	$Out[1]= i^2$
The local value for i in the block is used throughout the evaluation of i + m.	`In[2]:= Block[{i = a}, i + m]`
	$Out[2]= a + a^2$
Here only the i that appears explicitly in i + m is treated as a local variable.	`In[3]:= Module[{i = a}, i + m]`
	$Out[3]= a + i^2$

■ 2.6.8 Contexts

It is always a good idea to give variables and functions names that are as explicit as possible. Sometimes, however, such names may get inconveniently long.

In *Mathematica*, you can use the notion of "contexts" to organize the names of symbols. Contexts are particularly important in *Mathematica* packages which introduce symbols whose names must not conflict with those of any other symbols. If you write *Mathematica* packages, or make sophisticated use of packages that others have written, then you will need to know about contexts.

The basic idea is that the *full name* of any symbol is broken into two parts: a *context* and a *short name*. The full name is written as *context*`short, where the ` is the backquote or grave accent character (ASCII decimal code 96), called a "context mark" in *Mathematica*.

Here is a symbol with short name x, and context aaaa.	`In[1]:= aaaa`x`
	$Out[1]= aaaa`x$
You can use this symbol just like any other symbol.	`In[2]:= %^2 - %`
	$Out[2]= -aaaa`x + aaaa`x^2$
You can for example define a value for the symbol.	`In[3]:= aaaa`x = 78`
	$Out[3]= 78$

Mathematica treats a`x and b`x as completely different symbols.	*In[4]:=* **a`x == b`x**
	Out[4]= a`x == b`x

It is typical to have all the symbols that relate a particular topic in a particular context. Thus, for example, symbols that represent physical units might have a context PhysicalUnits`. Such symbols might have full names like PhysicalUnits`Joule or PhysicalUnits`Mole.

Although you can always refer to a symbol by its full name, it is often convenient to use a shorter name.

At any given point in a *Mathematica* session, there is always a *current context* $Context. You can refer to symbols that are in this context simply by giving their short names.

The default context for *Mathematica* sessions is Global`.	*In[5]:=* **$Context**
	Out[5]= Global`
Short names are sufficient for symbols that are in the current context.	*In[6]:=* **{x, Global`x}**
	Out[6]= {x, x}

Contexts in *Mathematica* work somewhat like file directories in many operating systems. You can always specify a particular file by giving its complete name, including its directory. But at any given point, there is usually a current working directory, analogous to the current *Mathematica* context. Files that are in this directory can then be specified just by giving their short names.

Like directories in many operating systems, contexts in *Mathematica* can be hierarchical. Thus, for example, the full name of a symbol can involve a sequence of context names, as in c_1`$c_2$`c_3`*name*.

context`*name*  or  $c_1$`c_2`  ...  `*name*	a symbol in an explicitly specified context
`*name*	a symbol in the current context
`*context*`*name* or `$c_1$`c_2`  ...  `*name*	a symbol in a specific context relative to the current context
name	a symbol in the current context, or found on the context search path

Specifying symbols in various contexts.

Here is a symbol in the context a`b`.	*In[7]:=* **a`b`x**
	Out[7]= a`b`x

When you start a *Mathematica* session, the default current context is Global`. Symbols that you introduce will usually be in this context. However, built-in symbols such as Pi are in the context System`.

In order to let you easily access not only symbols in the context `Global`, but also in contexts such as `System`, *Mathematica* supports the notion of a *context search path*. At any point in a *Mathematica* session, there is both a current context `$Context`, and also a current context search path `$ContextPath`. The idea of the search path is to allow you to type in the short name of a symbol, then have *Mathematica* search in a sequence of contexts to find a symbol with that short name.

The context search path for symbols in *Mathematica* is analogous to the "search path" for program files provided in operating systems such as Unix and MS-DOS.

The default context path includes the contexts for system-defined symbols.	`In[8]:= $ContextPath` `Out[8]= {Global`, System`}`
When you type in Pi, *Mathematica* interprets it as the symbol with full name System`Pi.	`In[9]:= Context[Pi]` `Out[9]= System``

`Context[s]`	the context of a symbol
`$Context`	the current context in a *Mathematica* session
`$ContextPath`	the current context search path
`Contexts[ ]`	a list of all contexts

Finding contexts and context search paths.

When you use contexts in *Mathematica*, there is no reason that two symbols which are in different contexts cannot have the same short name. Thus, for example, you can have symbols with the short name Mole both in the context `PhysicalUnits`` and in the context `BiologicalOrganisms``.

There is, however, then the question of which symbol you actually get when you type in only the short name Mole. The answer to this question is determined by which of the contexts comes first in the sequence of contexts listed in the context search path.

This introduces two symbols, both with short name Mole.	`In[10]:= {PhysicalUnits`Mole, BiologicalOrganisms`Mole}` `Out[10]= {PhysicalUnits`Mole, BiologicalOrganisms`Mole}`
This adds two additional contexts to $ContextPath.	`In[11]:= $ContextPath =` `        Join[$ContextPath,` `            {"PhysicalUnits`", "BiologicalOrganisms`"}]` `Out[11]= {Global`, System`, PhysicalUnits`,` ` BiologicalOrganisms`}`
Now if you type in Mole, you get the symbol in the context PhysicalUnits`.	`In[12]:= Context[Mole]` `Out[12]= PhysicalUnits``

In general, when you type in a short name for a symbol, *Mathematica* assumes that you want the symbol with that name whose context appears earliest in the context search path. As a result, symbols with the same short name whose contexts appear later in the context search path are effectively "shadowed". To refer to these symbols, you need to use their full names.

Mathematica always warns you when you introduce new symbols that "shadow" existing symbols with your current choice for $ContextPath.

This introduces a symbol with short name Mole in the context Global`. *Mathematica* warns you that the new symbol shadows existing symbols with short name Mole.	*In[13]:=* **Global`Mole**  Mole::shdw:     Symbol Mole appears in multiple contexts     {Global`, Ph<<11>>`, BiologicalOrganisms`}; definitions in context Global` may shadow or be shadowed by other definitions. *Out[13]=* Mole
Now when you type in Mole, you get the symbol in context Global`.	*In[14]:=* **Context[Mole]** *Out[14]=* Global`

If you once introduce a symbol which shadows existing symbols, it will continue to do so until you either rearrange $ContextPath, or explicitly remove the symbol. You should realize that it is not sufficient to clear the *value* of the symbol; you need to actually remove the symbol completely from *Mathematica*. You can do this using the function Remove[*s*].

Clear[*s*]	clear the values of a symbol
Remove[*s*]	remove a symbol completely from the system

Clearing and removing symbols in *Mathematica*.

This removes the symbol Global`Mole.	*In[15]:=* **Remove[Mole]**
Now if you type in Mole, you get the symbol PhysicalUnits`Mole.	*In[16]:=* **Context[Mole]** *Out[16]=* PhysicalUnits`

When *Mathematica* prints out the name of a symbol, it has to choose whether to give the full name, or just the short name. What it does is to give whatever version of the name you would have to type in to get the particular symbol, given your current settings for $Context and $ContextPath.

The short name is printed for the first symbol, so this would give that symbol if you typed it in.	*In[17]:=* **{PhysicalUnits`Mole, BiologicalOrganisms`Mole}** *Out[17]=* {Mole, BiologicalOrganisms`Mole}

If you type in a short name for which there is no symbol either in the current context, or in any context on the context search path, then *Mathematica* has to *create* a new symbol with this name. It always puts new symbols of this kind in the current context, as specified by $Context.

This introduces the new symbol with short name tree.	*In[18]:=* **tree** *Out[18]=* tree

Mathematica puts `tree` in the current context Global`.

```
In[19]:= Context[tree]
Out[19]= Global`
```

■ 2.6.9 Contexts and Packages

A typical package written in *Mathematica* introduces several new symbols intended for use outside the package. These symbols may correspond for example to new functions or new objects defined in the package.

There is a general convention that all new symbols introduced in a particular package are put into a context whose name is related to the name of the package. When you read in the package, it adds this context at the beginning of your context search path $ContextPath.

This reads in a package for doing Laplace transforms.

```
In[1]:= <<Calculus`LaplaceTransform`
```

The package prepends its context and related ones to $ContextPath.

```
In[2]:= $ContextPath
Out[2]= {Calculus`LaplaceTransform`,
          Calculus`Common`TransformCommon`,
          Calculus`DiracDelta`, Global`, System`}
```

The symbol LaplaceTransform is in the context set up by the package.

```
In[3]:= Context[LaplaceTransform]
Out[3]= Calculus`LaplaceTransform`
```

You can refer to the symbol using its short name.

```
In[4]:= LaplaceTransform[t^3, t, s]
```

$$Out[4]= \frac{6}{s^4}$$

The full names of symbols defined in packages are often quite long. In most cases, however, you will only need to use their short names. The reason for this is that after you have read in a package, its context is added to $ContextPath, so the context is automatically searched whenever you type in a short name.

There is a complication, however, when two symbols with the same short name appear in two different packages. In such a case, *Mathematica* will warn you when you read in the second package. It will tell you which symbols will be "shadowed" by the new symbols that are being introduced.

The symbol LaplaceTransform in the context Calculus`LaplaceTransform` is shadowed by the symbol with the same short name in the new package.

```
In[5]:= <<NewLaplace`
LaplaceTransform::shdw:
    Symbol LaplaceTransform appears in multiple contexts
    {NewLaplace`, Calculus`LaplaceTransform`}; definitions
        in context NewLaplace`
    may shadow or be shadowed by other definitions.
```

You can access the shadowed symbol by giving its full name.

```
In[6]:= Calculus`LaplaceTransform`LaplaceTransform[t^3, t, s]
```

$$Out[6]= \frac{6}{s^4}$$

Conflicts can occur not only between symbols in different packages, but also between symbols in packages and symbols that you introduce directly in your *Mathematica* session. If you define a symbol in your current context, then this symbol will shadow any other symbol with the same short name in packages that you read in. The reason for this is that *Mathematica* always searches for symbols in the current context before looking in contexts on the context search path.

This defines a function in the current context.	`In[7]:= Div[f_] = 1/f`
	$$Out[7]= \frac{1}{f}$$

Any other functions with short name Div will be shadowed by the one in your current context.	`In[8]:= <<Calculus`VectorAnalysis``
	Div::shdw: Symbol Div appears in multiple contexts {Calculus`VectorAnalysis`, Global`}; definitions in         context Calculus`VectorAnalysis` may shadow or be shadowed by other definitions.

This sets up the coordinate system for vector analysis.	`In[9]:= SetCoordinates[Cartesian[x, y, z]]`
	`Out[9]= Cartesian[x, y, z]`

This removes Div completely from the current context.	`In[10]:= Clear[Div]; Remove[Div]`

Now the Div from the package is used.	`In[11]:= Div[{x, y^2, x}]`
	`Out[11]= 1 + 2 y`

If you get into the situation where unwanted symbols are shadowing the symbols you want, the best thing to do is usually to get rid of the unwanted symbols using `Remove[s]`. An alternative that is sometimes appropriate is to rearrange the entries in `$ContextPath` and to reset the value of `$Context` so as to make the contexts that contain the symbols you want be the ones that are searched first.

`$Packages`	a list of the contexts corresponding to all packages loaded into your *Mathematica* session

Getting a list of packages.

■ 2.6.10 Setting Up *Mathematica* Packages

In a typical *Mathematica* package, there are generally two kinds of new symbols that are introduced. The first kind are ones that you want to "export" for use outside the package. The second kind are ones that you want to use only internally within the package. You can distinguish these two kinds of symbols by putting them in different contexts.

The usual convention is to put symbols intended for export in a context with a name *Package`* that corresponds to the name of the package. Whenever the package is read in, it adds this context to the context search path, so that the symbols in this context can be referred to by their short names.

Symbols that are not intended for export, but are instead intended only for internal use within the package, are conventionally put into a context with the name *Package*`Private`. This context is *not* added to the context search path. As a result, the symbols in this context cannot be accessed except by giving their full names.

Package`	symbols for export
Package`Private`	symbols for internal use only
System`	built-in *Mathematica* symbols
Needed₁`, *Needed₂*`, ...	other contexts needed in the package

Contexts conventionally used in *Mathematica* packages.

There is a standard sequence of *Mathematica* commands that is typically used to set up the contexts in a package. These commands set the values of $Context and $ContextPath so that the new symbols which are introduced are created in the appropriate contexts.

BeginPackage["*Package*`"]	set *Package*` to be the current context, and put only System` on the context search path
f::usage = "*text*", ...	introduce the objects intended for export (and no others)
Begin["`Private`"]	set the current context to *Package*`Private`
f[*args*] = *value*, ...	give the main body of definitions in the package
End[ ]	revert to the previous context (here *Package*`)
EndPackage[ ]	end the package, prepending the *Package*` to the context search path

The standard sequence of context control commands in a package.

```
BeginPackage["Collatz'"]

Collatz::usage =
      "Collatz[n] gives a list of the iterates in the 3n+1 problem,
      starting from n. The conjecture is that this sequence always
      terminates."

Begin["'Private'"]

Collatz[1] := {1}

Collatz[n_Integer]  := Prepend[Collatz[3 n + 1], n] /; OddQ[n] && n > 0

Collatz[n_Integer] := Prepend[Collatz[n/2], n] /; EvenQ[n] && n > 0

End[ ]

EndPackage[ ]
```

The sample package Collatz.m.

The convention of defining **usage** messages at the beginning of a package is essentially a trick for creating symbols you want to export in the appropriate context. The point is that in defining these messages, the only symbols you mention are exactly the ones you want to export. These symbols are then created in the context *Package*`, which is then current.

In the actual definitions of the functions in a package, there are typically many new symbols, introduced as parameters, temporary variables, and so on. The convention is to put all these symbols in the context *Package*`Private`, which is not put on the context search path when the package is read in.

This reads in the sample package given above.	*In[1]:=* **<<Collatz.m**
The EndPackage command in the package adds the context associated with the package to the context search path.	*In[2]:=* **$ContextPath** *Out[2]=* {Collatz`, Global`, System`}
The Collatz function was created in the context Collatz`.	*In[3]:=* **Context[Collatz]** *Out[3]=* Collatz`
The parameter n is put in the private context Collatz`Private`.	*In[4]:=* **?Collatz`Private`*** Collatz`Private`n

In the Collatz package, the functions that are defined depend only on built-in *Mathematica* functions. Often, however, the functions defined in one package may depend on functions defined in another package.

Two things are needed to make this work. First, the other package must be read in, so that the functions needed are defined. And second, the context search path must include the context that these functions are in.

You can explicitly tell *Mathematica* to read in a package at any point using the command <<*context*`. (Section 2.11.5 discusses the tricky issue of translation from system-independent context names to system-dependent file names.) Often, however, you want to set it up so that a particular package is read in only if it is needed. The command `Needs["`*context*`'"]` tells *Mathematica* to read in a package if the context associated with that package is not already in the list `$Packages`.

`Get["`*context*`'"]` or <<*context*`	read in the package corresponding to the specified context
`Needs["`*context*`'"]`	read in the package if the specified context is not already in `$Packages`
`BeginPackage["`*Package*`'", {"`*Needed₁*`'", ... }]`	begin a package, specifying that certain contexts in addition to `System'` are needed

Functions for specifying interdependence of packages.

If you use `BeginPackage["`*Package*`'"]` with a single argument, *Mathematica* puts on the context search path only the *Package*` context and the contexts for built-in *Mathematica* symbols. If the definitions you give in your package involve functions from other packages, you must make sure that the contexts for these packages are also included in your context search path. You can do this by giving a list of the additional contexts as a second argument to `BeginPackage`. `BeginPackage` automatically calls `Needs` on these contexts, reading in the corresponding packages if necessary, and then making sure that the contexts are on the context search path.

`Begin["`*context*`'"]`	switch to a new current context
`End[ ]`	revert to the previous context

Context manipulation functions.

Executing a function like `Begin` which manipulates contexts changes the way that *Mathematica* interprets names you type in. However, you should realize that the change is effective only in subsequent expressions that you type in. The point is that *Mathematica* always reads in a complete input expression, and interprets the names in it, before it executes any part of the expression. As a result, by the time `Begin` is executed in a particular expression, the names in the expression have already been interpreted, and it is too late for `Begin` to have an effect.

The fact that context manipulation functions do not have an effect until the *next* complete expression is read in means that you must be sure to give those functions as separate expressions, typically on separate lines, when you write *Mathematica* packages.

The name x is interpreted before this expression is executed, so the Begin has no effect.

In[5]:= **Begin["a`"]; Print[Context[x]]; End[ ]**

Global`

Out[5]= a`

Context manipulation functions are used primarily as part of packages intended to be read into *Mathematica*. Sometimes, however, you may find it convenient to use such functions interactively.

This can happen, for example, if you go into a dialog, say using TraceDialog, while executing a function defined in a package. The parameters and temporary variables in the function are typically in a private context associated with the package. Since this context is not on your context search path, *Mathematica* will print out the full names of the symbols, and will require you to type in these full names in order to refer to the symbols. You can however use Begin["*Package*`Private`"] to make the private context of the package your current context. This will make *Mathematica* print out short names for the symbols, and allow you to refer to the symbols by their short names.

■ 2.6.11 Automatic Loading of Packages

Previous sections have discussed explicit loading of *Mathematica* packages using <<*package* and Needs[*package*]. Sometimes, however, you may want to set *Mathematica* up so that it automatically loads a particular package when the package is needed.

You can use DeclarePackage to give the names of symbols which are defined in a particular package. Then, when one of these symbols is actually used, *Mathematica* will automatically load the package where the symbol is defined.

DeclarePackage["*context*`", {"*name*$_1$", "*name*$_2$", ... }]

declare that a package should automatically be loaded if a symbol with any of the names *name*$_i$ is used

---

Arranging for automatic loading of packages.

This specifies that the symbols Div, Grad and Curl are defined in Calculus`VectorAnalysis`.

In[1]:= **DeclarePackage["Calculus`VectorAnalysis`",**
                    {"Div", "Grad", "Curl"}]

Out[1]= Calculus`VectorAnalysis`

When you first use Grad, *Mathematica* automatically loads the package that defines it.

In[2]:= **Grad[x^2 + y^2, Cartesian[x, y, z]]**

Out[2]= {2x, 2y, 0}

When you set up a large collection of *Mathematica* packages, it is often a good idea to create an additional "names file" which contains a sequence of DeclarePackage commands, specifying packages to load when particular names are used. Within a particular *Mathematica* session, you then need to load explicitly only the names file. When you have done this, all the other packages will automatically be loaded if and when they are needed.

`DeclarePackage` works by immediately creating symbols with the names you specify, but giving each of these symbols the special attribute `Stub`. Whenever *Mathematica* finds a symbol with the `Stub` attribute, it automatically loads the package corresponding to the context of the symbol, in an attempt to find the definition of the symbol.

■ 2.6.12 Manipulating Symbols and Contexts by Name

+	`Symbol["name"]`	construct a symbol with a given name
+	`SymbolName[symb]`	find the name of a symbol

Converting between symbols and their names.

Here is the symbol x.

`In[1]:= x // InputForm`

`Out[1]//InputForm= x`

Its name is a string.

`In[2]:= SymbolName[x] // InputForm`

`Out[2]//InputForm= "x"`

This gives the symbol x again.

`In[3]:= Symbol["x"] // InputForm`

`Out[3]//InputForm= x`

Once you have made an assignment such as x = 2, then whenever x is evaluated, it is replaced by 2. Sometimes, however, you may want to continue to refer to x itself, without immediately getting the value of x.

You can do this by referring to x by name. The name of the symbol x is the string "x", and even though x itself may be replaced by a value, the string "x" will always stay the same.

The names of the symbols x and xp are the strings "x" and "xp".

`In[4]:= t = {SymbolName[x], SymbolName[xp]} // InputForm`

`Out[4]//InputForm= {"x", "xp"}`

This assigns a value to x.

`In[5]:= x = 2`

`Out[5]= 2`

Whenever you enter x it is now replaced by 2.

`In[6]:= {x, xp} // InputForm`

`Out[6]//InputForm= {2, xp}`

The name "x" is not affected, however.

`In[7]:= t // InputForm`

`Out[7]//InputForm= InputForm[{"x", "xp"}]`

NameQ["*form*"]	test whether any symbol has a name which matches *form*

Names["*form*"]	give a list of all symbol names which match *form*
Contexts["*form*`"]	give a list of all context names which match *form*

Referring to symbols and contexts by name.

x and xp are symbols that have been created in this *Mathematica* session; xpp is not.

```
In[8]:= {NameQ["x"], NameQ["xp"], NameQ["xpp"]}
Out[8]= {True, True, False}
```

You can specify the form of symbol names using *string patterns* of the kind discussed on page 390. "x*" stands, for example, for all names that start with x.

This gives a list of all symbol names in this *Mathematica* session that begin with x.

```
In[9]:= Names["x*"] // InputForm
Out[9]//InputForm= {"x", "xmax", "xmin", "xp", "x$"}
```

These names correspond to built-in functions in *Mathematica*.

```
In[10]:= Names["Qu*"] // InputForm
Out[10]//InputForm= {"Quartics", "QuasiMonteCarlo", "QuasiNewton",
                     "Quit", "Quotient"}
```

This asks for names "close" to WeierstrssP.

```
In[11]:= Names["WeierstrssP", SpellingCorrection->True]
Out[11]= {WeierstrassP}
```

Clear["*form*"]	clear the values of all symbols whose names match *form*
Clear["*context*`*"]	clear the values of all symbols in the specified context
Remove["*form*"]	remove completely all symbols whose names match *form*
Remove["*context*`*"]	remove completely all symbols in the specified context

Getting rid of symbols by name.

This clears the values of all symbols whose names start with x.

```
In[12]:= Clear["x*"]
```

The name "x" is still known, however.

```
In[13]:= Names["x*"]
Out[13]= {x, xmax, xmin, xp, x$}
```

But the value of x has been cleared.

```
In[14]:= {x, xp}
Out[14]= {x, xp}
```

This removes completely all symbols whose names start with x.

```
In[15]:= Remove["x*"]
```

Now not even the name "x" is known.   *In[16]:=* **Names["x*"]**

Out[16]= {}

Remove["Global`*"]	remove completely all symbols in the Global` context

Removing all symbols you have introduced.

If you do not set up any additional contexts, then all the symbols that you introduce in a *Mathematica* session will be placed in the Global` context. You can remove these symbols completely using **Remove["Global`*"]**. Built-in *Mathematica* objects are in the System` context, and are thus unaffected by this.

■ 2.6.13 Advanced Topic: Intercepting the Creation of New Symbols

Mathematica creates a new symbol when you first enter a particular name. Sometimes it is useful to "intercept" the process of creating a new symbol. *Mathematica* provides several ways to do this.

On[General::newsym]	print a message whenever a new symbol is created
Off[General::newsym]	switch off the message printed when new symbols are created

Printing a message when new symbols are created.

This tells *Mathematica* to print a message whenever a new symbol is created.

In[1]:= **On[General::newsym]**

Mathematica now prints a message about each new symbol that it creates.

In[2]:= **sin[k]**

General::newsym: Symbol sin is new.

General::newsym: Symbol k is new.

Out[2]= sin[k]

This switches off the message.

In[3]:= **Off[General::newsym]**

Generating a message when *Mathematica* creates a new symbol is often a good way to catch typing mistakes. *Mathematica* itself cannot tell the difference between an intentionally new name, and a misspelling of a name it already knows. But by reporting all new names it encounters, *Mathematica* allows you to see whether any of them are mistakes.

$NewSymbol	a function to be applied to the name and context of new symbols which are created

Performing operations when new symbols are created.

When *Mathematica* creates a new symbol, you may want it not just to print a message, but instead to perform some other action. Any function you specify as the value of the global variable $NewSymbol will automatically be applied to strings giving the name and context of each new symbol that *Mathematica* creates.

This defines a function to be applied to each new symbol which is created.

```
In[4]:= $NewSymbol = Print["Name: ", #1, "  Context: ", #2]&
Out[4]= Print[Name: , #1,  Context: , #2]&
```

The function is applied once to v and once to w.

```
In[5]:= v + w
Name: v  Context: Global`
Name: w  Context: Global`

Out[5]= v + w
```

2.7 Strings and Characters

■ 2.7.1 Properties of Strings

Much of what *Mathematica* does revolves around manipulating structured expressions. But you can also use *Mathematica* as a system for handling unstructured strings of text.

"text"	a string containing arbitrary text

Text strings.

When you input a string of text to *Mathematica* you must always enclose it in quotes. However, when *Mathematica* outputs the string it usually does not explicitly show the quotes.

You can see the quotes by asking for the input form of the string. In addition, in a *Mathematica* notebook, quotes will typically appear automatically as soon as you start to edit a string.

When *Mathematica* outputs a string, it usually does not explicitly show the quotes.

```
In[1]:= "This is a string."
Out[1]= This is a string.
```

You can see the quotes, however, by asking for the input form of the string.

```
In[2]:= InputForm[%]
Out[2]//InputForm= "This is a string."
```

The fact that *Mathematica* does not usually show explicit quotes around strings makes it possible for you to use strings to specify quite directly the textual output you want.

The strings are printed out here without explicit quotes.

```
In[3]:= Print["The value is ", 567, "."]
The value is 567.
```

You should understand, however, that even though the string "x" often appears as x in output, it is still a quite different object from the symbol x.

The string "x" is not the same as the symbol x.

```
In[4]:= "x" === x
Out[4]= False
```

You can test whether any particular expression is a string by looking at its head. The head of any string is always String.

All strings have head String.

```
In[5]:= Head["x"]
Out[5]= String
```

The pattern _String matches any string.

```
In[6]:= Cases[{"ab", x, "a", y}, _String]
Out[6]= {ab, a}
```

You can use strings just like other expressions as elements of patterns and transformations. Note, however, that you cannot assign values directly to strings.

This gives a definition for an expression that involves a string.	*In[7]:=* **z["gold"] = 79**
	Out[7]= 79
This replaces each occurrence of the string "aa" by the symbol x.	*In[8]:=* **{"aaa", "aa", "bb", "aa"} /. "aa" -> x**
	Out[8]= {aaa, x, bb, x}

■ 2.7.2 Operations on Strings

Mathematica provides a variety of functions for manipulating strings. Most of these functions are based on viewing strings as a sequence of characters, and many of the functions are analogous to ones for manipulating lists.

s_1 <> s_2 <> ... or StringJoin[{s_1, s_2, ... }]	join several strings together
StringLength[s]	give the number of characters in a string
StringReverse[s]	reverse the characters in a string

Operations on complete strings.

You can join together any number of strings using <>.	*In[1]:=* **"aaaaaaa" <> "bbb" <> "ccccccccc"**
	Out[1]= aaaaaaabbbccccccccc
StringLength gives the number of characters in a string.	*In[2]:=* **StringLength[%]**
	Out[2]= 20
StringReverse reverses the characters in a string.	*In[3]:=* **StringReverse["A string."]**
	Out[3]= .gnirts A

StringTake[s, n]	make a string by taking the first n characters from s
StringTake[s, {n}]	take the nth character from s
StringTake[s, {n_1, n_2}]	take characters n_1 through n_2
StringDrop[s, n]	make a string by dropping the first n characters in s
StringDrop[s, {n_1, n_2}]	drop characters n_1 through n_2

Taking and dropping substrings.

StringTake and StringDrop are the analogs for strings of Take and Drop for lists. Like Take and Drop, they use standard *Mathematica* sequence specifications, so that, for example, negative numbers count character positions from the end of a string. Note that the first character of a string is taken to have position 1.

Here is a sample string.	*In[4]:=* **alpha = "ABCDEFGHIJKLMNOPQRSTUVWXYZ"**
	Out[4]= ABCDEFGHIJKLMNOPQRSTUVWXYZ
This takes the first five characters from alpha.	*In[5]:=* **StringTake[alpha, 5]**
	Out[5]= ABCDE
Here is the fifth character in alpha.	*In[6]:=* **StringTake[alpha, {5}]**
	Out[6]= E
This drops the characters 10 through 2, counting from the end of the string.	*In[7]:=* **StringDrop[alpha, {-10, -2}]**
	Out[7]= ABCDEFGHIJKLMNOPZ

StringInsert[*s*, *snew*, *n*]	insert the string *snew* at position *n* in *s*
+ StringInsert[*s*, *snew*, {*n*₁, *n*₂, ... }]	
	insert several copies of *snew* into *s*

Inserting into a string.

StringInsert[*s*, *snew*, *n*] is set up to produce a string whose n^{th} character is the first character of *snew*.

This produces a new string whose fourth character is the first character of the string "XX".	*In[8]:=* **StringInsert["abcdefgh", "XX", 4]**
	Out[8]= abcXXdefgh
Negative positions are counted from the end of the string.	*In[9]:=* **StringInsert["abcdefgh", "XXX", -1]**
	Out[9]= abcdefghXXX
Each copy of "XXX" is inserted at the specified position in the original string.	*In[10]:=* **StringInsert["abcdefgh", "XXX", {2, 4, -1}]**
	Out[10]= aXXXbcXXXdefghXXX

+ `StringReplacePart[s, snew, {m, n}]`	
	replace the characters at positions *m* through *n* in *s* by the string *snew*
+ `StringReplacePart[s, snew, {{m₁, n₁}, {m₂, n₂}, ... }]`	
	replace several substrings in *s* by *snew*
+ `StringReplacePart[s, {snew₁, snew₂, ... }, {{m₁, n₁}, {m₂, n₂}, ... }]`	
	replace substrings in *s* by the corresponding *snew_i*

Replacing parts of a string.

This replaces characters 2 through 6 by the string `"XXX"`.

```
In[11]:= StringReplacePart["abcdefgh", "XXX", {2, 6}]
Out[11]= aXXXgh
```

This replaces two runs of characters by the string `"XXX"`.

```
In[12]:= StringReplacePart["abcdefgh", "XXX", {{2, 3}, {5, -1}}]
Out[12]= aXXXdXXX
```

Now the two runs of characters are replaced by different strings.

```
In[13]:= StringReplacePart["abcdefgh", {"XXX", "YYYY"},
                            {{2, 3}, {5, -1}}]
Out[13]= aXXXdYYYY
```

`StringPosition[s, sub]`	give a list of the starting and ending positions at which *sub* appears as a substring of *s*
`StringPosition[s, sub, k]`	include only the first *k* occurrences of *sub* in *s*
`StringPosition[s, {sub₁, sub₂, ... }]`	
	include occurrences of any of the *sub_i*

Finding positions of substrings.

You can use `StringPosition` to find where a particular substring appears within a given string. `StringPosition` returns a list, each of whose elements corresponds to an occurrence of the substring. The elements consist of lists giving the starting and ending character positions for the substring. These lists are in the form used as sequence specifications in `StringTake`, `StringDrop` and `StringReplacePart`.

This gives a list of the positions of the substring `"abc"`.

```
In[14]:= StringPosition["abcdabcdaabcabcd", "abc"]
Out[14]= {{1, 3}, {5, 7}, {10, 12}, {13, 15}}
```

This gives only the first occurrence of `"abc"`.

```
In[15]:= StringPosition["abcdabcdaabcabcd", "abc", 1]
Out[15]= {{1, 3}}
```

This shows where both "abc" and "cd" appear. Overlaps between these strings are taken into account.

`In[16]:= StringPosition["abcdabcdaabcabcd", {"abc", "cd"}]`

`Out[16]= {{1, 3}, {3, 4}, {5, 7}, {7, 8}, {10, 12},`
`            {13, 15}, {15, 16}}`

`StringReplace[s, {s₁ -> sp₁, s₂ -> sp₂, ... }]`
$\qquad$ replace the s_i by the corresponding sp_i whenever they appear as substrings of s

Replacing substrings according to rules.

`StringReplace` allows you to perform replacements for substrings within a string. `StringReplace` sequentially goes through a string, testing substrings that start at each successive character position. To each substring, it tries in turn each of the transformation rules you have specified. If any of the rules apply, it replaces the substring, then continues to go through the string, starting at the character position after the end of the substring.

This replaces all occurrences of the character a by the string XX.

`In[17]:= StringReplace["abcdabcdaabcabcd", "a" -> "XX"]`

`Out[17]= XXbcdXXbcdXXXXbcXXbcd`

This replaces abc by Y, and d by XXX.

`In[18]:= StringReplace["abcdabcdaabcabcd",`
`                        {"abc" -> "Y", "d" -> "XXX"}]`

`Out[18]= YXXXYXXXaYYXXX`

The first occurrence of cde is not replaced because it overlaps with abc.

`In[19]:= StringReplace["abcde abacde",`
`                        {"abc" -> "X", "cde" -> "Y"}]`

`Out[19]= Xde abaY`

`StringPosition[s, sub, IgnoreCase -> True]`
$\qquad$ find where *sub* occurs in *s*, treating lower- and upper-case letters as equivalent

`StringReplace[s, {s₁ -> sp₁, ... }, IgnoreCase -> True]`
$\qquad$ replace s_i by sp_i in *s*, treating lower- and upper-case letters as equivalent

Case-independent operations.

This replaces all occurrences of "the", independent of case.

`In[20]:= StringReplace["The cat in the hat.", "the" -> "a",`
`                                        IgnoreCase -> True]`

`Out[20]= a cat in a hat.`

> Sort[{s_1, s_2, s_3, ... }]   sort a list of strings

Sorting strings.

Sort sorts strings into standard dictionary order.	*In[21]:=* **Sort[{"cat", "fish", "catfish", "Cat"}]**
	Out[21]= {cat, Cat, catfish, fish}

■ 2.7.3 String Patterns

You can use the standard *Mathematica* equality test s_1 == s_2 to test whether two strings are identical. Sometimes, however, you may want to find out whether a particular string matches a certain *string pattern*.

Mathematica allows you to define *string patterns* which consist of ordinary strings in which certain characters are interpreted as special "metacharacters". You can then use the function **StringMatchQ** to find out whether a particular string matches a string pattern you have defined. You should realize however that string patterns have nothing to do with the ordinary *Mathematica* patterns for expressions that were discussed in Section 2.3.

> "*string*$_1$" == "*string*$_2$"   test whether two strings are identical
>
> StringMatchQ["*string*", "*pattern*"]   test whether a string matches a particular string pattern

Matching strings.

The character * can be used in a string pattern as a metacharacter to stand for any sequence of alphanumeric characters. Thus, for example, the string pattern "a*b" would match any string which begins with an a, ends with a b, and has any number of alphanumeric characters in between. Similarly, "a*b*" would match any string that starts with a, and has any number of other characters, including at least one b.

The string matches the string pattern you have given.	*In[1]:=* **StringMatchQ["aaaaabbbbcccbbb", "a*b*"]**
	Out[1]= True

The way * is used in *Mathematica* string patterns is analogous to the way it is used for file-name patterns in many operating systems. *Mathematica* however provides some other string pattern metacharacters that are tailored to matching different classes of *Mathematica* symbol names.

*	zero or more characters	
@	one or more characters which are not upper-case letters	
* etc.	literal * etc.	

Metacharacters used in string patterns.

In *Mathematica* there is a general convention that only built-in names should contain upper-case characters. Assuming that you follow this convention, you can use @ as a metacharacter to set up string patterns which match names you have defined, but avoid matching built-in names.

StringMatchQ["*string*", "*pattern*", SpellingCorrection -> True]	test whether *pattern* matches *string*, allowing a small fraction of characters to differ
StringMatchQ["*string*", "*pattern*", IgnoreCase -> True]	test whether *pattern* matches *string*, treating lower- and upper-case letters as equivalent

Options for matching strings.

These strings do not match.

```
In[2]:= StringMatchQ["platypus", "paltypus"]
Out[2]= False
```

Allowing for spelling correction, these strings are considered to match.

```
In[3]:= StringMatchQ["platypus", "paltypus",
                        SpellingCorrection -> True]
Out[3]= True
```

These strings match when lower- and upper-case letters are treated as equivalent.

```
In[4]:= StringMatchQ["AAaaBBbb", "a*b*", IgnoreCase -> True]
Out[4]= True
```

■ 2.7.4 Characters in Strings

Characters["*string*"]	convert a string to a list of characters
StringJoin[{"c_1", "c_2", ... }]	convert a list of characters to a string

Converting between strings and lists of characters.

This gives a list of the characters in the string.

```
In[1]:= Characters["A string."]
Out[1]= {A,  , s, t, r, i, n, g, .}
```

You can apply standard list manipulation operations to this list.

In[2]:= **RotateLeft[%, 3]**

Out[2]= {t, r, i, n, g, ., A, , s}

StringJoin converts the list of characters back to a single string.

In[3]:= **StringJoin[%]**

Out[3]= tring.A s

DigitQ[*string*]	test whether all characters in a string are digits
LetterQ[*string*]	test whether all characters in a string are letters
UpperCaseQ[*string*]	test whether all characters in a string are upper-case letters
LowerCaseQ[*string*]	test whether all characters in a string are lower-case letters

Testing characters in a string.

All characters in the string given are letters.

In[4]:= **LetterQ["Mixed"]**

Out[4]= True

Not all the letters are upper case, so the result is False.

In[5]:= **UpperCaseQ["Mixed"]**

Out[5]= False

ToUpperCase[*string*]	generate a string in which all letters are upper case
ToLowerCase[*string*]	generate a string in which all letters are lower case

Converting between upper and lower case.

This converts all letters to upper case.

In[6]:= **ToUpperCase["Mixed Form"]**

Out[6]= MIXED FORM

+ CharacterRange["c_1", "c_2"]	generate a list of all characters from c_1 and c_2

Generating ranges of characters.

This generates a list of lower-case letters in alphabetical order.

In[7]:= **CharacterRange["a", "h"]**

Out[7]= {a, b, c, d, e, f, g, h}

Here is a list of upper-case letters.

In[8]:= **CharacterRange["T", "Z"]**

Out[8]= {T, U, V, W, X, Y, Z}

Here are some digits.

In[9]:= **CharacterRange["0", "7"]**

Out[9]= {0, 1, 2, 3, 4, 5, 6, 7}

`CharacterRange` will usually give meaningful results for any range of characters that have a natural ordering. The way `CharacterRange` works is by using the character codes that *Mathematica* internally assigns to every character.

This shows the ordering defined by the internal character codes used by *Mathematica*.	*In[10]:=* **CharacterRange["T", "f"]**
	Out[10]= {T, U, V, W, X, Y, Z, [, \",], ^, _, `, a, b, c, d, e, f}

■ 2.7.5 Special Characters

In addition to the ordinary characters that appear on a standard keyboard, you can include in *Mathematica* strings any of the special characters that are supported by *Mathematica*.

Here is a string containing special characters.	*In[1]:=* **"α⊕β⊕…"**
	Out[1]= α⊕β⊕…
You can manipulate this string just as you would any other.	*In[2]:=* **StringReplace[%, "⊕" -> " ⊙⊙ "]**
	Out[2]= α ⊙⊙ β ⊙⊙ …
Here is the list of the characters in the string.	*In[3]:=* **Characters[%]**
	Out[3]= {α, , ⊙, ⊙, , β, , ⊙, ⊙, , …}

In a *Mathematica* notebook, a special character such as α can always be displayed directly. But if you use a text-based interface, then typically the only characters that can readily be displayed are the ones that appear on your keyboard.

As a result, what *Mathematica* does in such situations is to try to approximate special characters by similar-looking sequences of ordinary characters. And when this is not practical, *Mathematica* just gives the full name of the special character.

In a *Mathematica* notebook using `StandardForm`, special characters can be displayed directly.	*In[4]:=* **"Lamé → αβ+"**
	Out[4]= Lamé → αβ+
In `OutputForm`, however, the special characters are approximated when possible by sequences of ordinary ones.	*In[5]:=* **% // OutputForm**
	Out[5]//OutputForm= Lame' ─> \[Alpha]\[Beta]+

Mathematica always uses full names for special characters in `InputForm`. This means that when special characters are written out to files or external programs, they are by default represented purely as sequences of ordinary characters.

This uniform representation is crucial in allowing special characters in *Mathematica* to be used in a way that does not depend on the details of particular computer systems.

In `InputForm` the full names of all special characters are always written out explicitly.	*In[6]:=* **"Lamé → αβ+" // InputForm**
	Out[6]//InputForm= "Lam\[EAcute] \[LongRightArrow] \[Alpha]\[Beta]+"

a	a literal character
\[*Name*]	a character specified using its full name
\"	a " to be included in a string
\\	a \ to be included in a string

Ways to enter characters in a string.

You have to use \ to "escape" any " or \ characters in strings that you enter.

```
In[7]:= "Strings can contain \"quotes\" and \\ characters."
Out[7]= Strings can contain "quotes" and \ characters.
```

\\ produces a literal \ rather than forming part of the specification of α.

```
In[8]:= "\\[Alpha] is \[Alpha]."
Out[8]= \[Alpha] is α.
```

This breaks the string into a list of individual characters.

```
In[9]:= Characters[%]
Out[9]= {\, [, A, l, p, h, a, ], , i, s, , α, .}
```

This creates a list of the characters in the full name of α.

```
In[10]:= Characters[ ToString[InputForm["α"]] ]
Out[10]= {", \, [, A, l, p, h, a, ], "}
```

And this produces a string consisting of an actual α from its full name.

```
In[11]:= ToExpression[ "\"\\[" <> "Alpha" <> "]\""]
Out[11]= α
```

■ 2.7.6 Advanced Topic: Newlines and Tabs in Strings

\n	a newline (line feed) to be included in a string
\t	a tab to be included in a string

Explicit representations of newlines and tabs in strings.

This prints on two lines.

```
In[1]:= "First line.\nSecond line."
Out[1]= First line.
        Second line.
```

In InputForm there is an explicit \n to represent the newline.

```
In[2]:= InputForm[%]
Out[2]//InputForm= "First line.\nSecond line."
```

When you enter a long string in *Mathematica*, it is often convenient to break your input across several lines. *Mathematica* will by default ignore such breaks, so that if you subsequently output the string, it can then be broken in whatever way is appropriate.

Mathematica ignores the line break and any tabs that follow it.	*In[3]:=* **"A string on two lines."** *Out[3]=* A string on two lines.
There is no newline in the string.	*In[4]:=* **InputForm[%]** *Out[4]//InputForm=* "A string on two lines."

"text"	line breaks in *text* are ignored
"\\<*text*\\>"	line breaks in *text* are stored explicitly as \n

Input forms for strings.

Now *Mathematica* keeps the newline.	*In[5]:=* **"\\<A string on
	        two lines.\\>"**
	
	Out[5]= A string on
	        two lines.

In InputForm, the newline is shown as an explicit \n.	*In[6]:=* **InputForm[%]** *Out[6]//InputForm=* "A string on\ntwo lines."

You should realize that even though it is possible to achieve some formatting of *Mathematica* output by creating strings which contain raw tabs and newlines, this is rarely a good idea. Typically a much better approach is to use the higher-level *Mathematica* formatting primitives to be discussed in the next two sections. These primitives will always yield consistent output, independent of such issues as the positions of tab settings on a particular device.

In strings with newlines, text is always aligned on the left.	*In[7]:=* **{"Here is\na string\non several lines.",
	        "Here is\nanother"}**
	
	Out[7]= {Here is
	        a string
	        on several lines., Here is
	        another}

The ColumnForm formatting primitive gives more control. Here text is aligned on the right.	*In[8]:=* **ColumnForm[{"First line", "Second", "Third"}, Right]**
	Out[8]= First line
	             Second
	               Third

And here the text is centered.	*In[9]:=* **ColumnForm[{"First line", "Second", "Third"}, Center]**
	Out[9]= First line
	            Second
	             Third

Within *Mathematica* you can use formatting primitives to avoid raw tabs and newlines. But if you intend to send your output in textual form to external programs, then these programs will often expect to get raw tabs and newlines.

Note that you must either use `WriteString` or give your output in `OutputForm` in order for the raw tabs and newlines to show up. In `InputForm`, they will just be given as \t and \n.

This outputs a string to a file.	`In[10]:= "First line.\nSecond line." >> test`
Here are the contents of the file. By default, `>>` generates output in `InputForm`.	`In[11]:= !!test` `"First line.\nSecond line."`
This explicitly tells *Mathematica* to use `OutputForm` for the output.	`In[12]:= OutputForm["First line.\nSecond line."] >> test`

Now there is a raw newline in the file.	`In[13]:= !!test`
	`First line.`
	`Second line.`

■ 2.7.7 Advanced Topic: Character Codes

`ToCharacterCode["string"]`	give a list of the character codes for the characters in a string
`FromCharacterCode[n]`	construct a character from its character code
`FromCharacterCode[{n_1, n_2, ... }]`	construct a string of characters from a list of character codes

Converting to and from character codes.

Mathematica assigns every character that can appear in a string a unique *character code*. This code is used internally as a way to represent the character.

This gives the character codes for the characters in the string.	`In[1]:= ToCharacterCode["ABCD abcd"]` `Out[1]= {65, 66, 67, 68, 32, 97, 98, 99, 100}`
`FromCharacterCode` reconstructs the original string.	`In[2]:= FromCharacterCode[%]` `Out[2]= ABCD abcd`
Special characters also have character codes.	`In[3]:= ToCharacterCode["α⊕ΓΘ⊘"]` `Out[3]= {945, 8853, 915, 8854, 8709}`

+ `CharacterRange["c_1", "c_2"]`	generate a list of characters with successive character codes

Generating sequences of characters.

This gives part of the English alphabet.

In[4]:= **CharacterRange["a", "k"]**

Out[4]= {a, b, c, d, e, f, g, h, i, j, k}

Here is the Greek alphabet.

In[5]:= **CharacterRange["α", "ω"]**

Out[5]= {α, β, γ, δ, ε, ζ, η, θ, ι, κ, λ, μ, ν, ξ, ο, π, ρ, ς, σ, τ, υ, φ, χ, ψ, ω}

Mathematica assigns names such as \[Alpha] to a large number of special characters. This means that you can always refer to such characters just by giving their names, without ever having to know their character codes.

This generates a string of special characters from their character codes.

In[6]:= **FromCharacterCode[{8706, 8709, 8711, 8712}]**

Out[6]= ∂∅∇∈

You can always refer to these characters by their names, without knowing their character codes.

In[7]:= **InputForm[%]**

Out[7]//InputForm= "\[PartialD]\[EmptySet]\[Del]\[Element]"

Mathematica has names for all the common characters that are used in mathematical notation and in standard European languages. But for a language such as Japanese, there are more than 3,000 additional characters, and *Mathematica* does not assign an explicit name to each of them. Instead, it refers to such characters by standardized character codes.

Here is a string containing Japanese characters.

In[8]:= **"数学"**

Out[8]= 数学

In InputForm, these characters are referred to by standardized character codes. The character codes are given in hexadecimal.

In[9]:= **InputForm[%]**

Out[9]//InputForm= "\:a0fd\:a079"

The notebook front end for *Mathematica* is typically set up so that when you enter a character in a particular font, *Mathematica* will automatically work out the character code for that character.

Sometimes, however, you may find it convenient to be able to enter characters directly using character codes.

\0	null byte (code 0)
nnn	a character with octal code *nnn*
\.*nn*	a character with hexadecimal code *nn*
\:*nnnn*	a character with hexadecimal code *nnnn*

Ways to enter characters directly in terms of character codes.

For characters with character codes below 256, you can use *nnn* or \.*nn*. For characters with character codes above 256, you must use \:*nnnn*. Note that in all cases you must give a fixed number of octal or hexadecimal digits, padding with leading 0s if necessary.

This gives character codes in
hexadecimal for a few characters.

```
In[10]:= BaseForm[ToCharacterCode["Aàαℵ"], 16]
```

$Out[10]//BaseForm= \{41_{16}, e0_{16}, 3b1_{16}, 2135_{16}\}$

This enters the characters using their
character codes. Note the leading 0
inserted in the character code for α.

```
In[11]:= "\.41\.e0\:03b1\:2135"
```

$Out[11]= Aàαℵ$

In assigning codes to characters, *Mathematica* follows three compatible standards: ASCII, ISO Latin-1, and Unicode. ASCII covers the characters on a normal American English keyboard. ISO Latin-1 covers characters in many European languages. Unicode is a more general standard which defines character codes for several tens of thousands of characters used in languages and notations around the world.

0 – 127 (\000 – \177)	ASCII characters
1 – 31 (\001 – \037)	ASCII control characters
32 – 126 (\040 – \176)	printable ASCII characters
97 – 122 (\141 – \172)	lower-case English letters
129 – 255 (\201 – \377)	ISO Latin-1 characters
192 – 255 (\240 – \377)	letters in European languages
0 – 59391 (\:0000 – \:e7ff)	Unicode standard public characters
913 – 1009 (\:0391 – \:03f1)	Greek letters
12288 – 35839 (\:3000 – \:8bff)	Chinese, Japanese and Korean characters
8450 – 8504 (\:2102 – \:2138)	modified letters used in mathematical notation
8592 – 8677 (\:2190 – \:21e5)	arrows
8704 – 8945 (\:2200 – \:22f1)	mathematical symbols and operators
64256 – 64300 (\:fb00 – \:fb2c)	Unicode private characters defined specially by *Mathematica*

A few ranges of character codes used by *Mathematica*.

Here are all the printable ASCII characters.

```
In[12]:= FromCharacterCode[Range[32, 126]]
Out[12]= !"#$%&'()*+,-./0123456789:;<=>
         ?@ABCDEFGHIJKLMNOPQRSTUVWXYZ[\]^
         _`abcdefghijklmnopqrstuvwxyz{|}~
```

Here are some ISO Latin-1 letters.

```
In[13]:= FromCharacterCode[Range[192, 255]]
Out[13]= ÀÁÂÃÄÅÆÇÈÉÊËÌÍÎÏÐÑÒÓÔÕÖ×
         ØÙÚÛÜÝÞßàáâãäåæçèéêëìíîïðñòóôõö÷øùúûüýþÿ
```

Here are some special characters used in mathematical notation. The black blobs correspond to characters not available in the current font.

```
In[14]:= FromCharacterCode[Range[8704, 8750]]
Out[14]= ∀■∂∃∄∅∆∇∈∉■∋∌∍■∏∑■∓∔∕∖/\■∘∙√∛∜∝
         ∞∟∠∡∢∣∤∥∦∧∨■■∫∬■∮∯
```

Here are a few Japanese characters.

```
In[15]:= FromCharacterCode[Range[30000, 30030]]
Out[15]= 田由甲申■■■男■町画甼■■■■甾■甿■畋界畍畎■
```

+■ 2.7.8 Advanced Topic: Raw Character Encodings

Mathematica always allows you to refer to special characters by using names such as \[Alpha] or explicit hexadecimal codes such as \:03b1. And when *Mathematica* writes out files, it by default uses these names or hexadecimal codes.

But sometimes you may find it convenient to use raw encodings for at least some special characters. What this means is that rather than representing special characters by names or explicit hexadecimal codes, you instead represent them by raw bit patterns appropriate for a particular computer system or particular font.

$CharacterEncoding = None	use printable ASCII names for all special characters
+ $CharacterEncoding = "*name*"	use the raw character encoding specified by *name*
+ $SystemCharacterEncoding	the default raw character encoding for your particular computer system

Setting up raw character encodings.

When you press a key or combination of keys on your keyboard, the operating system of your computer sends a certain bit pattern to *Mathematica*. How this bit pattern is interpreted as a character within *Mathematica* will depend on the character encoding that has been set up.

The notebook front end for *Mathematica* typically takes care of setting up the appropriate character encoding automatically for whatever font you are using. But if you use *Mathematica* with a text-based interface or via files or pipes, then you may need to set $CharacterEncoding explicitly.

By specifying an appropriate value for $CharacterEncoding you will typically be able to get *Mathematica* to handle raw text generated by whatever language-specific text editor or operating system you use.

You should realize, however, that while the standard representation of special characters used in *Mathematica* is completely portable across different computer systems, any representation that involves raw character encodings will inevitably not be.

`"PrintableASCII"`	printable ASCII characters only (default)
`"ASCII"`	all ASCII including control characters
`"ISOLatin1"`	characters for common western European languages
`"ISOLatin2"`	characters for central and eastern European languages
`"ISOLatin3"`	characters for additional European languages (e.g. Catalan, Turkish)
`"ISOLatin4"`	characters for other additional European languages (e.g. Estonian, Lappish)
`"ISOLatinCyrillic"`	English and Cyrillic characters
`"AdobeStandard"`	Adobe standard PostScript font encoding
`"MacintoshRoman"`	Macintosh roman font encoding
`"WindowsANSI"`	Microsoft Windows standard font encoding
`"Symbol"`	symbol font encoding
`"ZapfDingbats"`	Zapf dingbats font encoding
`"ShiftJIS"`	shift-JIS for Japanese (mixture of 8- and 16-bit)
`"EUC"`	extended Unix code for Japanese (mixture of 8- and 16-bit)
`"Unicode"`	raw 16-bit Unicode bit patterns

Some raw character encodings supported by *Mathematica*.

Mathematica knows about various raw character encodings, appropriate for different computer systems and different languages.

Any character that is included in a particular raw encoding will be written out in raw form by *Mathematica* if you specify that encoding. But characters which are not included in the encoding will still be written out using standard *Mathematica* full names or hexadecimal codes.

In addition, any character included in a particular encoding can be given in raw form as input to *Mathematica* if you specify that encoding. *Mathematica* will automatically translate the character to its own standard internal form.

This writes a string to the file `tmp`.	`In[1]:= "a b c \[EAcute] \[Alpha] \[Pi] \:2766" >> tmp`
Special characters are by default written out using full names or explicit hexadecimal codes.	`In[2]:= !!tmp` `"a b c \[EAcute] \[Alpha] \[Pi] \:2766"`
This tells *Mathematica* to use a raw character encoding appropriate for Macintosh roman fonts.	`In[3]:= $CharacterEncoding = "MacintoshRoman"` `Out[3]= MacintoshRoman`
Now those special characters that can will be written out in raw form.	`In[4]:= "a b c \[EAcute] \[Alpha] \[Pi] \:2766" >> tmp`
You can only read the raw characters if you have a system that uses the Macintosh roman encoding.	`In[5]:= !!tmp` `"a b c é \[Alpha] \[Pi] \:2766"`
This tells *Mathematica* to use no raw encoding by default.	`In[6]:= $CharacterEncoding = None` `Out[6]= None`
You can still explicitly request raw encodings to be used in certain functions.	`In[7]:= Get["tmp", CharacterEncoding->"MacintoshRoman"]` `Out[7]= a b c È α π ∎`

Mathematica supports both 8- and 16-bit raw character encodings. In an encoding such as `"ISOLatin1"`, all characters are represented by bit patterns containing 8 bits. But in an encoding such as `"ShiftJIS"` some characters instead involve bit patterns containing 16 bits.

Most of the raw character encodings supported by *Mathematica* include basic ASCII as a subset. This means that even when you are using such encodings, you can still give ordinary *Mathematica* input in the usual way, and you can specify special characters using \[and \: sequences.

Some raw character encodings, however, do not include basic ASCII as a subset. An example is the `"Symbol"` encoding, in which the character codes normally used for a and b are instead used for α and β.

This gives the usual ASCII character codes for a few English letters.	`In[8]:= ToCharacterCode["abcdefgh"]` `Out[8]= {97, 98, 99, 100, 101, 102, 103, 104}`

In the "Symbol" encoding, these character codes are used for Greek letters.

In[9]:= **FromCharacterCode[%, "Symbol"]**

Out[9]= αβχδεφγη

ToCharacterCode["*string*"]   generate codes for characters using the standard *Mathematica* encoding

+ ToCharacterCode["*string*", "*encoding*"]
                  generate codes for characters using the specified encoding

FromCharacterCode[{n_1, n_2, ... }]
                  generate characters from codes using the standard *Mathematica* encoding

+ FromCharacterCode[{n_1, n_2, ... }, "*encoding*"]
                  generate characters from codes using the specified encoding

Handling character codes with different encodings.

This gives the codes assigned to various characters by *Mathematica*.

In[10]:= **ToCharacterCode["abc\[EAcute]\[Pi]"]**

Out[10]= {97, 98, 99, 233, 960}

Here are the codes assigned to the same characters in the Macintosh roman encoding.

In[11]:= **ToCharacterCode["abc\[EAcute]\[Pi]", "MacintoshRoman"]**

Out[11]= {97, 98, 99, 142, 960}

Here are the codes in the Windows standard encoding. There is no code for \[Pi] in that encoding.

In[12]:= **ToCharacterCode["abc\[EAcute]\[Pi]", "WindowsANSI"]**

Out[12]= {97, 98, 99, 233, 960}

The character codes used internally by *Mathematica* are based on Unicode. But externally *Mathematica* by default always uses plain ASCII sequences such as \[*Name*] or \:*xxxx* to refer to special characters. By telling it to use the raw "Unicode" character encoding, however, you can get *Mathematica* to read and write characters in raw 16-bit Unicode form.

2.8 Textual Input and Output

■ 2.8.1 Forms of Input and Output

Here is one way to enter a particular expression.

In[1]:= **x^2 + Sqrt[y]**

Out[1]= $x^2 + \sqrt{y}$

Here is another way to enter the same expression.

In[2]:= **Plus[Power[x, 2], Sqrt[y]]**

Out[2]= $x^2 + \sqrt{y}$

With a notebook front end, you can also enter the expression directly in this way.

In[3]:= **$x^2 + \sqrt{y}$**

Out[3]= $x^2 + \sqrt{y}$

Mathematica allows you to output expressions in many different ways.

In *Mathematica* notebooks, expressions are by default output in StandardForm.

In[4]:= **x^2 + Sqrt[y]**

Out[4]= $x^2 + \sqrt{y}$

OutputForm uses only ordinary keyboard characters and is the default for text-based interfaces to *Mathematica*.

In[5]:= **OutputForm[x^2 + Sqrt[y]]**

Out[5]//OutputForm= x^2 + Sqrt[y]

InputForm yields a form that can be typed directly on a keyboard.

In[6]:= **InputForm[x^2 + Sqrt[y]]**

Out[6]//InputForm= x^2 + Sqrt[y]

FullForm shows the internal form of an expression in explicit functional notation.

In[7]:= **FullForm[x^2 + Sqrt[y]]**

Out[7]//FullForm= Plus[Power[x, 2], Power[y, Rational[1, 2]]]

FullForm[*expr*]	the internal form of an expression
InputForm[*expr*]	a form suitable for direct keyboard input
OutputForm[*expr*]	a two-dimensional form using only keyboard characters
StandardForm[*expr*]	the default form used in *Mathematica* notebooks

Some output forms for expressions.

Output forms provide textual representations of *Mathematica* expressions. In some cases these textual representations are also suitable for input to *Mathematica*. But in other cases they are intended just to be looked at, or to be exported to other programs, rather than to be used as input to *Mathematica*.

TraditionalForm uses a large collection of ad hoc rules to produce an approximation to traditional mathematical notation.

In[8]:= **TraditionalForm[x^2 + Sqrt[y] + Gamma[z] EllipticK[z]]**

Out[8]//TraditionalForm= $x^2 + K(z)\,\Gamma(z) + \sqrt{y}$

TeXForm yields output suitable for export to TEX.

In[9]:= **TeXForm[x^2 + Sqrt[y]]**

Out[9]//TeXForm= {x^2} + {\sqrt{y}}

CForm yields output that can be included in a C program. Macros for objects like Power are included in the header file mdefs.h.

In[10]:= **CForm[x^2 + Sqrt[y]]**

Out[10]//CForm= Power(x,2) + Sqrt(y)

FortranForm yields output suitable for export to Fortran.

In[11]:= **FortranForm[x^2 + Sqrt[y]]**

Out[11]//FortranForm= x**2 + Sqrt(y)

+ TraditionalForm[*expr*]	traditional mathematical notation
TeXForm[*expr*]	output suitable for export to TEX
CForm[*expr*]	output suitable for export to C
FortranForm[*expr*]	output suitable for export to Fortran

Output forms not normally used for *Mathematica* input.

Section 2.8.17 will discuss how you can create your own output forms. You should realize however that in communicating with external programs it is often better to use *MathLink* to send expressions directly than to generate a textual representation for these expressions.

- Exchange textual representations of expressions.
- Exchange expressions directly via *MathLink*.

Two ways to communicate between *Mathematica* and other programs.

■ 2.8.2 How Input and Output Work

Input	convert from a textual form to an expression
Processing	do computations on the expression
Output	convert the resulting expression to textual form

Steps in the operation of *Mathematica*.

When you type something like x^2 what *Mathematica* at first sees is just the string of characters x, ^, 2. But with the usual way that *Mathematica* is set up, it immediately knows to convert this string of characters into the expression Power[x, 2].

Then, after whatever processing is possible has been done, *Mathematica* takes the expression Power[x, 2] and converts it into some kind of textual representation for output.

Mathematica reads the string of characters x, ^, 2 and converts it to the expression Power[x, 2].	In[1]:= **x ^ 2** Out[1]= x^2
This shows the expression in Fortran form.	In[2]:= **FortranForm[%]** Out[2]//FortranForm= x**2
FortranForm is just a "wrapper": the value of Out[2] is still the expression Power[x, 2].	In[3]:= **%** Out[3]= x^2

It is important to understand that in a typical *Mathematica* session In[n] and Out[n] record only the underlying expressions that are processed, not the textual representations that happen to be used for their input or output.

If you explicitly request a particular kind of output, say by using TraditionalForm[*expr*], then what you get will be labeled with Out[n]//TraditionalForm. This indicates that what you are seeing is *expr*//TraditionalForm, even though the value of Out[n] itself is just *expr*.

Mathematica also allows you to specify globally that you want output to be displayed in a particular form. And if you do this, then the form will no longer be indicated explicitly in the label for each line. But it is still the case that In[n] and Out[n] will record only underlying expressions, not the textual representations used for their input and output.

This sets t to be an expression with FortranForm explicitly wrapped around it.	In[4]:= **t = FortranForm[x^2 + y^2]** Out[4]//FortranForm= x**2 + y**2
The result on the previous line is just the expression.	In[5]:= **%** Out[5]= $x^2 + y^2$
But t contains the FortranForm wrapper, and so is displayed in FortranForm.	In[6]:= **t** Out[6]//FortranForm= x**2 + y**2
Wherever t appears, it is formatted in FortranForm.	In[7]:= **{t^2, 1/t}** Out[7]= $\left\{ \text{x**2 + y**2}^2, \ \dfrac{1}{\text{x**2 + y**2}} \right\}$

⁺■ 2.8.3 The Representation of Textual Forms

Like everything else in *Mathematica* the textual forms of expressions can themselves be represented as expressions. Textual forms that consist of one-dimensional sequences of characters can be represented directly as ordinary *Mathematica* strings. Textual forms that involve subscripts, superscripts and other two-dimensional constructs, however, can be represented by nested collections of two-dimensional boxes.

One-dimensional strings	`InputForm`, `FullForm`, etc.
Two-dimensional boxes	`StandardForm`, `TraditionalForm`, etc.

Typical representations of textual forms.

This generates the string corresponding to the textual representation of the expression in InputForm.

```
In[1]:= ToString[x^2 + y^3, InputForm]
Out[1]= x^2 + y^3
```

FullForm shows the string explicitly.

```
In[2]:= FullForm[%]
Out[2]//FullForm= "x^2 + y^3"
```

Here are the individual characters in the string.

```
In[3]:= Characters[%]
Out[3]= {x, ^, 2, , +, , y, ^, 3}
```

Here is the box structure corresponding to the expression in StandardForm.

```
In[4]:= ToBoxes[x^2 + y^3, StandardForm]
Out[4]= RowBox[
            {SuperscriptBox[x, 2], +, SuperscriptBox[y, 3]}]
```

Here is the InputForm of the box structure. In this form the structure is effectively represented by an ordinary string.

```
In[5]:= ToBoxes[x^2 + y^3, StandardForm] // InputForm
Out[5]//InputForm= \(x\^2 + y\^3\)
```

If you use the notebook front end for *Mathematica*, then you can see the expression that corresponds to the textual form of each cell by using the Show Expression menu item.

Here is a cell containing an expression in StandardForm.

$$\frac{1}{2(1+x^2)} + \text{Log}[x] - \frac{\text{Log}[1+x^2]}{2}$$

Here is the underlying representation of that expression in terms of boxes, displayed using the Show Expression menu item.

```
Cell[BoxData[
  RowBox[{
    FractionBox["1",
      RowBox[{"2", " ",
        RowBox[{"(",
          RowBox[{"1", "+",
            SuperscriptBox["x", "2"]}], ")"}]}]], "+",
    RowBox[{"Log", "[", "x", "]"}], "-",
    FractionBox[
      RowBox[{"Log", "[",
        RowBox[{"1", "+",
          SuperscriptBox["x", "2"]}], "]"}], "2"]}]], "Output"]
```

ToString[*expr*, *form*]	create a string representing the specified textual form of *expr*
ToBoxes[*expr*, *form*]	create a box structure representing the specified textual form of *expr*

Creating strings and boxes from expressions.

+ ■ 2.8.4 The Interpretation of Textual Forms

ToExpression[*input*]	create an expression by interpreting strings or boxes

Converting from strings or boxes to expressions.

This takes a string and interprets it as an expression.

$In[1]:=$ **ToExpression["2 + 3 + x/y"]**

$Out[1]= 5 + \dfrac{x}{y}$

Here is the box structure corresponding to the textual form of an expression in StandardForm.

$In[2]:=$ **ToBoxes[2 + x^2, StandardForm]**

$Out[2]=$ RowBox[{2, +, SuperscriptBox[x, 2]}]

ToExpression interprets this box structure and yields the original expression again.

$In[3]:=$ **ToExpression[%]**

$Out[3]= 2 + x^2$

In any *Mathematica* session, *Mathematica* is always effectively using ToExpression to interpret the textual form of your input as an actual expression to evaluate.

If you use the notebook front end for *Mathematica*, then the interpretation only takes place when the contents of a cell are sent to the kernel, say for evaluation. This means that within a notebook there is no need for the textual forms you set up to correspond to meaningful *Mathematica* expressions; this is only necessary if you want to send these forms to the kernel.

FullForm	explicit functional notation
InputForm	one-dimensional notation
StandardForm	two-dimensional notation

The hierarchy of forms for standard *Mathematica* input.

Here is an expression entered in
FullForm.

In[4]:= **Plus[1, Power[x, 2]]**

Out[4]= $1 + x^2$

Here is the same expression entered in
InputForm.

In[5]:= **1 + x^2**

Out[5]= $1 + x^2$

And here is the expression entered in
StandardForm.

In[6]:= **1 + x²**

Out[6]= $1 + x^2$

Built into *Mathematica* is a collection of standard rules for use by ToExpression in converting textual forms to expressions.

These rules define the *grammar* of *Mathematica*. They state, for example, that $x + y$ should be interpreted as Plus[x, y], and that x^y should be interpreted as Power[x, y]. If the input you give is in FullForm, then the rules for interpretation are very straightforward: every expression consists just of a head followed by a sequence of elements enclosed in brackets. The rules for InputForm are slightly more sophisticated: they allow operators such as +, =, and ->, and understand the meaning of expressions where these operators appear between operands. StandardForm involves still more sophisticated rules, which allow operators and operands to be arranged not just in a one-dimensional sequence, but in a full two-dimensional structure.

Mathematica is set up so that FullForm, InputForm and StandardForm form a strict hierarchy: anything you can enter in FullForm will also work in InputForm, and anything you can enter in InputForm will also work in StandardForm.

If you use a notebook front end for *Mathematica*, then you will typically want to use all the features of StandardForm. If you use a text-based interface, however, then you will typically be able to use only features of InputForm.

x^2	ordinary InputForm
\!\(x\^2\)	one-dimensional representation of StandardForm

Two versions of InputForm.

When you use StandardForm in a *Mathematica* notebook, you can enter directly two-dimensional forms such as x^2. But InputForm allows only one-dimensional forms. Nevertheless, even though the actual text you give in `InputForm` must be one-dimensional, it is still possible to make it represent a two-dimensional form. Thus, for example, \!\(x\^2\) represents the two-dimensional form x^2, and is interpreted by *Mathematica* as `Power[x, 2]`.

Here is ordinary one-dimensional input.	*In[7]:=* `x^2 + 1/y`
	Out[7]= $x^2 + \dfrac{1}{y}$
Here is input that represents a two-dimensional form.	*In[8]:=* `\!\( x\^2 + 1\/y \)`
	Out[8]= $x^2 + \dfrac{1}{y}$
Even though the input is given differently, the expressions obtained on the last two lines are exactly the same.	*In[9]:=* `% == %%`
	Out[9]= True

If you copy a two-dimensional form out of *Mathematica*, it is normally given in \!\(... \) form. When you paste this one-dimensional form back into a *Mathematica* notebook, it will automatically "snap" into two-dimensional form. If you simply type a \!\(... \) form into a notebook, you can get it to snap into two-dimensional form using the Make 2D menu item.

`ToExpression[`*input*`, `*form*`]`	attempt to create an expression assuming that *input* is given in the specified textual form

Importing from other textual forms.

`StandardForm` and its subsets `FullForm` and `InputForm` provide precise ways to represent any *Mathematica* expression in textual form. And given such a textual form, it is always possible to convert it unambiguously to the expression it represents.

`TraditionalForm` is an example of a textual form intended primarily for output. It is possible to take any *Mathematica* expression and display it in `TraditionalForm`. But `TraditionalForm` does not have the precision of `StandardForm`, and as a result there is in general no unambiguous way to go back from a `TraditionalForm` representation and get the expression it represents.

Nevertheless, `ToExpression[`*input*`, TraditionalForm]` takes text in `TraditionalForm` and attempts to interpret it as an expression.

This takes a string and interprets it as `TraditionalForm` input.	*In[10]:=* `ToExpression["f(6)", TraditionalForm]`
	Out[10]= f[6]
In `StandardForm` the same string would mean a product of terms.	*In[11]:=* `ToExpression["f(6)", StandardForm]`
	Out[11]= 6 f

When `TraditionalForm` output is generated as the result of a computation, the actual collection of boxes that represent the output typically contains special `InterpretationBox` and `TagBox` objects which specify how an expression can be reconstructed from the `TraditionalForm` output.

The same is true of `TraditionalForm` that is obtained by explicit conversion from `StandardForm`. But if you edit `TraditionalForm` extensively, or enter it from scratch, then *Mathematica* will have to try to interpret it without the benefit of any additional embedded information.

■ 2.8.5 Short and Shallow Output

When you generate a very large output expression in *Mathematica*, you often do not want to see the whole expression at once. Rather, you would first like to get an idea of the general structure of the expression, and then, perhaps, go in and look at particular parts in more detail.

The functions `Short` and `Shallow` allow you to see "outlines" of large *Mathematica* expressions.

`Short[`*expr*`]`	show a one-line outline of *expr*
`Short[`*expr*`, `*n*`]`	show an *n*-line outline of *expr*
`Shallow[`*expr*`]`	show the "top parts" of *expr*
`Shallow[`*expr*`, {`*depth*`, `*length*`}]`	show the parts of *expr* to the specified depth and length

Showing outlines of expressions.

This generates a long expression. If the whole expression were printed out here, it would go on for 23 lines.

```
In[1]:= t = Expand[(1 + x + y)^12] ;
```

This gives a one-line "outline" of t. The <<87>> indicates that 87 terms are omitted.

```
In[2]:= Short[t]
```
$Out[2]//Short= 1 + 12\,x + \ll 87 \gg + 12\,x\,y^{11} + y^{12}$

When *Mathematica* generates output, it first effectively writes the output in one long row. Then it looks at the width of text you have asked for, and it chops the row of output into a sequence of separate "lines". Each of the "lines" may of course contain superscripts and built-up fractions, and so may take up more than one actual line on your output device. When you specify a particular number of lines in `Short`, *Mathematica* takes this to be the number of "logical lines" that you want, not the number of actual physical lines on your particular output device.

Here is a four-line version of t. More terms are shown in this case.

```
In[3]:= Short[t, 4]
```
$Out[3]//Short= 1 + 12\,x + 66\,x^{2} + 220\,x^{3} + 495\,x^{4} +$
$792\,x^{5} + 924\,x^{6} + 792\,x^{7} + 495\,x^{8} + \ll 73 \gg +$
$660\,x\,y^{9} + 660\,x^{2}\,y^{9} + 220\,x^{3}\,y^{9} + 66\,y^{10} + 132\,x\,y^{10} +$
$66\,x^{2}\,y^{10} + 12\,y^{11} + 12\,x\,y^{11} + y^{12}$

You can use Short with other output
forms, such as InputForm.

In[4]:= **Short[InputForm[t]]**

Out[4]//Short= $1 + 12*x + << 88 >> + y \char`^ 12$

Short works by removing a sequence of parts from an expression until the output form of the result fits on the number of lines you specify. Sometimes, however, you may find it better to specify not how many final output lines you want, but which parts of the expression to drop. Shallow[*expr*, {*depth*, *length*}] includes only *length* arguments to any function, and drops all subexpressions that are below the specified depth.

Shallow shows a different outline of t.

In[5]:= **Shallow[t]**

Out[5]//Shallow= $1 + 12x + 66\,\mathrm{Power}[<<2>>] + 220\,\mathrm{Power}[<<2>>] +$
$495\,\mathrm{Power}[<<2>>] + 792\,\mathrm{Power}[<<2>>] +$
$924\,\mathrm{Power}[<<2>>] + 792\,\mathrm{Power}[<<2>>] +$
$495\,\mathrm{Power}[<<2>>] + 220\,\mathrm{Power}[<<2>>] + <<81>>$

This includes only 10 arguments to
each function, but allows any depth.

In[6]:= **Shallow[t, {Infinity, 10}]**

Out[6]//Shallow= $1 + 12x + 66x^2 + 220x^3 + 495x^4 + 792x^5 +$
$924x^6 + 792x^7 + 495x^8 + 220x^9 + <<81>>$

Shallow is particularly useful when you want to drop parts in a uniform way throughout a highly nested expression, such as a large list structure returned by Trace.

Here is the recursive definition of the
Fibonacci function.

In[7]:= **fib[n_] := fib[n-1] + fib[n-2] ; fib[0] = fib[1] = 1**

Out[7]= 1

This generates a large list structure.

In[8]:= **tr = Trace[fib[8]] ;**

You can use Shallow to see an outline
of the structure.

In[9]:= **Shallow[tr]**

Out[9]//Shallow= $\{\mathrm{fib}[<<1>>],$
$\mathrm{Plus}[<<2>>], \{\{<<2>>\}, <<1>>, <<1>>,$
$\{<<7>>\}, \{<<7>>\}, <<1>>, <<1>>\}, \{\{<<2>>\},$
$<<1>>, <<1>>, \{<<7>>\}, \{<<7>>\}, <<1>>, <<1>>\},$
$\mathrm{Plus}[<<2>>], 34\}$

Short gives you a less uniform outline,
which can be more difficult to
understand.

In[10]:= **Short[tr, 4]**

Out[10]//Short= $\{\mathrm{fib}[8], \mathrm{fib}[8-1] + \mathrm{fib}[8-2],$
$\{\{8-1, 7\}, \mathrm{fib}[7], \mathrm{fib}[7-1] + \mathrm{fib}[7-2], <<2>>,$
$13+8, 21\}<<1>>\{\{8-2, 6\}, \mathrm{fib}[6], <<4>>, 13\},$
$21+13, 34\}$

■ 2.8.6 String-Oriented Output Formats

"text"	a string containing arbitrary text

Text strings.

The quotes are not included in standard *Mathematica* output form.	*In[1]:=* **"This is a string."** *Out[1]=* This is a string.
In input form, the quotes are included.	*In[2]:=* **InputForm[%]** *Out[2]//InputForm=* "This is a string."

You can put any kind of text into a *Mathematica* string. This includes non-English characters, as well as newlines and other control information. Section 2.7 discusses in more detail how strings work.

StringForm["*cccc*``*cccc*", x_1, x_2, ...]

output a string in which successive `` are replaced by successive x_i

StringForm["*cccc*`*i*`*cccc*", x_1, x_2, ...]

output a string in which each `*i*` is replaced by the corresponding x_i

---

Using format strings.

In many situations, you may want to generate output using a string as a "template", but "splicing" in various *Mathematica* expressions. You can do this using StringForm.

This generates output with each successive `` replaced by an expression.	*In[3]:=* **StringForm["x = ``, y = ``", 3, (1 + u)^2]** *Out[3]=* x = 3, y = $(1+u)^2$
You can use numbers to pick out expressions in any order.	*In[4]:=* **StringForm["{`1`, `2`, `1`}", a, b]** *Out[4]=* {a, b, a}

The string in StringForm acts somewhat like a "format directive" in the formatted output statements of languages such as C and Fortran. You can determine how the expressions in StringForm will be formatted by wrapping them with standard output format functions.

You can specify how the expressions in StringForm are formatted using standard output format functions.	*In[5]:=* **StringForm["The `` of `` is ``.", TeXForm, a/b, TeXForm[a/b]]** *Out[5]=* The TeXForm of $\dfrac{a}{b}$ is $\{a\backslash\text{over } b\}$.

You should realize that StringForm is only an output format. It does not evaluate in any way. You can use the function ToString to create an ordinary string from a StringForm object.

StringForm generates formatted output in standard *Mathematica* output form.	*In[6]:=* **StringForm["Q: `` -> ``", a, b]** *Out[6]=* Q: a -> b
In input form, you can see the actual StringForm object.	*In[7]:=* **InputForm[%]** *Out[7]//InputForm=* StringForm["Q: `` -> ``", a, b]

This creates an ordinary string from the StringForm object.	*In[8]:=* **InputForm[ToString[%]]**
	Out[8]//InputForm= "Q: a -> b"

StringForm allows you to specify a "template string", then fill in various expressions. Sometimes all you want to do is to concatenate together the output forms for a sequence of expressions. You can do this using SequenceForm.

SequenceForm[*expr*₁, *expr*₂, ...]   give the output forms of the *expr*ᵢ concatenated together

Output of sequences of expressions.

SequenceForm prints as a sequence of expressions concatenated together.	*In[9]:=* **SequenceForm["[x = ", 56, "]"]**
	Out[9]= [x = 56]

ColumnForm[{*expr*₁, *expr*₂, ... }]   a left-aligned column of objects

ColumnForm[*list*, *h*, *v*]   a column with horizontal alignment *h* (Left, Center or Right), and vertical alignment *v* (Below, Center or Above)

Output of columns of expressions.

This arranges the two expressions in a column.	*In[10]:=* **ColumnForm[{a + b, x^2}]**
	Out[10]= a + b
	x^2

HoldForm[*expr*]   give the output form of *expr*, with *expr* maintained unevaluated

Output of unevaluated expressions.

Using text strings and functions like StringForm, you can generate pieces of output that do not necessarily correspond to valid *Mathematica* expressions. Sometimes, however, you want to generate output that corresponds to a valid *Mathematica* expression, but only so long as the expression is not evaluated. The function HoldForm maintains its argument unevaluated, but allows it to be formatted in the standard *Mathematica* output form.

HoldForm maintains 1 + 1 unevaluated.	*In[11]:=* **HoldForm[1 + 1]**
	Out[11]= 1 + 1
The HoldForm prevents the actual assignment from being done.	*In[12]:=* **HoldForm[x = 3]**
	Out[12]= x = 3

If it was not for the HoldForm, the   *In[13]:=* **HoldForm[34^78]**
power would be evaluated.
                                           Out[13]= 34^{78}

■ 2.8.7 Output Formats for Numbers

ScientificForm[*expr*]	print all numbers in scientific notation
EngineeringForm[*expr*]	print all numbers in engineering notation (exponents divisible by 3)
AccountingForm[*expr*]	print all numbers in standard accounting format

Output formats for numbers.

These numbers are given in the default   *In[1]:=* **{6.7^-4, 6.7^6, 6.7^8}**
output format. Large numbers are
given in scientific notation.   *Out[1]=* $\{0.00049625, 90458.4, 4.06068 \times 10^6\}$

This gives all numbers in scientific   *In[2]:=* **ScientificForm[%]**
notation.
                                           Out[2]//ScientificForm= $\{4.9625 \times 10^{-4}, 9.04584 \times 10^4, 4.06068 \times 10^6\}$

This gives the numbers in engineering   *In[3]:=* **EngineeringForm[%]**
notation, with exponents arranged to
be multiples of three.   *Out[3]//EngineeringForm=* $\{496.25 \times 10^{-6}, 90.4584 \times 10^3, 4.06068 \times 10^6\}$

In accounting form, negative numbers   *In[4]:=* **AccountingForm[{5.6, -6.7, 10.^7}]**
are given in parentheses, and scientific
notation is never used.   *Out[4]//AccountingForm=* {5.6, (6.7), 10000000.}

NumberForm[*expr, tot*]	print at most *tot* digits of all approximate real numbers in *expr*
ScientificForm[*expr, tot*]	use scientific notation with at most *tot* digits
EngineeringForm[*expr, tot*]	use engineering notation with at most *tot* digits

Controlling the printed precision of real numbers.

Here is π^9 to 30 decimal places.   *In[5]:=* **N[Pi^9, 30]**

                                           Out[5]= 29809.0993334462116665094 0240124

This prints just 10 digits of π^9.   *In[6]:=* **NumberForm[%, 10]**

                                           Out[6]//NumberForm= 29809.09933

This gives 12 digits, in engineering notation.

In[7]:= **EngineeringForm[%, 12]**

Out[7]//EngineeringForm= $29.8090993334 \times 10^3$

option name	default value	
DigitBlock	Infinity	maximum length of blocks of digits between breaks
NumberSeparator	{",", " "}	strings to insert at breaks between blocks of digits to the left and right of a decimal point
NumberPoint	"."	string to use for a decimal point
+ NumberMultiplier	"\[Times]"	string to use for the multiplication sign in scientific notation
NumberSigns	{"-", ""}	strings to use for signs of negative and positive numbers
NumberPadding	{"", ""}	strings to use for padding on the left and right
SignPadding	False	whether to insert padding after the sign
NumberFormat	Automatic	function to generate final format of number
ExponentFunction	Automatic	function to determine the exponent to use

Options for number formatting.

All the options in the table except the last one apply to both integers and approximate real numbers.

All the options can be used in any of the functions NumberForm, ScientificForm, EngineeringForm and AccountingForm. In fact, you can in principle reproduce the behavior of any one of these functions simply by giving appropriate option settings in one of the others. The default option settings listed in the table are those for NumberForm.

Setting DigitBlock->*n* breaks digits into blocks of length *n*.

In[8]:= **NumberForm[30!, DigitBlock->3]**

Out[8]//NumberForm= 265,252,859,812,191,058,636,308,480,000,000

You can specify any string to use as a separator between blocks of digits.

In[9]:= **NumberForm[30!, DigitBlock->5, NumberSeparator->" "]**

Out[9]//NumberForm= 265 25285 98121 91058 63630 84800 00000

This gives an explicit plus sign for positive numbers, and uses | in place of a decimal point.

In[10]:= **NumberForm[{4.5, -6.8}, NumberSigns->{"-", "+"},
        NumberPoint->"|"]**

Out[10]//NumberForm= {+4|5, -6|8}

When *Mathematica* prints an approximate real number, it has to choose whether scientific notation should be used, and if so, how many digits should appear to the left of the decimal point. What *Mathematica* does is first to find out what the exponent would be if scientific notation were used, and one digit were given to the left of the decimal point. Then it takes this exponent, and applies any function given as the setting for the option ExponentFunction. This function should return the actual exponent to be used, or Null if scientific notation should not be used.

The default is to use scientific notation for all numbers with exponents outside the range −5 to 5.

```
In[11]:= {8.^5, 11.^7, 13.^9}
```
$$Out[11]= \{32768., 1.94872 \times 10^7, 1.06045 \times 10^{10}\}$$

This uses scientific notation only for numbers with exponents of 10 or more.

```
In[12]:= NumberForm[%,
            ExponentFunction -> (If[-10 < # < 10, Null, #]&)]
```
$$Out[12]//NumberForm= \{32768., 19487171., 1.06045 \times 10^{10}\}$$

This forces all exponents to be multiples of 3.

```
In[13]:= NumberForm[%, ExponentFunction -> (3 Quotient[#, 3]&)]
```
$$Out[13]//NumberForm= \{32.768 \times 10^3, 19.4872 \times 10^6, 10.6045 \times 10^9\}$$

Having determined what the mantissa and exponent for a number should be, the final step is to assemble these into the object to print. The option NumberFormat allows you to give an arbitrary function which specifies the print form for the number. The function takes as arguments three strings: the mantissa, the base, and the exponent for the number. If there is no exponent, it is given as "".

This gives the exponents in Fortran-like "e" format.

```
In[14]:= NumberForm[{5.6^10, 7.8^20},
            NumberFormat -> (SequenceForm[#1, "e", #3]&) ]
```
$$Out[14]//NumberForm= \{3.03305e7, 6.94852e17\}$$

You can use FortranForm to print individual numbers in Fortran format.

```
In[15]:= FortranForm[7.8^20]
```
$$Out[15]//FortranForm= 6.948515870862151e17$$

PaddedForm[*expr*, *tot*]	print with all numbers having room for *tot* digits, padding with leading spaces if necessary
PaddedForm[*expr*, {*tot*, *frac*}]	print with all numbers having room for *tot* digits, with exactly *frac* digits to the right of the decimal point
NumberForm[*expr*, {*tot*, *frac*}]	print with all numbers having at most *tot* digits, exactly *frac* of them to the right of the decimal point
ColumnForm[{*expr*$_1$, *expr*$_2$, ... }]	print with the *expr*$_i$ left aligned in a column

Controlling the alignment of numbers in output.

Whenever you print a collection of numbers in a column or some other definite arrangement, you typically need to be able to align the numbers in a definite way. Usually you want all the numbers to be set up so that the digit corresponding to a particular power of 10 always appears at the same position within the region used to print a number.

You can change the positions of digits in the printed form of a number by "padding" it in various ways. You can pad on the right, typically adding zeros somewhere after the decimal. Or you can pad on the left, typically inserting spaces in place of leading zeros.

This pads with spaces to make room for up to 7 digits in each integer.

```
In[16]:= PaddedForm[{456, 12345, 12}, 7]

Out[16]//PaddedForm= {    456,   12345,      12}
```

This creates a column of integers.

```
In[17]:= PaddedForm[ColumnForm[{456, 12345, 12}], 7]

Out[17]//PaddedForm=    456
                      12345
                         12
```

This prints each number with room for a total of 7 digits, and with 4 digits to the right of the decimal point.

```
In[18]:= PaddedForm[{-6.7, 6.888, 6.99999}, {7, 4}]

Out[18]//PaddedForm= { -6.7000,   6.8880,   7.0000}
```

In NumberForm, the 7 specifies the maximum precision, but does not make *Mathematica* pad with spaces.

```
In[19]:= NumberForm[{-6.7, 6.888, 6.99999}, {7, 4}]

Out[19]//NumberForm= {-6.7, 6.888, 7.}
```

If you set the option SignPadding-> True, *Mathematica* will insert leading spaces *after* the sign.

```
In[20]:= PaddedForm[{-6.7, 6.888, 6.99999}, {7, 4},
                              SignPadding->True]

Out[20]//PaddedForm= {-  6.7000,   6.8880,   7.0000}
```

Only the mantissa portion is aligned when scientific notation is used.

```
In[21]:= PaddedForm[
             ColumnForm[{6.7 10^8, 48.7, -2.3 10^-16}], {4, 2}]

Out[21]//PaddedForm=   6.70×10^8
                      48.70
                      -2.30×10^{-16}
```

With the default setting for the option NumberPadding, both NumberForm and PaddedForm insert trailing zeros when they pad a number on the right. You can use spaces for padding on both the left and the right by setting NumberPadding -> {" ", " "}.

This uses spaces instead of zeros for padding on the right.

```
In[22]:= PaddedForm[{-6.7, 6.888, 6.99999}, {7, 4},
                        NumberPadding -> {" ", " "}]

Out[22]//PaddedForm= { -6.7  ,   6.888,   7.   }
```

| BaseForm[*expr*, *b*] | print with all numbers given in base *b* |

Printing numbers in other bases.

This prints a number in base 2.

```
In[23]:= BaseForm[2342424, 2]

Out[23]//BaseForm= 1000111011111000011000_2
```

In bases higher than 10, letters are used for the extra digits.	$In[24]:= $ **BaseForm[242345341, 16]** $Out[24]//BaseForm=$ e71e57d$_{16}$
BaseForm also works with approximate real numbers.	$In[25]:= $ **BaseForm[2.3, 2]** $Out[25]//BaseForm=$ 10.0101$_2$
You can even use BaseForm for numbers printed in scientific notation.	$In[26]:= $ **BaseForm[2.3 10^8, 2]** $Out[26]//BaseForm=$ 1.1011011010110000101$_2 \times 2^{27}$

Section 3.1.3 discusses how to enter numbers in arbitrary bases, and also how to get lists of the digits in a number.

■ 2.8.8 Tables and Matrices

TableForm[*list*]	print in tabular form
MatrixForm[*list*]	print in matrix form

Formatting lists as tables and matrices.

Here is a list.	$In[1]:= $ **Table[(i + 45)^j, {i, 3}, {j, 3}]** $Out[1]=$ {{46, 2116, 97336}, {47, 2209, 103823}, {48, 2304, 110592}}
TableForm displays the list in a tabular format.	$In[2]:= $ **TableForm[%]** $Out[2]//TableForm=$ 46 2116 97336 47 2209 103823 48 2304 110592
MatrixForm displays the list as a matrix.	$In[3]:= $ **MatrixForm[%]** $Out[3]//MatrixForm=$ $\begin{pmatrix} 46 & 2116 & 97336 \\ 47 & 2209 & 103823 \\ 48 & 2304 & 110592 \end{pmatrix}$

This displays an array of algebraic expressions as a matrix.

In[4]:= **MatrixForm[Table[x^i - y^j, {i, 3}, {j, 3}]]**

$$Out[4]//MatrixForm= \begin{pmatrix} x - y & x - y^2 & x - y^3 \\ x^2 - y & x^2 - y^2 & x^2 - y^3 \\ x^3 - y & x^3 - y^2 & x^3 - y^3 \end{pmatrix}$$

PaddedForm[TableForm[*list*], *tot*]	print a table with all numbers padded to have room for *tot* digits
PaddedForm[TableForm[*list*], {*tot*, *frac*}]	put *frac* digits to the right of the decimal point in all approximate real numbers

Printing tables of numbers.

Here is a list of numbers.

In[5]:= **fac = {10!, 15!, 20!}**

Out[5]= {3628800, 1307674368000, 2432902008176640000}

TableForm displays the list in a column.

In[6]:= **TableForm[fac]**

Out[6]//TableForm=
```
          3628800
       1307674368000
 2432902008176640000
```

This aligns the numbers by padding each one to leave room for up to 20 digits.

In[7]:= **PaddedForm[TableForm[fac], 20]**

Out[7]//PaddedForm=
```
              3628800
         1307674368000
   2432902008176640000
```

In this particular case, you could also align the numbers using the TableAlignments option.

In[8]:= **TableForm[fac, TableAlignments -> {Right}]**

Out[8]//TableForm=
```
              3628800
         1307674368000
   2432902008176640000
```

This lines up the numbers, padding each one to have room for 8 digits, with 5 digits to the right of the decimal point.

In[9]:= **PaddedForm[TableForm[{6.7, 6.888, 6.99999}], {8, 5}]**

Out[9]//PaddedForm=
```
 6.70000
 6.88800
 6.99999
```

You can use TableForm and MatrixForm to format lists that are nested to any depth, corresponding to arrays with any number of dimensions.

Here is the format for a 2×2 array of elements a[*i*, *j*].

In[10]:= **TableForm[Array[a, {2, 2}]]**

Out[10]//TableForm=
```
a[1, 1]    a[1, 2]
a[2, 1]    a[2, 2]
```

Here is a $2 \times 2 \times 2$ array.

```
In[11]:= TableForm[ { Array[a, {2, 2}], Array[b, {2, 2}] } ]
```

$$Out[11]//TableForm= \begin{array}{ll} a[1, 1] & a[2, 1] \\ a[1, 2] & a[2, 2] \\ b[1, 1] & b[2, 1] \\ b[1, 2] & b[2, 2] \end{array}$$

And here is a $2 \times 2 \times 2 \times 2$ array.

```
In[12]:= TableForm[ { {Array[a, {2, 2}], Array[b, {2, 2}]},
                      {Array[c, {2, 2}], Array[d, {2, 2}]} } ]
```

$$Out[12]//TableForm= \begin{array}{llll} a[1, 1] & a[1, 2] & b[1, 1] & b[1, 2] \\ a[2, 1] & a[2, 2] & b[2, 1] & b[2, 2] \\ c[1, 1] & c[1, 2] & d[1, 1] & d[1, 2] \\ c[2, 1] & c[2, 2] & d[2, 1] & d[2, 2] \end{array}$$

In general, when you print an *n*-dimensional table, successive dimensions are alternately given as columns and rows. By setting the option TableDirections -> {dir_1, dir_2, ... }, where the dir_i are Column or Row, you can specify explicitly which way each dimension should be given. By default, the option is effectively set to {Column, Row, Column, Row, ... }.

The option TableDirections allows you to specify explicitly how each dimension in a multidimensional table should be given.

```
In[13]:= TableForm[ { Array[a, {2, 2}], Array[b, {2, 2}] },
                    TableDirections -> {Row, Row, Column} ]
```

$$Out[13]//TableForm= \begin{array}{llll} a[1, 1] & a[2, 1] & b[1, 1] & b[2, 1] \\ a[1, 2] & a[2, 2] & b[1, 2] & b[2, 2] \end{array}$$

Whenever you make a table from a nested list such as {$list_1$, $list_2$, ... }, there is a question of whether it should be the $list_i$ or their elements which appear as the basic entries in the table. The default behavior is slightly different for MatrixForm and TableForm.

MatrixForm handles only arrays that are "rectangular". Thus, for example, to consider an array as two-dimensional, all the rows must have the same length. If they do not, MatrixForm treats the array as one-dimensional, with elements that are lists.

MatrixForm treats this as a one-dimensional array, since the rows are of differing lengths.

```
In[14]:= MatrixForm[{{a, a, a}, {b, b}}]
```

$$Out[14]//MatrixForm= \begin{pmatrix} \{a, a, a\} \\ \{b, b\} \end{pmatrix}$$

While MatrixForm can handle only "rectangular arrays", TableForm can handle arbitrary "ragged" arrays. It leaves blanks wherever there are no elements supplied.

TableForm can handle "ragged" arrays.

```
In[15]:= TableForm[{{a, a, a}, {b, b}}]
```

$$Out[15]//TableForm= \begin{array}{lll} a & a & a \\ b & b & \end{array}$$

You can include objects that behave as "subtables".

```
In[16]:= TableForm[{{a, {{p, q}, {r, s}}, a, a},
                    {{x, y}, b, b}}]
```

$$Out[16]//TableForm= \begin{array}{llll} a & \begin{array}{ll} p & q \\ r & s \end{array} & a & a \\ \begin{array}{l} x \\ y \end{array} & b & b & \end{array}$$

You can control the number of levels in a nested list to which both `TableForm` and `MatrixForm` go by setting the option `TableDepth`.

This tells `TableForm` only to go down to depth 2. As a result {x, y} is treated as a single table entry.

In[17]:= `TableForm[{{a, {x, y}}, {c, d}}, TableDepth -> 2]`

Out[17]//TableForm=
$$\begin{matrix} a & \{x, y\} \\ c & d \end{matrix}$$

option name	default value	
`TableDepth`	`Infinity`	maximum number of levels to include in the table
`TableDirections`	`{Column, Row, Column, ... }`	whether to arrange dimensions as rows or columns
`TableAlignments`	`{Left, Bottom, Left, ... }`	how to align the entries in each dimension
`TableSpacing`	`{1, 3, 0, 1, 0, ... }`	how many spaces to put between entries in each dimension
`TableHeadings`	`{None, None, ... }`	how to label the entries in each dimension

Options for `TableForm`.

With the option `TableAlignments`, you can specify how each entry in the table should be aligned with its row or column. For columns, you can specify `Left`, `Center` or `Right`. For rows, you can specify `Bottom`, `Center` or `Top`. If you set `TableAlignments -> Center`, all entries will be centered both horizontally and vertically. `TableAlignments -> Automatic` uses the default choice of alignments.

Entries in columns are by default aligned on the left.

In[18]:= `TableForm[{a, bbbb, ccccccc}]`

Out[18]//TableForm=
```
a
bbbb
ccccccc
```

This centers all entries.

In[19]:= `TableForm[{a, bbbb, ccccccc},`
        `TableAlignments -> Center]`

Out[19]//TableForm=
```
   a
 bbbb
ccccccc
```

You can use the option `TableSpacing` to specify how much horizontal space there should be between successive columns, or how much vertical space there should be between successive rows. A setting of 0 specifies that successive objects should abut.

This leaves 6 spaces between the entries in each row, and no space between successive rows.

```
In[20]:= TableForm[{{a, b}, {ccc, d}}, TableSpacing -> {0, 6}]
                  a              b
Out[20]//TableForm= ccc            d
```

None	no labels in any dimension
Automatic	successive integer labels in each dimension
$\{\{lab_{11}, lab_{12}, \dots\}, \dots\}$	explicit labels

Settings for the option `TableHeadings`.

This puts integer labels in a $2 \times 2 \times 2$ array.

```
In[21]:= TableForm[Array[a, {2, 2, 2}],
                     TableHeadings -> Automatic]

Out[21]//TableForm=              1              2

                    1    a[1, 1, 1]    a[1, 2, 1]
                  1 2    a[1, 1, 2]    a[1, 2, 2]

                    1    a[2, 1, 1]    a[2, 2, 1]
                  2 2    a[2, 1, 2]    a[2, 2, 2]
```

This gives a table in which the rows are labeled by integers, and the columns by a list of strings.

```
In[22]:= TableForm[{{a, b, c}, {ap, bp, cp}},
            TableHeadings ->
               {Automatic, {"first", "middle", "last"}}]

                       first     middle     last
Out[22]//TableForm= 1     a         b         c

                    2     ap        bp        cp
```

This labels the rows but not the columns. `TableForm` automatically inserts a blank row to go with the third label.

```
In[23]:= TableForm[{{2, 3, 4}, {5, 6, 1}},
            TableHeadings ->
               {{"row a", "row b", "row c"}, None}]

                    row a    2     3     4
Out[23]//TableForm= row b    5     6     1

                    row c
```

■ 2.8.9 Styles and Fonts in Output

| StyleForm[*expr*, *options*] | print with the specified style options |
| StyleForm[*expr*, *"style"*] | print with the specified cell style |

Specifying output styles.

The second x^2 is here shown in boldface.

```
In[1]:= {x^2, StyleForm[x^2, FontWeight->"Bold"]}

Out[1]= {x², x²}
```

This shows the word text in font sizes from 10 to 20 points.

In[2]:= **Table[StyleForm["text", FontSize->s], {s, 10, 20}]**

Out[2]= {text, text, text, text, text, text,

text, text, text, text, text}

This shows the text in the Tekton font.

In[3]:= **StyleForm["some text", FontFamily->"Tekton"]**

Out[3]//StyleForm= sometex

option	typical setting(s)	
FontSize	12	size of characters in printer's points
FontWeight	"Plain" or "Bold"	weight of characters
FontSlant	"Plain" or "Italic"	slant of characters
FontFamily	"Courier", "Times", "Helvetica"	font family
FontColor	GrayLevel[0]	color of characters
Background	GrayLevel[1]	background color for characters

A few options that can be used in StyleForm.

If you use the notebook front end for *Mathematica*, then each piece of output that is generated will by default be in the style of the cell in which the output appears. By using StyleForm[*expr*, "*style*"], however, you can tell *Mathematica* to output a particular expression in a different style.

Here is an expression output in the style normally used for section headings.

In[4]:= **StyleForm[x^2 + y^2, "Section"]**

Out[4]//StyleForm= $\mathbf{x^2 + y^2}$

Page 547 describes in more detail how cell styles work. By using StyleForm[*expr*, "*style*", *options*] you can generate output that is in a particular style, but with certain options modified.

■ 2.8.10 Representing Textual Forms by Boxes

All textual forms in *Mathematica* are ultimately represented in terms of nested collections of *boxes*. Typically the elements of these boxes correspond to objects that are to be placed at definite relative positions in two dimensions.

Here are the boxes corresponding to the expression a + b.

In[1]:= **ToBoxes[a + b]**

Out[1]= RowBox[{a, +, b}]

DisplayForm shows how these boxes would be displayed.

In[2]:= **DisplayForm[%]**

Out[2]//DisplayForm= a + b

DisplayForm[*boxes*]	show *boxes* as they would be displayed

Showing the displayed form of boxes.

This displays three strings in a row.

```
In[3]:= RowBox[{"a", "+", "b"}] // DisplayForm
Out[3]//DisplayForm= a + b
```

This displays one string as a subscript of another.

```
In[4]:= SubscriptBox["a", "i"] // DisplayForm
Out[4]//DisplayForm= a_i
```

This puts two subscript boxes in a row.

```
In[5]:= RowBox[{SubscriptBox["a", "1"], SubscriptBox["b", "2"]}] //
            DisplayForm
Out[5]//DisplayForm= a_1 b_2
```

"*text*"	literal text
RowBox[{*a*, *b*, ... }]	a row of boxes or strings $a\ b\ ...$
GridBox[{{*a*₁, *b*₁, ... }, {*a*₂, *b*₂, ... }, ... }]	a grid of boxes $\begin{matrix} a_1 & b_1 & ... \\ a_2 & b_2 & ... \\ \vdots & \vdots \end{matrix}$
SubscriptBox[*a*, *b*]	subscript a_b
SuperscriptBox[*a*, *b*]	superscript a^b
SubsuperscriptBox[*a*, *b*, *c*]	subscript and superscript a_b^c
UnderscriptBox[*a*, *b*]	underscript $\underset{b}{a}$
OverscriptBox[*a*, *b*]	overscript $\overset{b}{a}$
UnderoverscriptBox[*a*, *b*, *c*]	underscript and overscript $\underset{b}{\overset{c}{a}}$
FractionBox[*a*, *b*]	fraction $\dfrac{a}{b}$
SqrtBox[*a*]	square root $\sqrt{a}$
RadicalBox[*a*, *b*]	b^{th} root $\sqrt[b]{a}$

Some basic box types.

This nests a fraction inside a radical.

```
In[6]:= RadicalBox[FractionBox[x, y], n] // DisplayForm
Out[6]//DisplayForm= $\sqrt[n]{\dfrac{x}{y}}$
```

This puts a superscript on a subscripted object.

In[7]:= **SuperscriptBox[SubscriptBox[a, b], c] // DisplayForm**

Out[7]//DisplayForm= $a_b{}^c$

This puts both a subscript and a superscript on the same object.

In[8]:= **SubsuperscriptBox[a, b, c] // DisplayForm**

Out[8]//DisplayForm= a_b^c

FrameBox[*box*]	render *box* with a frame drawn around it
GridBox[*list*, RowLines->True]	put lines between rows in a GridBox
GridBox[*list*, ColumnLines->True]	put lines between columns in a GridBox
GridBox[*list*, RowLines->{True, False}]	put a line below the first row, but not subsequent ones

Inserting frames and grid lines.

This shows a fraction with a frame drawn around it.

In[9]:= **FrameBox[FractionBox["x", "y"]] // DisplayForm**

Out[9]//DisplayForm= $\boxed{\dfrac{x}{y}}$

This puts lines between rows and columns of an array.

In[10]:= **GridBox[Table[i+j, {i, 3}, {j, 3}], RowLines->True, ColumnLines->True] // DisplayForm**

Out[10]//DisplayForm=
$$\begin{array}{c|c|c} 2 & 3 & 4 \\ \hline 3 & 4 & 5 \\ \hline 4 & 5 & 6 \end{array}$$

And this also puts a frame around the outside.

In[11]:= **FrameBox[%] // DisplayForm**

Out[11]//DisplayForm=
$$\boxed{\begin{array}{c|c|c} 2 & 3 & 4 \\ \hline 3 & 4 & 5 \\ \hline 4 & 5 & 6 \end{array}}$$

StyleBox[*boxes*, *options*]	render *boxes* with the specified option settings
StyleBox[*boxes*, *"style"*]	render *boxes* in the specified style

Modifying the appearance of boxes.

StyleBox takes the same options as StyleForm. The difference is that StyleForm acts as a "wrapper" for any expression, while StyleBox represents underlying box structure.

This shows the string "name" in italics.

In[12]:= **StyleBox["name", FontSlant->"Italic"] // DisplayForm**

Out[12]//DisplayForm= *name*

This shows "name" in the style used for section headings in your current notebook.

In[13]:= **StyleBox["name", "Section"] // DisplayForm**

Out[13]//DisplayForm= name

This uses section heading style, but with characters shown in gray.

In[14]:= **StyleBox["name", "Section", FontColor->GrayLevel[0.5]] // DisplayForm**

Out[14]//DisplayForm= name

If you use a notebook front end for *Mathematica*, then you will be able to change the style and appearance of what you see on the screen directly by using menu items. Internally, however, these changes will still be recorded by the insertion of appropriate StyleBox objects.

FormBox[*boxes*, *form*]	interpret *boxes* using rules associated with the specified form
InterpretationBox[*boxes*, *expr*]	interpret *boxes* as representing the expression *expr*
TagBox[*boxes*, *tag*]	use *tag* to guide the interpretation of *boxes*
ErrorBox[*boxes*]	indicate an error and do not attempt further interpretation of *boxes*

Controlling the interpretation of boxes.

This prints as x with a superscript.

In[15]:= **SuperscriptBox["x", "2"] // DisplayForm**

Out[15]//DisplayForm= x^2

It is normally interpreted as a power.

In[16]:= **ToExpression[%] // InputForm**

Out[16]//InputForm= x^2

This again prints as x with a superscript.

In[17]:= **InterpretationBox[SuperscriptBox["x", "2"], vec[x, 2]] // DisplayForm**

Out[17]//DisplayForm= x^2

But now it is interpreted as vec[x, 2], following the specification given in the InterpretationBox.

In[18]:= **ToExpression[%] // InputForm**

Out[18]//InputForm= vec[x, 2]

If you edit the boxes given in an InterpretationBox, then there is no guarantee that the interpretation specified by the interpretation box will still be correct. As a result, *Mathematica* provides various options that allow you to control the selection and editing of InterpretationBox objects.

option	default value	
Editable	False	whether to allow the contents to be edited
Selectable	True	whether to allow the contents to be selected
Deletable	True	whether to allow the box to be deleted
DeletionWarning	False	whether to issue a warning if the box is deleted
BoxAutoDelete	False	whether to strip the box if its contents are modified
StripWrapperBoxes	False	whether to remove StyleBox etc. from within *boxes* in TagBox[*boxes*, ...]

Options for InterpretationBox and related boxes.

TagBox objects are used to store information that will not be displayed but which can nevertheless be used by the rules that interpret boxes. Typically the *tag* in TagBox[*boxes*, *tag*] is a symbol which gives the head of the expression corresponding to *boxes*. If you edit only the arguments of this expression then there is a good chance that the interpretation specified by the TagBox will still be appropriate. As a result, Editable->True is the default setting for a TagBox.

The rules that *Mathematica* uses for interpreting boxes are in general set up to ignore details of formatting, such as those defined by StyleBox objects. Thus, unless StripWrapperBoxes->False, a red x, for example, will normally not be distinguished from an ordinary black x.

A red x is usually treated as identical to an ordinary one.

```
In[19]:= ToExpression[
            StyleBox[x, FontColor->RGBColor[1,0,0]]] == x

Out[19]= True
```

ButtonBox[*boxes*]	display like *boxes* but perform an action whenever *boxes* are clicked on

Setting up active elements.

In a *Mathematica* notebook it is possible to set up elements which perform an action whenever you click on them. These elements are represented internally by ButtonBox objects. When you create an expression containing a ButtonBox, you will be able to edit the contents of the ButtonBox directly so long as the Active option is False for the cell containing the expression. As soon as you set Active->True, the ButtonBox will perform its action whenever you click on it.

Section 2.10.6 discusses how to set up actions for ButtonBox objects.

⁺■ 2.8.11 Adjusting Details of Formatting

Mathematica provides a large number of options for adjusting the details of how expressions are formatted. In most cases, the default settings for these options will be quite adequate. But sometimes special features in the expressions you are dealing with may require you to change the options.

option	default value	
ColumnAlignments	Center	how to align columns
RowAlignments	Baseline	how to align rows
ColumnSpacings	1	spacings between columns in ems
RowSpacings	0.5	spacings between rows in x-heights
ColumnsEqual	False	whether to make all columns equal width
RowsEqual	False	whether to make all rows equal total height
ColumnWidths	Automatic	the actual width of each column in ems
RowMinHeight	1	the minimum total height in units of font size assigned to each row
GridBaseline	Axis	with what part of the whole grid the baselines of boxes around it should be aligned
ColumnLines	False	whether to draw lines between columns
RowLines	False	whether to draw lines between rows
GridDefaultElement	"□"	what to insert when a new element is interactively created

Options to GridBox.

This sets up an array of numbers.

In[1]:= **t = Table[{i, (2i)!, (3i)!}, {i, 4}] ;**

Here is how the array is displayed with the default settings for all GridBox options.

In[2]:= **GridBox[t] // DisplayForm**

$$
Out[2]//DisplayForm=
\begin{array}{lll}
1 & 2 & 6 \\
2 & 24 & 720 \\
3 & 720 & 362880 \\
4 & 40320 & 479001600
\end{array}
$$

This right justifies all the columns.

```
In[3]:= GridBox[t, ColumnAlignments->Right] // DisplayForm
```

```
             1      2        6
             2     24      720
Out[3]//DisplayForm= 3    720    362880
             4  40320  479001600
```

This left justifies the first two columns and right justifies the last one.

```
In[4]:= GridBox[t,
        ColumnAlignments->{Left, Left, Right}] // DisplayForm
```

```
             1 2          6
             2 24        720
Out[4]//DisplayForm= 3 720     362880
             4 40320  479001600
```

This sets the gutters between columns.

```
In[5]:= GridBox[t, ColumnSpacings->{5, 10}] // DisplayForm
```

```
             1          2                  6
             2         24                720
Out[5]//DisplayForm= 3        720              362880
             4       40320             479001600
```

This forces all columns to be the same width.

```
In[6]:= GridBox[t, ColumnsEqual->True] // DisplayForm
```

```
             1      2       6
             2     24     720
Out[6]//DisplayForm=  3    720   362880
             4   40320  479001600
```

Usually a GridBox leaves room for any character in the current font to appear in each row. But with RowMinHeight->0 it packs rows in more tightly.

```
In[7]:= {GridBox[{{x, x}, {x, x}}],
         GridBox[{{x, x}, {x, x}}, RowMinHeight->0]} // DisplayForm
```

$$Out[7]//DisplayForm= \left\{ \begin{matrix} x & x \\ x & x \end{matrix} , \begin{matrix} x & x \\ x & x \end{matrix} \right\}$$

Center	centered (default)
Left	left justified (aligned on left edge)
Right	right justified (aligned on right edge)
"."	aligned at decimal points
"c"	aligned at the first occurrence of the specified character
{pos_1, pos_2, ... }	separate specifications for each column in the grid

Settings for the ColumnAlignments option.

In formatting complicated tables, it is often important to be able to control in detail the alignment of table entries. By setting `ColumnAlignments->"c"` you tell *Mathematica* to arrange the elements in each column so that the first occurrence of the character `"c"` in each entry is aligned.

Choosing `ColumnAlignments->"."` will therefore align numbers according to the positions of their decimal points. *Mathematica* also provides a special `\[AlignmentMarker]` character, which can be entered as ⦂am⦂. This character does not display explicitly, but can be inserted in entries in a table to mark which point in these entries should be lined up.

Center	centered
Top	tops aligned
Bottom	bottoms aligned
Baseline	baselines aligned (default)
Axis	axes aligned
{pos_1, pos_2, ... }	separate specifications for each row in the grid

Settings for the `RowAlignments` option.

This is the default alignment of elements in a row of a GridBox.

In[8]:= `GridBox[{{SuperscriptBox[x, 2], FractionBox[y, z]}}] // DisplayForm`

Out[8]//DisplayForm= $x^2 \ \frac{y}{z}$

Here is what happens if the bottom of each element is aligned.

In[9]:= `GridBox[{{SuperscriptBox[x, 2], FractionBox[y, z]}}, RowAlignments->Bottom] // DisplayForm`

Out[9]//DisplayForm= $x^2 \ \frac{y}{z}$

In a piece of ordinary text, successive characters are normally positioned so that their baselines are aligned. For many characters, such as m and x, the baseline coincides with the bottom of the character. But in general the baseline is the bottom of the main part of the character, and for example, in most fonts g and y have "descenders" that extend below the baseline.

This shows the alignment of characters with the default setting `RowAlignments->Baseline`.

In[10]:= `GridBox[{{"x", "m", "g", "y"}}] // DisplayForm`

Out[10]//DisplayForm= x m g y

This is what happens if instead the bottom of each character is aligned.

In[11]:= `GridBox[{{"x", "m", "g", "y"}}, RowAlignments->Bottom] // DisplayForm`

Out[11]//DisplayForm= x m g y

Like characters in ordinary text, *Mathematica* will normally position sequences of boxes so that their baselines are aligned. For many kinds of boxes the baseline is simply taken to be the baseline of the main element of the box. Thus, for example, the baseline of a `SuperScript` box x^y is taken to be the baseline of x.

For a `FractionBox` $\dfrac{x}{y}$, the fraction bar defines the *axis* of the box. In text in a particular font, one can also define an axis—a line going through the centers of symmetrical characters such as + and (. The baseline for a `FractionBox` is then taken to be the same distance below its axis as the baseline for text in the current font is below its axis.

For a `GridBox`, you can use the option `GridBaseline` to specify where the baseline should be taken to lie. The possible settings are the same as the ones for `RowAlignments`. The default is `Axis`, which makes the center of the `GridBox` be aligned with the axis of text around it.

The `GridBaseline` option specifies where the baseline of the `GridBox` should be assumed to be.

```
In[12]:= {GridBox[{{x,x},{x,x}}, GridBaseline->Top],
            GridBox[{{x,x},{x,x}}, GridBaseline->Bottom]} //
          DisplayForm
```

$$Out[12]//DisplayForm= \left\{ \begin{smallmatrix} x & x \\ x & x \end{smallmatrix} , \begin{smallmatrix} x & x \\ x & x \end{smallmatrix} \right\}$$

option	default value	
Background	GrayLevel[0.8]	button background color
ButtonFrame	"Palette"	the type of frame for the button
ButtonExpandable	True	whether a button should expand to fill a position in a GridBox
ButtonMargins	3	the margin in printer's points around the contents of a button
ButtonMinHeight	1	the minimum total height of a button in units of font size
ButtonStyle	"Paste"	the style from which properties of the button not explicitly specified should be inherited

Formatting options for ButtonBox objects.

This makes a button that looks like an element of a dialog box.

```
In[13]:= ButtonBox["abcd",
            ButtonFrame->"DialogBox"] // DisplayForm
```

Out[13]//DisplayForm= abcd

Palettes are typically constructed using grids of ButtonBox objects with zero row and column spacing.

```
In[14]:= GridBox[{{ButtonBox["abc"], ButtonBox["xyz"]}},
            ColumnSpacings->0] // DisplayForm
```

Out[14]//DisplayForm= abc xyz

Buttons usually expand to be aligned in a GridBox.

In[15]:= **GridBox[{{ButtonBox["abcd"]},**
                  {ButtonBox["x"]}}] // DisplayForm

Out[15]//DisplayForm=

Here the lower button is made not to expand.

In[16]:= **GridBox[{{ButtonBox["abcd"]}, {ButtonBox["x",**
                  ButtonExpandable->False]}}] // DisplayForm

Out[16]//DisplayForm=

Section 2.10.6 will discuss how to set up actions for ButtonBox objects.

printer's point	approximately 1/72 inch (or sometimes the size of a pixel on a display)
pica	12 printer's points, or 1/6 inch
font point size	the maximum distance in printer's points between the top and bottom of any character in a particular font
em	a width equal to the point font size—approximately the width of an "M"
en	half an em
x-height	the height of an "x" character in the current font

Units of distance.

full name	alias	
\[InvisibleSpace]	⋮is⋮	zero-width space
\[VeryThinSpace]	⋮␣⋮	1/18 em (xx)
\[ThinSpace]	⋮␣␣⋮	3/18 em (x x)
\[MediumSpace]	⋮␣␣␣⋮	4/18 em (x x)
\[ThickSpace]	⋮␣␣␣␣⋮	5/18 em (x x)
\[NegativeVeryThinSpace]	⋮-␣⋮	−1/18 em (xx)
\[NegativeThinSpace]	⋮-␣␣⋮	−3/18 em (xx)
\[NegativeMediumSpace]	⋮-␣␣␣⋮	−4/18 em (x)
\[NegativeThickSpace]	⋮-␣␣␣␣⋮	−5/18 em (x)
\[RawSpace]	␣	keyboard space character
\[SpaceIndicator]	⋮space⋮	the ␣ character indicating a space

Spacing characters of various widths. ␣ indicates the space key on your keyboard.

When you enter input such as x+y, *Mathematica* will automatically convert this to RowBox[{"x","+","y"}]. When the RowBox is output, *Mathematica* will then try to insert appropriate space between each element. Typically, it will put more space around characters such as + that are usually used as operators, and less space around characters such as x that are not. You can however always modify spacing by inserting explicit spacing characters. Positive spacing characters will move successive elements further apart, while negative ones will bring them closer together.

Mathematica by default leaves more space around characters such as + and − that are usually used as operators.

```
In[17]:= RowBox[{"a", "b", "+", "c", "-", "+"}] // DisplayForm
Out[17]//DisplayForm= ab + c - +
```

You can explicitly insert positive and negative spacing characters to change spacing.

```
In[18]:= RowBox[{"a", "\[ThickSpace]", "b", "+",
         "\[NegativeMediumSpace]", "c", "-", "+"}] // DisplayForm
Out[18]//DisplayForm= a b +c - +
```

StyleBox[*boxes*, AutoSpacing->False]
        leave the same space around every character in *boxes*

Inhibiting automatic spacing in *Mathematica*.

This makes *Mathematica* leave the same
space between successive characters.

`In[19]:= StyleBox[RowBox[{"a", "b", "+", "c", "-", "+"}],`
`          AutoSpacing->False] // DisplayForm`

`Out[19]//DisplayForm= ab+c-+`

When you have an expression displayed on the screen, the notebook front end allows you interactively to make detailed adjustments to the positions of elements. Typically CTRL[←], CTRL[→], CTRL[↑],
CTRL[↓] "nudge" whatever you have selected by one pixel at your current screen magnification. Such
adjustments are represented within *Mathematica* using AdjustmentBox objects.

AdjustmentBox[*box*, BoxMargins->{{*left*, *right*}, {*bottom*, *top*}}]
                    draw margins of the specified widths around *box*

AdjustmentBox[*box*, BoxBaselineShift->*up*]
                    shift the height at which baselines of boxes around *box*
                    should be aligned

Adjusting the position of a box.

This adds space to the left of the B and
removes space to its right.

`In[20]:= RowBox[{"A", AdjustmentBox["B", BoxMargins->`
`          {{1, -0.3}, {0, 0}}], "C", "D"}] // DisplayForm`

`Out[20]//DisplayForm= A ᗷD`

By careful adjustment, you can set
things up to put two characters on top
of each other.

`In[21]:= RowBox[{"C", AdjustmentBox["/",`
`          BoxMargins->{{-.8, .8}, {0, 0}}]}] // DisplayForm`

`Out[21]//DisplayForm= ₵`

The left and right margins in an AdjustmentBox are given in ems; the bottom and top ones in
x-heights. By giving positive values for margins you can force there to be space around a box. By
giving negative values you can effectively trim space away, and force other boxes to be closer. Note
that in a RowBox, vertical alignment is determined by the position of the baseline; in a FractionBox
or an OverscriptBox, for example, it is instead determined by top and bottom margins.

StyleBox[*boxes*, ShowContents->False]
                    leave space for *boxes* but do not display them

---

Leaving space for boxes without displaying them.

If you are trying to line up different elements of your output, you can use ShowContents->False
in StyleBox to leave space for boxes without actually displaying them.

This leaves space for the Y, but does
not display it.

`In[22]:= RowBox[{"X", StyleBox["Y", ShowContents->False], "Z"}] //`
`          DisplayForm`

`Out[22]//DisplayForm= X  Z`

The sizes of most characters are determined solely by what font they are in, as specified for example by the `FontSize` option in `StyleBox`. But there are some special expandable characters whose size can change even within a particular font. Examples are parentheses, which by default are taken to expand so as to span any expression they contain.

Parentheses by default expand to span whatever expressions they contain.

In[23]:= `{RowBox[{"(", "X", ")"}],`
        `RowBox[{"(", FractionBox["X", "Y"], ")"}]} // DisplayForm`

$$Out[23]//DisplayForm= \left\{ (X), \left(\frac{X}{Y} \right) \right\}$$

option	default value	
SpanMinSize	Automatic	minimum size of expandable characters in units of font size
SpanMaxSize	Automatic	maximum size of expandable characters in units of font size
SpanSymmetric	True	whether vertically expandable characters should be symmetric about the axis of the box they are in
SpanLineThickness	Automatic	thickness in printer's points of fraction lines etc.

`StyleBox` options for controlling expandable characters.

Parentheses within a single `RowBox` by default grow to span whatever other objects appear in the `RowBox`.

In[24]:= `RowBox[{"(", "(", GridBox[{{X},{Y},{Z}}]}] // DisplayForm`

$$Out[24]//DisplayForm= \left(\left(\begin{matrix} X \\ Y \\ Z \end{matrix} \right. \right.$$

Some expandable characters, however, grow by default only to a limited extent.

In[25]:= `RowBox[{"{", "[", "(",`
        `GridBox[{{X},{Y},{Z}}]}] // DisplayForm`

$$Out[25]//DisplayForm= \left\{ \left[\left(\begin{matrix} X \\ Y \\ Z \end{matrix} \right. \right. \right.$$

This specifies that all characters inside the `StyleBox` should be allowed to grow as large as they need.

In[26]:= `StyleBox[%, SpanMaxSize->Infinity] // DisplayForm`

$$Out[26]//DisplayForm= \left\{ \left[\left(\begin{matrix} X \\ Y \\ Z \end{matrix} \right. \right. \right.$$

By default, expandable characters grow symmetrically.

$In[27]:=$ `RowBox[{"(", GridBox[{{X},{Y}},`
$\qquad\qquad$ `GridBaseline->Bottom], ")"}] // DisplayForm`

$Out[27]//DisplayForm=$ $\begin{pmatrix} X \\ Y \end{pmatrix}$

Setting SpanSymmetric->False allows expandable characters to grow asymmetrically.

$In[28]:=$ `{X, StyleBox[%, SpanSymmetric->False]} // DisplayForm`

$Out[28]//DisplayForm=$ $\left\{ X, \binom{X}{Y} \right\}$

The notebook front end typically provides a Spanning Characters menu which allows you to change the spanning characteristics of all characters within your current selection.

parentheses, arrows, bracketing bars	grow without bound
brackets, braces, slash	grow to limited size

Default characteristics of expandable characters.

The top bracket by default grows to span the OverscriptBox.

$In[29]:=$ `OverscriptBox["xxxxxx", "\[OverBracket]"] // DisplayForm`

$Out[29]//DisplayForm=$ $\overline{\text{xxxxxx}}$

The right arrow by default grows horizontally to span the column it is in.

$In[30]:=$ `GridBox[{{"a", "xxxxxxx", "b"},`
$\qquad\qquad$ `{"a", "\[RightArrow]", "b"}}] // DisplayForm`

$Out[30]//DisplayForm=$ $\begin{array}{ccc} a & \text{xxxxxxx} & b \\ a & \longrightarrow & b \end{array}$

The up arrow similarly grows vertically to span the row it is in.

$In[31]:=$ `GridBox[{{FractionBox[X, Y],`
$\qquad\qquad$ `"\[UpArrow]"}}] // DisplayForm`

$Out[31]//DisplayForm=$ $\frac{X}{Y}$ $\uparrow$

option	default value	
ScriptSizeMultipliers	0.71	how much smaller to make each level of subscripts, etc.
ScriptMinSize	4	the minimum point size to use for subscripts, etc.
ScriptBaselineShifts	{Automatic, Automatic}	the distance in x-heights to shift subscripts and superscripts

StyleBox options for controlling the size and positioning of subscripts, etc.

This sets up a collection of nested `SuperscriptBox` objects.

$In[32]:=$ `b = ToBoxes[X^X^X^X^X]`

$Out[32]=$ SuperscriptBox[X, SuperscriptBox[X,
  SuperscriptBox[X, SuperscriptBox[X, X]]]]

By default, successive superscripts get progressively smaller.

$In[33]:=$ `b // DisplayForm`

$Out[33]//DisplayForm=$ $X^{X^{X^{X^X}}}$

This tells *Mathematica* to make all levels of superscripts the same size.

$In[34]:=$ `StyleBox[b, ScriptSizeMultipliers->1] // DisplayForm`

$Out[34]//DisplayForm=$ $X^{X^{X^{X^X}}}$

Here successive levels of superscripts are smaller, but only down to 5-point size.

$In[35]:=$ `StyleBox[b, ScriptMinSize->5] // DisplayForm`

$Out[35]//DisplayForm=$ $X^{X^{X^{X^X}}}$

Mathematica will usually optimize the position of subscripts and superscripts in a way that depends on their environment. If you want to line up several different subscripts or superscripts you therefore typically have to use the option `ScriptBaselineShifts` to specify an explicit distance to shift each one.

The second subscript is by default shifted down slightly more than the first.

$In[36]:=$ `RowBox[{SubscriptBox["x", "0"], "+",`
`        SubsuperscriptBox["x", "0", "2"]}] // DisplayForm`

$Out[36]//DisplayForm=$ $x_0 + x_0^2$

This tells *Mathematica* to apply exactly the same shift to both subscripts.

$In[37]:=$ `StyleBox[%, ScriptBaselineShifts->{1, Automatic}] //`
`                                        DisplayForm`

$Out[37]//DisplayForm=$ $x_0 + x_0^2$

option	default value	
LimitsPositioning	Automatic	whether to change positioning in the way conventional for limits

An option to `UnderoverscriptBox` and related boxes.

The limits of a sum are usually displayed as underscripts and overscripts.

$In[38]:=$ `Sum[f[i], {i, 0, n}]`

$Out[38]=$ $\sum_{i=0}^{n} f[i]$

When the sum is shown smaller, however, it is conventional for the limits to be displayed as subscripts and superscripts.

$In[39]:=$ `1/%`

$Out[39]=$ $\dfrac{1}{\sum_{i=0}^{n} f[i]}$

Here low and high still display directly above and below XX.

In[40]:= **UnderoverscriptBox["XX", "low", "high", LimitsPositioning->True] // DisplayForm**

$Out[40]//DisplayForm= \overset{\text{high}}{\underset{\text{low}}{XX}}$

But now low and high are moved to subscript and superscript positions.

In[41]:= **FractionBox["a", %] // DisplayForm**

$Out[41]//DisplayForm= \dfrac{a}{XX_{\text{low}}^{\text{high}}}$

LimitsPositioning->Automatic will act as if LimitsPositioning->True when the first argument of the box is an object such as \[Sum] or \[Product]. You can specify the list of such characters by setting the option LimitsPositioningTokens.

option	default value	
MultilineFunction	Automatic	what to do when a box breaks across several lines

Line breaking options for boxes.

When you are dealing with long expressions it is inevitable that they will continue beyond the length of a single line. Many kinds of boxes change their display characteristics when they break across several lines.

This displays as a built-up fraction on a single line.

In[42]:= **Expand[(1 + x)^5]/Expand[(1 + y)^5]**

$Out[42]= \dfrac{1 + 5x + 10x^2 + 10x^3 + 5x^4 + x^5}{1 + 5y + 10y^2 + 10y^3 + 5y^4 + y^5}$

This breaks across several lines.

In[43]:= **Expand[(1 + x)^10]/Expand[(1 + y)^5]**

$Out[43]= (1 + 10x + 45x^2 + 120x^3 +$
$\quad\quad 210x^4 + 252x^5 + 210x^6 + 120x^7 + 45x^8 + 10x^9 + x^{10}) /$
$\quad\quad (1 + 5y + 10y^2 + 10y^3 + 5y^4 + y^5)$

You can use the option MultilineFunction to specify how a particular box should be displayed if it breaks across several lines. The setting MultilineFunction->None prevents the box from breaking at all.

You can to some extent control where expressions break across lines by inserting \[NoBreak] and \[NonBreakingSpace] characters. *Mathematica* will try to avoid ever breaking an expression at the position of such characters.

You can force *Mathematica* to break a line by explicitly inserting a \[NewLine] character, obtained in the standard notebook front end simply by typing RETURN. With default settings for options, *Mathematica* will automatically indent the next line after you type a RETURN. However, the level of indenting used will be fixed as soon as the line is started, and will not change when you edit around it. By inserting an \[IndentingNewLine] character, you can tell *Mathematica* always to maintain the correct level of indenting based on the actual environment in which a line occurs.

full name	alias	
\[NoBreak]	⠿nb⠿	inhibit a line break
\[NonBreakingSpace]	⠿nbs⠿	insert a space, inhibiting a line break on either side of it
\[NewLine]	RET	insert a line break, setting the indenting level at the time the new line is started
\[IndentingNewLine]	⠿nl⠿	insert a line break, always maintaining the correct indenting level

Characters for controlling line breaking.

When *Mathematica* breaks an expression across several lines, it indents intermediate lines by an amount proportional to the nesting level in the expression at which the break occurred.

The line breaks here occur only at level 1.

```
In[44]:= Range[30]
Out[44]= {1, 2, 3, 4, 5, 6,
            7, 8, 9, 10, 11, 12, 13, 14, 15, 16, 17, 18,
            19, 20, 21, 22, 23, 24, 25, 26, 27, 28, 29, 30}
```

But here the break is at a much deeper level.

```
In[45]:= Nest[List, x+y, 30]
Out[45]= {{{{{{{{{{{{{{{{{{{{{{{{{{{{{{{x +
                      y}}}}}}}}}}}}}}}}}}}}}}}}}}}}}}}
```

+■ 2.8.12 String Representation of Boxes

Mathematica provides a compact way of representing boxes in terms of strings. This is particularly convenient when you want to import or export specifications of boxes as ordinary text.

This generates an InputForm string that represents the SuperscriptBox.

```
In[1]:= ToString[SuperscriptBox["x", "2"], InputForm]
Out[1]= \(x\^2\)
```

This creates the SuperscriptBox.

```
In[2]:= \( x \^ 2 \)
Out[2]= SuperscriptBox[x, 2]
```

ToExpression interprets the SuperscriptBox as a power.

```
In[3]:= ToExpression[%] // FullForm
Out[3]//FullForm= Power[x, 2]
```

It is important to distinguish between forms that represent just raw boxes, and forms that represent the *meaning* of the boxes.

This corresponds to a raw
SuperscriptBox.

In[4]:= \(x \^ 2 \)

Out[4]= SuperscriptBox[x, 2]

This corresponds to the power that the
SuperscriptBox represents.

In[5]:= \!\(x \^ 2 \)

Out[5]= x^2

The expression generated here is a
power.

In[6]:= **FullForm[** \!\(x \^ 2 \) **]**

Out[6]//FullForm= Power[x, 2]

\(*input*\)	raw boxes
\!\(*input*\)	the meaning of the boxes

Distinguishing raw boxes from the expressions they represent.

If you copy the contents of a StandardForm cell into another program, such as a text editor, *Mathematica* will automatically generate a \!\(... \) form. This is done so that if you subsequently paste the form back into *Mathematica*, the original contents of the StandardForm cell will automatically be re-created. Without the \!, only the raw boxes corresponding to these contents would be obtained.

With default settings for options, \!\(... \) forms pasted into *Mathematica* notebooks are automatically displayed in two-dimensional form. \!\(... \) forms entered directly from the keyboard can be displayed in two-dimensional form using the Make 2D item in the Edit menu.

"\(*input*\)"	a raw character string
"\!\(*input*\)"	a string containing boxes

Embedding two-dimensional box structures in strings.

Mathematica will usually treat a \(... \) form that appears within a string just like any other sequence of characters. But by inserting a \! you can tell *Mathematica* instead to treat this form like the boxes it represents. In this way you can therefore embed box structures within ordinary character strings.

Mathematica treats this as an ordinary
character string.

In[7]:= "\(x \^ 2 \)"

Out[7]= \(x \^ 2 \)

The \! tells *Mathematica* that this string
contains boxes.

In[8]:= "\!\(x \^ 2 \)"

Out[8]= x^2

You can mix boxes with ordinary text.

In[9]:= "**box 1:** \!\(x\^2\)**; box 2:** \!\(y\^3\)"

Out[9]= box 1: x^2; box 2: y^3

$\backslash(box_1, box_2, \dots \backslash)$	RowBox[box_1, box_2, ...]
$box_1 \ \backslash^\wedge box_2$	SuperscriptBox[box_1, box_2]
$box_1 \ \backslash\_ box_2$	SubscriptBox[box_1, box_2]
$box_1 \ \backslash\_ box_2 \ \backslash\% box_3$	SubsuperscriptBox[box_1, box_2, box_3]
$box_1 \ \backslash\& box_2$	OverscriptBox[box_1, box_2]
$box_1 \ \backslash+ box_2$	UnderscriptBox[box_1, box_2]
$box_1 \ \backslash+ box_2 \ \backslash\% box_3$	UnderoverscriptBox[box_1, box_2, box_3]
$box_1 \ \backslash/ box_2$	FractionBox[box_1, box_2]
$\backslash@ \ box$	SqrtBox[box]
$\backslash@ \ box_1 \ \backslash\% box_2$	RadicalBox[box_1, box_2]
$form \ \backslash` \ box$	FormBox[box, $form$]
$\backslash* \ input$	construct boxes from $input$

Input forms for boxes.

Mathematica requires that any input forms you give for boxes be enclosed within \(and \). But within these outermost \(and \) you can use additional \(and \) to specify grouping.

Here ordinary parentheses are used to indicate grouping.

```
In[10]:= \( x \/ (y + z) \) // DisplayForm
```
$$Out[10]//DisplayForm= \frac{x}{(y+z)}$$

Without the parentheses, the grouping would be different.

```
In[11]:= \( x \/ y + z \) // DisplayForm
```
$$Out[11]//DisplayForm= \frac{x}{y} + z$$

\(and \) specify grouping, but are not displayed as explicit parentheses.

```
In[12]:= \( x \/ \(y + z\) \) // DisplayForm
```
$$Out[12]//DisplayForm= \frac{x}{y+z}$$

The inner \(and \) lead to the construction of a RowBox.

```
In[13]:= \( x \/ \(y + z\) \)
```
$$Out[13]= \text{FractionBox}[x, \text{RowBox}[\{y, +, z\}]]$$

When you type aa+bb as input to *Mathematica*, the first thing that happens is that aa, + and bb are recognized as being separate "tokens". The same separation into tokens is done when boxes are constructed from input enclosed in \(... \). However, inside the boxes each token is given as a string, rather than in its raw form.

The RowBox has aa, + and bb broken into separate strings.

```
In[14]:= \( aa+bb \) // FullForm
```
$$Out[14]//FullForm= \text{RowBox}[\text{List}["aa", "+", "bb"]]$$

The spaces around the + are by default discarded.	`In[15]:= \( aa + bb \) // FullForm`
	
	`Out[15]//FullForm= RowBox[List["aa", "+", "bb"]]`

Backslash-space inserts a literal space.	`In[16]:= \( aa \ + \ bb \) // FullForm`
	
	`Out[16]//FullForm= RowBox[List["aa", " ", "+", " ", "bb"]]`

Here two nested RowBox objects are formed.	`In[17]:= \( aa+bb/cc \) // FullForm`
	
	`Out[17]//FullForm= RowBox[`
	`              List["aa", "+", RowBox[List["bb", "/", "cc"]]]]`

The same box structure is formed even when the string given does not correspond to a complete *Mathematica* expression.	`In[18]:= \( aa+bb/ \) // FullForm`
	
	`Out[18]//FullForm= RowBox[List["aa", "+", RowBox[List["bb", "/"]]]]`

Within \(... \) sequences, you can set up certain kinds of boxes by using backslash notations such as \^ and \@. But for other kinds of boxes, you need to give ordinary *Mathematica* input, prefaced by *.

This constructs a GridBox.	`In[19]:= \( \*GridBox[{{"a", "b"}, {"c", "d"}}] \) // DisplayForm` `Out[19]//DisplayForm=` $\begin{array}{cc} a & b \\ c & d \end{array}$
This constructs a StyleBox.	`In[20]:= \( \*StyleBox["text", FontWeight->Bold] \) // DisplayForm` `Out[20]//DisplayForm=` **text**

* in effect acts like an escape: it allows you to enter ordinary *Mathematica* syntax even within a \(... \) sequence. Note that the input you give after a * can itself in turn contain \(... \) sequences.

You can alternate nested * and \(... \). Explicit quotes are needed outside of \(... \).	`In[21]:= \( x + \*GridBox[{{"a", "b"}, {\(c \^ 2\), \(d \/`
	`            \*GridBox[{{"x","y"},{"x","y"}}] \)}}] \) // DisplayForm`
	
	`Out[21]//DisplayForm= x + c`^{2} $\dfrac{d}{\begin{array}{cc} a & b \\ x & y \\ x & y \end{array}}$

In the notebook front end, you can typically use CTRL * or CTRL 8 to get a dialog box in which you can enter raw boxes—just as you do after *.

\!\(*input*\)	interpret input in the current form
\!\(*form* \` *input*\)	interpret input using the specified form

Controlling the way input is interpreted.

In a StandardForm cell, this will be interpreted in StandardForm, yielding a product.	`In[22]:= \!\( c(1+x) \)`
	
	`Out[22]= c (1 + x)`

The backslash backquote sequence tells *Mathematica* to interpret this in `TraditionalForm`.

```
In[23]:= \!\(TraditionalForm\' c(1+x) \)
Out[23]= c[1 + x]
```

When you copy the contents of a cell from a notebook into a program such as a text editor, no explicit backslash backquote sequence is usually included. But if you expect to paste what you get back into a cell of a different type from the one it came from, then you will typically need to include a backslash backquote sequence in order to ensure that everything is interpreted correctly.

■ 2.8.13 Converting between Strings, Boxes and Expressions

`ToString[`*expr*`, `*form*`]`	create a string representing the specified textual form of *expr*
`ToBoxes[`*expr*`, `*form*`]`	create boxes representing the specified textual form of *expr*
`ToExpression[`*input*`, `*form*`]`	create an expression by interpreting a string or boxes as input in the specified textual form
`ToString[`*expr*`]`	create a string using `OutputForm`
`ToBoxes[`*expr*`]`	create boxes using `StandardForm`
`ToExpression[`*input*`]`	create an expression using `StandardForm`

Converting between strings, boxes and expressions.

Here is a simple expression.

```
In[1]:= x^2 + y^2
Out[1]= x² + y²
```

This gives the `InputForm` of the expression as a string.

```
In[2]:= ToString[x^2 + y^2, InputForm]
Out[2]= x^2 + y^2
```

In `FullForm` explicit quotes are shown around the string.

```
In[3]:= FullForm[%]
Out[3]//FullForm= "x^2 + y^2"
```

This gives a string representation for the `StandardForm` boxes that correspond to the expression.

```
In[4]:= ToString[x^2 + y^2, StandardForm] // FullForm
Out[4]//FullForm= "\!\(x\^2 + y\^2\)"
```

`ToBoxes` yields the boxes themselves.

```
In[5]:= ToBoxes[x^2 + y^2, StandardForm]
Out[5]= RowBox[
            {SuperscriptBox[x, 2], +, SuperscriptBox[y, 2]}]
```

In generating data for files and external programs, it is sometimes necessary to produce two-dimensional forms which use only ordinary keyboard characters. You can do this using `OutputForm`.

This produces a string which gives a two-dimensional rendering of the expression, using only ordinary keyboard characters.	*In[6]:=* **ToString[x^2 + y^2, OutputForm]** *Out[6]=* 2 2 x + y
The string consists of two lines, separated by an explicit \n newline.	*In[7]:=* **FullForm[%]** *Out[7]//FullForm=* " 2 2\nx + y"
The string looks right only in a monospaced font.	*In[8]:=* **StyleBox[%, FontFamily->"Times"] // DisplayForm** *Out[8]//DisplayForm=* 2 2 x + y

If you operate only with one-dimensional structures, you can effectively use `ToString` to do string manipulation with formatting functions.

This generates a string corresponding to the OutputForm of StringForm.	*In[9]:=* **ToString[StringForm["`^10 = `", 4, 4^10]] // InputForm** *Out[9]//InputForm=* "4^10 = 1048576"

InputForm	strings corresponding to keyboard input
+ StandardForm	strings or boxes corresponding to standard two-dimensional input (default)
+ TraditionalForm	strings or boxes mimicking traditional mathematical notation

Some forms handled by `ToExpression`.

This creates an expression from an InputForm string.	*In[10]:=* **ToExpression["x^2 + y^2"]** *Out[10]=* $x^2 + y^2$
This creates the same expression from StandardForm boxes.	*In[11]:=* **ToExpression[RowBox[{SuperscriptBox["x", "2"], "+",** **SuperscriptBox["y", "2"]}]]** *Out[11]=* $x^2 + y^2$
Here the boxes are represented in InputForm.	*In[12]:=* **ToExpression[\(x\^2 + y\^2\)]** *Out[12]=* $x^2 + y^2$
This returns raw boxes.	*In[13]:=* **ToExpression["\(x\^2 + y\^2\)"]** *Out[13]=* RowBox[{SuperscriptBox[x, 2], +, SuperscriptBox[y, 2]}]
This interprets the boxes.	*In[14]:=* **ToExpression["\!\(x\^2 + y\^2\)"]** *Out[14]=* $x^2 + y^2$
In TraditionalForm these are interpreted as functions.	*In[15]:=* **ToExpression["c(1 + x) + log(x)", TraditionalForm]** *Out[15]=* c[1 + x] + Log[x]

ToExpression[*input*, *form*, *h*]	create an expression, then wrap it with head *h*

Creating expressions wrapped with special heads.

This creates an expression, then immediately evaluates it.

In[16]:= **ToExpression["1 + 1"]**

Out[16]= 2

This creates an expression using StandardForm rules, then wraps it in Hold.

In[17]:= **ToExpression["1 + 1", StandardForm, Hold]**

Out[17]= Hold[1 + 1]

You can get rid of the Hold using ReleaseHold.

In[18]:= **ReleaseHold[%]**

Out[18]= 2

SyntaxQ["*string*"]	determine whether a string represents syntactically correct *Mathematica* input
SyntaxLength["*string*"]	find out how long a sequence of characters starting at the beginning of a string is syntactically correct

Testing correctness of strings as input.

ToExpression will attempt to interpret any string as *Mathematica* input. But if you give it a string that does not correspond to syntactically correct input, then it will print a message, and return $Failed.

This is not syntactically correct input, so ToExpression does not convert it to an expression.

In[19]:= **ToExpression["1 +/+ 2"]**

ToExpression::sntx: Syntax error in or before "1 +/+ 2".
                                                    ^

Out[19]= $Failed

ToExpression requires that the string correspond to a *complete Mathematica* expression.

In[20]:= **ToExpression["1 + 2 + "]**

ToExpression::sntxi:
    Incomplete expression; more input is needed.

Out[20]= $Failed

You can use the function SyntaxQ to test whether a particular string corresponds to syntactically correct *Mathematica* input. If SyntaxQ returns False, you can find out where the error occurred using SyntaxLength. SyntaxLength returns the number of characters which were successfully processed before a syntax error was detected.

SyntaxQ shows that this string does not correspond to syntactically correct *Mathematica* input.

In[21]:= **SyntaxQ["1 +/+ 2"]**

Out[21]= False

SyntaxLength reveals that an error
was detected after the third character
in the string.

```
In[22]:= SyntaxLength["1 +/+ 2"]
Out[22]= 3
```

Here SyntaxLength returns a value
greater than the length of the string,
indicating that the input was correct so
far as it went, but needs to be
continued.

```
In[23]:= SyntaxLength["1 + 2 + "]
Out[23]= 10
```

┼■ 2.8.14 The Syntax of the *Mathematica* Language

Mathematica uses various syntactic rules to interpret input that you give, and to convert strings and
boxes into expressions. The version of these rules that is used for StandardForm and InputForm in effect defines the basic *Mathematica* language. The rules used for other forms, such as TraditionalForm,
follow the same overall principles, but differ in many details.

a, xyz, $\alpha\beta\gamma$	symbols
"some text", "$\alpha + \beta$"	strings
123.456, 3*^45	numbers
+, ->, $\neq$	operators
(* comment *)	input to be ignored

Types of tokens in the *Mathematica* language.

When you give text as input to *Mathematica*, the first thing that *Mathematica* does is to break the
text into a sequence of *tokens*, with each token representing a separate syntactic unit.

Thus, for example, if you give the input xx+yy-zzzz, *Mathematica* will break this into the sequence
of tokens xx, +, yy, - and zzzz. Here xx, yy and zzzz are tokens that correspond to symbols, while
+ and - are operators.

Operators are ultimately what determine the structure of the expression formed from a particular
piece of input. The *Mathematica* language involves several general classes of operators, distinguished
by the different positions in which they appear with respect to their operands.

prefix	$!x$	Not[x]
postfix	$x!$	Factorial[x]
infix	$x + y + z$	Plus[x, y, z]
matchfix	{x, y, z}	List[x, y, z]
compound	x /: $y = z$	TagSet[x, y, z]
overfix	$\hat{x}$	OverHat[x]

Examples of classes of operators in the *Mathematica* language.

Operators typically work by picking up operands from definite positions around them. But when a string contains more than one operator, the result can in general depend on which operator picks up its operands first.

Thus, for example, a*b+c could potentially be interpreted either as (a*b)+c or as a*(b+c) depending on whether * or + picks up its operands first.

To avoid such ambiguities, *Mathematica* assigns a *precedence* to each operator that can appear. Operators with higher precedence are then taken to pick up their operands first.

Thus, for example, the multiplication operator * is assigned higher precedence than +, so that it picks up its operands first, and a*b+c is interpreted as (a*b)+c rather than a*(b+c).

The * operator has higher precedence than +, so in both cases Times is the innermost function.

In[1]:= **{FullForm[a * b + c], FullForm[a + b * c]}**

Out[1]= {Plus[Times[a, b], c], Plus[a, Times[b, c]]}

The // operator has rather low precedence.

In[2]:= **a * b + c // f**

Out[2]= f[a b + c]

The @ operator has high precedence.

In[3]:= **f @ a * b + c**

Out[3]= c + b f[a]

Whatever the precedence of the operators you are using, you can always specify the structure of the expressions you want to form by explicitly inserting appropriate parentheses.

Inserting parentheses makes Plus rather than Times the innermost function.

In[4]:= **FullForm[a * (b + c)]**

Out[4]//FullForm= Times[a, Plus[b, c]]

Extensions of symbol names	$x\_$, #2, $e::s$, etc.
Function application variants	$e[e]$, e @@ e, etc.
Power-related operators	$\sqrt{e}$, $e\verb|^|e$, etc.
Multiplication-related operators	∇e, e/e, $e \otimes e$, $e\ e$, etc.
Addition-related operators	$e \oplus e$, $e + e$, $e \cup e$, etc.
Relational operators	$e == e$, $e \sim e$, $e \lessdot e$, $e \vartriangleleft e$, $e \in e$, etc.
Arrow and vector operators	$e \rightarrow e$, $e \nearrow e$, $e \rightleftharpoons e$, $e \twoheadrightarrow e$, etc.
Logic operators	$\forall_e\, e$, e && e, $e \vee e$, $e \vdash e$, etc.
Pattern and rule operators	$e..$, $e \mid e$, $e \rightarrow e$, $e\ /.\ e$, etc.
Pure function operator	e &
Assignment operators	$e = e$, $e := e$, etc.
Compound expression	$e; e$

Outline of operators in order of decreasing precedence.

The table on pages 972–977 gives the complete ordering by precedence of all operators in *Mathematica*. Much of this ordering, as in the case of * and +, is determined directly by standard mathematical usage. But in general the ordering is simply set up to make it less likely for explicit parentheses to have to be inserted in typical pieces of input.

Operator precedences are such that this requires no parentheses.

```
In[5]:= ∀x ∃y x ⊗ y > y ∧ m ≠ 0 ⇒ n ⋫ m

Out[5]= Implies[∀x ∃y x ⊗ y > y && m ≠ 0, n ⋫ m]
```

FullForm shows the structure of the expression that was constructed.

```
In[6]:= FullForm[%]

Out[6]//FullForm= Implies[And[ForAll[x,
                    Exists[y, Succeeds[CircleTimes[x, y], y]]],
                Unequal[m, 0]],
            NotRightTriangleBar[n, m]]
```

Note that the first and second forms here are identical; the third requires explicit parentheses.

```
In[7]:= {x -> #^2 &, (x -> #^2)&, x -> (#^2 &)}

Out[7]= {x → #1² &, x → #1² &, x → (#1² &)}
```

flat	$x + y + z$	$x + y + z$
left grouping	$x \, / \, y \, / \, z$	$(x \, / \, y) \, / \, z$
right grouping	$x \wedge y \wedge z$	$x \wedge (y \wedge z)$

Types of grouping for infix operators.

Plus is a Flat function, so no grouping is necessary here.

```
In[8]:= FullForm[a + b + c + d]
Out[8]//FullForm= Plus[a, b, c, d]
```

Power is not Flat, so the operands have to be grouped in pairs.

```
In[9]:= FullForm[a ^ b ^ c ^ d]
Out[9]//FullForm= Power[a, Power[b, Power[c, d]]]
```

The syntax of the *Mathematica* language is defined not only for characters that you can type on a typical keyboard, but also for all the various special characters that *Mathematica* supports.

Letters such as γ, $\mathcal{L}$ and $\aleph$ from any alphabet are treated just like ordinary English letters, and can for example appear in the names of symbols. The same is true of letter-like forms such as ∞, $\hbar$ and ι.

But many other special characters are treated as operators. Thus, for example, $\oplus$ and $\uplus$ are infix operators, while $\neg$ is a prefix operator, and $\langle$ and $\rangle$ are matchfix operators.

$\oplus$ is an infix operator.

```
In[10]:= a ⊕ b ⊕ c // FullForm
Out[10]//FullForm= CirclePlus[a, b, c]
```

$\times$ is an infix operator which means the same as *.

```
In[11]:= a × a × a × b × b × c
Out[11]= a³ b² c
```

Some special characters form elements of fairly complicated compound operators. Thus, for example, $\int f \, \mathrm{d}x$ contains the compound operator with elements $\int$ and d.

The $\int$ and d form parts of a compound operator.

```
In[12]:= ∫ k[x] dx // FullForm
Out[12]//FullForm= Integrate[k[x], x]
```

No parentheses are needed here: the "inner precedence" of $\int \ldots \mathrm{d}$ is lower than Times.

```
In[13]:= ∫ a[x] b[x] dx + c[x]
Out[13]= c[x] + ∫ a[x] b[x] dx
```

Parentheses are needed here, however.

```
In[14]:= ∫ (a[x] + b[x]) dx + c[x]
Out[14]= c[x] + ∫ (a[x] + b[x]) dx
```

Input to *Mathematica* can be given not only in the form of one-dimensional strings, but also in the form of two-dimensional boxes. The syntax of the *Mathematica* language covers not only one-dimensional constructs but also two-dimensional ones.

This superscript is interpreted as a power.	$In[15]:= \mathbf{x^{a+b}}$ $Out[15]= x^{a+b}$
$\partial_x f$ is a two-dimensional compound operator.	$In[16]:= \mathbf{\partial_x x^n}$ $Out[16]= n\, x^{-1+n}$
$\sum$ is part of a more complicated two-dimensional compound operator.	$In[17]:= \displaystyle\sum_{n=1}^{\infty} \frac{1}{n^s}$ $Out[17]= \text{Zeta[s]}$
The $\sum$ operator has higher precedence than +.	$In[18]:= \displaystyle\sum_{n=1}^{\infty} \frac{1}{n^s} + \mathbf{n}$ $Out[18]= n + \text{Zeta[s]}$

■ 2.8.15 Operators without Built-in Meanings

When you enter a piece of input such as 2 + 2, *Mathematica* first recognizes the + as an operator and constructs the expression Plus[2, 2], then uses the built-in rules for Plus to evaluate the expression and get the result 4.

But not all operators recognized by *Mathematica* are associated with functions that have built-in meanings. *Mathematica* also supports several hundred additional operators that can be used in constructing expressions, but for which no evaluation rules are initially defined.

You can use these operators as a way to build up your own notation within the *Mathematica* language.

The $\oplus$ is recognized as an infix operator, but has no predefined value.	$In[1]:= \mathbf{2 \oplus 3 \,//\, FullForm}$ $Out[1]//FullForm= \text{CirclePlus[2, 3]}$
In StandardForm, $\oplus$ prints as an infix operator.	$In[2]:= \mathbf{2 \oplus 3}$ $Out[2]= 2 \oplus 3$
You can define a value for $\oplus$.	$In[3]:= \mathbf{x\_ \oplus y\_ := Mod[x + y, 2]}$
Now $\oplus$ is not only recognized as an operator, but can also be evaluated.	$In[4]:= \mathbf{2 \oplus 3}$ $Out[4]= 1$

$$
\begin{array}{ll}
x \oplus y & \texttt{CirclePlus[}x, y\texttt{]} \\
x \approx y & \texttt{TildeTilde[}x, y\texttt{]} \\
x \notin y & \texttt{NotElement[}x, y\texttt{]} \\
x \leftrightarrow y & \texttt{LeftRightArrow[}x, y\texttt{]} \\
\nabla\, x & \texttt{Del[}x\texttt{]} \\
\square\, x & \texttt{Square[}x\texttt{]} \\
\langle x, y, \ldots\, \rangle & \texttt{AngleBracket[}x, y, \ldots\ \texttt{]}
\end{array}
$$

A few *Mathematica* operators corresponding to functions without predefined values.

Mathematica follows the general convention that the function associated with a particular operator should have the same name as the special character that represents that operator.

\[Congruent] is displayed as $\equiv$.	*In[5]:=* **x \[Congruent] y**
	Out[5]= x $\equiv$ y
It corresponds to the function Congruent.	*In[6]:=* **FullForm[%]**
	Out[6]//FullForm= Congruent[x, y]

$$
\begin{array}{ll}
x \,\backslash[\textit{name}]\, y & \textit{name}[x, y] \\
\backslash[\textit{name}]\, x & \textit{name}[x] \\
\backslash[\text{Left}\textit{name}]\, x, y, \ldots \backslash[\text{Right}\textit{name}] & \textit{name}[x, y, \ldots\ ]
\end{array}
$$

The conventional correspondence in *Mathematica* between operator names and function names.

You should realize that even though the functions `CirclePlus` and `CircleTimes` do not have built-in evaluation rules, the operators $\oplus$ and $\otimes$ do have built-in precedences. Pages 972–977 list all the operators recognized by *Mathematica*, in order of their precedence.

The operators $\otimes$ and $\oplus$ have definite precedences—with $\otimes$ higher than $\oplus$.	*In[7]:=* **x $\otimes$ y $\oplus$ z // FullForm**
	Out[7]//FullForm= Mod[Plus[z, CircleTimes[x, y]], 2]

x_y	`Subscript[x, y]`	$\overset{y}{x}$	`Overscript[x, y]`
x_+	`SubPlus[x]`	$\underset{y}{x}$	`Underscript[x, y]`
x_-	`SubMinus[x]`	$\overline{x}$	`OverBar[x]`
x_*	`SubStar[x]`	$\vec{x}$	`OverVector[x]`
x^+	`SuperPlus[x]`	$\tilde{x}$	`OverTilde[x]`
x^-	`SuperMinus[x]`	$\hat{x}$	`OverHat[x]`
x^*	`SuperStar[x]`	$\dot{x}$	`OverDot[x]`
$x^\dagger$	`SuperDagger[x]`	$\underline{x}$	`UnderBar[x]`

Some two-dimensional forms without built-in meanings.

Subscripts have no built-in meaning in *Mathematica*.

```
In[8]:= x₂ + y₂ // InputForm
Out[8]//InputForm= Subscript[x, 2] + Subscript[y, 2]
```

Most superscripts are however interpreted as powers by default.

```
In[9]:= x² + y² // InputForm
Out[9]//InputForm= x^2 + y^2
```

A few special superscripts are not interpreted as powers.

```
In[10]:= x† + y⁺ // InputForm
Out[10]//InputForm= SuperDagger[x] + SuperPlus[y]
```

Bar and hat are interpreted as `OverBar` and `OverHat`.

```
In[11]:= x̄ + ŷ // InputForm
Out[11]//InputForm= OverBar[x] + OverHat[y]
```

■ 2.8.16 Defining Output Formats

Just as *Mathematica* allows you to define how expressions should be evaluated, so also it allows you to define how expressions should be formatted for output. The basic idea is that whenever *Mathematica* is given an expression to format for output, it first calls Format[*expr*] to find out whether any special rules for formatting the expression have been defined. By assigning a value to Format[*expr*] you can therefore tell *Mathematica* that you want a particular kind of expression to be output in a special way.

This tells *Mathematica* to format bin objects in a special way.

```
In[1]:= Format[bin[x_, y_]] := MatrixForm[{{x}, {y}}]
```

Now bin objects are output to look like binomial coefficients.

```
In[2]:= bin[i + j, k]
Out[2]= ( i + j )
          (  k  )
```

Internally, however, bin objects are still exactly the same.

```
In[3]:= FullForm[%]
Out[3]//FullForm= bin[Plus[i, j], k]
```

> $$\text{Format}[expr_1] := expr_2 \qquad \text{define } expr_1 \text{ to be formatted like } expr_2$$
>
> $$\text{Format}[expr_1, form] := expr_2 \qquad \text{give a definition only for a particular output form}$$

Defining your own rules for formatting.

By making definitions for Format, you can tell *Mathematica* to format a particular expression so as to look like another expression. You can also tell *Mathematica* to run a program to determine how a particular expression should be formatted.

This specifies that *Mathematica* should run a simple program to determine how xrep objects should be formatted.

```
In[4]:= Format[xrep[n_]] := StringJoin[Table["x", {n}]]
```

The strings are created when each xrep is formatted.

```
In[5]:= xrep[1] + xrep[4] + xrep[9]
Out[5]= x + xxxx + xxxxxxxxx
```

Internally however the expression still contains xrep objects.

```
In[6]:= % /. xrep[n_] -> x^n
Out[6]= x + x^4 + x^9
```

> | | |
> |---|---|
> | $\text{Prefix}[f[x], h]$ | prefix form $h\ x$ |
> | $\text{Postfix}[f[x], h]$ | postfix form $x\ h$ |
> | $\text{Infix}[f[x, y, \ldots], h]$ | infix form $x\ h\ y\ h\ \ldots$ |
> | $\text{Prefix}[f[x]]$ | standard prefix form $f\ @\ x$ |
> | $\text{Postfix}[f[x]]$ | standard postfix form $x\ /\!/\ \#f$ |
> | $\text{Infix}[f[x, y, \ldots]]$ | standard infix form $x \sim f \sim y \sim f \sim \ldots$ |
> | $\text{PrecedenceForm}[expr, n]$ | an object to be parenthesized with a precedence level n |

Output forms for operators.

This prints with f represented by the "prefix operator" <>.

```
In[7]:= Prefix[f[x], "<>"]
Out[7]= <>x
```

Here is output with the "infix operator" <>.

```
In[8]:= s = Infix[{a, b, c}, "<>"]
Out[8]= a<>b<>c
```

By default, the "infix operator" <> is assumed to have "higher precedence" than ^, so no parentheses are inserted.

```
In[9]:= s^2
Out[9]= a<>b<>c^2
```

When you have an output form involving operators, the question arises of whether the arguments of some of them should be parenthesized. As discussed in Section 2.1.3, this depends on the "precedence" of the operators. When you set up output forms involving operators, you can use `PrecedenceForm` to specify the precedence to assign to each operator. *Mathematica* uses integers from 1 to 1000 to represent "precedence levels". The higher the precedence level for an operator, the less it needs to be parenthesized.

Here `<>` is treated as an operator with precedence 100. This precedence turns out to be low enough that parentheses are inserted.

In[10]:= `PrecedenceForm[s, 100]^2`

Out[10]= $(a \texttt{<>} b \texttt{<>} c)^2$

When you make an assignment for `Format[`*expr*`]`, you are defining the output format for *expr* in all standard types of *Mathematica* output. By making definitions for `Format[`*expr*`,` *form*`]`, you can specify formats to be used in specific output forms.

This specifies the TeXForm for the symbol x.

In[11]:= `Format[x, TeXForm] := "{\\bf x}"`

The output format for x that you specified is now used whenever the TₑX form is needed.

In[12]:= `TeXForm[1 + x^2]`

Out[12]//TeXForm= `1 + {{{\bf x}}^2}`

■ 2.8.17 Advanced Topic: Low-Level Input and Output Rules

`MakeBoxes[`*expr*`,` *form*`]`	construct boxes to represent *expr* in the specified form
`MakeExpression[`*boxes*`,` *form*`]`	construct an expression corresponding to *boxes*

Low-level functions for converting between expressions and boxes.

MakeBoxes generates boxes without evaluating its input.

In[1]:= `MakeBoxes[2 + 2, StandardForm]`

Out[1]= `RowBox[{2, +, 2}]`

MakeExpression interprets boxes but uses HoldComplete to prevent the resulting expression from being evaluated.

In[2]:= `MakeExpression[%, StandardForm]`

Out[2]= `HoldComplete[2 + 2]`

Built into *Mathematica* are a large number of rules for generating output and interpreting input. Particularly in `StandardForm`, these rules are carefully set up to be consistent, and to allow input and output to be used interchangeably.

It is fairly rare that you will need to modify these rules. The main reason is that *Mathematica* already has built-in rules for the input and output of many operators to which it does not itself assign specific meanings.

Thus, if you want to add, for example, a generalization form of addition, you can usually just use an operator like ⊕ for which *Mathematica* already has built-in input and output rules.

This outputs using the ⊕ operator.	*In[3]:=* **CirclePlus[u, v, w]**
	Out[3]= u ⊕ v ⊕ w
Mathematica understands ⊕ on input.	*In[4]:=* **u ⊕ v ⊕ w // FullForm**
	Out[4]//FullForm= CirclePlus[u, v, w]

In dealing with output, you can make definitions for Format[*expr*] to change the way that a particular expression will be formatted. You should realize, however, that as soon as you do this, there is no guarantee that the output form of your expression will be interpreted correctly if it is given as *Mathematica* input.

If you want to, *Mathematica* allows you to redefine the basic rules that it uses for the input and output of all expressions. You can do this by making definitions for MakeBoxes and MakeExpression. You should realize, however, that unless you make such definitions with great care, you are likely to end up with inconsistent results.

This defines how gplus objects should be output in StandardForm.	*In[5]:=* **gplus /: MakeBoxes[gplus[x_, y_, n_], StandardForm] :=**
	     RowBox[{MakeBoxes[x, StandardForm],
	       SubscriptBox["\[CirclePlus]", MakeBoxes[n, StandardForm]],
	       MakeBoxes[y, StandardForm]}]

gplus is now output using a subscripted ⊕.	*In[6]:=* **gplus[a, b, m+n]** *Out[6]=* a ⊕$_{m+n}$ b
Mathematica cannot however interpret this as input.	*In[7]:=* **a ⊕$_{m+n}$ b** Syntax::sntxi: Incomplete expression; more input is needed.

This tells *Mathematica* to interpret a subscripted ⊕ as a specific piece of FullForm input.	*In[7]:=* **MakeExpression[RowBox[{x_, SubscriptBox[**
	       "\[CirclePlus]", n_], y_}], StandardForm] :=
	     MakeExpression[RowBox[
	       {"gplus", "[", x, ",", y, ",", n, "]"}], StandardForm]

Now the subscripted ⊕ is interpreted as a gplus.	*In[8]:=* **a ⊕$_{m+n}$ b // FullForm** *Out[8]//FullForm=* gplus[a, b, Plus[m, n]]

When you give definitions for MakeBoxes, you can think of this as essentially a lower-level version of giving definitions for Format. An important difference is that MakeBoxes does not evaluate its argument, so you can define rules for formatting expressions without being concerned about how these expressions would evaluate.

In addition, while Format is automatically called again on any results obtained by applying it, the same is not true of MakeBoxes. This means that in giving definitions for MakeBoxes you explicitly have to call MakeBoxes again on any subexpressions that still need to be formatted.

- Break input into tokens.

- Strip spacing characters.

- Construct boxes using built-in operator precedences.

- Strip `StyleBox` and other boxes not intended for interpretation.

- Apply rules defined for `MakeExpression`.

Operations done on *Mathematica* input.

■ 2.8.18 Generating Unstructured Output

The functions described so far in this section determine *how* expressions should be formatted when they are printed, but they do not actually cause anything to be printed.

In the most common way of using *Mathematica* you never in fact explicitly have to issue a command to generate output. Usually, *Mathematica* automatically prints out the final result that it gets from processing input you gave. Sometimes, however, you may want to get *Mathematica* to print out expressions at intermediate stages in its operation. You can do this using the function `Print`.

`Print[`*expr*$_1$`, `*expr*$_2$`, ... ]`	print the *expr*$_i$, with no spaces in between, but with a newline (line feed) at the end

Printing expressions.

Print prints its arguments, with no spaces in between, but with a newline (line feed) at the end.

```
In[1]:= Print[a, b]; Print[c]
ab
c
```

This prints a table of the first five integers and their squares.

```
In[2]:= Do[Print[i, " ", i^2], {i, 5}]
1  1
2  4
3  9
4  16
5  25
```

Print simply takes the arguments you give, and prints them out one after the other, with no spaces in between. In many cases, you will need to print output in a more complicated format. You can do this by giving an output form as an argument to `Print`.

This prints the matrix in the form of a table.

```
In[3]:= Print[TableForm[{{1, 2}, {3, 4}}]]
1    2

3    4
```

Here the output format is specified using `StringForm`.

$In[4]:=$ `Print[StringForm["x = ``, y = ``", a^2, b^2]]`

$$x = a^2, y = b^2$$

The output generated by `Print` is usually given in the standard *Mathematica* output format. You can however explicitly specify that some other output format should be used.

This prints output in *Mathematica* input form.

$In[5]:=$ `Print[InputForm[a^2 + b^2]]`

`a^2 + b^2`

You should realize that `Print` is only one of several mechanisms available in *Mathematica* for generating output. Another is the function `Message` described in Section 2.8.21, used for generating named messages. There are also a variety of lower-level functions described in Section 2.11.3 which allow you to produce output in various formats both as part of an interactive session, and for files and external programs.

◼ 2.8.19 Generating Styled Output in Notebooks

+	`StylePrint[`*expr*`, "`*style*`"]`	create a new cell containing *expr* in the specified style
+	`StylePrint[`*expr*`]`	use the default style for the notebook

Generating styled output in notebooks.

This generates a cell in section heading style.

$In[1]:=$ `StylePrint["The heading", "Section"];`

◼ **The heading**

This generates a cell in input style.

$In[2]:=$ `StylePrint[x^2 + y^2, "Input"]`

◼ **The heading**
$x^2 + y^2$

Mathematica provides many capabilities for manipulating the contents of notebooks, as discussed in Section 2.10. `StylePrint` handles the simple case when all you want to do is to add a cell of a particular style.

■ 2.8.20 Requesting Input

Mathematica usually works by taking whatever input you give, and then processing it. Sometimes, however, you may want to have a program you write explicitly request more input. You can do this using Input and InputString.

Input[ ]	read an expression as input
InputString[ ]	read a string as input
Input["*prompt*"]	issue a prompt, then read an expression
InputString["*prompt*"]	issue a prompt then read a string

Interactive input.

Exactly how Input and InputString work depends on the computer system and *Mathematica* interface you are using. With a text-based interface, they typically just wait for standard input, terminated with a newline. With a notebook interface, however, they typically get the front end to put up a "dialog box", in which the user can enter input.

In general, Input is intended for reading complete *Mathematica* expressions. InputString, on the other hand, is for reading arbitrary strings.

■ 2.8.21 Messages

Mathematica has a general mechanism for handling messages generated during computations. Many built-in *Mathematica* functions use this mechanism to produce error and warning messages. You can also use the mechanism for messages associated with functions you write.

The basic idea is that every message has a definite name, of the form *symbol*::*tag*. You can use this name to refer to the message. (The object *symbol*::*tag* has head MessageName.)

Off[*s*::*tag*]	switch off a message, so it is not printed
On[*s*::*tag*]	switch on a message

Controlling the printing of messages.

As discussed in Section 1.3.11, you can use On and Off to control the printing of particular messages. Most messages associated with built-in functions are switched on by default. You can use Off to switch them off if you do not want to see them.

This prints a warning message.	*In[1]:=* **Log[a, b, c]**
	Log::argt: Log called with 3 arguments; 1 or 2 arguments are expected.
	Out[1]= Log[a, b, c]
You can switch off the message like this.	*In[2]:=* **Off[Log::argt]**
Now no warning message is produced.	*In[3]:=* **Log[a, b, c]**
	Out[3]= Log[a, b, c]

Although most messages associated with built-in functions are switched on by default, there are some which are switched off by default, and which you will see only if you explicitly switch them on. An example is the message General::newsym, discussed in Section 2.6.13, which tells you every time a new symbol is created.

s::tag	give the text of a message
s::tag = string	set the text of a message
Messages[*s*]	show all messages associated with *s*

Manipulating messages.

The text of a message with the name *s::tag* is stored simply as the value of *s::tag*, associated with the symbol *s*. You can therefore see the text of a message simply by asking for *s::tag*. You can set the text by assigning a value to *s::tag*.

If you give LinearSolve a singular matrix, it prints a warning message.	*In[4]:=* **LinearSolve[{{1, 1}, {2, 2}}, {3, 5}]**
	LinearSolve::nosol: Linear equation encountered which has no solution.
	Out[4]= LinearSolve[{{1, 1}, {2, 2}}, {3, 5}]
Here is the text of the message.	*In[5]:=* **LinearSolve::nosol**
	Out[5]= Linear equation encountered which has no solution.
This redefines the message.	*In[6]:=* **LinearSolve::nosol = "Matrix encountered is not invertible."**
	Out[6]= Matrix encountered is not invertible.
Now the new form will be used.	*In[7]:=* **LinearSolve[{{1, 1}, {2, 2}}, {3, 5}]**
	LinearSolve::nosol: Matrix encountered is not invertible.
	Out[7]= LinearSolve[{{1, 1}, {2, 2}}, {3, 5}]

Messages are always stored as strings suitable for use with StringForm. When the message is printed, the appropriate expressions are "spliced" into it. The expressions are wrapped with HoldForm to prevent evaluation. In addition, any function that is assigned as the value of the global variable

`$MessagePrePrint` is applied to the resulting expressions before they are given to `StringForm`. The default for `$MessagePrePrint` is `Short`.

Most messages are associated directly with the functions that generate them. There are, however, some "general" messages, which can be produced by a variety of functions.

If you give the wrong number of arguments to a function F, *Mathematica* will warn you by printing a message such as `F::argx`. If *Mathematica* cannot find a message named `F::argx`, it will use the text of the "general" message `General::argx` instead. You can use `Off[F::argx]` to switch off the argument count message specifically for the function F. You can also use `Off[General::argx]` to switch off all messages that use the text of the general message.

<table>
<tr><td>Mathematica prints a message if you give the wrong number of arguments to a built-in function.</td><td><code>In[8]:= Sqrt[a, b]</code>

<code>Sqrt::argx:</code>
<code>   Sqrt called with 2 arguments; 1 argument is expected.</code>

<code>Out[8]= Sqrt[a, b]</code></td></tr>
<tr><td>This argument count message is a general one, used by many different functions.</td><td><code>In[9]:= General::argx</code>

<code>Out[9]= `1` called with `2`</code>
<code>   arguments; 1 argument is expected.</code></td></tr>
</table>

If something goes very wrong with a calculation you are doing, it is common to find that the same warning message is generated over and over again. This is usually more confusing than useful. As a result, *Mathematica* keeps track of all messages that are produced during a particular calculation, and stops printing a particular message if it comes up more than three times. Whenever this happens, *Mathematica* prints the message `General::stop` to let you know. If you really want to see all the messages that *Mathematica* tries to print, you can do this by switching off `General::stop`.

`$MessageList`	a list of the messages produced during a particular computation
`MessageList[n]`	a list of the messages produced during the processing of the nth input line in a *Mathematica* session

Finding out what messages were produced during a computation.

In every computation you do, *Mathematica* maintains a list `$MessageList` of all the messages that are produced. In a standard *Mathematica* session, this list is cleared after each line of output is generated. However, during a computation, you can access the list. In addition, when the nth output line in a session is generated, the value of `$MessageList` is assigned to `MessageList[n]`.

This returns $MessageList, which gives a list of the messages produced.	*In[10]:=* **Sqrt[a, b, c]; Exp[a, b]; $MessageList**

Sqrt::argx:
   Sqrt called with 3 arguments; 1 argument is expected.

Exp::argx: Exp called with 2
    arguments; 1 argument is expected.

Out[10]= {Sqrt::argx, Exp::argx}

The message names are wrapped in HoldForm to stop them from evaluating.	*In[11]:=* **InputForm[%]**

Out[11]//InputForm= {HoldForm[Sqrt::argx], HoldForm[Exp::argx]}

In writing programs, it is often important to be able to check automatically whether any messages were generated during a particular calculation. If messages were generated, say as a consequence of producing indeterminate numerical results, then the result of the calculation may be meaningless.

Check[*expr*, *failexpr*]   if no messages are generated during the evaluation of *expr*, then return *expr*, otherwise return *failexpr*

Check[*expr*, *failexpr*, s_1::t_1, s_2::t_2, ...]
                          check only for the messages s_i::t_i

---

Checking for warning messages.

Evaluating 1^0 produces no messages, so the result of the evaluation is returned.	*In[12]:=* **Check[1^0, err]** *Out[12]=* 1

Evaluating 0^0 produces a message, so the second argument of Check is returned.	*In[13]:=* **Check[0^0, err]**

                                                         0
Power::indet: Indeterminate expression 0   encountered.

Out[13]= err

Check[*expr*, *failexpr*] tests for all messages that are actually printed out. It does not test for messages whose output has been suppressed using Off.

In some cases you may want to test only for a specific set of messages, say ones associated with numerical overflow. You can do this by explicitly telling Check the names of the messages you want to look for.

The message generated by Sin[1, 2] is ignored by Check, since it is not the one specified.	*In[14]:=* **Check[Sin[1, 2], err, General::ind]**

Sin::argx: Sin called with 2
    arguments; 1 argument is expected.

Out[14]= Sin[1, 2]

Message[*s*::*tag*]	print a message
Message[*s*::*tag*, *expr*$_1$, ...]	print a message, with the *expr*$_i$ spliced into its string form

Generating messages.

By using the function Message, you can mimic all aspects of the way in which built-in *Mathematica* functions generate messages. You can for example switch on and off messages using On and Off, and Message will automatically look for General::*tag* if it does not find the specific message *s*::*tag*.

This defines the text of a message associated with f.	*In[15]:=* **f::overflow = "Factorial argument `1` too large."**
	Out[15]= Factorial argument `1` too large.
Here is the function f.	*In[16]:=* **f[x_] :=**
	If[x > 10,
	(Message[f::overflow, x]; Infinity), x!]
When the argument of f is greater than 10, the message is generated.	*In[17]:=* **f[20]**
	f::overflow: Factorial argument 20 too large.
	Out[17]= ∞
This switches off the message.	*In[18]:=* **Off[f::overflow]**
Now the message is no longer generated.	*In[19]:=* **f[20]**
	Out[19]= ∞

When you call Message, it first tries to find a message with the explicit name you have specified. If this fails, it tries to find a message with the appropriate tag associated with the symbol General. If this too fails, then *Mathematica* takes any function you have defined as the value of the global variable $NewMessage, and applies this function to the symbol and tag of the message you have requested.

By setting up the value of $NewMessage appropriately, you can, for example, get *Mathematica* to read in the text of a message from a file when that message is first needed.

■ 2.8.22 International Messages

The standard set of messages for built-in *Mathematica* functions are written in American English. In some versions of *Mathematica*, messages are also available in other languages. In addition, if you set up messages yourself, you can give ones in other languages.

Languages in *Mathematica* are conventionally specified by strings. The languages are given in English, in order to avoid the possibility of needing special characters. Thus, for example, the French language is specified in *Mathematica* as "French".

$Language = "*lang*"   set the language to use

$Language = {"*lang*₁", "*lang*₂", ... }
                        set a sequence of languages to try

Setting the language to use for messages.

This tells *Mathematica* to use French-language versions of messages.	`In[1]:= $Language = "French"`
	`Out[1]= French`
If your version of *Mathematica* has French-language messages, the message generated here will be in French.	`In[2]:= Sqrt[a, b, c]`
	`Sqrt::argx: Sqrt est appelée avec 3 arguments;`
	`      il faut y avoir 1.`

symbol::*tag*   the default form of a message

symbol::*tag*::*Language*   a message in a particular language

Messages in different languages.

When built-in *Mathematica* functions generate messages, they look first for messages of the form *s*::*t*::*Language*, in the language specified by $Language. If they fail to find any such messages, then they use instead the form *s*::*t* without an explicit language specification.

The procedure used by built-in functions will also be followed by functions you define if you call **Message** with message names of the form *s*::*t*. If you give explicit languages in message names, however, only those languages will be used.

■ 2.8.23 Documentation Constructs

When you write programs in *Mathematica*, there are various ways to document your code. As always, by far the best thing is to write clear code, and to name the objects you define as explicitly as possible.

Sometimes, however, you may want to add some "commentary text" to your code, to make it easier to understand. You can add such text at any point in your code simply by enclosing it in matching (* and *). Notice that in *Mathematica*, "comments" enclosed in (* and *) can be nested in any way.

You can use comments anywhere in the *Mathematica* code you write.	`In[1]:= If[a > b, (* then *) p, (* else *) q]`
	`Out[1]= If[a > b, p, q]`

(* *text* *)	a comment that can be inserted anywhere in *Mathematica* code

Comments in *Mathematica*.

There is a convention in *Mathematica* that all functions intended for later use should be given a definite "usage message", which documents their basic usage. This message is defined as the value of f::usage, and is retrieved when you type $?f$.

f::usage = "*text*"	define the usage message for a function
$?f$	get information about a function
$??f$	get more information about a function

Usage messages for functions.

Here is the definition of a function f.	*In[2]:=* **f[x_] := x^2**
Here is a "usage message" for f.	*In[3]:=* **f::usage = "f[x] gives the square of x."**
	Out[3]= f[x] gives the square of x.
This gives the usage message for f.	*In[4]:=* **?f**
	f[x] gives the square of x.
??f gives all the information *Mathematica* has about f, including the actual definition.	*In[5]:=* **??f**
	f[x] gives the square of x.
	f[x_] := x^2

When you define a function f, you can usually display its value using $?f$. However, if you give a usage message for f, then $?f$ just gives the usage message. Only when you type $??f$ do you get all the details about f, including its actual definition.

If you ask for information using ? about just one function, *Mathematica* will print out the complete usage messages for the function. If you ask for information on several functions at the same time, however, *Mathematica* will just give you the name of each function.

f::usage	main usage message
f::notes	notes about the function
f::usage::*Language*, etc.	messages in a particular language

Some typical documentation messages.

In addition to the usage message, there are some messages such as `notes` and `qv` that are often defined to document functions.

If you use *Mathematica* with a text-based interface, then messages and comments are the primary mechanisms for documenting your definitions. However, if you use *Mathematica* with a notebook interface, then you will be able to give much more extensive documentation in text cells in the notebook.

2.9 The Structure of Graphics and Sound

■ 2.9.1 The Structure of Graphics

Section 1.9 discussed how to use functions like Plot and ListPlot to plot graphs of functions and data. In this section, we discuss how *Mathematica* represents such graphics, and how you can program *Mathematica* to create more complicated images.

The basic idea is that *Mathematica* represents all graphics in terms of a collection of *graphics primitives*. The primitives are objects like Point, Line and Polygon, that represent elements of a graphical image, as well as directives such as RGBColor, Thickness and SurfaceColor.

This generates a plot of a list of points.   *In[1]:=* **ListPlot[Table[Prime[n], {n, 20}]]**

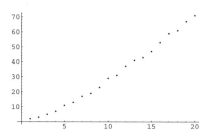

InputForm shows how *Mathematica* represents the graphics. Each point is represented as a Point graphics primitive. All the various graphics options used in this case are also given.

In[2]:= **InputForm[%]**

```
Out[2]//InputForm= Graphics[{Point[{1, 2}], Point[{2, 3}],
              Point[{3, 5}], Point[{4, 7}], Point[{5, 11}],
              Point[{6, 13}], Point[{7, 17}], Point[{8, 19}],
              Point[{9, 23}], Point[{10, 29}], Point[{11, 31}],
              Point[{12, 37}], Point[{13, 41}], Point[{14, 43}],
              Point[{15, 47}], Point[{16, 53}], Point[{17, 59}],
              Point[{18, 61}], Point[{19, 67}], Point[{20, 71}]},
          {PlotRange -> Automatic,
           AspectRatio -> GoldenRatio^(-1),
           DisplayFunction :> $DisplayFunction,
           ColorOutput -> Automatic, Axes -> Automatic,
           AxesOrigin -> Automatic, PlotLabel -> None,
           AxesLabel -> None, Ticks -> Automatic,
           GridLines -> None, Prolog -> {}, Epilog -> {},
           AxesStyle -> Automatic, Background -> Automatic,
           DefaultColor -> Automatic,
           DefaultFont :> $DefaultFont, RotateLabel -> True,
           Frame -> False, FrameStyle -> Automatic,
           FrameTicks -> Automatic, FrameLabel -> None,
           PlotRegion -> Automatic, ImageSize -> Automatic,
           TextStyle :> $TextStyle, FormatType :> $FormatType}]
```

Each complete piece of graphics in *Mathematica* is represented as a *graphics object*. There are several different kinds of graphics object, corresponding to different types of graphics. Each kind of graphics object has a definite head which identifies its type.

Graphics[*list*]	general two-dimensional graphics
DensityGraphics[*list*]	density plot
ContourGraphics[*list*]	contour plot
SurfaceGraphics[*list*]	three-dimensional surface
Graphics3D[*list*]	general three-dimensional graphics
GraphicsArray[*list*]	array of other graphics objects

Graphics objects in *Mathematica*.

The functions like Plot and ListPlot discussed in Section 1.9 all work by building up *Mathematica* graphics objects, and then displaying them.

Graphics	Plot, ListPlot, ParametricPlot
DensityGraphics	DensityPlot, ListDensityPlot
ContourGraphics	ContourPlot, ListContourPlot
SurfaceGraphics	Plot3D, ListPlot3D
Graphics3D	ParametricPlot3D

Generating graphics objects by plotting functions and data.

You can create other kinds of graphical images in *Mathematica* by building up your own graphics objects. Since graphics objects in *Mathematica* are just symbolic expressions, you can use all the standard *Mathematica* functions to manipulate them.

Once you have created a graphics object, you must then display it. The function Show allows you to display any *Mathematica* graphics object.

Show[g]	display a graphics object
Show[g_1, g_2, ...]	display several graphics objects combined
Show[GraphicsArray[{{g_{11}, g_{12}, ... }, ... }]]	
	display an array of graphics objects

Displaying graphics objects.

This uses Table to generate a polygon graphics primitive.

```
In[3]:= poly = Polygon[
            Table[N[{Cos[n Pi/5], Sin[n Pi/5]}], {n, 0, 5}] ]
Out[3]= Polygon[{{1., 0}, {0.809017, 0.587785},
           {0.309017, 0.951056}, {-0.309017, 0.951056},
           {-0.809017, 0.587785}, {-1., 0}}]
```

This creates a two-dimensional graphics object that contains the polygon graphics primitive. In standard output format, the graphics object is given simply as -Graphics-.

```
In[4]:= Graphics[ poly ]
Out[4]= -Graphics-
```

InputForm shows the complete graphics object.

```
In[5]:= InputForm[%]
Out[5]//InputForm=
        Graphics[Polygon[{{1., 0},
            {0.8090169943749474, 0.5877852522924732},
            {0.3090169943749474, 0.9510565162951536},
            {-0.3090169943749474, 0.9510565162951536},
            {-0.8090169943749474, 0.5877852522924732}, {-1., 0}}]]
```

This displays the graphics object you have created.

```
In[6]:= Show[%]
```

Graphics directives	Examples: RGBColor, Thickness, SurfaceColor
Graphics options	Examples: PlotRange, Ticks, AspectRatio, ViewPoint

Local and global ways to modify graphics.

Given a particular list of graphics primitives, *Mathematica* provides two basic mechanisms for modifying the final form of graphics you get. First, you can insert into the list of graphics primitives certain *graphics directives*, such as RGBColor, which modify the subsequent graphical elements in the list. In this way, you can specify how a particular set of graphical elements should be rendered.

This takes the list of graphics primitives created above, and adds the graphics directive GrayLevel[0.3].

```
In[7]:= Graphics[ {GrayLevel[0.3], poly} ]
Out[7]= -Graphics-
```

Now the polygon is rendered in gray.   *In[8]:=* **Show[%]**

By inserting graphics directives, you can specify how particular graphical elements should be rendered. Often, however, you want to make global modifications to the way a whole graphics object is rendered. You can do this using *graphics options*.

By adding the graphics option Frame   *In[9]:=* **Show[%, Frame -> True]**
you can modify the overall appearance
of the graphics.

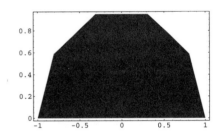

Show returns a graphics object with the   *In[10]:=* **InputForm[%]**
options in it.

Out[10]//InputForm=
```
Graphics[{GrayLevel[0.3],
    Polygon[{{1., 0}, {0.8090169943749474,
        0.5877852522924732},
      {0.3090169943749474, 0.9510565162951536},
      {-0.3090169943749474, 0.9510565162951536},
      {-0.8090169943749474, 0.5877852522924732}, {-1., 0}}
]}, {Frame -> True}]
```

You can specify graphics options in Show. As a result, it is straightforward to take a single graphics object, and show it with many different choices of graphics options.

Notice however that Show always returns the graphics objects it has displayed. If you specify graphics options in Show, then these options are automatically inserted into the graphics objects that Show returns. As a result, if you call Show again on the same objects, the same graphics options will be used, unless you explicitly specify other ones. Note that in all cases new options you specify will overwrite ones already there.

Options[*g*]	give a list of all graphics options for a graphics object
Options[*g*, *opt*]	give the setting for a particular option
FullOptions[*g*, *opt*]	give the actual value used for a particular option, even if the setting is Automatic

Finding the options for a graphics object.

Some graphics options work by requiring you to specify a particular value for a parameter related to a piece of graphics. Other options allow you to give the setting Automatic, which makes *Mathematica* use internal algorithms to choose appropriate values for parameters. In such cases, you can find out the values that *Mathematica* actually used by applying the function FullOptions.

Here is a plot.

$In[11]:=$ **zplot = Plot[Abs[Zeta[1/2 + I x]], {x, 0, 10}]**

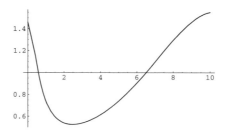

The option PlotRange is set to its default value of Automatic, specifying that *Mathematica* should use internal algorithms to determine the actual plot range.

$In[12]:=$ **Options[zplot, PlotRange]**

$Out[12]=$ {PlotRange → Automatic}

FullOptions gives the actual plot range determined by *Mathematica* in this case.

$In[13]:=$ **FullOptions[zplot, PlotRange]**

$Out[13]=$ {{-0.25, 10.25}, {0.50068, 1.57477}}

FullGraphics[*g*]	translate objects specified by graphics options into lists of explicit graphics primitives

Finding the complete form of a piece of graphics.

When you use a graphics option such as Axes, *Mathematica* effectively has to construct a list of graphics elements to represent the objects such as axes that you have requested. Usually *Mathematica* does not explicitly return the list it constructs in this way. Sometimes, however, you may find it useful to get this list. The function FullGraphics gives the complete list of graphics primitives needed to generate a particular plot, without any options being used.

This plots a list of values.   *In[14]:=* **ListPlot[Table[EulerPhi[n], {n, 10}]]**

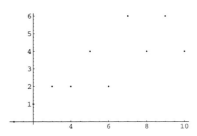

FullGraphics yields a graphics object   *In[15]:=* **Short[InputForm[FullGraphics[%]], 6]**
that includes graphics primitives
representing axes and so on.   *Out[15]//Short=* Graphics[{{Point[{1, 0}], Point[{2, 1}],
                                                          Point[{3, 2}], Point[{4, 2}],
                                                          Point[{5, 4}], Point[{6, 2}],
                                                          Point[{7, 6}], Point[{8, 4}],
                                                          Point[{9, 6}], Point[{10, 4}]},
                                                       << 1 >>}]

With their default option settings, functions like `Plot` and `Show` actually cause *Mathematica* to generate graphical output. In general, the actual generation of graphical output is controlled by the graphics option `DisplayFunction`. The default setting for this option is the value of the global variable `$DisplayFunction`.

In most cases, `$DisplayFunction` and the `DisplayFunction` option are set to use the lower-level rendering function `Display` to produce output, perhaps after some preprocessing. Sometimes, however, you may want to get a function like `Plot` to produce a graphics object, but you may not immediately want that graphics object actually rendered as output. You can tell *Mathematica* to generate the object, but not render it, by setting the option `DisplayFunction -> Identity`. Section 2.9.14 will explain exactly how this works.

`Plot[f, ... , DisplayFunction -> Identity]`, etc.	generate a graphics object for a plot, but do not actually display it
`Show[g, DisplayFunction -> $DisplayFunction]`	show a graphics object using the default display function

Generating and displaying graphics objects.

This generates a graphics object, but does not actually display it.

```
In[16]:= Plot[BesselJ[0, x], {x, 0, 10},
                            DisplayFunction -> Identity]

Out[16]= -Graphics-
```

This modifies the graphics object, but still does not actually display it.

```
In[17]:= Show[%, Frame -> True]
Out[17]= -Graphics-
```

To display the graphic, you explicitly have to tell *Mathematica* to use the default display function.

```
In[18]:= Show[%, DisplayFunction -> $DisplayFunction]
```

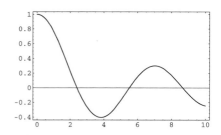

■ 2.9.2 Two-Dimensional Graphics Elements

Point[{x, y}]	point at position x, y
Line[{{x_1, y_1}, {x_2, y_2}, ... }]	line through the points {x_1, y_1}, {x_2, y_2}, ...
Rectangle[{$xmin$, $ymin$}, {$xmax$, $ymax$}]	
	filled rectangle
Polygon[{{x_1, y_1}, {x_2, y_2}, ... }]	
	filled polygon with the specified list of corners
Circle[{x, y}, r]	circle with radius r centered at x, y
Disk[{x, y}, r]	filled disk with radius r centered at x, y
Raster[{{a_{11}, a_{12}, ... }, {a_{21}, ... }, ... }]	
	rectangular array of gray levels between 0 and 1
Text[*expr*, {x, y}]	the text of *expr*, centered at x, y (see Section 2.9.16)

Basic two-dimensional graphics elements.

Here is a line primitive.

```
In[1]:= sawline = Line[Table[{n, (-1)^n}, {n, 6}]]

Out[1]= Line[{{1, -1}, {2, 1}, {3, -1}, {4, 1},
        {5, -1}, {6, 1}}]
```

This shows the line as a two-dimensional graphics object.

In[2]:= **sawgraph = Show[Graphics[sawline]]**

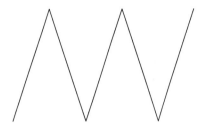

This redisplays the line, with axes added.

In[3]:= **Show[%, Axes -> True]**

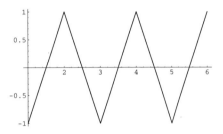

You can combine graphics objects that you have created explicitly from graphics primitives with ones that are produced by functions like Plot.

This produces an ordinary *Mathematica* plot.

In[4]:= **Plot[Sin[Pi x], {x, 0, 6}]**

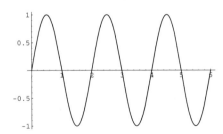

This combines the plot with the sawtooth picture made above.

$In[5]:=$ **Show[%, sawgraph]**

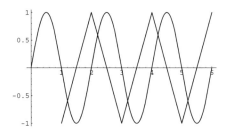

You can combine different graphical elements simply by giving them in a list. In two-dimensional graphics, *Mathematica* will render the elements in exactly the order you give them. Later elements are therefore effectively drawn on top of earlier ones.

Here is a list of two Rectangle graphics elements.

$In[6]:=$ **{Rectangle[{1, -1}, {2, -0.6}],**
                    Rectangle[{4, .3}, {5, .8}]}

$Out[6]=$ {Rectangle[{1, -1}, {2, -0.6}],
            Rectangle[{4, 0.3}, {5, 0.8}]}

This draws the rectangles on top of the line that was defined above.

$In[7]:=$ **Show[Graphics[{sawline, %}]]**

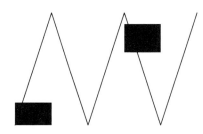

The Polygon graphics primitive takes a list of x, y coordinates, corresponding to the corners of a polygon. *Mathematica* joins the last corner with the first one, and then fills the resulting area.

Here are the coordinates of the corners of a regular pentagon.

$In[8]:=$ **pentagon = Table[{Sin[2 Pi n/5], Cos[2 Pi n/5]}, {n, 5}]**

$Out[8]= \left\{\left\{\frac{1}{2}\sqrt{\frac{1}{2}(5+\sqrt{5})}, \frac{1}{4}(-1+\sqrt{5})\right\},\right.$

$\left\{\frac{1}{2}\sqrt{\frac{1}{2}(5-\sqrt{5})}, \frac{1}{4}(-1-\sqrt{5})\right\},$

$\left\{-\frac{1}{2}\sqrt{\frac{1}{2}(5-\sqrt{5})}, \frac{1}{4}(-1-\sqrt{5})\right\},$

$\left.\left\{-\frac{1}{2}\sqrt{\frac{1}{2}(5+\sqrt{5})}, \frac{1}{4}(-1+\sqrt{5})\right\}, \{0, 1\}\right\}$

This displays the pentagon. With the default choice of aspect ratio, the pentagon looks somewhat squashed.

In[9]:= **Show[Graphics[Polygon[pentagon]]]**

This chooses the aspect ratio so that the shape of the pentagon is preserved.

In[10]:= **Show[%, AspectRatio -> Automatic]**

Mathematica can handle polygons which fold over themselves.

In[11]:= **Show[Graphics[**
Polygon[{{-1, -1}, {1, 1}, {1, -1}, {-1, 1}}]]]

Circle[{x, y}, r]	a circle with radius r centered at the point {x, y}
Circle[{x, y}, {r_x, r_y}]	an ellipse with semi-axes r_x and r_y
Circle[{x, y}, r, {$theta_1$, $theta_2$}]	
	a circular arc
Circle[{x, y}, {r_x, r_y}, {$theta_1$, $theta_2$}]	
	an elliptical arc
Disk[{x, y}, r], etc.	filled disks

Circles and disks.

This shows two circles with radius 2. Setting the option AspectRatio -> Automatic makes the circles come out with their natural aspect ratio.

```
In[12]:= Show[ Graphics[
              {Circle[{0, 0}, 2], Circle[{1, 1}, 2]} ],
                        AspectRatio -> Automatic ]
```

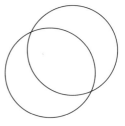

This shows a sequence of disks with progressively larger semi-axes in the x direction, and progressively smaller ones in the y direction.

```
In[13]:= Show[ Graphics[
              Table[Disk[{3n, 0}, {n/4, 2-n/4}], {n, 4}] ],
                        AspectRatio -> Automatic ]
```

Mathematica allows you to generate arcs of circles, and segments of ellipses. In both cases, the objects are specified by starting and finishing angles. The angles are measured counterclockwise in radians with zero corresponding to the positive x direction.

This draws a 140° wedge centered at the origin.

In[14]:= **Show[Graphics[Disk[{0, 0}, 1, {0, 140 Degree}]],**
            AspectRatio -> Automatic]

Raster[{{a_{11}, a_{12}, ... }, {a_{21}, ... }, ... }]
        array of gray levels between 0 and 1

Raster[*array*, {{*xmin*, *ymin*}, {*xmax*, *ymax*}}, {*zmin*, *zmax*}]
        array of gray levels between *zmin* and *zmax* drawn in the
        rectangle defined by {*xmin*, *ymin*} and {*xmax*, *ymax*}

RasterArray[{{g_{11}, g_{12}, ... }, {g_{21}, ... }, ... }]
        rectangular array of cells colored according to the graphics
        directives g_{ij}

Raster-based graphics elements.

Here is a 4×4 array of values between 0 and 1.

In[15]:= **modtab = Table[Mod[i, j]/3, {i, 4}, {j, 4}] // N**

Out[15]= {{0, 0.333333, 0.333333, 0.333333},
       {0, 0, 0.666667, 0.666667}, {0, 0.333333, 0, 1.},
       {0, 0, 0.333333, 0}}

This uses the array of values as gray levels in a raster.

In[16]:= **Show[Graphics[Raster[%]]]**

This shows two overlapping copies of the raster.

In[17]:= **Show[Graphics[{Raster[modtab, {{0, 0}, {2, 2}}],**
Raster[modtab, {{1.5, 1.5}, {3, 2}}]}]]

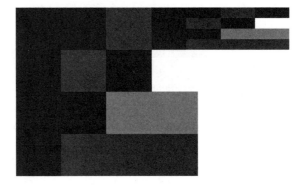

In the default case, Raster always generates an array of gray cells. As described on page 497, you can use the option ColorFunction to apply a "coloring function" to all the cells.

You can also use the graphics primitive RasterArray. While Raster takes an array of *values*, RasterArray takes an array of *Mathematica graphics directives*. The directives associated with each cell are taken to determine the color of that cell. Typically the directives are chosen from the set GrayLevel, RGBColor or Hue. By using RGBColor and Hue directives, you can create color rasters using RasterArray.

■ 2.9.3 Graphics Directives and Options

When you set up a graphics object in *Mathematica*, you typically give a list of graphical elements. You can include in that list *graphics directives* which specify how subsequent elements in the list should be rendered.

In general, the graphical elements in a particular graphics object can be given in a collection of nested lists. When you insert graphics directives in this kind of structure, the rule is that a particular graphics directive affects all subsequent elements of the list it is in, together with all elements of sublists that may occur. The graphics directive does not, however, have any effect outside the list it is in.

The first sublist contains the graphics directive GrayLevel.

```
In[1]:= {{GrayLevel[0.5], Rectangle[{0, 0}, {1, 1}]},
            Rectangle[{1, 1}, {2, 2}]}

Out[1]= {{GrayLevel[0.5], Rectangle[{0, 0}, {1, 1}]},
            Rectangle[{1, 1}, {2, 2}]}
```

Only the rectangle in the first sublist is affected by the GrayLevel directive.

```
In[2]:= Show[Graphics[ % ]]
```

Mathematica provides various kinds of graphics directives. One important set is those for specifying the colors of graphical elements. Even if you have a black-and-white display device, you can still give color graphics directives. The colors you specify will be converted to gray levels at the last step in the graphics rendering process. Note that you can get gray-level display even on a color device by setting the option ColorOutput -> GrayLevel.

GrayLevel[*i*]	gray level between 0 (black) and 1 (white)
RGBColor[*r*, *g*, *b*]	color with specified red, green and blue components, each between 0 and 1
Hue[*h*]	color with hue *h* between 0 and 1
Hue[*h*, *s*, *b*]	color with specified hue, saturation and brightness, each between 0 and 1

Basic *Mathematica* color specifications.

On a color display, the two curves would be shown in color. Here they are shown in gray.

In[3]:= `Plot[{BesselI[1, x], BesselI[2, x]}, {x, 0, 5},`
`            PlotStyle ->`
`                {{RGBColor[1, 0, 0]}, {RGBColor[0, 1, 0]}}]`

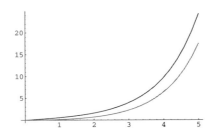

The function `Hue[h]` provides a convenient way to specify a range of colors using just one parameter. As *h* varies from 0 to 1, `Hue[h]` runs through red, yellow, green, cyan, blue, magenta, and back to red again. `Hue[h, s, b]` allows you to specify not only the "hue", but also the "saturation" and "brightness" of a color. Taking the saturation to be equal to one gives the deepest colors; decreasing the saturation toward zero leads to progressively more "washed out" colors.

The end of the Graphics Gallery later in this book shows examples of colors generated with various color specifications.

For most purposes, you will be able to specify the colors you need simply by giving appropriate `RGBColor` or `Hue` directives. However, if you need very precise or repeatable colors, particularly for color printing, there are a number of subtleties which arise, as discussed in Section 2.9.17.

When you give a graphics directive such as `RGBColor`, it affects *all* subsequent graphical elements that appear in a particular list. *Mathematica* also supports various graphics directives which affect only specific types of graphical elements.

The graphics directive `PointSize[d]` specifies that all `Point` elements which appear in a graphics object should be drawn as circles with diameter *d*. In `PointSize`, the diameter *d* is measured as a fraction of the width of your whole plot.

Mathematica also provides the graphics directive `AbsolutePointSize[d]`, which allows you to specify the "absolute" diameter of points, measured in fixed units. The units are approximately printer's points, equal to $\frac{1}{72}$ of an inch.

`PointSize[d]`	give all points a diameter *d* as a fraction of the width of the whole plot
`AbsolutePointSize[d]`	give all points a diameter *d* measured in absolute units

Graphics directives for points.

Here is a list of points.

```
In[4]:= Table[Point[{n, Prime[n]}], {n, 6}]

Out[4]= {Point[{1, 2}], Point[{2, 3}], Point[{3, 5}],
            Point[{4, 7}], Point[{5, 11}], Point[{6, 13}]}
```

This makes each point have a diameter equal to one-tenth of the width of the plot.

```
In[5]:= Show[Graphics[{PointSize[0.1], %}], PlotRange -> All]
```

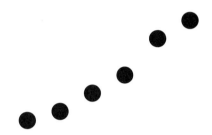

Here each point has size 3 in absolute units.

```
In[6]:= ListPlot[Table[Prime[n], {n, 20}],
                Prolog -> AbsolutePointSize[3]]
```

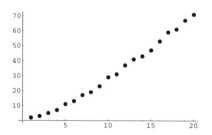

Thickness[w]	give all lines a thickness w as a fraction of the width of the whole plot
AbsoluteThickness[w]	give all lines a thickness w measured in absolute units
Dashing[{w_1, w_2, ... }]	show all lines as a sequence of dashed segments, with lengths w_1, w_2, ...
AbsoluteDashing[{w_1, w_2, ... }]	use absolute units to measure dashed segments

Graphics directives for lines.

This generates a list of lines with different absolute thicknesses.

```
In[7]:= Table[
          {AbsoluteThickness[n], Line[{{0, 0}, {n, 1}}]}, {n, 4}]

Out[7]= {{AbsoluteThickness[1], Line[{{0, 0}, {1, 1}}]},
          {AbsoluteThickness[2], Line[{{0, 0}, {2, 1}}]},
          {AbsoluteThickness[3], Line[{{0, 0}, {3, 1}}]},
          {AbsoluteThickness[4], Line[{{0, 0}, {4, 1}}]}}
```

Here is a picture of the lines.

```
In[8]:= Show[Graphics[%]]
```

The `Dashing` graphics directive allows you to create lines with various kinds of dashing. The basic idea is to break lines into segments which are alternately drawn and omitted. By changing the lengths of the segments, you can get different line styles. Dashing allows you to specify a sequence of segment lengths. This sequence is repeated as many times as necessary in drawing the whole line.

This gives a dashed line with a succession of equal-length segments.

```
In[9]:= Show[Graphics[ {Dashing[{0.05, 0.05}],
                Line[{{-1, -1}, {1, 1}}]} ]]
```

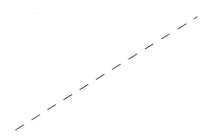

This gives a dot-dashed line.

```
In[10]:= Show[Graphics[{Dashing[{0.01, 0.05, 0.05, 0.05}],
            Line[{{-1, -1}, {1, 1}}]}]]
```

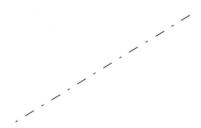

One way to use *Mathematica* graphics directives is to insert them directly into the lists of graphics primitives used by graphics objects. Sometimes, however, you want the graphics directives to be applied more globally, and for example to determine the overall "style" with which a particular type of graphical element should be rendered. There are typically graphics options which can be set to specify such styles in terms of lists of graphics directives.

PlotStyle -> *style*	specify a style to be used for all curves in Plot
PlotStyle -> {{*style₁*}, {*style₂*}, ... }	specify styles to be used (cyclically) for a sequence of curves in Plot
MeshStyle -> *style*	specify a style to be used for a mesh in density and surface graphics
BoxStyle -> *style*	specify a style to be used for the bounding box in three-dimensional graphics

Some graphics options for specifying styles.

This generates a plot in which the curve is given in a style specified by graphics directives.

```
In[11]:= Plot[BesselJ[2, x], {x, 0, 10},
            PlotStyle -> {{Thickness[0.02], GrayLevel[0.5]}}]
```

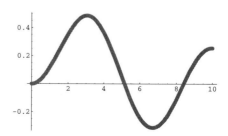

GrayLevel[0.5]	gray
RGBColor[1, 0, 0], etc.	red, etc.
Thickness[0.05]	thick
Dashing[{0.05, 0.05}]	dashed
Dashing[{0.01, 0.05, 0.05, 0.05}]	dot-dashed

Some typical styles.

The various "style options" allow you to specify how particular graphical elements in a plot should be rendered. *Mathematica* also provides options that affect the rendering of the whole plot.

Background -> *color*	specify the background color for a plot
DefaultColor -> *color*	specify the default color for a plot
Prolog -> *g*	give graphics to render before a plot is started
Epilog -> *g*	give graphics to render after a plot is finished

Graphics options that affect whole plots.

This draws the whole plot on a gray background.

```
In[12]:= Plot[Sin[Sin[x]], {x, 0, 10},
              Background -> GrayLevel[0.6]]
```

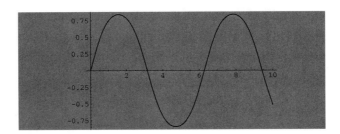

This makes the default color white.   *In[13]:=* **Show[%, DefaultColor -> GrayLevel[1]]**

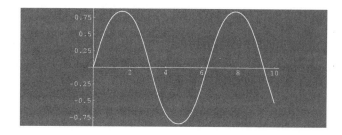

~■ 2.9.4 Coordinate Systems for Two-Dimensional Graphics

When you set up a graphics object in *Mathematica*, you give coordinates for the various graphical elements that appear. When *Mathematica* renders the graphics object, it has to translate the original coordinates you gave into "display coordinates" which specify where each element should be placed in the final display area.

Sometimes, you may find it convenient to specify the display coordinates for a graphical element directly. You can do this by using "scaled coordinates" Scaled[{*sx*, *sy*}] rather than {*x*, *y*}. The scaled coordinates are defined to run from 0 to 1 in *x* and *y*, with the origin taken to be at the lower-left corner of the display area.

{*x*, *y*}	original coordinates
Scaled[{*sx*, *sy*}]	scaled coordinates

Coordinate systems for two-dimensional graphics.

The rectangle is drawn at a fixed position relative to the display area, independent of the original coordinates used for the plot.

In[1]:= **Plot[Tan[x], {x, 0, 2Pi},**
           Prolog ->
               Rectangle[Scaled[{0.7, 0.7}], Scaled[{1, 1}]]]

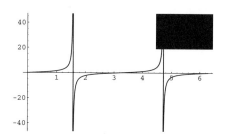

When you use {x, y} or Scaled[{sx, sy}], you are specifying position either completely in original coordinates, or completely in scaled coordinates. Sometimes, however, you may need to use a combination of these coordinate systems. For example, if you want to draw a line at a particular point whose length is a definite fraction of the width of the plot, you will have to use original coordinates to specify the basic position of the line, and scaled coordinates to specify its length.

You can use Scaled[{dsx, dsy}, {x, y}] to specify a position using a mixture of original and scaled coordinates. In this case, {x, y} gives a position in original coordinates, and {dsx, dsy} gives the offset from the position in scaled coordinates.

Note that you can use Scaled with either one or two arguments to specify radii in Disk and Circle graphics elements.

Scaled[{sdx, sdy}, {x, y}]	scaled offset from original coordinates
+ Offset[{adx, ady}, {x, y}]	absolute offset from original coordinates
+ Offset[{adx, ady}, Scaled[{sx, sy}]]	absolute offset from scaled coordinates

Positions specified as offsets.

Each line drawn here has an absolute length of 6 printer's points.

```
In[2]:= Show[Graphics[Table[
            Line[{{x, x^2}, Offset[{0, 6}, {x, x^2}]}],
            {x, 10}], Frame->True]]
```

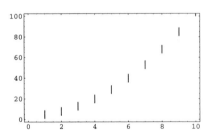

You can also use Offset inside Circle
with just one argument to create a
circle with a certain absolute radius.

```
In[3]:= Show[Graphics[Table[
           Circle[{x, x^2}, Offset[{2, 2}]],
           {x, 10}], Frame->True]]
```

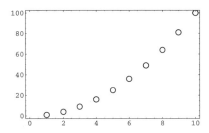

In most kinds of graphics, you typically want the relative positions of different objects to adjust automatically when you change the coordinates or the overall size of your plot. But sometimes you may instead want the offset from one object to another to be constrained to remain fixed. This can be the case, for example, when you are making a collection of plots in which you want certain features to remain consistent, even though the different plots have different forms.

Offset[{*adx*, *ady*}, *position*] allows you to specify the position of an object by giving an absolute offset from a position that is specified in original or scaled coordinates. The units for the offset are printer's points, equal to $\frac{1}{72}$ of an inch.

When you give text in a plot, the size of the font that is used is also specified in printer's points. A 10-point font, for example, therefore has letters whose basic height is 10 printer's points. You can use Offset to move text around in a plot, and to create plotting symbols or icons which match the size of text.

PlotRange -> {{*xmin*, *xmax*}, {*ymin*, *ymax*}}
> the range of original coordinates to include in the plot

PlotRegion -> {{*sxmin*, *sxmax*}, {*symin*, *symax*}}
> the region of the display specified in scaled coordinates which the plot fills

---

Options which determine translation from original to display coordinates.

When *Mathematica* renders a graphics object, one of the first things it has to do is to work out what range of original x and y coordinates it should actually display. Any graphical elements that are outside this range will be "clipped", and not shown.

The option PlotRange specifies the range of original coordinates to include. As discussed on page 135, the default setting is PlotRange -> Automatic, which makes *Mathematica* try to choose a range which includes all "interesting" parts of a plot, while dropping "outliers". By setting

PlotRange -> All, you can tell *Mathematica* to include everything. You can also give explicit ranges of coordinates to include.

This sets up a polygonal object whose corners have coordinates between roughly ±1.

```
In[4]:= obj = Polygon[
            Table[{Sin[n Pi/10], Cos[n Pi/10]} + 0.05 (-1)^n,
                                          {n, 20}]] ;
```

In this case, the polygonal object fills almost the whole display area.

```
In[5]:= Show[Graphics[obj]]
```

With the default PlotRange -> Automatic, the outlying point is not included, but does affect the range of coordinates chosen.

```
In[6]:= Show[ Graphics[{obj, Point[{20, 20}]}] ]
```

With PlotRange -> All, the outlying point is included, and the coordinate system is correspondingly modified.

```
In[7]:= Show[%, PlotRange -> All]
```

The option PlotRange allows you to specify a rectangular region in the original coordinate system, and to drop any graphical elements that lie outside this region. In order to render the remaining elements, however, *Mathematica* then has to determine how to position this rectangular region with respect to the final display area.

The option `PlotRegion` allows you to specify where the corners of the rectangular region lie within the final display area. The positions of the corners are specified in scaled coordinates, which are defined to run from 0 to 1 across the display area. The default is `PlotRegion -> {{0, 1}, {0, 1}}`, which specifies that the rectangular region should fill the whole display area.

By specifying `PlotRegion`, you can effectively add "margins" around your plot.

```
In[8]:= Plot[ArcTan[x], {x, 0, 10},
              PlotRegion -> {{0.2, 0.8}, {0.3, 0.7}}]
```

`AspectRatio -> r`	make the ratio of height to width for the display area equal to *r*
`AspectRatio -> Automatic`	determine the shape of the display area from the original coordinate system

Specifying the shape of the display area.

What we have discussed so far is how *Mathematica* translates the original coordinates you specify into positions in the final display area. What remains to discuss, however, is what the final display area is like.

On most computer systems, there is a certain fixed region of screen or paper into which the *Mathematica* display area must fit. How it fits into this region is determined by its "shape" or aspect ratio. In general, the option `AspectRatio` specifies the ratio of height to width for the final display area.

It is important to note that the setting of `AspectRatio` does not affect the meaning of the scaled or display coordinates. These coordinates always run from 0 to 1 across the display area. What `AspectRatio` does is to change the shape of this display area.

This generates a graphic object corresponding to a hexagon.

```
In[9]:= hex = Graphics[Polygon[
              Table[{Sin[n Pi/3], Cos[n Pi/3]}, {n, 6}] ]] ;
```

This renders the hexagon in a display area whose height is three times its width.

In[10]:= **Show[hex, AspectRatio -> 3]**

For two-dimensional graphics, AspectRatio is set by default to the fixed value of 1/GoldenRatio. Sometimes, however, you may want to determine the aspect ratio for a plot from the original co-ordinate system used in the plot. Typically what you want is for one unit in the x direction in the original coordinate system to correspond to the same distance in the final display as one unit in the y direction. In this way, objects that you define in the original coordinate system are displayed with their "natural shape". You can make this happen by setting the option AspectRatio -> Automatic.

With AspectRatio -> Automatic, the aspect ratio of the final display area is determined from the original coordinate system, and the hexagon is shown with its "natural shape".

In[11]:= **Show[hex, AspectRatio -> Automatic]**

Using scaled coordinates, you can specify the sizes of graphical elements as fractions of the size of the display area. You cannot, however, tell *Mathematica* the actual physical size at which a particular graphical element should be rendered. Of course, this size ultimately depends on the details of your graphics output device, and cannot be determined for certain within *Mathematica*. Nevertheless, graph-ics directives such as AbsoluteThickness discussed on page 481 do allow you to indicate "absolute sizes" to use for particular graphical elements. The sizes you request in this way will be respected by most, but not all, output devices. (For example, if you optically project an image, it is neither possible nor desirable to maintain the same absolute size for a graphical element within it.)

■ 2.9.5 Labeling Two-Dimensional Graphics

Axes -> True	give a pair of axes
GridLines -> Automatic	draw grid lines on the plot
Frame -> True	put axes on a frame around the plot
PlotLabel -> "*text*"	give an overall label for the plot

Ways to label two-dimensional plots.

Here is a plot, using the default Axes -> True.

In[1]:= **bp = Plot[BesselJ[2, x], {x, 0, 10}]**

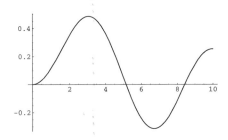

Setting Frame -> True generates a frame with axes, and removes tick marks from the ordinary axes.

In[2]:= **Show[bp, Frame -> True]**

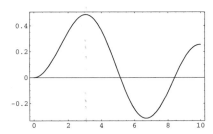

This includes grid lines, which are shown in light blue on color displays.

In[3]:= **Show[%, GridLines -> Automatic]**

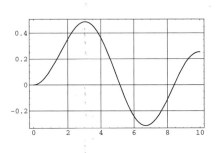

`Axes -> False`	draw no axes
`Axes -> True`	draw both x and y axes
`Axes -> {False, True}`	draw a y axis but no x axis
`AxesOrigin -> Automatic`	choose the crossing point for the axes automatically
`AxesOrigin -> {x, y}`	specify the crossing point
`AxesStyle -> `*style*	specify the style for axes
`AxesStyle -> {{`*xstyle*`}, {`*ystyle*`}}`	specify individual styles for axes
`AxesLabel -> None`	give no axis labels
`AxesLabel -> `*ylabel*	put a label on the y axes
`AxesLabel -> {`*xlabel*`, `*ylabel*`}`	put labels on both x and y axes

Options for axes.

This makes the axes cross at the point {5, 0}, and puts a label on each axis.

`In[4]:= Show[bp, AxesOrigin->{5, 0}, AxesLabel->{"x", "y"}]`

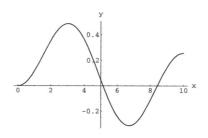

`Ticks -> None`	draw no tick marks
`Ticks -> Automatic`	place tick marks automatically
`Ticks -> {`*xticks*`, `*yticks*`}`	tick mark specifications for each axis

Settings for the `Ticks` option.

With the default setting `Ticks -> Automatic`, *Mathematica* creates a certain number of major and minor tick marks, and places them on axes at positions which yield the minimum number of decimal digits in the tick labels. In some cases, however, you may want to specify the positions and properties of tick marks explicitly. You will need to do this, for example, if you want to have tick marks at multiples of π, or if you want to put a nonlinear scale on an axis.

None	draw no tick marks
Automatic	place tick marks automatically
$\{x_1, x_2, \ldots\}$	draw tick marks at the specified positions
$\{\{x_1, label_1\}, \{x_2, label_2\}, \ldots\}$	draw tick marks with the specified labels
$\{\{x_1, label_1, len_1\}, \ldots\}$	draw tick marks with the specified scaled lengths
$\{\{x_1, label_1, \{plen_1, mlen_1\}\}, \ldots\}$	draw tick marks with the specified lengths in the positive and negative directions
$\{\{x_1, label_1, len_1, style_1\}, \ldots\}$	draw tick marks with the specified styles
func	a function to be applied to *xmin, xmax* to get the tick mark option

Tick mark options for each axis.

This gives tick marks at specified positions on the *x* axis, and chooses the tick marks automatically on the *y* axis.

In[5]:= **Show[bp, Ticks -> {{0, Pi, 2Pi, 3Pi}, Automatic}]**

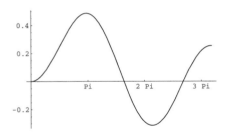

This adds tick marks with no labels at multiples of $\pi/2$.

In[6]:= **Show[bp,**
**   Ticks -> {{0, {Pi/2, ""}, Pi, {3Pi/2, ""},**
**   2Pi, {5Pi/2, ""}, 3Pi}, Automatic}]**

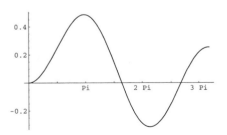

Particularly when you want to create complicated tick mark specifications, it is often convenient to define a "tick mark function" which creates the appropriate tick mark specification given the minimum and maximum values on a particular axis.

This defines a function which gives a list of tick mark positions with a spacing of 1.

In[7]:= `units[xmin_, xmax_] :=`
          `Range[Floor[xmin], Floor[xmax], 1]`

This uses the units function to specify tick marks for the *x* axis.

In[8]:= `Show[bp, Ticks -> {units, Automatic}]`

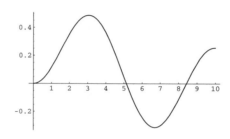

Sometimes you may want to generate tick marks which differ only slightly from those produced automatically with the setting `Ticks -> Automatic`. You can get the complete specification for tick marks that were generated automatically in a particular plot by using `FullOptions[g, Ticks]`, as discussed on page 470.

`Frame -> False`	draw no frame
`Frame -> True`	draw a frame around the plot
`FrameStyle -> `*style*	specify a style for the frame
`FrameStyle -> {{`*xmstyle*`}, {`*ymstyle*`}, ... }`	specify styles for each edge of the frame
`FrameLabel -> None`	give no frame labels
`FrameLabel -> {`*xmlabel*`, `*ymlabel*`, ... }`	put labels on edges of the frame
`RotateLabel -> False`	do not rotate text in labels
`FrameTicks -> None`	draw no tick marks on frame edges
`FrameTicks -> Automatic`	position tick marks automatically
`FrameTicks -> {{`*xmticks*`, `*ymticks*`, ... }}`	specify tick marks for frame edges

Options for frame axes.

The **Axes** option allows you to draw a single pair of axes in a plot. Sometimes, however, you may instead want to show the scales for a plot on a frame, typically drawn around the whole plot. The option **Frame** allows you effectively to draw four axes, corresponding to the four edges of the frame around a plot. These four axes are ordered clockwise, starting from the one at the bottom.

This draws frame axes, and labels each of them.

```
In[9]:= Show[bp, Frame -> True,
            FrameLabel -> {"label 1", "label 2",
                          "label 3", "label 4"}]
```

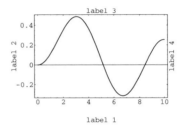

GridLines -> None	draw no grid lines
GridLines -> Automatic	position grid lines automatically
GridLines -> {*xgrid*, *ygrid*}	specify grid lines in analogy with tick marks

Options for grid lines.

Grid lines in *Mathematica* work very much like tick marks. As with tick marks, you can specify explicit positions for grid lines. There is no label or length to specify for grid lines. However, you can specify a style.

This generates *x* but not *y* grid lines.

```
In[10]:= Show[bp, GridLines -> {Automatic, None}]
```

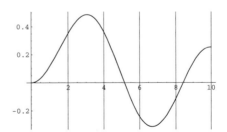

■ 2.9.6 Making Plots within Plots

Section 1.9.4 described how you can make regular arrays of plots using `GraphicsArray`. Using the `Rectangle` graphics primitive, however, you can combine and superimpose plots in any way.

`Rectangle[{xmin, ymin}, {xmax, ymax}, graphics]`
                                        render a graphics object within the specified rectangle

---

Creating a subplot.

Here is a three-dimensional plot.   *In[1]:=* **p3 = Plot3D[Sin[x] Exp[y], {x, -5, 5}, {y, -2, 2}]**

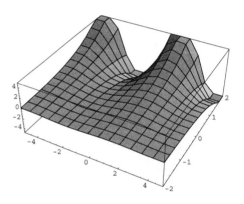

This creates a two-dimensional   *In[2]:=* **Show[Graphics[{Rectangle[{0, 0}, {1, 1}, p3],**
graphics object which contains two   **Rectangle[{0.8, 0.8}, {1.2, 1.4}, p3]}]]**
copies of the three-dimensional plot.

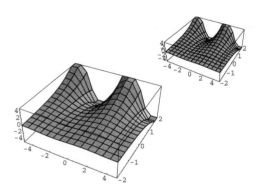

Mathematica can render any graphics object within a `Rectangle`. In all cases, what it puts in the rectangle is a scaled down version of what would be obtained if you displayed the graphics object on its own. Notice that in general the display area for the graphics object will be sized so as to touch at least one pair of edges of the rectangle.

■ 2.9.7 Density and Contour Plots

DensityGraphics[*array*]	density plot
ContourGraphics[*array*]	contour plot

Graphics objects that represent density and contour plots.

The functions DensityPlot and ContourPlot discussed in Section 1.9.6 work by creating ContourGraphics and DensityGraphics objects containing arrays of values.

Most of the options for density and contour plots are the same as those for ordinary two-dimensional plots. There are, however, a few additional options.

option name	default value	
ColorFunction	Automatic	how to assign colors to each cell
Mesh	True	whether to draw a mesh
MeshStyle	Automatic	a style for the mesh

Additional options for density plots.

In a density plot, the color of each cell represents its value. By default, each cell is assigned a gray level, running from black to white as the value of the cell increases. In general, however, you can specify other "color maps" for the relation between the value of a cell and its color. The option ColorFunction allows you to specify a function which is applied to each cell value to find the color of the cell. The cell values are scaled so as to run between 0 and 1 in a particular density plot. The function you give as the setting for ColorFunction may return any *Mathematica* color directive, such as GrayLevel, Hue or RGBColor. A common setting to use is ColorFunction -> Hue.

Here is a density plot with the default
ColorFunction.

In[1]:= **DensityPlot[Sin[x y], {x, -1, 1}, {y, -1, 1}]**

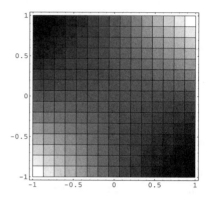

This gives a density plot with a
different "color map".

In[2]:= **Show[%, ColorFunction -> (GrayLevel[#^3]&)]**

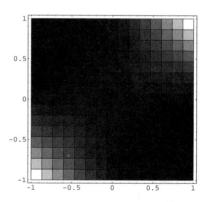

option name	default value	
Contours	10	what contours to use
ContourLines	True	whether to draw contour lines
ContourStyle	Automatic	style to use for contour lines
ContourShading	True	whether to shade regions in the plot
ColorFunction	Automatic	how to assign colors to contour levels

Options for contour plots.

In constructing a contour plot, the first issue is what contours to use. With the default setting `Contours -> 10`, *Mathematica* uses a sequence of 10 contour levels equally spaced between the minimum and maximum values defined by the `PlotRange` option.

`Contours -> `n	use a sequence of n equally spaced contours
`Contours -> {`z_1`, `z_2`, ... }`	use contours with values $z_1, z_2, \ldots$

Specifying contours.

This creates a contour plot with two contours.

`In[3]:= ContourPlot[Sin[x y], {x, -1, 1}, {y, -1, 1},`
`        Contours -> {-.5, .5}]`

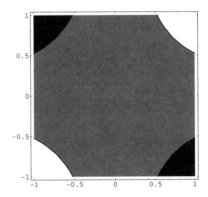

There are some slight subtleties associated with labeling density and contour plots. Both the `Axes` and `Frame` options from ordinary two-dimensional graphics can be used. But setting `AxesOrigin -> Automatic` keeps the axes outside the plot in both cases.

■ 2.9.8 Three-Dimensional Graphics Primitives

One of the most powerful aspects of graphics in *Mathematica* is the availability of three-dimensional as well as two-dimensional graphics primitives. By combining three-dimensional graphics primitives, you can represent and render three-dimensional objects in *Mathematica*.

Point[{x, y, z}]	point with coordinates x, y, z
Line[{{x_1, y_1, z_1}, {x_2, y_2, z_2}, ... }]	
	line through the points {x_1, y_1, z_1}, {x_2, y_2, z_2}, ...
Polygon[{{x_1, y_1, z_1}, {x_2, y_2, z_2}, ... }]	
	filled polygon with the specified list of corners
Cuboid[{$xmin$, $ymin$, $zmin$}, {$xmax$, $ymax$, $zmax$}]	
	cuboid
Text[$expr$, {x, y, z}]	text at position {x, y, z} (see Section 2.9.16)

Three-dimensional graphics elements.

Every time you evaluate rcoord, it generates a random coordinate in three dimensions.

```
In[1]:= rcoord := {Random[ ], Random[ ], Random[ ]}
```

This generates a list of 20 random points in three-dimensional space.

```
In[2]:= pts = Table[Point[rcoord], {20}] ;
```

Here is a plot of the points.

```
In[3]:= Show[ Graphics3D[ pts ] ]
```

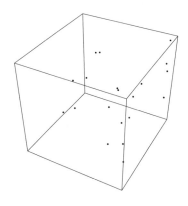

This gives a plot showing a line through 10 random points in three dimensions.

In[4]:= **Show[Graphics3D[Line[Table[rcoord, {10}]]]]**

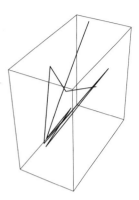

If you give a list of graphics elements in two dimensions, *Mathematica* simply draws each element in turn, with later elements obscuring earlier ones. In three dimensions, however, *Mathematica* collects together all the graphics elements you specify, then displays them as three-dimensional objects, with the ones in front in three-dimensional space obscuring those behind.

Every time you evaluate rantri, it generates a random triangle in three-dimensional space.

In[5]:= **rantri := Polygon[Table[rcoord, {3}]]**

This draws a single random triangle.

In[6]:= **Show[Graphics3D[rantri]]**

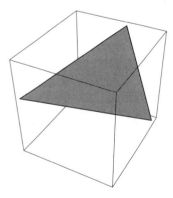

This draws a collection of 5 random triangles. The triangles in front obscure those behind.

`In[7]:= Show[ Graphics3D[ Table[rantri, {5}] ] ]`

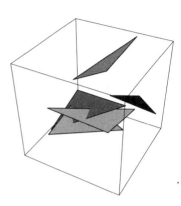

By creating an appropriate list of polygons, you can build up any three-dimensional object in *Mathematica*. Thus, for example, all the surfaces produced by `ParametricPlot3D` are represented simply as lists of polygons.

The package `Graphics'Polyhedra'` contains examples of lists of polygons which correspond to polyhedra in three dimensions.

This loads a package which defines various polyhedra.

`In[8]:= <<Graphics'Polyhedra'`

Here is the list of polygons corresponding to a tetrahedron centered at the origin.

```
In[9]:= Tetrahedron[ ]
Out[9]= {Polygon[{{0, 0, 1.73205}, {0, 1.63299, -0.57735},
            {-1.41421, -0.816497, -0.57735}}],
         Polygon[{{0, 0, 1.73205},
            {-1.41421, -0.816497, -0.57735},
            {1.41421, -0.816497, -0.57735}}],
         Polygon[{{0, 0, 1.73205},
            {1.41421, -0.816497, -0.57735},
            {0, 1.63299, -0.57735}}],
         Polygon[{{0, 1.63299, -0.57735},
            {1.41421, -0.816497, -0.57735},
            {-1.41421, -0.816497, -0.57735}}]}
```

This displays the tetrahedron as a three-dimensional object.

In[10]:= **Show[Graphics3D[%]]**

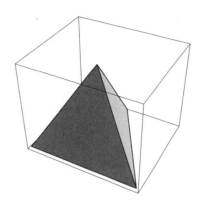

Dodecahedron[ ] is another three-dimensional object defined in the polyhedra package.

In[11]:= **Show[Graphics3D[Dodecahedron[ ]]]**

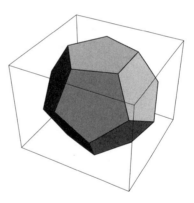

This shows four intersecting dodecahedra.

In[12]:= **Show[Graphics3D[**
Table[Dodecahedron[0.8 {k, k, k}], {k, 0, 3}]]]

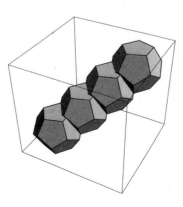

Mathematica allows polygons in three dimensions to have any number of vertices. However, these vertices should lie in a plane, and should form a convex figure. If they do not, then *Mathematica* will break the polygon into triangles, which are planar by definition, before rendering it.

Cuboid[{x, y, z}]   a unit cube with opposite corners having coordinates {x, y, z} and {x+1, y+1, z+1}

Cuboid[{xmin, ymin, zmin}, {xmax, ymax, zmax}]
                      a cuboid (rectangular parallelepiped) with opposite corners having the specified coordinates

---

Cuboid graphics elements.

This draws 20 random unit cubes in three-dimensional space.

In[13]:= **Show[Graphics3D[Table[Cuboid[10 rcoord], {20}]]]**

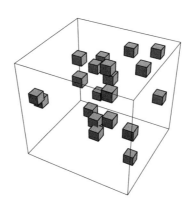

■ 2.9.9 Three-Dimensional Graphics Directives

In three dimensions, just as in two dimensions, you can give various graphics directives to specify how the different elements in a graphics object should be rendered.

All the graphics directives for two dimensions also work in three dimensions. There are however some additional directives in three dimensions.

Just as in two dimensions, you can use the directives PointSize, Thickness and Dashing to tell *Mathematica* how to render Point and Line elements. Note that in three dimensions, the lengths that appear in these directives are measured as fractions of the total width of the display area for your plot.

This generates a list of 20 random points in three dimensions.

In[1]:= **pts = Table[Point[Table[Random[ ], {3}]], {20}];**

This displays the points, with each one being a circle whose diameter is 5% of the display area width.

In[2]:= **Show[Graphics3D[{ PointSize[0.05], pts }]]**

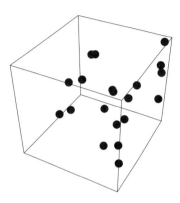

As in two dimensions, you can use **AbsolutePointSize**, **AbsoluteThickness** and **AbsoluteDashing** if you want to measure length in absolute units.

This generates a line through 10 random points in three dimensions.

In[3]:= **line = Line[Table[Random[ ], {10}, {3}]] ;**

This shows the line dashed, with a thickness of 2 printer's points.

In[4]:= **Show[Graphics3D[{ AbsoluteThickness[2],**
AbsoluteDashing[{5, 5}], line }]]

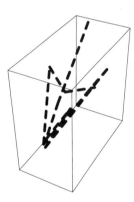

For **Point** and **Line** objects, the color specification directives also work the same in three dimensions as in two dimensions. For **Polygon** objects, however, they can work differently.

In two dimensions, polygons are always assumed to have an intrinsic color, specified directly by graphics directives such as **RGBColor**. In three dimensions, however, *Mathematica* also provides the option of generating colors for polygons using a more physical approach based on simulated illumination. With the default option setting **Lighting -> True** for **Graphics3D** objects, *Mathematica* ignores explicit colors specified for polygons, and instead determines all polygon colors using the simulated illumination model. Even in this case, however, explicit colors are used for points and lines.

Lighting -> False	intrinsic colors
Lighting -> True	colors based on simulated illumination (default)

The two schemes for coloring polygons in three dimensions.

This loads a package which defines various polyhedra.

```
In[5]:= <<Graphics`Polyhedra`
```

This draws an icosahedron, using the same gray level for all faces.

```
In[6]:= Show[Graphics3D[{GrayLevel[0.7], Icosahedron[ ]}],
                                          Lighting -> False]
```

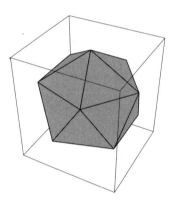

With the default setting Lighting -> True, the colors of polygons are determined by the simulated illumination model, and explicit color specifications are ignored.

```
In[7]:= Show[%, Lighting -> True]
```

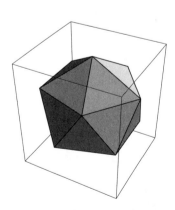

Explicit color directives are, however, always followed for points and lines.

```
In[8]:= Show[{%, Graphics3D[{GrayLevel[0.5], Thickness[0.05],
            Line[{{0, 0, -2}, {0, 0, 2}}]]}]]
```

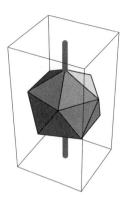

EdgeForm[ ]	draw no lines at the edges of polygons
EdgeForm[g]	use the graphics directives g to determine how to draw lines at the edges of polygons

Giving graphics directives for all the edges of polygons.

When you render a three-dimensional graphics object in *Mathematica*, there are two kinds of lines that can appear. The first kind are lines from explicit Line primitives that you included in the graphics object. The second kind are lines that were generated as the edges of polygons.

You can tell *Mathematica* how to render all lines of the second kind by giving a list of graphics directives inside EdgeForm.

This renders a dodecahedron with its edges shown as thick gray lines.

```
In[9]:= Show[Graphics3D[
            {EdgeForm[{GrayLevel[0.5], Thickness[0.02]}],
             Dodecahedron[ ]}]]
```

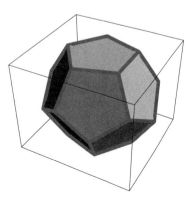

FaceForm[*gfront*, *gback*]	use *gfront* graphics directives for the front face of each polygon, and *gback* for the back

Rendering the fronts and backs of polygons differently.

An important aspect of polygons in three dimensions is that they have both front and back faces. *Mathematica* uses the following convention to define the "front face" of a polygon: if you look at a polygon from the front, then the corners of the polygon will appear counterclockwise, when taken in the order that you specified them.

This defines a dodecahedron with one face removed.

In[10]:= **d = Drop[Dodecahedron[ ], {6}] ;**

You can now see inside the dodecahedron.

In[11]:= **Show[Graphics3D[d]]**

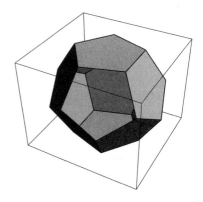

This makes the front (outside) face of each polygon light gray, and the back (inside) face dark gray.

In[12]:= **Show[Graphics3D[**
{FaceForm[GrayLevel[0.8], GrayLevel[0.3]], d}],
Lighting -> False]

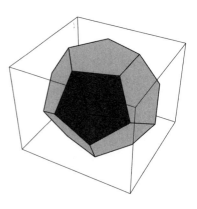

■ 2.9.10 Coordinate Systems for Three-Dimensional Graphics

Whenever *Mathematica* draws a three-dimensional object, it always effectively puts a cuboidal box around the object. With the default option setting Boxed -> True, *Mathematica* in fact draws the edges of this box explicitly. But in general, *Mathematica* automatically "clips" any parts of your object that extend outside of the cuboidal box.

The option PlotRange specifies the range of *x*, *y* and *z* coordinates that *Mathematica* should include in the box. As in two dimensions the default setting is PlotRange -> Automatic, which makes *Mathematica* use an internal algorithm to try and include the "interesting parts" of a plot, but drop outlying parts. With PlotRange -> All, *Mathematica* will include all parts.

This loads a package defining various polyhedra.

In[1]:= **<<Graphics`Polyhedra`**

This creates a stellated icosahedron.

In[2]:= **stel = Stellate[Icosahedron[ ]] ;**

Here is the stellated icosahedron, drawn in a box.

In[3]:= **Show[Graphics3D[stel], Axes -> True]**

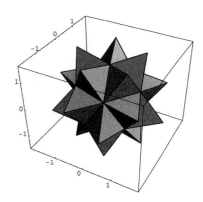

With this setting for PlotRange, many parts of the stellated icosahedron lie outside the box, and are clipped.

In[4]:= **Show[%, PlotRange -> {-1, 1}]**

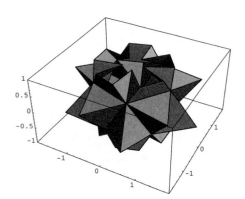

Much as in two dimensions, you can use either "original" or "scaled" coordinates to specify the positions of elements in three-dimensional objects. Scaled coordinates, specified as Scaled[{sx, sy, sz}] are taken to run from 0 to 1 in each dimension. The coordinates are set up to define a right-handed coordinate system on the box.

{x, y, z}	original coordinates
Scaled[{sx, sy, sz}]	scaled coordinates, running from 0 to 1 in each dimension

Coordinate systems for three-dimensional objects.

This puts a cuboid in one corner of the box.	In[5]:= **Show[Graphics3D[{stel,**
	    Cuboid[Scaled[{0, 0, 0}],
	        Scaled[{0.2, 0.2, 0.2}]]}]]

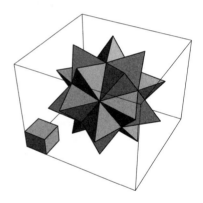

Once you have specified where various graphical elements go inside a three-dimensional box, you must then tell *Mathematica* how to draw the box. The first step is to specify what shape the box should be. This is analogous to specifying the aspect ratio of a two-dimensional plot. In three dimensions, you can use the option BoxRatios to specify the ratio of side lengths for the box. For Graphics3D objects, the default is BoxRatios -> Automatic, specifying that the shape of the box should be determined from the ranges of actual coordinates for its contents.

BoxRatios -> {xr, yr, zr}	specify the ratio of side lengths for the box
BoxRatios -> Automatic	determine the ratio of side lengths from the range of actual coordinates (default for Graphics3D)
BoxRatios -> {1, 1, 0.4}	specify a fixed shape of box (default for SurfaceGraphics)

Specifying the shape of the bounding box for three-dimensional objects.

This displays the stellated icosahedron in a tall box.

In[6]:= **Show[Graphics3D[stel], BoxRatios -> {1, 1, 5}]**

To produce an image of a three-dimensional object, you have to tell *Mathematica* from what view point you want to look at the object. You can do this using the option `ViewPoint`.

Some common settings for this option were given on page 152. In general, however, you can tell *Mathematica* to use any view point, so long as it lies outside the box.

View points are specified in the form `ViewPoint -> {`*sx*, *sy*, *sz*`}`. The values *si* are given in a special coordinate system, in which the center of the box is {0, 0, 0}. The special coordinates are scaled so that the longest side of the box corresponds to one unit. The lengths of the other sides of the box in this coordinate system are determined by the setting for the `BoxRatios` option. For a cubical box, therefore, each of the special coordinates runs from $-1/2$ to $1/2$ across the box. Note that the view point must always lie outside the box.

This generates a picture using the default view point {1.3, -2.4, 2}.

In[7]:= **surf = Plot3D[(2 + Sin[x]) Cos[2 y],**
   {x, -2, 2}, {y, -3, 3},
   AxesLabel -> {"x", "y", "z"}]

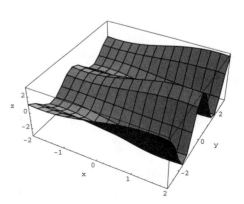

This is what you get with a view point close to one of the corners of the box.

In[8]:= **Show[surf, ViewPoint -> {1.2, 1.2, 1.2}]**

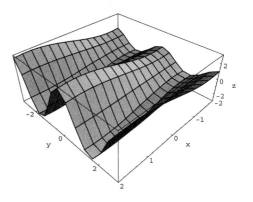

As you move away from the box, the perspective effect gets smaller.

In[9]:= **Show[surf, ViewPoint -> {5, 5, 5}]**

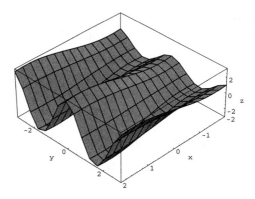

option name	default value	
ViewPoint	{1.3, -2.4, 2}	the point in a special scaled coordinate system from which to view the object
ViewCenter	Automatic	the point in the scaled coordinate system which appears at the center of the final image
ViewVertical	{0, 0, 1}	the direction in the scaled coordinate system which appears as vertical in the final image

Specifying the position and orientation of three-dimensional objects.

In making a picture of a three-dimensional object you have to specify more than just *where* you want to look at the object from. You also have to specify how you want to "frame" the object in your final image. You can do this using the additional options `ViewCenter` and `ViewVertical`.

`ViewCenter` allows you to tell *Mathematica* what point in the object should appear at the center of your final image. The point is specified by giving its scaled coordinates, running from 0 to 1 in each direction across the box. With the setting `ViewCenter -> {1/2, 1/2, 1/2}`, the center of the box will therefore appear at the center of your final image. With many choices of view point, however, the box will not appear symmetrical, so this setting for `ViewCenter` will not center the whole box in the final image area. You can do this by setting `ViewCenter -> Automatic`.

`ViewVertical` specifies which way up the object should appear in your final image. The setting for `ViewVertical` gives the direction in scaled coordinates which ends up vertical in the final image. With the default setting `ViewVertical -> {0, 0, 1}`, the *z* direction in your original coordinate system always ends up vertical in the final image.

With this setting for `ViewCenter`, a corner of the box appears in the center of your image.

In[10]:= `Show[surf, ViewCenter -> {1, 1, 1}]`

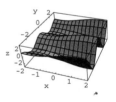

This setting for `ViewVertical` makes the *x* axis of the box appear vertical in your image.

In[11]:= `Show[surf, ViewVertical -> {1, 0, 0}]`

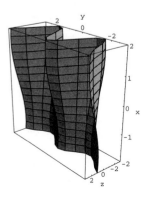

When you set the options `ViewPoint`, `ViewCenter` and `ViewVertical`, you can think about it as specifying how you would look at a physical object. `ViewPoint` specifies where your head is relative to the object. `ViewCenter` specifies where you are looking (the center of your gaze). And `ViewVertical` specifies which way up your head is.

In terms of coordinate systems, settings for `ViewPoint`, `ViewCenter` and `ViewVertical` specify how coordinates in the three-dimensional box should be transformed into coordinates for your image in the final display area.

For some purposes, it is useful to think of the coordinates in the final display area as three dimensional. The x and y axes run horizontally and vertically, respectively, while the z axis points into the page. Positions specified in this "display coordinate system" remain fixed when you change `ViewPoint` and so on. The positions of light sources discussed in the next section are defined in this display coordinate system.

Box coordinate system	measured relative to the box around your object
Display coordinate system	measured relative to your final display area

Coordinate systems for three-dimensional graphics.

Once you have obtained a two-dimensional image of a three-dimensional object, there are still some issues about how this image should be rendered. The issues however are identical to those that occur for two-dimensional graphics. Thus, for example, you can modify the final shape of your image by changing the `AspectRatio` option. And you specify what region of your whole display area your image should take up by setting the `PlotRegion` option.

This modifies the aspect ratio of the   *In[12]:=* `Show[surf, Axes -> False, AspectRatio -> 0.3]`
final image.

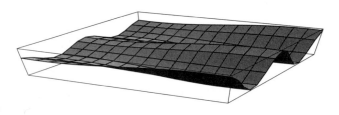

Mathematica usually scales the images of three-dimensional objects to be as large as possible, given the display area you specify. Although in most cases this scaling is what you want, it does have the consequence that the size at which a particular three-dimensional object is drawn may vary with the orientation of the object. You can set the option `SphericalRegion -> True` to avoid such variation. With this option setting, *Mathematica* effectively puts a sphere around the three-dimensional bounding box, and scales the final image so that the whole of this sphere fits inside the display area you specify. The sphere has its center at the center of the bounding box, and is drawn so that the bounding box just fits inside it.

This draws a rather elongated version of the plot.

In[13]:= `Show[surf, BoxRatios -> {1, 5, 1}]`

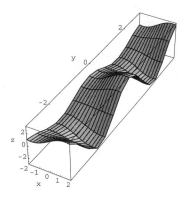

With `SphericalRegion -> True`, the final image is scaled so that a sphere placed around the bounding box would fit in the display area.

In[14]:= `Show[%, SphericalRegion -> True]`

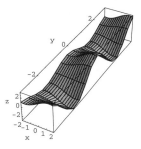

By setting `SphericalRegion -> True`, you can make the scaling of an object consistent for all orientations of the object. This is useful if you create animated sequences which show a particular object in several different orientations.

| SphericalRegion -> False | scale three-dimensional images to be as large as possible |
| SphericalRegion -> True | scale images so that a sphere drawn around the three-dimensional bounding box would fit in the final display area |

Changing the magnification of three-dimensional images.

■ 2.9.11 Plotting Three-Dimensional Surfaces

By giving an appropriate list of graphics primitives, you can represent essentially any three-dimensional object in *Mathematica* with Graphics3D. You can represent three-dimensional surfaces with Graphics3D by giving explicit lists of polygons with adjacent edges.

If you need to represent arbitrary surfaces which can fold over and perhaps intersect themselves, there is no choice but to use explicit lists of polygons with Graphics3D, as ParametricPlot3D does.

However, there are many cases in which you get simpler surfaces. For example, Plot3D and ListPlot3D yield surfaces which never fold over, and have a definite height at every x, y point. You can represent simple surfaces like these in *Mathematica* without giving an explicit list of polygons. Instead, all you need do is to give an array which specifies the z height at every point in an x, y grid. The graphics object SurfaceGraphics[*array*] represents a surface constructed in this way.

| Graphics3D[*primitives*] | arbitrary three-dimensional objects, including folded surfaces |
| SurfaceGraphics[*array*] | simple three-dimensional surfaces |

Three-dimensional graphics objects.

Here is a 4×4 array of values.

```
In[1]:= moda = Table[Mod[i, j], {i, 4}, {j, 4}]
Out[1]= {{0, 1, 1, 1}, {0, 0, 2, 2}, {0, 1, 0, 3},
         {0, 0, 1, 0}}
```

This uses the array to give the height of each point on the surface.

In[2]:= **Show[SurfaceGraphics[moda]]**

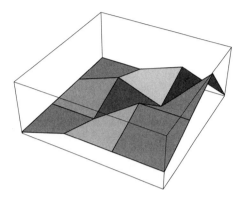

Both `Plot3D` and `ListPlot3D` work by creating `SurfaceGraphics` objects.

`Graphics3D[`*surface*`]`	convert `SurfaceGraphics` to `Graphics3D`

Converting between representations of surfaces.

If you apply `Graphics3D` to a `SurfaceGraphics` object, *Mathematica* will generate a `Graphics3D` object containing an explicit list of polygons representing the surface in the `SurfaceGraphics` object. Whenever you ask *Mathematica* to combine two `SurfaceGraphics` objects together, it automatically converts them both to `Graphics3D` objects.

Here is a surface represented by a `SurfaceGraphics` object.

In[3]:= **Plot3D[(1 - Sin[x]) (2 - Cos[2 y]),**
                 {x, -2, 2}, {y, -2, 2}]

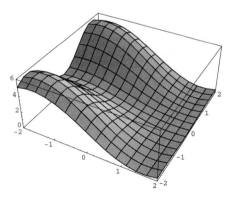

Here is another surface.

In[4]:= `Plot3D[(2 + Sin[x]) (1 + Cos[2 y]),`
`                                          {x, -2, 2}, {y, -2, 2}]`

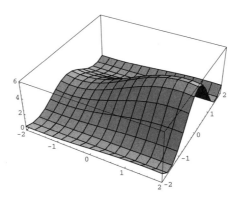

Mathematica shows the two surfaces together by converting each of them to a `Graphics3D` object containing an explicit list of polygons.

In[5]:= `Show[%, %%]`

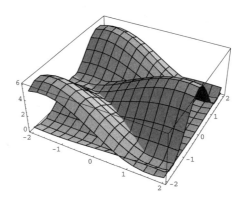

option name	default value	
Mesh	True	whether to draw a mesh on the surface
MeshStyle	Automatic	graphics directives specifying how to render the mesh
MeshRange	Automatic	the original range of coordinates corresponding to the mesh

Mesh options in `SurfaceGraphics`.

When you create a surface using `SurfaceGraphics`, the default is to draw a rectangular mesh on the surface. As discussed on page 153, including this mesh typically makes it easier for one to see the shape of the surface. You can nevertheless get rid of the mesh by setting the option `Mesh -> False`. You can also set the option `MeshStyle` to a list of graphics directives which specify thickness, color or other properties of the mesh lines.

A `SurfaceGraphics` object contains an array of values which specify the height of a surface at points in an x, y grid. By setting the option `MeshRange`, you can give the range of original x and y coordinates that correspond to the points in this grid. When you use
`Plot3D[f, {x, xmin, xmax}, {y, ymin, ymax}]` to generate a `SurfaceGraphics` object, the setting
`MeshRange -> {{xmin, xmax}, {ymin, ymax}}` is automatically generated. The setting for `MeshRange` is used in labeling the x and y axes in surface plots, and in working out polygon coordinates if you convert a `SurfaceGraphics` object to an explicit list of polygons in a `Graphics3D` object.

`None`	leave out clipped parts of the surface, so that you can see through
`Automatic`	show the clipped part of the surface with the same shading as an actual surface in the same position would have (default setting)
`GrayLevel[i]`, `RGBColor[r, g, b]`, etc.	show the clipped part of the surface with a particular gray level, color, etc.
`{bottom, top}`	give different specifications for parts that are clipped at the bottom and top

Settings for the `ClipFill` option.

The option `PlotRange` works for `SurfaceGraphics` as it does for other *Mathematica* graphics objects. Any parts of a surface that lie outside the range of coordinates defined by `PlotRange` will be "clipped". The option `ClipFill` allows you to specify what should happen to the parts of a surface that are clipped.

Here is a three-dimensional plot in which the top and bottom of the surface are clipped. With the default setting for ClipFill, the clipped parts are shown as they would be if they were part of the actual surface.

In[6]:= **Plot3D[Sin[x y], {x, 0, 3}, {y, 0, 3},**
                   PlotRange -> {-.5, .5}]

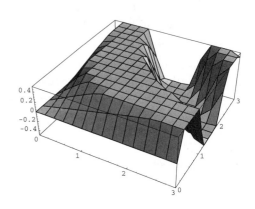

With ClipFill->None, parts of the surface which are clipped are left out, so that you can "see through" the surface there. *Mathematica* always leaves out parts of the surface that correspond to places where the value of the function you are plotting is not a real number.

In[7]:= **Show[%, ClipFill -> None]**

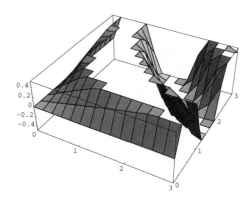

This makes the bottom clipped face white (gray level 1), and the top one black.

In[8]:= **Show[%, ClipFill -> {GrayLevel[1], GrayLevel[0]}]**

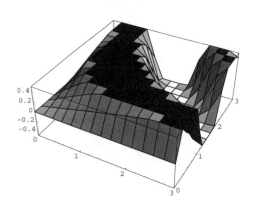

Whenever *Mathematica* draws a surface, it has to know not only the height, but also the color of the surface at each point. With the default setting `Lighting -> True`, *Mathematica* colors the surface using a simulated lighted model. However, with `Lighting -> False`, *Mathematica* uses a "color function" to determine how to color the surface.

The default color function takes the height of the surface, normalized to run from 0 to 1, and colors each part of the surface with a gray level corresponding to this height. There are two ways to change the default.

First, if you set the option `ColorFunction -> c`, then *Mathematica* will apply the function *c* to each height value to determine the color to use at that point. With `ColorFunction -> Hue`, *Mathematica* will for example color the surface with a range of hues.

`Plot3D[`*f*`, ... , ColorFunction -> `*c*`]`
  apply *c* to the normalized values of *f* to determine the color of each point on a surface

`ListPlot3D[`*array*`, ColorFunction -> `*c*`]`
  apply *c* to the elements of *array* to determine color

`SurfaceGraphics[`*array*`, ColorFunction -> `*c*`]`
  apply *c* to the elements of *array* to determine color

Specifying functions for coloring surfaces.

With `Lighting -> False`, the default is to color surfaces with gray scales determined by height.

In[9]:= `exp = Plot3D[Exp[-Sqrt[x^2 + y^2]],`
          `{x, -2, 2}, {y, -2, 2}, Lighting -> False,`
                           `PlotPoints -> 25]`

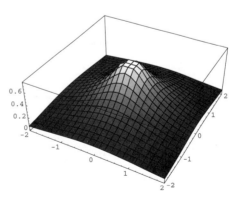

This defines a function which maps alternating ranges of values into black and white.

In[10]:= `stripes[f_] :=`
          `If[Mod[f, 1] > 0.5, GrayLevel[1], GrayLevel[0]]`

This shows the surface colored with black and white stripes.

`In[11]:= Show[exp, ColorFunction -> (stripes[5 #]&)]`

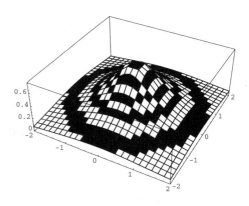

The second way to change the default coloring of surfaces is to supply an explicit second array along with the array of heights. ColorFunction is then applied to the elements of this second array, rather than the array of heights, to find the color directives to use. In the second array, you can effectively specify the value of another coordinate for each point on the surface. This coordinate will be plotted using color, rather than position.

You can generate an array of color values automatically using Plot3D[{f, s}, ...]. If you give the array explicitly in ListPlot3D or SurfaceGraphics, you should realize that with an $n \times n$ array of heights, you need an $(n-1) \times (n-1)$ array to specify colors. The reason is that the heights are specified for *points* on a grid, whereas the colors are specified for *squares* on the grid.

When you supply a second function or array to Plot3D, ListPlot3D, and so on, the default setting for the ColorFunction option is Automatic. This means that the function or array should contain explicit *Mathematica* color directives, such as GrayLevel or RGBColor. However, if you give another setting, such as ColorFunction -> Hue, then the function or array can yield pure numbers or other data which are converted to color directives when the function specified by ColorFunction is applied.

Plot3D[{f, s}, {x, $xmin$, $xmax$}, {y, $ymin$, $ymax$}]	
	plot a surface whose height is determined by f and whose color is determined by s
ListPlot3D[*height*, *color*]	generate a colored surface plot from an array of heights and colors
SurfaceGraphics[*height*, *color*]	a graphics object representing a surface with a specified array of heights and colors

Specifying arrays of colors for surfaces.

This plots a surface with gray level determined by the *y* coordinate.

In[12]:= **Plot3D[{Sin[x] Sin[y]^2, GrayLevel[y/3]},**
                              {x, 0, 3}, {y, 0, 3}]

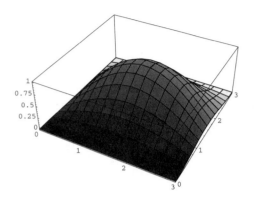

This puts a random gray level in each grid square. Notice that the array of grid squares is 9×9, whereas the array of grid points is 10×10.

In[13]:= **ListPlot3D[Table[i/j, {i, 10}, {j, 10}],**
              Table[GrayLevel[Random[ ]], {i, 9}, {j, 9}]]

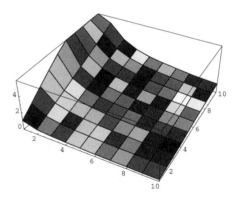

■ 2.9.12 Lighting and Surface Properties

With the default option setting Lighting -> True, *Mathematica* uses a simulated lighting model to determine how to color polygons in three-dimensional graphics.

Mathematica allows you to specify two components to the illumination of an object. The first is "ambient lighting", which produces uniform shading all over the object. The second is light from a collection of point sources, each with a particular position and color. *Mathematica* adds together the light from all of these sources in determining the total illumination of a particular polygon.

> AmbientLight -> *color*   diffuse isotropic lighting
>
> LightSources -> {{*pos₁*, *col₁*}, {*pos₂*, *col₂*}, ... }
>   point light sources with specified positions and colors

Options for simulated illumination.

The default lighting used by *Mathematica* involves three point light sources, and no ambient component. The light sources are colored respectively red, green and blue, and are placed at 45° angles on the right-hand side of the object.

Here is a surface, shaded using simulated lighting using the default set of lights.

In[1]:= **Plot3D[Sin[x + Sin[y]], {x, -3, 3}, {y, -3, 3}, Lighting -> True]**

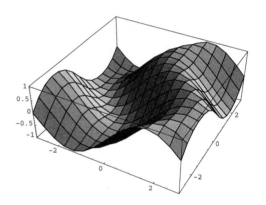

This shows the result of adding ambient light, and removing all point light sources.

In[2]:= **Show[%, AmbientLight -> GrayLevel[0.5], LightSources -> {}]**

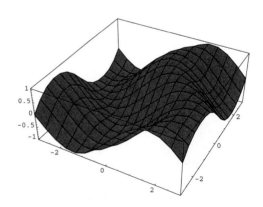

This adds a single point light source at the left-hand side of the image.

```
In[3]:= Show[%,
            LightSources -> {{{-1, 0, 0.5}, GrayLevel[0.5]}}]
```

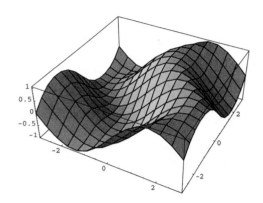

The positions of light sources in *Mathematica* are specified in the *display* coordinate system. The x and y coordinates are in the plane of the final display, and the z coordinate goes into the plane. Using this coordinate system ensures that the light sources remain fixed with respect to the viewer, even when the relative positions of the viewer and object change.

The end of the Graphics Gallery later in this book shows some examples of results obtained with various different arrangements of light sources.

Even though the view point is changed, the light source is kept fixed on the left-hand side of the image.

```
In[4]:= Show[%, ViewPoint -> {2, 2, 6}]
```

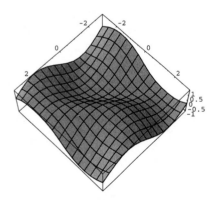

The perceived color of a polygon depends not only on the light which falls on the polygon, but also on how the polygon reflects that light. You can use the graphics directive **SurfaceColor** to specify the way that polygons reflect light.

If you do not explicitly use `SurfaceColor` directives, *Mathematica* effectively assumes that all polygons have matte white surfaces. Thus the polygons reflect light of any color incident on them, and do so equally in all directions. This is an appropriate model for materials such as uncoated white paper.

Using `SurfaceColor`, however, you can specify more complicated models. The basic idea is to distinguish two kinds of reflection: *diffuse* and *specular*.

In diffuse reflection, light incident on a surface is scattered equally in all directions. When this kind of reflection occurs, a surface has a "dull" or "matte" appearance. Diffuse reflectors obey Lambert's Law of light reflection, which states that the intensity of reflected light is $\cos(\alpha)$ times the intensity of the incident light, where α is the angle between the incident light direction and the surface normal vector. Note that when $\alpha > 90°$, there is no reflected light.

In specular reflection, a surface reflects light in a mirror-like way. As a result, the surface has a "shiny" or "gloss" appearance. With a perfect mirror, light incident at a particular angle is reflected at exactly the same angle. Most materials, however, scatter light to some extent, and so lead to reflected light that is distributed over a range of angles. *Mathematica* allows you to specify how broad the distribution is by giving a *specular exponent*, defined according to the Phong lighting model. With specular exponent n, the intensity of light at an angle θ away from the mirror reflection direction is assumed to vary like $\cos(\theta)^n$. As $n \to \infty$, therefore, the surface behaves like a perfect mirror. As n decreases, however, the surface becomes less "shiny", and for $n = 0$, the surface is a completely diffuse reflector. Typical values of n for actual materials range from about 1 to several hundred.

Most actual materials show a mixture of diffuse and specular reflection. In addition, they typically behave as if they have a certain intrinsic color. When the incident light is white, the reflected light has the color of the material. When the incident light is not white, each color component in the reflected light is a product of the corresponding component in the incident light and in the intrinsic color of the material.

In *Mathematica*, you can specify reflection properties by giving an intrinsic color associated with diffuse reflection, and another one associated with specular reflection. To get no reflection of a particular kind, you must give the corresponding intrinsic color as black, or `GrayLevel[0]`. For materials that are effectively "white", you can specify intrinsic colors of the form `GrayLevel[a]`, where a is the reflectance or albedo of the surface.

The end of the Graphics Gallery shows examples of results obtained with various choices of reflection parameters.

`SurfaceColor[GrayLevel[a]]`	matte surface with albedo a
`SurfaceColor[RGBColor[r, g, b]]`	matte surface with intrinsic color
`SurfaceColor[diff, spec]`	surface with diffuse intrinsic color *diff* and specular intrinsic color *spec*
`SurfaceColor[diff, spec, n]`	surface with specular exponent n

Specifying surface properties of lighted polygons.

This loads a package containing various graphics objects.

```
In[5]:= <<Graphics`Shapes`
```

`Sphere` creates a graphics object which represents a sphere.

```
In[6]:= s = Sphere[ ] ;
```

This shows the sphere with the default matte white surface.

```
In[7]:= Show[Graphics3D[s]]
```

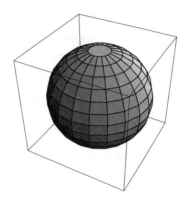

This makes the sphere have low diffuse reflectance, but high specular reflectance. As a result, the sphere has a "specular highlight" near the light sources, and is quite dark elsewhere.

```
In[8]:= Show[Graphics3D[{
            SurfaceColor[GrayLevel[0.2],
                GrayLevel[0.8], 5], s}]]
```

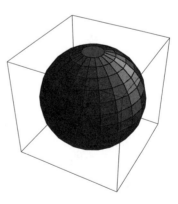

When you set up light sources and surface colors, it is important to make sure that the total intensity of light reflected from a particular polygon is never larger than 1. You will get strange effects if the intensity is larger than 1.

■ 2.9.13 Labeling Three-Dimensional Graphics

Mathematica provides various options for labeling three-dimensional graphics. Some of these options are directly analogous to those for two-dimensional graphics, discussed in Section 2.9.5. Others are different.

Boxed -> True	draw a cuboidal bounding box around the graphics (default)
Axes -> True	draw *x*, *y* and *z* axes on the edges of the box (default for SurfaceGraphics)
Axes -> {False, False, True}	draw the *z* axis only
FaceGrids -> All	draw grid lines on the faces of the box
PlotLabel -> *text*	give an overall label for the plot

Some options for labeling three-dimensional graphics.

This loads a package containing various polyhedra.

In[1]:= `<<Graphics'Polyhedra'`

The default for Graphics3D is to include a box, but no other forms of labeling.

In[2]:= `Show[Graphics3D[Dodecahedron[ ]]]`

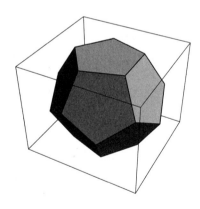

Setting `Axes -> True` adds *x*, *y* and *z* axes.

In[3]:= **Show[%, Axes -> True]**

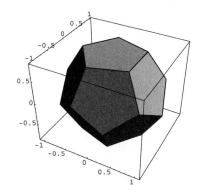

This adds grid lines to each face of the box.

In[4]:= **Show[%, FaceGrids -> All]**

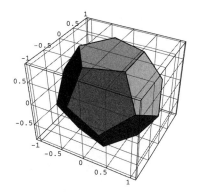

`BoxStyle -> ` *style*	specify the style for the box
`AxesStyle -> ` *style*	specify the style for axes
`AxesStyle -> {{`*xstyle*`}, {`*ystyle*`}, {`*zstyle*`}}`	
	specify separate styles for each axis

Style options.

This makes the box dashed, and draws axes which are thicker than normal.

```
In[5]:= Show[Graphics3D[Dodecahedron[ ]],
            BoxStyle -> Dashing[{0.02, 0.02}],
            Axes -> True, AxesStyle -> Thickness[0.01]]
```

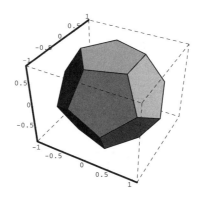

By setting the option `Axes -> True`, you tell *Mathematica* to draw axes on the edges of the three-dimensional box. However, for each axis, there are in principle four possible edges on which it can be drawn. The option `AxesEdge` allows you to specify on which edge to draw each of the axes.

`AxesEdge -> Automatic`	use an internal algorithm to choose where to draw all axes
`AxesEdge -> {xspec, yspec, zspec}`	
	give separate specifications for each of the *x*, *y* and *z* axes
`None`	do not draw this axis
`Automatic`	decide automatically where to draw this axis
`{dir_i, dir_j}`	specify on which of the four possible edges to draw this axis

Specifying where to draw three-dimensional axes.

This draws the *x* on the edge with larger *y* and *z* coordinates, draws no *y* axis, and chooses automatically where to draw the *z* axis.

`In[6]:= Show[Graphics3D[Dodecahedron[ ]], Axes -> True,`
`            AxesEdge -> {{1, 1}, None, Automatic}]`

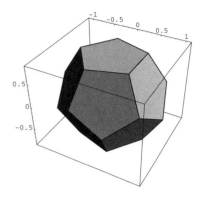

When you draw the *x* axis on a three-dimensional box, there are four possible edges on which the axis can be drawn. These edges are distinguished by having larger or smaller *y* and *z* coordinates. When you use the specification {*dir_y*, *dir_z*} for where to draw the *x* axis, you can set the *dir_i* to be +1 or −1 to represent larger or smaller values for the *y* and *z* coordinates.

AxesLabel -> None	give no axis labels
AxesLabel -> *zlabel*	put a label on the *z* axis
AxesLabel -> {*xlabel*, *ylabel*, *zlabel*}	
	put labels on all three axes

Axis labels in three-dimensional graphics.

You can use AxesLabel to label edges of the box, without necessarily drawing scales on them.

`In[7]:= Show[Graphics3D[Dodecahedron[ ]], Axes -> True,`
`            AxesLabel -> {"x", "y", "z"}, Ticks -> None]`

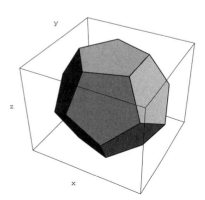

`Ticks -> None`	draw no tick marks
`Ticks -> Automatic`	place tick marks automatically
`Ticks -> {`*xticks*, *yticks*, *zticks*`}`	tick mark specifications for each axis

Settings for the `Ticks` option.

You can give the same kind of tick mark specifications in three dimensions as were described for two-dimensional graphics in Section 2.9.5.

`FaceGrids -> None`	draw no grid lines on faces
`FaceGrids -> All`	draw grid lines on all faces
`FaceGrids -> {`*face*$_1$, *face*$_2$, ... `}`	draw grid lines on the faces specified by the *face*$_i$
`FaceGrids -> {{`*face*$_1$, `{`*xgrid*$_1$, *ygrid*$_1$`}}`, ... `}`	use *xgrid*$_i$, *ygrid*$_i$ to determine where and how to draw grid lines on each face

Drawing grid lines in three dimensions.

Mathematica allows you to draw grid lines on the faces of the box that surrounds a three-dimensional object. If you set `FaceGrids -> All`, grid lines are drawn in gray on every face. By setting `FaceGrids -> {`*face*$_1$, *face*$_2$, ... `}` you can tell *Mathematica* to draw grid lines only on specific faces. Each face is specified by a list `{`*dir*$_x$, *dir*$_y$, *dir*$_z$`}`, where two of the *dir*$_i$ must be 0, and the third one is +1 or −1. For each face, you can also explicitly tell *Mathematica* where and how to draw the grid lines, using the same kind of specifications as you give for the `GridLines` option in two-dimensional graphics.

This draws grid lines only on the top
and bottom faces of the box.

In[8]:= `Show[Graphics3D[Dodecahedron[ ]],`
                    `FaceGrids -> {{0, 0, 1}, {0, 0, -1}}]`

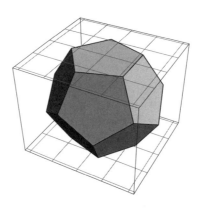

■ 2.9.14 Advanced Topic: Low-Level Graphics Rendering

All *Mathematica* graphics functions such as Show and Plot have an option DisplayFunction, which specifies how the *Mathematica* graphics objects they produce should actually be displayed. The way this works is that the setting you give for DisplayFunction is automatically applied to each graphics object that is produced.

DisplayFunction -> $DisplayFunction	
	default setting
DisplayFunction -> Identity	generate no display
DisplayFunction -> *f*	apply *f* to graphics objects to produce display

Settings for the DisplayFunction option.

Within the *Mathematica* kernel, graphics are always represented by graphics objects involving graphics primitives. When you actually render graphics, however, they must be converted to a lower-level form which can be processed by a *Mathematica* front end, such as a notebook interface, or by other external programs.

The standard low-level form that *Mathematica* uses for graphics is *PostScript*. The *Mathematica* function Display takes any *Mathematica* graphics object, and converts it into a block of PostScript code. It can then send this code to a file, an external program, or in general any output stream.

Display["*file*", *graphics*]	store the PostScript for a piece of *Mathematica* graphics in a file
Display["!*program*", *graphics*]	send the PostScript to an external program
Display[*stream*, *graphics*]	send the PostScript to an arbitrary stream
DisplayString[*graphics*]	generate a string of PostScript

Converting *Mathematica* graphics to PostScript.

The default value of the global variable $DisplayFunction is Function[Display[$Display, #]]. With this default, graphics objects produced by functions like Show and Plot are automatically converted to PostScript, and sent to whatever stream is specified by the value of the global variable $Display. The variable $Display is typically set during the initialization of a particular *Mathematica* session.

> PostScript["*string*$_1$", "*string*$_2$", ...]
> a two-dimensional graphics primitive giving PostScript code
> to include verbatim

Inserting verbatim PostScript code.

With the standard two-dimensional graphics primitives in *Mathematica* you can produce most of the effects that can be obtained with PostScript. Sometimes, however, you may find it necessary to give PostScript code directly. You can do this using the special two-dimensional graphics primitive `PostScript`.

The strings you specify in the `PostScript` primitive will be inserted verbatim into the final PostScript code generated by `Display`. You should use the `PostScript` primitive with care. For example, it is crucial that the code you give restores the PostScript stack to exactly its original state when it is finished. In addition, to specify positions of objects, you will have to understand the coordinate scaling that *Mathematica* does in its PostScript output. Finally, any PostScript primitives that you insert can only work if they are supported in the final PostScript interpreter that you use to display your graphics.

The `PostScript` primitive gives raw PostScript code which draws a Bézier curve.

```
In[1]:= Show[Graphics[ {
            PostScript[".008 setlinewidth"],
            PostScript[".1 .1 moveto"],
            PostScript["1.1 .6 -.1 .6 .9 .1 curveto stroke"] },
                Frame -> True]]
```

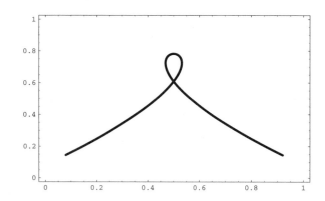

In most cases, a particular *Mathematica* graphics object always generates PostScript of a particular form. For `Graphics3D` objects, the option `RenderAll` allows you to choose between two different forms.

The main issue is how the polygons which make up three-dimensional objects should be rendered. With the default setting `RenderAll -> True`, all polygons you specify are drawn in full, but those behind are drawn first. When all the polygons are drawn, only those in front are visible. However, while an object is being drawn on a display, you can typically see the polygons inside it.

The problem with this approach is that for an object with many layers, you may generate a large amount of spurious PostScript code associated with polygons that are not visible in the final image. You can potentially avoid this by setting `RenderAll -> False`. In this case, *Mathematica* works out exactly which polygons or parts of polygons will actually be visible in your final image, and renders only these. So long as there are fairly few intersections between polygons, this approach will typically yield less PostScript code, though it may be much slower.

RenderAll -> True	draw all polygons, starting from the back (default)
RenderAll -> False	draw only those polygons or parts of polygons that are visible in the final image

An option for rendering three-dimensional pictures.

When you generate a PostScript representation of a three-dimensional object, you lose all information about the depths of the parts of the object. Sometimes, you may want to send to external programs a representation which includes depth information. Often, the original `Graphics3D` object in *Mathematica* form is then the appropriate representation. But some external programs cannot handle intersecting polygons. To deal with this, `Graphics3D` includes the option `PolygonIntersections`. If you set `PolygonIntersections -> False`, then `Show` will return not your original `Graphics3D` object, but rather one in which intersecting polygons have been broken into disjoint pieces, at least with the setting for `ViewPoint` and so on that you have given.

■ 2.9.15 Formats for Text in Graphics

+	$TextStyle = *value*	set the default text style for all graphics
+	$FormatType = *value*	set the default text format type for all graphics
+	TextStyle -> *value*	an option for the text style in a particular graphic
+	FormatType -> *value*	an option for the text format type in a particular graphic

Specifying formats for text in graphics.

Here is a plot with default settings for all formats.

`In[1]:= Plot[Sin[x]^2, {x, 0, 2 Pi}, PlotLabel->Sin[x]^2]`

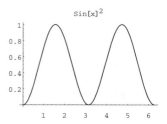

Here is the same plot, but now using a 7-point italic font.

`In[2]:= Plot[Sin[x]^2, {x, 0, 2 Pi}, PlotLabel->Sin[x]^2,`
`        TextStyle->{FontSlant->"Italic", FontSize->7}]`

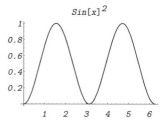

This uses `TraditionalForm` rather than `StandardForm`.

`In[3]:= Plot[Sin[x]^2, {x, 0, 2 Pi}, PlotLabel->Sin[x]^2,`
`        FormatType -> TraditionalForm]`

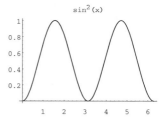

This tells *Mathematica* what default text style to use for all subsequent plots.

`In[4]:= $TextStyle = {FontFamily -> "Times", FontSize -> 7}`

`Out[4]= {FontFamily → Times, FontSize → 7}`

Now all the text is in 7-point Times font.

In[5]:= `Plot[Sin[x]^2, {x, 0, 2 Pi}, PlotLabel->Sin[x]^2]`

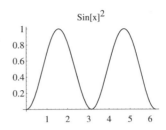

"style"	a cell style in your current notebook
`FontSize ->` *n*	the size of font to use in printer's points
`FontSlant -> "Italic"`	use an italic font
`FontWeight -> "Bold"`	use a bold font
`FontFamily ->` *"name"*	specify the name of the font family to use (e.g. `"Times"`, `"Courier"`, `"Helvetica"`)

Typical elements used in the setting for `TextStyle` or `$TextStyle`.

If you use the standard notebook front end for *Mathematica*, then you can set `$TextStyle` or `TextStyle` to be the name of a cell style in your current notebook. This tells *Mathematica* to use that cell style as the default for formatting any text that appears in graphics.

You can also explicitly specify how text should be formatted by using options such as `FontSize` and `FontFamily`. Note that `FontSize` gives the absolute size of the font to use, measured in units of printer's points, with one point being $\frac{1}{72}$ inches. If you resize a plot, the text in it will not by default change size: to get text of a different size you must explicitly specify a new value for the `FontSize` option.

`StyleForm[`*expr*`, "style"]`	output *expr* in the specified cell style
`StyleForm[`*expr*`, options]`	output *expr* using the specified font and style options
`TraditionalForm[`*expr*`]`	output *expr* in `TraditionalForm`

Changing the formats of individual pieces of output.

This outputs the plot label using the section heading style in your current notebook.

```
In[6]:= Plot[Sin[x]^2, {x, 0, 2 Pi},
            PlotLabel->StyleForm[Sin[x]^2, "Section"]]
```

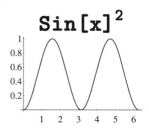

This uses the section heading style, but modified to be in italics.

```
In[7]:= Plot[Sin[x]^2, {x, 0, 2 Pi},
            PlotLabel->StyleForm[Sin[x]^2, "Section",
                FontSlant->"Italic"]]
```

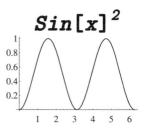

This produces TraditionalForm output, with a 12-point font.

```
In[8]:= Plot[Sin[x]^2, {x, 0, 2 Pi},
            PlotLabel->StyleForm[TraditionalForm[Sin[x]^2],
                FontSize->12]]
```

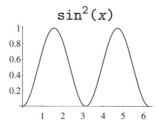

You should realize that the ability to refer to cell styles such as "Section" depends on using the standard *Mathematica* notebook front end. Even if you are just using a text-based interface to *Mathematica*, however, you can still specify formatting of text in graphics using options such as FontSize. The complete collection of options that you can use is given on page 587.

■ 2.9.16 Graphics Primitives for Text

With the `Text` graphics primitive, you can insert text at any position in two- or three-dimensional *Mathematica* graphics. Unless you explicitly specify a style or font using `StyleForm`, the text will be given in your current default style.

`Text[`*expr*`, {`*x*`, `*y*`}]`	text centered at the point {*x*, *y*}
`Text[`*expr*`, {`*x*`, `*y*`}, {-1, 0}]`	text with its left-hand end at {*x*, *y*}
`Text[`*expr*`, {`*x*`, `*y*`}, {1, 0}]`	right-hand end at {*x*, *y*}
`Text[`*expr*`, {`*x*`, `*y*`}, {0, -1}]`	centered above {*x*, *y*}
`Text[`*expr*`, {`*x*`, `*y*`}, {0, 1}]`	centered below {*x*, *y*}
`Text[`*expr*`, {`*x*`, `*y*`}, {`*dx*`, `*dy*`}]`	text positioned so that {*x*, *y*} is at relative coordinates {*dx*, *dy*} within the box that bounds the text
`Text[`*expr*`, {`*x*`, `*y*`}, {`*dx*`, `*dy*`}, {0, 1}]`	text oriented vertically to read from bottom to top
`Text[`*expr*`, {`*x*`, `*y*`}, {`*dx*`, `*dy*`}, {0, -1}]`	text that reads from top to bottom
`Text[`*expr*`, {`*x*`, `*y*`}, {`*dx*`, `*dy*`}, {-1, 0}]`	text that is upside-down

Two-dimensional text.

This generates five pieces of text, and displays them in a plot.

```
In[1]:= Show[Graphics[
            Table[ Text[Expand[(1 + x)^n], {n, n}], {n, 5} ] ],
            PlotRange -> All]
```

$$1 + 5x + 10x^2 + 10x^3 + 5x^4 + x^5$$

$$1 + 4x + 6x^2 + 4x^3 + x^4$$

$$1 + 3x + 3x^2 + x^3$$

$$1 + 2x + x^2$$

$$1 + x$$

Here is some vertically oriented text with its left-hand side at the point {2, 2}.

```
In[2]:= Show[Graphics[Text[
            StyleForm["Some text", FontSize->14, FontWeight->"Bold"],
                {2, 2}, {-1, 0}, {0, 1}]], Frame -> True]
```

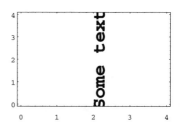

When you specify an offset for text, the relative coordinates that are used are taken to run from -1 to 1 in each direction across the box that bounds the text. The point {0, 0} in this coordinate system is defined to be center of the text. Note that the offsets you specify need not lie in the range -1 to 1.

Note that you can specify the color of a piece of text by preceding the Text graphics primitive with an appropriate RGBColor or other graphics directive.

Text[*expr*, {*x*, *y*, *z*}]	text centered at the point {*x*, *y*, *z*}
Text[*expr*, {*x*, *y*, *z*}, {*sdx*, *sdy*}]	
	text with a two-dimensional offset

Three-dimensional text.

This loads a package containing definitions of polyhedra.

```
In[3]:= <<Graphics`Polyhedra`
```

This puts text at the specified position in three dimensions.

```
In[4]:= Show[Graphics3D[{Dodecahedron[ ],
            Text["a point", {2, 2, 2}, {1, 1}]}]]
```

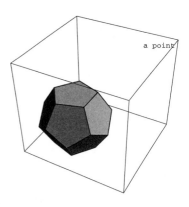

Note that when you use text in three-dimensional graphics, *Mathematica* assumes that the text is never hidden by any polygons or other objects.

option name	default value	
+ Background	None	background color
+ TextStyle	{}	style or font specification
+ FormatType	StandardForm	format type

Options for Text.

By default the text is just put straight on top of whatever graphics have already been drawn.

```
In[5]:= Show[Graphics[{{GrayLevel[0.5],
              Rectangle[{0, 0}, {1, 1}]},
           Text["Some text", {0.5, 0.5}]}]]
```

Now there is a rectangle with the background color of the whole plot enclosing the text.

```
In[6]:= Show[Graphics[{{GrayLevel[0.5],
              Rectangle[{0, 0}, {1, 1}]},
           Text["Some text", {0.5, 0.5},
              Background->Automatic]}]]
```

■ 2.9.17 Advanced Topic: Color Output

Monochrome displays	gray levels
Color displays	red, green and blue mixtures
Color printing	cyan, magenta, yellow and black mixtures

Specifications of color for different kinds of output devices.

When you generate graphics output in *Mathematica*, there are different specifications of color which are natural for different kinds of output devices. Sometimes output devices may automatically convert from one form of color specification to another. But *Mathematica* provides graphics directives which allow you directly to produce color specifications appropriate for particular devices.

GrayLevel[*i*]	gray level (setgray in PostScript)
RGBColor[*r*, *g*, *b*]	red, green and blue components for a display (setrgbcolor)
Hue[*h*, *s*, *b*]	hue, saturation and brightness components for a display (setrgbcolor)
CMYKColor[*c*, *m*, *y*, *k*]	cyan, magenta, yellow and black components for four-color process printing (setcmykcolor)

Color directives in *Mathematica*.

Each color directive in *Mathematica* yields a definite color directive in the PostScript code that *Mathematica* sends to your output device. Thus, for example, the RGBColor directive in *Mathematica* yields setrgbcolor in PostScript. The final treatment of the PostScript color directives is determined by your output device, and the PostScript interpreter that is used.

Nevertheless, in most cases, the parameters specified in the *Mathematica* color directives will be used fairly directly to set the intensities or densities of the components of the color output.

When this is done, it is important to realize that a given set of parameters in a *Mathematica* color directive may yield different perceived colors on different output devices. For example, the actual intensities of red, green and blue components will often differ between different color displays even when the settings for these components are the same. Such differences also occur when the brightness or contrast of a particular color display is changed.

In addition, you should realize that the complete "gamut" of colors that you can produce by varying parameters on a particular output device is smaller, often substantially so, than the gamut of colors which can be perceived by the human visual system. Even though the space of colors that we can perceive can be described with three parameters, it is not possible to reach all parts of this space with mixtures of a fixed number of "primary colors".

Different choices of primary colors are typically made for different types of output devices. Color displays, which work with emitted or transmitted light, typically use red, green and blue primary colors. However, color printing, which works with reflected light, typically uses cyan, magenta, yellow and black as primary colors. When a color image is printed, four separate passes are typically made, each time laying down one of these primary colors.

Thus, while RGBColor and Hue are natural color specifications for color displays, CMYKColor is the natural specification for color printing.

By default, *Mathematica* takes whatever color specifications you give, and uses them directly. The option ColorOutput, however, allows you to make *Mathematica* always convert the color specifications you give to ones appropriate for a particular kind of output device.

ColorOutput -> Automatic	use color specifications as given (default)
ColorOutput -> None	convert to monochrome
ColorOutput -> GrayLevel	convert all color specifications to gray levels
ColorOutput -> RGBColor	convert to RGBColor form
ColorOutput -> CMYKColor	convert to CMYKColor form
ColorOutput -> f	apply f to each color directive

Color output conversions.

One of the most complicated issues in color output is performing the "color separation" necessary to take a color specified using red, green and blue primaries, and render the color using cyan, magenta, yellow and black printing inks. *Mathematica* has a built-in algorithm for doing this conversion. The algorithm is based on an approximation to typical monitor colors and the standard set of four-color process printing inks. Note that the colors of these printing inks are not even close to complementary to typical monitor colors, and the actual transformation is quite nonlinear.

While *Mathematica* has built-in capabilities for various color conversions, you can also specify your own color conversions using ColorOutput -> f. With this option setting, the function f is automatically applied to each color directive generated by *Mathematica*.

Note that while any of the color directives given above can be used in setting up graphics objects, simulated lighting calculations in *Mathematica* are always done using RGBColor, and so all color directives are automatically converted to this form when simulated lighting is used.

This defines a transformation on RGBColor objects, which extracts the red component, and squares it.

```
In[1]:= red[RGBColor[r_, g_, b_]] = GrayLevel[r^2]
Out[1]= GrayLevel[r²]
```

This specifies that red should simply square any GrayLevel specification.

```
In[2]:= red[GrayLevel[g_]] = GrayLevel[g^2]
Out[2]= GrayLevel[g²]
```

This plots the squared red component, rather than using the usual transformation from color to black and white.

In[3]:= **Plot3D[Sin[x + y], {x, -3, 3}, {y, -3, 3},
                    ColorOutput -> red]**

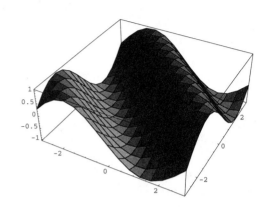

Note that if you give your own ColorOutput transformation, you must specify how the transformation acts on every color directive that arises in the image you are producing. For three-dimensional plots shaded with simulated lighting, you must typically specify the transformation at least for RGBColor and GrayLevel.

■ 2.9.18 The Representation of Sound

Section 1.9.13 described how you can take functions and lists of data and produce sounds from them. This subsection discusses how sounds are represented in *Mathematica*.

Mathematica treats sounds much like graphics. In fact, *Mathematica* allows you to combine graphics with sound to create pictures with "sound tracks".

In analogy with graphics, sounds in *Mathematica* are represented by symbolic sound objects. The sound objects have head Sound, and contain a list of sound primitives, which represent sounds to be played in sequence.

Sound[{s_1, s_2, ... }]   a sound object containing a list of sound primitives

The structure of a sound object.

The functions Play and ListPlay discussed in Section 1.9.13 return Sound objects.

Play returns a Sound object. On appropriate computer systems, it also produces sound.

In[1]:= **Play[Sin[300 t + 2 Sin[400 t]], {t, 0, 2}]**

Out[1]= -Sound-

The Sound object contains a SampledSoundFunction primitive which uses a compiled function to generate amplitude samples for the sound.

```
In[2]:= Short[ InputForm[%] ]

Out[2]//Short= Sound[SampledSoundFunction[<<3>>]]
```

SampledSoundList[{a_1, a_2, ... }, r]	a sound with a sequence of amplitude levels, sampled at rate r
SampledSoundFunction[f, n, r]	a sound whose amplitude levels sampled at rate r are found by applying the function f to n successive integers

Mathematica sound primitives.

At the lowest level, all sounds in *Mathematica* are represented as a sequence of amplitude samples. In SampledSoundList, these amplitude samples are given explicitly in a list. In SampledSoundFunction, however, they are generated when the sound is output, by applying the specified function to a sequence of integer arguments. In both cases, all amplitude values obtained must be between -1 and 1.

ListPlay generates SampledSoundList primitives, while Play generates SampledSoundFunction primitives. With the default option setting Compiled -> True, Play will produce a SampledSoundFunction object containing a CompiledFunction.

Once you have generated a Sound object containing various sound primitives, you must then output it as a sound. Much as with graphics, the basic scheme is to take the *Mathematica* representation of the sound, and convert it to a lower-level form that can be handled by an external program, such as a *Mathematica* front end.

The low-level representation of sound used by *Mathematica* consists of a sequence of hexadecimal numbers specifying amplitude levels. Within *Mathematica*, amplitude levels are given as approximate real numbers between -1 and 1. In producing the low-level form, the amplitude levels are "quantized". You can use the option SampleDepth to specify how many bits should be used for each sample. The default is SampleDepth -> 8, which yields 256 possible amplitude levels, sufficient for most purposes.

You can use the option SampleDepth in any of the functions Play, ListPlay and PlaySound. In sound primitives, you can specify the sample depth by replacing the sample rate argument by the list {*rate*, *depth*}.

Since graphics and sound can be combined in *Mathematica*, their low-level representations must not conflict. As discussed in Section 2.9.14, all graphics in *Mathematica* are generated in the PostScript language. Sounds are also generated as a special PostScript function, which can be ignored by PostScript interpreters on devices which do not support sound output.

Display[*stream*, *sound*]   output sound to a stream

Display[*stream*, {*graphics*, *sound*}]   output graphics and sound to a stream

Sending sound to a stream.

Mathematica uses the same function Display to output sound, graphics, and combinations of the two.

In Play, ListPlay and Sound, the option DisplayFunction specifies how the sound should ultimately be output. The default for this option is the global variable $SoundDisplayFunction. Typically, this is set to an appropriate call to Display.

2.10 Manipulating Notebooks

+■ 2.10.1 Cells as *Mathematica* Expressions

Like other objects in *Mathematica*, the cells in a notebook, and in fact the whole notebook itself, are all ultimately represented as *Mathematica* expressions. With the standard notebook front end, you can use the command Show Expression to see the text of the *Mathematica* expression that corresponds to any particular cell.

Show Expression menu item	toggle between displayed form and underlying *Mathematica* expression
CTRL*** or CTRL8 (between existing cells)	put up a dialog box to allow input of a cell in *Mathematica* expression form

Handling Cell expressions in the notebook front end.

Here is a cell displayed in its usual way in the front end.

> This is a text cell.

Here is the underlying *Mathematica* expression that corresponds to the cell.

> Cell["This is a text cell.", "Text"]

Cell[*contents*, "*style*"]	a cell with a specific style
Cell[*contents*, "*style*", *options*]	a cell with additional options specified

Mathematica expressions corresponding to cells in notebooks.

Within a given notebook, there is always a collection of *styles* that can be used to determine the appearance and behavior of cells. Typically the styles are named so as to reflect what role cells which have them will play in the notebook.

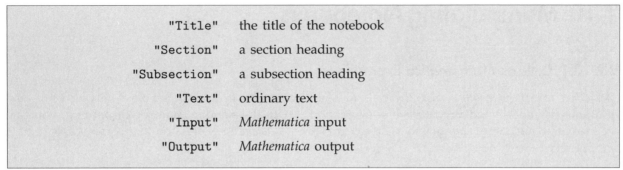

"Title"	the title of the notebook
"Section"	a section heading
"Subsection"	a subsection heading
"Text"	ordinary text
"Input"	*Mathematica* input
"Output"	*Mathematica* output

Some typical cell styles defined in notebooks.

Here are several cells in different styles.

■ **This is in Section style.**

This is in Text style.

      This is in Input style.

Here are the expressions that correspond to these cells.

```
Cell["This is in Section style.", "Section"]
Cell["This is in Text style.", "Text"]
Cell["This is in Input style.", "Input"]
```

A particular style such as "Section" or "Text" defines various settings for the options associated with a cell. You can override these settings by explicitly setting options within a specific cell.

Here is the expression for a cell in which options are set to use a gray background and to put a frame around the cell.

```
Cell["This is some text.", "Text", CellFrame->True,
  Background->GrayLevel[.8]]
```

This is how the cell looks in a notebook.

This is some text.

option	default value	
CellFrame	False	whether to draw a frame around the cell
Background	GrayLevel[1]	what color to draw the background for the cell
Editable	True	whether to allow the contents of the cell to be edited
TextAlignment	Left	how to align text in the cell
FontSize	12	the point size of the font for text
CellTags	{ }	tags to be associated with the cell

A few of the large number of possible options for cells.

The standard notebook front end for *Mathematica* provides several ways to change the options of a cell. In simple cases, such as changing the size or color of text, there will often be a specific menu item for the purpose. But in general you can use the *option inspector* that is built into the front end. This is typically accessed using the Option Inspector menu item in the Format menu.

- ■ Change settings for specific options with menus.
- ■ Look at and modify all options with the option inspector.
- ■ Edit the textual form of the expression corresponding to the cell.

- ■ Change the settings for all cells with a particular style.

Ways to manipulate cells in the front end.

Sometimes you will want just to change the options associated with a specific cell. But often you may want to change the options associated with all cells in your notebook that have a particular style. You can do this by using the Edit Style Sheet command in the front end to open up the style sheet associated with your notebook, and then modifying the options for the cells in this style sheet that represent the style you want to change.

`CellPrint[Cell[... ]]`	insert a cell into your currently selected notebook
`CellPrint[{Cell[... ], Cell[... ], ... }]`	insert a sequence of cells into your currently selected notebook

Inserting cells into a notebook.

This inserts a section cell into the current notebook.

In[1]:= `CellPrint[Cell["The heading", "Section"]]`

■ **The heading**

This inserts a text cell with a frame around it.

In[2]:= `CellPrint[Cell["Some text", "Text", CellFrame->True]]`

■ **The heading**

Some text

CellPrint allows you to take a raw `Cell` expression and insert it into your current notebook. Sometimes, however, you may find it more convenient to give an ordinary *Mathematica* expression, and then have *Mathematica* convert it into a `Cell` of a certain style, and insert this cell into a notebook. You can do this using the function `StylePrint`.

`StylePrint[`*expr*`, "`*style*`"]`	create a new cell of the specified style, and write *expr* into it
`StylePrint[`*contents*`, "`*style*`", `*options*`]`	use the specified options for the new cell

Writing expressions into cells with specified styles.

This inserts a cell in section style into your current notebook.

In[3]:= `StylePrint["The heading", "Section"]`

■ **The heading**

This creates several cells in output style.

$In[4]:=$ `Do[StylePrint[Factor[x^i - 1], "Output"], {i, 7, 10}]`

> **■ The heading**
>
> $(-1+x)(1+x+x^2+x^3+x^4+x^5+x^6)$
>
> $(-1+x)(1+x)(1+x^2)(1+x^4)$
>
> $(-1+x)(1+x+x^2)(1+x^3+x^6)$
>
> $(-1+x)(1+x)(1-x+x^2-x^3+x^4)(1+x+x^2+x^3+x^4)$

You can use any cell options in StylePrint.

$In[5]:=$ `StylePrint["Another heading", "Section", CellFrame->True, FontSize->28]`

> **■ The heading**
>
> $(-1+x)(1+x+x^2+x^3+x^4+x^5+x^6)$
>
> $(-1+x)(1+x)(1+x^2)(1+x^4)$
>
> $(-1+x)(1+x+x^2)(1+x^3+x^6)$
>
> $(-1+x)(1+x)(1-x+x^2-x^3+x^4)(1+x+x^2+x^3+x^4)$
>
> **■ Another heading**

CellPrint and StylePrint provide simple ways to modify open notebooks in the front end from within the kernel. Later in this section we will discuss more sophisticated and flexible ways to do this.

■ 2.10.2 Notebooks as *Mathematica* Expressions

Notebook[{*cell*$_1$, *cell*$_2$, ... }]	a notebook containing a sequence of cells
Notebook[*cells*, *options*]	a notebook with options specified

Expressions corresponding to notebooks.

Here is a simple *Mathematica* notebook.

> **■ Section heading**
>
> Some text.
>
> More text.

Here is the expression that corresponds
to this notebook.

```
Notebook[{
    Cell["Section heading", "Section"],
    Cell["Some text.", "Text"],
    Cell["More text.", "Text"]}]
```

Just like individual cells, notebooks in *Mathematica* can also have options. You can look at and modify these options using the options inspector in the standard notebook front end.

option	default value	
WindowSize	$\{nx, ny\}$	the size in pixels of the window used to display the notebook
WindowFloating	False	whether the window should float on top of others
WindowToolbars	{ }	what toolbars to include at the top of the window
ShowPageBreaks	False	whether to show where page breaks would occur if the notebook were printed
CellGrouping	Automatic	how to group cells in the notebook
Evaluator	"Local"	what kernel should be used to do evaluations in the notebook

A few of the large number of possible options for notebooks.

In addition to notebook options, you can also set any cell option at the notebook level. Doing this tells *Mathematica* to use that option setting as the default for all the cells in the notebook. You can override the default by explicitly setting the options within a particular cell.

Here is the expression corresponding to
a notebook with a ruler displayed in
the toolbar at the top of the window.

```
Notebook[{
    Cell["Section heading", "Section"],
    Cell["Some text.", "Text"]},
      WindowToolbars->{"RulerBar"}]
```

This is what the notebook looks like in
the front end.

This sets the default background color for all cells in the notebook.

```
Notebook[{
    Cell["Section heading", "Section"],
    Cell["Some text.", "Text"]},
        Background->GrayLevel[.7]]
```

Now each cell has a gray background.

■ Section heading

Some text.

If you go outside of *Mathematica* and look at the raw text of the file that corresponds to a *Mathematica* notebook, you will find that what is in the file is just the textual form of the expression that represents the notebook. One way to create a *Mathematica* notebook is therefore to construct an appropriate expression and put it in a file.

In notebook files that are written out by *Mathematica*, some additional information is typically included to make it faster for *Mathematica* to read the file in again. The information is enclosed in *Mathematica* comments indicated by (∗ ... ∗) so that it does not affect the actual expression stored in the file.

NotebookOpen["*file*.nb"]	open a notebook file in the front end
NotebookPut[*expr*]	create a notebook corresponding to *expr* in the front end
NotebookGet[*obj*]	get the expression corresponding to an open notebook in the front end

Setting up notebooks in the front end from the kernel.

This writes a notebook expression out to the file `sample.nb`.

```
In[1]:= Notebook[{Cell["Section heading", "Section"],
            Cell["Some text.", "Text"]}] >> "sample.nb"
```

This reads the notebook expression back from the file.

```
In[2]:= <<sample.nb
Out[2]= Notebook[{Cell[Section heading, Section],
            Cell[Some text., Text]}]
```

This opens `sample.nb` as a notebook in the front end.

```
In[3]:= NotebookOpen["sample.nb"]
```

■ Section heading

Some text.

Once you have set up a notebook in the front end using NotebookOpen, you can then manipulate the notebook interactively just as you would any other notebook. But in order to use NotebookOpen, you have to explicitly have a notebook expression in a file. With `NotebookPut`, however, you can take a notebook expression that you have created in the kernel, and immediately display it as a notebook in the front end.

Here is a notebook expression in the kernel.

```
In[4]:= Notebook[{Cell["Section heading", "Section"],
            Cell["Some text.", "Text"]}]

Out[4]= Notebook[{Cell[Section heading, Section],
            Cell[Some text., Text]}]
```

This uses the expression to set up a notebook in the front end.

```
In[5]:= NotebookPut[%]
```

> ■ **Section heading**
>
> Some text.

```
Out[5]= -NotebookObject-
```

You can use `NotebookGet` to get the notebook corresponding to a particular `NotebookObject` back into the kernel.

```
In[6]:= NotebookGet[%]
Out[6]= Notebook[{Cell[CellGroupData[
            {Cell[TextData[heading Section], Section],
            Cell[TextData[Some text.], Text]},
            Open]]}]
```

⁺■ 2.10.3 Manipulating Notebooks from the Kernel

If you want to do simple operations on *Mathematica* notebooks, then you will usually find it convenient just to use the interactive capabilities of the standard *Mathematica* front end. But if you want to do more complicated and systematic operations, then you will often find it better to use the kernel.

Notebooks[ ]	a list of all your open notebooks
Notebooks["*name*"]	a list of all open notebooks with the specified name
SelectedNotebook[ ]	the notebook that is currently selected
InputNotebook[ ]	the notebook into which typed input will go
EvaluationNotebook[ ]	the notebook in which this function is being evaluated
ButtonNotebook[ ]	the notebook containing the button (if any) which initiated this evaluation

Functions that give the notebook objects corresponding to particular notebooks.

Within the *Mathematica* kernel, notebooks that you have open in the front end are referred to by *notebook objects* of the form `NotebookObject[fe, id]`. The first argument of `NotebookObject` specifies the `FrontEndObject` for the front end in which the notebook resides, while the second argument gives a unique serial number for the notebook.

Here is a notebook set to be the currently selected one in the front end.	▪ **First Heading** ⌐ ▪ **Second Heading** ⌐
This gives the notebook object corresponding to the selected notebook in the front end.	`In[1]:= SelectedNotebook[ ]` `Out[1]= -NotebookObject-`

This gets the expression corresponding to the selected notebook into the kernel.	`In[2]:= NotebookGet[%]`
	`Out[2]= Notebook[`
	`        {Cell[TextData[FirstHeading], Section],`
	`         Cell[TextData[HeadingSecond], Section]}]`

This replaces every occurrence of the string "Section" by "Text".	`In[3]:= % /. "Section" -> "Text"`
	`Out[3]= Notebook[{Cell[TextData[FirstHeading], Text],`
	`         Cell[TextData[HeadingSecond], Text]}]`

This replaces the currently selected notebook by the modified form.	`In[4]:= NotebookPut[%, SelectedNotebook[ ]]` First Heading ⌐ Second Heading ⌐

`NotebookGet[obj]`	get the notebook expression corresponding to the notebook object *obj*
`NotebookPut[expr, obj]`	make *expr* the expression corresponding to the notebook object *obj*
`NotebookPut[expr]`	make *expr* the expression corresponding to the currently selected notebook

Exchanging whole notebook expressions between the kernel and front end.

If you want to do extensive manipulations on a particular notebook you will usually find it convenient to use `NotebookGet` to get the whole notebook into the kernel as a single expression. But if instead you want to do a sequence of small operations on a notebook, then it is often better to leave the notebook in the front end, and then to send specific commands from the kernel to the front end to tell it what operations to do.

Mathematica is set up so that anything you can do interactively to a notebook in the front end you can also do by sending appropriate commands to the front end from the kernel.

Options[*obj*]	give a list of all options set for the notebook corresponding to notebook object *obj*
Options[*obj, option*]	give the value of a specific option
FullOptions[*obj, option*]	give explicit option values even when the actual setting is Automatic
SetOptions[*obj, option->value*]	set the value of an option

Finding and setting options for notebooks.

This gives the setting of the WindowSize option for your currently selected notebook.

In[5]:= **Options[SelectedNotebook[ ], WindowSize]**

Out[5]= {WindowSize → {520., 600.}}

This changes the size of the currently selected notebook on the screen.

In[6]:= **SetOptions[SelectedNotebook[ ], WindowSize -> {250, 100}]**

Out[6]= {WindowSize → {250., 100.}}

Within any open notebook, the front end always maintains a *current selection*. The selection can consist for example of a region of text within a cell or of a complete cell. Usually the selection is indicated on the screen by some form of highlighting. The selection can also be between two characters of text, or between two cells, in which case it is usually indicated on the screen by a vertical or horizontal insertion bar.

You can modify the current selection in an open notebook by issuing commands from the kernel.

`SelectionMove[`*obj*`, Next, `*unit*`]`	move the current selection to make it be the next unit of the specified type
`SelectionMove[`*obj*`, Previous, `*unit*`]`	move to the previous unit
`SelectionMove[`*obj*`, After, `*unit*`]`	move to just after the end of the present unit of the specified unit
`SelectionMove[`*obj*`, Before, `*unit*`]`	move to just before the beginning of the present unit
`SelectionMove[`*obj*`, All, `*unit*`]`	extend the current selection to cover the whole unit of the specified type

Moving the current selection in a notebook.

`Character`	individual character
`Word`	word or other token
`Expression`	complete subexpression
`TextLine`	line of text
`TextParagraph`	paragraph of text
`CellContents`	the contents of the cell
`Cell`	complete cell
`CellGroup`	cell group
`EvaluationCell`	cell associated with the current evaluation
`ButtonCell`	cell associated with any button that initiated the evaluation
`GeneratedCell`	cell generated by the current evaluation
`Notebook`	complete notebook

Units used in specifying selections.

Here is a simple notebook.

> ■ **Here is a first cell.** ⌉
>
> ■ **Here is a second one.** ⌉

This sets nb to be the notebook object corresponding to the currently selected notebook.

In[7]:= **nb = SelectedNotebook[ ];**

This moves the current selection within the notebook to be the next word.

In[8]:= **SelectionMove[nb, Next, Word]**

> ■ **Here is a first cell.** ⌉
>
> ■ **Here is a second one.** ⌉

This extends the selection to the complete first cell.

In[9]:= **SelectionMove[nb, All, Cell]**

> ■ **Here is a first cell.** ▮
>
> ■ **Here is a second one.** ⌉

This puts the selection at the end of the whole notebook.

In[10]:= **SelectionMove[nb, After, Notebook]**

> ■ **Here is a first cell.** ⌉
>
> ■ **Here is a second one.** ⌉

NotebookFind[*obj*, *data*]	move the current selection to the next occurrence of the specified data in a notebook
NotebookFind[*obj*, *data*, Previous]	move to the previous occurrence
NotebookFind[*obj*, *data*, All]	make the current selection cover all occurrences
NotebookFind[*obj*, *data*, *dir*, *elems*]	search in the specified elements of each cell, going in direction *dir*
NotebookFind[*obj*, "*text*", IgnoreCase->True]	do not distinguish upper- and lower-case letters in text

Searching the contents of a notebook.

This moves the current selection to the position of the previous occurrence of the word cell.

In[11]:= **NotebookFind[nb, "cell", Previous]**

■ **Here is a first cell.**

■ **Here is a second one.**

Out[11]= NotebookSelection[-NotebookObject-]

The letter α does not appear in the current notebook, so $Failed is returned, and the selection is not moved.

In[12]:= **NotebookFind[nb, "\[Alpha]", Next]**

■ **Here is a first cell.**

■ **Here is a second one.**

Out[12]= $Failed

`CellContents`	contents of each cell
`CellStyle`	the name of the style for each cell
`CellLabel`	the label for each cell
`CellTags`	tags associated with each cell
$\{elem_1, elem_2, \dots\}$	several kinds of elements

Possible elements of cells to be searched by `NotebookFind`.

In setting up large notebooks, it is often convenient to insert tags which are not usually displayed, but which mark particular cells in such a way that they can be found using `NotebookFind`. You can set up tags for cells either interactively in the front end, or by explicitly setting the `CellTags` option for a cell.

`NotebookLocate["`*tag*`"]`	go to the next cell with the specified tag in the current notebook
`NotebookLocate[{"`*file*`", "`*tag*`"}]`	
	open another notebook if necessary

Globally locating cells in notebooks.

`NotebookLocate` is the underlying function that *Mathematica* calls when you follow a hyperlink in a notebook. The menu item Create Hyperlink sets up the appropriate `NotebookLocate` as part of the script for a particular hyperlink button.

`NotebookWrite[`*obj*`, `*data*`]`	write *data* into a notebook at the current selection
`NotebookApply[`*obj*`, `*data*`]`	write *data* into a notebook, inserting the current selection in place of the first ■ that appears in *data*
`NotebookDelete[`*obj*`]`	delete whatever is currently selected in a notebook
`NotebookRead[`*obj*`]`	get the expression that corresponds to the current selection in a notebook

Writing and reading in notebooks.

`NotebookWrite[`*obj*`, `*data*`]` is similar to a Paste operation in the front end: it replaces the current selection in your notebook by *data*. If the current selection is a cell `NotebookWrite[`*obj*`, `*data*`]` will replace the cell with *data*. If the current selection lies between two cells, however, then NotebookWrite[*obj*, *data*] will create an appropriate new cell or cells.

Here is a notebook with a word of text selected.

■ **Here is a first cell.**   ]

■ **Here is a second one.**   ]

This replaces the selected word by new text.

In[13]:= **NotebookWrite[nb, "<<inserted text>>"]**

■ **Here is a first <<inserted text>>.**   ]

■ **Here is a second one.**   ]

This moves the current selection to just after the first cell in the notebook.

In[14]:= **SelectionMove[nb, After, Cell]**

■ **Here is a first <<inserted text>>.**   ]

■ **Here is a second one.**   ]

This now inserts a text cell after the first cell in the notebook.

In[15]:= **NotebookWrite[nb,**
               Cell["This cell contains text.", "Text"]]

■ **Here is a first <<inserted text>>.**   ]
This cell contains text.   ]

■ **Here is a second one.**   ]

This makes the current selection be the next cell in the notebook.

In[16]:= **SelectionMove[nb, Next, Cell]**

■ **Here is a first <<inserted text>>.**   ]
This cell contains text.   ]

■ **Here is a second one.**

This reads the current selection, returning it as an expression in the kernel.

In[17]:= **NotebookRead[nb]**

■ **Here is a first <<inserted text>>.**

This cell contains text.

■ **Here is a second one.**

Out[17]= Cell[Here is a second one., Section]

NotebookWrite[*obj, data*] just discards the current selection and replaces it with *data*. But particularly if you are setting up palettes, it is often convenient first to modify *data* by inserting the current selection somewhere inside it. You can do this using *selection placeholders* and NotebookApply. The first time the character ■, entered as \[SelectionPlaceholder] or ⎋spl⎋, appears anywhere in *data*, NotebookApply will replace this character by the current selection.

Here is a simple notebook with the current selection being the contents of a cell.

In[18]:= **nb = SelectedNotebook[ ] ;**

Expand[(1 + x)^4]

This replaces the current selection by a string that contains a copy of its previous form.

In[19]:= **NotebookApply[nb, "x + 1/■"]**

x + 1 / Expand[(1 + x)^4]

SelectionEvaluate[*obj*]	evaluate the current selection in place
SelectionCreateCell[*obj*]	create a new cell containing just the current selection
SelectionEvaluateCreateCell[*obj*]	
	evaluate the current selection and create a new cell for the result
SelectionAnimate[*obj*]	animate graphics in the current selection
SelectionAnimate[*obj, t*]	animate graphics for *t* seconds

Operations on the current selection.

This makes the current selection be the whole cell.

In[20]:= **SelectionMove[nb, All, CellContents]**

x + 1 / Expand[(1 + x)^4]

This evaluates the current selection in place.

In[21]:= **SelectionEvaluate[nb]**

$$x + \frac{1}{1 + 4x + 6x^2 + 4x^3 + x^4}$$

SelectionEvaluate allows you to take material from a notebook and send it through the kernel for evaluation. On its own, however, SelectionEvaluate always overwrites the material you took. But by using functions like SelectionCreateCell you can maintain a record of the sequence of forms that are generated—just like in a standard *Mathematica* session.

This makes the current selection be the whole cell.

In[22]:= **SelectionMove[nb, All, Cell]**

$$x + \frac{1}{1 + 4x + 6x^2 + 4x^3 + x^4}$$

This creates a new cell, and copies the current selection into it.

In[23]:= **SelectionCreateCell[nb]**

$$x + \frac{1}{1 + 4x + 6x^2 + 4x^3 + x^4}$$

$$x + \frac{1}{1 + 4x + 6x^2 + 4x^3 + x^4}$$

This wraps Factor around the contents of the current cell.

In[24]:= **NotebookApply[nb, "Factor[■]"]**

$$x + \frac{1}{1 + 4x + 6x^2 + 4x^3 + x^4}$$

$$\text{Factor}\left[x + \frac{1}{1 + 4x + 6x^2 + 4x^3 + x^4}\right]$$

This evaluates the contents of the current cell, and creates a new cell to give the result.

In[25]:= **SelectionEvaluateCreateCell[nb]**

$$x + \frac{1}{1 + 4x + 6x^2 + 4x^3 + x^4}$$

$$\text{Factor}\left[x + \frac{1}{1 + 4x + 6x^2 + 4x^3 + x^4}\right]$$

$$\frac{1 + x + 4x^2 + 6x^3 + 4x^4 + x^5}{(1 + x)^4}$$

Functions like NotebookWrite and SelectionEvaluate by default leave the current selection just after whatever material they insert into your notebook. You can then always move the selection by explicitly using SelectionMove. But functions like NotebookWrite and SelectionEvaluate can also take an additional argument which specifies where the current selection should be left after they do their work.

NotebookWrite[*obj*, *data*, *sel*]	write *data* into a notebook, leaving the current selection as specified by *sel*
NotebookApply[*obj*, *data*, *sel*]	write *data* replacing ■ by the previous current selection, then leaving the current selection as specified by *sel*
SelectionEvaluate[*obj*, *sel*]	evaluate the current selection, making the new current selection be as specified by *sel*
SelectionCreateCell[*obj*, *sel*]	create a new cell containing just the current selection, and make the new current selection be as specified by *sel*
SelectionEvaluateCreateCell[*obj*, *sel*]	evaluate the current selection, make a new cell for the result, and make the new current selection be as specified by *sel*

Performing operations and specifying what the new current selection should be.

After	immediately after whatever material is inserted (default)
Before	immediately before whatever material is inserted
All	the inserted material itself
Placeholder	the first ■ in the inserted material
None	leave the current selection unchanged

Specifications for the new current selection.

Here is a blank notebook.	*In[26]:=* **nb = SelectedNotebook[ ] ;**
This writes 10! into the notebook, making the current selection be what was written.	*In[27]:=* **NotebookWrite[nb, "10!", All]**
	10!
This evaluates the current selection, creating a new cell for the result, and making the current selection be the whole of the result.	*In[28]:=* **SelectionEvaluateCreateCell[nb, All]**
	10! 3628800

This wraps `FactorInteger` around the current selection.

In[29]:= **NotebookApply[nb, "FactorInteger[■]", All]**

> 10!
>
> **FactorInteger[3628800]**

This evaluates the current selection, leaving the selection just before the result.

In[30]:= **SelectionEvaluate[nb, Before]**

> 10!
>
> |{{2, 8}, {3, 4}, {5, 2}, {7, 1}}

This now inserts additional text at the position of the current selection.

In[31]:= **NotebookWrite[nb, "a = "]**

> 10!
>
> a = {{2, 8}, {3, 4}, {5, 2}, {7, 1}}

`Options[`*obj, option*`]`	find the value of an option for a complete notebook
`Options[NotebookSelection[`*obj*`]], `*option*`]`	find the value for the current selection
`SetOptions[`*obj, option->value*`]`	set the value of an option for a complete notebook
`SetOptions[NotebookSelection[`*obj*`], `*option->value*`]`	set the value for the current selection

Finding and setting options for whole notebooks and for the current selection.

Make the current selection be a complete cell.

In[32]:= **SelectionMove[nb, All, Cell]**

> 10!
>
> a = {{2, 8}, {3, 4}, {5, 2}, {7, 1}}

Put a frame around the cell that is the current selection.

In[33]:= **SetOptions[NotebookSelection[nb], CellFrame->True]**

> 10!
>
> a = {{2, 8}, {3, 4}, {5, 2}, {7, 1}}

NotebookCreate[ ]	create a new notebook
NotebookCreate[*options*]	create a notebook with specified options
NotebookOpen["*name*"]	open an existing notebook
NotebookOpen["*name*", *options*]	open a notebook with specified options
SetSelectedNotebook[*obj*]	make the specified notebook the selected one
NotebookPrint[*obj*]	send a notebook to your printer
NotebookPrint[*obj*, "*file*"]	send a PostScript version of a notebook to a file
NotebookPrint[*obj*, "!*command*"]	send a PostScript version of a notebook to an external command
NotebookSave[*obj*]	save the current version of a notebook in a file
NotebookSave[*obj*, "*file*"]	save the notebook in a file with the specified name
NotebookClose[*obj*]	close a notebook

Operations on whole notebooks.

If you call NotebookCreate[ ] a new empty notebook will appear on your screen.

By executing commands like SetSelectedNotebook and NotebookOpen, you tell the *Mathematica* front end to change the windows you see. Sometimes you may want to manipulate a notebook without ever having it displayed on the screen. You can do this by using the option setting Visible->False in NotebookOpen or NotebookCreate.

■ 2.10.4 Manipulating the Front End from the Kernel

$FrontEnd	the front end currently in use
Options[$FrontEnd, *option*]	the setting for a global option in the front end
FullOptions[$FrontEnd, *option*]	the explicit setting for an option
SetOptions[$FrontEnd, *option*->value*]	reset an option in the front end

Manipulating global options in the front end.

Just like cells and notebooks, the complete *Mathematica* front end has various options, which you can look at and manipulate from the kernel.

This gives the object corresponding to
the front end currently in use.

In[1]:= **$FrontEnd**

Out[1]= FrontEndObject[LinkObject[ParentLink, 1, 1]]

This gives the current directory used
by the front end for notebook files.

In[2]:= **Options[$FrontEnd, NotebookDirectory]**

Out[2]= {NotebookDirectory → ~$}

option	default value	
NotebookDirectory	"~$"	the current directory for notebook files
NotebookPath	(system dependent)	the path to search when trying to open notebooks
Language	"English"	language for system-generated text
MessageOptions	(list of settings)	how to handle various help and warning messages

A few global options for the *Mathematica* front end.

By using NotebookWrite you can effectively input to the front end any ordinary text that you can
enter on the keyboard. FrontEndTokenExecute allows you to send from the kernel any command
that the front end can execute. These commands include both menu items and control sequences.

FrontEndTokenExecute["*name*"]	execute a named command in the front end

Executing a named command in the front end.

"Indent"	indent all selected lines by one tab
"NotebookStatisticsDialog"	display statistics about the current notebook
"OpenCloseGroup"	toggle a cell group between open and closed
"CellSplit"	split a cell in two at the current insertion point
"DuplicatePreviousInput"	create a new cell which is a duplicate of the nearest input cell above
"FindDialog"	bring up the find dialog
"ColorSelectorDialog"	bring up the color selector dialog
"GraphicsAlign"	align selected graphics
"CompleteSelection"	complete the command name that is the current selection

A few named commands that can be given to the front end. These commands usually correspond to menu items.

■ 2.10.5 Advanced Topic: Executing Notebook Commands Directly in the Front End

When you execute a command like NotebookWrite[*obj*, *data*] the actual operation of inserting data into your notebook is performed in the front end. Normally, however, the kernel is needed in order to evaluate the original command, and to construct the appropriate request to send to the front end. But it turns out that the front end is set up to execute a limited collection of commands directly, without ever involving the kernel.

NotebookWrite[*obj*, *data*]	version of NotebookWrite to be executed in the kernel
FrontEnd`NotebookWrite[*obj*, *data*]	
	version of NotebookWrite to be executed directly in the front end

Distinguishing kernel and front end versions of commands.

The basic way that *Mathematica* distinguishes between commands to be executed in the kernel and to be executed directly in the front end is by using contexts. The kernel commands are in the usual System` context, but the front end commands are in the FrontEnd` context.

FrontEndExecute[*expr*]	send *expr* to be executed in the front end

Sending an expression to be executed in the front end.

Here is a blank notebook.

This uses kernel commands to write data into the notebook.

$In[1]:=$ `NotebookWrite[SelectedNotebook[ ], "x + y + z"]`

In the kernel, these commands do absolutely nothing.

$In[2]:=$ `FrontEnd`NotebookWrite[FrontEnd`SelectedNotebook[ ], "a + b + c + d"]`

$Out[2]=$ FrontEnd`NotebookWrite[
FrontEnd`SelectedNotebook[], a + b + c + d]

If they are sent to the front end, however, they cause data to be written into the notebook.

$In[3]:=$ `FrontEndExecute[%]`

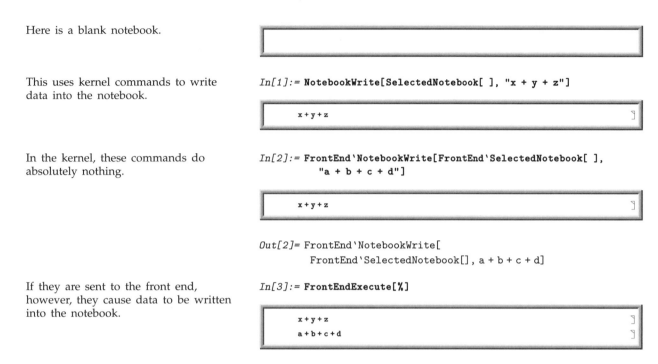

If you write sophisticated programs for manipulating notebooks, then you will have no choice but to execute these programs primarily in the kernel. But for the kinds of operations typically performed by simple buttons, you may find that it is possible to execute all the commands you need directly in the front end—without the kernel even needing to be running.

■ 2.10.6 Button Boxes and Active Elements in Notebooks

Within any cell in a notebook it is possible to set up ButtonBox objects that perform actions whenever you click on them. ButtonBox objects are the way that palette buttons, hyperlinks and other active elements are implemented in *Mathematica* notebooks.

When you first enter a ButtonBox object in a cell, it will behave just like any other expression, and by clicking on it you can select it, edit it, and so on. But if you set the Active option for the cell, say by choosing the Active item in the Cell Properties menu, then the ButtonBox will become active, and when you click on it, it will perform whatever action you have specified for it.

Here is a button.

$In[1]:=$ `ButtonBox["Expand[■]"] // DisplayForm`

$Out[1]//DisplayForm=$ Expand[■]

When the button appears in an active cell, it will paste its contents whenever you click on it.

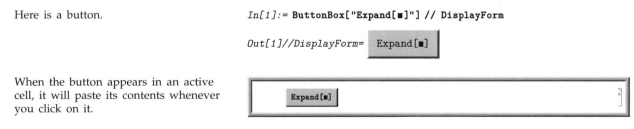

Here is a typical palette.

In the expression corresponding to the
palette each button corresponds to a
ButtonBox object.

```
Cell[BoxData[GridBox[{
    {
      ButtonBox["abc"],
      ButtonBox["xy"]}
    },
   ColumnSpacings->0]], "Input", Active->True]
```

ButtonBox[*boxes*]	a button that will paste its contents when it appears in an active cell
ButtonBox[*boxes*, Active->True]	a button that will always be active
ButtonBox[*boxes*, ButtonStyle->"*style*"]	a button whose properties are taken from the specified style

Basic ButtonBox objects.

By setting the ButtonStyle you can specify defaults both for how a button will be displayed, and
what its action will be. The notebook front end provides a number of standard ButtonStyle settings,
which you can access from the Create Button and Edit Button menu items.

"Paste"	paste the contents of the button (default)
"Evaluate"	paste then evaluate in place what has been pasted
"EvaluateCell"	paste then evaluate the whole cell
"CopyEvaluate"	copy the current selection into a new cell, then paste and evaluate in place
"CopyEvaluateCell"	copy the current selection into a new cell, then paste and evaluate the whole cell
"Hyperlink"	jump to a different location in the notebook

Standard settings for the ButtonStyle option.

Here is the expression corresponding to
a CopyEvaluateCell button.

```
Cell[BoxData[
  ButtonBox[
   RowBox[{"Expand", "[", "\[SelectionPlaceholder]", "]"}],
   ButtonStyle->"CopyEvaluateCell"]], "Input",
  Active->True]
```

This is what the button looks like.

$$\boxed{\texttt{Expand[∎]}}$$

Here is a notebook with a selection made.

$$(1+x)^6$$

This is what happens when one then clicks on the button.

$$(1+x)^6$$

In[1]:= **Expand[$(1+x)^6$]**

Out[1]= $1 + 6x + 15x^2 + 20x^3 + 15x^4 + 6x^5 + x^6$

option	default value	
ButtonFunction	(pasting function)	the function to apply when the button is clicked
ButtonSource	Automatic	where to get the first argument of the button function from
ButtonData	Null	the second argument to supply to the button function
ButtonEvaluator	None	where to send the button function for evaluation
ButtonNote	ButtonData	what to display in the window status line when the cursor is over the button

Options that affect the action of buttons.

A particular `ButtonStyle` setting will specify defaults for all other button options. Some of these options will affect the display of the button, as discussed on page 431. Others affect the action it performs.

What ultimately determines the action of a button is the setting for the `ButtonFunction` option. This setting gives the *Mathematica* function which is to be executed whenever the button is clicked. Typically this function will be a combination of various notebook manipulation commands.

Thus, for example, in its most basic form, a `Paste` button will have a `ButtonFunction` given effectively by `NotebookApply[SelectedNotebook[ ], #]&`, while a `Hyperlink` button will have a `ButtonFunction` given effectively by `NotebookLocate[#2]&`.

When a button is clicked, two arguments are supplied to its `ButtonFunction`. The first is specified by `ButtonSource`, and the second by `ButtonData`.

Typically `ButtonData` is set to be a fixed expression, defined when the button was first created. `ButtonSource`, on the other hand, usually changes with the contents of the button, or the environment in which the button appears.

`Automatic`	`ButtonData` if it is set, otherwise `ButtonContents`
`ButtonContents`	the expression displayed on the button
`ButtonData`	the setting for the `ButtonData` option
`CellContents`	the contents of the cell in which the button appears
`Cell`	the whole cell in which the button appears
`Notebook`	the whole notebook in which the button appears
n	the expression n levels up from the button in the notebook

Possible settings for the `ButtonSource` option.

For a simple `Paste` button, the setting for `ButtonSource` is typically `ButtonContents`. This means that whatever is displayed in the button will be what is passed as the first argument of the button function. The button function can then take this argument and feed it to `NotebookApply`, thereby actually pasting it into the notebook.

By using settings other than `ButtonContents` for `ButtonSource`, you can create buttons which effectively pull in various aspects of their environment for processing. Thus, for example, with the setting `ButtonSource->Cell`, the first argument to the button function will be the expression that represents the whole cell in which the button appears. By having the button function manipulate this expression you can then make the button have a global effect on the whole cell, say by restructuring it in some specified way.

`None`	the front end
`Automatic`	the current kernel
`"name"`	a kernel with the specified name

Settings for the `ButtonEvaluator` option.

Once the arguments to a `ButtonFunction` have been found, and an expression has been constructed, there is then the question of where that expression should be sent for evaluation. The `ButtonEvaluator` option for a `ButtonBox` allows you to specify this.

In general, if the expression involves a range of *Mathematica* functions, then there will be no choice but to evaluate it in an actual *Mathematica* kernel. But if the expression involves only simple notebook manipulation commands, then it may be possible to execute the expression directly in the front end, without ever involving the kernel. You can specify that this should be done by setting the option `ButtonEvaluator->None`.

`FrontEndExecute[`*expr*`]`	execute an expression in the front end
`FrontEnd`NotebookApply[`... `]`, etc.	
	front end versions of notebook commands

Expressions to be executed directly in the front end.

As discussed in the previous section, the standard notebook front end can handle only a limited set of commands, all identified as being in the `FrontEnd`` context. But these commands are sufficient to be able to implement all of the actions associated with standard button styles such as `Paste`, `EvaluateCell` and `Hyperlink`.

Note that even if an expression is sent to the front end, it will be executed only if it is wrapped in a `FrontEndExecute`.

■ 2.10.7 Advanced Topic: The Structure of Cells

`Cell[`*contents*`, "style"]`	a cell in a particular style
`Cell[`*contents*`, "style", `*options*`]`	a cell with additional options set

Expressions corresponding to cells.

Here is a notebook containing a text cell and a *Mathematica* input cell.

> Here is some ordinary text.
>
> x^{α} / y

Here are the expressions corresponding to these cells.

```
Cell["Here is some ordinary text.", "Text"]
Cell[BoxData[
  RowBox[{
    SuperscriptBox["x", "\[Alpha]"], "/", "y"}]], "Input"]
```

Here is a notebook containing a text cell with *Mathematica* input inside.

> Text with the formula xyz^{α} inside.

This is the expression corresponding to the cell. The *Mathematica* input is in a cell embedded inside the text.

```
Cell[TextData[{
 "Text with the formula ",
 Cell[BoxData[
  FormBox[
   SuperscriptBox["xyz", "\[Alpha]"], TraditionalForm]]],
 " inside."
}], "Text"]
```

"*text*"	plain text
TextData[{*text₁*, *text₂*, ... }]	text potentially in different styles, or containing cells
BoxData[*boxes*]	formatted *Mathematica* expressions
GraphicsData["*type*", *data*]	graphics or sounds
OutputFormData["*itext*", "*otext*"]	text as generated by InputForm and OutputForm
RawData["*data*"]	unformatted expressions as obtained using Show Expression
CellGroupData[{*cell₁*, *cell₂*, ... }, Open]	an open group of cells
CellGroupData[{*cell₁*, *cell₂*, ... }, Closed]	a closed group of cells
StyleData["*style*"]	a style definition cell

Expressions representing possible forms of cell contents.

+■ 2.10.8 Styles and the Inheritance of Option Settings

Global	the complete front end and all open notebooks
Notebook	the current notebook
Style	the style of the current cell
Cell	the specific current cell
Selection	a selection within a cell

The hierarchy of levels at which options can be set.

Here is a notebook containing three cells.

> ### ■ First Section
> Some text in the first section.
> Some more text in the first section.

This is what happens when the setting `CellFrame->True` is made specifically for the third cell.

> ### ■ First Section
> Some text in the first section.
> | Some more text in the first section. |

This is what happens when the setting `CellFrame->True` is made globally for the whole notebook.

This is what happens when the setting is made for the `"Section"` style.

> ### | ■ First Section |
> Some text in the first section.
> Some more text in the first section.

In the standard notebook front end, you can check and set options at any level by using the Option Inspector menu item. If you do not set an option at a particular level, then its value will always be inherited from the level above. Thus, for example, if a particular cell does not set the `CellFrame` option, then the value used will be inherited from its setting for the style of the cell or for the whole notebook that contains the cell.

As a result, if you set `CellFrame->True` at the level of a whole notebook, then all the cells in the notebook will have frames drawn around them—unless the style of a particular cell, or the cell itself, explicitly overrides this setting.

- Choose the basic default styles for a notebook
- Choose the styles for screen and printing style environments
- Edit specific styles for the notebook

Ways to set up styles in a notebook.

Depending on what you intend to use your *Mathematica* notebook for, you may want to choose different basic default styles for the notebook. In the standard notebook front end, you can do this using the Edit Style Sheet menu item.

`"Report"`	styles for everyday work and for reports
`"Tutorial"`	styles for tutorial-type material
`"Book"`	styles for books such as this one

Some typical choices of basic default styles.

With each choice of basic default styles, the styles that are provided will change. Thus, for example, only in the Book default styles is there a Box style which sets up the gray boxes used in this book.

Here is a notebook that uses Book default styles.

■**Calculus ` DiracDelta `**

This package defines the function `UnitStep` and its generalized derivative `DiracDelta`. The Dirac delta function $\delta(x)$ is not a true function in the usual mathematical sense since it is not defined for every value of x. However, it is commonly used to represent ideal distributions in problems in physics and engineering. The unit step function $\mu(x)$ may be used to represent piecewise continuous functions.

`UnitStep[x]`	unit step function with discontinuity located at $x = 0$
`DiracDelta[x]`	Dirac delta function with singularity located at $x = 0$

option	default value	
`ScreenStyleEnvironment`	`"Working"`	the style environment to use for display on the screen
`PrintingStyleEnvironment`	`"Printout"`	the style environment to use for printed output

Options for specifying style environments.

Within a particular set of basic default styles, *Mathematica* allows for two different style environments: one for display on the screen, and another for output to a printer. The existence of separate screen and printing style environments allows you to set up styles which are separately optimized both for low-resolution display on a screen, and high-resolution printing.

`"Working"`	on-screen working environment
`"Presentation"`	on-screen environment for presentations
`"Condensed"`	on-screen environment for maximum display density
`"Printout"`	paper printout environment

Some typical settings for style environments.

Here is a notebook with the usual Working screen style environment.

$$\int \frac{\log(x)}{x^3 - 1} dx$$

$$-\frac{-\log(1-x)\log(x) - \text{Li}_2(x)}{\left(1 + \sqrt[3]{-1}\right)(1 - (-1)^{2/3})} + \frac{-\log(x)\log(\sqrt[3]{-1}\,x + 1) - \text{Li}_2(-\sqrt[3]{-1}\,x)}{(1 - (-1)^{2/3})\left(\sqrt[3]{-1} + (-1)^{2/3}\right)} +$$

$$\frac{-\log(x)\log(1 - (-1)^{2/3}\,x) - \text{Li}_2((-1)^{2/3}\,x)}{\left(1 + \sqrt[3]{-1}\right)\left(-\sqrt[3]{-1} - (-1)^{2/3}\right)}$$

Here is the same notebook with the Condensed screen style environment.

$$\int \frac{\log(x)}{x^3 - 1} dx$$

$$-\frac{-\log(1-x)\log(x) - \text{Li}_2(x)}{\left(1 + \sqrt[3]{-1}\right)(1 - (-1)^{2/3})} + \frac{-\log(x)\log(\sqrt[3]{-1}\,x + 1) - \text{Li}_2(-\sqrt[3]{-1}\,x)}{(1 - (-1)^{2/3})\left(\sqrt[3]{-1} + (-1)^{2/3}\right)} +$$

$$\frac{-\log(x)\log(1 - (-1)^{2/3}\,x) - \text{Li}_2((-1)^{2/3}\,x)}{\left(1 + \sqrt[3]{-1}\right)\left(-\sqrt[3]{-1} - (-1)^{2/3}\right)}$$

The way that *Mathematica* actually sets up the definitions for styles is by using *style definition cells*. These cells can either be given in separate *style definition notebooks*, or can be included in the options of a specific notebook. In either case, you can access style definitions by using the Style Definitions menu item in the standard notebook front end.

`"name.nb"`	get definitions from the specified notebook
`{cell₁, cell₂, ... }`	get definitions from the explicit cells given

Settings for the `StyleDefinitions` option for a `Notebook`.

Here is an example of a typical style definition cell.

> ■ Prototype for style: **"Section"**:
> ## Section

This is the expression corresponding to the cell. Any cell in Section style will inherit the option settings given here.

```
Cell[StyleData["Section"], NotebookDefault,
  CellFrame->False,
  CellDingbat->"\[GraySquare]",
  CellMargins->{{22, Inherited}, {Inherited, 20}},
  CellGroupingRules->{"SectionGrouping", 30},
  PageBreakBelow->False,
  CounterIncrements->"Section",
  CounterAssignments->{{"Subsection", 0}, {"Subsubection", 0}},
  FontFamily->"Times",
  FontSize->18,
  FontWeight->"Bold"]
```

`Cell[StyleData["style"], options]`	a cell specifying option settings for a particular style
`Cell[StyleData["style", "env"], options]`	a cell specifying additional options for a particular style environment

Expressions corresponding to style definition cells.

■ 2.10.9 Options for Cells

Mathematica provides a large number of options for cells. All of these options can be accessed through the Option Inspector menu item in the front end. They can be set either directly at the level of individual cells or at a higher level, to be inherited by individual cells.

option	typical default value	
CellDingbat	""	a dingbat to use to emphasize the cell
CellFrame	False	whether to draw a frame around the cell
Background	GrayLevel[1]	the background color for the cell
ShowCellBracket	True	whether to display the cell bracket
Magnification	1	the magnification at which to display the cell
CellOpen	True	whether to display the contents of the cell

Some basic cell display options.

This creates a cell in Section style with default settings for all options.

In[1]:= `CellPrint[Cell["A Heading", "Section"]]`

■ **A Heading**

This creates a cell with dingbat and background options modified.

In[2]:= `CellPrint[Cell["A Heading", "Section",`
`        CellDingbat->"\[FilledCircle]", Background->GrayLevel[.7]]]`

option	typical default value	
CellMargins	{7, 0}, {4, 4}	outer margins in printer's points to leave around the contents of the cell
CellFrameMargins	8	margins to leave inside the cell frame
CellElementSpacings	list of rules	details of the layout of cell elements
CellBaseline	Baseline	how to align the baseline of an inline cell with text around it

Options for cell positioning.

The option `CellMargins` allow you to specify both horizontal and vertical margins to put around a cell. You can set the horizontal margins interactively by using the margin stops in the ruler displayed when you choose the Show Ruler menu item in the front end.

Whenever an option can refer to all four edges of a cell, *Mathematica* follows the convention that the setting for the option takes the form {{*left*, *right*}, {*bottom*, *top*}}. By giving nonzero values for the *top* and *bottom* elements, `CellMargins` can specify gaps to leave above and below a particular cell. The values are always taken to be in printer's points.

This leaves 50 points of space on the left of the cell, and 20 points above and below.

```
In[3]:= CellPrint[Cell["First text", "Text",
            CellMargins->{{50, 0}, {20, 20}}]]
```

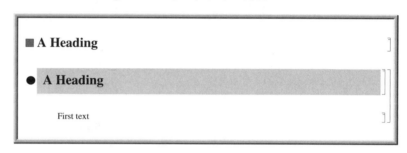

Almost every aspect of *Mathematica* notebooks can be controlled by some option or another. More detailed aspects are typically handled by "aggregate options" such as `CellElementSpacings`. The settings for these options are lists of *Mathematica* rules, which effectively give values for a sequence of suboptions. The names of these suboptions are usually strings rather than symbols.

This shows the settings for all the suboptions associated with `CellElementSpacings`.

```
In[4]:= Options[SelectedNotebook[ ], CellElementSpacings]

Out[4]= {CellElementSpacings →
            {CellMinHeight → 12., ClosedCellHeight → 19.,
             ClosedGroupTopMargin → 4.,
             GroupIconTopMargin → 3.,
             GroupIconBottomMargin → 12.}}
```

Mathematica allows you to embed cells inside pieces of text. The option `CellBaseline` determines how such "inline cells" will be aligned vertically with respect to the text around them. In direct analogy with the option `GridBaseline` for a `GridBox`, the option `CellBaseline` specifies what aspect of the cell should be considered its baseline.

Here is a cell containing an inline formula. The baseline of the formula is aligned with the baseline of the text around it.

■ the $\frac{x}{y}$ fraction

Here is a cell in which the bottom of the formula is aligned with the baseline of the text around it.

■ the $\frac{x}{y}$ fraction

This alignment is specified using the
CellBaseline->Bottom setting.

```
Cell[TextData[{
  "the ",
  Cell[BoxData[
    RowBox[{
      FractionBox["x", "y"], " "}]],
    CellBaseline->Bottom],
  "fraction "
}], "Section"]
```

option	typical default value	
CellLabel	" "	a label for a cell
ShowCellLabel	True	whether to show the label for a cell
CellLabelAutoDelete	True	whether to delete the label if the cell is modified
CellTags	{ }	tags for a cell
ShowCellTags	False	whether to show tags for a cell
ConversionRules	{ }	rules for external conversions

Options for ancillary data associated with cells.

In addition to the actual contents of a cell, it is often useful to associate various kinds of ancillary data with cells.

In a standard *Mathematica* session, cells containing successive lines of kernel input and output are given labels of the form In[n]:= and Out[n]=. The option ShowCellLabel determines whether such labels should be displayed. CellLabelAutoDelete determines whether the label on a cell should be removed if the contents of the cell are modified. Doing this ensures that In[n]:= and Out[n]= labels are only associated with unmodified pieces of kernel input and output.

Cell tags are typically used to associate keywords or other attributes with cells, that can be searched for using functions like NotebookFind. Destinations for hyperlinks in *Mathematica* notebooks are usually implemented using cell tags.

The option ConversionRules allows you to give a list containing entries such as "TeX" -> *data* which specify how the contents of a cell should be converted to external formats. This is particularly relevant if you want to keep a copy of the original form of a cell that has been converted in *Mathematica* notebook format from some external format.

option	typical default value	
Deletable	True	whether to allow a cell to be deleted interactively with the front end
Copyable	True	whether to allow a cell to be copied
Selectable	True	whether to allow the contents of a cell to be selected
Editable	True	whether to allow the contents of a cell to be edited
CellEditDuplicate	False	whether to make a copy of a cell if its contents are edited
Active	False	whether buttons in the cell are active

Options for controlling interactive operations on cells.

The options `Deletable`, `Copyable`, `Selectable` and `Editable` allow you to control what interactive operations should be allowed on cells. By setting these options to `False` at the notebook level, you can protect all the cells in a notebook.

Even if you allow a particular cell to be edited, you can set `CellEditDuplicate->True` to get *Mathematica* to make a copy of the contents of the cell before they are actually changed. Styles for cells that contain output from *Mathematica* kernel evaluations usually make use of this option.

option	typical default value	
Evaluator	"Local"	the name of the kernel to use for evaluations
Evaluatable	False	whether to allow the contents of a cell to be evaluated
CellEvaluationDuplicate	False	whether to make a copy of a cell if it is evaluated
CellAutoOverwrite	False	whether to overwrite previous output when new output is generated
GeneratedCell	False	whether this cell was generated from the kernel
InitializationCell	False	whether this cell should automatically be evaluated when the notebook is opened

Options for evaluation.

Mathematica makes it possible to specify a different evaluator for each cell in a notebook. But most often, the `Evaluator` option is set only at the notebook level, typically using the Kernel menu item in the front end.

The option `CellAutoOverwrite` is typically set to `True` for styles that represent *Mathematica* output. Doing this means that when you re-evaluate a particular piece of input, *Mathematica* will automatically delete the output that was previously generated from that input, and will overwrite it with new output.

The option `GeneratedCell` is set whenever a cell is generated by an external request to the front end rather than by an interactive operation within the front end. Thus, for example, any cell obtained as output from a kernel evaluation, or created using a function like `CellPrint` or `NotebookWrite`, will have `GeneratedCell->True`.

option	typical default value	
PageBreakAbove	Automatic	whether to put a page break just above a particular cell
PageBreakWithin	False	whether to allow a page break within a particular cell
PageBreakBelow	Automatic	whether to put a page break just below a particular cell
GroupPageBreakWithin	False	whether to allow a page break within a particular group of cells

Options for controlling page breaks when cells are printed.

When you display a notebook on the screen, you can scroll continuously through it. But if you print the notebook out, you have to decide where page breaks will occur. A setting of `Automatic` for a page break option tells *Mathematica* to make a page break if necessary; `True` specifies that a page break should always be made, while `False` specifies that it should never be.

◾ 2.10.10 Text and Font Options

option	typical default value	
PageWidth	WindowWidth	how wide to assume the page to be
TextAlignment	Left	how to align successive lines of text
TextJustification	0	how much to allow lines of text to be stretched to make them fit
ParagraphIndent	0	how many printer's points to indent the first line in each paragraph

General options for text formatting.

If you have a large block of text containing no explicit RETURN characters, then *Mathematica* will automatically break your text into a sequence of lines. The option PageWidth specifies how long each line should be allowed to be.

WindowWidth	the width of the window on the screen
PaperWidth	the width of the page as it would be printed
Infinity	an infinite width (no linebreaking)
n	explicit width given in ems

Settings for the PageWidth option.

The option TextAlignment allows you to specify how you want successive lines of text to be aligned. Since *Mathematica* normally breaks text only at space or punctuation characters, it is common to end up with lines of different lengths. Normally the variation in lengths will give your text a ragged boundary. But *Mathematica* allows you to adjust the spaces in successive lines of text so as to make the lines more nearly equal in length. The setting for TextJustification gives the fraction of extra space which *Mathematica* is allowed to add. TextJustification->1 leads to "full justification" in which all complete lines of text are adjusted to be exactly the same length.

Left	aligned on the left
Right	aligned on the right
Center	centered
x	aligned at a position x running from −1 to +1 across the page

Settings for the `TextAlignment` option.

Here is text with
`TextAlignment->Left` and
`TextJustification->0`.

> Like other objects in *Mathematica*, the cells in a notebook, and in fact the whole notebook itself, are all ultimately represented as *Mathematica* expressions. With the standard notebook front end, you can use the command Show Expression to see the text of the *Mathematica* expression that corresponds to any particular cell.

With `TextAlignment->Center` the text
is centered.

> Like other objects in *Mathematica*, the cells in a notebook, and in fact the whole notebook itself, are all ultimately represented as *Mathematica* expressions. With the standard notebook front end, you can use the command Show Expression to see the text of the *Mathematica* expression that corresponds to any particular cell.

`TextJustification->1` adjusts word
spacing so that both the left and right
edges line up.

> Like other objects in *Mathematica*, the cells in a notebook, and in fact the whole notebook itself, are all ultimately represented as *Mathematica* expressions. With the standard notebook front end, you can use the command Show Expression to see the text of the *Mathematica* expression that corresponds to any particular cell.

`TextJustification->0.5` reduces the
degree of raggedness, but does not
force the left and right edges to be
precisely lined up.

> Like other objects in *Mathematica*, the cells in a notebook, and in fact the whole notebook itself, are all ultimately represented as *Mathematica* expressions. With the standard notebook front end, you can use the command Show Expression to see the text of the *Mathematica* expression that corresponds to any particular cell.

When you enter a block of text in a *Mathematica* notebook, *Mathematica* will treat any explicit Return characters that you type as paragraph breaks. The option `ParagraphIndent` allows you to specify how much you want to indent the first line in each paragraph. By giving a negative setting for `ParagraphIndent`, you can make the first line stick out to the left.

LineSpacing->{c, 0}	leave space so that the total height of each line is c times the height of its contents
LineSpacing->{0, n}	make the total height of each line exactly n printer's points
LineSpacing->{c, n}	make the total height c times the height of the contents plus n printer's points
ParagraphSpacing->{c, 0}	leave an extra space of c times the height of the font before the beginning of each paragraph
ParagraphSpacing->{0, n}	leave an extra space of exactly n printer's points before the beginning of each paragraph
ParagraphSpacing->{c, n}	leave an extra space of c times the height of the font plus n printer's points

Options for spacing between lines of text.

Here is some text with the default setting LineSpacing->{1, 1}, which inserts just 1 printer's point of extra space between successive lines.

> Like other objects in *Mathematica*, the cells in a notebook, and in fact the whole notebook itself, are all ultimately represented as *Mathematica* expressions. With the standard notebook front end, you can use the command Show Expression to see the text of the *Mathematica* expression that corresponds to any particular cell.

With LineSpacing->{1, 5} the text is "looser".

> Like other objects in *Mathematica*, the cells in a notebook, and in fact the whole notebook itself, are all ultimately represented as *Mathematica* expressions. With the standard notebook front end, you can use the command Show Expression to see the text of the *Mathematica* expression that corresponds to any particular cell.

LineSpacing->{2, 0} makes the text double-spaced.

> Like other objects in *Mathematica*, the cells in a notebook, and in fact the whole notebook itself, are all ultimately represented as *Mathematica* expressions. With the standard notebook front end, you can use the command Show Expression to see the text of the *Mathematica* expression that corresponds to any particular cell.

With LineSpacing->{1, -2} the text is tight.

> Like other objects in *Mathematica*, the cells in a notebook, and in fact the whole notebook itself, are all ultimately represented as *Mathematica* expressions. With the standard notebook front end, you can use the command Show Expression to see the text of the *Mathematica* expression that corresponds to any particular cell.

option	typical default value	
FontFamily	"Courier"	the family of font to use
FontSubstitutions	{ }	a list of substitutions to try for font family names
FontSize	12	the maximum height of characters in printer's points
FontWeight	"Bold"	the weight of characters to use
FontSlant	"Plain"	the slant of characters to use
FontTracking	"Plain"	the horizontal compression or expansion of characters
FontColor	GrayLevel[0]	the color of characters
Background	GrayLevel[1]	the color of the background for each character

Options for fonts.

"Courier"	text like this
"Times"	text like this
"Helvetica"	text like this

Some typical font family names.

FontWeight->"Plain"	text like this
FontWeight->"Bold"	**text like this**
FontWeight->"ExtraBold"	**text like this**
FontSlant->"Italic"	*text like this*
FontTracking->"Condensed"	text like this

Some settings of font options.

Mathematica allows you to specify the font that you want to use in considerable detail. Sometimes, however, the particular combination of font families and variations that you request may not be available on your computer system. In such cases, *Mathematica* will try to find the closest approximation it can. There are various additional options, such as `FontPostScriptName` and `FontNativeNames` that you can set to help *Mathematica* find an appropriate font. In addition, you can set `FontSubstitutions` to be a list of rules that give replacements to try for font family names.

There are a great many fonts available for ordinary text. But for special technical characters, and even for Greek letters, far fewer fonts are available. The *Mathematica* system includes fonts that were built to support all of the various special characters that are used by *Mathematica*. There are three versions of these fonts: ordinary (like Times), monospaced (like Courier), and sans serif (like Helvetica).

For a given text font, *Mathematica* tries to choose the special character font that matches it best. You can help *Mathematica* to make this choice by giving rules for `"FontSerifed"` and `"FontMonospaced"` in the setting for the `FontProperties` option. You can also give rules for `"FontEncoding"` to specify explicitly from what font each character is to be taken.

■ 2.10.11 Advanced Topic: Options for Expression Input and Output

option	typical default value	
`AutoIndent`	`True`	whether to indent after an explicit RETURN character is entered
`DelimiterFlashTime`	`0.3`	the time in seconds to flash a delimiter when a matching one is entered
`ShowSpecialCharacters`	`True`	whether to replace \[*Name*] by a special character as soon as the] is entered
`ShowStringCharacters`	`False`	whether to display " when a string is entered
`SingleLetterItalics`	`False`	whether to put single-letter symbol names in italics
`ZeroWidthTimes`	`False`	whether to represent multiplication by a zero width character
`AutoItalicWords`	`{"Mathematica", ... }`	words to automatically put in italics

Options associated with the interactive entering of expressions.

The options `SingleLetterItalics` and `ZeroWidthTimes` are typically set whenever a cell uses `TraditionalForm`.

Here is an expression entered with default options for a StandardForm input cell.

$$x^6 + 6x^5y + 15x^4y^2 + 20x^3y^3 + 15x^2y^4 + 6xy^5 + y^6$$

Here is the same expression entered in a cell with SingleLetterItalics->True and ZeroWidthTimes->True.

$$x^6 + 6x^5y + 15x^4y^2 + 20x^3y^3 + 15x^2y^4 + 6xy^5 + y^6$$

option	typical default value	
StructuredSelection	False	whether to allow only complete subexpressions to be selected
DragAndDrop	False	whether to allow drag-and-drop editing

Options associated with interactive manipulation of expressions.

Mathematica normally allows you to select any part of an expression that you see on the screen. Occasionally, however, you may find it useful to get *Mathematica* to allow only selections which correspond to complete subexpressions. You can do this by setting the option StructuredSelection->True.

Here is an expression with a piece selected.

$$(-1+x)\,(1+x)\,(1-x+x^2-x^3+x^4)\,(1+x+x^2+x^3+x^4)$$

With StructuredSelection->True only complete subexpressions can ever be selected.

$$(-1+x)\,(1+x)\,(1-x+x^2-x^3+x^4)\,(1+x+x^2+x^3+x^4)$$
$$(-1+x)\,(1+x)\,(1-x+x^2-x^3+x^4)\,(1+x+x^2+x^3+x^4)$$
$$(-1+x)\,(1+x)\,(1-x+x^2-x^3+x^4)\,(1+x+x^2+x^3+x^4)$$

GridBox[*data*, *opts*]	give options that apply to a particular grid box
StyleBox[*boxes*, *opts*]	give options that apply to all boxes in *boxes*
Cell[*contents*, *opts*]	give options that apply to all boxes in *contents*
Cell[*contents*, GridBoxOptions->*opts*]	give default options settings for all GridBox objects in *contents*

Examples of specifying options for the display of expressions.

As discussed in Section 2.8, *Mathematica* provides many options for specifying how expressions should be displayed. By using `StyleBox[boxes, opts]` you can apply such options to collections of boxes. But *Mathematica* is set up so that any option that you can give to a `StyleBox` can also be given to a complete `Cell` object, or even a complete `Notebook`. Thus, for example, options like `Background` and `LineIndent` can be given to complete cells as well as to individual `StyleBox` objects.

There are some options that apply only to a particular type of box, such as `GridBox`. Usually these options are best given separately in each `GridBox` where they are needed. But sometimes you may want to specify default settings to be inherited by all `GridBox` objects that appear in a particular cell. You can do this by giving these default settings as the value of the option `GridBoxOptions` for the whole cell.

For each box type named *XXX*`Box`, *Mathematica* provides a cell option *XXX*`BoxOptions` that allows you to specify the default options settings for that type of box.

■ 2.10.12 Options for Graphics Cells

option	typical default value	
AspectRatioFixed	True	whether to keep a fixed aspect ratio if the image is resized
ImageSize	{288, 288}	the absolute width and height of the image in printer's points
ImageMargins	{{0, 0}, {0, 0}}	the widths of margins in printer's points to leave around the image

Options for displaying images in notebooks.

Here is a graphic displayed in a notebook.

With the default setting
`AspectRatioFixed->True` resizing the graphic does not change its shape.

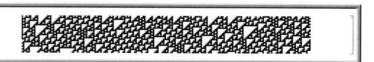

If you set `AspectRatioFixed->False` then you can change the shape.

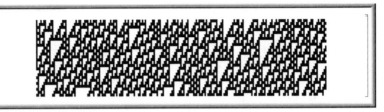

Mathematica allows you to specify the final size of a graphic by setting the `ImageSize` option in kernel graphics functions such as `Plot` and `Display`. Once a graphic is in a notebook, you can then typically resize or move it just by using the mouse.

- Use the Animate Selected Graphics menu item in the front end.

- Use the kernel command `SelectionAnimate[obj]`.

Ways to generate animations in a notebook.

Mathematica generates animated graphics by taking a sequence of graphics cells, and then treating them like frames in a movie. The option `AnimationDisplayTime` specifies how long a particular cell should be displayed as part of the movie.

option	typical default value	
AnimationDisplayTime	0	minimum time in seconds to display this cell during an animation
AnimationDirection	Forward	which direction to run an animation starting with this cell

Options for animations.

+■ 2.10.13 Options for Notebooks

- Use the Option Inspector menu to change options interactively.

- Use `SetOptions[obj, options]` from the kernel.

- Use `NotebookCreate[options]` to create a new notebook with specified options.

Ways to change the overall options for a notebook.

This creates a notebook displayed in a 40 × 30 window with a thin frame.

```
In[1]:= NotebookCreate[WindowFrame->"ThinFrame",
                         WindowSize->{40, 30}]
```

option	typical default value	
StyleDefinitions	"DefaultStyles.nb"	the basic style sheet to use for the notebook
ScreenStyleEnvironment	"Working"	the style environment to use for screen display
PrintingStyleEnvironment	"Printout"	the style environment to use for printing

Style options for a notebook.

In giving style definitions for a particular notebook, *Mathematica* allows you either to reference another notebook, or explicitly to include the Notebook expression that defines the styles.

option	typical default value	
CellGrouping	Automatic	how to group cells in the notebook
ShowPageBreaks	False	whether to show where page breaks would occur if the notebook were printed
NotebookAutoSave	False	whether to automatically save the notebook after each evaluation

General options for notebooks.

Without CellGrouping->Automatic, cells are automatically grouped based on their style.

■ **Section heading**

First text cell.

Second text cell.

With CellGrouping->Manual, you have to group cells by hand.

■ **Section heading**

First text cell.

Second text cell.

option	typical default value	
DefaultNewCellStyle	"Input"	the default style for new cells created in the notebook
DefaultDuplicateCellStyle	"Input"	the default style for cells created by automatic duplication of existing cells

Options specifying default styles for cells created in a notebook.

Mathematica allows you to take any cell option and set it at the notebook level, thereby specifying a global default for that option throughout the notebook.

option	typical default value	
Editable	True	whether to allow cells in the notebook to be edited
Selectable	True	whether to allow cells to be selected
Deletable	True	whether to allow cells to be deleted
Background	GrayLevel[1]	what background color to use for the notebook
Magnification	1	at what magnification to display the notebook
PageWidth	WindowWidth	how wide to allow the contents of cells to be

A few cell options that are often set at the notebook level.

Here is a notebook with the Background option set at the notebook level.

Here is some text.

option	typical default value	
Visible	True	whether the window should be visible on the screen
WindowSize	{Automatic, Automatic}	the width and height of the window in printer's points
WindowMargins	Automatic	the margins to leave around the window when it is displayed on the screen
WindowFrame	"Normal"	the type of frame to draw around the window
WindowElements	{"StatusArea", ... }	elements to include in the window
WindowTitle	Automatic	what title should be displayed for the window
WindowToolbars	{ }	toolbars to display at the top of the window
WindowMovable	True	whether to allow the window to be moved around on the screen
WindowFloating	False	whether the window should always float on top of other windows
WindowClickSelect	True	whether the window should become selected if you click in it

Characteristics of the notebook window.

WindowSize allows you to specify how large you want a window to be; WindowMargins allows you to specify where you want the window to be placed on your screen. The setting WindowMargins->{{*left*, *right*}, {*bottom*, *top*}} gives the margins in printer's points to leave around your window on the screen. Often only two of the margins will be set explicitly; the others will be Automatic, indicating that these margins will be determined from the particular size of screen that you use.

`"Normal"`	an ordinary window
`"Palette"`	a palette window
`"ModelessDialog"`	a modeless dialog box window
`"ModalDialog"`	a modal dialog box window
`"MovableModalDialog"`	a modal dialog box window that can be moved around the screen
`"ThinFrame"`	an ordinary window with a thin frame
`"Frameless"`	an ordinary window with no frame at all
`"Generic"`	a window with a generic border, as used for the examples in this book

Typical possible settings for `WindowFrame`.

Mathematica allows many different types of windows. The details of how particular windows are rendered may differ slightly from one computer system to another, but their general form is always the same. `WindowFrame` specifies the type of frame to draw around the window. `WindowElements` gives a list of specific elements to include in the window.

`"StatusArea"`	an area used to display status messages, such as those from `ButtonNote` options
`"MagnificationPopUp"`	a pop-up menu of common magnifications
`"HorizontalScrollBar"`	a scroll bar for horizontal motion
`"VerticalScrollBar"`	a scroll bar for vertical motion

Some typical possible entries in the `WindowElements` list.

Here is a window with a status area and horizontal scroll bar, but no magnification pop-up or vertical scroll bar.

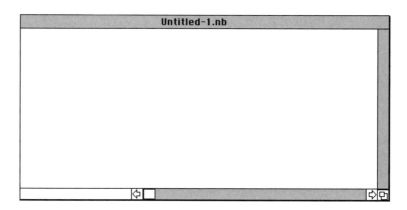

"RulerBar"	a ruler showing margin settings
"EditBar"	buttons for common editing operations
"LinksBar"	buttons for hyperlink operations

Some typical possible entries in the WindowToolbars list.

Here is a window with ruler and edit toolbars.

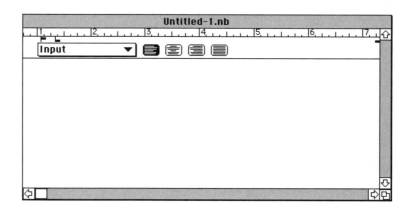

+ ■ 2.10.14 Advanced Topic: Global Options for the Front End

In the standard notebook front end, *Mathematica* allows you to set a large number of global options. The values of all these options are by default saved in a "preferences file", and are automatically reused when you run *Mathematica* again.

style definitions	default style definitions to use for new notebooks
file locations	directories for finding notebooks and system files
data export options	how to export data in various formats
character encoding options	how to encode special characters
language options	what language to use for text
message options	how to handle messages generated by *Mathematica*
menu settings	items displayed in modifiable menus
dialog settings	choices made in dialog boxes
system configuration	private options for specific computer systems

Some typical categories of global options for the front end.

As discussed on page 566, you can access global front end options from the kernel by using `Options[$FrontEnd, `*name*`]`. But more often, you will want to access these options interactively using the Option Inspector in the front end.

2.11 Files and Streams

■ 2.11.1 Reading and Writing *Mathematica* Files

Particularly if you use a text-based *Mathematica* interface, you will often need to read and write files containing definitions and results from *Mathematica*. Section 1.11.1 gave a general discussion of how to do this. This section gives some more details.

<<*file* or Get["*file*"]	read in a file of *Mathematica* input, and return the last expression in the file
!!*file*	display the contents of a file

Reading files.

This shows the contents of the file factors.

```
In[1]:= !!factors
(* Factors of x^20 - 1 *)
  (-1 + x)*(1 + x)*(1 + x^2)*(1 - x + x^2 - x^3 + x^4)*
  (1 + x + x^2 + x^3 + x^4)*(1 - x^2 + x^4 - x^6 + x^8)
```

This reads in the file, and returns the last expression in it.

$In[2]:=$ <<factors

$Out[2]=$ $(-1 + x)\,(1 + x)\,(1 + x^2)\,(1 - x + x^2 - x^3 + x^4)$
$(1 + x + x^2 + x^3 + x^4)\,(1 - x^2 + x^4 - x^6 + x^8)$

If *Mathematica* cannot find the file you ask it to read, it prints a message, then returns the symbol $Failed.

$In[3]:=$ <<faxors

Get::noopen: Can't open faxors.

$Out[3]=$ $Failed

Mathematica input files can contain any number of expressions. Each expression, however, must start on a new line. The expressions may however continue for as many lines as necessary. Just as in a standard interactive *Mathematica* session, the expressions are processed as soon as they are complete. Note, however, that in a file, unlike an interactive session, you can insert a blank line at any point without effect.

When you read in a file with <<*file*, *Mathematica* returns the last expression it evaluates in the file. You can avoid getting any visible result from reading a file by ending the last expression in the file with a semicolon, or by explicitly adding Null after that expression.

If *Mathematica* encounters a syntax error while reading a file, it reports the error, skips the remainder of the file, then returns $Failed. If the syntax error occurs in the middle of a package which uses BeginPackage and other context manipulation functions, then *Mathematica* tries to restore the context to what it was before the package was read.

expr >> *file* or Put[*expr*, "*file*"]	
	write an expression to a file
expr >>> *file* or PutAppend[*expr*, "*file*"]	
	append an expression to a file

Writing expressions to files.

This writes an expression to the file tmp.	*In[4]:=* **Factor[x^6 - 1] >> tmp**
Here are the contents of the file.	*In[5]:=* **!!tmp**
	(-1 + x)*(1 + x)*(1 - x + x^2)*(1 + x + x^2)
This appends another expression to the same file.	*In[6]:=* **Factor[x^8 - 1] >>> tmp**
Both expressions are now in the file.	*In[7]:=* **!!tmp**
	(-1 + x)*(1 + x)*(1 - x + x^2)*(1 + x + x^2)
	(-1 + x)*(1 + x)*(1 + x^2)*(1 + x^4)

When you use *expr* >>> *file*, *Mathematica* appends each new expression you give to the end of your file. If you use *expr* >> *file*, however, then *Mathematica* instead wipes out anything that was in the file before, and then puts *expr* into the file.

When you use either >> or >>> to write expressions to files, the expressions are usually given in *Mathematica* input format, so that you can read them back into *Mathematica*. Sometimes, however, you may want to save expressions in other formats. You can do this by explicitly wrapping a format directive such as OutputForm around the expression you write out.

This writes an expression to the file tmp in output format.	*In[8]:=* **OutputForm[Factor[x^6 - 1]] >> tmp**
The expression in tmp is now in output format.	*In[9]:=* **!!tmp**
	(-1 + x) (1 + x) (1 - x + x^2) (1 + x + x^2)

One of the most common reasons for using files is to save definitions of *Mathematica* objects, to be able to read them in again in a subsequent *Mathematica* session. The operators >> and >>> allow you to save *Mathematica* expressions in files. You can use the function Save to save complete definitions of *Mathematica* objects, in a form suitable for execution in subsequent *Mathematica* sessions.

Save["*file*", *symbol*]	save the complete definitions for a symbol in a file
Save["*file*", "*form*"]	save definitions for symbols whose names match the string pattern *form*
Save["*file*", "*context*`"]	save definitions for all symbols in the specified context
Save["*file*", {*object*$_1$, *object*$_2$, ... }]	
	save definitions for several objects

Writing out definitions.

This assigns a value to the symbol a.	*In[10]:=* **a = 2 - x^2**
	Out[10]= $2 - x^2$
You can use Save to write the definition of a to a file.	*In[11]:=* **Save["afile", a]**
Here is the definition of a that was saved in the file.	*In[12]:=* **!!afile**
	a = 2 - x^2

When you define a new object in *Mathematica*, your definition will often depend on other objects that you defined before. If you are going to be able to reconstruct the definition of your new object in a subsequent *Mathematica* session, it is important that you store not only its own definition, but also the definitions of other objects on which it depends. The function Save looks through the definitions of the objects you ask it to save, and automatically also saves all definitions of other objects on which it can see that these depend. However, in order to avoid saving a large amount of unnecessary material, Save never includes definitions for symbols that have the attribute Protected. It assumes that the definitions for these symbols are also built in. Nevertheless, with such definitions taken care of, it should always be the case that reading the output generated by Save back into a new *Mathematica* session will set up the definitions of your objects exactly as you had them before.

This defines a function f which depends on the symbol a defined above.	*In[13]:=* **f[z_] := a^2 - 2**
This saves the complete definition of f in a file.	*In[14]:=* **Save["ffile", f]**
The file contains not only the definition of f itself, but also the definition of the symbol a on which f depends.	*In[15]:=* **!!ffile**
	f[z_] := a^2 - 2
	a = 2 - x^2

The function Save makes use of the output forms Definition and FullDefinition, which print as definitions of *Mathematica* symbols. In some cases, you may find it convenient to use these output forms directly.

The output form Definition[*f*] prints as the sequence of definitions that have been made for *f*.

In[16]:= **Definition[f]**

Out[16]= f[z_] := a² - 2

FullDefinition[*f*] includes definitions of the objects on which *f* depends.

In[17]:= **FullDefinition[f]**

Out[17]= f[z_] := a² - 2

a = 2 - x²

When you create files for input to *Mathematica*, you usually want them to contain only "plain text", which can be read or modified directly. Sometimes, however, you may want the contents of a file to be "encoded" so that they cannot be read or modified directly as plain text, but can be loaded into *Mathematica*. You can create encoded files using the *Mathematica* function Encode.

Encode["*source*", "*dest*"]	write an encoded version of the file *source* to the file *dest*
<<*dest*	read in an encoded file
Encode["*source*", "*dest*", "*key*"]	encode with the specified key
Get["*dest*", "*key*"]	read in a file that was encoded with a key
Encode["*source*", "*dest*", MachineID -> "*ID*"]	create an encoded file which can only be read on a machine with a particular ID

Creating and reading encoded files.

This writes an expression in plain text to the file tmp.

In[18]:= **Factor[x^2 - 1] >> tmp**

This writes an encoded version of the file tmp to the file tmp.x.

In[19]:= **Encode["tmp", "tmp.x"]**

Here are the contents of the encoded file. The only recognizable part is the special *Mathematica* comment at the beginning.

In[20]:= **!!tmp.x**

(*!1N!*)mcm
_QZ9tcI1cfre*Wo8:) P

Even though the file is encoded, you can still read it into *Mathematica* using the << operator.

In[21]:= **<<tmp.x**

Out[21]= (-1 + x) (1 + x)

DumpSave["*file*.mx", *symbol*]	save definitions for a symbol in internal *Mathematica* format
DumpSave["*file*.mx", "*context*`"]	save definitions for all symbols in a context
DumpSave["*file*.mx", {*object*$_1$, *object*$_2$, ... }]	
	save definitions for several symbols or contexts
DumpSave["*package*`", *objects*]	save definitions in a file with a specially chosen name

Saving definitions in internal *Mathematica* format.

If you have to read in very large or complicated definitions, you will often find it more efficient to store these definitions in internal *Mathematica* format, rather than as text. You can do this using DumpSave.

This saves the definition for f in internal *Mathematica* format.	*In[22]:=* **DumpSave["ffile.mx", f]**
	Out[22]= {f}
You can still use << to read the definition in.	*In[23]:=* **<<ffile.mx**

<< recognizes when a file contains definitions in internal *Mathematica* format, and operates accordingly. One subtlety is that the internal *Mathematica* format differs from one computer system to another. As a result, .mx files created on one computer cannot typically be read on another.

If you use DumpSave["*package*`", ...] then *Mathematica* will write out definitions to a file with a name like *package*.mx/*system*/*package*.mx, where *system* identifies your type of computer system.

This creates a file with a name that reflects the name of the computer system being used.	*In[24]:=* **DumpSave["gffile`", f]**
	Out[24]= {f}
<< automatically picks out the file with the appropriate name for your computer system.	*In[25]:=* **<<gffile`**

DumpSave["*file*.mx"]	save all definitions in your current *Mathematica* session
DumpSave["*package*`"]	save all definitions in a file with a specially chosen name

Saving the complete state of a *Mathematica* session.

■ 2.11.2 External Programs

On most computer systems, you can execute external programs or commands from within *Mathematica*. Often you will want to take expressions you have generated in *Mathematica*, and send them to an external program, or take results from external programs, and read them into *Mathematica*.

Mathematica supports two basic forms of communication with external programs: *structured* and *unstructured*.

Structured communication	use *MathLink* to exchange expressions with *MathLink*-compatible external programs
Unstructured communication	use file reading and writing operations to exchange ordinary text

Two kinds of communication with external programs in *Mathematica*.

The idea of structured communication is to exchange complete *Mathematica* expressions to external programs which are specially set up to handle such objects. The basis for structured communication is the *MathLink* system, discussed in Section 2.12.

Unstructured communication consists in sending and receiving ordinary text from external programs. The basic idea is to treat an external program very much like a file, and to support the same kinds of reading and writing operations.

expr >> "!*command*"	send the text of an expression to an external program
<< "!*command*"	read in text from an external program as *Mathematica* input

Reading and writing to external programs.

In general, wherever you might use an ordinary file name, *Mathematica* allows you instead to give a *pipe*, written as an external command, prefaced by an exclamation point. When you use the pipe, *Mathematica* will execute the external command, and send or receive text from it.

This sends the result from FactorInteger to the external program lpr. On many Unix systems, this program generates a printout.

`In[1]:= FactorInteger[2^31 - 1] >> !lpr`

This executes the external command echo $TERM, then reads the result as *Mathematica* input.

`In[2]:= <<"!echo $TERM"`

`Out[2]= vt100`

One point to notice is that you can get away with dropping the double quotes around the name of a pipe on the right-hand side of << or >> if the name does not contain any spaces or other special characters.

Pipes in *Mathematica* provide a very general mechanism for unstructured communication with external programs. On many computer systems, *Mathematica* pipes are implemented using pipe mechanisms in the underlying operating system; in some cases, however, other interprocess communication mechanisms are used. One restriction of unstructured communication in *Mathematica* is that a given pipe can only be used for input or for output, and not for both at the same time. In order to do genuine two-way communication, you need to use *MathLink*.

Even with unstructured communication, you can nevertheless set up somewhat more complicated arrangements by using temporary files. The basic idea is to write data to a file, then to read it as needed.

`OpenTemporary[ ]`	open a temporary file with a unique name

Opening a temporary file.

Particularly when you work with temporary files, you may find it useful to be able to execute external commands which do not explicitly send or receive data from *Mathematica*. You can do this using the *Mathematica* function Run.

`Run["`*command*`", `*arg*$_1$`, ... ]`	run an external command from within *Mathematica*

Running external commands without input or output.

This executes the external Unix command `date`. The returned value is an "exit code" from the operating system.

```
In[3]:= Run["date"]

Wed Mar 27 16:51:55 CST 1996

Out[3]= 0
```

Note that when you use Run, you must not preface commands with exclamation points. Run simply takes the textual forms of the arguments you specify, then joins them together with spaces in between, and executes the resulting string as an external command.

It is important to realize that Run never "captures" any of the output from an external command. As a result, where this output goes is purely determined by your operating system. Similarly, Run does not supply input to external commands. This means that the commands can get input through any mechanism provided by your operating system. Sometimes external commands may be able to access the same input and output streams that are used by *Mathematica* itself. In some cases, this may be what you want. But particularly if you are using *Mathematica* with a front end, this can cause considerable trouble.

`!`*command*	intercept a line of *Mathematica* input, and run it as an external command

Shell escapes in *Mathematica*.

If you use *Mathematica* with a text-based interface, there is usually a special mechanism for executing external commands. With such an interface, *Mathematica* takes any line of input that starts with an exclamation point, and executes the text on the remainder of the line as an external command.

The way *Mathematica* uses !*command* is typical of the way "shell escapes" work in programs running under the Unix operating system. In most versions of *Mathematica*, you will be able to start an interactive shell from *Mathematica* simply by typing a single exclamation point on its own on a line.

This line is taken as a "shell escape", and executes the Unix command date.	*In[4]:= !***date** `Wed Mar 27 16:52:00 CST 1996` *Out[4]=* 0

`RunThrough["command", expr]`	run *command*, using *expr* as input, and reading the output back into *Mathematica*

Running *Mathematica* expressions through external programs.

As discussed above, `<<` and `>>` cannot be used to both send and receive data from an external program at the same time. Nevertheless, by using temporary files, you can effectively both send and receive data from an external program while still using unstructured communication.

The function `RunThrough` writes the text of an expression to a temporary file, then feeds this file as input to an external program, and captures the output as input to *Mathematica*. Note that in `RunThrough`, like `Run`, you should not preface the names of external commands with exclamation points.

This feeds the expression 789 to the external program cat, which in this case simply echoes the text of the expression. The output from cat is then read back into *Mathematica*.	*In[5]:=* **RunThrough["cat", 789]** *Out[5]=* 789

■ 2.11.3 Advanced Topic: Streams and Low-Level Input and Output

Files and pipes are both examples of general *Mathematica* objects known as *streams*. A stream in *Mathematica* is a source of input or output. There are many operations that you can perform on streams.

You can think of `>>` and `<<` as "high-level" *Mathematica* input-output functions. They are based on a set of lower-level input-output primitives that work directly with streams. By using these primitives, you can exercise more control over exactly how *Mathematica* does input and output. You will often need to do this, for example, if you write *Mathematica* programs which store and retrieve intermediate data from files or pipes.

The basic low-level scheme for writing output to a stream in *Mathematica* is as follows. First, you call `OpenWrite` or `OpenAppend` to "open the stream", telling *Mathematica* that you want to write output to a particular file or external program, and in what form the output should be written. Having opened a stream, you can then call `Write` or `WriteString` to write a sequence of expressions or strings to the stream. When you have finished, you call `Close` to "close the stream".

"name"	a file, specified by name
"!name"	a command, specified by name
`InputStream["`*name*`", `*n*`]`	an input stream
`OutputStream["`*name*`", `*n*`]`	an output stream

Streams in *Mathematica*.

When you open a file or a pipe, *Mathematica* creates a "stream object" that specifies the open stream associated with the file or pipe. In general, the stream object contains the name of the file or the external command used in a pipe, together with a unique number.

The reason that the stream object needs to include a unique number is that in general you can have several streams connected to the same file or external program at the same time. For example, you may start several different instances of the same external program, each connected to a different stream.

Nevertheless, when you have opened a stream, you can still refer to it using a simple file name or external command name so long as there is only one stream associated with this object.

This opens an output stream to the file tmp.

```
In[1]:= stmp = OpenWrite["tmp"]
Out[1]= OutputStream[tmp, 5]
```

This writes a sequence of expressions to the file.

```
In[2]:= Write[stmp, a, b, c]
```

Since you only have one stream associated with file tmp, you can refer to it simply by giving the name of the file.

```
In[3]:= Write["tmp", x]
```

This closes the stream.

```
In[4]:= Close[stmp]
Out[4]= tmp
```

Here is what was written to the file.

```
In[5]:= !!tmp
abc
x
```

OpenWrite["*file*"]	open an output stream to a file, wiping out the previous contents of the file
OpenAppend["*file*"]	open an output stream to a file, appending to what was already in the file
OpenWrite["!*command*"]	open an output stream to an external command
Write[*stream*, *expr*₁, *expr*₂, ...]	write a sequence of expressions to a stream, ending the output with a newline (line feed)
WriteString[*stream*, *str*₁, *str*₂, ...]	
	write a sequence of character strings to a stream, with no extra newlines
Display[*stream*, *graphics*]	write graphics or sound output to a stream, in PostScript form
Close[*stream*]	tell *Mathematica* that you are finished with a stream

Low-level output functions.

When you call Write[*stream*, *expr*], it writes an expression to the specified stream. The default is to write the expression in *Mathematica* input form. If you call Write with a sequence of expressions, it will write these expressions one after another to the stream. In general, it leaves no space between the successive expressions. However, when it has finished writing all the expressions, Write always ends its output with a newline.

This re-opens the file tmp.

```
In[6]:= stmp = OpenWrite["tmp"]
Out[6]= OutputStream[tmp, 8]
```

This writes a sequence of expressions to the file, then closes the file.

```
In[7]:= Write[stmp, a^2, 1 + b^2]; Write[stmp, c^3]; Close[stmp]
Out[7]= tmp
```

All the expressions are written in input form. The expressions from a single Write are put on the same line.

```
In[8]:= !!tmp
a^21 + b^2
c^3
```

Write provides a way of writing out complete *Mathematica* expressions. Sometimes, however, you may want to write out less structured data. WriteString allows you to write out any character string. Unlike Write, WriteString adds no newlines or other characters.

This opens the stream.

```
In[9]:= stmp = OpenWrite["tmp"]
Out[9]= OutputStream[tmp, 11]
```

This writes two strings to the stream.

```
In[10]:= WriteString[stmp, "Arbitrary output.\n", "More output."]
```

This writes another string, then closes the stream.

```
In[11]:= WriteString[stmp, " Second line.\n"]; Close[stmp]
Out[11]= tmp
```

Here are the contents of the file. The strings were written exactly as specified, including only the newlines that were explicitly given.

```
In[12]:= !!tmp

Arbitrary output.
More output.  Second line.
```

Write[{*stream*₁, *stream*₂, ... }, *expr*₁, ...]
  write expressions to a list of streams

WriteString[{*stream*₁, *stream*₂, ... }, *str*₁, ...]
  write strings to a list of streams

Writing output to lists of streams.

An important feature of the functions Write and WriteString is that they allow you to write output not just to a single stream, but also to a list of streams.

In using *Mathematica*, it is often convenient to define a *channel* which consists of a list of streams. You can then simply tell *Mathematica* to write to the channel, and have it automatically write the same object to several streams.

In a standard interactive *Mathematica* session, there are several output channels that are usually defined. These specify where particular kinds of output should be sent. Thus, for example, $Output specifies where standard output should go, while $Messages specifies where messages should go. The function Print then works essentially by calling Write with the $Output channel. Message works in the same way by calling Write with the $Messages channel. Page 678 lists the channels used in a typical *Mathematica* session.

Note that when you run *Mathematica* through *MathLink*, a different approach is usually used. All output is typically written to a single *MathLink* link, but each piece of output appears in a "packet" which indicates what type it is.

In most cases, the names of files or external commands that you use in *Mathematica* correspond exactly with those used by your computer's operating system. On some systems, however, *Mathematica* supports various streams with special names.

"stdout"   standard output

"stderr"   standard error

Special streams used on some computer systems.

The special stream "stdout" allows you to give output to the "standard output" provided by the operating system. Note however that you can use this stream only with simple text-based interfaces to *Mathematica*. If your interaction with *Mathematica* is more complicated, then this stream will not work, and trying to use it may cause considerable trouble.

option name	default value	
FormatType	InputForm	the default output format to use
PageWidth	78	the width of the page in characters
+ NumberMarks	$NumberMarks	whether to include ` marks in approximate numbers
CharacterEncoding	$CharacterEncoding	encoding to be used for special characters

Some options for output streams.

You can associate a number of options with output streams. You can specify these options when you first open a stream using OpenWrite or OpenAppend.

This opens a stream, specifying that the default output format used should be OutputForm.	*In[13]:=* **stmp = OpenWrite["tmp", FormatType -> OutputForm]** *Out[13]=* OutputStream[tmp, 14]
This writes expressions to the stream, then closes the stream.	*In[14]:=* **Write[stmp, x^2 + y^2, " ", z^2]; Close[stmp]** *Out[14]=* tmp
The expressions were written to the stream in OutputForm.	*In[15]:=* **!!tmp** 2 2 2 x + y z

Note that you can always override the output format specified for a particular stream by wrapping a particular expression you write to the stream with an explicit *Mathematica* format directive, such as OutputForm or TeXForm.

The option PageWidth gives the width of the page available for textual output from *Mathematica*. All lines of output are broken so that they fit in this width. If you do not want any lines to be broken, you can set PageWidth -> Infinity. Usually, however, you will want to set PageWidth to the value appropriate for your particular output device. On many systems, you will have to run an external program to find out what this value is. Using SetOptions, you can make the default rule for PageWidth be, for example, PageWidth :> <<"!devicewidth", so that an external program is run automatically to find the value of the option.

This opens a stream, specifying that the page width is 20 characters.	*In[16]:=* **stmp = OpenWrite["tmp", PageWidth -> 20]** *Out[16]=* OutputStream[tmp, 17]
This writes out an expression, then closes the stream.	*In[17]:=* **Write[stmp, Expand[(1 + x)^5]]; Close[stmp]** *Out[17]=* tmp

The lines in the expression written out are all broken so as to be at most 20 characters long.	*In[18]:=* **!!tmp**
	1 + 5*x + 10*x^2 +
	   10*x^3 + 5*x^4 +
	   x^5

The option `StringConversion` allows you to give a function that will be applied to all strings containing special characters which are sent to a particular output stream, whether by `Write` or `WriteString`. You will typically need to use `StringConversion` if you want to modify an international character set, or prevent a particular output device from receiving characters that it cannot handle.

`Options[`*stream*`]`	find the options that have been set for a stream
`SetOptions[`*stream*`, `*opt*$_1$` -> `*val*$_1$`, ... ]`	reset options for an open stream

Manipulating options of streams.

This opens a stream with the default settings for options.	`In[19]:= stmp = OpenWrite["tmp"]`
	
	`Out[19]= OutputStream[tmp, 20]`

This changes the `FormatType` option for the open stream.	`In[20]:= SetOptions[stmp, FormatType -> TeXForm];`

Options shows the options you have set for the open stream.	`In[21]:= Options[stmp]`
	
	`Out[21]= {DOSTextFormat → True,`
	`          FormatType → TeXForm, PageWidth → 78,`
	`          PageHeight → 22, TotalWidth → ∞, TotalHeight → ∞,`
	`          CharacterEncoding :→ $CharacterEncoding,`
	`          NumberMarks :→ $NumberMarks}`

This closes the stream again.	`In[22]:= Close[stmp]`
	
	`Out[22]= tmp`

`Options[$Output]`	find the options set for all streams in the channel `$Output`
`SetOptions[$Output, `*opt*$_1$` -> `*val*$_1$`, ... ]`	set options for all streams in the channel `$Output`

Manipulating options for the standard output channel.

At every point in your session, *Mathematica* maintains a list `Streams[ ]` of all the input and output streams that are currently open, together with their options. In some cases, you may find it useful to look at this list directly. *Mathematica* will not, however, allow you to modify the list, except indirectly through `OpenRead` and so on.

■ 2.11.4 Naming and Finding Files

The precise details of the naming of files differ from one computer system to another. Nevertheless, *Mathematica* provides some fairly general mechanisms that work on all systems.

As mentioned in Section 1.11.2, *Mathematica* assumes that all your files are arranged in a hierarchy of *directories*. To find a particular file, *Mathematica* must know both what the name of the file is, and what sequence of directories it is in.

At any given time, however, you have a *current working directory*, and you can refer to files or other directories by specifying where they are relative to this directory. Typically you can refer to files or directories that are actually *in* this directory simply by giving their names, with no directory information.

Directory[ ]	your current working directory
SetDirectory["*dir*"]	set your current working directory
ResetDirectory[ ]	revert to your previous working directory

Manipulating directories.

This gives a string representing your current working directory.

In[1]:= **Directory[ ]**

Out[1]= /users/sw

This sets your current working directory to be the Packages subdirectory.

In[2]:= **SetDirectory["Packages"]**

Out[2]= /users/sw/Packages

Now your current working directory is different.

In[3]:= **Directory[ ]**

Out[3]= /users/sw/Packages

This reverts to your previous working directory.

In[4]:= **ResetDirectory[ ]**

Out[4]= /users/sw

When you call SetDirectory, you can give any directory name that is recognized by your operating system. Thus, for example, on Unix-based systems, you can specify a directory one level up in the directory hierarchy using the notation . ., and you can specify your "home" directory as ~.

Whenever you go to a new directory using SetDirectory, *Mathematica* always remembers what the previous directory was. You can return to this previous directory using ResetDirectory. In general, *Mathematica* maintains a stack of directories, given by DirectoryStack[ ]. Every time you call SetDirectory, it adds a new directory to the stack, and every time you call ResetDirectory it removes a directory from the stack.

	`ParentDirectory[ ]`	give the parent of your current working directory
+	`$TopDirectory`	the top-level directory in which *Mathematica* system files are installed
+	`$LaunchDirectory`	the directory in which the copy of *Mathematica* being run resides
+	`$InitialDirectory`	the current directory at the time *Mathematica* was started
+	`$HomeDirectory`	your home directory, if this is defined

Special directories.

Whenever you ask for a particular file, *Mathematica* in general goes through several steps to try and find the file you want. The first step is to use whatever standard mechanisms exist in your operating system or shell.

Mathematica scans the full name you give for a file, and looks to see whether it contains any of the "metacharacters" *, $, ~, ?, [, ", \ and '. If it finds such characters, then it passes the full name to your operating system or shell for interpretation. This means that if you are using a Unix-based system, then constructions like *name*∗ and $*VAR* will be expanded at this point. But in general, *Mathematica* takes whatever was returned by your operating system or shell, and treats this as the full file name.

For output files, this is the end of the processing that *Mathematica* does. If *Mathematica* cannot find a unique file with the name you specified, then it will proceed to create the file.

If you are trying to get input from a file, however, then there is another round of processing that *Mathematica* does. What happens is that *Mathematica* looks at the value of the `Path` option for the function you are using to determine the names of directories relative to which it should search for the file. The default setting for the `Path` option is the global variable `$Path`.

`$Path`	a default list of directories relative to which to search for input files

Search path for files.

In general, the global variable `$Path` is defined to be a list of strings, with each string representing a directory. Every time you ask for an input file, what *Mathematica* effectively does is temporarily to make each of these directories in turn your current working directory, and then from that directory to try and find the file you have requested.

Here is a typical setting for $Path. The current directory (.) and your home directory (~) are listed first.

```
In[5]:= $Path

Out[5]= {., ~, /users/math/bin, /users/math/Packages}
```

FileNames[ ]	list all files in your current working directory
FileNames["*form*"]	list all files in your current working directory whose names match the string pattern *form*
FileNames[{"*form*$_1$", "*form*$_2$", ... }]	list all files whose names match any of the *form*$_i$
FileNames[*forms*, {"*dir*$_1$", "*dir*$_2$", ... }]	give the full names of all files whose names match *forms* in any of the directories *dir*$_i$
FileNames[*forms*, *dirs*, *n*]	include files that are in subdirectories up to *n* levels down
FileNames[*forms*, *dirs*, Infinity]	include files in all subdirectories
FileNames[*forms*, $Path, Infinity]	give all files whose names match *forms* in any subdirectory of the directories in $Path

Getting lists of files in particular directories.

Here is a list of all files in the current working directory whose names end with .m.

```
In[6]:= FileNames["*.m"]
Out[6]= {alpha.m, control.m, signals.m, test.m}
```

This lists files whose names start with a in the current directory, and in subdirectories with names that start with P.

```
In[7]:= FileNames["a*", {".", "P*"}]
Out[7]= {alpha.m, Packages/astrodata, Packages/astro.m,
                Previous/atmp}
```

FileNames returns a list of strings corresponding to file names. When it returns a file that is not in your current directory, it gives the name of the file relative to the current directory. Note that all names are given in the format appropriate for the particular computer system on which they were generated.

+	DirectoryName["*file*"] extract the directory name from a file name
+	ToFileName["*directory*", "*name*"]
	assemble a full file name from a directory name and a file name
	ParentDirectory["*directory*"] give the parent of a directory
+	ToFileName[{"*dir1*", "*dir2*", ... }, "*name*"]
	assemble a full file name from a hierarchy of directory names
+	ToFileName[{"*dir1*", "*dir2*", ... }]
	assemble a single directory name from a hierarchy of directory names

Manipulating file names.

You should realize that different computer systems may give file names in different ways. Thus, for example, Unix systems typically give names in the form *dir/dir/name*, Macintosh systems in the form :*dir*:*dir*:*name*, and VMS systems in the form [*dir*]*name*. The function ToFileName assembles file names in the appropriate way for the particular computer system you are using.

This gives the directory portion of the file name.	*In[8]:=* **DirectoryName["Packages/Math/test.m"]**
	Out[8]= Packages/Math/
This constructs the full name of another file in the same directory as test.m.	*In[9]:=* **ToFileName[%, "abc.m"]**
	Out[9]= Packages/Math/abc.m

If you want to set up a collection of related files, it is often convenient to be able to refer to one file when you are reading another one. The global variable $Input gives the name of the file from which input is currently being taken. Using DirectoryName and ToFileName you can then conveniently specify the names of other related files.

$Input	the name of the file or stream from which input is currently being taken

Finding out how to refer to a file currently being read by *Mathematica*.

■ 2.11.5 Files for Packages

When you create or use *Mathematica* packages, you will often want to refer to files in a system-independent way. You can use contexts to do this.

The basic idea is that on every computer system there is a convention about how files corresponding to *Mathematica* contexts should be named. Then, when you refer to a file using a context, the particular version of *Mathematica* you are using converts the context name to the file name appropriate for the computer system you are on.

<<*context*`	read in the file corresponding to the specified context

Using contexts to specify files.

This reads in one of the standard packages that come with *Mathematica*.

In[1]:= **<<Graphics`Colors`**

+	*name*.mx	file in DumpSave format
+	*name*.mx/$SystemID/*name*.mx	file in DumpSave format for your computer system
	name.m	file in *Mathematica* source format
+	*name*/init.m	initialization file for a particular directory
	dir/...	files in other directories specified by $Path

The typical sequence of files looked for by **<<***name*`.

Mathematica is set up so that **<<***name*` will automatically try to load the appropriate version of a file. It will first try to load a *name*.mx file that is optimized for your particular computer system. If it finds no such file, then it will try to load a *name*.m file containing ordinary system-independent *Mathematica* input.

If *name* is a directory, then *Mathematica* will try to load the initialization file init.m in that directory. The purpose of the init.m file is to provide a convenient way to set up *Mathematica* packages that involve many separate files.

The idea is to allow you to give just the command **<<***name*`, but then to load init.m to initialize the whole package, reading in whatever other files are necessary.

This reads in the file Graphics/init.m, which initializes all standard *Mathematica* graphics packages.

In[2]:= **<<Graphics`**

■ 2.11.6 Manipulating Files and Directories

CopyFile["*file*₁", "*file*₂"]	copy *file*₁ to *file*₂
RenameFile["*file*₁", "*file*₂"]	give *file*₁ the name *file*₂
DeleteFile["*file*"]	delete a file
FileByteCount["*file*"]	give the number of bytes in a file
FileDate["*file*"]	give the modification date for a file
SetFileDate["*file*"]	set the modification date for a file to be the current date
FileType["*file*"]	give the type of a file as File, Directory or None

Functions for manipulating files.

Different operating systems have different commands for manipulating files. *Mathematica* provides a simple set of file manipulation functions, intended to work in the same way under all operating systems.

Notice that CopyFile and RenameFile give the final file the same modification date as the original one. FileDate returns modification dates in the {*year*, *month*, *day*, *hour*, *minute*, *second*} format used by Date.

CreateDirectory["*name*"]	create a new directory
DeleteDirectory["*name*"]	delete an empty directory
DeleteDirectory["*name*", DeleteContents -> True]	
	delete a directory and all files and directories it contains
RenameDirectory["*name*₁", "*name*₂"]	
	rename a directory
CopyDirectory["*name*₁", "*name*₂"]	
	copy a directory and all the files in it

Functions for manipulating directories.

■ 2.11.7 Reading Data

With <<, you can read files which contain *Mathematica* expressions given in input form. Sometimes, however, you may instead need to read files of *data* in other formats. For example, you may have data generated by an external program which consists of a sequence of numbers separated by spaces.

This data cannot be read directly as *Mathematica* input. However, the function ReadList can take such data from a file or input stream, and convert it to a *Mathematica* list.

ReadList["*file*", Number]	read a sequence of numbers from a file, and put them in a *Mathematica* list

Reading numbers from a file.

Here is a file of numbers.	*In[1]:=* `!!numbers`
	
	`11.1    22.2    33.3`
	`44.4    55.5    66.6`

This reads all the numbers in the file, and returns a list of them.	*In[2]:=* `ReadList["numbers", Number]` *Out[2]=* `{11.1, 22.2, 33.3, 44.4, 55.5, 66.6}`

ReadList["*file*", {Number, Number}]	
	read numbers from a file, putting each successive pair into a separate list
ReadList["*file*", Table[Number, {*n*}]]	
	put each successive block of *n* numbers in a separate list
ReadList["*file*", Number, RecordLists -> True]	
	put all the numbers on each line of the file into a separate list

Reading blocks of numbers.

This puts each successive pair of numbers from the file into a separate list.	*In[3]:=* `ReadList["numbers", {Number, Number}]` *Out[3]=* `{{11.1, 22.2}, {33.3, 44.4}, {55.5, 66.6}}`
This makes each line in the file into a separate list.	*In[4]:=* `ReadList["numbers", Number, RecordLists -> True]` *Out[4]=* `{{11.1, 22.2, 33.3}, {44.4, 55.5, 66.6}}`

ReadList can handle numbers which are given in Fortran-like "E" notation. Thus, for example, ReadList will read 2.5E+5 as 2.5×10^5. Note that ReadList can handle numbers with any number of digits of precision.

Here is a file containing numbers in Fortran-like "E" notation.	*In[5]:=* `!!bignum`
	
	`4.5E-5       7.8E4`
	`2.5E2       -8.9`

ReadList can handle numbers in this form.	*In[6]:=* `ReadList["bignum", Number]` *Out[6]=* `{0.000045, 78000., 250., -8.9}`

ReadList["*file*", *type*]	read a sequence of objects of a particular type
ReadList["*file*", *type*, *n*]	read at most *n* objects

Reading objects of various types.

ReadList can read not only numbers, but also a variety of other types of object. Each type of object is specified by a symbol such as Number.

Here is a file containing text.

```
In[7]:= !!strings
Here is text.
And more text.
```

This produces a list of the characters in the file, each given as a one-character string.

```
In[8]:= ReadList["strings", Character]
Out[8]= {H, e, r, e,  , i, s,  , t, e, x, t, .,  ,
          , A, n, d,  , m, o, r, e,  , t, e, x, t, .,
         }
```

Here are the integer codes corresponding to each of the bytes in the file.

```
In[9]:= ReadList["strings", Byte]
Out[9]= {72, 101, 114, 101, 32, 105,
         115, 32, 116, 101, 120, 116, 46,
         32, 10, 65, 110, 100, 32, 109, 111, 114, 101,
         32, 116, 101, 120, 116, 46, 10}
```

This puts the data from each line in the file into a separate list.

```
In[10]:= ReadList["strings", Byte, RecordLists -> True]
Out[10]= {{72, 101, 114, 101, 32, 105,
           115, 32, 116, 101, 120, 116, 46, 32},
          {65, 110, 100, 32, 109, 111, 114,
           101, 32, 116, 101, 120, 116, 46}}
```

Byte	single byte of data, returned as an integer
Character	single character, returned as a one-character string
Real	approximate number in Fortran-like notation
Number	exact or approximate number in Fortran-like notation
Word	sequence of characters delimited by word separators
Record	sequence of characters delimited by record separators
String	string terminated by a newline
Expression	complete *Mathematica* expression
Hold[Expression]	complete *Mathematica* expression, returned inside Hold

Types of objects to read.

This returns a list of the "words" in
the file strings.

In[11]:= **ReadList["strings", Word]**

Out[11]= {Here, is, text., And, more, text.}

ReadList allows you to read "words" from a file. It considers a "word" to be any sequence of characters delimited by word separators. You can set the option **WordSeparators** to specify the strings you want to treat as word separators. The default is to include spaces and tabs, but not to include, for example, standard punctuation characters. Note that in all cases successive words can be separated by any number of word separators. These separators are never taken to be part of the actual words returned by **ReadList**.

option name	default value	
RecordLists	False	whether to make a separate list for the objects in each record
RecordSeparators	{"\n"}	separators for records
WordSeparators	{" ", "\t"}	separators for words
NullRecords	False	whether to keep zero-length records
NullWords	False	whether to keep zero-length words
TokenWords	{}	words to take as tokens

Options for ReadList.

This reads the text in the file strings
as a sequence of words, using the
letter e and . as word separators.

In[12]:= **ReadList["strings", Word, WordSeparators -> {"e", "."}]**

Out[12]= {H, r, is t, xt, , And mor, t, xt}

Mathematica considers any data file to consist of a sequence of *records*. By default, each line is considered to be a separate record. In general, you can set the option **RecordSeparators** to give a list of separators for records. Note that words can never cross record separators. As with word separators, any number of record separators can exist between successive records, and these separators are not considered to be part of the records themselves.

By default, each line of the file is
considered to be a record.

In[13]:= **ReadList["strings", Record] // InputForm**

Out[13]//InputForm= {"Here is text. ", "And more text."}

Here is a file containing three
"sentences" ending with periods.

In[14]:= **!!sentences**

Here is text. And more.
And a second line.

This allows both periods and newlines
as record separators.

In[15]:= **ReadList["sentences", Record,**
                    RecordSeparators -> {".", "\n"}]

Out[15]= {Here is text, And more, And a second line}

This puts the words in each "sentence" into a separate list.

```
In[16]:= ReadList["sentences", Word, RecordLists -> True,
                  RecordSeparators -> {".", "\n"}]

Out[16]= {{Here, is, text}, {And, more}, {And, a, second, line}}
```

```
ReadList["file", Record, RecordSeparators -> { }]
                     read the whole of a file as a single string

ReadList["file", Record, RecordSeparators -> {{"lsep_1", ... }, {"rsep_1", ... }}]
                     make a list of those parts of a file which lie between the lsep_i
                     and the rsep_i
```

Settings for the RecordSeparators option.

Here is a file containing some text.

```
In[17]:= !!source

f[x] (: function f :)
g[x] (: function g :)
```

This reads all the text in the file source, and returns it as a single string.

```
In[18]:= InputForm[
              ReadList["source", Record, RecordSeparators -> { }]
              ]

Out[18]//InputForm=
              {"f[x] (: function f :)\ng[x] (: function g :)\n"}
```

This gives a list of the parts of the file that lie between (: and :) separators.

```
In[19]:= ReadList["source", Record,
                  RecordSeparators -> {{"(: "}, {" :)"}}]

Out[19]= {function f, function g}
```

By choosing appropriate separators, you can pick out specific parts of files.

```
In[20]:= ReadList[ "source", Record,
             RecordSeparators ->
                     {{"(: function ", "["}, {" :)", "]"}} ]

Out[20]= {x, f, x, g}
```

Mathematica usually allows any number of appropriate separators to appear between successive records or words. Sometimes, however, when several separators are present, you may want to assume that a "null record" or "null word" appears between each pair of adjacent separators. You can do this by setting the options NullRecords -> True or NullWords -> True.

Here is a file containing "words" separated by colons.

```
In[21]:= !!words

first:second::fourth:::seventh
```

Here the repeated colons are treated as single separators.

```
In[22]:= ReadList["words", Word, WordSeparators -> {":"}]

Out[22]= {first, second, fourth, seventh}
```

Now repeated colons are taken to have null words in between.

```
In[23]:= ReadList["words", Word, WordSeparators -> {":"},
                                 NullWords -> True]

Out[23]= {first, second, , fourth, , , seventh}
```

In most cases, you want words to be delimited by separators which are not themselves considered as words. Sometimes, however, it is convenient to allow words to be delimited by special "token words", which are themselves words. You can give a list of such token words as a setting for the option TokenWords.

Here is some text.

In[24]:= **!!language**

22*a*b+56*c+13*a*d

This reads the text, using the specified token words to delimit words in the text.

In[25]:= **ReadList["language", Word, TokenWords -> {"+", "*"}]**

Out[25]= {22, *, a, *, b, +, 56, *, c, +, 13, *, a, *, d}

You can use ReadList to read *Mathematica* expressions from files. In general, each expression must end with a newline, although a single expression may go on for several lines.

Here is a file containing text that can be used as *Mathematica* input.

In[26]:= **!!exprs**

x + y +
z
2^8

This reads the text in exprs as *Mathematica* expressions.

In[27]:= **ReadList["exprs", Expression]**

Out[27]= {x + y + z, 256}

This prevents the expressions from being evaluated.

In[28]:= **ReadList["exprs", Hold[Expression]]**

Out[28]= {Hold[x + y + z], Hold[2^8]}

ReadList can insert the objects it reads into any *Mathematica* expression. The second argument to ReadList can consist of any expression containing symbols such as Number and Word specifying objects to read. Thus, for example, ReadList["*file*", {Number, Number}] inserts successive pairs of numbers that it reads into lists. Similarly, ReadList["*file*", Hold[Expression]] puts expressions that it reads inside Hold.

If ReadList reaches the end of your file before it has finished reading a particular set of objects you have asked for, then it inserts the special symbol EndOfFile in place of the objects it has not yet read.

Here is a file of numbers.

In[29]:= **!!numbers**

11.1   22.2   33.3
44.4   55.5   66.6

The symbol EndOfFile appears in place of numbers that were needed after the end of the file was reached.

In[30]:= **ReadList["numbers", {Number, Number, Number, Number}]**

Out[30]= {{11.1, 22.2, 33.3, 44.4},
            {55.5, 66.6, EndOfFile, EndOfFile}}

| ReadList["!*command*", *type*] | execute a command, and read its output |
| ReadList[*stream*, *type*] | read any input stream |

Reading from commands and streams.

This executes the Unix command date,   *In[31]:=* **ReadList["!date", String]**
and reads its output as a string.
                                          Out[31]= {Wed Mar 27 16:56:12 CST 1996}

OpenRead["*file*"]	open a file for reading
OpenRead["!*command*"]	open a pipe for reading
Read[*stream*, *type*]	read an object of the specified type from a stream
Skip[*stream*, *type*]	skip over an object of the specified type in an input stream
Skip[*stream*, *type*, *n*]	skip over *n* objects of the specified type in an input stream
Close[*stream*]	close an input stream

Functions for reading from input streams.

ReadList allows you to read *all* the data in a particular file or input stream. Sometimes, however, you want to get data a piece at a time, perhaps doing tests to find out what kind of data to expect next.

When you read individual pieces of data from a file, *Mathematica* always remembers the "current point" that you are at in the file. When you call OpenRead, *Mathematica* sets up an input stream from a file, and makes your current point the beginning of the file. Every time you read an object from the file using Read, *Mathematica* sets your current point to be just after the object you have read. Using Skip, you can advance the current point past a sequence of objects without actually reading the objects.

Here is a file of numbers.   *In[32]:=* **!!numbers**

                                          11.1   22.2   33.3
                                          44.4   55.5   66.6

This opens an input stream from the   *In[33]:=* **snum = OpenRead["numbers"]**
file.
                                          Out[33]= InputStream[numbers, 47]

This reads the first number from the   *In[34]:=* **Read[snum, Number]**
file.
                                          Out[34]= 11.1

This reads the second pair of numbers.   *In[35]:=* **Read[snum, {Number, Number}]**

                                          Out[35]= {22.2, 33.3}

This skips the next number.   *In[36]:=* **Skip[snum, Number]**

And this reads the remaining numbers.   *In[37]:=* **ReadList[snum, Number]**

                                          Out[37]= {55.5, 66.6}

This closes the input stream.   *In[38]:=* **Close[snum]**

                                          Out[38]= numbers

You can use the options `WordSeparators` and `RecordSeparators` in `Read` and `Skip` just as you do in `ReadList`.

Note that if you try to read past the end of file, `Read` returns the symbol `EndOfFile`.

■ 2.11.8 Searching Files

`FindList["`*file*`", "`*text*`"]`	get a list of all the lines in the file that contain the specified text
`FindList["`*file*`", "`*text*`", n]`	get a list of the first *n* lines that contain the specified text
`FindList["`*file*`", {"`*text*$_1$`", "`*text*$_2$`", ... }]`	get lines that contain any of the *text*$_i$

Finding lines that contain specified text.

Here is a file containing some text.	*In[1]:=* `!!textfile`
	
	`Here is the first line of text.`
	`And the second.`
	`And the third. Here is the end.`

This returns a list of all the lines in the file containing the text `is`.	*In[2]:=* `FindList["textfile", "is"]` *Out[2]=* `{Here is the first line of text.,` `           And the third. Here is the end.}`
The text `fourth` appears nowhere in the file.	*In[3]:=* `FindList["textfile", "fourth"]` *Out[3]=* `{}`

By default, `FindList` scans successive lines of a file, and returns those lines which contain the text you specify. In general, however, you can get `FindList` to scan successive *records*, and return complete records which contain specified text. As in `ReadList`, the option `RecordSeparators` allows you to tell *Mathematica* what strings you want to consider as record separators. Note that by giving a pair of lists as the setting for `RecordSeparators`, you can specify different left and right separators. By doing this, you can make `FindList` search only for text which is between specific pairs of separators.

This finds all "sentences" ending with a period which contain `And`.	*In[4]:=* `FindList["textfile", "And", RecordSeparators -> {"."}]`
	
	Out[4]= `{`
	`        And the second,`
	`        And the third}`

option name	default value	
RecordSeparators	{"\n"}	separators for records
AnchoredSearch	False	whether to require the text searched for to be at the beginning of a record
WordSeparators	{" ", "\t"}	separators for words
WordSearch	False	whether to require that the text searched for appear as a word
IgnoreCase	False	whether to treat lower- and upper-case letters as equivalent

Options for FindList.

This finds only the occurrence of Here which is at the beginning of a line in the file.

```
In[5]:= FindList["textfile", "Here", AnchoredSearch -> True]
Out[5]= {Here is the first line of text.}
```

In general, FindList finds text that appears anywhere inside a record. By setting the option WordSearch -> True, however, you can tell FindList to require that the text it is looking for appears as a separate *word* in the record. The option WordSeparators specifies the list of separators for words.

The text th does appear in the file, but not as a word. As a result, the FindList fails.

```
In[6]:= FindList["textfile", "th", WordSearch -> True]
Out[6]= {}
```

FindList[{"*file*₁", "*file*₂", ... }, "*text*"]
  search for occurrences of the text in any of the *file*ᵢ

Searching in multiple files.

This searches for third in two copies of textfile.

```
In[7]:= FindList[{"textfile", "textfile"}, "third"]
Out[7]= {And the third. Here is the end.,
         And the third. Here is the end.}
```

It is often useful to call FindList on lists of files generated by functions such as FileNames.

FindList["!*command*", ...]   run an external command, and find text in its output

Finding text in the output from an external program.

This runs the external Unix command date.	*In[8]:=* **!date** Wed Mar 27 16:56:53 CST 1996 *Out[8]=* 0
This finds the time-of-day field in the date.	*In[9]:=* **FindList["!date", ":", RecordSeparators -> {" "}]** *Out[9]=* {16:56:55}

OpenRead["*file*"]	open a file for reading
OpenRead["!*command*"]	open a pipe for reading
Find[*stream*, *text*]	find the next occurrence of *text*
Close[*stream*]	close an input stream

Finding successive occurrences of text.

FindList works by making one pass through a particular file, looking for occurrences of the text you specify. Sometimes, however, you may want to search incrementally for successive occurrences of a piece of text. You can do this using Find.

In order to use Find, you first explicitly have to open an input stream using OpenRead. Then, every time you call Find on this stream, it will search for the text you specify, and make the current point in the file be just after the record it finds. As a result, you can call Find several times to find successive pieces of text.

This opens an input stream for textfile.	*In[10]:=* **stext = OpenRead["textfile"]** *Out[10]=* InputStream[textfile, 22]
This finds the first line containing And.	*In[11]:=* **Find[stext, "And"]** *Out[11]=* And the second.
Calling Find again gives you the next line containing And.	*In[12]:=* **Find[stext, "And"]** *Out[12]=* And the third. Here is the end.
This closes the input stream.	*In[13]:=* **Close[stext]** *Out[13]=* textfile

Once you have an input stream, you can mix calls to Find, Skip and Read. If you ever call FindList or ReadList, *Mathematica* will immediately read to the end of the input stream.

This opens the input stream.	*In[14]:=* **stext = OpenRead["textfile"]** *Out[14]=* InputStream[textfile, 27]

This finds the first line which contains second, and leaves the current point in the file at the beginning of the next line.

```
In[15]:= Find[stext, "second"]
Out[15]= And the second.
```

Read can then read the word that appears at the beginning of the line.

```
In[16]:= Read[stext, Word]
Out[16]= And
```

This skips over the next three words.

```
In[17]:= Skip[stext, Word, 3]
```

Mathematica finds is in the remaining text, and prints the entire record as output.

```
In[18]:= Find[stext, "is"]
Out[18]= And the third. Here is the end.
```

This closes the input stream.

```
In[19]:= Close[stext]
Out[19]= textfile
```

StreamPosition[*stream*]	find the position of the current point in an open stream
SetStreamPosition[*stream*, *n*]	set the position of the current point
SetStreamPosition[*stream*, 0]	set the current point to the beginning of a stream
SetStreamPosition[*stream*, Infinity]	set the current point to the end of a stream

Finding and setting the current point in a stream.

Functions like Read, Skip and Find usually operate on streams in an entirely sequential fashion. Each time one of the functions is called, the current point in the stream moves on.

Sometimes, you may need to know where the current point in a stream is, and be able to reset it. On most computer systems, StreamPosition returns the position of the current point as an integer giving the number of bytes from the beginning of the stream.

This opens the stream.

```
In[20]:= stext = OpenRead["textfile"]
Out[20]= InputStream[textfile, 33]
```

When you first open the file, the current point is at the beginning, and StreamPosition returns 0.

```
In[21]:= StreamPosition[stext]
Out[21]= 0
```

This reads the first line in the file.

```
In[22]:= Read[stext, Record]
Out[22]= Here is the first line of text.
```

Now the current point has advanced.

```
In[23]:= StreamPosition[stext]
Out[23]= 31
```

This sets the stream position back.	*In[24]:=* **SetStreamPosition[stext, 5]**
	Out[24]= 5
Now Read returns the remainder of the first line.	*In[25]:=* **Read[stext, Record]**
	Out[25]= is the first line of text.
This closes the stream.	*In[26]:=* **Close[stext]**
	Out[26]= textfile

■ 2.11.9 Searching and Reading Strings

Functions like Read and Find are most often used for processing text and data from external files. In some cases, however, you may find it convenient to use these same functions to process strings within *Mathematica*. You can do this by using the function StringToStream, which opens an input stream that takes characters not from an external file, but instead from a *Mathematica* string.

StringToStream["*string*"]	open an input stream for reading from a string
Close[*stream*]	close an input stream

Treating strings as input streams.

This opens an input stream for reading from the string.	*In[1]:=* **str = StringToStream["A string of words."]**
	Out[1]= InputStream[String, 5]
This reads the first "word" from the string.	*In[2]:=* **Read[str, Word]**
	Out[2]= A
This reads the remaining words from the string.	*In[3]:=* **ReadList[str, Word]**
	Out[3]= {string, of, words.}
This closes the input stream.	*In[4]:=* **Close[str]**
	Out[4]= String

Input streams associated with strings work just like those with files. At any given time, there is a current position in the stream, which advances when you use functions like Read. The current position is given as the number of bytes from the beginning of the string by the function StreamPosition[*stream*]. You can explicitly set the current position using SetStreamPosition[*stream*, *n*].

Here is an input stream associated with a string.	*In[5]:=* **str = StringToStream["123 456 789"]**
	Out[5]= InputStream[String, 10]
The current position is initially 0 bytes from the beginning of the string.	*In[6]:=* **StreamPosition[str]**
	Out[6]= 0

This reads a number from the stream.	*In[7]:=* **Read[str, Number]**
	Out[7]= 123
The current position is now 3 bytes from the beginning of the string.	*In[8]:=* **StreamPosition[str]**
	Out[8]= 3
This sets the current position to be 1 byte from the beginning of the string.	*In[9]:=* **SetStreamPosition[str, 1]**
	Out[9]= 1
If you now read a number from the string, you get the 23 part of 123.	*In[10]:=* **Read[str, Number]**
	Out[10]= 23
This sets the current position to the end of the string.	*In[11]:=* **SetStreamPosition[str, Infinity]**
	Out[11]= 11
If you now try to read from the stream, you will always get EndOfFile.	*In[12]:=* **Read[str, Number]**
	Out[12]= EndOfFile
This closes the stream.	*In[13]:=* **Close[str]**
	Out[13]= String

Particularly when you are processing large volumes of textual data, it is common to read fairly long strings into *Mathematica*, then to use **StringToStream** to allow further processing of these strings within *Mathematica*. Once you have created an input stream using **StringToStream**, you can read and search the string using any of the functions discussed for files above.

This puts the whole contents of textfile into a string.	*In[14]:=* **s = First[ReadList["textfile", Record,** **RecordSeparators -> {}]]**

	Out[14]= Here is the first line of text.
	                 And the second.
	                 And the third. Here is the end.

This opens an input stream for the string.	*In[15]:=* **str = StringToStream[s]**
	Out[15]= InputStream[String, 22]
This gives the lines of text in the string that contain is.	*In[16]:=* **FindList[str, "is"]**
	Out[16]= {Here is the first line of text., And the third. Here is the end.}
This resets the current position back to the beginning of the string.	*In[17]:=* **SetStreamPosition[str, 0]**
	Out[17]= 0
This finds the first occurrence of the in the string, and leaves the current point just after it.	*In[18]:=* **Find[str, "the", RecordSeparators -> {" "}]**
	Out[18]= the

This reads the "word" which appears immediately after the.

In[19]:= **Read[str, Word]**

Out[19]= first

This closes the input stream.

In[20]:= **Close[str]**

Out[20]= String

2.12 *MathLink* and External Program Communication

+■ 2.12.1 How *MathLink* Is Used

Most of this book has been concerned with how human users interact with *Mathematica*. *MathLink* provides a mechanism through which *programs* rather than human users can interact with *Mathematica*.

- Calling functions in an external program from within *Mathematica*.

- Calling *Mathematica* from within an external program.

- Setting up alternative front ends to *Mathematica*.

- Exchanging data between *Mathematica* and external programs.

- Exchanging data between concurrent *Mathematica* processes.

Some typical uses of *MathLink*.

MathLink provides a general interface for external programs to communicate with *Mathematica*. Many standard software systems now have *MathLink* compatibility either built in or available in add-on modules.

In addition, the *MathLink* Developer's Kit bundled with most versions of *Mathematica* provides the tools you need to create your own *MathLink*-compatible programs.

Once you have a *MathLink*-compatible program, you can transparently establish a link between it and *Mathematica*.

The link can either be on a single computer, or it can be over a network, potentially with a different type of computer at each end.

- Implementing inner loops in a low-level language.

- Handling large volumes of data external to *Mathematica*.

- Sending *Mathematica* graphics or other data for special processing.

- Connecting to a system with an existing user interface.

A few uses of *MathLink*-compatible programs.

MathLink-compatible programs range from very simple to very complex. A minimal *MathLink*-compatible program is just a few lines long. But it is also possible to build very large and sophisticated *MathLink*-compatible programs. Indeed, the *Mathematica* notebook front end is one example of a sophisticated *MathLink*-compatible program.

> ■ *MathLink* is a mechanism for exchanging *Mathematica* expressions between programs.

The basic idea of *MathLink*.

Much of the power of *MathLink* comes from its use of *Mathematica* expressions. The basic idea is that *MathLink* provides a way to exchange *Mathematica* expressions between programs, and such expressions can represent absolutely any kind of data.

> ■ An array of numbers.
>
> ■ A collection of geometrical objects.
>
> ■ A sequence of commands.
>
> ■ A stream of text.
>
> ■ Records in a database.
>
> ■ The cells of a *Mathematica* notebook.

A few examples of data represented by *Mathematica* expressions in *MathLink*.

The *MathLink* library consists of a collection of routines that allow external programs to send and receive *Mathematica* expressions.

The *MathLink* Developer's Kit provides utilities for incorporating these routines into external programs. The utilities are primarily intended for programs written in the C programming language, although by adding the appropriate links to the *MathLink* library it is possible to make any program *MathLink* compatible.

An important feature of the *MathLink* library is that it is completely platform independent: it can transparently use any interprogram communication mechanism that exists on your computer system.

■ 2.12.2 Installing Existing *MathLink*-Compatible Programs

One of the most common uses of *MathLink* is to allow you to call functions in an external program from within *Mathematica*. Once the external program has been set up, all you need do to be able to use it is to "install" it in your current *Mathematica* session.

Install["*prog*"]	install a *MathLink*-compatible external program
Uninstall[*link*]	uninstall the program

Setting up external programs with functions to be called from within *Mathematica*.

This installs a *MathLink*-compatible external program called bitprog.	*In[1]:=* **Install["bitprog"]**	
	Out[1]= LinkObject[bitprog, 4, 4]	
BitAnd is one of the functions inside bitprog.	*In[2]:=* **BitAnd[65535, 2047]**	
	Out[2]= 2047	
You can use it just as you would a function within *Mathematica*.	*In[3]:=* **Table[BitAnd[65535, i], {i, 2046, 2049}]**	
	Out[3]= {2046, 2047, 2048, 2049}	

When you have a package written in the *Mathematica* language a single version will run unchanged on any computer system. But external programs typically need to be compiled separately for every different type of computer.

Mathematica has a convention of keeping versions of external programs in directories that are named after the types of computers on which they will run. And assuming that this convention has been followed, Install["*prog*"] should always install the version of *prog* appropriate for the particular kind of computer that you are currently using.

Install["name`"]	install a program found anywhere on $Path

Using context names to specify programs to install.

When you ask to read in a *Mathematica* language file using <<*name*`, *Mathematica* will automatically search all directories in the list $Path in order to find a file with the appropriate name. Similarly, if you use Install["*name*`"] *Mathematica* will automatically search all directories in $Path in order to find an external program with the name *name*.exe. Install["*name*`"] allows you to install programs that are stored in a central directory without explicitly having to specify their location.

▪ 2.12.3 Setting Up External Functions to Be Called from *Mathematica*

If you have a function defined in an external program, then what you need to do in order to make it possible to call the function from within *Mathematica* is to add appropriate *MathLink* code that passes arguments to the function, and takes back the results it produces.

In simple cases, you can generate the necessary code just by giving an appropriate *MathLink template* for each external function.

```
:Begin:
:Function:      f
:Pattern:       f[x_Integer, y_Integer]
:Arguments:     {x, y}
:ArgumentTypes: {Integer, Integer}
:ReturnType:    Integer
:End:
```

A file `f.tm` containing a *MathLink* template for an external function `f`.

`:Begin:`	begin the template for a particular function
`:Function:`	the name of the function in the external program
`:Pattern:`	the pattern to be defined to call the function
`:Arguments:`	the arguments to the function
`:ArgumentTypes:`	the types of the arguments to the function
`:ReturnType:`	the type of the value returned by the function
`:End:`	end the template for a particular function
`:Evaluate:`	*Mathematica* input to evaluate when the function is installed

The elements of a *MathLink* template.

Once you have constructed a *MathLink* template for a particular external function, you have to combine this template with the actual source code for the function. Assuming that the source code is written in the C programming language, you can do this just by adding a line to include the standard *MathLink* header file, and then inserting a small **main** program.

Include the standard *MathLink* header file.	`#include "mathlink.h"`

Here is the actual source code for the function `f`.	`int f(int x, int y) {`
	`    return x+y;`
	`}`

This sets up the external program to be ready to take requests from *Mathematica*.	`int main(int argc, char *argv[]) {`
	`    return MLMain(argc, argv);`
	`}`

A file `f.c` containing C source code.

Note that the form of `main` required on different systems may be slightly different. The release notes included in the *MathLink* Developer's Kit on your particular computer system should give the appropriate form.

`mcc`	preprocess and compile *MathLink* source files
`mprep`	preprocess *MathLink* source files

Typical external programs for processing *MathLink* source files.

MathLink templates are conventionally put in files with names of the form *file*`.tm`. Such files can also contain C source code, interspersed between templates for different functions.

Once you have set up the appropriate files, you then need to process the *MathLink* template information, and compile all of your source code. Typically you do this by running various external programs, but the details will depend on your computer system.

Under Unix, for example, the *MathLink Developer's Kit* includes a program named `mcc` which will preprocess *MathLink* templates in any file whose name ends with `.tm`, and then call `cc` on the resulting C source code. `mcc` will pass command-line options and other files directly to `cc`.

This preprocesses `f.tm`, then compiles the resulting C source file.	`mcc -o f.exe f.tm`

This installs the binary in the current *Mathematica* session.	`In[1]:= Install["f.exe"]` `Out[1]= LinkObject[f.exe, 4, 4]`
Now `f[x, y]` calls the external function `f(int x, int y)` and adds two integers together.	`In[2]:= f[6, 9]` `Out[2]= 15`
The external program handles only machine integers, so this gives a peculiar result.	`In[3]:= f[2^31-1, 5]` `Out[3]= -2147483644`

On systems other than Unix, the *MathLink Developer's Kit* typically includes a program named `mprep`, which you have to call directly, giving as input all of the `.tm` files that you want to preprocess. `mprep` will generate C source code as output, which you can then feed to a C compiler.

Install["*prog*"]	install an external program
Uninstall[*link*]	uninstall an external program
Links["*prog*"]	show active links associated with "*prog*"
Links[ ]	show all active links
LinkPatterns[*link*]	show patterns that can be evaluated on a particular link

Handling links to external programs.

This finds the link to the f.exe
program.

```
In[4]:= Links["f.exe"]
Out[4]= {LinkObject[./f.exe, 4, 4]}
```

This shows the *Mathematica* patterns
that can be evaluated using the link.

```
In[5]:= LinkPatterns[%[[1]]]
Out[5]= {f[x_Integer, y_Integer]}
```

Install sets up the actual function f
to execute an appropriate
ExternalCall function.

```
In[6]:= ?f
Global`f

f[x_Integer, y_Integer] :=
    ExternalCall[LinkObject["./f.exe", 4, 4],
        CallPacket[0, {x, y}]]
```

When a *MathLink* template file is processed, two basic things are done. First, the :Pattern: and
:Arguments: specifications are used to generate a *Mathematica* definition that calls an external function
via *MathLink*. And second, the :Function:, :ArgumentTypes: and :ReturnType: specifications are
used to generate C source code that calls your function within the external program.

	:Begin:	
This gives the name of the actual C function to call in the external program.	:Function:	prog_add
This gives the *Mathematica* pattern for which a definition should be set up.	:Pattern:	SkewAdd[x_Integer, y_Integer:1]
The values of the two list elements are the actual arguments to be passed to the external function.	:Arguments:	{x, If[x > 1, y, y + x - 2]}
This specifies that the arguments should be passed as integers to the C function.	:ArgumentTypes:	{Integer, Integer}
This specifies that the return value from the C function will be an integer.	:ReturnType:	Integer
	:End:	

Both the :Pattern: and :Arguments: specifications in a *MathLink* template can be any *Mathematica* expressions. Whatever you give as the :Arguments: specification will be evaluated every time you call the external function. The result of the evaluation will be used as the list of arguments to pass to the function.

Sometimes you may want to set up *Mathematica* expressions that should be evaluated not when an external function is called, but instead only when the external function is first installed.

You can do this by inserting :Evaluate: specifications in your *MathLink* template. The expression you give after :Evaluate: can go on for several lines: it is assumed to end when there is first a blank line, or a line that does not begin with spaces or tabs.

This specifies that a usage message for SkewAdd should be set up when the external program is installed.	```:Evaluate: SkewAdd::usage = "SkewAdd[x, y] performs a skew addition in an external program."```

When an external program is installed, the specifications in its *MathLink* template file are used in the order they were given. This means that any expressions given in :Evaluate: specifications that appear before :Begin: will have been evaluated before definitions for the external function are set up.

Here are *Mathematica* expressions to be evaluated before the definitions for external functions are set up.	```:Evaluate: BeginPackage["XPack`"]:Evaluate:  XF1::usage = "XF1[x, y] is one external function.":Evaluate:  XF2::usage = "XF2[x] is another external function.":Evaluate:  Begin["`Private`"]```
This specifies that the function XF1 in *Mathematica* should be set up to call the function f in the external C program.	```:Begin::Function: f:Pattern: XF1[x_Integer, y_Integer]:Arguments: {x, y}:ArgumentTypes: {Integer, Integer}:ReturnType: Integer:End:```
This specifies that XF2 in *Mathematica* should call g. Its argument and return value are taken to be approximate real numbers.	```:Begin::Function: g:Pattern: XF2[x_?NumberQ]:Arguments: {x}:ArgumentTypes: {Real}:ReturnType: Real:End:```
These *Mathematica* expressions are evaluated after the definitions for the external functions. They end the special context used for the definitions.	```:Evaluate: End[ ]:Evaluate: EndPackage[ ]```

Here is the actual source code for the function f. There is no need for the arguments of this function to have the same names as their *Mathematica* counterparts.	```int f(int i, int j) {
return i + j;
}```
Here is the actual source code for g. Numbers that you give in *Mathematica* will automatically be converted into C double types before being passed to g.	```double g(double x) {
return x*x;
}```

By using :Evaluate: specifications, you can evaluate *Mathematica* expressions when an external program is first installed. You can also execute code inside the external program at this time simply by inserting the code in main() before the call to MLMain(). This is sometimes useful if you need to initialize the external program before any functions in it are used.

MLEvaluateString(stdlink, "*string*")	evaluate a string as *Mathematica* input

Executing a command in *Mathematica* from within an external program.

This evaluates a *Mathematica* Print function if i < j.	```int diff(int i, int j) {

    if (i < j) MLEvaluateString(stdlink, "Print[\"negative\"]");

    return i - j;
}``` |

This installs an external program containing the diff function defined above.	*In[7]:=* **Install["diffprog"]**
	Out[7]= LinkObject[diffprog, 5, 5]
Calling diff causes Print to be executed.	*In[8]:=* **diff[4, 7]**
	negative
	Out[8]= -3

Note that any results generated in the evaluation requested by MLEvaluateString() are ignored. To make use of such results requires full two-way communication between *Mathematica* and external programs, as discussed on page 660.

◾ 2.12.4 Handling Lists, Arrays and Other Expressions

MathLink allows you to exchange data of any type with external programs. For more common types of data, you simply need to give appropriate `:ArgumentTypes:` or `:ReturnType:` specifications in your *MathLink* template file.

Mathematica specification		C specification
Integer	integer	int
Real	floating-point number	double
IntegerList	list of integers	int *, long
RealList	list of floating-point numbers	double *, long
String	character string	char *
Symbol	symbol name	char *
Manual	call *MathLink* routines directly	void

Basic type specifications.

Here is the *MathLink* template for a function that takes a list of integers as its argument.	`:Begin:`
	`:Function:       h`
	`:Pattern:        h[a_List]`
	`:Arguments:      {a}`
	`:ArgumentTypes:  {IntegerList}`
	`:ReturnType:     Integer`
	`:End:`	

Here is the template for a function that takes a list of integers as its argument.

```
:Begin:
:Function:       h
:Pattern:        h[a_List]
:Arguments:      {a}
:ArgumentTypes:  {IntegerList}
:ReturnType:     Integer
:End:
```

Here is the C source code for the function. Note the extra argument `alen` which is used to pass the length of the list.

```
int h(int *a, long alen) {

    int i, tot=0;

    for(i=0; i<alen; i++)
        tot += a[i];

    return tot;
}
```

This installs an external program containing the specifications for the function `h`.

```
In[1]:= Install["hprog"]
Out[1]= LinkObject[hprog, 4, 4]
```

This calls the external code.	*In[2]:=* **h[{3, 5, 6}]**
	Out[2]= 14
This does not match the pattern h[a_List] so does not call the external code.	*In[3]:=* **h[67]**
	Out[3]= h[67]
The pattern is matched, but the elements in the list are of the wrong type for the external code, so $Failed is returned.	*In[4]:=* **h[{a, b, c}]**
	Out[4]= $Failed

You can mix basic types of arguments in any way you want. Whenever you use IntegerList or RealList, however, you have to include an extra argument in your C program to represent the length of the list.

Here is an :ArgumentTypes: specification.	:ArgumentTypes: {IntegerList, RealList, Integer}
Here is a possible corresponding C function declaration.	void f(int *a, long alen, double *b, long blen, int c)

Note that when a list is passed to a C program by *MathLink* its first element is assumed to be at position 0, as is standard in C, rather than at position 1, as is standard in *Mathematica*.

In addition, following C standards, character strings specified by String are passed as char * objects, terminated by \0 null bytes. Page 652 discusses how to handle special characters.

`MLPutInteger(stdlink, int i)`	put a single integer
`MLPutReal(stdlink, double x)`	put a single floating-point number

`MLPutIntegerList(stdlink, int *a, long n)`
                   put a list of *n* integers starting from location *a*

`MLPutRealList(stdlink, double *a, long n)`
                   put a list of *n* floating-point numbers starting from
                   location *a*

`MLPutIntegerArray(stdlink, int *a, long *dims, NULL, long d)`
                   put an array of integers to form a depth *d* list with
                   dimensions *dims*

`MLPutRealArray(stdlink, double *a, long *dims, NULL, long d)`
                   put an array of floating-point numbers

`MLPutString(stdlink, char *s)`	put a character string
`MLPutSymbol(stdlink, char *s)`	put a character string as a symbol name

`MLPutFunction(stdlink, char *s, long n)`
                   begin putting a function with head *s* and *n* arguments

MathLink functions for sending data to *Mathematica*.

When you use a *MathLink* template file, what `mprep` and `mcc` actually do is to create a C program that includes explicit calls to *MathLink* library functions. If you want to understand how *MathLink* works, you can look at the source code of this program. Note when you use `mcc`, you typically need to give a `-g` option, otherwise the source code that is generated is automatically deleted.

If your external function just returns a single integer or floating-point number, then you can specify this just by giving `Integer` or `Real` as the `:ReturnType:` in your *MathLink* template file. But because of the way memory allocation and deallocation work in C, you cannot directly give `:ReturnType:` specifications such as `IntegerList` or `RealList`. And instead, to return such structures, you must explicitly call *MathLink* library functions within your C program, and give `Manual` as the `:ReturnType:` specification.

| Here is the *MathLink* template for a function that takes an integer as an argument, and returns its value using explicit *MathLink* functions. | ```
:Begin:
:Function:       bits
:Pattern:        bits[i_Integer]
:Arguments:      {i}
:ArgumentTypes:  {Integer}
:ReturnType:     Manual
:End:
``` |
| The function is declared as void. | ```
void bits(int i) {

    int a[32], k;
``` |
| This puts values into the C array a. | ```
    for(k=0; k<32; k++) {
        a[k] = i%2;
        i >>= 1;
        if (i==0) break;
    }

    if (k<32) k++;
``` |
| This sends k elements of the array a back to *Mathematica*. | ```
    MLPutIntegerList(stdlink, a, k);
    return ;
}
``` |

This installs the program containing the external function bits.	*In[5]:=* **Install["bitsprog"]** *Out[5]=* LinkObject[bitsprog, 5, 5]
The external function now returns a list of bits.	*In[6]:=* **bits[14]** *Out[6]=* {0, 1, 1, 1}

If you declare an array in C as int $a[n1][n2][n3]$ then you can use MLPutIntegerArray() to send it to *Mathematica* as a depth 3 list.

. . .

| Here is a declaration for a 3-dimensional C array. | `int a[8][16][100];` |
| This sets up the array dims and initializes it to the dimensions of a. | `long dims[] = {8, 16, 100};` |

. . .

| This sends the 3-dimensional array a to *Mathematica*, creating a depth 3 list. | `MLPutIntegerArray(stdlink, a, dims, NULL, 3);` |

. . .

You can use *MathLink* functions to create absolutely any *Mathematica* expression. The basic idea is to call a sequence of *MathLink* functions that correspond directly to the **FullForm** representation of the *Mathematica* expression.

This sets up the *Mathematica* function Plus with 2 arguments.	`MLPutFunction(stdlink, "Plus", 2);`
This specifies that the first argument is the integer 77.	`MLPutInteger(stdlink, 77);`
And this specifies that the second argument is the symbol x.	`MLPutSymbol(stdlink, "x");`

In general, you first call `MLPutFunction()`, giving the head of the *Mathematica* function you want to create, and the number of arguments it has. Then you call other *MathLink* functions to fill in each of these arguments in turn. Section 2.1 discusses the general structure of *Mathematica* expressions and the notion of heads.

This creates a *Mathematica* list with 2 elements.	`MLPutFunction(stdlink, "List", 2);`
The first element of the list is a list of 10 integers from the C array r.	`MLPutIntegerList(stdlink, r, 10);`
The second element of the main list is itself a list with 2 elements.	`MLPutFunction(stdlink, "List", 2);`
The first element of this sublist is a floating-point number.	`MLPutReal(stdlink, 4.5);`
The second element is an integer.	`MLPutInteger(stdlink, 11);`

`MLPutIntegerArray()` and `MLPutRealArray()` allow you to send arrays which are laid out in memory in the one-dimensional way that C pre-allocates them. But if you create arrays during the execution of a C program, it is more common to set them up as nested collections of pointers. You can send such arrays to *Mathematica* by using a sequence of `MLPutFunction()` calls, ending with an `MLPutIntegerList()` call.

	`...`
This declares a to be a nested list of lists of lists of integers.	`int ***a;`
	`...`
This creates a *Mathematica* list with n1 elements.	`MLPutFunction(stdlink, "List", n1);`
	`for (i=0; i<n1; i++) {`
This creates a sublist with n2 elements.	`    MLPutFunction(stdlink, "List", n2);`
	`    for (j=0; j<n2; j++) {`
This writes out lists of integers.	`        MLPutIntegerList(stdlink, a[i][j], n3);`
	`    }`
	`}`
	`...`

It is important to realize that any expression you create using *MathLink* functions will be evaluated as soon as it is sent to *Mathematica*. This means, for example, that if you wanted to transpose an array that you were sending back to *Mathematica*, all you would need to do is to wrap a `Transpose` around the expression representing the array. You can then do this simply by calling `MLPutFunction(stdlink, "Transpose", 1);` just before you start creating the expression that represents the array.

The idea of post-processing data that you send back to *Mathematica* has many uses. One example is as a way of sending lists whose length you do not know in advance.

This creates a list in *Mathematica* by explicitly appending successive elements.	`In[7]:= t = {}; Do[t = Append[t, i^2], {i, 5}]; t` `Out[7]= {1, 4, 9, 16, 25}`
This creates a list in which each successive element is in a nested sublist.	`In[8]:= t = {}; Do[t = {t, i^2}, {i, 5}]; t` `Out[8]= {{{{{{}, 1}, 4}, 9}, 16}, 25}`
Flatten flattens out the list.	`In[9]:= Flatten[t]` `Out[9]= {1, 4, 9, 16, 25}`

Sequence automatically flattens itself.   *In[10]:=* **{Sequence[1, Sequence[4, Sequence[ ]]]}**

Out[10]= {1, 4}

In order to call `MLPutIntegerList()`, you need to know the length of the list you want to send. But by creating a sequence of nested `Sequence` objects, you can avoid having to know the length of your whole list in advance.

This sets up the List around your result.	`MLPutFunction(stdlink, "List", 1);`
	`while(`*condition*`) {` *generate an element*
Create the next level Sequence object.	`MLPutFunction(stdlink, "Sequence", 2);`
Put the element.	`MLPutInteger(stdlink, `*i*`);`
	`}`
This closes off your last Sequence object.	`MLPutFunction(stdlink, "Sequence", 0);`

`MLGetInteger(stdlink, int *`*i*`)`	get an integer, storing it at address *i*
`MLGetReal(stdlink, double *`*x*`)`	get a floating-point number, storing it at address *x*

Basic functions for explicitly getting data from *Mathematica*.

Just as *MathLink* provides functions like `MLPutInteger()` to send data from an external program into *Mathematica*, so also *MathLink* provides functions like `MLGetInteger()` that allow you to get data from *Mathematica* into an external program.

The list that you give for `:ArgumentTypes:` in a *MathLink* template can end with `Manual`, indicating that after other arguments have been received, you will call *MathLink* functions to get additional expressions.

	:Begin:	
	:Function:	f
The function f in *Mathematica* takes 3 arguments.	:Pattern:	f[i_Integer, x_Real, y_Real]
All these arguments are passed directly to the external program.	:Arguments:	{i, x, y}
Only the first argument is sent directly to the external function.	:ArgumentTypes:	{Integer, Manual}
	:ReturnType:	Real
	:End:	

```
The external function only takes one        double f(int i) {
explicit argument.

This declares the variables x and y.            double x, y;

MLGetReal() explicitly gets data from           MLGetReal(stdlink, &x);
the link.                                        MLGetReal(stdlink, &y);

                                                return i+x+y;
                                            }
```

MathLink functions such as `MLGetInteger(link, pi)` work much like standard C library functions such as `fscanf(fp, "%d", pi)`. The first argument specifies the link from which to get data. The last argument gives the address at which the data that is obtained should be stored.

`MLCheckFunction(stdlink, "name", long *n)`
                                check the head of a function and store how many arguments it has

---

Getting a function via *MathLink*.

	:Begin:	
	:Function:	f
The function f in *Mathematica* takes a list of integers as an argument.	:Pattern:	f[a:{___Integer}]
The list is passed directly to the external program.	:Arguments:	{a}
The argument is to be retrieved manually by the external program.	:ArgumentTypes:	{Manual}
	:ReturnType:	Integer
	:End:	

```
The external function takes no explicit        int f(void) {
arguments.

This declares local variables.                    long n, i;
                                                   int a[MAX];

This checks that the function being                MLCheckFunction(stdlink, "List", &n);
sent is a list, and stores how many
elements it has in n.

This gets each element in the list,                for (i=0; i<n; i++)
storing it in a[i].                                   MLGetInteger(stdlink, a+i);

                                                   ...
                                               }
```

In simple cases, it is usually possible to ensure on the *Mathematica* side that the data you send to an external program has the structure that is expected. But in general the return value from MLCheckFunction() will be non-zero only if the data consists of a function with the name you specify.

Note that if you want to get a nested collection of lists or other objects, you can do this by making an appropriate sequence of calls to MLCheckFunction().

> `MLGetIntegerList(stdlink, int **`*a*`, long *`*n*`)`
>> get a list of integers, allocating the memory needed to store it
>
> `MLGetRealList(stdlink, double **`*a*`, long *`*n*`)`
>> get a list of floating-point numbers
>
> ---
>
> `MLDisownIntegerList(stdlink, int *`*a*`, long `*n*`)`
>> disown the memory associated with a list of integers
>
> `MLDisownRealList(stdlink, double *`*a*`, long `*n*`)`
>> disown the memory associated with a list of floating-point numbers

Getting lists of numbers.

When an external program gets data from *Mathematica*, it must set up a place to store the data. If the data consists of a single integer, as in `MLGetInteger(stdlink, &n)`, then it suffices just to have declared this integer using `int n`.

But when the data consists of a list of integers of potentially any length, memory must be allocated to store this list at the time when the external program is actually called.

`MLGetIntegerList(stdlink, &a, &n)` will automatically do this allocation, setting *a* to be a pointer to the result. Note that memory allocated by functions like `MLGetIntegerList()` is always in a special reserved area, so you cannot modify or free it directly.

Here is an external program that will be sent a list of integers.	`int f(void) {`
This declares local variables. a is an array of integers.	`    long n;` `    int *a;`
This gets a list of integers, making a be a pointer to the result.	`    MLGetIntegerList(stdlink, &a, &n);`
	`    . . .`
This disowns the memory used to store the list of integers.	`    MLDisownIntegerList(stdlink, a, n);`
	`    . . .`
	`}`

If you use `IntegerList` as an `:ArgumentTypes:` specification, then *MathLink* will automatically disown the memory used for the list after your external function exits. But if you get a list of integers explicitly using `MLGetIntegerList()`, then you must not forget to disown the memory used to store the list after you have finished with it.

`MLGetIntegerArray(stdlink, int **`*a*`, long **`*dims*`, char ***`*heads*`, long *`*d*`)`	
get an array of integers of any depth	
`MLGetRealArray(stdlink, double **`*a*`, long **`*dims*`, char ***`*heads*`, long *`*d*`)`	
get an array of floating-point numbers of any depth	
`MLDisownIntegerArray(stdlink, int *`*a*`, long *`*dims*`, char **`*heads*`, long `*d*`)`	
disown memory associated with an integer array	
`MLDisownRealArray(stdlink, double *`*a*`, long *`*dims*`, char **`*heads*`, long `*d*`)`	
disown memory associated with a floating-point array	

Getting arrays of numbers.

`MLGetIntegerList()` extracts a one-dimensional array of integers from a single *Mathematica* list. `MLGetIntegerArray()` extracts an array of integers from a collection of lists or other *Mathematica* functions nested to any depth.

The name of the *Mathematica* function at level i in the structure is stored as a string in *heads*[i]. The size of the structure at level i is stored in *dims*[i], while the total depth is stored in d.

If you pass a list of complex numbers to your external program, then `MLGetRealArray()` will create a two-dimensional array containing a sequence of pairs of real and imaginary parts. In this case, *heads*[0] will be "List" while *heads*[1] will be "Complex".

Note that you can conveniently exchange arbitrary-precision numbers with external programs by converting them to lists of digits in *Mathematica* using `IntegerDigits` and `RealDigits`.

`MLGetString(stdlink, char **`*s*`)`	get a character string
`MLGetSymbol(stdlink, char **`*s*`)`	get a symbol name
`MLDisownString(stdlink, char *`*s*`)`	disown memory associated with a character string
`MLDisownSymbol(stdlink, char *`*s*`)`	disown memory associated with a symbol name

Getting character strings and symbol names.

If you use `String` as an `:ArgumentTypes:` specification, then *MathLink* will automatically disown the memory that is used to store the string after your function exits. This means that if you want to continue to refer to the string, you must allocate memory for it, and explicitly copy each character in it.

If you get a string using `MLGetString()`, however, then *MathLink* will not automatically disown the memory used for the string when your function exits. As a result, you can continue referring to the string. When you no longer need the string, you must nevertheless explicitly call `MLDisownString()` in order to disown the memory associated with it.

`MLGetFunction(stdlink, char **s, long *n)`
  begin getting a function, storing the name of the head in *s* and the number of arguments in *n*

`MLDisownSymbol(stdlink, char *s)`
  disown memory associated with a function name

Getting an arbitrary function.

If you know what function to expect in your external program, then it is usually simpler to call `MLCheckFunction()`. But if you do not know what function to expect, you have no choice but to call `MLGetFunction()`. If you do this, you need to be sure to call `MLDisownSymbol()` to disown the memory associated with the name of the function that is found by `MLGetFunction()`.

+■ 2.12.5 Special Topic: Portability of *MathLink* Programs

The *Mathematica* side of a *MathLink* connection is set up to work exactly the same on all computer systems. But inevitably there are differences between external programs on different computer systems.

For a start, different computer systems almost always require different executable binaries. When you call `Install["prog"]`, therefore, you must be sure that *prog* corresponds to a program that can be executed on your particular computer system.

`Install["file"]`   try to execute *file* directly

`Install["file", LinkProtocol->"type"]`
  use the specified protocol for low-level data transport

`$SystemID`   identify the type of computer system being used

`Install["dir"]`   try to execute a file with a name of the form
  dir/`$SystemID`/*dir*

Installing programs on different computer systems.

Mathematica follows the convention that if *prog* is an ordinary file, then `Install["`*prog*`"]` will just try to execute it. But if *prog* is a directory, then *Mathematica* will look for a subdirectory of that directory whose name agrees with the current value of `$SystemID`, and will then try to execute a file named *prog* within that subdirectory.

`mcc -o` *prog* ...	put compiled code in the file *prog* in the current directory
`mcc -xo` *prog* ...	put compiled code in *prog*`/$SystemID/`*prog*

Typical Unix commands for compiling external programs.

Even though the executable binary of an external program is inevitably different on different computer systems, it can still be the case that the source code in a language such as C from which this binary is obtained can be essentially the same.

But to achieve portability in your C source code there are several points that you need to watch.

For a start, you should never make use of extra features of the C language or C run-time libraries that happen to be provided on a particular system, but are not part of standard C. In addition, you should try to avoid dealing with segmented or otherwise special memory models.

The include file `mathlink.h` contains standard C prototypes for all the functions in the *MathLink* library. If your compiler does not support such prototypes, you can ignore them by giving the directive `#define MLPROTOTYPES 0` before `#include "mathlink.h"`. But assuming that it does support prototypes, your compiler will always be able to check that the calls you make to functions in the *MathLink* library have arguments of appropriate types.

MLPutInteger()	MLGetInteger()	default integer of type int; sometimes 16 bits, sometimes 32 bits
MLPutShortInteger()	MLGetShortInteger()	short integer of type short; usually 16 bits
MLPutLongInteger()	MLGetLongInteger()	long integer of type long; usually 32 bits
MLPutReal()	MLGetReal()	default real number of type double; usually at least 64 bits
MLPutFloat()	MLGetFloat()	single-precision floating-point number of type float; often 32 bits
MLPutDouble()	MLGetDouble()	double-precision floating-point number of type double; usually at least 64 bits

MathLink functions that use specific C types.

On some computer systems and with some compilers, a C language int may be equivalent to a long. But the standard for the C language equally well allows int to be equivalent to short. And if you are going to call *MathLink* library functions in a portable way, it is essential that you use the same types as they do.

Once you have passed your data into the *MathLink* library functions, these functions then take care of all further issues associated with differences between data representations on different computer systems. Thus, for example, *MathLink* automatically swaps bytes when it sends data between big and little endian machines, and converts floating-point formats losing as little precision as possible.

> `MLPutString(stdlink, char *s)`   put a string without special characters
>
> `MLPutUnicodeString(stdlink, unsigned short *s, long n)`
> put a string encoded in terms of 16-bit Unicode characters
>
> `MLPutByteString(stdlink, unsigned char *s, long n)`
> put a string containing only 8-bit character codes
>
> ---
>
> `MLGetString(stdlink, char **s)`   get a string without special characters
>
> `MLGetUnicodeString(stdlink, unsigned short **s, long *n)`
> get a string encoded in terms of 16-bit Unicode characters
>
> `MLGetByteString(stdlink, unsigned char **s, long *n, long spec)`
> get a string containing only 8-bit character codes, using
> *spec* as the code for all 16-bit characters

Manipulating general strings.

In simple C programs, it is typical to use strings that contain only ordinary ASCII characters. But in *Mathematica* it is possible to have strings containing all sorts of special characters. These characters are specified within *Mathematica* using Unicode character codes, as discussed on page 399.

C language `char *` strings typically use only 8 bits to store the code for each character. Unicode character codes, however, require 16 bits. As a result, the functions `MLPutUnicodeString()` and `MLGetUnicodeString()` work with arrays of `unsigned short` integers.

If you know that your program will not have to handle special characters, then you may find it convenient to use `MLPutByteString()` and `MLGetByteString()`. These functions represent all characters directly using 8-bit character codes. If a special character is sent from *Mathematica*, then it will be converted by `MLGetByteString()` to a fixed code that you specify.

> ■ `main()` may need to be different on different computer systems

A point to watch in creating portable *MathLink* programs.

Computer systems and compilers that have C run-time libraries based on the Unix model allow *MathLink* programs to have a main program of the form `main(argc, argv)` which simply calls `MLMain(argc, argv)`.

Some computer systems or compilers may however require main programs of a different form. You should realize that you can do whatever initialization you want inside `main()` before calling `MLMain()`. Once you have called `MLMain()`, however, your program will effectively go into an infinite loop, responding to requests from *Mathematica* until the link to it is closed.

+■ 2.12.6 Using *MathLink* to Communicate between *Mathematica* Sessions

LinkCreate["*name*"]	create a link for another program to connect to
LinkConnect["*name*"]	connect to a link created by another program
LinkClose[*link*]	close a *MathLink* connection
LinkWrite[*link*, *expr*]	write an expression to a *MathLink* connection
LinkRead[*link*]	read an expression from a *MathLink* connection
LinkRead[*link*, Hold]	read an expression and immediately wrap it with Hold
LinkReadyQ[*link*]	find out whether there is data ready to be read from a link

MathLink connections between *Mathematica* sessions.

Session A

This starts up a link on port number 5000.

```
In[1]:= link = LinkCreate["5000"]
Out[1]= LinkObject[5000@frog.wolfram.com, 4, 4]
```

Session B

This connects to the link on port 5000.

```
In[1]:= link = LinkConnect["5000"]
Out[1]= LinkObject[5000@frog.wolfram.com, 4, 4]
```

Session A

This evaluates 15! and writes it to the link.

```
In[2]:= LinkWrite[link, 15!]
```

Session B

This reads from the link, getting the 15! that was sent.

```
In[2]:= LinkRead[link]
Out[2]= 1307674368000
```

This writes data back on the link.

```
In[3]:= LinkWrite[link, N[%^6]]
```

Session A

And this reads the data written in session B.

```
In[3]:= LinkRead[link]
Out[3]= 5.00032×10^72
```

One use of *MathLink* connections between *Mathematica* sessions is simply as a way to transfer data without using intermediate files.

Another use is as a way to dispatch different parts of a computation to different sessions.

Session A

This writes the expression 2 + 2
without evaluating it.

In[4]:= **LinkWrite[link, Unevaluated[2 + 2]]**

Session B

This reads the expression from the link,
immediately wrapping it in Hold.

In[4]:= **LinkRead[link, Hold]**

Out[4]= Hold[2 + 2]

This evaluates the expression.

In[5]:= **ReleaseHold[%]**

Out[5]= 4

When you call LinkWrite, it writes an expression to the *MathLink* connection and immediately returns. But when you call LinkRead, it will not return until it has read a complete expression from the *MathLink* connection.

You can tell whether anything is ready to be read by calling LinkReadyQ[*link*]. If LinkReadyQ returns True, then you can safely call LinkRead and expect immediately to start reading an expression. But if LinkReadyQ returns False, then LinkRead would block until an expression for it to read had been written by a LinkWrite in your other *Mathematica* session.

Session A

There is nothing waiting to be read on
the link, so if LinkRead were to be
called, it would block.

In[5]:= **LinkReadyQ[link]**

Out[5]= False

Session B

This writes an expression to the link.

In[6]:= **LinkWrite[link, x + y]**

Session A

Now there is an expression waiting to
be read on the link.

In[6]:= **LinkReadyQ[link]**

Out[6]= True

LinkRead can thus be called without
fear of blocking.

In[7]:= **LinkRead[link]**

Out[7]= x + y

LinkCreate[ ]	pick any unused port on your computer
LinkCreate["*number*"]	use a specific port
LinkConnect["*number*"]	connect to a port on the same computer
LinkConnect["*number@host*"]	connect a port on another computer

Ways to set up *MathLink* links.

MathLink can use whatever mechanism for interprogram communication your computer system supports. In setting up connections between concurrent *Mathematica* sessions, the most common mechanism is internet TCP ports.

Most computer systems have a few thousand possible numbered ports, some of which are typically allocated to standard system services.

You can use any of the unallocated ports for *MathLink* connections.

Session on frog.wolfram.com

This finds an unallocated port on
frog.wolfram.com.

```
In[8]:= link = LinkCreate[ ]
Out[8]= LinkObject[2981@frog.wolfram.com, 5, 5]
```

Session on toad.wolfram.com

This connects to the port on
frog.wolfram.com.

```
In[7]:= link = LinkConnect["2981@frog.wolfram.com"]
Out[7]= LinkObject[2981@frog.wolfram.com, 5, 5]
```

This sends the current machine name
over the link.

```
In[8]:= LinkWrite[link, $MachineName]
```

Session on frog.wolfram.com

This reads the expression written on
toad.

```
In[9]:= LinkRead[link]
Out[9]= toad
```

By using internet ports for *MathLink* connections, you can easily transfer data between *Mathematica* sessions on different machines. All that is needed is that an internet connection exists between the machines.

Note that because *MathLink* is completely system independent, the computers at each end of a *MathLink* connection do not have to be of the same type. *MathLink* nevertheless notices when they are, and optimizes data transmission in this case.

+■ 2.12.7 Calling Subsidiary *Mathematica* Processes

LinkLaunch["*prog*"]	start an external program and open a connection to it

Connecting to a subsidiary program via *MathLink*.

This starts a subsidiary *Mathematica* process on the computer system used here.	In[1]:= **link = LinkLaunch["math -mathlink"]** Out[1]= LinkObject[math -mathlink, 4, 4]
Here is a packet representing the first input prompt from the subsidiary *Mathematica* process.	In[2]:= **LinkRead[link]** Out[2]= InputNamePacket[In[1]:=]
This writes a packet representing text to enter in the subsidiary *Mathematica* process.	In[3]:= **LinkWrite[link, EnterTextPacket["10!"]]**
Here is a packet representing the output prompt from the subsidiary *Mathematica* process.	In[4]:= **LinkRead[link]** Out[4]= OutputNamePacket[Out[1]=]
And here is the actual result from the computation.	In[5]:= **LinkRead[link]** Out[5]= ReturnTextPacket[3628800]

The basic way that the various different objects involved in a *Mathematica* session are kept organized is by using *MathLink packets*. A *MathLink* packet is simply an expression with a definite head that indicates its role or meaning.

EnterTextPacket["*input*"]	text to enter corresponding to an input line
ReturnTextPacket["*output*"]	text returned corresponding to an output line
InputNamePacket["*name*"]	text returned for the name of an input line
OutputNamePacket["*name*"]	text returned for the name of an output line

Basic packets used in *Mathematica* sessions.

The fact that LinkRead returns an InputNamePacket indicates that the subsidiary *Mathematica* is now ready for new input.	In[6]:= **LinkRead[link]** Out[6]= InputNamePacket[In[2]:=]
This enters two Print commands as input.	In[7]:= **LinkWrite[link, EnterTextPacket["Print[a]; Print[b];"]]**

Here is the text from the first Print.

In[8]:= **LinkRead[link]**

Out[8]= TextPacket[a
]

And here is the text from the second Print.

In[9]:= **LinkRead[link]**

Out[9]= TextPacket[b
]

No output line is generated, so the new packet is an InputNamePacket.

In[10]:= **LinkRead[link]**

Out[10]= InputNamePacket[In[3]:=]

TextPacket["*string*"]   text from Print etc.

MessagePacket[*symb*, "*tag*", "*string*"]
a message

DisplayPacket["*string*"]   parts of PostScript graphics

DisplayEndPacket["*string*"]   the end of PostScript graphics

Some additional packets generated in *Mathematica* sessions.

If you enter input to *Mathematica* using EnterTextPacket["*input*"], then *Mathematica* will automatically generate a string version of your output, and will respond with ReturnTextPacket["*output*"]. But if you instead enter input using EnterExpressionPacket[*expr*] then *Mathematica* will respond with ReturnExpressionPacket[*expr*] and will not turn your output into a string.

EnterExpressionPacket[*expr*]   an expression to enter corresponding to an input line

ReturnExpressionPacket[*expr*]   an expression returned corresponding to an output line

Packets for representing input and output lines using expressions.

This enters an expression into the subsidiary *Mathematica* session without evaluating it.

In[11]:= **LinkWrite[link, Unevaluated[EnterExpressionPacket[**
     Factor[x^6 - 1]]]]

Here are the next 3 packets that come back from the subsidiary *Mathematica* session.

In[12]:= **Table[LinkRead[link], {3}]**

Out[12]= {OutputNamePacket[Out[3]=],
     ReturnExpressionPacket[
         $(-1 + x) (1 + x) (1 - x + x^2) (1 + x + x^2)$],
     InputNamePacket[In[4]:=]}

InputNamePacket and OutputNamePacket packets are often convenient for making it possible to tell the current state of a subsidiary *Mathematica* session. But you can suppress the generation of these

packets by calling the subsidiary *Mathematica* session with a string such as
`"math -mathlink -batchoutput"`.

Even if you suppress the explicit generation of `InputNamePacket` and `OutputNamePacket` packets, *Mathematica* will still process any input that you give with `EnterTextPacket` or `EnterExpressionPacket` as if you were entering an input line. This means for example that *Mathematica* will call `$Pre` and `$Post`, and will assign values to `In[$Line]` and `Out[$Line]`.

`EvaluatePacket[`*expr*`]`	an expression to be sent purely for evaluation
`ReturnPacket[`*expr*`]`	an expression returned from an evaluation

Evaluating expressions without explicit input and output lines.

This sends an EvaluatePacket. The Unevaluated prevents evaluation before the packet is sent.	`In[13]:= LinkWrite[link, Unevaluated[EvaluatePacket[10!]]]`
The result is a pure ReturnPacket.	`In[14]:= LinkRead[link]` `Out[14]= ReturnPacket[3628800]`
This sends an EvaluatePacket requesting evaluation of Print[x].	`In[15]:= LinkWrite[link, Unevaluated[EvaluatePacket[Print[x]]]]`

The first packet to come back is a TextPacket representing text generated by the Print.	`In[16]:= LinkRead[link]`
	`Out[16]= TextPacket[x`
	`           ]`

After that, the actual result of the Print is returned.	`In[17]:= LinkRead[link]` `Out[17]= ReturnPacket[Null]`

In most cases, it is reasonable to assume that sending an `EvaluatePacket` to *Mathematica* will simply cause *Mathematica* to do a computation and to return various other packets, ending with a `ReturnPacket`. However, if the computation involves a function like Input, then *Mathematica* will have to request additional input before it can proceed with the computation.

This sends a packet whose evaluation involves an Input function.	`In[18]:= LinkWrite[link,` `            Unevaluated[EvaluatePacket[2 + Input["data ="]]]]`
What comes back is an InputPacket which indicates that further input is required.	`In[19]:= LinkRead[link]` `Out[19]= InputPacket[data =]`
There is nothing more to be read on the link at this point.	`In[20]:= LinkReadyQ[link]` `Out[20]= False`
This enters more input.	`In[21]:= LinkWrite[link, EnterTextPacket["x + y"]]`

| Now the Input function can be evaluated, and a ReturnPacket is generated. | *In[22]:=* **LinkRead[link]** |
| | *Out[22]=* ReturnPacket[2 + x + y] |

| **LinkInterrupt[*link*]** | send an interrupt to a *MathLink*-compatible program |

Interrupting a *MathLink*-compatible program.

| This sends a very time-consuming calculation to the subsidiary process. | *In[23]:=* **LinkWrite[link,** |
| | **EnterTextPacket["FactorInteger[2^777-1]"]]** |

| The calculation is still going on. | *In[24]:=* **LinkReadyQ[link]** |
| | *Out[24]=* False |

| This sends an interrupt. | *In[25]:=* **LinkInterrupt[link]** |

| Now the subsidiary process has stopped, and is sending back an interrupt menu. | *In[26]:=* **LinkRead[link]** |
| | *Out[26]=* MenuPacket[1, Interrupt>] |

+■ 2.12.8 Special Topic: Communication with *Mathematica* Front Ends

The *Mathematica* kernel uses *MathLink* to communicate with *Mathematica* front ends. If you start a *Mathematica* kernel from within a front end, therefore, the kernel will be controlled through a *MathLink* connection to this front end.

| **$ParentLink** | the *MathLink* connection to use for kernel input and output |

The link to the front end for a particular kernel.

The global variable $ParentLink specifies the *MathLink* connection that a particular kernel will use for input and output.

It is sometimes useful to reset $ParentLink in the middle of a *Mathematica* session, thereby effectively changing the front end to which the kernel is connected.

	Session A
This creates a link on port 6000.	*In[1]:=* **link = LinkCreate["6000"]**
	Out[1]= LinkObject[6000@frog.wolfram.com, 4, 4]

	Session B
This connects to the link opened in session A.	*In[1]:=* **LinkConnect["6000"]**
	Out[1]= LinkObject[6000@frog.wolfram.com, 4, 4]

This tells session B that it should use session A as a front end.

In[2]:= **$ParentLink = %**

Session A

Session A now acts as a front end to session B and gets all output from it.

In[2]:= **Table[LinkRead[link], 4]**

Out[2]= {ResumePacket[LinkObject[ParentLink, 1, 1]],
            OutputNamePacket[Out[2]=], ReturnTextPacket[
            LinkObject[6000@frog.wolfram.com, 4, 4]],
            InputNamePacket[In[3]:=]}

This releases session B again.

In[3]:= **LinkWrite[link, EnterTextPacket["$ParentLink=."]]**

Much like the *Mathematica* kernel, the standard notebook front end for *Mathematica* is set up to handle a certain set of *MathLink* packets.

Usually it is best to use functions like NotebookWrite and FrontEndExecute if you want to control the *Mathematica* front end from the kernel. But in some cases you may find it convenient to send packets directly to the front end using LinkWrite.

■ 2.12.9 Two-Way Communication with External Programs

When you install a *MathLink*-compatible external program using Install, the program is set up to behave somewhat like a simplified *Mathematica* kernel. Every time you call a function in the external program, a CallPacket is sent to the program, and the program responds by sending back a result wrapped in a ReturnPacket.

This installs an external program, returning the LinkObject used for the connection to that program.

In[1]:= **link = Install["bitsprog"]**

Out[1]= LinkObject[bitsprog, 4, 4]

The function ExternalCall sends a CallPacket to the external program.

In[2]:= **?bits**

Global`bits

bits[i_Integer] :=
   ExternalCall[LinkObject["bitsprog", 4, 4],
   CallPacket[0, {i}]]

You can send the CallPacket explicitly using LinkWrite. The first argument of the CallPacket specifies which function in the external program to call.

In[3]:= **LinkWrite[link, CallPacket[0, {67}]]**

Here is the response to the CallPacket from the external program.

In[4]:= **LinkRead[link]**

Out[4]= {1, 1, 0, 0, 0, 0, 1}

If you use Install several times on a single external program, *Mathematica* will open several *MathLink* connections to the program. Each connection will however always correspond to a unique

LinkObject. Note that on some computer systems, you may need to make an explicit copy of the file containing the external program in order to be able to call it multiple times.

$CurrentLink	the *MathLink* connection to the external program currently being run

Identifying different instances of a single external program.

<table>
<tr><td></td><td>:Begin:</td><td></td></tr>
<tr><td></td><td>:Function:</td><td>addto</td></tr>
<tr><td>This gives $CurrentLink as an argument to addto.</td><td>:Pattern:</td><td>addto[$CurrentLink, n_Integer]</td></tr>
<tr><td></td><td>:Arguments:</td><td>{n}</td></tr>
<tr><td></td><td>:ArgumentTypes:</td><td>{Integer}</td></tr>
<tr><td></td><td>:ReturnType:</td><td>Integer</td></tr>
<tr><td></td><td>:End:</td><td></td></tr>
</table>

This zeros the global variable counter every time the program is started.

```
int counter = 0;

int addto(int n) {
    counter += n;
    return counter;
}
```

This installs one instance of the external program containing addto.

```
In[5]:= ct1 = Install["addtoprog"]
Out[5]= LinkObject[addtoprog, 5, 5]
```

This installs another instance.

```
In[6]:= ct2 = Install["addtoprog"]
Out[6]= LinkObject[addtoprog, 6, 6]
```

This adds 10 to the counter in the first instance of the external program.

```
In[7]:= addto[ct1, 10]
Out[7]= 10
```

This adds 15 to the counter in the second instance of the external program.

```
In[8]:= addto[ct2, 15]
Out[8]= 15
```

This operates on the first instance of the program again.

```
In[9]:= addto[ct1, 20]
Out[9]= 30
```

If an external program maintains information about its state then you can use different instances of the program to represent different states. $CurrentLink then provides a way to refer to each instance of the program.

The value of $CurrentLink is temporarily set every time a particular instance of the program is called, as well as when each instance of the program is first installed.

MLEvaluateString(stdlink, "*string*")

   send input to *Mathematica* but return no results

Sending a string for evaluation by *Mathematica*.

The two-way nature of *MathLink* connections allows you not only to have *Mathematica* call an external program, but also to have that external program call back to *Mathematica*.

In the simplest case, you can use the *MathLink* function MLEvaluateString() to send a string to *Mathematica*. *Mathematica* will evaluate this string, producing whatever effects the string specifies, but it will not return any results from the evaluation back to the external program.

To get results back you need explicitly to send an EvaluatePacket to *Mathematica*, and then read the contents of the ReturnPacket that comes back.

. . .

This starts an EvaluatePacket.	`MLPutFunction(stdlink, "EvaluatePacket", 1);`
This constructs the expression Factorial[7] or 7!.	`MLPutFunction(stdlink, "Factorial", 1);` `  MLPutInteger(stdlink, 7);`
This specifies that the packet you are constructing is finished.	`MLEndPacket(stdlink);`
This checks the ReturnPacket that comes back.	`MLCheckFunction(stdlink, "ReturnPacket", &n);`
This extracts the integer result for 7! from the packet.	`MLGetInteger(stdlink, &ans);`

. . .

MLEndPacket(stdlink)   specify that a packet is finished and ready to be sent to *Mathematica*

Sending a packet to *Mathematica*.

At any stage in the execution of an external program, you can send EvaluatePacket[*input*] to *Mathematica*. In general, *Mathematica* may produce many packets in response, but the final packet should be ReturnPacket[*output*]. Page 668 will discuss how to handle sequences of packets and expressions whose structure you do not know in advance.

+ ■ 2.12.10 Special Topic: Running Programs on Remote Computers

MathLink allows you to call an external program from within *Mathematica* even when that program is running on a remote computer. Typically, you need to start the program directly from the operating system on the remote computer. But then you can connect to it using commands within your *Mathematica* session.

	Operating system on `toad.wolfram.com`
This starts the program `fprog` and tells it to create a new link.	**`fprog -linkcreate`**
The program responds with the specification of the link it has created.	`Link created on: 2976@toad.wolfram.com`

	Mathematica session on `frog.wolfram.com`
This connects to the link that has been created.	*In[1]:=* **`Install[LinkConnect["2976@toad.wolfram.com"]]`**
	Out[1]= `LinkObject[2976@toad.wolfram.com, 1]`
This now executes code in the external program on `toad.wolfram.com`.	*In[2]:=* **`f[16]`**
	Out[2]= `561243`

External programs that are created using `mcc` or `mprep` always contain the code that is needed to set up *MathLink* connections. If you start such programs directly from your operating system, they will prompt you to specify what kind of connection you want. Alternatively, if your operating system supports it, you can also give this information as a command-line argument to the external program.

prog `-linkcreate`	operating system command to run a program and have it create a link
`Install[LinkConnect["`*port@host*`"]]`	
	Mathematica command to connect to the external program

Running an external program on a remote computer.

+ ■ 2.12.11 Special Topic: Running External Programs under a Debugger

MathLink allows you to run external programs under whatever debugger is provided in your software environment.

MathLink-compatible programs are typically set up to take arguments, usually on the command line, which specify what *MathLink* connections they should use.

| In debugger: | `run -linkcreate` |
| In *Mathematica*: | `Install[LinkConnect["`*port*`"]]` |

Running an external program under a debugger.

Note that in order to get a version of an external program that can be run under a debugger, you may need to specify -g or other flags when you compile the program.

	Debugger
Set a breakpoint in the C function f.	*(debug)* **break f** Breakpoint set: f: line 1
Start the external program.	*(debug)* **run -linkcreate**
The program responds with what port it is listening on.	Link created on: 2981@frog.wolfram.com

	Mathematica session
This connects to the program running under the debugger.	*In[1]:=* **Install[LinkConnect["2981@frog.wolfram.com"]]** *Out[1]=* LinkObject[2981@frog.wolfram.com, 1]
This calls a function which executes code in the external program.	*In[2]:=* **f[16]**

	Debugger
The external program stops at the breakpoint.	*(debug)* Breakpoint: f(16)
This tells the debugger to continue.	*(debug)* **continue**

	Mathematica session
Now f returns.	*Out[2]=* 561243

+■ 2.12.12 Manipulating Expressions in External Programs

Mathematica expressions provide a very general way to handle all kinds of data, and you may sometimes want to use such expressions inside your external programs. A language like C, however, offers no direct way to store general *Mathematica* expressions. But it is nevertheless possible to do this by using the *loopback links* provided by the *MathLink* library. A loopback link is a local *MathLink* connection inside your external program, to which you can write expressions that can later be read back.

> MLINK MLLoopbackOpen(stdenv, long *errno*)
> open a loopback link
>
> void MLClose(MLINK *link*)   close a link
>
> ---
>
> int MLTransferExpression(MLINK *dest*, MLINK *src*)
> get an expression from *src* and put it onto *dest*

Functions for manipulating loopback links.

	. . .
This opens a loopback link.	`ml = MLLoopbackOpen(stdenv, &errno);`

This puts the expression `Power[x, 3]` onto the loopback link.	`MLPutFunction(ml, "Power", 2);`
	`  MLPutSymbol(ml, "x");`
	`  MLPutInteger(ml, 3);`

	. . .

This gets the expression back from the loopback link.	`MLGetFunction(ml, &head, &n);`
	`  MLGetSymbol(ml, &sname);`
	`  MLGetInteger(ml, &k);`

	. . .
This closes the loopback link again.	`MLClose(ml);`

You can use `MLTransferExpression()` to take an expression that you get via `stdlink` from *Mathematica*, and save it in a local loopback link for later processing.

You can also use `MLTransferExpression()` to take an expression that you have built up on a local loopback link, and transfer it back to *Mathematica* via `stdlink`.

<table>
<tr><td></td><td>. . .</td></tr>
</table>

This puts 21! onto a local loopback link.	`MLPutFunction(ml, "Factorial", 1);` `  MLPutInteger(ml, 21);`
This sends the head `FactorInteger` to *Mathematica*.	`MLPutFunction(stdlink, "FactorInteger", 1);`
This transfers the 21! from the loopback link to `stdlink`.	`MLTransferExpression(stdlink, ml);`

You can put any sequence of expressions onto a loopback link. Usually you get the expressions off the link in the same order as you put them on.

And once you have got an expression off the link it is usually no longer saved. But by using `MLCreateMark()` you can mark a particular position in a sequence of expressions on a link, forcing *MathLink* to save every expression after the mark so that you can go back to it later.

`MLMARK MLCreateMark(MLINK` *link*`)`	create a mark at the current position in a sequence of expressions on a link
`MLSeekMark(MLINK` *link*`, MLMARK` *mark*`, long` *n*`)`	go back to a position *n* expressions after the specified mark on a link
`MLDestroyMark(MLINK` *link*`, MLMARK` *mark*`)`	destroy a mark in a link

Setting up marks in *MathLink* links.

· · ·

This puts the integer 45 onto a loopback link.	`MLPutInteger(ml, 45);`
This puts 33 onto the link.	`MLPutInteger(ml, 33);`
And this puts 76.	`MLPutInteger(ml, 76);`
This will read 45 from the link. The 45 will no longer be saved.	`MLGetInteger(ml, &i);`
This creates a mark at the current position on the link.	`mark = MLCreateMark(ml);`
This will now read 33.	`MLGetInteger(ml, &i);`
And this will read 76.	`MLGetInteger(ml, &i);`
This goes back to the position of the mark.	`MLSeekMark(ml, mark, 0);`
Now this will read 33 again.	`MLGetInteger(ml, &i);`
It is important to destroy marks when you have finished with them, so no unnecessary expressions will be saved.	`MLDestroyMark(ml, mark);`

The way the *MathLink* library is implemented, it is very efficient to open and close loopback links, and to create and destroy marks in them. The only point to remember is that as soon as you create a mark on a particular link, *MathLink* will save subsequent expressions that are put on that link, and will go on doing this until the mark is destroyed.

`int MLGetNext(MLINK `*link*`)`	find the type of the next object on a link
`int MLGetArgCount(MLINK `*link*`, long *`*n*`)`	store in *n* the number of arguments for a function on a link
`int MLGetSymbol(MLINK `*link*`, char **`*name*`)`	get the name of a symbol
`int MLGetInteger(MLINK `*link*`, int *`*i*`)`	get a machine integer
`int MLGetReal(MLINK `*link*`, double *`*x*`)`	get a machine floating-point number
`int MLGetString(MLINK `*link*`, char **`*string*`)`	get a character string

Functions for getting pieces of expressions from a link.

MLTKFUNC	composite function—head and arguments
MLTKSYM	*Mathematica* symbol
MLTKINT	integer
MLTKREAL	floating-point number
MLTKSTR	character string

Constants returned by MLGetNext().

```
                                       switch(MLGetNext(ml)) {

This reads a composite function.        case MLTKFUNC:
                                        MLGetArgCount(ml, &n);
                                        recurse for head
                                        for (i = 0; i < n; i++) {
                                            recurse for each argument
                                        }
                                        ...

This reads a single symbol.             case MLTKSYM:
                                        MLGetSymbol(ml, &name);
                                        ...

This reads a machine integer.           case MLTKINT:
                                        MLGetInteger(ml, &i);
                                        ...

                                       }
```

By using `MLGetNext()` it is straightforward to write programs that can read any expression. The way *MathLink* works, the head and arguments of a function appear as successive expressions on the link, which you read one after another.

Note that if you know that the head of a function will be a symbol, then you can use `MLGetFunction()` instead of `MLGetNext()`. In this case, however, you still need to call `MLDisownSymbol()` to disown the memory used to store the symbol name.

int MLPutNext(MLINK *link*, int *type*)	prepare to put an object of the specified type on a link
int MLPutArgCount(MLINK *link*, long *n*)	give the number of arguments for a composite function
int MLPutSymbol(MLINK *link*, char **name*)	put a symbol on the link
int MLPutInteger(MLINK *link*, int *i*)	put a machine integer
int MLPutReal(MLINK *link*, double *x*)	put a machine floating-point number
int MLPutString(MLINK *link*, char **string*)	put a character string

Functions for putting pieces of expressions onto a link.

MLPutNext() specifies types of expressions using constants such as MLTKFUNC from the mathlink.h header file—just like MLGetNext().

+■ 2.12.13 Advanced Topic: Error and Interrupt Handling

When you are putting and getting data via *MathLink* various kinds of errors can occur. Whenever any error occurs, *MathLink* goes into a completely inactive state, and all *MathLink* functions you call will return 0 immediately.

long MLError(MLINK *link*)	return a number identifying the current error, or 0 if none has occurred
char *MLErrorMessage(MLINK *link*)	return a character string describing the current error
int MLClearError(MLINK *link*)	clear the current error, returning *MathLink* if possible to an active state

Handling errors in *MathLink* programs.

When you do complicated operations, it is often convenient to check for errors only at the end. If you find that an error occurred, you must then call MLClearError() to activate *MathLink* again.

int `MLNewPacket(MLINK `*`link`*`)`   skip to the end of the current packet

Clearing out the remains of a packet.

After an error, it is common to want to discard the remainder of the packet or expression that you are currently processing. You can do this using `MLNewPacket()`.

In some cases, you may want to set it up so that if an error occurs while you are processing particular data, you can then later go back and reprocess the data in a different way. You can do this by calling `MLCreateMark()` to create a mark before you first process the data, and then calling `MLSeekMark()` to seek back to the mark if you need to reprocess the data. You should not forgot to call `MLDestroyMark()` when you have finally finished with the data—otherwise *MathLink* will continue to store it.

int `MLAbort`   a global variable set when a program set up by `Install` is sent an abort interrupt

Aborting an external program.

If you interrupt *Mathematica* while it is in the middle of executing an external function, it will typically give you the opportunity to try to abort the external function. If you choose to do this, what will happen is that the global variable `MLAbort` will be set to 1 inside your external program.

MathLink cannot automatically back out of an external function call that has been made. So if you have a function that can take a long time, you should explicitly check `MLAbort` every so often, returning from the function if you find that the variable has been set.

■ 2.12.14 Running *Mathematica* from Within an External Program

To run *Mathematica* from within an external program requires making use of many general features of *MathLink*. The first issue is how to establish a *MathLink* connection to *Mathematica*.

When you use *MathLink* templates to create external programs that can be called from *Mathematica*, source code to establish a *MathLink* connection is automatically generated, and all you have to do in your external program is to call `MLMain(`*`argc`*`, `*`argv`*`)`. But in general you need to call several functions to establish a *MathLink* connection.

`MLENV MLInitialize(0)`	initialize *MathLink* library functions
`MLINK MLOpenArgv(MLENV` *env*`, char **`*argv0*`, char **`*argv1*`, long *`*errno*`)`	open a *MathLink* connection taking parameters from an `argv` array
`MLINK MLOpenString(MLENV` *env*`, char *`*string*`, long *`*errno*`)`	open a *MathLink* connection taking parameters from a single character string
`int MLActivate(MLINK` *link*`)`	activate a *MathLink* connection, waiting for the program at the other end to respond
`void MLClose(MLINK` *link*`)`	close a *MathLink* connection
`void MLDeinitialize(MLENV` *env*`)`	deinitialize *MathLink* library functions

Opening and closing *MathLink* connections.

Include the standard *MathLink* header file.

```
#include "mathlink.h"

int main(int argc, char *argv[]) {

    MLENV env;
    MLINK link;
    long errno;
```

This initializes *MathLink* library functions.

```
    env = MLInitialize(0);
```

This opens a *MathLink* connection, using the same arguments as were passed to the main program.

```
    link = MLOpenArgv(env, argv, argv+argc, &errno);
```

This activates the connection, waiting for the other program to respond.

```
    MLActivate(link);

    . . .
}
```

Often the `argv` that you pass to `MLOpenArgv()` will come directly from the `argv` that is passed to `main()` when your whole program is started. Note that `MLOpenArgv()` takes pointers to the beginning and end of the `argv` array. By not using `argc` directly it avoids having to know the size of an `int`.

The elements in the `argv` array are character strings which mirror the arguments and options used in the *Mathematica* functions `LinkLaunch`, `LinkCreate` and `LinkConnect`.

`"-linklaunch"`	operate like `LinkLaunch["`*name*`"]`
`"-linkcreate"`	operate like `LinkCreate["`*name*`"]`
`"-linkconnect"`	operate like `LinkConnect["`*name*`"]`
`"-linkname"`, `"`*name*`"`	give the name to use
`"-linkprotocol"`, `"`*protocol*`"`	give the link protocol to use (`tcp`, `pipes`, etc.)

Possible elements of the `argv` array passed to `MLOpenArgv()`.

As an alternative to `MLOpenArgv()` you can use `MLOpenString()`, which takes parameters concatenated into a single character string with spaces in between.

Once you have successfully opened a *MathLink* connection to the *Mathematica* kernel, you can then use standard *MathLink* functions to exchange data with it.

`int MLEndPacket(MLINK` *link*`)`	indicate the end of a packet
`int MLNextPacket(MLINK` *link*`)`	find the head of the next packet
`int MLNewPacket(MLINK` *link*`)`	skip to the end of the current packet

Functions often used in communicating with the *Mathematica* kernel.

Once you have sent all the pieces of a packet using `MLPutFunction()` etc., *MathLink* requires you to call `MLEndPacket()` to ensure synchronization and consistency.

One of the main issues in writing an external program which communicates directly with the *Mathematica* kernel is handling all the various kinds of packets that the kernel can generate.

The function `MLNextPacket()` finds the head of the next packet that comes from the kernel, and returns a constant that indicates the type of the packet.

Mathematica packet	*constant*	
ReturnPacket[*expr*]	RETURNPKT	result from a computation
ReturnTextPacket["*string*"]	RETURNTEXTPKT	textual form of a result
InputNamePacket["*name*"]	INPUTNAMEPKT	name of an input line
OutputNamePacket["*name*"]	OUTPUTNAMEPKT	name of an output line
TextPacket["*string*"]	TEXTPKT	textual output from functions like Print
MessagePacket[*symb*, "*tag*", "*string*"]	MESSAGEPKT	a message generated by *Mathematica*
DisplayPacket["*string*"]	DISPLAYPKT	part of PostScript graphics
DisplayEndPacket["*string*"]	DISPLAYENDPKT	end of PostScript graphics
InputPacket["*prompt*"]	INPUTPKT	request for a response to an Input function
CallPacket[*i*, *list*]	CALLPKT	request for a call to an external function

Some packets recognized by MLNextPacket().

This keeps on reading data from a link, discarding it until an error or a ReturnPacket is found.

```
while ((p = MLNextPacket(link)) && p != RETURNPKT)
    MLNewPacket(link);
```

If you want to write a complete front end to *Mathematica*, you will need to handle all of the possible types of packets that the kernel can generate. Typically you can do this by setting up an appropriate switch on the value returned by MLNextPacket().

The *MathLink* Developer's Kit contains sample source code for several simple but complete front ends.

int MLReady(MLINK *link*)	test whether there is data waiting to be read on a link
int MLFlush(MLINK *link*)	flush out buffers containing data waiting to be sent on a link

Flow of data on links.

One feature of more sophisticated external programs such as front ends is that they may need to perform operations while they are waiting for data to be sent to them by *Mathematica*. When you call a standard *MathLink* library function such as MLNextPacket() your program will normally block until all the data needed by this function is available.

You can avoid blocking by repeatedly calling MLReady(), and only calling functions like MLNextPacket() when MLReady() no longer returns 0. MLReady() is the analog of the *Mathematica* function LinkReadyQ.

Note that *MathLink* sometimes buffers the data that you tell it to send. To make sure that all necessary data has been sent you should call MLFlush(). Only after doing this does it make sense to call MLReady() and wait for data to be sent back.

2.13 Global Aspects of *Mathematica* Sessions

■ 2.13.1 The Main Loop

In any interactive session, *Mathematica* effectively operates in a loop. It waits for your input, processes the input, prints the result, then goes back to waiting for input again. As part of this "main loop", *Mathematica* maintains and uses various global objects. You will often find it useful to work with these objects.

You should realize, however, that if you use *Mathematica* through a special front end, your front end may set up its own main loop, and what is said in this section may not apply.

In[n]	the expression on the nth input line
InString[n]	the textual form of the nth input line
%n or Out[n]	the expression on the nth output line
Out[{n_1, n_2, ... }]	a list of output expressions
%% ... % (n times) or Out[-n]	the expression on the nth previous output line
MessageList[n]	a list of messages produced while processing the nth line
$Line	the current line number (resettable)

Input and output expressions.

In a standard interactive session, there is a sequence of input and output lines. *Mathematica* stores the values of the expressions on these lines in In[n] and Out[n].

As indicated by the usual In[n]:= prompt, the input expressions are stored with delayed assignments. This means that whenever you ask for In[n], the input expression will always be re-evaluated in your current environment.

This assigns a value to x.	*In[1]:=* **x = 7**
	Out[1]= 7
Now the value for x is used.	*In[2]:=* **x - x^2 + 5x - 1**
	Out[2]= -8
This removes the value assigned to x.	*In[3]:=* **x =.**
This is re-evaluated in your current environment, where there is no value assigned to x.	*In[4]:=* **In[2]**
	Out[4]= $-1 + 6x - x^2$

This gives the textual form of the second input line, appropriate for editing or other textual manipulation.

```
In[5]:= InString[2] // InputForm

Out[5]//InputForm= "x - x^2 + 5x - 1"
```

+	$HistoryLength	the number of previous lines of input and output to keep

Specifying the length of session history to keep.

Mathematica by default stores *all* your input and output lines for the duration of the session. In a very long session, this may take up a large amount of computer memory. You can nevertheless get rid of the input and output lines by explicitly clearing the values of In and Out, using Unprotect[In, Out], followed by Clear[In, Out]. You can also tell *Mathematica* to keep only a limited number of lines of history by setting the global variable $HistoryLength.

Note that at any point in a session, you can reset the line number counter $Line, so that for example new lines are numbered so as to overwrite previous ones.

$PreRead	a function applied to each input string before being fed to *Mathematica*
$Pre	a function applied to each input expression before evaluation
$Post	a function applied to each expression after evaluation
$PrePrint	a function applied after Out[n] is assigned, but before the result is printed
$SyntaxHandler	a function applied to any input line that yields a syntax error

Global functions used in the main loop.

Mathematica provides a variety of "hooks" that allow you to insert functions to be applied to expressions at various stages in the main loop. Thus, for example, any function you assign as the value of the global variable $Pre will automatically be applied before evaluation to any expression you give as input.

For a particular input line, the standard main loop begins by getting a text string of input. Particularly if you need to deal with special characters, you may want to modify this text string before it is further processed by *Mathematica*. You can do this by assigning a function as the value of the global variable $PreRead. This function will be applied to the text string, and the result will be used as the actual input string for the particular input line.

This tells *Mathematica* to replace << ... >> by { ... } in every input string.	`In[6]:= $PreRead = StringReplace[#, {"<<" -> "{", ">>" -> "}"}]&`
	
	`Out[6]= StringReplace[#1, {<< → {, >> → }}]&`

You can now enter braces as double angle brackets.	`In[7]:= <<4, 5, 6>>`
	
	`Out[7]= {4, 5, 6}`

You can remove the value for $PreRead like this, at least so long as your definition for $PreRead does not modify this very input string.	`In[8]:= $PreRead =.`

Once any $PreRead processing on an input string is finished, the string is read by *Mathematica*. At this point, *Mathematica* may find that there is a syntax error in the string. If this happens, then *Mathematica* calls whatever function you have specified as the value of $SyntaxHandler. It supplies two arguments: the input string, and the character position at which the syntax error was detected. With $SyntaxHandler you can, for example, generate an analysis of the syntax error, or call an editor. If your function returns a string, then *Mathematica* will use this string as a new input string.

This specifies what *Mathematica* should do when it gets a syntax error.	`In[9]:= $SyntaxHandler =`
	`            (Print[StringForm["Error at char `1` in `2`",`
	`                                #2, #1]]; $Failed)&`
	
	`Out[9]= (Print[Error at char #2 in #1];`
	`          $Failed)&`

This input generates a syntax error.	`In[10]:= 3 +/+ 5`
	
	`Syntax::sntxf: "3 +" cannot be followed by "/+ 5".`
	
	`Error at char 4 in 3 +/+ 5`

Once *Mathematica* has successfully read an input expression, it then evaluates this expression. Before doing the evaluation, *Mathematica* applies any function you have specified as the value of $Pre, and after the evaluation, it applies any function specified as the value of $Post. Note that unless the $Pre function holds its arguments unevaluated, the function will have exactly the same effect as $Post.

$Post allows you to specify arbitrary "post processing" to be done on results obtained from *Mathematica*. Thus, for example, to make *Mathematica* get a numerical approximation to every result it generates, all you need do is to set $Post = N.

This tells *Mathematica* to apply N to every result it generates.	`In[10]:= $Post = N`
	
	`Out[10]= N`

Now *Mathematica* gets a numerical approximation to anything you type in.	`In[11]:= Sqrt[7]`
	
	`Out[11]= 2.64575`

This removes the post-processing function you specified.	`In[12]:= $Post =.`

As soon as *Mathematica* has generated a result, and applied any $Post function you have specified, it takes the result, and assigns it as the value of Out[$Line]. The next step is for *Mathematica* to print the result. However, before doing this, it applies any function you have specified as the value of $PrePrint.

This tells *Mathematica* to shorten all output to two lines.	*In[13]:=* **$PrePrint = Short[#, 2]& ;**

Only a two-line version of the output is now shown.

In[14]:= **Expand[(x + y)^40]**

$Out[14]= x^{40} + 40\,x^{39}\,y + 780\,x^{38}\,y^2 + 9880\,x^{37}\,y^3 + \ll 33 \gg +$
$9880\,x^3\,y^{37} + 780\,x^2\,y^{38} + 40\,x\,y^{39} + y^{40}$

This removes the value you assigned to $PrePrint.	*In[15]:=* **$PrePrint =.**

There are various kinds of output generated in a typical *Mathematica* session. In general, each kind of output is sent to a definite *output channel*, as discussed on page 608. Associated with each output channel, there is a global variable which gives a list of the output streams to be included in that output channel.

$Output	standard output and text generated by Print
$Echo	an echo of each input line (as stored in InString[n])
$Urgent	input prompts and other urgent output
$Messages	standard messages and output generated by Message
$Display	graphics output generated by the default $DisplayFunction
$SoundDisplay	sound output generated by the default $SoundDisplayFunction

Output channels in a standard *Mathematica* session.

By modifying the list of streams in a given output channel, you can redirect or copy particular kinds of *Mathematica* output. Thus, for example, by opening an output stream to a file, and including that stream in the $Echo list, you can get each piece of input you give to *Mathematica* saved in a file.

Streams[ ]	list of all open streams
Streams["*name*"]	list of all open streams with the specified name
$Input	the name of the current input stream

Open streams in a *Mathematica* session.

The function Streams shows you all the input, output and other streams that are open at a particular point in a *Mathematica* session. The variable $Input gives the name of the current stream from which *Mathematica* input is being taken at a particular point. $Input is reset, for example, during the execution of a Get command.

$MessagePrePrint	a function to be applied to expressions that are given in messages
$Language	list of default languages to use for messages

Parameters for messages.

There are various global parameters which determine the form of messages generated by *Mathematica*.

As discussed in Section 2.8.21, typical messages include a sequence of expressions which are combined with the text of the message through StringForm. $MessagePrePrint gives a function to be applied to the expressions before they are printed. The default value of $MessagePrePrint is Short.

As discussed in Section 2.8.22, *Mathematica* allows you to specify the language in which you want messages to be produced. In a particular *Mathematica* session, you can assign a list of language names as the value of $Language.

Exit[ ] or Quit[ ]	terminate your *Mathematica* session
$Epilog	a global variable to be evaluated before termination

Terminating *Mathematica* sessions.

Mathematica will continue in its main loop until you explicitly tell it to exit. Most *Mathematica* interfaces provide special ways to do this. Nevertheless, you can always do it by explicitly calling Exit or Quit.

Mathematica allows you to give a value to the global variable $Epilog to specify operations to perform just before *Mathematica* actually exits. In this way, you can for example make *Mathematica* always save certain objects before exiting.

$IgnoreEOF	whether to ignore the end-of-file character

A global variable that determines the treatment of end-of-file characters.

As discussed in Section 2.7.5, *Mathematica* usually does not treat special characters in a special way. There is one potential exception, however. With the default setting $IgnoreEOF = False, *Mathematica* recognizes end-of-file characters. If *Mathematica* receives an end-of-file character as the only thing on a particular input line in a standard interactive *Mathematica* session, then it will exit the session.

Exactly how you enter an end-of-file character depends on the computer system you are using. Under Unix, for example, you typically press CONTROL-D.

Note that if you use *Mathematica* in a "batch mode", with all its input coming from a file, then it will automatically exit when it reaches the end of the file, regardless of the value of $IgnoreEOF.

■ 2.13.2 Dialogs

Within a standard interactive session, you can create "subsessions" or *dialogs* using the *Mathematica* command `Dialog`. Dialogs are often useful if you want to interact with *Mathematica* while it is in the middle of doing a calculation. As mentioned in Section 2.5.10, `TraceDialog` for example automatically calls `Dialog` at specified points in the evaluation of a particular expression. In addition, if you interrupt *Mathematica* during a computation, you can typically "inspect" its state using a dialog.

`Dialog[ ]`	initiate a *Mathematica* dialog
`Dialog[expr]`	initiate a dialog with *expr* as the current value of %
`Return[ ]`	return from a dialog, taking the current value of % as the return value
`Return[expr]`	return from a dialog, taking *expr* as the return value

Initiating and returning from dialogs.

This initiates a dialog.	`In[1]:= Dialog[ ]`
You can do computations in a dialog just as you would in any *Mathematica* session.	`In[2]:= 2^41` `Out[2]= 2199023255552`
You can use `Return` to exit from a dialog.	`In[3]:= Return[ ]` `Out[1]= 2199023255552`

When you exit a dialog, you can return a value for the dialog using `Return[expr]`. If you do not want to return a value, and you have set `$IgnoreEOF = False`, then you can also exit a dialog simply by giving an end-of-file character, at least on systems with text-based interfaces.

To evaluate this expression, *Mathematica* initiates a dialog.	`In[2]:= 1 + Dialog[ ]^2`
The value a + b returned from the dialog is now inserted in the original expression.	`In[3]:= Return[a + b]` `Out[2]= 1 + (a + b)^2`

In starting a dialog, you will often find it useful to have some "initial expression". If you use `Dialog[expr]`, then *Mathematica* will start a dialog, using *expr* as the initial expression, accessible for example as the value of %.

This first starts a dialog with initial expression a^2.	*In[3]:=* **Map[Dialog, {a^2, b + c}]** *Out[4]=* a^2
% is the initial expression in the dialog.	*In[5]:=* **%^2 + 1** *Out[5]=* $1 + a^4$
This returns a value from the first dialog, and starts the second dialog, with initial expression b + c.	*In[6]:=* **Return[%]** *Out[4]=* $b + c$
This returns a value from the second dialog. The final result is the original expression, with values from the two dialogs inserted.	*In[5]:=* **Return[444]** *Out[3]=* $\{1 + a^4, 444\}$

Dialog effectively works by running a subsidiary version of the standard *Mathematica* main loop. Each dialog you start effectively "inherits" various values from the overall main loop. Some of the values are, however, local to the dialog, so their original values are restored when you exit the dialog.

Thus, for example, dialogs inherit the current line number $Line when they start. This means that the lines in a dialog have numbers that follow the sequence used in the main loop. Nevertheless, the value of $Line is local to the dialog. As a result, when you exit the dialog, the value of $Line reverts to what it was in the main loop.

If you start a dialog on line 10 of your *Mathematica* session, then the first line of the dialog will be labeled *In[11]*. Successive lines of the dialog will be labeled *In[12]*, *In[13]* and so on. Then, when you exit the dialog, the next line in your main loop will be labeled *In[11]*. At this point, you can still refer to results generated within the dialog as *Out[11]*, *Out[12]* and so on. These results will be overwritten, however, when you reach lines *In[12]*, *In[13]*, and so on in the main loop.

In a standard *Mathematica* session, you can tell whether you are in a dialog by seeing whether your input and output lines are indented. If you call a dialog from within a dialog, you will get two levels of indentation. In general, the indentation you get inside *d* nested dialogs is determined by the output form of the object **DialogIndent[*d*]**. By defining the format for this object, you can specify how dialogs should be indicated in your *Mathematica* session.

DialogSymbols :> {*x*, *y*, ... }	symbols whose values should be treated as local to the dialog
DialogSymbols :> {*x* = x_0, *y* = y_0, ... }	symbols with initial values
DialogProlog :> *expr*	an expression to evaluate before starting the dialog

Options for **Dialog**.

Whatever setting you give for DialogSymbols, Dialog will always treat the values of $Line, $Epilog and $MessageList as local. Note that if you give a value for $Epilog, it will automatically be evaluated when you exit the dialog.

When you call Dialog, its first step is to localize the values of variables. Then it evaluates any expression you have set for the option DialogProlog. If you have given an explicit argument to the Dialog function, this is then evaluated next. Finally, the actual dialog is started.

When you exit the dialog, you can explicitly specify the return value using Return[*expr*]. If you do not do this, the return value will be taken to be the last value generated in the dialog.

■ 2.13.3 Date and Time Functions

Date[ ]	give the current local date and time in the form {*year*, *month*, *day*, *hour*, *minute*, *second*}
Date[*z*]	give the current date and time in time zone *z*
TimeZone[ ]	give the time zone assumed by your computer system

Finding the date and time.

This gives the current date and time.

```
In[1]:= Date[ ]
Out[1]= {1996, 3, 27, 16, 38, 53}
```

The *Mathematica* Date function returns whatever your computer system gives as the current date and time. It assumes that any corrections for daylight saving time and so on have already been done by your computer system. In addition, it assumes that your computer system has been set for the appropriate time zone.

The function TimeZone[ ] returns the current time zone assumed by your computer system. The time zone is given as the number of hours which must be added to Greenwich mean time (GMT) to obtain the correct local time. Thus, for example, U.S. eastern standard time (EST) corresponds to time zone −5. Note that daylight saving time corrections must be included in the time zone, so U.S. eastern daylight time (EDT) corresponds to time zone −4.

This gives the current time zone assumed by your computer system.

```
In[2]:= TimeZone[ ]
Out[2]= -6
```

This gives the current date and time in time zone +9, the time zone for Japan.

```
In[3]:= Date[9]
Out[3]= {1996, 3, 28, 7, 38, 56}
```

`AbsoluteTime[ ]`	total number of seconds since the beginning of January 1, 1900
`SessionTime[ ]`	total number of seconds elapsed since the beginning of your current *Mathematica* session
`TimeUsed[ ]`	total number of seconds of CPU time used in your current *Mathematica* session
`$TimeUnit`	the minimum time interval recorded on your computer system

Time functions.

You should realize that on any computer system, there is a certain "granularity" in the times that can be measured. This granularity is given as the value of the global variable $TimeUnit. Typically it is about $\frac{1}{60}$ of a second.

`Pause[n]`	pause for at least *n* seconds

Pausing during a calculation.

This gives various time functions.

```
In[4]:= {AbsoluteTime[ ], SessionTime[ ], TimeUsed[ ]}

Out[4]= {3.036933537730713×10⁹, 22.738351, 3.61667}
```

This pauses for 10 seconds, then re-evaluates the time functions. Note that TimeUsed[ ] is not affected by the pause.

```
In[5]:= Pause[10]; {AbsoluteTime[ ], SessionTime[ ],
                                          TimeUsed[ ]}

Out[5]= {3.03693353994321×10⁹, 24.950748, 3.81667}
```

`FromDate[date]`	convert from date to absolute time
`ToDate[time]`	convert from absolute time to date

Converting between dates and absolute times.

This sets d to be the current date.

```
In[6]:= d = Date[ ]

Out[6]= {1996, 3, 27, 16, 39, 1}
```

This adds one month to the current date.

```
In[7]:= Date[ ] + {0, 1, 0, 0, 0, 0}

Out[7]= {1996, 4, 27, 16, 39, 2}
```

This gives the number of seconds in the additional month.

```
In[8]:= FromDate[%] - FromDate[d]

Out[8]= 2678401
```

Timing[*expr*]	evaluate *expr*, and return a list of the CPU time needed, together with the result obtained

Timing *Mathematica* operations.

Timing allows you to measure the CPU time, corresponding to the increase in TimeUsed, associated with the evaluation of a single *Mathematica* expression. Note that only CPU time associated with the actual evaluation of the expression within the *Mathematica* kernel is included. The time needed to format the expression for output, and any time associated with external programs, is not included.

You should realize that the time reported by Timing for a particular calculation depends on many factors.

First, the time depends in detail on the computer system you are using. It depends not only on instruction times, but also on memory caching, as well as on the details of the optimization done in compiling the parts of the internal code of *Mathematica* used in the calculation.

The time also depends on the precise state of your *Mathematica* session when the calculation was done. Many of the internal optimizations used by *Mathematica* depend on details of preceding calculations. For example, *Mathematica* often uses previous results it has obtained, and avoids unnecessarily re-evaluating expressions. In addition, some *Mathematica* functions build internal tables when they are first called in a particular way, so that if they are called in that way again, they run much faster. For all of these kinds of reasons, it is often the case that a particular calculation may not take the same amount of time if you run it at different points in the same *Mathematica* session.

This gives the CPU time needed for the calculation. The semicolon causes the result of the calculation to be given as Null.

```
In[9]:= Timing[1000!;]
Out[9]= {0.433333 Second, Null}
```

Now *Mathematica* has built internal tables for factorial functions, and the calculation takes much less time.

```
In[10]:= Timing[1000!;]
Out[10]= {0. Second, Null}
```

Note that the results you get from Timing are only accurate to the timing granularity $TimeUnit of your computer system. Thus, for example, a timing reported as 0 could in fact be as much as $TimeUnit.

TimeConstrained[*expr*, *t*]	try to evaluate *expr*, aborting the calculation after *t* seconds
TimeConstrained[*expr*, *t*, *failexpr*]	return *failexpr* if the time constraint is not met

Time-constrained calculation.

When you use *Mathematica* interactively, it is quite common to try doing a calculation, but to abort the calculation if it seems to be taking too long. You can emulate this behavior inside a program by using `TimeConstrained`. `TimeConstrained` tries to evaluate a particular expression for a specified amount of time. If it does not succeed, then it aborts the evaluation, and returns either `$Aborted`, or an expression you specify.

You can use `TimeConstrained`, for example, to have *Mathematica* try a particular approach to a problem for a certain amount of time, and then to switch to another approach if the first one has not yet succeeded. You should realize however that `TimeConstrained` may overrun the time you specify if *Mathematica* cannot be interrupted during a particular part of a calculation. In addition, you should realize that because different computer systems run at different speeds, programs that use `TimeConstrained` will often give different results on different systems.

■ 2.13.4 Memory Management

`MemoryInUse[ ]`	number of bytes of memory currently being used by *Mathematica*
`MaxMemoryUsed[ ]`	maximum number of bytes of memory used by *Mathematica* in this session

Finding memory usage.

Particularly for symbolic computations, memory is usually the primary resource which limits the size of computations you can do. If a computation runs slowly, you can always potentially let it run longer. But if the computation generates intermediate expressions which simply cannot fit in the memory of your computer system, then you cannot proceed with the computation.

Mathematica is careful about the way it uses memory. Every time an intermediate expression you have generated is no longer needed, *Mathematica* immediately reclaims the memory allocated to it. This means that at any point in a session, *Mathematica* stores only those expressions that are actually needed; it does not keep unnecessary objects which have to be "garbage collected" later.

This gives the number of bytes of memory currently being used by *Mathematica*.

```
In[1]:= MemoryInUse[ ]
Out[1]= 713040
```

This generates a 10000-element list.

```
In[2]:= Range[10000] // Short
Out[2]//Short= {1, 2, 3, 4, 5, 6, 7, 8, «9985», 9994, 9995,
                9996, 9997, 9998, 9999, 10000}
```

Additional memory is needed to store the list.

```
In[3]:= MemoryInUse[ ]
Out[3]= 883516
```

This list is kept because it is the value of Out[2]. If you clear Out[2], the list is no longer needed.	*In[4]:=* **Unprotect[Out]; Out[2]=.**
The memory in use goes down again.	*In[5]:=* **MemoryInUse[ ]** *Out[5]=* 727668
This shows the maximum memory needed at any point in the session.	*In[6]:=* **MaxMemoryUsed[ ]** *Out[6]=* 1314252

One issue that often comes up is exactly how much memory *Mathematica* can actually use on a particular computer system. Usually there is a certain amount of memory available for *all* processes running on the computer at a particular time. Sometimes this amount of memory is equal to the physical number of bytes of RAM in the computer. Often, it includes a certain amount of "virtual memory", obtained by swapping data on and off a mass storage device.

When *Mathematica* runs, it needs space both for data and for code. The complete code of *Mathematica* is typically several megabytes in size. For any particular calculation, only a small fraction of this code is usually used. However, in trying to work out the total amount of space available for *Mathematica* data, you should not forget what is needed for *Mathematica* code. In addition, you must include the space that is taken up by other processes running in the computer. If there are fewer jobs running, you will usually find that your job can use more memory.

It is also worth realizing that the time needed to do a calculation can depend very greatly on how much physical memory you have. Although virtual memory allows you in principle to use large amounts of memory space, it is usually hundreds or even thousands of times slower to access than physical memory. As a result, if your calculation becomes so large that it needs to make use of virtual memory, it may run *much* more slowly.

MemoryConstrained[*expr*, *b*]	try to evaluate *expr*, aborting if more than *b* additional bytes of memory are requested
MemoryConstrained[*expr*, *b*, *failexpr*]	return *failexpr* if the memory constraint is not met

Memory-constrained computation.

MemoryConstrained works much like TimeConstrained. If more than the specified amount of memory is requested, MemoryConstrained attempts to abort your computation. As with TimeConstrained, there may be some overshoot in the actual amount of memory used before the computation is aborted.

ByteCount[*expr*]	the maximum number of bytes of memory needed to store *expr*
LeafCount[*expr*]	the number of terminal nodes in the expression tree for *expr*

Finding the size of expressions.

Although you may find ByteCount useful in estimating how large an expression of a particular kind you can handle, you should realize that the specific results given by ByteCount can differ substantially from one version of *Mathematica* to another.

Another important point is that ByteCount always gives you the *maximum* amount of memory needed to store a particular expression. Often *Mathematica* will actually use a much smaller amount of memory to store the expression. The main issue is how many of the subexpressions in the expression can be *shared*.

In an expression like f[1 + x, 1 + x], the two subexpressions 1 + x are identical, but they may or may not actually be stored in the same piece of computer memory. ByteCount gives you the number of bytes needed to store expressions with the assumption that no subexpressions are shared. You should realize that the sharing of subexpressions is often destroyed as soon as you use an operation like the /. operator.

Nevertheless, you can explicitly tell *Mathematica* to share subexpressions using the function Share. In this way, you can significantly reduce the actual amount of memory needed to store a particular expression.

Share[*expr*]	share common subexpressions in the storage of *expr*
Share[ ]	share common subexpressions throughout memory

Optimizing memory usage.

On most computer systems, the memory used by a running program is divided into two parts: memory explicitly allocated by the program, and "stack space". Every time an internal routine is called in the program, a certain amount of stack space is used to store parameters associated with the call. On many computer systems, the maximum amount of stack space that can be used by a program must be specified in advance. If the specified stack space limit is exceeded, the program usually just exits.

In *Mathematica*, one of the primary uses of stack space is in handling the calling of one *Mathematica* function by another. All such calls are explicitly recorded in the *Mathematica* Stack discussed in Section 2.5.11. You can control the size of this stack by setting the global parameter $RecursionLimit. You should be sure that this parameter is set small enough that you do not run out of stack space on your particular computer system.

■ 2.13.5 Advanced Topic: Global System Information

In order to write the most general *Mathematica* programs you will sometimes need to find out global information about the setup under which your program is being run.

Thus, for example, to tell whether your program should be calling functions like `NotebookWrite`, you need to find out whether the program is being run in a *Mathematica* session that is using the notebook front end. You can do this by testing the global variable `$Notebooks`.

`$Notebooks`	whether a notebook front end is being used

Determining whether a notebook front end is being used.

Mathematica is usually used interactively, but it can also operate in a batch mode—say taking input from a file and writing output to a file. In such a case, a program cannot for example expect to get interactive input from the user.

`$BatchInput`	whether input is being given in batch mode
`$BatchOutput`	whether output should be given in batch mode, without labeling, etc.

Variables specifying batch mode operation.

The *Mathematica* kernel is a process that runs under the operating system on your computer. Within *Mathematica* there are several global variables that allow you to find the characteristics of this process and its environment.

$CommandLine	the original command line used to invoke the *Mathematica* kernel
$ParentLink	the *MathLink* LinkObject specifying the program that invoked the kernel (or Null if the kernel was invoked directly)
$ProcessID	the ID assigned to the *Mathematica* kernel process by the operating system
$ParentProcessID	the ID of the process that invoked the *Mathematica* kernel
$UserName	the login name of the user running the *Mathematica* kernel
Environment["*var*"]	the value of a variable defined by the operating system

Variables associated with the *Mathematica* kernel process.

If you have a variable such as x in a particular *Mathematica* session, you may or may not want that variable to be the same as an x in another *Mathematica* session. In order to make it possible to maintain distinct objects in different sessions, *Mathematica* supports the variable $SessionID, which uses information such as starting time, process ID and machine ID to try to give a different value for every single *Mathematica* session, whether it is run on the same computer or a different one.

$SessionID	a number set up to be different for every *Mathematica* session

A unique number different for every *Mathematica* session.

Mathematica provides various global variables that allow you to tell which version of the kernel you are running. This is important if you write programs that make use of features that are, say, new in Version 3.0. You can then check $VersionNumber to find out if these features will be available.

$Version	a string giving the complete version of *Mathematica* in use
$VersionNumber	the *Mathematica* kernel version number (e.g. 3.0)
$ReleaseNumber	the release number for your version of the *Mathematica* kernel on your particular computer system
$CreationDate	the date, in Date format, on which your particular *Mathematica* release was created
$InstallationDate	the date on which your copy of *Mathematica* was installed

Variables specifying the version of *Mathematica* used.

Mathematica itself is set up to be as independent of the details of the particular computer system on which it is run as possible. However, if you want to access external aspects of your computer system, then you will often need to find out its characteristics.

$System	a full string describing the computer system in use
$SystemID	a short string specifying the computer system in use
$ProcessorType	the architecture of the processor in your computer system
$MachineType	the general type of your computer system
$OperatingSystem	the basic operating system in use
$SystemCharacterEncoding	the default raw character encoding used by your operating system

Variables specifying the characteristics of your computer system.

Mathematica uses the values of $SystemID to label directories that contain versions of files for different computer systems, as discussed on pages 602 and 650. Computer systems for which $SystemID is the same will normally be binary compatible.

$OperatingSystem has values such as "Unix" and "MacOS". By testing $OperatingSystem you can determine whether a particular external program is likely to be available on your computer system.

This gives some characteristics of the computer system used to generate the examples for this book.

```
In[1]:= {$System, $ProcessorType, $OperatingSystem}

Out[1]= {NeXT, 680x0, Unix}
```

$MachineName	the name of the computer on which *Mathematica* is running
$MachineDomain	the network domain for the computer
$MachineID	the unique ID assigned by *Mathematica* to the computer

Variables identifying the computer on which *Mathematica* is running.

$LicenseID	the ID for the license under which *Mathematica* is running
$LicenseExpirationDate	the date on which the license expires
$NetworkLicense	whether this is a network license
$LicenseServer	the full name of the machine serving the license
$LicenseProcesses	the number of *Mathematica* processes currently being run under the license
$MaxLicenseProcesses	the maximum number of processes provided by the license
$PasswordFile	password file used when the kernel was started

Variables associated with license management.

~■ 2.13.6 Advanced Topic: Customizing Your *Mathematica* Configuration

- Load system-wide `init.m` initialization files
- Load `init.m`, `Kernel/init.m` and `FrontEnd/init.m` files in subdirectories of `Autoload` directories

Operations performed whenever *Mathematica* starts up.

You will often find it convenient to customize your copy of *Mathematica* by having *Mathematica* execute particular commands or load specific packages every time it starts up. You can do this by setting up system-wide `init.m` files, or by placing items in an `Autoload` directory.

- Load special or user-specific customization files
- Load customization files shared by all users of this copy of *Mathematica*

The order of loading customization files.

All versions of *Mathematica* allow shared customization files to be placed in a central `Configuration` directory. However, special or user-specific customization files are typically placed in directories that differ from one computer system to another.

Microsoft Windows	`Config` subdirectory of main *Mathematica* folder
Macintosh	`Mathematica 3.0 Prefs` folder in the `System Folder`
Unix	`.Mathematica3.0` subdirectory of each user's home directory
NeXT	`Library/Mathematica3.0` subdirectory of each user's home directory
all systems	`Configuration` subdirectory of the main *Mathematica* directory

Typical locations for customization files.

Section A.8 describes the arrangement of customization files for the *Mathematica* kernel and front end in more detail.

Part 3

Part 1 described how to do basic mathematics with Mathematica. For many kinds of calculations, you will need to know nothing more. But if you do want to use more advanced mathematics, this part discusses how to do it in Mathematica.

This part goes through the various mathematical functions and methods that are built into Mathematica. Some calculations can be done just by using these built-in mathematical capabilities. For many specific calculations, however, you will need to use application packages that have been written in Mathematica. These packages build on the mathematical capabilities discussed in this part, but add new functions for doing special kinds of calculations.

Much of what is said in this part assumes a knowledge of mathematics at an advanced undergraduate level. If you do not understand a particular section, then you can probably assume that you will not need to use that section.

Part 3

Advanced Mathematics in *Mathematica*

3.1 Numbers

■ 3.1.1 Types of Numbers

Four underlying types of numbers are built into *Mathematica*.

Integer	arbitrary-length exact integer
Rational	*integer/integer* in lowest terms
Real	approximate real number, with any specified precision
Complex	complex number of the form *number* + *number* I

Intrinsic types of numbers in *Mathematica*.

Rational numbers always consist of a ratio of two integers, reduced to lowest terms.

$In[1]:=$ **12344/2222**

$Out[1]=$ $\dfrac{6172}{1111}$

Approximate real numbers are distinguished by the presence of an explicit decimal point.

$In[2]:=$ **5456.**

$Out[2]=$ 5456.

An approximate real number can have any number of digits.

$In[3]:=$ **4.5454352345454352345345234523454543**

$Out[3]=$ 4.5454352345454352345345234523454543

Complex numbers can have integer or rational components.

$In[4]:=$ **4 + 7/8 I**

$Out[4]=$ $4 + \dfrac{7\,I}{8}$

They can also have approximate real number components.

$In[5]:=$ **4 + 5.6 I**

$Out[5]=$ $4 + 5.6\,I$

123	an exact integer
123.	an approximate real number
123.0000000000000	an approximate real number with a certain precision
123. + 0. I	a complex number with approximate real number components

Several versions of the number 123.

You can distinguish different types of numbers in *Mathematica* by looking at their heads. (Although numbers in *Mathematica* have heads like other expressions, they do not have explicit elements which you can extract.)

The object 123 is taken to be an exact integer, with head `Integer`.	*In[6]:=* **Head[123]** *Out[6]=* Integer
The presence of an explicit decimal point makes *Mathematica* treat 123. as an approximate real number, with head `Real`.	*In[7]:=* **Head[123.]** *Out[7]=* Real

NumberQ[*x*]	test whether *x* is any kind of number
IntegerQ[*x*]	test whether *x* is an integer
EvenQ[*x*]	test whether *x* is even
OddQ[*x*]	test whether *x* is odd
PrimeQ[*x*]	test whether *x* is a prime integer
Head[*x*]===*type*	test the type of a number

Tests for different types of numbers.

NumberQ[*x*] tests for any kind of number.	*In[8]:=* **NumberQ[5.6]** *Out[8]=* True
5. is treated as a Real, so IntegerQ gives False.	*In[9]:=* **IntegerQ[5.]** *Out[9]=* False

If you use complex numbers extensively, there is one subtlety you should be aware of. When you enter a number like 123., *Mathematica* treats it as an approximate real number, but assumes that its imaginary part is exactly zero. Sometimes you may want to enter approximate complex numbers with imaginary parts that are zero, but only to a certain precision.

When the imaginary part is the exact integer 0, *Mathematica* simplifies complex numbers to real ones.	*In[10]:=* **Head[123 + 0 I]** *Out[10]=* Integer
Here the imaginary part is only zero to a certain precision, so *Mathematica* retains the complex number form.	*In[11]:=* **Head[123. + 0. I]** *Out[11]=* Complex

The distinction between complex numbers whose imaginary parts are exactly zero, or are only zero to a certain precision, may seem like a pedantic one. However, when we discuss, for example, the interpretation of powers and roots of complex numbers in Section 3.2.7, the distinction will become significant.

One way to find out the type of a number in *Mathematica* is just to pick out its head using `Head[expr]`. For many purposes, however, it is better to use functions like `IntegerQ` which explicitly test for particular types. Functions like this are set up to return `True` if their argument is manifestly of the required type, and to return `False` otherwise. As a result, `IntegerQ[x]` will give `False`, unless you have assigned x an explicit integer value.

In doing symbolic computations, however, you may sometimes want to treat x as an integer, even though you have not assigned an explicit integer value to it. You can override the assumption that the symbol x is not an integer by explicitly making an assignment of the form `x/: IntegerQ[x] = True`. This assignment specifies that whenever you specifically test x with `IntegerQ`, it will give the result `True`. You should realize, however, that the assignment does not actually change the head of x, so that, for example, x will still not match `n_Integer`. *Mathematica* also does not automatically make inferences based on the assignment. Thus, for example, it cannot determine solely on the basis of this assignment that `IntegerQ[x^2]` is also `True`.

x does not explicitly have head `Integer`, so `IntegerQ` returns `False`.	*In[12]:=* `IntegerQ[x]` *Out[12]=* False
This specifies that x is in fact an integer. The `x/:` specifies that the rule is associated with x, not `IntegerQ`.	*In[13]:=* `x/: IntegerQ[x] = True` *Out[13]=* True
The definition overrides the default assumption that x is not an integer.	*In[14]:=* `IntegerQ[x]` *Out[14]=* True

■ 3.1.2 Numeric Quantities

`NumberQ[`*expr*`]`	test whether *expr* is explicitly a number
`NumericQ[`*expr*`]`	test whether *expr* has a numerical value

Testing for numeric quantities.

Pi is a symbol, so Pi + 3 is not explicitly a number.	*In[1]:=* `NumberQ[Pi + 3]` *Out[1]=* False
It does however have a numerical value.	*In[2]:=* `NumericQ[Pi + 3]` *Out[2]=* True
This finds the explicit numerical value of Pi + 3.	*In[3]:=* `N[Pi + 3]` *Out[3]=* 6.14159

Mathematica knows that constants such as Pi are numeric quantities. It also knows that standard mathematical functions such as Log and Sin have numerical values when their arguments are numerical.

Log[2 + x] contains x, and is therefore not a numeric quantity.

```
In[4]:= {NumericQ[Log[2]], NumericQ[Log[2 + x]]}
Out[4]= {True, False}
```

Many functions implicitly use the numerical values of numeric quantities.

```
In[5]:= Min[Exp[2], Log[2], Sqrt[2]]
Out[5]= Log[2]
```

In general, *Mathematica* assumes that any function which has the attribute `NumericFunction` will yield numerical values when its arguments are numerical. All standard mathematical functions in *Mathematica* already have this attribute. But when you define your own functions, you can explicitly set the attribute to tell *Mathematica* to assume that these functions will have numerical values when their arguments are numerical.

■ 3.1.3 Converting between Different Forms of Numbers

N[x, n]	convert x to an approximate real number with n digits of precision
Rationalize[x]	give a rational number approximation to x
Rationalize[x, dx]	give a rational number approximation to within tolerance dx

Functions that convert between different types of numbers.

This gives a 30-digit real number approximation to 3/7.

```
In[1]:= N[3/7, 30]
Out[1]= 0.428571428571428571428571428571
```

This takes the 30-digit number you have just generated, and reduces it to 20-digit precision.

```
In[2]:= N[%, 20]
Out[2]= 0.428571428571428571429
```

This converts the result back to a rational number.

```
In[3]:= Rationalize[%]
```
$$Out[3]= \frac{3}{7}$$

The numerical value of π is not "sufficiently close" to a rational number to be converted.

```
In[4]:= Rationalize[ N[Pi] ]
Out[4]= 3.14159
```

If you give a specific tolerance, Rationalize will give you a rational number approximation accurate to within that tolerance.

```
In[5]:= Rationalize[ N[Pi], 10^-5 ]
```
$$Out[5]= \frac{355}{113}$$

With a tolerance of 0, Rationalize yields the best possible rational approximation given the precision of your input.

In[6]:= **Rationalize[N[Pi], 0]**

$$Out[6]= \frac{245850922}{78256779}$$

IntegerDigits[n]	a list of the decimal digits in the integer n
IntegerDigits[n, b]	the digits of n in base b
IntegerDigits[n, b, *len*]	the list of digits padded on the left with zeros to give total length *len*
RealDigits[x]	a list of the decimal digits in the approximate real number x, together with the number of digits to the left of the decimal point
RealDigits[x, b]	the digits of x in base b
RealDigits[x, b, *len*]	the first *len* digits of x in base b
RealDigits[x, b, *len*, n]	the first *len* digits starting with the coefficient of b^n
FromDigits[*list*]	reconstruct a number from its decimal digit sequence
FromDigits[*list*, b]	reconstruct a number from its digits sequence in base b

Converting between numbers and lists of digits.

Here is the list of base 16 digits for an integer.

In[7]:= **IntegerDigits[1234135634, 16]**
Out[7]= {4, 9, 8, 15, 6, 10, 5, 2}

This gives a list of digits, together with the number of digits that appear to the left of the decimal point.

In[8]:= **RealDigits[123.45678901234567890123456]**
Out[8]= {{1, 2, 3, 4, 5, 6, 7, 8, 9, 0, 1, 2, 3, 4, 5, 6, 7, 8, 9, 0, 1, 2, 3, 4, 5, 7}, 3}

Here is the binary digit sequence for 56, padded with zeros so that it is of total length 8.

In[9]:= **IntegerDigits[56, 2, 8]**
Out[9]= {0, 0, 1, 1, 1, 0, 0, 0}

This reconstructs the original number from its binary digit sequence.

$In[10]:=$ **FromDigits[%, 2]**

$Out[10]=$ 56

b^^*nnnn*	a number in base b
BaseForm[x, b]	print with x in base b

Numbers in other bases.

When the base is larger than 10, extra digits are represented by letters a–z.

The number 100101_2 in base 2 is 37 in base 10.

$In[11]:=$ **2^^100101**

$Out[11]=$ 37

This prints 37 in base 2.

$In[12]:=$ **BaseForm[37, 2]**

$Out[12]//BaseForm=$ 100101_2

Here is a number in base 16.

$In[13]:=$ **16^^ffffaa00**

$Out[13]=$ 4294945280

You can do computations with numbers in base 16. Here the result is given in base 10.

$In[14]:=$ **16^^fffaa2 + 16^^ff - 1**

$Out[14]=$ 16776096

This gives the result in base 16.

$In[15]:=$ **BaseForm[%, 16]**

$Out[15]//BaseForm=$ $fffba0_{16}$

You can give approximate real numbers, as well as integers, in other bases.

$In[16]:=$ **2^^101.100101**

$Out[16]=$ 5.58

Here are the first few digits of $\sqrt{2}$ in octal.

$In[17]:=$ **BaseForm[N[Sqrt[2], 30], 8]**

$Out[17]//BaseForm=$ $1.32404746317716746220426276611546 7_8$

This gives an explicit list of the first 15 octal digits.

$In[18]:=$ **RealDigits[Sqrt[2], 8, 15]**

$Out[18]=$ {{1, 3, 2, 4, 0, 4, 7, 4, 6, 3, 1, 7, 7, 1, 6}, 1}

This gives 15 octal digits starting with the coefficient of 8^{-10}.

$In[19]:=$ **RealDigits[Sqrt[2], 8, 15, -10]**

$Out[19]=$ {{1, 7, 7, 1, 6, 7, 4, 6, 2, 2, 0, 4, 2, 6, 2}, -9}

Section 2.8.7 describes how to print numbers in various formats. If you want to create your own formats, you will often need to use MantissaExponent to separate the pieces of approximate real numbers.

MantissaExponent[*x*]	give a list containing the mantissa and exponent of *x*
MantissaExponent[*x*, *b*]	give the mantissa and exponent in base *b*

Separating the mantissa and exponent of numbers.

<table>
<tr><td>This gives a list in which the mantissa and exponent of the number are separated.</td><td>In[20]:= MantissaExponent[3.45 10^125]
Out[20]= {0.345, 126}</td></tr>
</table>

■ 3.1.4 Numerical Precision

As discussed in Section 1.1.2, *Mathematica* can handle approximate real numbers with any number of digits. In general, the *precision* of an approximate real number is the number of decimal digits in it which are treated as significant for computations. The *accuracy* of an approximate real number is the number of these digits which appear to the right of the decimal point. Precision is thus a measure of the relative error in a number, while accuracy is a measure of absolute error.

Precision[*x*]	the total number of significant decimal digits in *x*
Accuracy[*x*]	the number of significant decimal digits to the right of the decimal point in *x*

Precision and accuracy of real numbers.

<table>
<tr><td>Here is an approximate real number.</td><td>In[1]:= xacc = 431.123145333555141444
Out[1]= 431.123145333555141444</td></tr>
<tr><td>This gives the total number of digits entered to specify the real number.</td><td>In[2]:= Precision[xacc]
Out[2]= 21</td></tr>
<tr><td>This gives the number of digits which appear to the right of the decimal point.</td><td>In[3]:= Accuracy[xacc]
Out[3]= 18</td></tr>
</table>

When you use N[*expr*, *n*], *Mathematica* tries to evaluate the expression *expr* to *n* digits of precision. And so long as your input has sufficient precision, *Mathematica* will usually succeed in getting a result with the requested precision.

<table>
<tr><td>This asks for Pi^25 to be evaluated to 30 digits of precision.</td><td>In[4]:= N[Pi^25, 30]
Out[4]= 2.68377941431776454900992812439$\times 10^{12}$</td></tr>
<tr><td>The result indeed has 30 digits of precision.</td><td>In[5]:= Precision[%]
Out[5]= 30</td></tr>
</table>

N[*expr*, *n*]	evaluate *expr* numerically to *n*-digit precision using arbitrary-precision numbers if necessary
N[*expr*]	evaluate *expr* numerically using only machine-precision numbers

Numerical evaluation.

If you use N[*expr*], and do not explicitly specify the precision of numbers to use, *Mathematica* will use *machine-precision* numbers.

In general, *Mathematica* distinguishes two kinds of approximate real numbers: *arbitrary-precision* ones, and *machine-precision* ones. Arbitrary-precision numbers can contain any number of digits, and their precision is adjusted during computations. Machine-precision numbers, on the other hand, contain a fixed number of digits, and their precision remains unchanged throughout computations.

As discussed in more detail below, machine-precision numbers work by making direct use of the numerical capabilities of your underlying computer system. As a result, computations with them can be done quickly. However, machine-precision numbers are much less flexible than arbitrary-precision ones.

This evaluates Pi using machine precision.	*In[6]:=* **N[Pi]** *Out[6]=* 3.14159
On the computer system used to generate this example, the machine precision is 16 decimal digits.	*In[7]:=* **Precision[%]** *Out[7]=* 16
This gives the machine precision on the computer system.	*In[8]:=* **$MachinePrecision** *Out[8]=* 16

$MachinePrecision	the machine precision on your computer system
MachineNumberQ[*x*]	give True if *x* is a machine-precision number, and False otherwise

Machine-precision numbers.

When you enter an approximate real number, *Mathematica* has to decide whether to treat it as machine precision or arbitrary precision. Unless you specify otherwise, then if you give less than $MachinePrecision digits, *Mathematica* will treat the number as machine precision, and if you give more digits, it will treat the number as arbitrary precision.

123.4	a machine-precision number
123.45678901234567890	an arbitrary-precision number on some computer systems
123.45678901234567890`	a machine-precision number on all computer systems
123.456`200	an arbitrary-precision number with 200 digits of precision
123.456``200	an arbitrary-precision number with 200 digits of accuracy
1.234*^6	a machine-precision number in scientific notation (1.234×10^6)
1.234`200*^6	a number in scientific notation with 200 digits of precision
2^^101.111`200	a number in base 2 with 200 binary digits of precision
2^^101.111`200*^6	a number in base 2 scientific notation $(101.111_2 \times 2^6)$

Input forms for numbers.

When *Mathematica* prints out numbers, it usually tries to give them in a form that will be as easy as possible to read. But if you want to take numbers that are printed out by *Mathematica*, and then later use them as input to *Mathematica*, you need to make sure that no information gets lost.

In standard output form, *Mathematica* prints a number like this to six digits.

```
In[9]:= N[Pi]
Out[9]= 3.14159
```

In input form, *Mathematica* prints all the digits it knows.

```
In[10]:= InputForm[%]
Out[10]//InputForm= 3.141592653589793
```

Here is an arbitrary-precision number in standard output form.

```
In[11]:= N[Pi, 20]
Out[11]= 3.14159265358979323846
```

In input form, *Mathematica* explicitly indicates the precision of the number, and gives extra digits to make sure the number can be reconstructed correctly.

```
In[12]:= InputForm[%]
Out[12]//InputForm= 3.1415926535897932384626433832795`20
```

This makes *Mathematica* not explicitly indicate precision.

```
In[13]:= InputForm[%, NumberMarks->False]
Out[13]//InputForm= 3.14159265358979323846
```

+	`InputForm[`*expr*`, NumberMarks->True]`	
		use ` marks in all approximate numbers
+	`InputForm[`*expr*`, NumberMarks->Automatic]`	
		use ` only in arbitrary-precision numbers
	`InputForm[`*expr*`, NumberMarks->False]`	
		never use ` marks

Controlling printing of numbers.

The default setting for the `NumberMarks` option, both in `InputForm` and in functions such as `ToString` and `OpenWrite` is given by the value of `$NumberMarks`. By resetting `$NumberMarks`, therefore, you can globally change the way that numbers are printed in `InputForm`.

This makes *Mathematica* by default always include number marks in input form.	`In[14]:= $NumberMarks = True`
	
	`Out[14]= True`

Even a machine-precision number is now printed with an explicit number mark.	`In[15]:= InputForm[N[Pi]]`
	
	`Out[15]//InputForm= 3.14159265358979311``

Even with no number marks, `InputForm` still uses `*^` for scientific notation.	`In[16]:= InputForm[N[Exp[600], 20], NumberMarks->False]`
	
	`Out[16]//InputForm= 3.7730203009299398234*^260`

In doing numerical computations, it is inevitable that you will sometimes end up with results that are less precise than you want. Particularly when you get numerical results that are very close to zero, you may well want to *assume* that the results should be exactly zero. The function `Chop` allows you to replace approximate real numbers that are close to zero by the exact integer 0.

`Chop[`*expr*`]`	replace all approximate real numbers in *expr* with magnitude less than 10^{-10} by 0
`Chop[`*expr*`, dx]`	replace numbers with magnitude less than *dx* by 0

Removing numbers close to zero.

This computation gives a small imaginary part.	`In[17]:= Exp[ N[2 Pi I] ]`
	
	`Out[17]= 1. - 2.44921 \times 10^{-16} I`

You can get rid of the imaginary part using `Chop`.	`In[18]:= Chop[%]`
	
	`Out[18]= 1.`

■ 3.1.5 Arbitrary-Precision Numbers

When you do calculations with arbitrary-precision numbers, *Mathematica* keeps track of precision at all points. In general, *Mathematica* tries to give you results which have the highest possible precision, given the precision of the input you provided.

Mathematica treats arbitrary-precision numbers as representing the values of quantities where a certain number of digits are known, and the rest are unknown. In general, an arbitrary-precision number x is taken to have Precision[x] digits which are known exactly, followed by an infinite number of digits which are completely unknown.

When you do a computation, *Mathematica* keeps track of which digits in your result could be affected by unknown digits in your input. It sets the precision of your result so that no affected digits are ever included. This procedure ensures that all digits returned by *Mathematica* are correct, whatever the values of the unknown digits may be.

This evaluates $\Gamma(1/7)$ trying to get 30-digit precision.	In[1]:= **N[Gamma[1/7], 30]** Out[1]= 6.54806294024782443771409334929
In this case, the result has a precision of exactly 30 digits.	In[2]:= **Precision[%]** Out[2]= 30
If you give input only to a few digits of precision, *Mathematica* cannot give you such high-precision output.	In[3]:= **N[Gamma[0.142], 30]** Out[3]= 6.589647294920398
If you want *Mathematica* to assume that 0.142 is *exactly* 142/1000, then you have to show this explicitly.	In[4]:= **N[Gamma[142/1000], 30]** Out[4]= 6.58964729492039788328481917496

In many computations, the precision of the results you get progressively degrades as a result of "roundoff error". A typical case of this occurs if you subtract two numbers that are close together. The result you get depends on high-order digits in each number, and typically has far fewer digits of precision than either of the original numbers.

Both input numbers have a precision of 20 digits, but the result has a precision of only 3 digits.	In[5]:= **1.11111111111111111111 -** **1.11111111111111111000** Out[5]= 1.11×10^{-18}
Adding extra digits in one number but not the other is not sufficient to allow extra digits to be found in the result.	In[6]:= **1.1111111111111111111345 -** **1.11111111111111111000** Out[6]= 1.11×10^{-18}

The precision of the output from a function can depend in a complicated way on the precision of the input. Functions that vary rapidly typically give less precise output, since the variation of the output associated with uncertainties in the input is larger. Functions that are close to constants can actually give output that is more precise than their input.

Functions like Sin that vary rapidly typically give output that is less precise than their input.

In[7]:= **Sin[111111111.0000000000000000]**

Out[7]= -0.29753510333494323

Here is e^{-40} evaluated to 20-digit precision.

In[8]:= **N[Exp[-40], 20]**

Out[8]= 4.2483542552915889533 × 10^{-18}

The result you get by adding the exact integer 1 has a higher precision.

In[9]:= **1 + %**

Out[9]= 1.0000000000000000042483542552915889953

It is worth realizing that different ways of doing the same calculation can end up giving you results with very different precisions. Typically, if you once lose precision in a calculation, it is essentially impossible to regain it; in losing precision, you are effectively losing information about your result.

Here is a 40-digit number that is close to 1.

In[10]:= **x = N[1 - 10^-30, 40]**

Out[10]= 0.9999999999999999999999999999999999999999

Adding 1 to it gives another 40-digit number.

In[11]:= **1 + x**

Out[11]= 1.999999999999999999999999999999999999999

The original precision has been maintained.

In[12]:= **Precision[%]**

Out[12]= 40

This way of computing 1 + x loses precision.

In[13]:= **(x^2 - 1) / (x - 1)**

Out[13]= 2.

The result obtained in this way has quite low precision.

In[14]:= **Precision[%]**

Out[14]= 10

The fact that different ways of doing the same calculation can give you different numerical answers means, among other things, that comparisons between approximate real numbers must be treated with care. In testing whether two real numbers are "equal", *Mathematica* effectively finds their difference, and tests whether the result is "consistent with zero" to the precision given.

These numbers are equal to the precision given.

In[15]:= **3 == 3.000000000000000000**

Out[15]= True

The internal algorithms that *Mathematica* uses to evaluate mathematical functions are set up to maintain as much precision as possible. In most cases, built-in *Mathematica* functions will give you results that have as much precision as can be justified on the basis of your input. In some cases, however, it is simply impractical to do this, and *Mathematica* will give you results that have lower precision. If you give higher-precision input, *Mathematica* will use higher precision in its internal calculations, and you will usually be able to get a higher-precision result.

N[*expr*]	evaluate *expr* numerically to give a machine-precision result
N[*expr*, *n*]	evaluate *expr* numerically trying to get a result with *n* digits of precision

Numerical evaluation.

If you start with an expression that contains only integers and other exact numeric quantities, then N[*expr*, *n*] will in almost all cases succeed in giving you a result to *n* digits of precision. You should realize, however, that to do this *Mathematica* sometimes has to perform internal intermediate calculations to much higher precision.

The global variable $MaxExtraPrecision specifies how many additional digits should be allowed in such intermediate calculations.

Mathematica automatically increases the precision that it uses internally in order to get the correct answer here.

```
In[16]:= N[Sin[10^40], 30]

Out[16]= -0.569633400953636327308034181815736
```

Using the default setting $MaxExtraPrecision=50 *Mathematica* cannot get the correct answer here.

```
In[17]:= N[Sin[10^100], 30]

$MaxExtraPrecision::mepr:
   In attempting to evaluate
     Sin[10000000000000000000<<71>>0000000000],
      $MaxExtraPrecision 50.
      was encountered. Increasing the value of
      $MaxExtraPrecision may help resolve the uncertainty.

Out[17]= 0.0
```

The precision is zero, indicating that no digits can be expected to be correct.

```
In[18]:= Precision[%]

Out[18]= 0
```

This tells *Mathematica* that it can use more digits in its internal calculations.

```
In[19]:= $MaxExtraPrecision = 100

Out[19]= 100
```

Now it gets the correct answer.

```
In[20]:= N[Sin[10^100], 30]

Out[20]= -0.372376123661276688262086955532
```

This resets $MaxExtraPrecision to its default value.

```
In[21]:= $MaxExtraPrecision = 50

Out[21]= 50
```

Mathematica saves its previous result, so still gives the correct answer here.

```
In[22]:= N[Sin[10^100], 30]

Out[22]= -0.372376123661276688262086955532
```

Even when you are doing computations that give exact results, *Mathematica* still occasionally uses approximate numbers for some of its internal calculations, so that the value of $MaxExtraPrecision can thus have an effect.

Mathematica works this out using bounds from approximate numbers.	`In[23]:= Sin[Exp[100]] > 0`
	
	`Out[23]= True`

With the default value of `$MaxExtraPrecision`, *Mathematica* cannot work this out.	`In[24]:= Sin[Exp[200]] > 0`
	
	`$MaxExtraPrecision::mepr:`
	    In attempting to evaluate Sin[E^{200}], $MaxExtraPrecision
	    50. was encountered. Increasing the value of
	    $MaxExtraPrecision may help resolve the uncertainty.
	
	`Out[24]= Sin[E`^{200}`] > 0`

Temporarily resetting `$MaxExtraPrecision` allows *Mathematica* to get the result.	`In[25]:= Block[{$MaxExtraPrecision = 100},`
	           `Sin[Exp[200]] > 0 ]`
	
	`Out[25]= False`

variable	default value	
+ `$MaxExtraPrecision`	50	maximum additional precision to be used
+ `$MaxPrecision`	50000	maximum total precision to be used
+ `$MinPrecision`	0	minimum precision to be used

Global precision parameters.

When *Mathematica* works out the potential effect of unknown digits in arbitrary-precision numbers, it assumes by default that these digits are completely independent in different numbers. While this assumption will never yield too high a precision in a result, it may lead to unnecessary loss of precision.

In particular, if two numbers are generated in the same way in a computation, some of their unknown digits may be equal. Then, when these numbers are, for example, subtracted, the unknown digits may cancel. By assuming that the unknown digits are always independent, however, *Mathematica* will miss such cancellations.

Here is a number computed to 20-digit precision.	`In[26]:= delta = N[3^-30, 20]` `Out[26]= 4.85693574961886113791×10`$^{-15}$

The quantity 1 + delta has 34-digit precision.	`In[27]:= Precision[1 + delta]`
	
	`Out[27]= 34`

This quantity also has only 34-digit precision, since *Mathematica* assumes that the unknown digits in each number delta are independent.	`In[28]:= Precision[(1 + delta) - delta]`
	
	`Out[28]= 34`

Numerical algorithms sometimes rely on cancellations between unknown digits in different numbers yielding results of higher precision. If you can be sure that certain unknown digits will eventually cancel, then you can explicitly introduce arbitrary digits in place of the unknown ones. You can carry these arbitrary digits through your computation, then let them cancel, and get a result of higher precision.

SetPrecision[x, n]	create a number with n decimal digits of precision, padding with zeros if necessary
SetAccuracy[x, n]	create a number with n decimal digits of accuracy

Functions for modifying precision and accuracy.

This adds 10 arbitrary digits to delta.

In[29]:= **delta = SetPrecision[delta, 30]**

Out[29]= $4.856935749618861137906242664975 \times 10^{-15}$

The digits that were added cancel out here.

In[30]:= **(1 + delta) - delta**

Out[30]= 1.

The precision of the result is now 44, rather than 34, digits.

In[31]:= **Precision[%]**

Out[31]= 44

SetPrecision works by adding digits which are zero in base 2. Sometimes, *Mathematica* stores slightly more digits in an arbitrary-precision number than it displays, and in such cases, SetPrecision will use these extra digits before introducing zeros.

This creates a number with a precision of 40 decimal digits. The extra digits come from conversion to base 10.

In[32]:= **SetPrecision[0.300000000000000, 40]**

Out[32]= 0.2999999999999999988897769753748434459576368

By making the global assignment $MinPrecision = n, you can effectively apply SetPrecision[*expr*, n] at every step in a computation. This means that even when the number of correct digits in an arbitrary-precision number drops below n, the number will always be padded to have n digits.

If you set $MaxPrecision = n as well as $MinPrecision = n, then you can force all arbitrary-precision numbers to have a fixed precision of n digits. In effect, what this does is to make *Mathematica* treat arbitrary-precision numbers in much the same way as it treats machine numbers—but with more digits of precision.

Fixed-precision computation can make some calculations more efficient, but without careful analysis you can never be sure how many digits are correct in the results you get.

Here is a small number with 20-digit precision.

In[33]:= **k = N[Exp[-60], 20]**

Out[33]= $8.7565107626965203849 \times 10^{-27}$

With *Mathematica*'s usual arithmetic, this works fine.

In[34]:= **Evaluate[1 + k] - 1**

Out[34]= $8.7565107626965203849 \times 10^{-27}$

This tells *Mathematica* to use fixed-precision arithmetic.

In[35]:= **$MinPrecision = $MaxPrecision = 20**

Out[35]= 20

The first few digits are correct, but the rest are wrong.

In[36]:= **Evaluate[1 + k] - 1**

Out[36]= $8.7565107001277653351 \times 10^{-27}$

■ 3.1.6 Machine-Precision Numbers

Whenever machine-precision numbers appear in a calculation, the whole calculation is typically done in machine precision. *Mathematica* will then give machine-precision numbers as the result.

Whenever the input contains any machine-precision numbers, *Mathematica* does the computation to machine precision.

In[1]:= **1.4444444444444444444 ^ 5.7**

Out[1]= 8.13382

Zeta[5.6] yields a machine-precision result, so the N is irrelevant.

In[2]:= **N[Zeta[5.6], 30]**

Out[2]= 1.02337547922703

This gives a higher-precision result.

In[3]:= **N[Zeta[56/10], 30]**

Out[3]= 1.0233754792270299108604417881026

When you do calculations with arbitrary-precision numbers, as discussed in the previous section, *Mathematica* always keeps track of the precision of your results, and gives only those digits which are known to be correct, given the precision of your input. When you do calculations with machine-precision numbers, however, *Mathematica* always gives you a machine-precision result, whether or not all the digits in the result can, in fact, be determined to be correct on the basis of your input.

This subtracts two machine-precision numbers.

In[4]:= **diff = 1.11111111 - 1.11111000**

Out[4]= 1.11×10^{-6}

The result is taken to have machine precision.

In[5]:= **Precision[diff]**

Out[5]= 16

Here are all the digits in the result.

In[6]:= **InputForm[diff]**

Out[6]//InputForm= 1.109999999915345*^-6

The fact that you can get spurious digits in machine-precision numerical calculations with *Mathematica* is in many respects quite unsatisfactory. The ultimate reason, however, that *Mathematica* uses fixed precision for these calculations is a matter of computational efficiency.

Mathematica is usually set up to insulate you as much as possible from the details of the computer system you are using. In dealing with machine-precision numbers, you would lose too much, however, if *Mathematica* did not make use of some specific features of your computer.

The important point is that almost all computers have special hardware or microcode for doing floating-point calculations to a particular fixed precision. *Mathematica* makes use of these features when doing machine-precision numerical calculations.

The typical arrangement is that all machine-precision numbers in *Mathematica* are represented as "double-precision floating-point numbers" in the underlying computer system. On most current computers, such numbers contain a total of 64 binary bits, typically yielding 16 decimal digits of mantissa.

The main advantage of using the built-in floating-point capabilities of your computer is speed. Arbitrary-precision numerical calculations, which do not make such direct use of these capabilities, are usually many times slower than machine-precision calculations.

There are several disadvantages of using built-in floating-point capabilities. One already mentioned is that it forces all numbers to have a fixed precision, independent of what precision can be justified for them.

A second disadvantage is that the treatment of machine-precision numbers can vary slightly from one computer system to another. In working with machine-precision numbers, *Mathematica* is at the mercy of the floating-point arithmetic system of each particular computer. If floating-point arithmetic is done differently on two computers, you may get slightly different results for machine-precision *Mathematica* calculations on those computers.

$MachinePrecision	the number of decimal digits of precision
$MachineEpsilon	the minimum positive machine-precision number which can be added to 1.0 to give a result distinguishable from 1.0
$MaxMachineNumber	the maximum machine-precision number
$MinMachineNumber	the minimum positive machine-precision number
+ $MaxNumber	the maximum magnitude of an arbitrary-precision number
+ $MinNumber	the minimum magnitude of a positive arbitrary-precision number

Properties of numbers on a particular computer system.

Since machine-precision numbers on any particular computer system are represented by a definite number of binary bits, numbers which are too close together will have the same bit pattern, and so cannot be distinguished. The parameter $MachineEpsilon gives the distance between 1.0 and the closest number which has a distinct binary representation.

This gives the value of $MachineEpsilon for the computer system on which these examples are run.

In[7]:= **$MachineEpsilon**

Out[7]= 2.22045×10^{-16}

Although this prints as 1., *Mathematica* knows that the result is larger than 1.	*In[8]:=* **1. + $MachineEpsilon** *Out[8]=* 1.
Subtracting 1 gives $MachineEpsilon.	*In[9]:=* **% - 1.** *Out[9]=* 2.22045×10^{-16}
This again prints as 1.	*In[10]:=* **1. + $MachineEpsilon/2** *Out[10]=* 1.
In this case, however, subtracting 1 yields 0, since 1 + $MachineEpsilon/2 is not distinguished from 1. to machine precision.	*In[11]:=* **% - 1.** *Out[11]=* 0.

Machine-precision numbers have not only limited precision, but also limited magnitude. If you generate a number which lies outside the range specified by $MinMachineNumber and $MaxMachineNumber, *Mathematica* will automatically convert the number to arbitrary-precision form.

This is the maximum machine-precision number which can be handled on the computer system used for this example.	*In[12]:=* **$MaxMachineNumber** *Out[12]=* 1.79769×10^{308}
Mathematica automatically converts the result of this computation to arbitrary precision.	*In[13]:=* **Exp[1000.]** *Out[13]=* $1.970071114017 \times 10^{434}$

■ 3.1.7 Advanced Topic: Interval Arithmetic

+ **Interval[{***min, max***}]**	the interval from *min* to *max*
+ **Interval[{***min₁, max₁***}, {***min₂, max₂***}, ...]**	the union of intervals from min_1 to max_1, min_2 to max_2, ...

Representations of real intervals.

This represents all numbers between −2 and +5.	*In[1]:=* **Interval[{-2, 5}]** *Out[1]=* Interval[{-2, 5}]
The square of any number between −2 and +5 is always between 0 and 25.	*In[2]:=* **Interval[{-2, 5}]^2** *Out[2]=* Interval[{0, 25}]
Taking the reciprocal gives two distinct intervals.	*In[3]:=* **1/Interval[{-2, 5}]** *Out[3]=* Interval$\left[\left\{-\infty, -\frac{1}{2}\right\}, \left\{\frac{1}{5}, \infty\right\}\right]$

Abs folds the intervals back together again.

$In[4]:=$ **Abs[%]**

$Out[4]=$ $\text{Interval}\left[\left\{\frac{1}{5}, \infty\right\}\right]$

You can use intervals in many kinds of functions.

$In[5]:=$ **Solve[3 x + 2 == Interval[{-2, 5}], x]**

$Out[5]=$ $\left\{\left\{x \to \text{Interval}\left[\left\{-\frac{4}{3}, 1\right\}\right]\right\}\right\}$

Some functions automatically generate intervals.

$In[6]:=$ **Limit[Sin[1/x], x -> 0]**

$Out[6]=$ $\text{Interval}[\{-1, 1\}]$

+	IntervalUnion[*interval$_1$*, *interval$_2$*, ...]	
		find the union of several intervals
+	IntervalIntersection[*interval$_1$*, *interval$_2$*, ...]	
		find the intersection of several intervals
+	IntervalMemberQ[*interval*, *x*]	test whether the point *x* lies within an interval
+	IntervalMemberQ[*interval$_1$*, *interval$_2$*]	
		test whether *interval$_2$* lies completely within *interval$_1$*

Operations on intervals.

This finds the overlap of the two intervals.

$In[7]:=$ **IntervalIntersection[Interval[{3, 7}], Interval[{-2, 5}]]**

$Out[7]=$ $\text{Interval}[\{3, 5\}]$

You can use Max and Min to find the end points of intervals.

$In[8]:=$ **Max[%]**

$Out[8]=$ 5

This finds out which of a list of intervals contains the point 7.

$In[9]:=$ **IntervalMemberQ[**
            Table[Interval[{i, i+1}], {i, 1, 20, 3}], 7]

$Out[9]=$ {False, False, True, False, False, False, False}

You can use intervals not only with exact quantities but also with approximate numbers. Even with machine-precision numbers, *Mathematica* always tries to do rounding in such a way as to preserve the validity of results.

This shows explicitly the interval treated by *Mathematica* as the machine-precision number 0.

$In[10]:=$ **Interval[0.]**

$Out[10]=$ $\text{Interval}[\{-2.22507 \times 10^{-308}, 2.22507 \times 10^{-308}\}]$

This shows the corresponding interval around 100., shifted back to zero.

$In[11]:=$ **Interval[100.] - 100**

$Out[11]=$ $\text{Interval}[\{-1.42108 \times 10^{-14}, 1.42108 \times 10^{-14}\}]$

The same kind of thing works with numbers of any precision.

$In[12]:=$ **Interval[N[Pi, 50]] - Pi**

$Out[12]=$ $\text{Interval}[\{-8. \times 10^{-50}, 8. \times 10^{-50}\}]$

With ordinary machine-precision arithmetic, this computation gives an incorrect result.

```
In[13]:= Sin[N[Pi]]
Out[13]= 1.22461×10⁻¹⁶
```

The interval generated here, however, includes the correct value of 0.

```
In[14]:= Sin[Interval[N[Pi]]]
Out[14]= Interval[{-3.21629×10⁻¹⁶, 5.6655×10⁻¹⁶}]
```

■ 3.1.8 Advanced Topic: Indeterminate and Infinite Results

If you type in an expression like 0/0, *Mathematica* prints a message, and returns the result Indeterminate.

```
In[1]:= 0/0
                                    1
Power::infy: Infinite expression - encountered.
                                    0

Infinity::indet:
     Indeterminate expression 0 ComplexInfinity encountered.

Out[1]= Indeterminate
```

An expression like 0/0 is an example of an *indeterminate numerical result*. If you type in 0/0, there is no way for *Mathematica* to know what answer you want. If you got 0/0 by taking the limit of x/x as $x \to 0$, then you might want the answer 1. On the other hand, if you got 0/0 instead as the limit of $2x/x$, then you probably want the answer 2. The expression 0/0 on its own does not contain enough information to choose between these and other cases. As a result, its value must be considered indeterminate.

Whenever an indeterminate result is produced in an arithmetic computation, *Mathematica* prints a warning message, and then returns Indeterminate as the result of the computation. If you ever try to use Indeterminate in an arithmetic computation, you always get the result Indeterminate. A single indeterminate expression effectively "poisons" any arithmetic computation. (The symbol Indeterminate plays a role in *Mathematica* similar to the "not a number" object in the IEEE Floating Point Standard.)

The usual laws of arithmetic simplification are suspended in the case of Indeterminate.

```
In[2]:= Indeterminate - Indeterminate
Out[2]= Indeterminate
```

Indeterminate "poisons" any arithmetic computation, and leads to an indeterminate result.

```
In[3]:= 2 Indeterminate - 7
Out[3]= Indeterminate
```

When you do arithmetic computations inside *Mathematica* programs, it is often important to be able to tell whether indeterminate results were generated in the computations. You can do this by using the function Check discussed on page 461 to test whether any warning messages associated with indeterminate results were produced.

You can use Check inside a program to test whether warning messages are generated in a computation.

```
In[4]:= Check[(7 - 7)/(8 - 8), meaningless]
```
$$\frac{1}{0}$$
```
Power::infy: Infinite expression - encountered.
```
$$\frac{1}{0}$$
```
Infinity::indet:
    Indeterminate expression 0 ComplexInfinity encountered.
```
```
Out[4]= meaningless
```

Indeterminate	an indeterminate numerical result
Infinity	a positive infinite quantity
-Infinity	a negative infinite quantity (DirectedInfinity[-1])
DirectedInfinity[r]	an infinite quantity with complex direction r
ComplexInfinity	an infinite quantity with an undetermined direction
DirectedInfinity[ ]	equivalent to ComplexInfinity

Indeterminate and infinite quantities.

There are many situations where it is convenient to be able to do calculations with infinite quantities. The symbol Infinity in *Mathematica* represents a positive infinite quantity. You can use it to specify such things as limits of sums and integrals. You can also do some arithmetic calculations with it.

Here is an integral with an infinite limit.

```
In[5]:= Integrate[1/x^3, {x, 1, Infinity}]
```
$$Out[5]= \frac{1}{2}$$

Mathematica knows that $1/\infty = 0$.

```
In[6]:= 1/Infinity
```
```
Out[6]= 0
```

If you try to find the difference between two infinite quantities, you get an indeterminate result.

```
In[7]:= Infinity - Infinity
```
```
Infinity::indet:
    Indeterminate expression (-Infinity) + (Infinity)
      encountered.
```
```
Out[7]= Indeterminate
```

There are a number of subtle points that arise in handling infinite quantities. One of them concerns the "direction" of an infinite quantity. When you do an infinite integral, you typically think of performing the integration along a path in the complex plane that goes to infinity in some direction. In this case, it is important to distinguish different versions of infinity that correspond to different directions in the complex plane. $+\infty$ and $-\infty$ are two examples, but for some purposes one also needs $i\infty$ and so on.

In *Mathematica*, infinite quantities can have a "direction", specified by a complex number. When you type in the symbol `Infinity`, representing a positive infinite quantity, this is converted internally to the form `DirectedInfinity[1]`, which represents an infinite quantity in the +1 direction. Similarly, `-Infinity` becomes `DirectedInfinity[-1]`, and `I Infinity` becomes `DirectedInfinity[I]`. Although the `DirectedInfinity` form is always used internally, the standard output format for `DirectedInfinity[r]` is *r* `Infinity`.

Infinity is converted internally to `DirectedInfinity[1]`.	*In[8]:=* **Infinity // FullForm**
	Out[8]//FullForm= DirectedInfinity[1]

Although the notion of a "directed infinity" is often useful, it is not always available. If you type in 1/0, you get an infinite result, but there is no way to determine the "direction" of the infinity. *Mathematica* represents the result of 1/0 as `DirectedInfinity[ ]`. In standard output form, this undirected infinity is printed out as `ComplexInfinity`.

1/0 gives an undirected form of infinity.

In[9]:= **1/0**

Power::infy: Infinite expression $\dfrac{1}{0}$ encountered.

Out[9]= ComplexInfinity

■ 3.1.9 Advanced Topic: Controlling Numerical Evaluation

+	`NHoldAll`	prevent any arguments of a function from being affected by `N`
+	`NHoldFirst`	prevent the first argument from being affected
+	`NHoldRest`	prevent all but the first argument from being affected

Attributes for controlling numerical evaluation.

Usually `N` goes inside functions and gets applied to each of their arguments.	*In[1]:=* **N[f[2/3, Pi]]**
	Out[1]= f[0.666667, 3.14159]
This tells *Mathematica* not to apply `N` to the first argument of `f`.	*In[2]:=* **SetAttributes[f, NHoldFirst]**
Now the first argument of `f` is left in its exact form.	*In[3]:=* **N[f[2/3, Pi]]**
	Out[3]= $f\left[\dfrac{2}{3}, 3.14159\right]$

3.2 Mathematical Functions

■ 3.2.1 Naming Conventions

Mathematical functions in *Mathematica* are given names according to definite rules. As with most *Mathematica* functions, the names are usually complete English words, fully spelled out. For a few very common functions, *Mathematica* uses the traditional abbreviations. Thus the modulo function, for example, is Mod, not Modulo.

Mathematical functions that are usually referred to by a person's name have names in *Mathematica* of the form *PersonSymbol*. Thus, for example, the Legendre polynomials $P_n(x)$ are denoted LegendreP[n, x]. Although this convention does lead to longer function names, it avoids any ambiguity or confusion.

When the standard notation for a mathematical function involves both subscripts and superscripts, the subscripts are given *before* the superscripts in the *Mathematica* form. Thus, for example, the associated Legendre polynomials $P_n^m(x)$ are denoted LegendreP[n, m, x].

■ 3.2.2 Numerical Functions

IntegerPart[x]	integer part of x
FractionalPart[x]	fractional part of x
Round[x]	integer $\langle x \rangle$ closest to x
Floor[x]	greatest integer $\lfloor x \rfloor$ not larger than x
Ceiling[x]	least integer $\lceil x \rceil$ not smaller than x
Sign[x]	1 for $x > 0$, -1 for $x < 0$
Abs[x]	absolute value $|x|$ of x
Max[x_1, x_2, ...] or Max[{x_1, x_2, ... }, ...]	the maximum of x_1, x_2, ...
Min[x_1, x_2, ...] or Min[{x_1, x_2, ... }, ...]	the minimum of x_1, x_2, ...

Some numerical functions of real variables.

x	IntegerPart[x]	FractionalPart[x]	Round[x]	Floor[x]	Ceiling[x]
2.4	2	0.4	2	2	3
2.5	2	0.5	2	2	3
2.6	2	0.6	3	2	3
-2.4	-2	-0.4	-2	-3	-2
-2.5	-2	-0.5	-2	-3	-2
-2.6	-2	-0.6	-3	-3	-2

Extracting integer and fractional parts.

IntegerPart[x] and FractionalPart[x] can be thought of as extracting digits to the left and right of the decimal point. Round[x] is often used for forcing numbers that are close to integers to be exactly integers. Floor[x] and Ceiling[x] often arise in working out how many elements there will be in sequences of numbers with non-integer spacings.

x + I y	the complex number $x + iy$
Re[z]	the real part $\mathrm{Re}\, z$
Im[z]	the imaginary part $\mathrm{Im}\, z$
Conjugate[z]	the complex conjugate z^* or $\bar{z}$
Abs[z]	the absolute value $|z|$
Arg[z]	the argument ϕ such that $z = |z|e^{i\phi}$

Numerical functions of complex variables.

■ 3.2.3 Pseudorandom Numbers

Random[ ]	a pseudorandom real between 0 and 1
Random[Real, *xmax*]	a pseudorandom real between 0 and *xmax*
Random[Real, {*xmin*, *xmax*}]	a pseudorandom real between *xmin* and *xmax*
Random[Complex]	a pseudorandom complex number in the unit square
Random[Complex, {*zmin*, *zmax*}]	a pseudorandom complex number in the rectangle defined by *zmin* and *zmax*
Random[*type*, *range*, *n*]	an *n*-digit pseudorandom number
Random[Integer]	0 or 1 with probability $\frac{1}{2}$
Random[Integer, {*imin*, *imax*}]	a pseudorandom integer between *imin* and *imax*, inclusive
SeedRandom[ ]	reseed the pseudorandom generator, with the time of day
SeedRandom[*s*]	reseed with the integer *s*
$RandomState	the current state of the pseudorandom generator

Pseudorandom number generation.

This gives a list of 3 pseudorandom numbers.

```
In[1]:= Table[Random[ ], {3}]
Out[1]= {0.0560708, 0.6303, 0.359894}
```

Here is a 30-digit pseudorandom real number in the range 0 to 1.

```
In[2]:= Random[Real, {0, 1}, 30]
Out[2]= 0.748823044099679773836330229377
```

This gives a list of 8 pseudorandom integers between 100 and 200 (inclusive).

```
In[3]:= Table[Random[Integer, {100, 200}], {8}]
Out[3]= {120, 108, 109, 147, 146, 189, 188, 187}
```

If you call Random[ ] repeatedly, you should get a "typical" sequence of numbers, with no particular pattern. There are many ways to use such numbers.

One common way to use pseudorandom numbers is in making numerical tests of hypotheses. For example, if you believe that two symbolic expressions are mathematically equal, you can test this by plugging in "typical" numerical values for symbolic parameters, and then comparing the numerical results. (If you do this, you should be careful about numerical accuracy problems and about functions of complex variables that may not have unique values.)

| Here is a symbolic equation. | *In[4]:=* **Sin[Cos[x]] == Cos[Sin[x]]** |
| | *Out[4]=* Sin[Cos[x]] == Cos[Sin[x]] |

| Substituting in a random numerical value shows that the equation is not always True. | *In[5]:=* **% /. x -> Random[ ]** |
| | *Out[5]=* False |

Other common uses of pseudorandom numbers include simulating probabilistic processes, and sampling large spaces of possibilities. The pseudorandom numbers that *Mathematica* generates are always uniformly distributed over the range you specify.

Random is unlike almost any other *Mathematica* function in that every time you call it, you potentially get a different result. If you use Random in a calculation, therefore, you may get different answers on different occasions.

The sequences that you get from Random[ ] are not in most senses "truly random", although they should be "random enough" for practical purposes. The sequences are in fact produced by applying a definite mathematical algorithm, starting from a particular "seed". If you give the same seed, then you get the same sequence.

When *Mathematica* starts up, it takes the time of day (measured in small fractions of a second) as the seed for the pseudorandom number generator. Two different *Mathematica* sessions will therefore almost always give different sequences of pseudorandom numbers.

If you want to make sure that you always get the same sequence of pseudorandom numbers, you can explicitly give a seed for the pseudorandom generator, using SeedRandom.

| This reseeds the pseudorandom generator. | *In[6]:=* **SeedRandom[143]** |

| Here are three pseudorandom numbers. | *In[7]:=* **Table[Random[ ], {3}]** |
| | *Out[7]=* {0.952311, 0.93591, 0.813754} |

| If you reseed the pseudorandom generator with the same seed, you get the same sequence of pseudorandom numbers. | *In[8]:=* **SeedRandom[143]; Table[Random[ ], {3}]** |
| | *Out[8]=* {0.952311, 0.93591, 0.813754} |

Every single time Random is called, the internal state of the pseudorandom generator that it uses is changed. This means that calls to Random made in subsidiary calculations will have an effect on the numbers returned by Random in your main calculation. To avoid any problems associated with this, you can save the value of $RandomState before you do subsidiary calculations, and then restore it afterwards.

| By localizing the value of $RandomState using Block, the internal state of the pseudorandom generator is restored after generating the first list. | *In[9]:=* **{Block[{$RandomState}, {Random[ ], Random[ ]}],** **{Random[ ], Random[ ]}}** |
| | *Out[9]=* {{0.1169, 0.783447}, {0.1169, 0.783447}} |

■ 3.2.4 Integer and Number-Theoretical Functions

Mod[k, n]	k modulo n (remainder from dividing k by n)
Quotient[m, n]	the quotient of m and n (integer part of m/n)
GCD[n_1, n_2, ...]	the greatest common divisor of n_1, n_2, ...
LCM[n_1, n_2, ...]	the least common multiple of n_1, n_2, ...
IntegerDigits[n, b]	the digits of n in base b

Some integer functions.

The remainder on dividing 17 by 3.	*In[1]:=* **Mod[17, 3]**
	Out[1]= 2
The integer part of 17/3.	*In[2]:=* **Quotient[17, 3]**
	Out[2]= 5
Mod also works with real numbers.	*In[3]:=* **Mod[5.6, 1.2]**
	Out[3]= 0.8
The result from Mod always has the same sign as the second argument.	*In[4]:=* **Mod[-5.6, 1.2]**
	Out[4]= 0.4

For any integers a and b, it is always true that b*Quotient[a, b] + Mod[a, b] is equal to a.

The **greatest common divisor** function GCD[n_1, n_2, ...] gives the largest integer that divides all the n_i exactly. When you enter a ratio of two integers, *Mathematica* effectively uses GCD to cancel out common factors, and give a rational number in lowest terms.

The **least common multiple** function LCM[n_1, n_2, ...] gives the smallest integer that contains all the factors of each of the n_i.

The largest integer that divides both 24 and 15 is 3.	*In[5]:=* **GCD[24, 15]**
	Out[5]= 3

FactorInteger[n]	a list of the prime factors of n, and their exponents
Divisors[n]	a list of the integers that divide n
Prime[k]	the kth prime number
PrimePi[x]	the number of primes less than or equal to x
PrimeQ[n]	give True if n is a prime, and False otherwise
FactorInteger[n, GaussianIntegers->True]	a list of the Gaussian prime factors of the Gaussian integer n, and their exponents
PrimeQ[n, GaussianIntegers->True]	give True if n is a Gaussian prime, and False otherwise

Integer factoring and related functions.

This gives the factors of 24 as 2^3, 3^1.
The first element in each list is the factor; the second is its exponent.

```
In[6]:= FactorInteger[24]
Out[6]= {{2, 3}, {3, 1}}
```

Here are the factors of a larger integer.

```
In[7]:= FactorInteger[111111111111111111]
Out[7]= {{3, 2}, {7, 1}, {11, 1}, {13, 1}, {19, 1},
         {37, 1}, {52579, 1}, {333667, 1}}
```

You should realize that according to current mathematical thinking, integer factoring is a fundamentally difficult computational problem. As a result, you can easily type in an integer that *Mathematica* will not be able to factor in anything short of an astronomical length of time. As long as the integers you give are less than about 20 digits long, FactorInteger should have no trouble. Only in special cases, however, will it be able to deal with much longer integers. (You can make some factoring problems go faster by setting the option FactorComplete->False, so that FactorInteger[n] tries to pull out only easy factors from n.)

Here is a rather special long integer.

```
In[8]:= 30!
Out[8]= 265252859812191058636308480000000
```

Mathematica can easily factor this special integer.

```
In[9]:= FactorInteger[%]
Out[9]= {{2, 26}, {3, 14}, {5, 7}, {7, 4}, {11, 2}, {13, 2},
         {17, 1}, {19, 1}, {23, 1}, {29, 1}}
```

Although *Mathematica* may not be able to factor a large integer, it can often still test whether or not the integer is a prime. In addition, *Mathematica* has a fast way of finding the kth prime number.

It is often much faster to test whether a number is prime than to factor it.

```
In[10]:= PrimeQ[234242423]
Out[10]= False
```

Here is a plot of the first 100 primes.   *In[11]:=* **ListPlot[Table[Prime[n], {n, 100}]]**

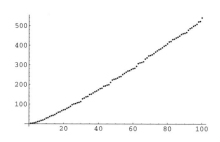

This is the millionth prime.   *In[12]:=* **Prime[1000000]**

Out[12]= 15485863

Particularly in number theory, it is often more important to know the distribution of primes than their actual values. The function `PrimePi[x]` gives the number of primes $\pi(x)$ that are less than or equal to x.

This gives the number of primes less   *In[13]:=* **PrimePi[10^9]**
than a billion.
                                                 Out[13]= 50847534

By default, `FactorInteger` allows only real integers. But with the option setting `GaussianIntegers -> True`, it also handles **Gaussian integers**, which are complex numbers with integer real and imaginary parts. Just as it is possible to factor uniquely in terms of real primes, it is also possible to factor uniquely in terms of Gaussian primes. There is nevertheless some potential ambiguity in the choice of Gaussian primes. In *Mathematica*, they are always chosen to have positive real parts, and non-negative imaginary parts, except for a possible initial factor of -1 or $\pm i$.

Over the Gaussian integers, 2 can be   *In[14]:=* **FactorInteger[2, GaussianIntegers -> True]**
factored as $(-i)(1 + i)^2$.
                                                 Out[14]= {{-I, 1}, {1 + I, 2}}

Here are the factors of a Gaussian   *In[15]:=* **FactorInteger[111 + 78 I, GaussianIntegers -> True]**
integer.
                                                 Out[15]= {{2 + I, 1}, {3, 1}, {20 + 3 I, 1}}

PowerMod[*a*, *b*, *n*]	the power a^b modulo *n*
EulerPhi[*n*]	the Euler totient function $\phi(n)$
MoebiusMu[*n*]	the Möbius function $\mu(n)$
DivisorSigma[*k*, *n*]	the divisor function $\sigma_k(n)$
JacobiSymbol[*n*, *m*]	the Jacobi symbol $\left(\frac{n}{m}\right)$
ExtendedGCD[*m*, *n*]	the extended gcd of *m* and *n*
LatticeReduce[{v_1, v_2, ... }]	the reduced lattice basis for the set of integer vectors v_i

Some functions from number theory.

The **modular power function** PowerMod[*a*, *b*, *n*] gives exactly the same results as Mod[*a*^*b*, *n*] for $b > 0$. PowerMod is much more efficient, however, because it avoids generating the full form of *a*^*b*.

You can use PowerMod not only to find positive modular powers, but also to find **modular inverses**. For negative *b*, PowerMod[*a*, *b*, *n*] gives, if possible, an integer *k* such that $ka^{-b} \equiv 1 \bmod n$. (Whenever such an integer exists, it is guaranteed to be unique modulo *n*.) If no such integer *k* exists, *Mathematica* leaves PowerMod unevaluated.

PowerMod is equivalent to using Power, then Mod, but is much more efficient.

```
In[16]:= PowerMod[2, 13451, 3]
Out[16]= 2
```

This gives the modular inverse of 3 modulo 7.

```
In[17]:= PowerMod[3, -1, 7]
Out[17]= 5
```

Multiplying the inverse by 3 modulo 7 gives 1, as expected.

```
In[18]:= Mod[3 %, 7]
Out[18]= 1
```

The **Euler totient function** $\phi(n)$ gives the number of integers less than *n* that are relatively prime to *n*. An important relation (Fermat's Little Theorem) is that $a^{\phi(n)} \equiv 1 \bmod n$ for all *a* relatively prime to *n*.

The **Möbius function** $\mu(n)$ is defined to be $(-1)^k$ if *n* is a product of *k* distinct primes, and 0 if *n* contains a squared factor (other than 1). An important relation is the Möbius inversion formula, which states that if $g(n) = \sum_{d|n} f(d)$ for all *n*, then $f(n) = \sum_{d|n} \mu(d)g(n/d)$, where the sums are over all positive integers *d* that divide *n*.

The **divisor function** $\sigma_k(n)$ is the sum of the kth powers of the divisors of *n*. The function $\sigma_0(n)$ gives the total number of divisors of *n*, and is often denoted $d(n)$. The function $\sigma_1(n)$, equal to the sum of the divisors of *n*, is often denoted $\sigma(n)$.

For prime *n*, $\phi(n) = n - 1$.

```
In[19]:= EulerPhi[17]
Out[19]= 16
```

The result is 1, as guaranteed by
Fermat's Little Theorem.

`In[20]:= PowerMod[3, %, 17]`

`Out[20]= 1`

This gives a list of all the divisors of
24.

`In[21]:= Divisors[24]`

`Out[21]= {1, 2, 3, 4, 6, 8, 12, 24}`

$\sigma_0(n)$ gives the total number of distinct
divisors of 24.

`In[22]:= DivisorSigma[0, 24]`

`Out[22]= 8`

The **Jacobi symbol** `JacobiSymbol[n, m]` reduces to the **Legendre symbol** $\left(\frac{n}{m}\right)$ when m is an odd prime. The Legendre symbol is equal to zero if n is divisible by m, otherwise it is equal to 1 if n is a quadratic residue modulo the prime m, and to -1 if it is not. An integer n relatively prime to m is said to be a quadratic residue modulo m if there exists an integer k such that $k^2 \equiv n \bmod m$. The full Jacobi symbol is a product of the Legendre symbols $\left(\frac{n}{p_i}\right)$ for each of the prime factors p_i such that $m = \prod_i p_i$.

The **extended gcd** `ExtendedGCD[m, n]` gives a list $\{g, \{r, s\}\}$ where g is the greatest common divisor of m and n, and r and s are integers such that $g = rm + sn$. The extended gcd is important in finding integer solutions to linear (Diophantine) equations.

The first number in the list is the gcd
of 105 and 196.

`In[23]:= ExtendedGCD[105, 196]`

`Out[23]= {7, {15, -8}}`

The second pair of numbers satisfies
$g = rm + sn$.

`In[24]:= 15 105 - 8 196`

`Out[24]= 7`

The lattice reduction function `LatticeReduce[{v_1, v_2, ... }]` is used in several kinds of modern algorithms. The basic idea is to think of the vectors v_k of integers as defining a mathematical *lattice*. The vector representing each point in the lattice can be written as a linear combination of the form $\sum c_k v_k$, where the c_k are integers. For a particular lattice, there are many possible choices of the "basis vectors" v_k. What `LatticeReduce` does is to find a reduced set of basis vectors $\bar{v}_k$ for the lattice, with certain special properties.

Three unit vectors along the three
coordinate axes already form a reduced
basis.

`In[25]:= LatticeReduce[{{1,0,0},{0,1,0},{0,0,1}}]`

`Out[25]= {{1, 0, 0}, {0, 1, 0}, {0, 0, 1}}`

This gives the reduced basis for a
lattice in four-dimensional space
specified by three vectors.

`In[26]:= LatticeReduce[{{1,0,0,12345}, {0,1,0,12435},`
`                {0,0,1,12354}}]`

`Out[26]= {{-1, 0, 1, 9}, {9, 1, -10, 0}, {85, -143, 59, 6}}`

Notice that in the last example, `LatticeReduce` replaces vectors that are nearly parallel by vectors that are more perpendicular. In the process, it finds some quite short basis vectors.

■ 3.2.5 Combinatorial Functions

$n!$	factorial $n(n-1)(n-2) \times \ldots \times 1$
$n!!$	double factorial $n(n-2)(n-4) \times \ldots$
Binomial[n, m]	binomial coefficient $\binom{n}{m} = n!/[m!(n-m)!]$
Multinomial[n_1, n_2, ...]	multinomial coefficient $(n_1 + n_2 + \ldots)!/(n_1!n_2!\ldots)$
Fibonacci[n]	Fibonacci number F_n
Fibonacci[n, x]	Fibonacci polynomial $F_n(x)$
BernoulliB[n]	Bernoulli number B_n
BernoulliB[n, x]	Bernoulli polynomial $B_n(x)$
EulerE[n]	Euler number E_n
EulerE[n, x]	Euler polynomial $E_n(x)$
StirlingS1[n, m]	Stirling number of the first kind $S_n^{(m)}$
StirlingS2[n, m]	Stirling number of the second kind $s_n^{(m)}$
PartitionsP[n]	the number $p(n)$ of unrestricted partitions of the integer n
PartitionsQ[n]	the number $q(n)$ of partitions of n into distinct parts
Signature[$\{i_1, i_2, \ldots \}$]	the signature of a permutation

Combinatorial functions.

The **factorial function** $n!$ gives the number of ways of ordering n objects. For non-integer n, the numerical value of $n!$ is obtained from the gamma function, discussed in Section 3.2.10.

The **binomial coefficient** Binomial[n, m] can be written as $\binom{n}{m} = n!/[m!(n-m)!]$. It gives the number of ways of choosing m objects from a collection of n objects, without regard to order. The **Catalan numbers**, which appear in various tree enumeration problems, are given in terms of binomial coefficients as $c_n = \binom{2n}{n}/(n+1)$.

The **multinomial coefficient** Multinomial[n_1, n_2, ...], denoted $(N; n_1, n_2, \ldots, n_m) = N!/(n_1!n_2!\ldots n_m!)$, gives the number of ways of partitioning N distinct objects into m sets of sizes n_i (with $N = \sum_{i=1}^{m} n_i$).

Mathematica gives the exact integer result for the factorial of an integer.	$In[1]:=$ **30!**
	$Out[1]=$ 265252859812191058636308480000000

For non-integers, *Mathematica* evaluates factorials using the gamma function.	$In[2]:=$ **3.6!**
	$Out[2]=$ 13.3813

Mathematica can give symbolic results for some binomial coefficients.	$In[3]:=$ **Binomial[n, 2]**
	$Out[3]= \dfrac{(-1+n)\,n}{2}$

This gives the number of ways of partitioning $6 + 5 = 11$ objects into sets containing 6 and 5 objects.	$In[4]:=$ **Multinomial[6, 5]**
	$Out[4]=$ 462

The result is the same as $\binom{11}{6}$.	$In[5]:=$ **Binomial[11, 6]**
	$Out[5]=$ 462

The **Fibonacci numbers** Fibonacci[n] satisfy the recurrence relation $F_n = F_{n-1} + F_{n-2}$ with $F_1 = F_2 = 1$. They appear in a wide range of discrete mathematical problems. For large n, F_n/F_{n-1} approaches the golden ratio.

The **Fibonacci polynomials** Fibonacci[n, x] appear as the coefficients of t^n in the expansion of $t/(1 - xt - t^2) = \sum_{n=0}^{\infty} F_n(x)t^n/n!$.

The **Bernoulli polynomials** BernoulliB[n, x] satisfy the generating function relation $te^{xt}/(e^t - 1) = \sum_{n=0}^{\infty} B_n(x)t^n/n!$. The **Bernoulli numbers** BernoulliB[n] are given by $B_n = B_n(0)$. The B_n appear as the coefficients of the terms in the Euler-Maclaurin summation formula for approximating integrals.

Numerical values for Bernoulli numbers are needed in many numerical algorithms. You can always get these numerical values by first finding exact rational results using BernoulliB[n], and then applying N.

The **Euler polynomials** EulerE[n, x] have generating function $2e^{xt}/(e^t + 1) = \sum_{n=0}^{\infty} E_n(x)t^n/n!$, and the **Euler numbers** EulerE[n] are given by $E_n = 2^n E_n(\frac{1}{2})$. The Euler numbers are related to the **Genocchi numbers** by $G_n = 2^{2-2n}nE_{2n-1}$.

This gives the second Bernoulli polynomial $B_2(x)$.	$In[6]:=$ **BernoulliB[2, x]**
	$Out[6]= \dfrac{1}{6} - x + x^2$

You can also get Bernoulli polynomials by explicitly computing the power series for the generating function.	$In[7]:=$ **Series[t Exp[x t]/(Exp[t] - 1), {t, 0, 4}]**

$$Out[7]= 1 + \left(-\frac{1}{2} + x\right)t + \left(\frac{1}{12} - \frac{x}{2} + \frac{x^2}{2}\right)t^2 + \left(\frac{x}{12} - \frac{x^2}{4} + \frac{x^3}{6}\right)t^3 + \left(-\frac{1}{720} + \frac{x^2}{24} - \frac{x^3}{12} + \frac{x^4}{24}\right)t^4 + O[t]^5$$

BernoulliB[n] gives exact rational-number results for Bernoulli numbers.

$In[8]:=$ **BernoulliB[20]**

$Out[8]= -\dfrac{174611}{330}$

Stirling numbers show up in many combinatorial enumeration problems. For **Stirling numbers of the first kind** StirlingS1[n, m], $(-1)^{n-m}S_n^{(m)}$ gives the number of permutations of n elements which contain exactly m cycles. These Stirling numbers satisfy the generating function relation $x(x-1)\ldots(x-n+1) = \sum_{m=0}^{n} S_n^{(m)}x^m$. Note that some definitions of the $S_n^{(m)}$ differ by a factor $(-1)^{n-m}$ from what is used in *Mathematica*.

Stirling numbers of the second kind StirlingS2[n, m] give the number of ways of partitioning a set of n elements into m non-empty subsets. They satisfy the relation $x^n = \sum_{m=0}^{n} S_n^{(m)}x(x-1)\ldots(x-m+1)$.

The **partition function** PartitionsP[n] gives the number of ways of writing the integer n as a sum of positive integers, without regard to order. PartitionsQ[n] gives the number of ways of writing n as a sum of positive integers, with the constraint that all the integers in each sum are distinct.

This gives a table of Stirling numbers of the first kind.

$In[9]:=$ **Table[StirlingS1[5, i], {i, 5}]**

$Out[9]= \{24, -50, 35, -10, 1\}$

The Stirling numbers appear as coefficients in this product.

$In[10]:=$ **Expand[Product[x - i, {i, 0, 4}]]**

$Out[10]= 24\,x - 50\,x^2 + 35\,x^3 - 10\,x^4 + x^5$

This gives the number of partitions of 100, with and without the constraint that the terms should be distinct.

$In[11]:=$ **{PartitionsQ[100], PartitionsP[100]}**

$Out[11]= \{444793, 190569292\}$

The partition function $p(n)$ increases asymptotically like $e^{\sqrt{n}}$. Note that you cannot simply use Plot to generate a plot of a function like PartitionsP because the function can only be evaluated with integer arguments.

$In[12]:=$ **ListPlot[Table[**
N[Log[PartitionsP[n]]], {n, 100}]]

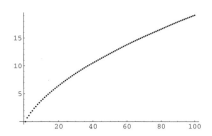

The functions in this section allow you to *enumerate* various kinds of combinatorial objects. Functions like Permutations, discussed in Section 1.8.13, allow you instead to *generate* lists of various combinations of elements.

The **signature function** Signature[{i_1, i_2, ... }] gives the signature of a permutation. It is equal to +1 for even permutations (composed of an even number of transpositions), and to -1 for odd permutations. The signature function can be thought of as a totally antisymmetric tensor, **Levi-Civita symbol** or **epsilon symbol**.

ClebschGordan[{j_1, m_1}, {j_2, m_2}, {j, m}]
                     Clebsch-Gordan coefficient

ThreeJSymbol[{j_1, m_1}, {j_2, m_2}, {j_3, m_3}]
                     Wigner 3-j symbol

SixJSymbol[{j_1, j_2, j_3}, {j_4, j_5, j_6}]
                     Racah 6-j symbol

Rotational coupling coefficients.

Clebsch-Gordan coefficients and *n*-j symbols arise in the study of angular momenta in quantum mechanics, and in other applications of the rotation group. The **Clebsch-Gordan coefficients** ClebschGordan[{j_1, m_1}, {j_2, m_2}, {j, m}] give the coefficients in the expansion of the quantum mechanical angular momentum state $|j, m\rangle$ in terms of products of states $|j_1, m_1\rangle |j_2, m_2\rangle$.

The **3-j symbols** or **Wigner coefficients** ThreeJSymbol[{j_1, m_1}, {j_2, m_2}, {j_3, m_3}] are a more symmetrical form of Clebsch-Gordan coefficients. In *Mathematica*, the Clebsch-Gordan coefficients are given in terms of 3-j symbols by $C^{j_1 j_2 j_3}_{m_1 m_2 m_3} = (-1)^{m_3 + j_1 - j_2} \sqrt{2j_3 + 1} \begin{pmatrix} j_1 & j_2 & j_3 \\ m_1 & m_2 & -m_3 \end{pmatrix}$.

The **6-j symbols** SixJSymbol[{j_1, j_2, j_3}, {j_4, j_5, j_6}] give the couplings of three quantum mechanical angular momentum states. The **Racah coefficients** are related by a phase to the 6-j symbols.

You can give symbolic parameters in
3-j symbols.

In[13]:= **ThreeJSymbol[{j, m}, {j+1/2, -m-1/2}, {1/2, 1/2}]**

Out[13]= $-\dfrac{(-1)^{-j+m} \sqrt{1 + j + m}}{\sqrt{1 + 2j}\ \sqrt{2 + 2j}}$

■ 3.2.6 Elementary Transcendental Functions

Exp[z]	exponential function e^z
Log[z]	logarithm $\log_e(z)$
Log[b, z]	logarithm $\log_b(z)$ to base b
Sin[z], Cos[z], Tan[z], Csc[z], Sec[z], Cot[z]	trigonometric functions (with arguments in radians)
ArcSin[z], ArcCos[z], ArcTan[z], ArcCsc[z], ArcSec[z], ArcCot[z]	inverse trigonometric functions (giving results in radians)
ArcTan[x, y]	the argument of $x + iy$
Sinh[z], Cosh[z], Tanh[z], Csch[z], Sech[z], Coth[z]	hyperbolic functions
ArcSinh[z], ArcCosh[z], ArcTanh[z], ArcCsch[z], ArcSech[z], ArcCoth[z]	inverse hyperbolic functions

Elementary transcendental functions.

Mathematica gives exact results for logarithms whenever it can. Here is $\log_2 1024$.	*In[1]:=* **Log[2, 1024]** *Out[1]=* 10
You can find the numerical values of mathematical functions to any precision.	*In[2]:=* **N[Log[2], 40]** *Out[2]=* 0.6931471805599453094172321214581765680755
This gives a complex number result.	*In[3]:=* **N[Log[-2]]** *Out[3]=* 0.693147 + 3.14159 I
Mathematica can evaluate logarithms with complex arguments.	*In[4]:=* **N[Log[2 + 8 I]]** *Out[4]=* 2.10975 + 1.32582 I
The arguments of trigonometric functions are always given in radians.	*In[5]:=* **Sin[Pi/2]** *Out[5]=* 1
You can convert from degrees by explicitly multiplying by the constant Degree.	*In[6]:=* **N[Sin[30 Degree]]** *Out[6]=* 0.5

Here is a plot of the hyperbolic tangent function. It has a characteristic "sigmoidal" form.

$In[7]:=$ **Plot[Tanh[x], {x, -8, 8}]**

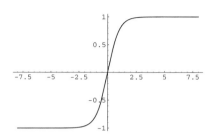

There are a number of additional trigonometric and hyperbolic functions that are sometimes used. The **versine** function is defined as $\text{vers}(z) = 1 - \cos(z)$. The **haversine** is simply $\text{hav}(z) = \frac{1}{2}\text{vers}(z)$. The complex exponential e^{ix} is sometimes written as $\text{cis}(x)$. The **gudermannian function** is defined as $\text{gd}(z) = 2\tan^{-1}(e^z) - \frac{\pi}{2}$. The **inverse gudermannian** is $\text{gd}^{-1}(z) = \log[\sec(z) + \tan(z)]$. The gudermannian satisfies such relations as $\sinh(z) = \tan[\text{gd}(x)]$.

■ 3.2.7 Functions That Do Not Have Unique Values

When you ask for the square root s of a number a, you are effectively asking for the solution to the equation $s^2 = a$. This equation, however, in general has two different solutions. Both $s = 2$ and $s = -2$ are, for example, solutions to the equation $s^2 = 4$. When you evaluate the "function" $\sqrt{4}$, however, you usually want to get a single number, and so you have to choose one of these two solutions. A standard choice is that $\sqrt{x}$ should be positive for $x > 0$. This is what the *Mathematica* function Sqrt[x] does.

The need to make one choice from two solutions means that Sqrt[x] cannot be a true *inverse function* for x^2. Taking a number, squaring it, and then taking the square root can give you a different number than you started with.

$\sqrt{4}$ gives +2, not −2.

$In[1]:=$ **Sqrt[4]**

$Out[1]=$ 2

Squaring and taking the square root does not necessarily give you the number you started with.

$In[2]:=$ **Sqrt[(-2)^2]**

$Out[2]=$ 2

When you evaluate $\sqrt{-2i}$, there are again two possible answers: $-1 + i$ and $1 - i$. In this case, however, it is less clear which one to choose.

There is in fact no way to choose $\sqrt{z}$ so that it is continuous for all complex values of z. There has to be a "branch cut"—a line in the complex plane across which the function $\sqrt{z}$ is discontinuous. *Mathematica* adopts the usual convention of taking the branch cut for $\sqrt{z}$ to be along the negative real axis.

This gives $1 - i$, not $-1 + i$.

```
In[3]:= N[ Sqrt[-2 I] ]
Out[3]= 1. - 1. I
```

The branch cut in Sqrt along the negative real axis means that values of Sqrt[z] with z just above and below the axis are very different.

```
In[4]:= {Sqrt[-2 + 0.1 I], Sqrt[-2 - 0.1 I]}
Out[4]= {0.0353443 + 1.41465 I, 0.0353443 - 1.41465 I}
```

Their squares are nevertheless close.

```
In[5]:= %^2
Out[5]= {-2. + 0.1 I, -2. - 0.1 I}
```

The discontinuity along the negative real axis is quite clear in this three-dimensional picture of the imaginary part of the square root function.

```
In[6]:= Plot3D[ Im[Sqrt[x + I y]], {x, -4, 4}, {y, -4, 4} ]
```

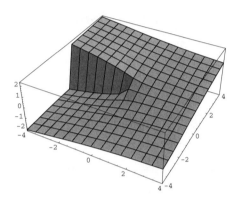

When you find an nth root using $z^{1/n}$, there are, in principle, n possible results. To get a single value, you have to choose a particular *principal root*. There is absolutely no guarantee that taking the nth root of an nth power will leave you with the same number.

This takes the tenth power of a complex number. The result is unique.

```
In[7]:= (2.5 + I)^10
Out[7]= -15781.1 - 12335.8 I
```

There are ten possible tenth roots. *Mathematica* chooses one of them. In this case it is not the number whose tenth power you took.

```
In[8]:= %^(1/10)
Out[8]= 2.61033 - 0.660446 I
```

There are many mathematical functions which, like roots, essentially give solutions to equations. The logarithm function and the inverse trigonometric functions are examples. In almost all cases, there are many possible solutions to the equations. Unique "principal" values nevertheless have to be chosen for the functions. The choices cannot be made continuous over the whole complex plane. Instead, lines of discontinuity, or branch cuts, must occur. The positions of these branch cuts are often quite arbitrary. *Mathematica* makes the most standard mathematical choices for them.

Sqrt[z] and z^s	$(-\infty, 0)$ for $\mathrm{Re}\, s > 0$, $(-\infty, 0]$ for $\mathrm{Re}\, s \leq 0$ (s not an integer)
Exp[z]	none
Log[z]	$(-\infty, 0]$
trigonometric functions	none
ArcSin[z] and ArcCos[z]	$(-\infty, -1)$ and $(+1, +\infty)$
ArcTan[z]	$(-i\infty, -i]$ and $[i, i\infty)$
ArcCsc[z] and ArcSec[z]	$(-1, +1)$
ArcCot[z]	$[-i, +i]$
hyperbolic functions	none
ArcSinh[z]	$(-i\infty, -i)$ and $(+i, +i\infty)$
ArcCosh[z]	$(-\infty, +1)$
ArcTanh[z]	$(-\infty, -1]$ and $[+1, +\infty)$
ArcCsch[z]	$(-i, i)$
ArcSech[z]	$(-\infty, 0]$ and $(+1, +\infty)$
ArcCoth[z]	$[-1, +1]$

Some branch-cut discontinuities in the complex plane.

ArcSin is a multiple-valued function, so there is no guarantee that it always gives the "inverse" of Sin.

```
In[9]:= ArcSin[Sin[4.5]]
Out[9]= -1.35841
```

Values of ArcSin[z] on opposite sides of the branch cut can be very different.

```
In[10]:= {ArcSin[2 + 0.1 I], ArcSin[2 - 0.1 I]}
Out[10]= {1.51316 + 1.31888 I, 1.51316 - 1.31888 I}
```

A three-dimensional picture, showing the two branch cuts for the function $\sin^{-1}(z)$.

In[11]:= **Plot3D[Im[ArcSin[x + I y]], {x, -4, 4}, {y, -4, 4}]**

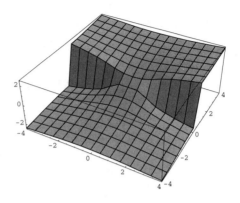

■ 3.2.8 Mathematical Constants

I	$i = \sqrt{-1}$
Infinity	∞
Pi	$\pi \simeq 3.14159$
Degree	$\pi/180$: degrees to radians conversion factor
GoldenRatio	$\phi = (1 + \sqrt{5})/2 \simeq 1.61803$
E	$e \simeq 2.71828$
EulerGamma	Euler's constant $\gamma \simeq 0.577216$
Catalan	Catalan's constant $\simeq 0.915966$

Mathematical constants.

Euler's constant EulerGamma is given by the limit $\gamma = \lim_{m \to \infty} \left(\sum_{k=1}^{m} \frac{1}{k} - \log m \right)$. It appears in many integrals, and asymptotic formulas. It is sometimes known as the **Euler-Mascheroni constant**, and denoted C.

Catalan's constant Catalan is given by the sum $\sum_{k=0}^{\infty} (-1)^k (2k+1)^{-2}$. It often appears in asymptotic estimates of combinatorial functions.

Mathematical constants can be evaluated to arbitrary precision.

In[1]:= **N[EulerGamma, 40]**

Out[1]= 0.5772156649015328606065120900824024310421

■ 3.2.9 Orthogonal Polynomials

LegendreP[n, x]	Legendre polynomials $P_n(x)$
LegendreP[n, m, x]	associated Legendre polynomials $P_n^m(x)$
SphericalHarmonicY[l, m, θ, ϕ]	
	spherical harmonics $Y_l^m(\theta, \phi)$
GegenbauerC[n, m, x]	Gegenbauer polynomials $C_n^{(m)}(x)$
ChebyshevT[n, x], ChebyshevU[n, x]	
	Chebyshev polynomials $T_n(x)$ and $U_n(x)$ of the first and second kinds
HermiteH[n, x]	Hermite polynomials $H_n(x)$
LaguerreL[n, x]	Laguerre polynomials $L_n(x)$
LaguerreL[n, a, x]	generalized Laguerre polynomials $L_n^a(x)$
JacobiP[n, a, b, x]	Jacobi polynomials $P_n^{(a,b)}(x)$

Orthogonal polynomials.

Legendre polynomials LegendreP[n, x] arise in studies of systems with three-dimensional spherical symmetry. They satisfy the differential equation $(1 - x^2)y'' - 2xy' + n(n + 1)y = 0$, and the orthogonality relation $\int_{-1}^{1} P_m(x)P_n(x)\, dx = 0$ for $m \neq n$.

The **associated Legendre polynomials** LegendreP[n, m, x] are obtained from derivatives of the Legendre polynomials according to $P_n^m(x) = (-1)^m(1-x^2)^{m/2}\, d^m[P_n(x)]/dx^m$. Notice that for odd integers $m \leq n$, the $P_n^m(x)$ contain powers of $\sqrt{1 - x^2}$, and are therefore not strictly polynomials. The $P_n^m(x)$ reduce to $P_n(x)$ when $m = 0$.

The **spherical harmonics** SphericalHarmonicY[l, m, θ, ϕ] are related to associated Legendre polynomials. They satisfy the orthogonality relation $\int Y_l^m(\theta, \phi)\bar{Y}_{l'}^{m'}(\theta, \phi)\, d\omega = 0$ for $l \neq l'$ or $m \neq m'$, where $d\omega$ represents integration over the surface of the unit sphere.

This gives the algebraic form of the Legendre polynomial $P_8(x)$.

In[1]:= **LegendreP[8, x]**

$$Out[1]= \frac{35}{128} - \frac{315\,x^2}{32} + \frac{3465\,x^4}{64} - \frac{3003\,x^6}{32} + \frac{6435\,x^8}{128}$$

The integral $\int_{-1}^{1} P_7(x)\,P_8(x)\, dx$ gives zero by virtue of the orthogonality of the Legendre polynomials.

In[2]:= **Integrate[LegendreP[7,x] LegendreP[8,x], {x, -1, 1}]**

Out[2]= 0

Integrating the square of a single Legendre polynomial gives a non-zero result.

In[3]:= **Integrate[LegendreP[8, x]^2, {x, -1, 1}]**

$$Out[3]= \frac{2}{17}$$

High-degree Legendre polynomials oscillate rapidly.

$In[4]:=$ **Plot[LegendreP[10, x], {x, -1, 1}]**

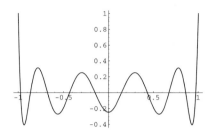

The associated Legendre "polynomials" contain pieces proportional to $\sqrt{1-x^2}$.

$In[5]:=$ **LegendreP[8, 3, x]**

$Out[5]=$ $\dfrac{3465}{8}\sqrt{1-x^2}\,(-1+x^2)\,(3x-26x^3+39x^5)$

Section 3.2.10 discusses the generalization of Legendre polynomials to Legendre functions, which can have non-integer degrees.

$In[6]:=$ **LegendreP[8.1, 0]**

$Out[6]=$ 0.268501

Gegenbauer polynomials GegenbauerC[n, m, x] can be viewed as generalizations of the Legendre polynomials to systems with $(m+2)$-dimensional spherical symmetry. They are sometimes known as **ultraspherical polynomials**.

GegenbauerC[n, 0, x] is always equal to zero. GegenbauerC[n, x] is however given by the limit $\lim_{m\to 0} C_n^{(m)}(x)/m$. This form is sometimes denoted $C_n^{(0)}(x)$.

Series of Chebyshev polynomials are often used in making numerical approximations to functions. The **Chebyshev polynomials of the first kind** ChebyshevT[n, x] are defined by $T_n(\cos\theta) = \cos(n\theta)$. They are normalized so that $T_n(1) = 1$. They satisfy the orthogonality relation $\int_{-1}^{1} T_m(x)T_n(x)(1-x^2)^{-1/2}\,dx = 0$ for $m \neq n$. The $T_n(x)$ also satisfy an orthogonality relation under summation at discrete points in x corresponding to the roots of $T_n(x)$.

The **Chebyshev polynomials of the second kind** ChebyshevU[n, z] are defined by $U_n(\cos\theta) = \sin[(n+1)\theta]/\sin\theta$. With this definition, $U_n(1) = n+1$. The U_n satisfy the orthogonality relation $\int_{-1}^{1} U_m(x)U_n(x)(1-x^2)^{1/2}\,dx = 0$ for $m \neq n$.

The name "Chebyshev" is a transliteration from the Cyrillic alphabet; several other spellings, such as "Tschebyscheff", are sometimes used.

Hermite polynomials HermiteH[n, x] arise as the quantum-mechanical wave functions for a harmonic oscillator. They satisfy the differential equation $y'' - 2xy' + 2ny = 0$, and the orthogonality relation $\int_{-\infty}^{\infty} H_m(x)H_n(x)e^{-x^2}\,dx = 0$ for $m \neq n$. An alternative form of Hermite polynomials sometimes used is $He_n(x) = 2^{-n/2}H_n(x/\sqrt{2})$ (a different overall normalization of the $He_n(x)$ is also sometimes used).

The Hermite polynomials are related to the **parabolic cylinder functions** or **Weber functions** $D_n(x)$ by $D_n(x) = 2^{-n/2}e^{-x^2/4}H_n(x/\sqrt{2})$.

<table>
<tr>
<td>

This gives the density for an excited state of a quantum-mechanical harmonic oscillator. The average of the wiggles is roughly the classical physics result.

</td>
<td>

$In[7]:=$ **Plot[(HermiteH[6, x] Exp[-x^2/2])^2, {x, -6, 6}]**

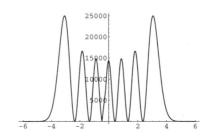

</td>
</tr>
</table>

Generalized Laguerre polynomials LaguerreL[n, a, x] are related to hydrogen atom wave functions in quantum mechanics. They satisfy the differential equation $xy'' + (a + 1 - x)y' + ny = 0$, and the orthogonality relation $\int_0^\infty L_m^a(x)L_n^a(x)x^a e^{-x}\,dx = 0$ for $m \neq n$. The **Laguerre polynomials** LaguerreL[n, x] correspond to the special case $a = 0$.

Jacobi polynomials JacobiP[n, a, b, x] occur in studies of the rotation group, particularly in quantum mechanics. They satisfy the orthogonality relation $\int_{-1}^1 P_m^{(a,b)}(x)P_n^{(a,b)}(x)(1 - x)^a(1 + x)^b\,dx = 0$ for $m \neq n$. Legendre, Gegenbauer and Chebyshev polynomials can all be viewed as special cases of Jacobi polynomials. The Jacobi polynomials are sometimes given in the alternative form $G_n(p, q, x) = n!\,\Gamma(n + p)/\Gamma(2n + p)\;P_n^{(p-q,q-1)}(2x - 1)$.

<table>
<tr>
<td>

You can get formulas for generalized Laguerre polynomials with arbitrary values of a.

</td>
<td>

$In[8]:=$ **LaguerreL[2, a, x]**

$Out[8]= \dfrac{1}{2}\,(2 + 3\,a + a^2 - 4\,x - 2\,a\,x + x^2)$

</td>
</tr>
</table>

■ 3.2.10 Special Functions

Mathematica includes all the common special functions of mathematical physics found in standard handbooks. We will discuss each of the various classes of functions in turn.

One point you should realize is that in the technical literature there are often several conflicting definitions of any particular special function. When you use a special function in *Mathematica*, therefore, you should be sure to look at the definition given here to confirm that it is exactly what you want.

<table>
<tr>
<td>

Mathematica gives exact results for some values of special functions.

</td>
<td>

$In[1]:=$ **Gamma[15/2]**

$Out[1]= \dfrac{135135}{128}\,\sqrt{\pi}$

</td>
</tr>
</table>

No exact result is known here.

In[2]:= **Gamma[15/7]**

Out[2]= $\text{Gamma}\left[\dfrac{15}{7}\right]$

A numerical result, to arbitrary precision, can nevertheless be found.

In[3]:= **N[%, 40]**

Out[3]= 1.0690715004486243979941376897026932673667

You can give complex arguments to special functions.

In[4]:= **Gamma[3 + 4I] //N**

Out[4]= 0.00522554 - 0.172547 I

Special functions automatically get applied to each element in a list.

In[5]:= **Gamma[{3/2, 5/2, 7/2}]**

Out[5]= $\left\{\dfrac{1}{2}\sqrt{\pi},\ \dfrac{3}{4}\sqrt{\pi},\ \dfrac{15}{8}\sqrt{\pi}\right\}$

Mathematica knows analytical properties of special functions, such as derivatives.

In[6]:= **D[Gamma[x], {x, 2}]**

Out[6]= Gamma[x] PolyGamma[0, x]^2 + Gamma[x] PolyGamma[1, x]

You can use FindRoot to find roots of special functions.

In[7]:= **FindRoot[BesselJ[0, x], {x, 1}]**

Out[7]= {x → 2.40482}

Special functions in *Mathematica* can usually be evaluated for arbitrary complex values of their arguments. Often, however, the defining relations given below apply only for some special choices of arguments. In these cases, the full function corresponds to a suitable extension or "analytic continuation" of these defining relations. Thus, for example, integral representations of functions are valid only when the integral exists, but the functions themselves can usually be defined elsewhere by analytic continuation.

As a simple example of how the domain of a function can be extended, consider the function represented by the sum $\sum_{k=0}^{\infty} x^k$. This sum converges only when $|x| < 1$. Nevertheless, it is easy to show analytically that for any x, the complete function is equal to $1/(1 - x)$. Using this form, you can easily find a value of the function for any x, at least so long as $x \neq 1$.

Gamma and Related Functions

Beta[a, b]	Euler beta function $B(a, b)$
Beta[z, a, b]	incomplete beta function $B_z(a, b)$
BetaRegularized[z, a, b]	regularized incomplete beta function $I(z, a, b)$
Gamma[z]	Euler gamma function $\Gamma(z)$
Gamma[a, z]	incomplete gamma function $\Gamma(a, z)$
Gamma[a, z_0, z_1]	generalized incomplete gamma function $\Gamma(a, z_0) - \Gamma(a, z_1)$
GammaRegularized[a, z]	regularized incomplete gamma function $Q(a, z)$
InverseBetaRegularized[s, a, b]	
	inverse beta function
InverseGammaRegularized[a, s]	
	inverse gamma function
Pochhammer[a, n]	Pochhammer symbol $(a)_n$
PolyGamma[z]	digamma function $\psi(z)$
PolyGamma[n, z]	n^{th} derivative of the digamma function $\psi^{(n)}(z)$

Gamma and related functions.

The **Euler gamma function** Gamma[z] is defined by the integral $\Gamma(z) = \int_0^\infty t^{z-1} e^{-t} dt$. For positive integer n, $\Gamma(n) = (n-1)!$. $\Gamma(z)$ can be viewed as a generalization of the factorial function, valid for complex arguments z.

There are some computations, particularly in number theory, where the logarithm of the gamma function often appears. For positive real arguments, you can evaluate this simply as Log[Gamma[z]]. For complex arguments, however, this form yields spurious discontinuities. *Mathematica* therefore includes the separate function LogGamma[z], which yields the **logarithm of the gamma function** with a single branch cut along the negative real axis.

The **Euler beta function** Beta[a, b] is $B(a, b) = \Gamma(a)\Gamma(b)/\Gamma(a + b) = \int_0^1 t^{a-1}(1 - t)^{b-1} dt$.

The **Pochhammer symbol** or **rising factorial** Pochhammer[a, n] is $(a)_n = a(a + 1) \ldots (a + n - 1) = \Gamma(a + n)/\Gamma(a)$. It often appears in series expansions for hypergeometric functions. Note that the Pochhammer symbol has a definite value even when the gamma functions which appear in its definition are infinite.

The **incomplete gamma function** Gamma[a, z] is defined by the integral $\Gamma(a, z) = \int_z^\infty t^{a-1} e^{-t} dt$. *Mathematica* includes a generalized incomplete gamma function Gamma[a, z_0, z_1] defined as $\int_{z_0}^{z_1} t^{a-1} e^{-t} dt$.

The alternative incomplete gamma function $\gamma(a, z)$ can therefore be obtained in *Mathematica* as Gamma[a, 0, z].

The **incomplete beta function** Beta[z, a, b] is given by $B_z(a, b) = \int_0^z t^{a-1}(1-t)^{b-1}dt$. Notice that in the incomplete beta function, the parameter z is an *upper* limit of integration, and appears as the *first* argument of the function. In the incomplete gamma function, on the other hand, z is a *lower* limit of integration, and appears as the *second* argument of the function.

In certain cases, it is convenient not to compute the incomplete beta and gamma functions on their own, but instead to compute *regularized forms* in which these functions are divided by complete beta and gamma functions. *Mathematica* includes the **regularized incomplete beta function** BetaRegularized[z, a, b] defined for most arguments by $I(z, a, b) = B(z, a, b)/B(a, b)$, but taking into account singular cases. *Mathematica* also includes the **regularized incomplete gamma function** GammaRegularized[a, z] defined by $Q(a, z) = \Gamma(a, z)/\Gamma(a)$, with singular cases taken into account.

The incomplete beta and gamma functions, and their inverses, are common in statistics. The **inverse beta function** InverseBetaRegularized[s, a, b] is the solution for z in $s = I(z, a, b)$. The **inverse gamma function** InverseGammaRegularized[a, s] is similarly the solution for z in $s = Q(a, z)$.

Derivatives of the gamma function often appear in summing rational series. The **digamma function** PolyGamma[z] is the logarithmic derivative of the gamma function, given by $\psi(z) = \Gamma'(z)/\Gamma(z)$. For integer arguments, the digamma function satisfies the relation $\psi(n) = -\gamma + \sum_{k=1}^{n-1} \frac{1}{k}$, where γ is Euler's constant (EulerGamma in *Mathematica*).

The **polygamma functions** PolyGamma[n, z] are given by $\psi^{(n)}(z) = d^n\psi(z)/dz^n$. Notice that the digamma function corresponds to $\psi^{(0)}(z)$. The general form $\psi^{(n)}(z)$ is the $(n+1)^{\text{th}}$, not the nth, logarithmic derivative of the gamma function. The polygamma functions satisfy the relation $\psi^{(n)}(z) = (-1)^{n+1}n! \sum_{k=0}^{\infty} 1/(z+k)^{n+1}$.

Many exact results for gamma and polygamma functions are built into *Mathematica*.

```
In[8]:= PolyGamma[6]
```

$$Out[8]= \frac{137}{60} - \text{EulerGamma}$$

Here is a contour plot of the gamma
function in the complex plane.

In[9]:= `ContourPlot[ Abs[Gamma[x + I y]], {x, -3, 3},`
`{y, -2, 2}, PlotPoints->40 ]`

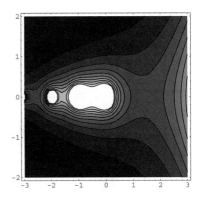

Zeta and Related Functions

`LerchPhi[z, s, a]`	Lerch's transcendent $\Phi(z, s, a)$
`PolyLog[n, z]`	polylogarithm function $\mathrm{Li}_n(z)$
`RiemannSiegelTheta[t]`	Riemann-Siegel function $\vartheta(t)$
`RiemannSiegelZ[t]`	Riemann-Siegel function $Z(t)$
`StieltjesGamma[n]`	Stieltjes constants γ_n
`Zeta[s]`	Riemann zeta function $\zeta(s)$
`Zeta[s, a]`	generalized Riemann zeta function $\zeta(s, a)$

Zeta and related functions.

The **Riemann zeta function** `Zeta[s]` is defined by the relation $\zeta(s) = \sum_{k=1}^{\infty} k^{-s}$ (for $s > 1$). Zeta functions with integer arguments arise in evaluating various sums and integrals. *Mathematica* gives exact results when possible for zeta functions with integer arguments.

There is an analytic continuation of $\zeta(s)$ for arbitrary complex $s \neq 1$. The zeta function for complex arguments is central to number-theoretical studies of the distribution of primes. Of particular importance are the values on the critical line $\mathrm{Re}\, s = \frac{1}{2}$.

In studying $\zeta(\frac{1}{2} + it)$, it is often convenient to define the two analytic **Riemann-Siegel functions** `RiemannSiegelZ[t]` and `RiemannSiegelTheta[z]` according to $Z(t) = e^{i\vartheta(t)}\zeta(\frac{1}{2} + it)$ and $\vartheta(t) =$

Im $\log \Gamma(\frac{1}{4} + it/2) - t \log(\pi)/2$ (for t real). Note that the Riemann-Siegel functions are both real as long as t is real.

The **Stieltjes constants** StieltjesGamma[n] are generalizations of Euler's constant which appear in the series expansion of $\zeta(s)$ around its pole at $s = 1$; the coefficient of $(1 - s)^n$ is $\gamma_n/n!$. Euler's constant is γ_0.

The **generalized Riemann zeta function** or **Hurwitz zeta function** Zeta[s, a] is given by $\zeta(s, a) = \sum_{k=0}^{\infty}(k + a)^{-s}$, where any term with $k + a = 0$ is excluded.

Mathematica gives exact results for $\zeta(2n)$.

$In[10]:=$ **Zeta[6]**

$Out[10]=$ $\dfrac{\pi^6}{945}$

Here is a three-dimensional picture of the Riemann zeta function in the complex plane.

$In[11]:=$ **Plot3D[Abs[Zeta[x + I y]], {x, -3, 3},**
           {y, 2, 35}, PlotPoints->30]

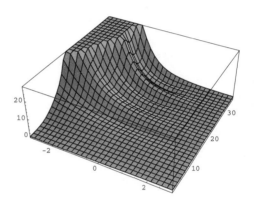

This is a plot of the absolute value of the Riemann zeta function on the critical line $\text{Re}\, z = \frac{1}{2}$. You can see the first few zeros of the zeta function.

$In[12]:=$ **Plot[Abs[Zeta[1/2 + I y]], {y, 0, 40}]**

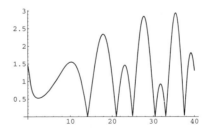

The **polylogarithm functions** PolyLog[n, z] are given by $\text{Li}_n(z) = \sum_{k=1}^{\infty} z^k/k^n$. The **dilogarithm** PolyLog[2, z] satisfies $\text{Li}_2(z) = \int_z^0 \log(1 - t)/t\, dt$. $\text{Li}_2(1 - z)$ is sometimes known as **Spence's integral**. Polylogarithms crop up in Feynman diagram integrals in elementary particle physics. The polylogarithm function is sometimes known as **Jonquière's function**.

The **Lerch transcendent** LerchPhi[z, s, a] is a generalization of the zeta and polylogarithm functions, given by $\Phi(z, s, a) = \sum_{k=0}^{\infty} z^k/(a + k)^s$, where any term with $a + k = 0$ is excluded. Many sums of reciprocal powers can be expressed in terms of the Lerch transcendent. For example, the **Catalan beta function** $\beta(s) = \sum_{k=0}^{\infty}(-1)^k(2k + 1)^{-s}$ can be obtained as $2^{-s}\Phi(-1, s, \frac{1}{2})$.

The Lerch transcendent is related to integrals of the **Fermi-Dirac** distribution in statistical mechanics by $\int_0^{\infty} k^s/(e^{k-\mu} + 1)\,dk = e^{\mu}\Gamma(s + 1)\Phi(-e^{\mu}, s + 1, 1)$.

The Lerch transcendent can also be used to evaluate **Dirichlet** *L*-series which appear in number theory. The basic *L*-series has the form $L(s, \chi) = \sum_{k=1}^{\infty} \chi(k)k^{-s}$, where the "character" $\chi(k)$ is an integer function with period *m*. *L*-series of this kind can be written as sums of Lerch functions with *z* a power of $e^{2\pi i/m}$.

LerchPhi[z, s, a, DoublyInfinite->True] gives the doubly infinite sum $\sum_{k=-\infty}^{\infty} z^k/(a + k)^s$.

Exponential Integral and Related Functions

	CosIntegral[z]	cosine integral function Ci(z)
+	CoshIntegral[z]	hyperbolic cosine integral function Chi(z)
	ExpIntegralE[n, z]	exponential integral $E_n(z)$
	ExpIntegralEi[z]	exponential integral Ei(z)
	LogIntegral[z]	logarithmic integral li(z)
	SinIntegral[z]	sine integral function Si(z)
+	SinhIntegral[z]	hyperbolic sine integral function Shi(z)

Exponential integral and related functions.

Mathematica has two forms of exponential integral: ExpIntegralE and ExpIntegralEi.

The **exponential integral function** ExpIntegralE[n, z] is defined by $E_n(z) = \int_1^{\infty} e^{-zt}/t^n\,dt$.

The second **exponential integral function** ExpIntegralEi[z] is defined by $\text{Ei}(z) = -\int_{-z}^{\infty} e^{-t}/t\,dt$ (for $z > 0$), where the principal value of the integral is taken.

The **logarithmic integral function** LogIntegral[z] is given by $\text{li}(z) = \int_0^z dt/\log t$ (for $z > 1$), where the principal value of the integral is taken. li(z) is central to the study of the distribution of primes in number theory. The logarithmic integral function is sometimes also denoted by Li(z). In some number-theoretical applications, li(z) is defined as $\int_2^z dt/\log t$, with no principal value taken. This differs from the definition used in *Mathematica* by the constant li(2).

The **sine and cosine integral functions** `SinIntegral[z]` and `CosIntegral[z]` are defined by $\mathrm{Si}(z) = \int_0^z \sin(t)/t\,dt$ and $\mathrm{Ci}(z) = -\int_z^\infty \cos(t)/t\,dt$. The **hyperbolic sine and cosine integral functions** `SinhIntegral[z]` and `CoshIntegral[z]` are defined by $\mathrm{Shi}(z) = \int_0^z \sinh(t)/t\,dt$ and $\mathrm{Chi}(z) = \gamma + \log(z) + \int_0^z (\cosh(t)-1)/t\,dt$.

Error Function and Related Functions

`Erf[z]`	error function erf(z)
`Erf[z0, z1]`	generalized error function $\mathrm{erf}(z_1) - \mathrm{erf}(z_0)$
`Erfc[z]`	complementary error function erfc(z)
`Erfi[z]`	imaginary error function erfi(z)
`FresnelC[z]`	Fresnel integral $C(z)$
`FresnelS[z]`	Fresnel integral $S(z)$
`InverseErf[s]`	inverse error function
`InverseErfc[s]`	inverse complementary error function

Error function and related functions.

The **error function** `Erf[z]` is the integral of the Gaussian distribution, given by $\mathrm{erf}(z) = 2/\sqrt{\pi}\int_0^z e^{-t^2}dt$. The **complementary error function** `Erfc[z]` is given simply by $\mathrm{erfc}(z) = 1 - \mathrm{erf}(z)$. The **imaginary error function** `Erfi[z]` is given by $\mathrm{erfi}(z) = \mathrm{erf}(iz)/i$. The generalized error function `Erf[z0, z1]` is defined by the integral $2/\sqrt{\pi}\int_{z_0}^{z_1} e^{-t^2}dt$. The error function is central to many calculations in statistics.

The **inverse error function** `InverseErf[s]` is defined as the solution for z in the equation $s = \mathrm{erf}(z)$. The inverse error function appears in computing confidence intervals in statistics as well as in some algorithms for generating Gaussian random numbers.

Closely related to the error function are the **Fresnel integrals** `FresnelC[z]` defined by $C(z) = \int_0^z \cos(\pi t^2/2)\,dt$ and `FresnelS[z]` defined by $S(z) = \int_0^z \sin(\pi t^2/2)\,dt$. Fresnel integrals occur in diffraction theory.

Bessel Functions

`AiryAi[z]` and `AiryBi[z]`	Airy functions Ai(z) and Bi(z)
`AiryAiPrime[z]` and `AiryBiPrime[z]`	derivatives of Airy functions Ai'(z) and Bi'(z)
`BesselJ[n, z]` and `BesselY[n, z]`	Bessel functions $J_n(z)$ and $Y_n(z)$
`BesselI[n, z]` and `BesselK[n, z]`	modified Bessel functions $I_n(z)$ and $K_n(z)$

Bessel functions.

The **Bessel functions** `BesselJ[n, z]` and `BesselY[n, z]` are linearly independent solutions to the differential equation $z^2 y'' + z y' + (z^2 - n^2) y = 0$. For integer n, the $J_n(z)$ are regular at $z = 0$, while the $Y_n(z)$ have a logarithmic divergence at $z = 0$.

Bessel functions arise in solving differential equations for systems with cylindrical symmetry.

$J_n(z)$ is often called the **Bessel function of the first kind,** or simply *the* Bessel function. $Y_n(z)$ is referred to as the **Bessel function of the second kind**, the **Weber function**, or the **Neumann function** (denoted $N_n(z)$).

The **Hankel functions** (or **Bessel functions of the third kind**) $H_n^{(1,2)}(z) = J_n(z) \pm i Y_n(z)$ give an alternative pair of solutions to the Bessel differential equation.

In studying systems with spherical symmetry, **spherical Bessel functions** arise, defined by $f_n(z) = \sqrt{\pi/2z} F_{n+\frac{1}{2}}(z)$, where f and F can be j and J, y and Y, or h^i and H^i. For integer n, *Mathematica* gives exact algebraic formulas for spherical Bessel functions.

The **modified Bessel functions** `BesselI[n, z]` and `BesselK[n, z]` are solutions to the differential equation $z^2 y'' + z y' - (z^2 + n^2) y = 0$. For integer n, $I_n(z)$ is regular at $z = 0$; $K_n(z)$ always has a logarithmic divergence at $z = 0$. The $I_n(z)$ are sometimes known as **hyperbolic Bessel functions**.

Particularly in electrical engineering, one often defines the **Kelvin functions**, according to $\mathrm{ber}_n(z) + i\,\mathrm{bei}_n(z) = e^{n\pi i} J_n(ze^{-\pi i/4})$, $\mathrm{ker}_n(z) + i\,\mathrm{kei}_n(z) = e^{-n\pi i/2} K_n(ze^{\pi i/4})$.

The **Airy functions** `AiryAi[z]` and `AiryBi[z]` are the two independent solutions Ai(z) and Bi(z) to the differential equation $y'' - z y = 0$. Ai(z) tends to zero for large positive z, while Bi(z) increases unboundedly. The Airy functions are related to modified Bessel functions with one-third-integer orders. The Airy functions often appear as the solutions to boundary value problems in electromagnetic theory and quantum mechanics. In many cases the **derivatives of the Airy functions** `AiryAiPrime[z]` and `AiryBiPrime[z]` also appear.

Here is a plot of $J_0(\sqrt{x})$. This is a curve that an idealized chain hanging from one end can form when you wiggle it.

In[13]:= **Plot[BesselJ[0, Sqrt[x]], {x, 0, 50}]**

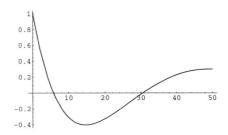

Mathematica generates explicit formulas for half-integer-order Bessel functions.

In[14]:= **BesselK[3/2, x]**

$$Out[14]= \frac{E^{-x}\sqrt{\frac{\pi}{2}}\left(1+\frac{1}{x}\right)}{\sqrt{x}}$$

The Airy function plotted here gives the quantum-mechanical amplitude for a particle in a potential that increases linearly from left to right. The amplitude is exponentially damped in the classically inaccessible region on the right.

In[15]:= **Plot[AiryAi[x], {x, -10, 10}]**

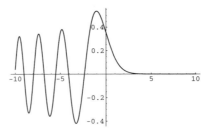

Legendre and Related Functions

LegendreP[n, z]	Legendre functions of the first kind $P_n(z)$
LegendreP[n, m, z]	associated Legendre functions of the first kind $P_n^m(z)$
LegendreQ[n, z]	Legendre functions of the second kind $Q_n(z)$
LegendreQ[n, m, z]	associated Legendre functions of the second kind $Q_n^m(z)$

Legendre and related functions.

The **Legendre functions** and **associated Legendre functions** satisfy the differential equation $(1-z^2)y'' - 2zy' + [n(n+1) - m^2/(1-z^2)]y = 0$. The **Legendre functions of the first kind**, LegendreP[n, z] and LegendreP[n, m, z], reduce to Legendre polynomials when n and m are integers. The **Legendre**

functions of the second kind LegendreQ[n, z] and LegendreQ[n, m, z] give the second linearly independent solution to the differential equation. For integer m they have logarithmic singularities at $z = \pm 1$. The $P_n(z)$ and $Q_n(z)$ solve the differential equation with $m = 0$.

Legendre functions arise in studies of quantum-mechanical scattering processes.

+ LegendreP[n, m, z] or LegendreP[n, m, 1, z]

  type 1 function containing $(1 - z^2)^{m/2}$

+   LegendreP[n, m, 2, z]   type 2 function containing $((1 + z)/(1 - z))^{m/2}$

+   LegendreP[n, m, 3, z]   type 3 function containing $((1 + z)/(-1 + z))^{m/2}$

Types of Legendre functions. Analogous types exist for LegendreQ.

Legendre functions of type 1 are defined only when z lies inside the unit circle in the complex plane. **Legendre functions of type 2** have the same numerical values as type 1 inside the unit circle, but are also defined outside. The type 2 functions have branch cuts from $-\infty$ to -1 and from $+1$ to $+\infty$. **Legendre functions of type 3**, sometimes denoted $\mathcal{P}_n^m(z)$ and $Q_n^m(z)$, have a single branch cut from $-\infty$ to $+1$.

Toroidal functions or **ring functions**, which arise in studying systems with toroidal symmetry, can be expressed in terms of the Legendre functions $P_{\nu - \frac{1}{2}}^{\mu}(\cosh \eta)$ and $Q_{\nu - \frac{1}{2}}^{\mu}(\cosh \eta)$.

Conical functions can be expressed in terms of $P_{-\frac{1}{2} + ip}^{\mu}(\cos \theta)$ and $Q_{-\frac{1}{2} + ip}^{\mu}(\cos \theta)$.

When you use the function LegendreP[n, x] with an integer n, you get a Legendre polynomial. If you take n to be an arbitrary complex number, you get, in general, a Legendre function.

In the same way, you can use the functions GegenbauerC and so on with arbitrary complex indices to get **Gegenbauer functions**, **Chebyshev functions**, **Hermite functions**, **Jacobi functions** and **Laguerre functions**. Unlike for associated Legendre functions, however, there is no need to distinguish different types in such cases.

Confluent Hypergeometric Functions

`HypergeometricOF1[a, z]`	hypergeometric function $_0F_1(;a;z)$
+ `HypergeometricOF1Regularized[a, z]`	regularized hypergeometric function $_0F_1(;a;z)/\Gamma(a)$
`Hypergeometric1F1[a, b, z]`	Kummer confluent hypergeometric function $_1F_1(a;b;z)$
+ `Hypergeometric1F1Regularized[a, b, z]`	regularized confluent hypergeometric function $_1F_1(a;b;z)/\Gamma(b)$
`HypergeometricU[a, b, z]`	confluent hypergeometric function $U(a,b,z)$

Confluent hypergeometric functions.

Many of the special functions that we have discussed so far can be viewed as special cases of the **confluent hypergeometric function** `Hypergeometric1F1[a, b, z]`.

The confluent hypergeometric function can be obtained from the series expansion $_1F_1(a;b;z) = 1 + az/b + a(a+1)/b(b+1)\, z^2/2! + \cdots = \sum_{k=0}^{\infty} (a)_k/(b)_k\, z^k/k!$. Some special results are obtained when a and b are both integers. If $a < 0$, and either $b > 0$ or $b < a$, the series yields a polynomial with a finite number of terms.

If b is zero or a negative integer, then $_1F_1(a;b;z)$ itself is infinite. But the **regularized confluent hypergeometric function** `Hypergeometric1F1Regularized[a, b, z]` given by $_1F_1(a;b;z)/\Gamma(b)$ has a finite value in all cases.

Among the functions that can be obtained from $_1F_1$ are the Bessel functions, error function, incomplete gamma function, and Hermite and Laguerre polynomials.

The function $_1F_1(a;b;z)$ is sometimes denoted $\Phi(a;b;z)$ or $M(a,b,z)$. It is often known as the **Kummer function**.

The $_1F_1$ function can be written in the integral representation $_1F_1(a;b;z) = \Gamma(b)/[\Gamma(b-a)\Gamma(a)] \int_0^1 e^{zt} t^{a-1} (1-t)^{b-a-1}\, dt$.

The $_1F_1$ confluent hypergeometric function is a solution to Kummer's differential equation $zy'' + (b-z)y' - ay = 0$, with the boundary conditions $_1F_1(a;b;0) = 1$ and $\partial[_1F_1(a;b;z)]/\partial z|_{z=0} = a/b$.

The function `HypergeometricU[a, b, z]` gives a second linearly independent solution to Kummer's equation. For $\mathrm{Re}\, b > 1$ this function behaves like z^{1-b} for small z. It has a branch cut along the negative real axis in the complex z plane.

The function $U(a,b,z)$ has the integral representation $U(a,b,z) = 1/\Gamma(a) \int_0^\infty e^{-zt} t^{a-1}(1+t)^{b-a-1}\, dt$.

$U(a,b,z)$, like $_1F_1(a;b;z)$, is sometimes known as the **Kummer function**. The U function is sometimes denoted by Ψ.

The **Whittaker functions** give an alternative pair of solutions to Kummer's differential equation. The Whittaker function $M_{\kappa,\mu}$ is related to ${}_1F_1$ by $M_{\kappa,\mu}(z) = e^{-z/2}z^{1/2+\mu}{}_1F_1(\frac{1}{2}+\mu-\kappa;1+2\mu;z)$. The second Whittaker function $W_{\kappa,\mu}$ obeys the same relation, with ${}_1F_1$ replaced by U.

The **parabolic cylinder functions** are related to Whittaker functions by $D_\nu(z) = 2^{1/4+\nu/2}z^{-1/2} \times W_{\frac{1}{4}+\frac{\nu}{2},-\frac{1}{4}}(z^2/2)$. For integer ν, the parabolic cylinder functions reduce to Hermite polynomials.

The **Coulomb wave functions** are also special cases of the confluent hypergeometric function. Coulomb wave functions give solutions to the radial Schrödinger equation in the Coulomb potential of a point nucleus. The regular Coulomb wave function is given by $F_L(\eta,\rho) = C_L(\eta)\rho^{L+1}e^{-i\rho}{}_1F_1(L+1-i\eta;2L+2;2i\rho)$, where $C_L(\eta) = 2^L e^{-\pi\eta/2}|\Gamma(L+1+i\eta)|/\Gamma(2L+2)$.

Other special cases of the confluent hypergeometric function include the **Toronto functions** $T(m,n,r)$, **Poisson-Charlier polynomials** $\rho_n(\nu,x)$, **Cunningham functions** $\omega_{n,m}(x)$ and **Bateman functions** $k_\nu(x)$.

A limiting form of the confluent hypergeometric function which often appears is `Hypergeometric0F1[a, z]`. This function is obtained as the limit ${}_0F_1(;a;z) = \lim_{q\to\infty} {}_1F_1(q;a;z/q)$.

The ${}_0F_1$ function has the series expansion ${}_0F_1(;a;z) = \sum_{k=0}^{\infty} 1/(a)_k z^k/k!$ and satisfies the differential equation $zy'' + ay' - y = 0$.

Bessel functions of the first kind can be expressed in terms of the ${}_0F_1$ function.

Hypergeometric Functions and Generalizations

`Hypergeometric2F1[a, b, c, z]`   hypergeometric function ${}_2F_1(a,b;c;z)$

+ `Hypergeometric2F1Regularized[a, b, c, z]`
                    regularized hypergeometric function ${}_2F_1(a,b;c;z)/\Gamma(c)$

+ `HypergeometricPFQ[{a_1, ... , a_p}, {b_1, ... , b_q}, z]`
                    generalized hypergeometric function ${}_pF_q(\mathbf{a};\mathbf{b};z)$

+ `HypergeometricPFQRegularized[{a_1, ... , a_p}, {b_1, ... , b_q}, z]`
                    regularized generalized hypergeometric function

+ `MeijerG[{{a_1, ... , a_n}, {a_{n+1}, ... , a_p}}, {{b_1, ... , b_m}, {b_{m+1}, ... , b_q}}, z]`
                    Meijer G function

Hypergeometric functions and generalizations.

The **hypergeometric function** `Hypergeometric2F1[a, b, c, z]` has series expansion ${}_2F_1(a,b;c;z) = \sum_{k=0}^{\infty} (a)_k(b)_k/(c)_k z^k/k!$. The function is a solution of the hypergeometric differential equation $z(1-z)y'' + [c-(a+b+1)z]y' - aby = 0$.

The hypergeometric function can also be written as an integral: ${}_2F_1(a,b;c;z) = \Gamma(c)/[\Gamma(b)\Gamma(c-b)] \times \int_0^1 t^{b-1}(1-t)^{c-b-1}(1-tz)^{-a}\, dt$.

The hypergeometric function is also sometimes denoted by F, and is known as the **Gauss series** or the **Kummer series**.

The Legendre functions, and the functions which give generalizations of other orthogonal polynomials, can be expressed in terms of the hypergeometric function. Complete elliptic integrals can also be expressed in terms of the $_2F_1$ function.

The **Riemann P function**, which gives solutions to Riemann's differential equation, is also a $_2F_1$ function.

The **generalized hypergeometric function** HypergeometricPFQ[$\{a_1, \ldots, a_p\}$, $\{b_1, \ldots, b_q\}$, z] has series expansion $_pF_q(\mathbf{a}; \mathbf{b}; z) = \sum_{k=0}^{\infty} (a_1)_k \ldots (a_p)_k / [(b_1)_k \ldots (b_q)_k] z^k / k!$.

The **Meijer G function** MeijerG[$\{\{a_1,\ldots,a_n\}, \{a_{n+1},\ldots,a_p\}\}$, $\{\{b_1,\ldots,b_m\}, \{b_{m+1},\ldots,b_q\}\}$, z] is defined by the contour integral representation $G_{pq}^{mn}\left(z \begin{vmatrix} a_1,\ldots,a_p \\ b_1,\ldots,b_q \end{vmatrix}\right) = 1/2\pi i \int \Gamma(1 - a_1 - s) \ldots \Gamma(1 - a_n - s) \times$ $\Gamma(b_1 + s) \ldots \Gamma(b_m + s) / \Gamma(a_{n+1} + s) \ldots \Gamma(a_p + s) \Gamma(1 - b_{m+1} - s) \ldots \Gamma(1 - b_q - s) z^{-s} ds$, where the contour of integration is set up to lie between the poles of $\Gamma(1 - a_i - s)$ and the poles of $\Gamma(b_i + s)$.

MeijerG is a very general function whose special cases cover most of the functions discussed in the past few sections.

The Product Log Function

+	ProductLog[z]	product log function $W(z)$

The product log function.

The **product log function** gives the solution for w in $z = we^w$. The function can be viewed as a generalization of a logarithm. It can be used to represent solutions to a variety of transcendental equations.

■ 3.2.11 Elliptic Integrals and Elliptic Functions

Even more so than for other special functions, you need to be very careful about the arguments you give to elliptic integrals and elliptic functions. There are several incompatible conventions in common use, and often these conventions are distinguished only by the specific names given to arguments or by the presence of separators other than commas between arguments.

■ Amplitude ϕ (used by *Mathematica*, in radians)

■ Argument u (used by *Mathematica*): related to amplitude by $\phi = \text{am}(u)$

■ Delta amplitude $\Delta(\phi)$: $\Delta(\phi) = \sqrt{1 - m \sin^2(\phi)}$

■ Coordinate x: $x = \sin(\phi)$

■ Characteristic n (used by *Mathematica* in elliptic integrals of the third kind)

■ Parameter m (used by *Mathematica*): preceded by |, as in $I(\phi\,|\,m)$

■ Complementary parameter m_1: $m_1 = 1 - m$

■ Modulus k: preceded by comma, as in $I(\phi, k)$; $m = k^2$

■ Modular angle α: preceded by \, as in $I(\phi\backslash\alpha)$; $m = \sin^2(\alpha)$

■ Nome q: preceded by comma in θ functions; $q = \exp[-\pi K(1 - m)/K(m)] = \exp(i\pi\omega'/\omega)$

■ Invariants g_2, g_3 (used by *Mathematica*)

■ Half-periods ω, ω': $g_2 = 60 \sum'_{r,s} w^{-4}$, $g_3 = 140 \sum'_{r,s} w^{-6}$, where $w = 2r\omega + 2s\omega'$

■ Ratio of periods τ: $\tau = \omega'/\omega$

■ Discriminant Δ: $\Delta = g_2^3 - 27g_3^2$

■ Parameters of curve a, b (used by *Mathematica*)

■ Coordinate y (used by *Mathematica*): related by $y^2 = x^3 + ax^2 + bx$

Common argument conventions for elliptic integrals and elliptic functions.

JacobiAmplitude[u, m]	give the amplitude ϕ corresponding to argument u and parameter m
EllipticNomeQ[m]	give the nome q corresponding to parameter m
InverseEllipticNomeQ[q]	give the parameter m corresponding to nome q
WeierstrassInvariants[{ω, ω'}]	give the invariants {g_2, g_3} corresponding to the half-periods {ω, ω'}
WeierstrassHalfPeriods[{g_2, g_3}]	give the half-periods {ω, ω'} corresponding to the invariants {g_2, g_3}

Converting between different argument conventions.

Elliptic Integrals

EllipticK[*m*]	complete elliptic integral of the first kind $K(m)$
EllipticF[ϕ, *m*]	elliptic integral of the first kind $F(\phi\|m)$
EllipticE[*m*]	complete elliptic integral of the second kind $E(m)$
EllipticE[ϕ, *m*]	elliptic integral of the second kind $E(\phi\|m)$
EllipticPi[*n*, *m*]	complete elliptic integral of the third kind $\Pi(n\|m)$
EllipticPi[*n*, ϕ, *m*]	elliptic integral of the third kind $\Pi(n;\phi\|m)$
JacobiZeta[ϕ, *m*]	Jacobi zeta function $Z(\phi\|m)$

Elliptic integrals.

Integrals of the form $\int R(x,y)\,dx$, where R is a rational function, and y^2 is a cubic or quartic polynomial in x, are known as **elliptic integrals**. Any elliptic integral can be expressed in terms of the three standard kinds of **Legendre-Jacobi elliptic integrals**.

The **elliptic integral of the first kind** EllipticF[ϕ, *m*] is given for $-\pi/2 < \phi < \pi/2$ by $F(\phi\|m) = \int_0^\phi [1 - m\sin^2(\theta)]^{-1/2}\,d\theta = \int_0^{\sin(\phi)}[(1 - t^2)(1 - mt^2)]^{-1/2}\,dt$. This elliptic integral arises in solving the equations of motion for a simple pendulum. It is sometimes known as an **incomplete elliptic integral of the first kind**.

Note that the arguments of the elliptic integrals are sometimes given in the opposite order from what is used in *Mathematica*.

The **complete elliptic integral of the first kind** EllipticK[*m*] is given by $K(m) = F(\frac{\pi}{2}\|m)$. Note that K is used to denote the *complete* elliptic integral of the first kind, while F is used for its incomplete form. In many applications, the parameter m is not given explicitly, and $K(m)$ is denoted simply by K. The **complementary complete elliptic integral of the first kind** $K'(m)$ is given by $K(1-m)$. It is often denoted K'. K and iK' give the "real" and "imaginary" quarter-periods of the corresponding Jacobi elliptic functions discussed below.

The **elliptic integral of the second kind** EllipticE[ϕ, *m*] is given for $-\pi/2 < \phi < \pi/2$ by $E(\phi\|m) = \int_0^\phi [1 - m\sin^2(\theta)]^{1/2}\,d\theta = \int_0^{\sin(\phi)}(1 - t^2)^{-1/2}(1 - mt^2)^{1/2}\,dt$.

The **complete elliptic integral of the second kind** EllipticE[*m*] is given by $E(m) = E(\frac{\pi}{2}\|m)$. It is often denoted E. The complementary form is $E'(m) = E(1-m)$.

The **Jacobi zeta function** JacobiZeta[ϕ, *m*] is given by $Z(\phi\|m) = E(\phi\|m) - E(m)F(\phi\|m)/K(m)$.

The **Heuman lambda function** is given by $\Lambda_0(\phi\|m) = F(\phi\|1-m)/K(1-m) + \frac{2}{\pi}K(m)Z(\phi\|1-m)$.

The **elliptic integral of the third kind** EllipticPi[n, ϕ, m] is given by $\Pi(n; \phi \mid m) = \int_0^\phi (1 - n \sin^2(\theta))^{-1} [1 - m \sin^2(\theta)]^{-1/2} d\theta$.

The **complete elliptic integral of the third kind** EllipticPi[n, m] is given by $\Pi(n \mid m) = \Pi(n; \frac{\pi}{2} \mid m)$.

Here is a plot of the complete elliptic integral of the second kind $E(m)$.

In[1]:= **Plot[EllipticE[m], {m, 0, 1}]**

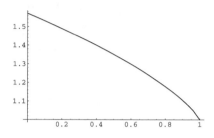

Here is $K(\alpha)$ with $\alpha = 30°$.

In[2]:= **EllipticK[Sin[30 Degree]^2] // N**
Out[2]= 1.68575

The elliptic integrals have a complicated structure in the complex plane.

In[3]:= **Plot3D[Im[EllipticF[px + I py, 2]],**
          {px, 0.5, 2.5}, {py, -1, 1}, PlotPoints->60]

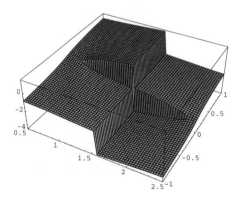